Professional
ASP XML

Mark Baartse
Richard Blair
Luca Bolognese
Dinar Dalvi
Steven Hahn
Corey Haines
Alex Homer
Bill Kropog
Brian Loesgen
Stephen Mohr
John Slater
Kevin Williams
Mario Zucca

Wrox Press Ltd.

Professional ASP XML

Published by Wrox Press Ltd
Arden House, 1102 Warwick Road, Acock's Green, Birmingham B27 6BH, UK
Printed in Canada
ISBN 1-861004-02-8

Trademark Acknowledgements

Wrox has endeavored to provide trademark information about all the companies and products mentioned in this book by the appropriate use of capitals. However, Wrox cannot guarantee the accuracy of this information.

Credits

Authors
Mark Baartse
Richard Blair
Luca Bolognese
Dinar Dalvi
Steven Hahn
Corey Haines
Alex Homer
Bill Kropog
Brian Loesgen
Stephen Mohr
John Slater
Kevin Williams
Mario Zucca

Additional Material
Steven Livingstone
Dave Sussman

Technical Architect
Chris Goode

Technical Editors
Catherine Alexander
Sarah Drew
Adrian Young

Development Editor
Greg Pearson

Category Manager
Joanna Mason

Author Agent
Sophie Edwards

Production Manager
Laurent Lafon

Technical Reviewers
Matthew Bullock
Carl Burnham
Kenneth Cox
Duncan Godwin
Stephen Kaufman
Gerry O'Brien
Robert Oliver
Mark Oswald
Matthew Reynolds
Kenn Scribner
Marc Simpkin
Steve Smith
Dino Esposito
Dinar Dalvi
John Timney
Steven Hahn

Production Project Coordinator
Tom Bartlett

Design and Layout
Tom Bartlett
Jonathan Jones
Laurent Lafon

Figures
William Fallon

Cover Design
Shelley Frazier

Index
Andrew Criddle

Project Administrator
Jake Manning

About the Authors

Richard Blair

Richard is a Systems Architect for Fry Multimedia, Inc. After earning degrees in English Literature and Theatre from the University of Michigan he realized that computers were much more interesting than waiting tables at the local eatery. Throughout his career he has specialized in distributed PC software doing everthing from design through implementation using Visual Basic, ASP, COM, Scripting, HTML, and XML. He enjoys learning new technologies and teaching them to others.

Richard can be reached by e-mail at rdblair@ix.netcom.com.

Acknowledgements

I would like to thank my wife and son for their patience and support while waiting up nights so I could fix "just one more bug". I would also like to thank the folks at Wrox for all their help and support, especially Chris who always answered my questions.

Luca Bolognese

I was born 30 years ago in Milan, and ever since I was very young I loved software. I started off writing assembler code, then moved on to C++, then to Java. My real interests have always been Software Design and Object Orientation; how to apply them to the present distributed component scenario, and how to use XML as a glue between different layers. I recently worked on these topics in projects undertaken in both Italy, and the USA.

I can be reached at l.bolognese@genoavalley.org.

Dinar Dalvi

Dinar Dalvi is an E-Commerce consultant with Compuware Professional Services Division (Cleveland, Ohio.). At Compuware, Dinar is responsible for prototyping and developing advanced Internet/Client Server (n-tier) using technologies like COM, COM+. His tools of choice include ASP, Visual Basic, SQL Server, XML and Visual C++.

Acknowledgements

Dinar wants to thank his wife Pallavi for the support and encouragement she gave in writing the case study. Dinar also wants to thank his programming posse – Corey Haines, John Ehrlinger, John Slater and Jerry Personen. Also, he would like to thank the Wrox staff, in particular Chris Goode, for going out of their way to help get the case study done.

Trademark Acknowledgements

Wrox has endeavored to provide trademark information about all the companies and products mentioned in this book by the appropriate use of capitals. However, Wrox cannot guarantee the accuracy of this information.

Credits

Authors
Mark Baartse
Richard Blair
Luca Bolognese
Dinar Dalvi
Steven Hahn
Corey Haines
Alex Homer
Bill Kropog
Brian Loesgen
Stephen Mohr
John Slater
Kevin Williams
Mario Zucca

Additional Material
Steven Livingstone
Dave Sussman

Technical Architect
Chris Goode

Technical Editors
Catherine Alexander
Sarah Drew
Adrian Young

Development Editor
Greg Pearson

Category Manager
Joanna Mason

Author Agent
Sophie Edwards

Production Manager
Laurent Lafon

Technical Reviewers
Matthew Bullock
Carl Burnham
Kenneth Cox
Duncan Godwin
Stephen Kaufman
Gerry O'Brien
Robert Oliver
Mark Oswald
Matthew Reynolds
Kenn Scribner
Marc Simpkin
Steve Smith
Dino Esposito
Dinar Dalvi
John Timney
Steven Hahn

Production Project Coordinator
Tom Bartlett

Design and Layout
Tom Bartlett
Jonathan Jones
Laurent Lafon

Figures
William Fallon

Cover Design
Shelley Frazier

Index
Andrew Criddle

Project Administrator
Jake Manning

About the Authors

Richard Blair

Richard is a Systems Architect for Fry Multimedia, Inc. After earning degrees in English Literature and Theatre from the University of Michigan he realized that computers were much more interesting than waiting tables at the local eatery. Throughout his career he has specialized in distributed PC software doing everthing from design through implementation using Visual Basic, ASP, COM, Scripting, HTML, and XML. He enjoys learning new technologies and teaching them to others.

Richard can be reached by e-mail at rdblair@ix.netcom.com.

Acknowledgements

I would like to thank my wife and son for their patience and support while waiting up nights so I could fix "just one more bug". I would also like to thank the folks at Wrox for all their help and support, especially Chris who always answered my questions.

Luca Bolognese

I was born 30 years ago in Milan, and ever since I was very young I loved software. I started off writing assembler code, then moved on to C++, then to Java. My real interests have always been Software Design and Object Orientation; how to apply them to the present distributed component scenario, and how to use XML as a glue between different layers. I recently worked on these topics in projects undertaken in both Italy, and the USA.

I can be reached at l.bolognese@genoavalley.org.

Dinar Dalvi

Dinar Dalvi is an E-Commerce consultant with Compuware Professional Services Division (Cleveland, Ohio.). At Compuware, Dinar is responsible for prototyping and developing advanced Internet/Client Server (n-tier) using technologies like COM, COM+. His tools of choice include ASP, Visual Basic, SQL Server, XML and Visual C++.

Acknowledgements

Dinar wants to thank his wife Pallavi for the support and encouragement she gave in writing the case study. Dinar also wants to thank his programming posse – Corey Haines, John Ehrlinger, John Slater and Jerry Personen. Also, he would like to thank the Wrox staff, in particular Chris Goode, for going out of their way to help get the case study done.

Steven Hahn

Steven Hahn works for a prominent investment firm developing Internet systems. He has been involved in the computer industry for almost 20 years. He lives in New York with his wife, Avital Louria, who is a journalist, two children and one (rather large) cat. Steve can be e-mailed at shahn@cybertechnic.com.

Steven Hahn's Cover photograph is by Danielle Louria.

Acknowledgements

I would like to thank a great development team for their support in developing awesome web and XML solutions – Roman Gorodetsky and Jayant Patwardhen. Thank you to the graphics guys who can make anything look good – Tim Camuti and Richie 'Bits' Feliciano. A special grazie to Freddy Tenaglia who once said 'you should check out this XML thing'.

And most of all thank you to my beloved family – Avital, Danielle and David.

Corey Haines

Corey Haines is a senior systems architect at Interactive Information Service in Cleveland, Ohio. When not architecting systems as a senior, he enjoys playing the guitar and practicing Wing Chun, although not necessarily in that order.

Acknowledgements

I'd like to dedicate this book to my father, Terrell Haines, without whom I most likely would not have ended up in computers. I'd also like to say a big hello to my programming posse: John Ehrlinger, John Slater, Jerry Personen, and Dinar Dalvi.

Alex Homer

Alex Homer is a software developer and technical author living and working in the idyllic rural surroundings of the Derbyshire Dales in England. He came to computing late in life – in fact, while he was at school people still thought that the LED wristwatch was a really cool idea. Since then he has obtained a Bachelor of Arts degree in Mathematics, and so looked destined for a career painting computers. Instead, while not busy developing ASP components for Stonebroom Software (http://www.stonebroom.com), he prefers to install and play with the latest and flakiest beta code he can find and then write about it. You can contact him at alex@stonebroom.com or alex@stonebroom.co.uk.

Bill Kropog

Bill Kropog is a full-time consultant for a Web and software development firm in New Orleans, Louisiana. William specializes in finding new and creative ways to display and manipulate data with Active Server Pages. He uses Visual InterDev 6.0 for most of what he develops, with frequent hops into Visual Basic 6.0. He also creates most of the graphics he uses in his projects (Corel Xara 2.0 and Adobe PhotoShop 5.0), making him a well-rounded developer. XML is the latest thing on William's plate, and, being a former journalist, he'd like to develop XML-based standards for online publications to make it easier to share news and to bring ordinary journalists into the online world.

Brian Loesgen

Brian Loesgen is a Principal Engineer at San Diego-based Stellcom Inc., a leader in end-to-end e-commerce, Internet and wireless solutions. At Stellcom, Brian is involved in some of the most advanced web application development projects being built today. Brian has spoken at numerous technical conferences worldwide, and has been known to seize every opportunity possible to promote new technologies. He enjoys playing with bleeding edge software and translating those new technologies into real world benefits.

In his spare moments, Brian enjoys outdoor activities such as cycling, hiking in the mountains, camping in the desert, or going to the beach with his wife Miriam and children Steven and Melissa.

Brian can be reached at bloesgen@msn.com.

Stephen Mohr

Stephen Mohr is a senior systems architect with Omicron Consulting. Over the last ten years, he has specialized in the PC computing platform, designing and developing systems using C++, Java, JavaScript, COM, and various internetworking standards and protocols. His latest efforts include the use of XML for application integration. Stephen holds BS and MS degrees in computer science from Rensselaer Polytechnic Institute. His research interests include distributed object-based computing and the practical applications of artificial intelligence.

John Slater

John Slater is a project manager at Management Reports International in Cleveland, Ohio. At MRI he is currently developing Windows applications for the property management industry. His tools of choice for web development include ASP, Visual Basic components, and, of course, XML. He spends his free time with his wife, Beth, and one year old daughter, Rachel. John wants to thank his wife for encouraging him to write this case study and making the process so much easier.

Kevin Williams

Kevin's first experience with computers was at the age of 10 (in 1980) when he took a BASIC class at a local community college on their PDP-9, and by the time he was 12, he stayed up for four days straight hand-assembling 6502 code on his Atari 400. His professional career has been focused on Windows development – first client server, then on to Internet work. He's done a little bit of everything, from VB to Powerbuilder to Delphi to C/C++ to MASM to ISAPI, CGI, ASP, HTML, XML, and any other acronym you might care to name, but these days, he's focusing on XML work. Kevin is currently working with the Mortgage Bankers' Association of Amercia to help them put together an XML standard for the mortgage industry.

Mario Zucca

My curriculum vitae is becoming longer and longer as years pass by; it means I'm becoming older, it's so bad! I sold my first sw programs to my companions when I was in high school; these programs ran on HP calculators, the mythical ones! Then I went to university and it was a hard life dealing with C programming language and also with some other programming languages such as Prolog and Smalltalk. From starting my career I've worked with databases. Oracle has been my "first love" since 1992 when I entered Datasiel S.p.A. Here I dealt with Client server applications developed in Microsoft Oracle environments.

In 1996 I passed from the relational world to the OO world. This was a difficult step to take. My favorite matters were COM and MTS/COM+ technologies and also C++ programming language. But lately "I've fallen in love" with XML. These three letters, **X M L**, have become so important to me! I usually spend 99% of my free time working at my PC, for I'm really engaged in this new adventure. I spend the remaining free time with those who are so important to me: my family and my little daughter; she loves the sea and so do I. In fact we live in Genoa, Italy.

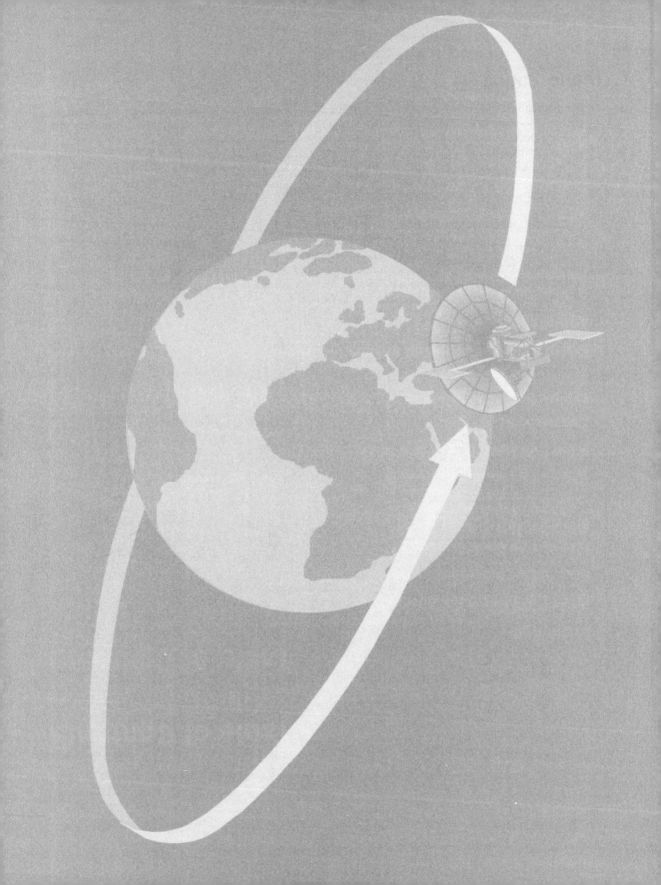

Table of Contents

Table of Contents

Chapter 5: Document Object Model

Chapter 15: Working with Emerging Standards in XML Technologies 337

Table of Contents

Introduction

XML, the Extensible Markup Language, is a platform-independent language for describing data. The XML and related specifications, as well as the Document Object Model, have all been developed with language independence in mind. This was done to allow *any* programmer to use these powerful protocols and object models in their own language of choice, thus providing a huge development potential for the XML community and offering a myriad of opportunities to developers working with established technologies. This, in essence, is the beauty of XML.

ASP has long been leading technology for server-side, dynamic web applications. And XML, as the newest markup language and a standard format for the universal sharing of data, is undoubtedly set to become an intrinsic part of all major development both on the Web, and in the wider business community. The next generation of web sites will inevitably combine these technologies as e-commerce matures and developers look for more efficient ways to integrate Internet presence with business systems. Consequently, it seems a timely and apt step in the progression of XML's evolution, that there should be a book to demonstrate how these popular and versatile technologies can be used together.

What Does this Book Cover?

We will cover the standards and ready-to-use components of XML in a step-by-step way. As we get to know more and more features of XML and related technologies, we will present more complex examples by incorporating these features.

The book will cover the XML 1.0 recommendation and the DOM 1.0 recommendation in detail, before it delves into the details of how to use XML in an ASP environment. We will cover styling XML for display in a web browser, covering both Cascading Style Sheets (CSS) and the Extensible Stylesheet Language (XSL), and also how XML can be used to persist ADO recordsets.

The book then shifts to a more practical standpoint with chapters covering Data Stores, Data Transfer and Server Manipulation. The final chapters are a combination of more advanced topics, such as data handling applications, which utilize data-binding techniques with XML, and XML-driven administration tools. A chapter is devoted to introducing the latest in XML-based technologies: BizTalk and the Simple Object Access Protocol (SOAP). The final section of the book covers real-world case studies including an online survey tool. Professional ASP XML allows Internet developers currently using ASP to expand their knowledge to the point where they can exploit the full potential of XML, thus allowing it to be employed effectively within integrated Internet systems.

Who Is this Book For?

This book is for intermediate to advanced ASP programmers, who have little or no knowledge of XML, and want to expand their programming ability by adding XML skills to their repertoire. XML will be explained from the ground up. However, other technologies will not be discussed in such detail and it is assumed that the user is familiar with other Internet techniques on the Microsoft platform, such as (D)HTML, client-side scripting with JScript, and programming in Visual Basic. You should have at least a *basic* understanding of three-tier architectures like Microsoft DNA.

If you have read or heard a bit about XML and wonder how to use it best, building on your existing programming skills, then this book is for you!

How is this Book Structured?

The book can be divided into four sections. The first part (Chapters 1 to 5) explains the background theory, using small code samples to illustrate how to use XML. Chapters 6 to 14 look more closely at how ASP and XML work together, and cover a range of topics including styling, data access, data binding, and procedure libraries. The section ends with a brief review on two exciting XML-based technologies that are emerging – BizTalk and SOAP. In the third section, six Case Studies are presented, illustrating the use of XML in ASP-based real-world applications. Finally, there are eight reference Appendices.

Section 1: Introdcution to XML

1: Introduction to Extensible Markup Language

This chapter introduces XML from first principles. It discusses the history of XML, how it improves on HTML and how it is more than just a web technology. The XML parser is introduced, as is the inbuilt ability of IE5 to display formatted XML in the browser and display syntax errors.

2: Understanding XML Structure and Syntax

This chapter follows on by discussing XML structure and syntax, covering elements, attributes, processing instructions, entities and namespaces. The concept of well-formedness, i.e. correctness, of XML documents is explained.

3: Validating XML with the DTD

In the first of two chapters on XML validation, we look at the established method of validating XML text against an external standard, the DTD. This chapter defines what a DTD is, how it is structured and how it is used.

4: Validating XML using Schemas

This chapter examines the proposed alternative to the DTD, the XML Schema. It defines what a Schema is, how it is structured and how it is used. At the end there is a brief comparison between DTDs and Schemas, to help you decide which technology would best fit your requirements.

5: Document Object Model

This chapter introduces the Document Object Model (DOM), discusses its syntax, properties and methods, and shows how it can be used to manipulate your XML data.

Section 2: Working with XML and ASP

6: Integrating ASP with XML

Having explained XML, DTDs, Schemas and the DOM, we present a series of simple ASP-based examples, which demonstrate what XML can do. Not much explanation of the mechanics is given at the stage, as the chapter is meant to provide an interlude between the chapters covering XML theory and the more complex ASP examples that follow.

7: Using CSS with XML

This chapter includes an overview of CSS syntax and structure, and includes a refresher course on how to use CSS with HTML. It then moves on to styling XML with CSS, and discusses the benefits and the drawbacks of such a technique, by comparing it with XSL.

8: XSL – Extensible Stylesheet Language

This chapter introduces the XML-based alternative to CSS – XSL. It reviews the limitations of CSS before delving into the structure and syntax of XSL, building upon the simple examples used earlier in the book.

9: Advanced XSL Techniques

This chapter follows on by discussing the various ways for transforming XML data using XSL, including converting to HTML on the server, then streaming HTML to the client as a way of overcoming browser compatibility issues. It also covers converting one XML document to another, thereby illustrating that XSL can do more than just styling. Finally, the bulk of this chapter is devoted to developing an XSL stylesheet that will create a collapsible navigation tree on the client.

10: Case Study: Data-Driven XSL

This chapter concludes the subsection on styling by demonstrating how you can create an XSL stylesheet on the fly from XML data.

11: Integrating ADO and XML

After a brief review of ADO, this chapter discusses how to relate ADO concepts to XML data, and shows how to convert ADO-driven applications into XML. Next, the important subject of recordset persistence with XML is discussed, including persistence of XML data to files or data streams, as well as persisting to and from ASP pages.

12: Client-side Data Binding with XML

This chapter, in conjunction with the next one, examines how IE4 and above can work with XML to create dynamic data management applications that are also network friendly. The basics of client-side data binding will be reviewed in theory and practice, and then the chapter will move on to show how this technique can be adapted for use with XML data.

13: Working with XML Data Binding

Continuing the theme from Chapter 12, this chapter will move on to look at some of the ways that data binding with XML can be used, and some of the technologies that allow us to make the most of its potential. The dynamic creation of XML documents for use with data binding techniques is considered before attention is turned to how source XML documents on the server can be updated. This chapter also covers the SQLXML Technology Preview.

14: Creating XML Procedure Libraries

Since XML is an evolving language, there are few tools and components available to take the work out of writing peripheral code that XML and its associated technologies require. This chapter shows how to create a set or library of XML-specific procedures to make applications cleaner and coding them potentially faster. The functions contained within the procedure library are demonstrated via an integrated sample page.

15: Working with Emerging Standards in XML Technologies

As the adoption of XML into the developer community increases at an incredibly fast pace, technologies that make the most of this flexible technology are constantly being developed and introduced. For example, Schema repositories are places where published XML Schemas are made generally available. This chapter reviews two of the currently leading repositories – BizTalk and OASIS, before examining BizTalk in more detail. Protocols for sending information over HTTP have also emerged that use XML as a communications medium. This chapter discusses Microsoft's contribution to this new world, XMLHTTPRequest and SOAP (Simple Object Access Protocol).

Section 3: Case Studies

Case Study 1: An On-Line Survey Tool

This case study presents a web application that enables you to create an on-line survey, get results and present them in report form. XML is used as the intermediate data storage format, and for styling the output to the browser.

Case Study 2: An On-line Documentation System

This case study describes a web front-end application that allows you to write documentation for components, and describe the methods and properties of components, using XML for the storage of the data.

Case Study 3: Shopping Cart

This case study presents an on-line shopping cart, linked to a database containing information on products. The user can then fill the cart with products and submit an order. The user's details are stored on the client as a cookie and are written to the database, so the items in the cart can persist between sessions.

Case Study 4: Workflow Application

This case study explains the concept of workflow, which is the process of passing messages and data along a chain of users, who each carry out an operation based on the message received. A web application is developed which reads in workflow data from a database, and allows the user to respond to messages at the click of a button. The messages are relayed in XML.

Case Study 5: Using XML and TIP for Distributed Web Transactions

This case study presents an application where the user can choose from a list of motor vehicles and submit an order. XML is used to pass the order details from the client to the server and to relay responses using the Transaction Internet Protocol (TIP). Note that support for TIP is restricted to Windows 2000.

Case Study 6: Data Transfer

This case study allows the user to choose from a selection of cheeses and make an order, which is stored as XML. The order can then be transformed using XSLT so that the details of the order can be presented as XML, and rendered either in the browser, or as a comma separated list. Note that this case study uses the more recent W3C Recommendations, XSLT and XPath, and as such requires the use of the very latest XML parser from Microsoft.

Section 4: Reference Appendices

Appendix A: XML 1.0 Specification

Appendix B: Microsoft XML v3.0 Reference

Appendix C: IE5 XSL Reference

Appendix D: CSS Reference

Appendix E: SAX 1.0: The Simple API for XML

Appendix F: XPath, XLink and XPointer Reference

Appendix G: IE5 XML Schemas and Data Types

Appendix H: XML Preview for SQL Server

Appendix I: Support and Errata

What You Need to Use this Book

As well as a thorough knowledge of ASP, basic familiarity with HTML is assumed, along with some knowledge of using SQL Server or Access, and a basic understanding of Visual Basic would be beneficial.

To develop and run all of the examples and case studies you'll need to have the following software:

- ❑   Windows 2000
- ❑   IIS 5.0
- ❑   Microsoft XML parser 2.0 (supplied with IE5)

- Visual Basic 6.0 (for the case studies)
- ADO 2.5
- SQL Server 7 and Access 97 Databases
- Microsoft Component Services
- Microsoft XML parser version 3.0 preview (for Case Study 6)

> **Note that if you are running Windows NT 4.0 with IIS 4.0 and MTS 2.0 you will be able to run some, but not all of the case studies in this book.**

The complete source code for this book is available for download from our website, at http://www.wrox.com

Conventions

To help you get the most from the text and keep track of what's happening, we've used a number of conventions throughout the book.

For instance:

> **These boxes hold important, not-to-be forgotten information that is directly relevant to the surrounding text.**

While the background style is used for asides to the current discussion.

As for styles in the text:

- When we introduce them, we **highlight** important words
- We show keyboard strokes like this: *Ctrl-A*
- We show filenames and code within the text like so: doGet()
- Text on user interfaces (and URLs) is shown as: Menu

We present code in two different ways:

```
In our code examples, the code foreground style shows new, important,
    pertinent code
while code background shows code that's less important in the present context,
    or which has been seen before.
```

Tell Us What You Think

We've worked hard to make this book as useful to you as possible, so we'd like to know what you think. We're always keen to know what it is you want and need to know.

We appreciate feedback on our efforts and take both criticism and praise on board in our future editorial efforts. If you've anything to say, let us know via e-mail:

feedback@wrox.com

or via the feedback links on our web site:

http://www.wrox.com

1

Introduction to eXtensible Markup Language

You've probably been told over and over that **eXtensible Markup Language** (**XML**) is going to change the Web and how we share data. You have most likely heard that XML is a cousin of **HTML** (Hypertext Markup Language), and perhaps that it's a subset of **SGML** – Standard Generalized Markup Language. In the most general sense both statements are true; but you certainly can't stop there in your understanding of XML if you plan to make significant use of it in your own applications.

As with any new language or technology, learning it is easier once you understand how it will fit into the grand scheme of things. Didn't you always hate those teachers who jumped right into a new subject without giving you an overview, and an explanation of how you could use it in the real world? However, the manner in which many developers found out about XML was by being told that they *had* to have it. Well, telling someone that they need to know something without clearly demonstrating why is not the most informative or enlightening approach to take, and quite different from how and why we usually go about learning something new.

For instance, I didn't get into Active Server Pages until a client of mine requested that their data be accessible on the Web. I barely knew anything about VBScript, much less server-side processing, but I knew I had this impossible task ahead of me, so I went out and found the right tool – or skill – for the job. And it was a similar situation too that pushed me into regular HTML in the days of battleship-gray HTML pages. I was a newspaper reporter who thought it would be cool to put my publication online.

So, in this introductory chapter I will try another tack. We'll start by taking a general overview of Markup languages in general, before going on to see what XML's mission in life is. We can then dive in and take our first look at the XML vista. Each successive chapter will dig a little deeper into the XML landscape and demonstrate how we can combine the power of this technology with Active Server Pagers (ASP).

ASP & XML?

But why ASP & XML, you might be asking. Well, I already mentioned that I got started with ASP because I had to meet the requirements of a business client, but with XML I didn't have a real task to complete. I just chose to learn it and then see how I could apply it to what I was already doing. I think it's still early enough in the evolution of XML that many of its possible applications simply haven't been adequately explored. Active Server Pages is one such road that we'll travel in this book.

With ASP, developers can create sophisticated applications that can be delivered via the Web. In every application I have worked on, there is always a data element to them. But ASP has many useful features for handling data that have nothing to do with XML, so why use the two technologies together? As the World Wide Web expands, and more and more companies start using Internet technologies to communicate and deliver applications (internal or external), data exchange becomes a crucial element. XML allows us to provide deliverable data easily without having to worry about the destination system. ASP allows us to wrap that delivery in a very usuable form.

So this first chapter is designed to introduce the experienced ASP developer to XML. If you're already comfortable with XML (particularly client-side), you should just use these first chapters as a means of revising your existing knowledge and ensuring there's nothing you've missed.

A Word on Markup Languages

Before we go any further, let's just do a quick refresher on what we define as a Markup language. The term markup is borrowed from the print world where electronic documents were, and still are, "marked up" with tags that tell a computer what to do. The markup generally serves one of two purposes: to determine the formatting, or to dictate structure or meaning. A markup language, therefore, is a standardized set of markup tags that conform to a defined syntax and grammar.

Our old friend markup

HTML might have been the first time you ever heard of markup, but word processors and text editors were using it long before the advent of the World Wide Web. If you have ever used WordPerfect and used the Reveal Codes command, or looked at the contents of a file stored in Rich Text Format (RTF), you have seen markup tags in a non-web context. However, unlike XML, trying to decipher either of the above examples was probably an exercise in futility.

RTF is a very general electronic document markup language that is still widely accepted as a means of sharing formatted documents today. In fact, it is the one format that can span word processor versions and operating systems. That is, WordPerfect is able to read a Word for Macintosh RTF document.

Journalists, who've been around a while, probably remember working on proprietary systems that used a special brand of markup to format stories. I myself used to write on one such dinosaur called the Mycroteck. It had a special keyboard with custom function keys that inserted strange-looking brackets around groups of letters, which would change the font, style or size of the text they surrounded.

The bottom line is, markup has been around for quite some time, but it wasn't until a small group of guys came up with HTML that it began receiving its notoriety and widespread use.

How Markup Works

On a rudimentary level, Markup languages old and new all work along very similar lines. Generally, they comprise a library of tag pairs that are placed around words or characters to alter their appearance or meaning. These tag pairs form what is called an element. For example, this snippet from an RTF document:

```
{\f0 Hello world! I use }{\b\f0\fs28 markup.}
```

would be interpreted by an RTF compliant word processor to look like this:

Hello world! I use **markup.**

The start tag, `{\f0`, sets the font for the text that follows. The end tag `}` tells the word processor to end the previously set formatting. Similarly, `{\b\f0\fs28` sets the font of the contained text, and also bolds and increases its size.

Significantly though, RTF does nothing to describe the structure of a document, only the formatting. HTML on the other hand does both.

Examine this HTML document:

```
<!DOCTYPE HTML PUBLIC "-//W3C//DTD HTML 3.2 FINAL//EN">
<HTML>
<HEAD>
<TITLE>Sample Page</TITLE>
</HEAD>
<BODY>
Hello, world! I use <FONT SIZE="5"><B>markup.</B></FONT>
</BODY>
</HTML>
```

This HTML produces a similar result as the RTF, in a browser window:

However, notice that the title of the window says "Sample Page", which is the value I gave to the Title tags. The document now describes, albeit very briefly, what it represents.

Obviously, as an ASP developer, you're familiar with HTML and how it works, but what you might not know is that the basis for the creation of HTML was the earlier-mentioned Standard Generalized Markup Language (SGML). SGML is actually a *metalanguage*; a language that allows you to describe other languages.

Languages and Metalanguages

SGML is an information-management standard adopted by the International Standards Organization (ISO) in 1986, although its roots extend much further back into history into the realms of Generalized Markup Language, for example. It was designed to provide a way to create platform-independent and application-independent documents that retain formatting, indexing and linked information. With a grammar-like mechanism, users can define the structure of their documents through the creation of custom tags.

As I noted earlier, SGML is a *metalanguage;* it can be used to create other languages. HTML is purely a language and cannot extend or create subsets of itself. Conversely, XML *is* a subset of SGML and can indeed be used to create other languages. This makes XML a metalanguage too. In plain English, XML is extensible as its name implies. We can use XML to create structures that describe the contents without regard to how those contents will be displayed. HTML, on the other hand, describes how the document will be displayed, but tells nothing of what the document is.

HTML's Place in the Universe

You'll have noticed that the very first line of our HTML document (often omitted by developers these days) is called the **Document Type Declaration**:

```
<!DOCTYPE HTML PUBLIC "-//W3C//DTD HTML 3.2 FINAL//EN">
...
```

It tells the processor (usually a Web browser for HTML) which **Document Type Definition** (DTD) to use. Even though both terms share the same initials (DTD), just remember that when we refer to a DTD later in this book, we're talking about the Document Type Definition, not the Document Type Declaration. The Document Type *Declaration* defines what type of document we have, in this case HTML 3.2. The Document Type *Definition* actually defines the syntax the document is validated against.

The DTD (Document Type *Definition*) can be thought of as a blueprint for the document, as it establishes rules for the parser to follow. It describes what kind of elements can exist in the document and what they do. The parser also uses the DTD to make sure the document's tags and organization conform to the pre-defined set of rules for HTML.

Most Web browsers, however, tend to run a bit loose with the HTML DTD, allowing developers to break some of the rules. For instance, does forgetting to close a <FONT> tag crash an HTML document? It might create an unwanted formatting effect, but it may not cause the processor to reject the whole document.

As we know, while HTML mainly deals with formatting documents for display, it also manages structure. The HTML language, or vocabulary, dictates that all documents must contain a body section set off by the <BODY></BODY> tags. The optional <HEAD></HEAD> element is reserved for information needed by the server and the browser; the <BODY></BODY> element is for visual display with special provisions for linking. And you're already aware that the <TITLE></TITLE> element, which generally appears within the <HEAD></HEAD> element tells the browser what to display in the title bar of the browser window.

Both the <HEAD> and <BODY> tags must be contained within the <HTML> element, which basically asserts that the document is indeed an HTML document. When dealing with a frameset page, the <FRAMESET></FRAMESET> tags replace the <BODY></BODY> tags. This is about the extent of structure in an HTML page.

You may have tried to create your own tags in an HTML document, such as:
`<GREETING>Howdy!</GREETING>` and found that your browser just ignored your entry, or printed the text as if the tags weren't even there. The browser is using the DTD to interpret or parse your document. `<GREETING>` is not defined in the DTD, and therefore the browser just ignores the tag. In a less forgiving browser, this action might generate an error or even cause the browser to crash. In my attempt to create a custom tag, you will notice that the tag says something about the values it should contain, although it says nothing about how the value should be displayed.

In Walks XML

The world needed a way to describe information, and the creators of XML attempted to fill that void with a metalanguage based on SGML, but without its complexity. The SGML specification is over 150 pages long while XML is only about 35 pages. This makes XML a much easier metalanguage to learn and apply. You can take a look at the specs for XML at http://www.w3c.org/xml, or you can refer to Appendix A.

The creators of XML also wanted it to possess a few capabilities that SGML did not have, such as the ability to work in conjunction with HTML in order to integrate and display data. And there are now a number of other initiatives coming out of the World Wide Web Consortium (W3C) to improve XML acceptance. Xlink, or the specification for how hyperlinks should be managed from XML documents, is one example. Another example that we will take a more detailed look at later, is the eXtensible Sytlesheet Language or XSL. This is used to transform XML documents into other XML documents, HTML documents, or just about anything you can dream up. You might want to think of XSL as Cascading Stylesheets (CSS) on steroids – not only can XSL style data like CSS, but it has the ability to transform the data. We'll meet CSS and XSL again in chapters 7 to 9.

More than A Little Something for the Web

The creators of XML wanted it to be used in far more places than just the Web. It was their intention that XML should become an accepted way of sharing data among many different applications. For example, if a newspaper editor wants to have his publication's stories appear on the Internet, as well as in print, plus perhaps share them with other newspapers, he could have them marked up according to an XML standard. Provided that the story was marked up in a standard way that was widely accepted, the story could easily be imported into these other media.

For this reason, the creators of XML established the following 10 design goals for the specification. These goals are part of the specification that can be found at http://www.w3c.org/TR/1998/REC-xml-19980210.

XML Shall be Straightforwardly Usable Over the Internet

This does not mean that XML should be limited to the Internet, but rather that the complexity involved in SGML should be removed. Doing so also served to remove much of the overhead needed in SGML parsers. By keeping XML simple, using it over the Internet or in an Enterprise network application becomes simple.

XML Shall Support a Wide Variety of Applications

XML can be used over the Web or in a more traditional Client/Server environment. There is no specific technology behind it, so just about any technology should be able to use it.

XML Shall be Compatible With SGML

XML is a subset of SGML, which means anything you can do in XML, you can do in SGML. Any SGML parser will be able to handle XML documents. You might think of XML as SGML lite.

It Shall be Easy to Write Programs That Process XML Documents

Only by making it easy for most programmers to write their own XML parser in a variety of different languages could they ensure that XML would gain rapid acceptance.

The Number of Optional Features in XML is to be Kept to the Absolute Minimum, Ideally Zero

SGML has quite a few options, many of which aren't used. Again, this contributes to unnecessary overhead in SGML processors. Potentially an application could be built based on one set of SGML options, and be unable to read a document from another SGML application. If XML has zero options, every XML processor can parse every XML document.

XML Documents Should be Human-Legible and Reasonably Clear

Because XML is text-based and follows a strict but simple formatting methodology, it is extremely easy for a human to get a true sense of what the document means. XML is designed to describe the structure of the contents. By looking at XML you should be able to tell that a particular document is a bill of sale, for example. However you won't know what that bill of sale will actually look like when displayed.

The XML Design Should be Prepared Quickly

The creators of XML needed to produce their finished product fast, while ensuring that no single vendor would own it. They were afraid that another group might beat them to the market with a proprietary solution.

The Design of XML Shall be Formal and Concise

The XML specification uses **Extended Backus-Naur Form** (EBNF) to formalize its wording. EBNF is a standard form used to describe programming languages, and keeps the specification concise. It is one of the more common notations for describing or specifying the syntax of a programming or metalanguage. The XML specification defines the character range as:

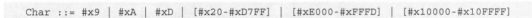

```
Char ::= #x9 | #xA | #xD | [#x20-#xD7FF] | [#xE000-#xFFFD] | [#x10000-#x10FFFF]
```

Which means that XML will interpret any Unicode character matching one of the above values or value ranges. If you are familiar with Regular expressions, then this format is nothing new.

XML Documents Shall be Easy to Create

XML documents can be created in a simple text editor, however, there are already various XML editors on the market. The simplicity in structure makes it even easier for various applications to generate XML on the fly.

Terseness in XML Markup is of Minimal Importance.

In XML, there cannot be any ambiguity. SGML and HTML both permit truncation techniques such as the omission of the closing tags of some elements. This makes it harder for humans to read the documents. When you include a closing tag for every opening tag, there is no room for confusion.

The Self-Describing Document

XML documents can be self-describing if the tag names are chosen appropriately. For example:

```
<customerFirstName>John</customerFirstName>
```

It is obvious that the value contained within the tags is a customer's first name, and not their address. XML doesn't stop you from putting an address between these tags, but it would make it difficult to really understand what is happening with the data. There are basically two criteria to which an XML document has to conform: a document must be **Well-formed**; and it must be **Valid**.

A Well-formed Document

Well-formed means that the document complies with the basic structure that all XML documents have. The basic rules for well-formed documents are:

- ❑ Like HTML and SGML, XML uses the less-than and greater-than characters (<...>) as its standard delimiters.

- ❑ Every opening tag must have an accompanying closing tag. The exception is an empty element (one that does not have a value). In this case the opening and closing tag can be the same, except the closing > is preceded by /. For example: `<custFirstName/>`.

- ❑ Attributes of tags must be in a set of quotes. In HTML we can have: `<FONT SIZE=3>`, and the 3 does not need to be in quotes. With XML, the same statement would have to be written like this: `<FONT SIZE="3">`.

- ❑ Elements must be appropriately nested. Every XML document has a root element and all other elements are children of that element. To continue with my customer element:

```
<customer>
    <customerFirstName salutation="Mr">John</customerFirstName>
    ...
</customer>
```

  The root element is `<customer>` and the first child is `<customerFirstName...>`. My document would not be well-formed without the customer tags. Also, note that the value of the salutation attribute is in quotes.

- ❑ Elements are case sensitive. Using the previous example `<customerFirstName>` is not the same as `<CUSTOMERFirstName>`. These would be interpreted by the XML parser as two separate tags.

If you're having trouble grasping this concept of XML, think of HTML tables with their generally strict nesting rules. HTML tables have cells, which contain "data" of a sort. All column elements (`<TD></TD>`) must be contained within row elements (`<TR></TR>`) and they in turn must reside within one all-encompassing table element (`<TABLE></TABLE>`). In fact, the new version of HTML, called XHTML, enforces all of these rules as it is an implementation of HTML in XML. You might want to check out the W3C's web site for more information: http://www.w3c.org/xhtml. All of this strict structure allows us to better define our data. XML is very good at wrapping up hierarchical data into a very neat package. The file system is one example of hierarchical data. Directories can have files and sub-directories, which in turn can contain other sub-directories and files. An XML representation of a file system might look like:

```
<myfiles>
   <directory>Windows
      <directory>Desktop
         <file>testhtml.htm</file>
         <file>test2html.htm</file>
      </directory>
      <file>...</file>
   </directory>
</myfiles>
```

This shows that the `Windows` directory contains some files and a directory named `Desktop`. `Desktop` contains two files, `testhtml.htm` and `test2html.htm`. This way of defining data can be very powerful when compared to the standard relational model. When you can keep child data with the parent data, the relationships are readily obvious when looking at the XML.

A Valid Document

Valid XML documents conform to the rules defined in their associated DTD or Schema. DTDs and Schemas define what each element can contain and the organizational structure of the XML document. These are very similar to defining a database schema in SQL Server or Oracle. The big difference with XML is its ability to have elements that contain elements. DTDs have their own unique syntax for describing the XML document, while Schemas use standard XML to define the document. When the parser compares your XML document to the DTD or Schema, all of the values have to comply with those rules. The XML is therefore *validated* by these rules. This will be covered in more detail in chapters 3 and 4. For now, I just want you to come to an understanding of the terms *well-formed* and *valid*.

Getting Started with XML

It doesn't take much to get started with XML. If you've ever tried to visualize a piece of data in your head, you're well on the road to writing XML. For example, think of a business client. That client has a name. That name has a first name and a last name. The client also has a phone number and an address. That address has a street name, city, state and zip code. You could go on and on. But, that's where XML comes in – to describe your data.

You Only Need a Text Editor

Now that you've had the basic ground rules laid out for you concerning XML, you're probably keen to have a go yourself. Let's start off with a very simple XML document:

```
<?xml version="1.0"?>
<CONTACT>
   <NAME>
      <FIRST_NAME>John</FIRST_NAME>
      <LAST_NAME>Doe</LAST_NAME>
   </NAME>
   <ADDRESS>
      <STREET_INFO>103 Eastern Avenue</STREET_INFO>
      <CITY>Pleasantville</CITY>
      <STATE>Indiana</STATE>
      <ZIP>30113</ZIP>
   </ADDRESS>
   <PHONE>555-5555</PHONE>
</CONTACT>
```

This is quite a simple XML document, that's fairly simple to understand. This is information pertaining to a contact. Three main pieces of information are shown for this contact: their name, address, and phone number. Before you arrive at the data itself, however, you'll notice the line at the very beginning of the document: `<?xml version="1.0"?>`. This is called the **prolog,** and we'll be covering it in more detail in the next chapter. As a means of introduction, though, you should just be aware that it is not a compulsory requirement, but it is a good idea to include it. This is because it instructs the parser as to what it is parsing, in this case, XML version 1.0. Notice also, that this directive is surrounded by special **processing instruction** tags `<?...?>`. These tags surround all instructions for the parser itself.

The Document Element

The `<CONTACT>` element serves as our document's root element or **document element**. Every XML document must have a document element. All other elements reside within the document element and are referred to as child nodes or child elements. Any child node can have children of its own.

As long as each set of child nodes is properly nested within its parent, you could theoretically nest as many levels deep as you desire. But how practical would a document be that holds 20 levels of nesting merely to describe simple contact information?

The XML Processor

This is where the XML processor comes into play. In simple terms, an XML processor, often referred to as a parser as you'll already know, does just that – it processes or parses the document. I probably don't have to point out that only well-formed XML documents will parse correctly. If you do not include a reference to a DTD or Schema, or your particular parser does not validate, well-formedness is the only criteria. Microsoft's Internet Explorer 5.0 has a native XML processor, although technically speaking, it is not a "built-in processor", because it is simply shipped with Internet Explorer. This parser lives in the file `msxml.dll`, which is why "built-in" is not correct. IE's parser does not validate your XML. Other browsers, such as Netscape Navigator 4.x and below, require you to provide your own XML parser. There are many available, such as the one from IBM.

The Microsoft XML processor is a COM component, and can be used by other applications, including Active Server Pages, which is obviously our primary concern in this book. Later on, we'll use this processor to parse XML documents on the server, but first we need to see how the client, or the Web browser, handles XML documents.

Internet Explorer 5.0 and XML

Microsoft Internet Explorer 5.0 has built-in support for XML, meaning that you can pass well-formed and valid XML documents directly to the browser.

When Internet Explorer 5.0 encounters a document with the `.xml` file name extension, it automatically attempts to parse the document. Let's take a look at how IE5 handles our earlier sample XML document. If you want, you can create the same document using Notepad. Type in the code exactly as it appears above, and then remember to save it with the `.xml` file extension rather than as a text file. You should also note that IE5 does not validate documents unless instructed to do so through code or script. We'll talk more about what it means to validate a document later.

If you then view the document in the browser, you'll see that IE5 displays it in very much the same way as we wrote it.

Chapter 1:

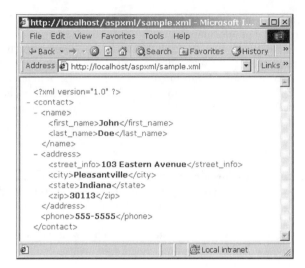

Notice the little dashes before each parent element. These dashes indicate a collapsible node. IE5 goes to the trouble of generating some dynamic HTML to give you a potentially more manageable display. In fact IE5 has a default XSL stylesheet that it applies as a default. We will look at this in more depth in a later chapter. If you selectively collapse a few of the nodes, you'll see how you can reduce the amount of space required to display the document:

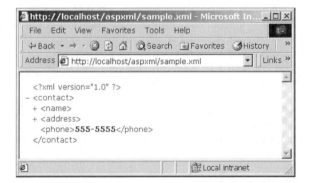

In this capacity, IE5's native support for XML is more of a convenience than a necessity. IE5 just provides a quick way to view your XML files within a browser. Since the whole point of XML is to remove the content from the display, it would be incredibly difficult to make display assumptions about your XML file. Therefore, the more useful display options are left to you. Again, we will be covering this in greater detail in the later chapter on XSL.

Parents, Children, Grand Children, and so on...

Generally speaking, child nodes help describe their parents, and you can use as many child nodes as necessary to describe a parent node. But be careful not to get too complicated. A good XML document should be easy to understand in its structure, regardless of how long it may be.

Notice that the <PHONE></PHONE> element doesn't contain any children, just data. This is perfectly acceptable; in fact, you may have the need for an XML document with only one tier of child nodes or elements. Elements that just contain data, or a value, are called leaf nodes. Just as the branch of a tree terminates with a leaf.

Watch what happens when we alter our document slightly with the following addition:

```
<?xml version="1.0"?>
<CONTACT>
    <TYPE>Personal
    <NAME>
        <FIRST_NAME>John</FIRST_NAME>
        <LAST_NAME>Doe</LAST_NAME>
    </NAME>
    <ADDRESS>
        <STREET_INFO>103 Eastern Avenue</STREET_INFO>
        <CITY>Pleasantville</CITY>
        <STATE>Indiana</STATE>
        <ZIP>30113</ZIP>
    </ADDRESS>
    <PHONE>555-5555</PHONE>
</CONTACT>
```

IE5 has a bit of a think, and eventually gives you the following message:

We are politely informed that we have just broken the cardinal rule of XML: close all tags! The browser is telling us that it talked to the XML processor and learned that `</CONTACT>` isn't an appropriate closing tag for `<TYPE>`. This can be corrected in two ways, depending how we want to structure the information: I could have closed the `<TYPE>` tag immediately after its value, `<TYPE>Personal</TYPE>`, or I could have inserted a closing `</TYPE>` tag immediately before the closing `</CONTACT>` tag. The first solution makes TYPE a leaf node, while the second turns the NAME, ADDRESS, and PHONE elements into children of the TYPE element.

Anatomy of an Error

The XML processor climbs down the structure of a document one element at a time. In our example, it started with the document element `<CONTACT>` and checked it for potential children where it found the opening `<TYPE>` tag. It checked `<TYPE>` for potential child elements, and found the opening `<NAME>` tag. It then checked it for potential child elements, finding both `<FIRST_NAME>John</FIRST_NAME>` and `<LAST_NAME>Doe</LAST_NAME>`. Since these both had matching closing tags and no child elements, it simply displayed the tags and data then moved on. The parser processed the `<ADDRESS>` tag with its children `<STREET_INFO>...</STREET_INFO>`, `<CITY>...</CITY>`, `<STATE>...</STATE>`, and `<ZIP>...</ZIP>` the same way. It then found the `<PHONE>...</PHONE>` tag with its data and processed it.

Here's were the problem occurred. The XML processor thinks it is still within the <TYPE> element, which means it's looking for either text data, more child elements or a closing </TYPE> tag. When it encounters a closing </CONTACT> tag instead, the processor throws an error.

In general, the XML processor follows this very simple procedure on all documents it handles, as well as doing some other things along the way, most of which we'll learn about in later chapters. But one of those additional duties that we'll discuss now concern the handling of attributes. You've seen them in HTML, and because of the similarities in the look of HTML and XML, I might as well put it on the table now. Any XML node or element can take on custom attributes, as long as you set them off in quotes. And as we mentioned earlier, unlike HTML, the values associated with attributes of XML elements must be contained within quotes or, you guessed it, an error will be generated.

If we alter our earlier XML example by making TYPE an attribute of the NAME element, but omit the quotes around the attribute value:

```
<?xml version="1.0"?>
<CONTACT>
   <NAME TYPE=Personal>
      ...
</CONTACT>
```

You'll see that an error like this is generated:

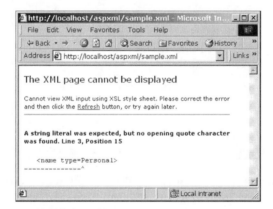

Incorporating Multiple Records

Let's go back to our <TYPE> element we had implemented incorrectly in our sample document earlier. Why not incorporate it as an attribute in our contact information? OK, but first we should expand our document structure so that it handles more than just one contact. Alter the code so that it looks like this:

```
<?xml version="1.0"?>
<CONTACT_INFO>
   <CONTACT TYPE="business">
      <NAME>
         <FIRST_NAME>John</FIRST_NAME>
         <LAST_NAME>Doe</LAST_NAME>
      </NAME>
      <ADDRESS>
         <STREET_INFO>103 Eastern Avenue</STREET_INFO>
         <CITY>Pleasantville</CITY>
```

```
            <STATE>Indiana</STATE>
            <ZIP>30113</ZIP>
        </ADDRESS>
        <PHONE>555-5555</PHONE>
    </CONTACT>
    <CONTACT TYPE="personal">
        <NAME>
            <FIRST_NAME>Alice</FIRST_NAME>
            <LAST_NAME>Smith</LAST_NAME>
        </NAME>
        <ADDRESS>
            <STREET_INFO>52B Wilkens Street</STREET_INFO>
            <CITY>Pleasantville</CITY>
            <STATE>Indiana</STATE>
            <ZIP>30113</ZIP>
        </ADDRESS>
        <PHONE>555-6666</PHONE>
    </CONTACT>
</CONTACT_INFO>
```

We've changed our document element to <CONTACT_INFO> and demoted <CONTACT> to the rank of child node. We also added another contact to keep John Doe from getting lonely. Finally, we added a TYPE attribute to each contact element, which could differentiate business contacts from personal contacts if our document were used in a real application.

Our document now takes on a more distinct look when parsed by IE5:

```
<?xml version="1.0" ?>
- <CONTACT_INFO>
  - <CONTACT TYPE="business">
    - <NAME>
        <FIRST_NAME>John</FIRST_NAME>
        <LAST_NAME>Doe</LAST_NAME>
      </NAME>
    - <ADDRESS>
        <STREET_INFO>103 Eastern Avenue</STREET_INFO>
        <CITY>Pleasantville</CITY>
        <STATE>Indiana</STATE>
        <ZIP>30113</ZIP>
      </ADDRESS>
      <PHONE>555-5555</PHONE>
    </CONTACT>
  - <CONTACT TYPE="personal">
    - <NAME>
        <FIRST_NAME>Alice</FIRST_NAME>
        <LAST_NAME>Smith</LAST_NAME>
      </NAME>
    - <ADDRESS>
        <STREET_INFO>52B Wilkens Street</STREET_INFO>
        <CITY>Pleasantville</CITY>
        <STATE>Indiana</STATE>
        <ZIP>30113</ZIP>
      </ADDRESS>
      <PHONE>555-6666</PHONE>
    </CONTACT>
  </CONTACT_INFO>
```

Summary

So why do you need XML? Well, you've just been given your first glimpse into the world of XML and have become acquainted with the fact that XML can describe all sorts of data and be used for varying purposes. While it may be nifty to see how IE5 renders our XML code as we saw in the previous figure, keep in mind that this is just the beginning. The future is pretty bright for XML. As we mentioned earlier in the chapter, the next version of HTML is called XHTML 1.0 and takes on some XML features.

The real power of XML is the way it can be used. In this book, we'll explore different ways to put XML to use with ASP. An alternative data source is just one of many possibilities. Later we will look at how to generate XML from an existing datasource via ADO and serve it through ASP to the client. We'll also explore how we can present XML data in a pleasant format, so that the user can use it directly as information. We will also look how to incorporate XML within your ASP pages through the use of the XML document object model.

We have undertaken a brief review of what a markup language is, and where XML came from. We have talked about the goals of the W3C in developing XML. And, we have started to look at the basic structure of XML documents and the rules governing their creation. XML is still emerging as a technology. As we will see in the following chapters, when combined with ASP, a tremendous amount of power exists for developing applications and exchanging information.

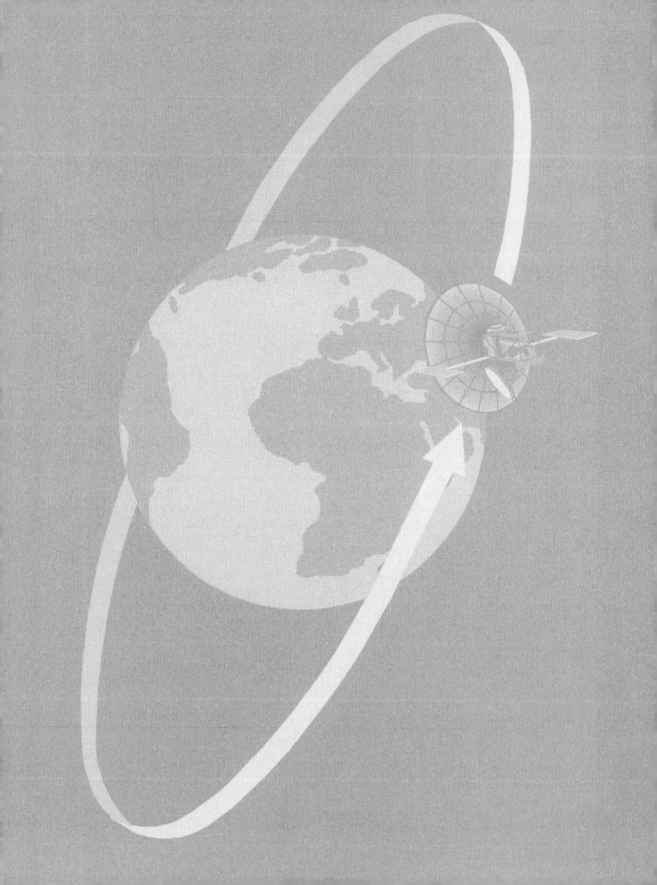

Understanding XML
Structure and Syntax

Now that you've had your first taste of XML in Chapter 1, it's time to discuss it in a little bit more depth. We mentioned very briefly in our introduction to XML, that XML documents must be properly structured and must follow strict syntax rules in order to work correctly. If a document is lacking in either of these areas, it simply won't get parsed; and even if it does, it will produce undesired results. Therefore, in this chapter we will look at the required parts of an XML document. First, we will examine the logical structure, and then we'll turn our attention to the actual physical implementation.

In sharp contrast, HTML is rather flexible in both structure and implementation. As we saw in Chapter 1, HTML was intended to be accessible and easy to learn and is designed to markup documents simply for the purpose of displaying data. There is no inherent way to extend the language in order to give special meaning to selected content. Even if you were to place custom tags around certain words in an HTML document, they would hold no special meaning for the HTML parser, and there is no way to instruct the parser that they should have special meaning.

That's where XML comes into the picture. XML provides a means to tell the parser exactly how data should be treated and what kind of meaning to attach to it. Hence, why XML is considered extensible. The catch is, however, you must adhere to proper syntax and structure to make it work.

There is also a wide selection of parsers. Remember from the previous chapter, that one of the design goals was to have parsers that were easy to write. Microsoft's Internet Explorer has had a parser for XML since version 4.0. IBM offers a parser, and the newest version of Netscape Navigator includes James Clark's non-validating ex-pat parser.

XML Structure

There are two types of structure in every XML document: logical and physical. The logical structure could be described as the framework of the document, while the physical structure is the actual data that fills it. In other words, you could say that when you design an XML document, you are really creating the logical structure, and when you populate it with data you are building its physical structure. I will be focusing on the logical structure, as the physical structure could be just about anything. We will look now at the parts that are required by an XML document.

Logical Structure

Every XML document has three logical parts: the Prolog, the Document Element, and the Epilog. These basically follow the rules of public speaking: first, tell 'em what you're gonna tell 'em; tell 'em; then tell 'em what you told 'em. The prolog and the epilog are optional. The prolog is used to instruct the parser how to interpret the Document Element. The epilog's purpose is unclear. Since there is no *end-of-document* tag in XML, most parsers use the closing tag of the document element. Therefore, it is unlikely that the epilog will even be interpreted correctly. Any instructions in the epilog could pertain to the preceding data, or to data that may follow. The basic structure looks like:

```
    <?xml version="1.0"?>
<!--The above line is the prolog -->

<!--The lines below are contained within the Document Element: CONTACT_INFO -->
<CONTACT_INFO>
    <CONTACT TYPE="business">
        <NAME>
            <FIRST_NAME>John</FIRST_NAME>
            <LAST_NAME>Doe</LAST_NAME>
        </NAME>
        <ADDRESS>
            <STREET_INFO>103 Eastern Avenue</STREET_INFO>
            <CITY>Pleasantville</CITY>
            <STATE>Indiana</STATE>
            <ZIP>30113</ZIP>
        </ADDRESS>
        <PHONE>555-5555</PHONE>
    </CONTACT>
</CONTACT_INFO>
<!--The epilog would go here -->
```

Even in HTML pages, you have the HTML, HEAD, and BODY elements, which all have a certain relation to one another. The HEAD and BODY elements must be contained within the HTML element. The BODY element usually follows the HEAD element. All of the information that you want displayed to the user has to be contained within the BODY element. The exception to this is the TITLE element. This tag is used to display text in the browser's title bar, and although it is standard practice to place it in the HEAD element, both Netscape Navigator and IE can interpret it no matter where it appears in the document.

The Prolog

The prolog is optional. However it gives the XML parser specific information about the document and its contents, and therefore should always be included. The prolog is made up of two parts: The *XML Declaration* and the *Document Type Declaration*. The XML Declaration basically tells the parser that it is dealing with an XML document, while the *Document Type Declaration* provides or points to any special rules that may be needed by the data. We'll be looking at these in greater detail next. Please note that the prolog contains the Document Type *Declaration* and not the Document Type *Definition*. The *declaration* contains a reference to the Document Type *Definition* (DTD) and/or a part of the DTD. I mentioned valid XML documents in the previous chapter; the Document Type Declaration is required in *all* valid XML documents. Additionally, comments can also be included in the prolog.

XML Declaration

This part of the Prolog does exactly what its name implies – it establishes that this is an XML document, and to which version of the XML specification it conforms. I strongly recommend that you include it in all your XML documents. A simple XML Declaration looks like this:

```
<?xml version="1.0"?>
```

This lets the parser know that your XML document complies with version 1.0 of the XML specification. Since things change so quickly when dealing with new technology, this information could mean success or failure when your document is parsed. The version attribute is required when using the XML Declaration.

The XML Declaration has to be the very first line of an XML document, with no preceding whitespace. Notice that it is written using lowercase letters – this is no accident. Always use lowercase letters when writing your XML declarations, since XML is case sensitive, as we mentioned in Chapter 1.

OK, so we have seen a simple XML declaration. So what does it mean and what does it do? Firstly, notice that its tag delimiters are a little different. It uses `<?...?>` instead of the expected `<.../>`. The `<?...?>` tags signify a processing instruction. This lets the parser know that it has to pay attention to this tag, as it is going to tell it something important, and that the parser is going to have to act on it. As I noted earlier, the declaration informs the parser that the XML document complies with the version 1.0 specification, but also has two further, optional, attributes. To expand our example:

```
<?xml version="1.0" encoding="UTF-16" standalone="yes"?>
```

Here we see the two additional attributes: `encoding` and `standalone`. When using all of these attributes, they must appear in this particular order: `version, encoding, standalone`. However, `version` is the only required attribute.

The `encoding` attribute dictates what character encoding the parser should use. This could be any accepted encoding scheme. By default, XML parsers will use "UTF-8" or "UTF-16" (Unicode Transformation Format) depending on the format of the XML Declaration. UTF-8 encoding works well for predominately ASCII data. However, since the Web is international, UTF-8 has a difficult time with foreign character sets (The 8 stands for 8 bit). UTF-16 is much more useful, as unicode characters are fully available in a 16 bit encoding scheme. If you want to be sure of what character encoding scheme is used with your XML documents, you should specify this attribute. Like the version information, the encoding scheme could mean success or failure when the document is parsed by your customers in say Taiwan or France. Also note, that the encoding attribute is the only part of XML that is *not* case sensitive. XML has to work with previously defined character encoding methods which may not have case sensitive names.

The `standalone` attribute lets the parser know whether the XML document can be validated on its own, or requires an external DTD or Schema. When the value is "yes" (yes is the default if the attribute is not included) all entity declaractions are included in the XML document. When "no", an external DTD or Schema is required.

Document Type Declaration

The Document Type Declaration establishes the grammar rules for the document, or it points to an external file where they can be found. The Document Type Declaration is optional, but, if included, it must appear immediately after the XML Declaration and before the Document Element. If it is excluded, the document can be well-formed, but it can never be valid (as there is nothing to validate the document against).

Examine the following Prolog:

```
<?xml version="1.0"?>
<!DOCTYPE Contacts SYSTEM "Contacts.dtd">
```

This Document Type Declaration points to the external file `Contacts.dtd`, which contains a *Document Type Definition.*

Also notice the use of a different tag delimeter: `<! ... >`. This delimeter is used to signify an entity reference. In this instance, the reference is for a DOCTYPE entity. This tells the XML parser that the document element is named `Contacts`, the actual DTD file can be found on the local system (by the `SYSTEM` directive), and is located in a file named: `Contacts.dtd`. DTDs will be discussed in greater detail later in Chapter 4, but for now just be aware that a DTD is nothing more than a means for you to establish very specific rules for the XML document. DTD's are optional, but as stated earlier they are required for valid XML documents. Another method for applying rules to an XML document is with a Schema, which will be explored in later chapters. Schemas are similar to DTDs in that they define the structure and acceptable content for the XML tags. The one big advantage of schemas is that, unlike DTDs, they use XML syntax to describe the document. The W3C should have Schemas finalized by the time you read this.

The Document Element

All the data in an XML document is contained inside this one element, which is named by the author of the document. Let's take another look at our sample XML document from Chapter 1:

```
<?xml version="1.0"?>
<CONTACT_ INFO>
   <CONTACT TYPE="business">
      <NAME>
         <FIRST_NAME>John</FIRST_NAME>
         <LAST_NAME>Doe</LAST_NAME>
      </NAME>
      <ADDRESS>
         <STREET_INFO>103 Eastern Avenue</STREET_INFO>
         <CITY>Pleasantville</CITY>
         <STATE>Indiana</STATE>
         <ZIP>30113</ZIP>
      </ADDRESS>
      <PHONE>555-5555</PHONE>
   </CONTACT>
   <CONTACT TYPE="personal">
      <NAME>
         <FIRST_NAME>Alice</FIRST_NAME>
         <LAST_NAME>Smith</LAST_NAME>
      </NAME>
      <ADDRESS>
         <STREET_INFO>52B Wilkens Street</STREET_INFO>
         <CITY>Pleasantville</CITY>
         <STATE>Indiana</STATE>
         <ZIP>30113</ZIP>
      </ADDRESS>
      <PHONE>555-6666</PHONE>
   </CONTACT>
</CONTACT_INFO>
```

The Document Element in our sample document is CONTACT_INFO. You *cannot* have more than one Document Element in the same document, but as we said in the earlier chapter, the Document Element can contain as many children as needed. This particular Document Element contains information relating to two different contacts. Each CONTACT element contains several child elements, and some of those children have child elements of their own. You might like to think of the Document Element in a similar way to the <HTML>...</HTML> element. All elements to your web page are contained within the HTML tag, and all elements of your XML documents are contained within your Document Element.

XML Syntax

As you're aware, HTML doesn't require strict adherence to its rules of syntax, but this is not the case with XML. It's rules are few and simple, yet unforgiving. HTML can be really forgiving because it's dealing with layout and formatting, allowing it to make certain assumptions when its rules aren't followed.

A great French philosopher once wrote, "If it isn't exact, it isn't French." The French people have long revered their language as being precise and devoid of ambiguities. In much the same way, the creators of XML insisted upon "exactness" in order to make the specification work.

I guess that leaves HTML in the same company as the English language – loose, full of ambiguities and changing by the minute. You will notice the similarities between XML and HTML, but rest assured these are only skin deep. The recently approved XHTML standard takes the similarity beyond the superficial. It is a HTML implementation in XML. The main difference between XHTML and HTML is the rules are a little stricter than they have been:

❑   Tags are case sensitive.

❑   All tags must be closed.

❑   Attribute values must be enclosed in quotes.

❑   The HEAD tag is required.

All of these rules – except the HEAD tag – apply to XML. For more information about XHTML you can check with the W3C at: http://www.w3c.org/xhtml.

Tags

Writing tags in XML isn't that different from writing them in HTML. We use the less-than and greater-than symbols (<...>) to delimit the tags, and the forward slash (/) is used to indicate closing tags. But, beyond these visual similarities there exits a far-reaching difference in the function of the overall XML specification, which starts with how the tags are used to mark up data.

Naming Conventions

Tag names, or element names, can begin with any acceptable letter, the underscore, or the colon. It is inadvisable to begin tag names with a colon as it might create confusion when reading the document. After the first character, any letter, digit, underscore, hyphen, colon, or period is acceptable. Remember that XML uses Unicode, so any letter means more than just standard ASCII; it means any letter in any language.

You will remember from Chapter 1 that XML is case sensitive. That means that `<NAME>`, `<Name>`, and `<name>` are three separate and unique tags. For this reason I strongly suggest that you create a standard for yourself: Either always use uppercase, or always use lowercase for your tag names. This will make case errors much easier to spot. It also will make your documents more consistent.

Open, Close, and Empty

XML tag pairs contain text, which is the data that they describe. This data must be contained within an opening tag and a closing tag to be accepted by the parser:

```
<NAME>John</NAME>
```

In the above example `<NAME>` is the opening tag and `</NAME>` is the closing tag. As you can see this is the same format for tags in HTML. However, unlike HTML the closing tag is required. The opening and closing tags along with their value make up an element.

There may be times when you want an element without a value (as a place holder, for instance). In this case, you can create an **Empty** tag. An empty tag is an open and close tag combined into one. an empy tag looks like this:

```
<NAME />
```

This empty tag will just hold a place for a name element without it actually having a value.

This form of truncation isn't needed with HTML tags, because the HTML processor doesn't generally interpret meaning from nested elements. In HTML, for example, the following code is acceptable:

```
The dog <B>jumped over the <I>moon.</B></I>
```

Granted, HTML does require a limited amount of proper nesting in several fundamental areas: the general structure of the document, tables and table elements, and form elements. But violating these rules doesn't result in a catastrophic page error, as it would in XML. The page may not render as expected, but it probably won't crash.

Elements

As I have already mentioned, elements are the kernels on the cob of your XML document. We have looked at the document element as the parent of all other elements, and noticed that elements can contain other elements. So what exactly is a child element, and what is nesting?

Child Elements

Every element apart from the document element is a child element. Child elements come in four flavors, or content types: If the child element only contains other child elements, then it is said to have **element content.** If it contains only a value, then it has **character content.** If it contains both elements and values, then it is of **mixed content**. And to wrap things up, it could be **empty**. To get a better understanding of how child elements fit together we need to talk about **nesting**.

Nesting

Nesting is the way the XML document fits its elements into a hierarchical tree. The rules for how this nesting occurs are strictly enforced. Browsers may allow you to get away without properly nesting some of your HTML tags, but XML will not.

Most data that you encounter has some sort of tree-like pattern. Companies have customers, customers have orders, orders have line items. Or since we are talking about trees and nests: Trees have branches, branches have nests, nests have birds, birds have feathers. This can be described in XML with:

```
<tree>
    <branch>
        <nest>
            <bird>
                <feather>...</feather>
                <feather>...</feather>
            </bird>
        </nest>
    </branch>
</tree>
```

What this hierarchy means is that a feather belongs to a bird, not a branch or a nest. Also, a particular feather cannot be on (in) more than one bird. A different bird will have feathers of its own.

Improper Nesting

We said a minute ago that when writing HTML, nesting is only important on certain tags, such as forms or tables. And, even when implementing these tags incorrectly, the browser will still try guessing what you meant, and rendering what it can. When you are dealing strictly with formatting, this is acceptable behavior. However, when trying to interpret *data*, guessing can be disastrous. Let's introduce a nesting error into our bird tree:

```
<tree>
    <branch>
        <nest>
            <bird>
                <feather>...</feather>
                <feather>...
        </nest>
                </feather>
    </branch>
                </bird>
</tree>
```

The first problem we come to is that the second feather is closed after the nest is closed. So, does the feather belong to the bird or the branch? Then the bird tag is closed after the branch. Does the nest have a bird or does the tree? This is a trivial example, but it is not too difficult to understand how this sort of thing can get out of hand. If I am processing orders for customers, it becomes critical that all order information for a particular customer is contained within that customer.

Comments

Comments can appear anywhere in your XML document, except at the very beginning which is reserved for the XML Declaration. XML Comments follow the same format as HTML comments. That is, they are surrounded by `<!--...-->` delimiters. Comments are commonly used to add reminders or other types of information to the document. However, one great feature of comments is their ability to *comment out* parts of the document. This works well when you are developing and testing, as you can effectively shrink the size of your test data. For example:

```
<?xml version="1.0" encoding="UTF-16" standalone="yes"?>
<CONTACT_ INFO>
   <CONTACT TYPE="business">
      <NAME>
         <FIRST_NAME>John</FIRST_NAME>
         <LAST_NAME>Doe</LAST_NAME>
      </NAME>
      <ADDRESS>
         <STREET_INFO>103 Eastern Avenue</STREET_INFO>
         <CITY>Pleasantville</CITY>
         <STATE>Indiana</STATE>
         <ZIP>30113</ZIP>
      </ADDRESS>
      <PHONE>555-5555</PHONE>
   </CONTACT>
<!--get rid of some extraneous records
   <CONTACT TYPE="personal">
      <NAME>
         <FIRST_NAME>Alice</FIRST_NAME>
         <LAST_NAME>Smith</LAST_NAME>
      </NAME>
      <ADDRESS>
         <STREET_INFO>52B Wilkens Street</STREET_INFO>
         <CITY>Pleasantville</CITY>
         <STATE>Indiana</STATE>
         <ZIP>30113</ZIP>
      </ADDRESS>
      <PHONE>555-6666</PHONE>
   </CONTACT>
...
-->
</CONTACT_INFO>
```

Only the first contact element will be used. Remember not to comment out the closing tag for the document element or you will receive an error from the parser.

Attribute

I'm sure you have seen attributes before. They are used to tell us something about an element that its value alone either does not, or cannot tell us, and they allow us to add description to an element, without affecting its value. In fact, you could design your XML documents to use only attributes with no explicit values. When we look at ADO and XML in a following chapter, you will see that the *records* are empty tags with the field values stored in attributes. In the contact list example I have been using, you will notice that the CONTACT Tag has an attribute named TYPE. It is used to describe the type of contact: Personal or Business:

```
<CONTACT TYPE="business">
      <NAME>...</NAME>
```

We could add an attribute to the name tag to indicate how the person should be addressed:

```
<NAME prefix='Dr.'>...</NAME>
```

Notice that the value for the attribute is enclosed within quotation marks. These quotes are required. When creating such string literals you can use either apostrophies ('...') or double quotes ("...") to delimit your string. If you need to have an apostrophy or a double quote appear in the literal, just use the different one to the delimiter. If both have to appear you must escape the one matching the delimiter:

```
"Sting delimited with double quotes"
'String delimited with single quote or apostrophies'
"Can't use single quotes on this string"
'"Cannot use double quotes to delimit here", he said'
'"Rich&apos;s string must escape the apostrophy", he said'
```

You can create attributes to help you describe your tags giving them any name/value pair that you deem appropriate. However, there are two special attributes that are defined by XML version 1.0: `xml:space` and `xml:lang`. We'll turn our attention to these next.

Special Attributes

You can use the special attributes to pass information from your document to the parser. These attributes use XML Namespace syntax.

Namespaces prevent problems of ambiguity and duplication with names. The W3C describe them as "... a collection of names, identified by a URI reference, which are used in XML documents as element types and attribute names." For example, an DTD can be a namespace, and you'll come across them in later chapters as you go on to look at DTDs.

xml:space

This attribute, although well documented and formally specified, breaks the *ownership* rule for attributes. If this attribute is specified in an element tag it applies to all of the children belonging to that element as well. This attribute signals that formatting should be retained in the element's data:

```
<companyName xml:space>
The
    Coding Cat</companyName>
```

This is similar to the `<pre>` tag in HTML. However, there is no absolute rule whether this functionality has to be implemented by the XML application or parser. Which means, it may not work as you intended.

xml:lang

This attribute allows you to specify the language of an element's content. It also applies not only to the element that specifies it, but all of its children as well:

```
<systemPrompt>
    <color xml:lang="en-GB">Choose a colour</color>
    <color xml:lang="en-US">Choose a color</color>
    ...
</systemPrompt>
```

One thing to think about: Although this attribute is specified in the XML recommendation, XML applications are under no obligation to implement its functionality. So again, use with caution.

CDATA

CDATA sections of an XML document get passed through the parser unmodified. This is important when your content may contain characters or other information that would normally be parsed, that is, viewed as markup. You could put examples of your XML in a CDATA section and they would not be interpreted by the parser. When using XSL stylesheets to transform your XML into HTML, any scripting must be in CDATA sections. To create a CDATA section use the syntax:

```
<![CDATA[..your data here…]]>

<SCRIPT>
   <![CDATA[
      function blowup()
      {
         alert("Uh Oh");
      }
   ]]>
</SCRIPT>
```

The above example shows how you might include a function in your XSL stylesheet so it will be sent to the client without modification. We will discuss XSL more in depth in Chapter 8.

Processing Instructions

Processing Instructions, or PIs, are used to direct the XML application or parser. As we saw earlier in our discussion of the prolog, the XML declaration is a processing instruction. All PIs take the format `<?receiver instruction?>`. Look at a simple XML declaration:

```
<?xml version="1.0"?>
```

The receiver is the XML parser, or application, and the instruction identifies this document as being compliant with version 1.0 of the XML specificiation. Another much used processing instruction is including the XSL stylesheet reference:

```
<?xml-stylesheet type="text/xsl" href="contacts.xsl"?>
```

Here we are telling the XML stylesheet parser that the stylesheet is of type, `"text/xsl"` and can be found in the file `contacts.xsl`.

Generally, these are the only two processing instructions that you really need to worry about.

Entities

There are two types of entities in XML: Character references and Entity references.

Character References

Character references are ways of inserting character data that you cannot actually type, such as ©, ®, ™, or ¶. Character references could also represent any of the Unicode characters. To insert a character reference you precede the character code with a number format prefix and follow it by semi-colon. There are two number format prefixes: "&#" for decimal codes, and "&#x" for hexidecimal codes. For example:

Character	Description	Decimal Reference	Hex Reference
«	Left Double Chevron	«	«
£	English Pounds	£	£
¥	Japanese Yen	¥	¥

You can use these character references anywhere in the content of your elements.

Entity References

Entities are a way of encapsulating repetitious static content, such as boiler plate text, or numeric constants. There are five pre-defined entities in XML:

Entity	Description
'	' - an apostrophe
&	& - an ampersand
>	> - greater than sign
<	< - less than sign
"	" - double quote

It is also possible to define your own entities. These must be defined in a DTD, however. This is discussed in detail in Chapter 3.

Well-Formed Documents

When all of your elements conform to the XML-specification, your document is considered well-formed. This means that you have chosen valid names for your element tags, nested them appropriately, properly escaped any special characters in your content, paid attention to your use of case, and used quotes (' or ") to delimit your attribute values. According to the XML-specification, every well-formed document should be parsable. Which means, that no errors should be generated. When the parser finds an exception to the rules governing well-formedness, then a *fatal* must be generated. However, even when your XML is well-formed, it is not necessary *valid*.

Valid XML Documents

If your document does not specify a DTD or Schema, then it is considered to be standalone, and well-formed is all it can ever hope to be. If you do specify a DTD or Schema, then your XML document can be valid (or not!) as well. As I mentioned earlier in the section about the prolog, the DTD or Schema specifies the structure of your XML document. It also can specify what type of data each element can contain. This will be covered in more depth in Chapter 3 for DTDs, and Chapter 4 for Schemas.

Summary

We have looked at the basic syntax and structure of XML documents. There are three parts to every XML document: prolog, document element, epilog. The epilog is completely optional, and should probably be avoided. You should have a good understanding of the naming conventions used for element tags, and know that all well-formed XML documents are properly nested.

You should now have a good-enough grasp of the basic XML syntax to move forward into the other areas such as DTDs, Schemas, and XSL. Then we can move on and show how you can gain tremendous functionality out of your ASP web applications by using XML for your data.

3

Validating XML with the DTD

Until now, we've only been dealing with well-formed XML documents, which means that our sole concern has been to ensure that the XML document follows the syntactical rules of XML. We've seen in earlier chapters how a document will fail the test if, for example, a closing tag is missing. And, as discussed, we know that a document that conforms to XML syntax is said to be **well-formed**. But, although the XML document is well-formed, it isn't necessarily a **valid** document. We have already come across the term **valid**, although very briefly, in the introductory chapter to this book. So in this chapter, we'll look at how we **validate** an XML document using the Document Type Definition or DTD.

So first, what is a DTD and why do we need to have documents that are well-formed and valid? Well, consider that we create our own XML elements, supply them with whatever meaning we like, and order them without having to follow a universally prescribed structure. Establishing our own pre-defined structure for an XML document means that we can ensure the data will display correctly in a browser, or will meet the requirements of the application that is going to work with the data, for example. The parser or application processing the data can compare the XML document against its defined structure, and check that it conforms. That pre-defined structure is known as the DTD, and an XML document that adheres to its DTD is a valid document.

A DTD is built as a special collection of markup declarations, which can take the form of either an internal subset (in the text of the XML) or an external entity, (or both). These markup declarations are special characters, which define the structure of the XML document by, simply speaking, specifying which elements are required or optional and also the order in which they should be nested. It is these markup declarations that we will be examining in this chapter.

Introducing the DTD

Just to get us going on the DTD path, let's take a look at two simple examples. In the first example, we use an internal DTD to describe the document:

```
<?xml version="1.0"?>
<!DOCTYPE greeting [
    <!ELEMENT greeting (#PCDATA) >
]>

<greeting> Hello World! </greeting>
```

By a quick inspection of the above code, it is possible to deduce that the DTD (the second through fourth lines) is defining an element called 'greeting'. On the last line (the XML data itself), sure enough, we find the famous greeting.

An external subset would be identified using the following format:

```
<?xml version="1.0"?>
<!DOCTYPE greeting SYSTEM "hello.dtd">

<greeting> Hello World! </greeting>
```

We will be seeing exactly what will need to be in the "hello.dtd" file very shortly. We will also discuss the order of precedence if both subsets are present. But first, let's underline the crux of the matter as far as DTDs are concerned. As a defining rule:

> **A document that conforms to its DTD specifications is referred to as valid.**

Suppose a group of newspaper publishers wanted to agree on an XML standard, which would enable them to share stories with one another. Consider the problems they may encounter; If one newspaper used the STORY tag to describe the document element, while another used the ARTICLE tag, the lack of agreement would cause a serious problem. Since the first user would not be able to understand the data of the second user, without some means of recognizing that <STORY> and <ARTICLE> are equivalent, it would be a futile exercise. Both newspapers would have to use the same set of tags for the system to work. Similarly, even if all of the tags were the same, but ordered slightly differently, the unifying goal behind the system would fail. Clearly, everyone has to use the same structural rules (the same tags, with the same meaning, in the same order) for it to be called beneficial.

While the ideas behind DTD validation are rather simple, the actual writing of the DTD can be a little daunting. It uses a very different syntax from most things that we've encountered and, because it needs to be a unifying factor among diverse interests, interpretation of the rules is rather strict.

At the time of writing this, the DTD is the only W3C-approved method for establishing structural organization in an XML document. As always, more information about the current release of any official specification can be found at www.w3.org. Another proposal, called Schemas, will be discussed in the next chapter.

So when do we produce our DTD? There are two practical ways to reach the completed DTD stage:

❑   Write the DTD before the XML is developed, by which it becomes useful as the specification for the XML.

❑   Write the DTD after the XML is developed, by which it becomes part of the XML documentation.

What often happens, unfortunately, is that both the DTD and the test XML are developed simultaneously, so that one or both have to be modified at a later time in order for the XML document to be valid.

Defining a DTD

As we found out in Chapter1, there are two phrases used in conjunction in XML with the initials DTD. The first is the **Document Type Declaration** (we'll call this one the DOCTYPE), and the second is the **Document Type Definition** (the real DTD). Only one of them is actually referred to as a DTD, and that's the Document Type Definition which we're concerned with in this chapter.

Remembering the basic logical structure of the XML document, we first have the prolog and then the document element (the data of the XML document). As we've seen before, it is in the prolog that we find the DOCTYPE declaration:

```
<?xml version="1.0"?>
<!DOCTYPE Presidents SYSTEM "Prez.dtd">
```

These statements identify the document as XML, and declare that it is of the 'Presidents' class. We will use this as the root-element name in the XML document. The SYSTEM keyword specifies that the DTD is for the private use of this document. In addition the processor knows to look at the Prez.dtd file for the specification rules to which the XML data must comply.

DOCTYPE can also use the PUBLIC keyword. This takes the form:

```
<!DOCTYPE root-element PUBLIC "name" "URI of DTD">
```

This form is used where the DTD has been made public (though this hasn't become very prevalent thus far). The XML will try to use the DTD by name, if it can. If the attempt fails, the XML will use the URI.

A completed PUBLIC declaration might look something like:

```
<!DOCTYPE AutoParts PUBLIC "-//AutoCo//DTD//EN"
          "http://xmlserver.AutoCo.com/dtd/AutoParts.dtd">
```

And as we mentioned earlier, we specify the DTD in two ways – an internal DTD subset or an external DTD subset. By 'subset', we mean that either or both may be present in the XML document, and that each plays a part in defining the contained XML data. The external DTD is usually used in the 'common DTD' scenario, where diverse systems need to share XML data. It would also be used in most production class applications, where segregating concepts and components assist in documentation and system maintenance. The internal DTD is most frequently found in smaller systems and in the testing and development phase. There is a real convenience to having a (simple) DTD in the XML document.

> If an internal and external DTD are used, the internal DTD is processed first and its
> information takes precedence over the external DTD.

The Basic Structure

The basic structure of the DTD is a top-down definition of the various elements that we need to find in
the XML document. This means that the DTD is processed from top to bottom, and that a parent
element (one that contains children) must be defined before any child elements. Each element appears
in an element declaration in the following format:

```
<!ELEMENT elementname rule >
```

We'll discuss the details of the declaration in the next section.

A Simple DTD

Lets begin by looking at a simple XML document and its accompanying DTD:

```
<?xml version="1.0"?>
<!DOCTYPE ARTICLE SYSTEM "example1.dtd">

<ARTICLE>
  <HEADLINE>
    <MAIN_HEAD>Main headline goes here</MAIN_HEAD>
    <SUB_HEAD>A subheadline goes here</SUB_HEAD>
  </HEADLINE>
  <BYLINE>
    <AUTHOR>John Doe</AUTHOR>
    <TITLE>Reporter</TITLE>
  </BYLINE>
  <STORY_DATE>February 19, 2000</STORY_DATE>
  <BODY>
    Content of story goes here...
  </BODY>
</ARTICLE>
```

First we'll compare these two files. It is (I hope) easy to see the similarities, and how the DTD is being
used to define the XML document. Just by looking at the element names below, which are indented for
clarity only, we can see how the DTD mirrors the XML.

We need to call this file example1.dtd, so that it can be found using the reference in the DOCTYPE:

```
<!ELEMENT ARTICLE (HEADLINE, BYLINE, STORY_DATE, BODY)>
  <!ELEMENT HEADLINE (MAIN_HEAD, SUB_HEAD)>
    <!ELEMENT MAIN_HEAD (#PCDATA)>
    <!ELEMENT SUB_HEAD (#PCDATA)>
  <!ELEMENT BYLINE (AUTHOR, TITLE)>
    <!ELEMENT AUTHOR (#PCDATA)>
    <!ELEMENT TITLE (#PCDATA)>
  <!ELEMENT STORY_DATE (#PCDATA)>
  <!ELEMENT BODY (#PCDATA)>
```

Our document element, ARTICLE, contains four child elements: HEADLINE, BYLINE, STORY_DATE and BODY, defined as a comma-separated list within parentheses:

```
<!ELEMENT ARTICLE (HEADLINE, BYLINE, STORY_DATE, BODY)>
```

Some of these elements have children of their own too, such as the HEADLINE element:

```
<!ELEMENT HEADLINE (MAIN_HEAD, SUB_HEAD)>
```

The elements that contain XML data are declared slightly differently:

```
<!ELEMENT MAIN_HEAD (#PCDATA)>
```

The #PCDATA term in parentheses does not refer to a child element at all, but to parsed character data, which is XML data that is processed by the XML parser, in contrast to CDATA which is not. We will discuss #PCDATA & CDATA more fully later on.

The Element Declarations

As we saw above, this is the general form of an element declaration:

```
<!ELEMENT elementname rule >
```

Every element that appears in a valid XML document will need to be first defined in the DTD. The rules for forming a 'proper' name are simple:

- ❏ Element names must start with a letter or underscore.

- ❏ They must not start with the string xml in upper or lower case, or any combination of cases.

- ❏ It can have any number of letters, numbers, underscores, dashes or periods. While the use of periods is legal, I find that it can become confusing in the actual code.

- ❏ Colons are reserved for experimentation with namespaces, which were not included in the original specification. Consequently, colons are 'legal characters', but should not be used in element names.

The ANY Rule

The first and most basic element declaration is the all-purpose ANY rule. An element that is defined using this rule can contain anything (or nothing) allowed by the DTD, in any order:

```
<!ELEMENT elementname ANY>
```

The ANY rule will allow other tags or general character data (or both) to be contained in the element.

The declaration of:

```
<!ELEMENT BitBucket ANY>
```

could result in the following XML:

```
<BitBucket> garbage </BitBucket>
```

or:

```
<BitBucket>
    <SmallBucket>
         trash
    </SmallBucket>
</BitBucket>
```

The EMPTY Rule

The EMPTY declaration specifies XML elements that must not contain any data.

```
<!ELEMENT elementname EMPTY>
```

At a first glance, having an element that cannot contain any data seems rather useless, but elements that are declared empty are still able to contain information in the form of attributes. We also encounter elements with no attributes that are useful, for example, in the HTML tag <BR>. We often use this tag without attributes (though, in the later releases of HTML attributes are defined). An example of a tag with no content but having attributes would be <HR>. We can use this element as it is, or modify it with a size attribute:

```
<HR size= "3" />
```

The Mixed Declaration

The mixed declaration contains a list of options enclosed by parentheses and separated by the pipe (|) operator. This provides for a set of alternative rules for the element:

```
<!ELEMENT elementname (ElementA | #PCDATA)>
```

A mixed declaration would be used when one of the options has child elements, but the other options do not.

```
<!ELEMENT Parent (Child | #PCDATA)>
<!ELEMENT Child  (ChildA, ChildB) >
<!ELEMENT ChildA (#PCDATA) >
<!ELEMENT ChildB (#PCDATA) >
```

In this example, the parent may have the information directly or have a child element, Child. That element would contain the two elements ChildA and ChildB.

The Multiple Declaration

As we've seen, the multiple element declaration allows for the nesting of elements. The order is important, and you must use commas between the listed elements. Because the DTD is a top-down definition, it is not necessary to declare an element prior to including it in the element list:

```
<!ELEMENT elementname (ElementA, ElementB)>
```

In this example both ElementA and ElementB are required.

The #PCDATA Rule

We have seen the expression #PCDATA several times. Just what is this? PCDATA stands for **parsed character data** and is one of the most common rules that we will encounter. Parsed characters are markedup character data – it contains markup tags. The parsing (reading) program will interpret these tags. We use the keyword CDATA to simply identify character data. This is text that can include characters reserved for markup (e.g. '<') but, because it is not parsed, it need not conform to the well-formed rules.

In the following example the `<test> show this </test>` will be treated as just another string sequence, and not as XML to be parsed.

```
<SampleDoc>
 <Data1> the data1 tag will be parsed </Data1>
 <Data2>
     <![CDATA[<test> show this </test>]]>
 </Data2>

</SampleDoc>
```

As a test, copy the above as a simple XML document and view it with IE 5.0. Then remove the `<![CDATA [ ` sequence (don't forget the `]]>` at the end) and view the document. Try it both ways after changing the `'/test'` to `'/TEST'`.

Grouping, Occurrence and Element Symbols

When creating the rules for the element declarations, there are several symbols or operators that are used. Some of these we've just seen and are included here for completeness.

The occurrence symbols are used in multiple declarations to further define the structure of the XML.

Symbol	Description	Example
Parentheses	Encloses a sequence or set of alternatives	(ElementA | #PCDATA)
Comma	Separates elements in sequence – order critical	(ElementA, ElementB)
Pipe	Separates elements in a set of alternatives	(ElementA | #PCDATA)
Question mark	Must appear never or once (0, 1)	ElementA?
Asterisk	Must appear never or many times (0, 1, 2, 3, ...)	ElementA*
Plus	Must appear one or more times (1, 2, 3, ...)	ElementA+
(None)	Must appear once only (1)	ElementA

We'll use the familiar email message as an example of the occurrence symbols:

```
<!ELEMENT EMAIL (To+, From, CC*, Subject?, Body?)>
```

43

This declares that an `EMAIL` element has:

❏ A required `To` element and that we can optionally send to more than one person

❏ A required `From` element (one only)

❏ An optional `CC` element, but it can have one or more addresses

❏ An optional `Subject` line

❏ An optional `Body` section

The Attribute Declarations

Anyone who works with HTML becomes familiar with adding attributes to tag elements. Most of the directives in a page today are attribute values: the `HREF` of the anchor (`A`) tag containing the URL, the `SIZE` of the `FONT`, or anything contained in the `SPAN` or `DIV` tags (e.g. ID, CLASS, etc) are attributes. Attributes contain information that is not a part of the XML content between the tags. For instance, the `<P>...</P>` delimits one paragraph of text. However, the attribute, such as the `ALIGN` in `<P ALIGN="CENTER">`, defines how the paragraph is displayed.

The syntax for the attribute definitions is:

```
<!ATTLIST targetElement AttrName attrType defaults >
```

While attributes can appear anywhere in the DTD, it would probably be a good idea to keep them in the same area as the element that they are targeting. This should be done for ease of readability and maintainability.

Since this chapter is designed as a brief overview, we wont be touching upon all attributes appearing in this list. Once you have read this introductory chapter to the DTD you may wish to consult Professional XML published by Wrox Press, ISBN 1861003-11-0.

Attribute Types

Type	Description
CDATA	Only character data can be used, which will be ignored by the XML parser
ENTITY	Value must refer to external entity declared in the DTD
ENTITIES	Same as above but multiple values separated by white space
ID	Unique element identifier
IDREF	Value of unique ID type attribute
IDREFS	Same as above but multiple values separated by white space
NMTOKEN	A valid XML token name (see rules for element naming)
NMTOKENS	Same as above but multiple values separated by white space
NOTATION	Value must refer to notation declaration in the DTD
Enumerated	Attribute value must match one of the included values

We can set the default values of the declaration by using one of the following four values:

Defaults

Type	Description
#REQUIRED	The value must be specified
#IMPLIED	The attribute value is optional
#FIXED value	The attribute must have the supplied value – it may not be changed by the user
Default	The supplied value is the default

Lets look again at the email ELEMENT that we've seen above:

```
<!ELEMENT EMAIL (To+, From, CC*, Subject?, Body?)>
```

We realize that something is missing, so BCC is added to the DTD, but it needs additional characteristics. It requires an attribute of 'hidden' set to 'TRUE' so that the contents of the element are not exposed to the email recipient. Additionally, users should not be able to change that attribute to 'false' thus exposing the BCC list:

```
<!ELEMENT EMAIL (To+, From, CC*, BCC*, Subject?, Body?)>
...
<!ELEMENT BCC (#PCDATA)>
<!ATTLIST BCC Hidden CDATA #FIXED "TRUE">
...
```

Here are some examples of other attributes:

Defaults:
```
<!ATTLIST Address country CDATA "US">
<!ATTLIST BoilingPoint scale CDATA 'C'>
...
```

Enumeration:
```
<!ATTLIST Employee gender (male | female) #REQUIRED>
<!ATTLIST Employee marital (single | married | divorced | widowed ) #REQUIRED>
...
```

There are also a few points to remember when dealing with attributes:

❑ If an attribute is defined more than once, only the first definition is used.

❑ Since attribute data is not parsed, we use the CDATA (character data) and not the PCDATA type that we've use previously.

❑ Remember that attributes are not ordered. Unlike XML elements, there is no concept of "a must be before b" in the list.

The ENTITY Declarations

The entity declarations in the DTD enable the author to create substitution entries for included text. Perhaps it helps to think of them as containers for content – similar to substitution macros. While there are several pre-defined entities in XML, the ENTITY declaration enables us to define as many additional entities as we need. This is the general form of the definition:

```
<!ENTITY entityname entitydefinition>
```

The use of the entity is delimited by the ampersand (&) and the semi-colon (;). The five pre-defined entities are:

Entity	Character
&	&
<	<
>	>
"	"
'	'

General or Internal Entities

The general entity is one that substitutes a name with a pre-defined string of replacement characters. It takes the form:

```
<!ENTITY name replacementCharacters>
```

These are simple common substitution entries similar to the pre-defined entitles listed above. A commonly added entity is the copyright symbol – ©:

```
<!ENTITY copyright "&#xA9">
```

This assigns the hexadecimal 0xA9 (Unicode 169, print/display as a circle-C) to the 'copyright' expression.

This entity would be used in the XML:

```
<copyrightNotice>
   &copyright; 2000 by WROX, Inc.
</copyrightNotice>
```

Entity replacement characters may include defined entities, but it is important not to create circular references while doing so. Take the following example:

```
<!ENTITY itemA "I can include another entity like this: &itemB; !" >
```

This is valid if the 'itemB' below contains just the string 'itemA.

```
<!ENTITY itemB "to include itemA here, is ok" >
```

But in this next example the itemA is a reference to the entity and is therefore invalid:

```
<!ENTITY itemB "to include &itemA; here, is ok" >
```

External Entities

External entities are a very powerful tool in the XML world. It is possible to dynamically import data from an offsite URI into the XML document. Two common examples of this are the importing of frequently changing data (such as the weather report) from a remote site or retrieving a picture or a shared binary file for local use.

For the first example we might code something like the following into the DTD:

```
<!ENTITY weatherA  SYSTEM "http://myserver1/London/current.xml">
<!ENTITY weatherB SYSTEM "http://myserver2/NewYork/current.xml">
```

And this is how it is used in the XML document:

```
<WeatherReport>
  <Title> The Current Weather Report </Title>
  &weatherA;
  &weatherB;
</WeatherReport>
```

The data that is in each 'current.xml' is processed by the XML parser. If the XML document contains very dynamic data from diverse sources, it would be possible to carry this concept to some rather complex extremes. Since data is being retrieved from external sources, be aware of bandwidth and other scalability issues when using these techniques.

Some data (binary images, for example) should not be processed by the parser. If we would like to prevent this parsing from taking place, we have to specify the NDATA (notation data) keyword:

```
<!ENTITY Image1 SYSTEM "MapOfLondon.gif" NDATA GIF>
<!ENTITY Image2 SYSTEM "MapOfNewYork.gif" NDATA GIF>
```

This entity, Image1, will be used in the XML in an unparsed state, typically as a value of the attribute of an element:

```
<WeatherReport>
  <Title> The Current Weather Report </Title>
  <map src="Image1;"/>
  &weatherA;
  <map src="Image2"/>
  &weatherB;
</WeatherReport>
```

Parameter Entities

Parameter entities are very similar to the general entities that we've just looked at and work in essentially the same way. Their purpose is, however, restricted to the DTD only. We would use these in the case of repetitive text in the DTD. The entities must be declared before they are used. Syntactically they look like:

```
<!ENTITY % name "replacementCharacters">
```

Please note that a space is on either side of the % in the declaration:

```
<!ENTITY % ng "NDATA GIF">
```

But, when using the parameter entities, a space does not follow the %:

```
<!ENTITY Image1 SYSTEM "Image1.gif" %ng;>
```

Also remember that circular references are not resolvable, and are invalid.

Other DTD Keywords

In addition to the elements, entities and attributes described above there are several DTD keywords that don't fall into these categories. We will cover them here.

IGNORE and INCLUDE

There are two directives that can be used to turn blocks of DTD content on or off. This can be very useful especially when developing and testing the DTD structures. The basic syntax of these directives is:

```
<![ IGNORE [
  DTD block not processed
]]>
```

The complement of the IGNORE directive is the INCLUDE directive:

```
<![ INCLUDE [
  DTD block processed
]]>
```

The DTD block within the directive must be a complete declaration or multiple declarations.

For example, consider this code:

```
<!ENTITY % doTest "INCLUDE">
...

<![ %doTest; [
  <!ELEMENT BYLINE (AUTHOR, TITLE)>
    <!ELEMENT AUTHOR (#PCDATA)>
    <!ELEMENT TITLE (#PCDATA)>
]]>
...
```

You can see that by changing only the value of the doTest parameter entity to IGNORE, we can control the inclusion of multiple blocks of DTD from a single location:

```
<!ENTITY % doTest "IGNORE">
```

Using these in the development process is much easier than commenting out lines of DTD.

Comments

Commenting a DTD is similar to using comments in HTML:

```
<!-- This is a comment -->
```

As developers, we know how much we enjoy this part of our task. As the comment tags cannot be nested, many developers do not add comments within blocks of code because if they did, the whole block cannot be temporarily commented out. Of course, by the time the DTD is designed, it's usually too late to go back and add all these comments.

The obvious solution to all this is to use the comments in the DTD structures and use the INCLUDE and IGNORE directives, which we just met, to comment out blocks of code.

We cannot easily comment out the BYLINE element because of the internal usage notes. We will ask the processor to include or ignore the block of code by changing the value of 'doTest':

```
<!ENTITY % doTest "INCLUDE">
...

<![ %doTest; [
  <!ELEMENT BYLINE (AUTHOR, TITLE)>
    <!-- Last name, First Name -->
    <!ELEMENT AUTHOR (#PCDATA)>
    <!-- Use corporate titles only -->
    <!ELEMENT TITLE (#PCDATA)>
]]>
...
```

Combining Internal and External DTDs

As we've discussed, the DTD may comprise both an internal subset as well as an external subset. A common DTD that is shared is the starting point for the rules that the XML document must follow. Each XML document may, optionally, modify those rules as necessary.

For Object Oriented Programmers: The common DTD that is shared by many XML documents is viewed as the base class DTD. The XML document inherits the rules of the base class, but it can also subclass the document and modify the behavior as necessary.

A common use of combining DTD subsets is to customize some XML entities:

```
<?xml version="1.0"?>
<!DOCTYPE newpaper SYSTEM "generic.dtd"[
  <!ENTITY company "WROX Press, Inc.">
]>
<newspaper>
  <papername> &company; </papername>
  ...
</newspaper>
```

The order of processing is as follows:

❏ The internal definition of the "Wrox Press, Inc" entity

❏ The contents of the `generic.dtd` file

Since the internal definition is processed first, it takes precedence, and the value of &company; in the XML document is the local name.

Client-Side Validation

Since the computer is the ultimate arbiter of our code, the best way to test for validation is to let a process do it. A downside of IE5 is that it does not check for the validity of an XML document, only if it is well–formed. A DTD can be checked either by script on the client, or on the server.

Microsoft has written and published an excellent tool for client-side verification. It accepts either the URL of the XML, or you can paste the XML into a text box. When a document is verified, a very nice tree view of the document is available on the page. If there are errors in the document, the code identifies the error and where it occurred. There are several interesting techniques on this page that may be of interest to ASP developers as well. At the time of writing this, this code can be found at http://msdn.microsoft.com/downloads/samples/Internet/xml/xml_validator/validate.htm under the title 'XML Validator'.

Server-Side Validation

This short piece of code has become a very useful tool in testing the validity of the XML documents that are being developed:

```
<% Language = VBScript %>
<HTML>
<HEAD>
  <TITLE> Verifire - an XML Verify utility</TITLE>
</HEAD>
<BODY>
```

This form will accept a local XML file for testing:

I'll leave it up to the reader to modify it to accept URLs. The VALUE= attribute in the INPUT tag allows for persistence of the submitted filename.

```
<FORM ACTION="verifire.asp" METHOD="POST">
  Enter File to Verify:
  <INPUT TYPE="TEXT" VALUE="<%=Request.Form("TestFile")%>" NAME="TestFile">
    <BR>Display the file (if it is ok?)
  <INPUT TYPE="CHECKBOX" NAME="Show"> <BR>
  <INPUT TYPE="SUBMIT" VALUE="Test This">
</FORM>


<%
If Request.Form("TestFile") <> "" Then
  Dim ObjXML, objRootElement
  Set objXML = Server.CreateObject("Microsoft.XMLDOM")
```

The XMLDOM in the `Server.CreateObject`, above is discussed in Chapter 5, but it essentially gives us access to the file as an XML document.

The XML processor will validate if this is set to `True`:

```
objXML.ValidateOnParse = True
objXML.Load(Server.MapPath(Request.Form("TestFile")))
```

The `.Load` will read the file into our object: `objXML`:

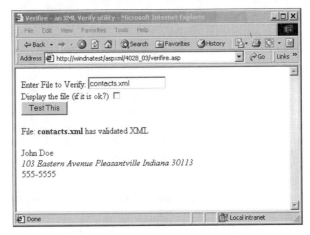

The `ParseError` object returns information about any parse error we may have just encountered, including the error number, line number, character position, and a text description. We will display this information if we receive an error code from the `.Load`:

```
If objXML.ParseError.errorCode <> 0 Then
  Response.Write ("Error: " & objXML.parseError.reason & "<BR>")
  Response.Write ("(code: 0x" _
                        & hex(objXML.parseError.errorCode) & ")<BR>")
  Response.Write ("At Line " & objXML.parseError.line & ", ")
  Response.Write ("Position " & objXML.parseError.linepos _
                        & " of XML document. <P>")
Else
  Response.Write ("File: <B>" & Request.Form("TestFile") _
                        & "</B> has validated XML <P>")

  If Request.Form("Show") = "on" Then
    Set objRootElement = objXML.documentElement
```

```
        Response.Write (objRootElement.xml)
      End If
    End If
End If
%>


</BODY>
</HTML>
```

So if we deliberately enter an XML document which we already know is invalid, we'll see something like the following:

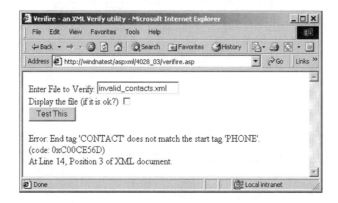

Summary

In this chapter we've looked at the details of the DTD and its component parts. We've seen how it relates to the XML document itself and how it verifies the validity of the XML. We've learned that the DTD can be used either as a design tool before the creation of the XML, or as a documentation of the XML once it is created. We looked at all of the major components of the DTD, and how they work to define and describe the XML document.

We also looked at how we can verify the validity of an XML document and its accompanying DTD with a simple ASP page.

In the next chapter, we'll look at the newer, XML-based method of XML validation – schemas.

4

Validating XML using Schemas

We've seen how the DTD can be used to define and describe the XML document. Recognizing several drawbacks of the DTD, the powers that be, in this case the W3C consortium (www.w3c.org), embarked on a process to accept ideas and propose for recommendation status a new method for "defining the structure, content and semantics of XML documents". Starting in early 1999, and still continuing today, the XML Schema Working Group is working to develop and ultimately recommend an XML Schema definition language.

Take a look at http://www.w3.org/TR/xmlschema-0/ for more information.

It is important to note that because schemas are not yet a recommendation, any information supplied at the time of writing is subject to change. Of course, most, if not all, of the concepts that will be in the final recommendation are in place now, and some of these concepts are even being used by a few software packages (such as XML Authority from Extensibility). While anything that we learn about schemas today will be able, I'm sure, to be used when the W3C releases the recommendation, it is very important to realize that, at present, it is still very much a work in progress. The candidate document (a step before recommendation) is expected in the first half of 2000.

One of the main drawbacks of DTDs is that because they are written in a different 'language' from XML, they require a different parser technology. This creates a burden on the toolmaker, who would need to code two parsers, one for XML and another for the DTD, which reduces the possibility of slim profile software. Additionally, the system developer needs to learn an additional language and its associated syntax just to work with the DTD. XML Schemas are written using standard XML rules, and as a result the learning curve is greatly reduced.

Another of the major DTD drawbacks is its lack of namespace support. As the computing world becomes more XML-centric, and the inter-connectedness of XML information becomes pervasive, the importance of namespace awareness will come to the fore and the DTD will become less usable. Other drawbacks of the DTD are its limited support for inheritance and sub-classing, which, since the advent of object-oriented design, have become critical concepts in the technological arena. The values of these concepts need not be preached here, but their absence when developing a system of DTDs is noticeable.

The last major drawback (that I'll mention) is that in the DTD there is no concept of data types (other than PCDATA and CDATA), that are used to help define the content of particular XML elements.

Ultimately, DTDs and Schemas will have to vie for supremacy. Owing to the limitations of the DTD concepts, the inherent value of being in the market first will probably not help in the long run. XML Schemas will, most likely, be the definitional methodology of the future.

In this chapter we will look at the basics of a schema. We'll examine the structure of the schema and its constituent parts. Please keep in mind that this is not meant to be an exhaustive tutorial on the topic. It will, hopefully, give us enough information so that when we are faced with an XML schema, we'll be able to understand what's going on.

The Components of a Schema

Like the DTD, the schema is used to describe the content and the structure of the XML data document. Similarly, it is the schema that is used to determine the validity of the XML (remember, saying that an XML document is valid implies that it is also well-formed).

When we use schemas, we will always be using a two-document model, the instance document (which is the well-formed XML that we're used to) and the schema document that we will develop here. The use of the term 'instance' is taken from the object-oriented world. The schema describes a class of XML documents, and the 'data document' is an instance of that class.

To help us investigate the schema, we will be using an instance document containing information related to a newspaper article:

```
<?xml version="1.0"?>

<article>
  <headline section="business">
    <MainHead>Main headline goes here</MainHead>
    <SubHead>A subheadline goes here</SubHead>
  </headline>
  <ByLine>
    <Author>John Doe</Author>
    <title>Reporter</title>
  </ByLine>
  <dateline>April 30, 2000</dateline>

  <body>
      Content of story goes here...
  </body>

  <stats>
    <submitted>2000-02-18</submitted>
    <wordCount>1532</wordCount>
    <bureauID>D-54</bureauID>
  </stats>
</article>
```

Looking at the XML document we notice several layers. Elements can contain other elements, and nesting can be several layers deep. Eventually, however, we'll arrive at the real information. If an element contains sub-elements or attributes, they are **complex types** (e.g. <ByLine>), or when an element contains just a number or string, it as a **simple type** (e.g. <DateLine>). A schema designer may also define a simple type using the simpleType declaration. As we've already learned, attributes cannot contain sub elements or other attributes, so they always have simple types.

The above example doesn't (yet) have the requisite link to any schema document; we'll add that later. First let's take a look at the Schema which describes the sample document:

```
<schema targetNamespace="http://www.MyCompany.com/news"
  xmlns:news="http://www.MyCompany.com/news"
  xmlns:xsd ="http://www.w3.org/1999/XMLSchema">

<element name="article" type="news:articleType" />
<element name="dateline" type="xsd:date" />
<element name="body" type="xsd:string" />

<complexType name="articleType">
  <element    name="headline"  type="news:headlineType" />
  <element    name="ByLine"     type="news:ByLineType" />
  <element    ref="dateline"   minOccurs="0" />
  <element    name="body"       type="xsd:string" />
  <element    name="stats"      type="xsd:statsType" />
    <attribute name="section"   type="xsd:string" />
</complexType>

<complexType name="headlineType">
  <element name="MainHead"     type="xsd:string" />
  <element name="SubHead"      type="xsd:string" />
</complexType>

<complexType name="ByLineType">
  <element name="Author"     type="xsd:string" />
  <element name="title"      type="xsd:string" />
</complexType>

<complexType name="statsType">
  <element name="submitted"      type="xsd:date" />
  <element name="wordCount"      type="xsd:decimal" />
  <element name="bureauID"        type="news:BureauIDType" />"
</complexType>

<simpleType name="BureauIDType" base="xsd:string">
  <pattern value="[A-Z]-d{2}" />
</simpleType>

</schema>
```

There are a few things that we should notice on the first view of a schema:

❑   It is a well-formed XML document. You may verify that they are well-formed by using a verifier program like the one we wrote in the last chapter. If you want to use IE 5.0 you can't use the (typical) extension of .xsd, since IE will not send it through its parser. First, rename the schema with an .xml extension, then try opening it with IE 5.0.

❑   We are using the schema namespace – elements in the schema that have the prefix .xsd are idenitfied as belonging to the XML Schema namespace by the decaration:
    xmlns:xsd ="http://www.w3.org/1999/XMLSchema

❑   Elements that are prefixed by news: belong to the vocabulary of the author:
    xmlns:news=http://www.MyCompany.com/news

❑   Elements are declared, then defined.

The xmlns namespace that we've used at the top of this document comes from the W3 XML specifications and *may* become the official XML Schema namespace in due course. Also note that we are using the xsd: prefix. Associating namespaces with common prefixes will help everyone viewing the document to follow what is going on easily. Other common prefixes would be: xmlns:dt for a data-types URI, and xmlns:xsi for the instance URI of the document to be validated.

We can map the datatypes namespace to :dt in order to use the built-in types in your schema definitions:

```
<schema xmlns='http://www.w3.org/1999/XMLSchema'
      xmlns:dt='http://www.w3.org/1999/XMLSchema/datatypes'
   targetNamespace=http://www.MyCompany.com/news >
```

By looking at the schema above, we see that elements, complex types, simple types and attributes are rather important concepts. We will be looking at each of these concepts, starting with the first lines of the document: the namespace.

Using Namespaces

As seen above, when creating a schema document (an XSD) we can give it a target namespace. Our developed schema can then be said to describe the particular namespace. To identify elements and attributes in the schema document we use:

```
xmlns:xsd="http://www.w3.org/1999/XMLSchema"
```

In the instance document we will use the following namespace declaration to identify the schema-related attributes in that document:

```
xmlns:xsi="http://www.w3.org/1999/XMLSchema/instance"
```

The namespace URI alone will not provide for validation mapping to the XSD from the XML instance document. We need to include the schemaLocation directive. Let's put it all together:

The Schema document (trade.xsd) looks like this:

```
<schema targetNamespace="urn:schemas-tradingCompany:trades"
        xmlns:xsd="http://www.w3.org/1999/XMLSchema">
  <!-- schema for <trades> and <accounts> -->
</schema>
```

The XML instance document (trades.xml) looks like this:

```
<tradedata xmlns="http://www.myCompany.com"
           xmlns:trd="urn:schemas-tradingCompany:trades"
           xmlns:xsi="http://www.w3.org/1999/XMLSchema/instance"
           xsi:schemaLocation="urn:schemas-tradingCompany:trades
                        http://www.myCompany.com/trade.xsd">

  <trd:trades />
  <trd:accounts />
</tradedata>
```

Using Multiple Schemas

We can also use the `schemaLocation` directive to `import` or `include` one schema document into another. We would use the `include` when the target namespaces of both the main document and the imported document are the same. If the target namespaces were different we would `import` the XSD instead.

The main schema document (mainSchema.xsd):

```
<schema targetNamespace="http://www.helloWorld.org"
        xmlns="http://www.w3.org/1999/XMLSchema">

  <import namespace="urn:some-other-space:foo"
          schemaLocation="http://www.someOther.com/schemas/foo.xsd" />
  <include schemaLocation="http://www.helloWorld.org/schemas/myTypes.xsd" />

</schema>
```

The included XSD (`myTypes.xsd`) has the same `targetNamespace`:

```
<schema targetNamespace="http://www.helloWorld.org"
        xmlns="http://www.w3.org/1999/XMLSchema">

  <!-- Some descriptions here -->

</schema>
```

The imported XSD (`foo.xsd`) uses a different `targetNamespace`:

```
<schema targetNamespace=""urn:some-other-space:foo"
        xmlns="http://www.w3.org/1999/XMLSchema">

  <!-- Some other descriptions here -->

</schema>
```

It's easy to see how we can use the `import` and `include` directives to organize and manage a complex collection of XSD information:

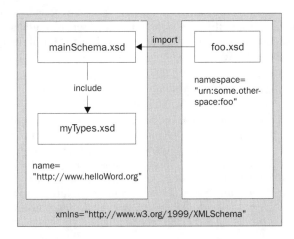

Complex Type Definitions

The basic container of all elements that we will see in a schema is the complex type. These types may have multiple elements and may have attributes. Simple types, on the other hand, must not have element content or attributes.

New complex types are built by using the `complexType` element. Most complex types will have several element and attribute declarations, though there is nothing that prohibits writing a `complexType` with only a single element.

This example declares that in the XML document, the instance of the element that is defined by `articleType` will have four elements, each a string. (If we look at the full schema, above, we see that each element resolves to a string lower in the chain). It also may have an optional element `dateline`, identified by the `minOccurs` attribute with a value of `0`. As this element is only a reference, we have to look elsewhere in the schema for its details:

```
<complexType name="articleType">
  <element    name="headline" type="news:headlineType" />
  <element    name="ByLine"   type="news:ByLineType" />
  <element    ref="dateline"  minOccurs="0" />
  <element    name="body"     type="string" />
  <element    name="stats"    type="news:statsType" />
    <attribute name="section"  type="string" />
</complexType>
```

We can imagine that when a complex type contains multiple complex types as well as attributes, the structure can become very elaborate. The elemental types that we see in the `complexType` are built into the XML schema definition and may be used to build other types, as we will see shortly.

Keep the attribute example in mind when we look at enumeration a little further in the chapter. Wouldn't it be better if we could limit the `section` options to the following: news, sport, business, and arts?

Using Existing Type Definitions

Often we need to use an existing type definition that we've already declared. To do this we use the `ref=` attribute. The caveat in using this is that the reference must be a **global element**. Global elements are those that are declared at the top of the document as a direct child of the root `schema` element. The dateline element was declared thus:

```
<element name="dateline" type="date" />
```

This element has also utilized the attribute `minOccurs` (minimum occurrences) with the value of 0, which, as we said earlier, defines an optional element. At the time of writing, the only acceptable value for this attribute is 0 or 1. (Though I think that it would be useful to have other options. For example, a `minOccurs` of 4 for AutoEngineCylinders). Another modifier that may be used is the attribute `maxOccurs` which can take the value of either 1 or a * (which means many). As you know, this pair of attributes can specify '*none*', '*one*', and '*many*' that are standard definitional values (if we had greater latitude, we could extend these standards to a `maxOccurs` of 12 for AutoEngineCylinders).

The default values for these two attributes are different depending where they are used. In an element, the default value of minOccurs is 1 and there is no default value for maxOccurs. The result of not specifying these attributes is that the element must then occur exactly once. In the case of attributes, however, the default value of minOccurs is 0, and maxOccurs is 1. The result of not specifying these attributes in the attribute declaration is that it becomes optional by default.

Here is a table of the various options:

minOccurs value	maxOccurs value	Description
0	1	Optional attribute or element; maximum of 1
0	*	Optional attribute or element; no maximum limit
1	1	A single mandatory attribute or element
1	*	Mandatory attribute or element; no maximum limit

Simple Types

If we take another look at the sample schema, we see that there are elements that are declared directly and, at the very end of the schema, a simpleType definition.

Simple types are the basic building blocks of the schema. These may either be of a type that is built in the schema, or a derived type that is created from (using a base of) one of the built in types. The built-in types are in the table below.

The type column refers to **P**rimitive or **D**erived data-type. Primitive types are the basic data types, while limiting or masking a type creates a Derived type. We will see how this is done in the next section:

Simple type	Type	Description / Example
string	P	"this is a test string"
boolean	P	true, false, 1, 0
float	P	A single-precision 32-bit floating point
double	P	A double-precision 64-bit floating point
decimal	P	-43.21, 0, 123.4, 1500.00
timeInstant	P	1989-07-17T11:30:00.000-05:00 (July 17th 1989 at 11.30am Eastern Standard Time.
timeDuration	P	P5Y3M2DT11H30M42.4S (5 year, 3 months, 2 days, 11 hours, 30 minutes, 42.4 seconds)
recurringInstant	P	--11-302T23:30:00 (Novmber 2nd every year at 11:30PM. - format similar to timeInstant)
binary	P	110010100110111

Table continued on following page

61

Simple type	Type	Description / Example
uri-reference	P	http://www.wrox.com/ http://www.w3.org/
integer	D	-123456, -1, 0, 1, 123456
non-positive-integer	D	-123456, -1, 0
negative-integer	D	-123456, -1
long	D	-1, 12345654321 from −9223372036854775808 to 9223372036854775807
int	D	-1, 1234567 from −2147483648 to 2147483647
short	D	-1, 12345 from 32768 to 32767
byte	D	-1, 126 from −128 to 127
non-negative-integer	D	0, 1, 123456
unsigned-long	D	0, 12345654321 Max value: 18446744073709551615
unsigned-int	D	0, 12345678 Max Value: 4294967295
unsigned-short	D	0, 12678 Max value: 65535
unsigned-byte	D	0, 126 Max Value: 255
positive-integer	D	1, 126789
date	D	1983-06-03, (June 3rd, 1983)
time	D	15:25:57.000, 15:25:57.000-05:00
ID	P	An XML 1.0 ID attribute type
IDREF	P	An XML 1.0 IDREF attribute type
ENTITY	P	An XML 1.0 ENTITY attribute type
NOTATION	P	An XML 1.0 NOTATION attribute type
Language	D	A valid xml:lang values as defined in XML 1.0
IDREFS	D	An XML 1.0 IDREFS attribute type
ENTITIES	D	An XML 1.0 ENTITIES attribute type
NMTOKEN	D	An XML 1.0 NMTOKEN attribute type
NMTOKENS	D	An XML 1.0 NMTOKENS attribute type
Name	D	An XML 1.0 Name type
QName	D	An XML Namespace QName
NCName	D	An XML Namespace NCName, i.e. is a QName without the prefix and colon

> *Since this chapter is designed to serve as an introduction to the concept of schemas, details of some of these types are beyond the current scope. Once you've gone beyond this introduction please refer to the XML documentation at www.w3.org for more detailed studies about these types, or take a look at Appendix G. Alternatively, check out Professional XML published by Wrox Press, ISBN 1861003-11-0.*

As you can see, this list of possible data types is rather extensive. Compare this with the type possibilities that are available in the DTDs (PCDATA and CDATA).

Facets

It is when we wish to create a new simple type that things can get very interesting. We can use what are called 'facets' to modify a base type. Some of the facets were developed to work primarily with numeric data, while others work mostly on string-type data representations. minExclusive, maxExclusive and their inclusive counterparts are applicable to all types. The length, minLength and maxlength facets are used on the string and the XML 1.0 derived types, while precision and scale are for the numeric type only.

Some simple examples of these facets are:

```
<!--Taken from a hospital system -->
<simpleType name="patientAges" base="double">
  <minInclusive value='0' />
  <maxInclusive value='150' />
</simpleType>
```

```
<!--Taken from a security system -->
<simpleType name="UserName" base="string">
  <minLength value='4' />
  <maxLength value='32' />
</simpleType>
```

This example is an excerpt from the schema and defines the simple type of short. It is from the W3C data-types documentation. While we will not delve into all of the details of this document, it is interesting to note the self-defining aspects of the XML schema environment (the annotation and appinfo will be discussed later on in this chapter):

```
<simpleType name="short" base="int">
  <annotation>
    <appinfo>
      <has-facet name="precision"/>
      <has-facet name="scale"/>
      <has-facet name="pattern"/>
      <has-facet name="enumeration"/>
      <has-facet name="maxInclusive"/>
      <has-facet name="maxExclusive"/>
      <has-facet name="minInclusive"/>
      <has-facet name="minExclusive"/>
      <has-property name="ordered" value="true"/>
      <has-property name="bounded" value="true"/>
      <has-property name="cardinality" value="finite"/>
      <has-property name="numeric" value="true"/>
    </appinfo>
```

```
    </annotation>
    <minInclusive value="-32768"/>
    <maxInclusive value="32767"/>
  </simpleType>
```

In the above example, we see how the defined type short is derived from the base int, but has an upper and lower allowable limit. It is very easy to determine the available facets for that type, as well as the limits of allowable values. But if we look at the data type table, we notice that int is also a derived type. Working our way through the schema definition for the schema we can discover the whole tree, with each successive derivation getting more specific:

❑   decimal – The primitive type.

❑   integer – a scale-value=0. The scale value is the number of digits in the fractional part datatype that is derived from a decimal. A scale value of 0 must then be a whole number.

❑   long –   minInclusive value="-9223372036854775808"
              maxInclusive value="9223372036854775807"

❑   int –   minInclusive value="-2147483648"
              maxInclusive value="2147483647"

❑   short – minInclusive value="-32768"
              maxInclusive value="32767"

❑   byte –   minInclusive value="-128"
              maxInclusive value="127"

By using the technique of applying facets the derived data types are built from the primitive types.

The Pattern Facet

Another major aspect of facets is the use of regular expressions to create masks for the data. These masks would be used in creating telephone numbers, zip or postal codes that are non-integer (i.e. contain a mixture of numerals and letters, for example) etc. For those unfamiliar with regular expressions, they are a symbolic shorthand for describing patterns of text. Similar to an arithmetic expression, small units (x+y) can be combined into complex expressions.

> *The pattern facet uses a language that is similar to the regular expression language used in the Perl programming language. There are some differences though, and it would be best to refer to the official schema specification, or the implementation that you are using for details.*

A simple example of pattern usage is:

```
<simpleType name="BureauIDType" base:"string">
  <pattern value="[A-Z]-d{2}" />
</simpleType>
```

The new BureauIDType will consist of the pattern: one uppercase letter, one dash, two digits.

The Enumeration Facet

Another one of the more useful facets is enumeration. While it is most often thought of as a string facet, it can prove to be very useful for numeric elements as well. In fact, it may be used in all of the simple types except Boolean (after all, what would we enumerate – the Boolean universe only consists of two values). In the following example, we would like to accept only valid gender types:

```
<simpleType name="gender" base:"string">
  <enumeration value="male" />
  <enumeration value="female" />
</simpleType>
```

For a numeric example, you might use:

```
<simpleType name="attack" base:"decimal">
  <enumeration value="1" />  <!-- By Land -->
  <enumeration value="2" />  <!-- By Sea  -->
</simpleType>
```

In all of these cases, if the instance data in the XML document is not schema-valid according to the rules that are defined, an error is generated.

Attributes

Most of the elements that we've described have not contained **attributes** although by now you will be familiar with the term. In XML we often use attributes to clarify some aspect of the element. One simple guideline for using attributes versus elements is that attributes are unordered while elements *are* ordered. For example:

The XML parser will see:

```
<ElementA  Value1="x" Value2="y" />
```

as equivalent to:

```
<ElementA  Value2="y" Value1="x" />
```

However to the XML parser, this:

```
<ElementA>
  <Value1> x </Value1>
  <Value2> y </Value2>
</ElementA>
```

is very different from this:

```
<ElementA>
  <Value2> y </Value2>
  <Value1> x </Value1>
</ElementA>
```

Another consideration is that attributes can't contain elements or have attributes themselves. In a stable, well-designed environment, this is not a problem, but if the schema is evolving, the options of elements may be useful. It tends to become a philosophical discussion as to the details after that. Nonetheless, attributes are a major aspect of the XML environment, so we ought not to leave them out.

Let's look at the following XML code fragment:

```
<weight units="lbs">24.5</weight>
```

This will be found (without any reference to the attribute) in the associated schema as:

```
<element name="weight" type="decimal" />
```

However, the above line of code defines a simple element, and, as you recall from the beginning of this chapter, simple elements may not have attributes. So specifying the attribute in the schema requires more text because all elements that have attributes must be defined as complex types:

```
<element name="weight">
  <complexType base="decimal" derivedBy="extension">
    <attribute name="units" type="string" />
  </complexType>
</element>
```

By examining the above schema snippet, we can see how the attribute is added to the element. Don't worry about the derivedBy, we'll cover that soon in the derivation section.

What do we do in the case of an element that only has attributes and no textual content? We'll use the following XML example:

```
<weight units="lbs" amount="24.5" />
```

In this case, we would need two attributes but no base:

```
<element name="weight">
  <complexType content="empty">
    <attribute name="units" type="xsd:string" />
    <attribute name="amount" type="xsd:decimal" />
  </complexType>
</element>
```

We need to use the content attribute of the complex type to accomplish this goal. The above example neatly introduces the next topic.

The Content Attribute

The complexType has, in its schema definition, the content attribute. This describes the intended content model of the described element. The default value of content is elementOnly. This directs that the complexType may contain only elements and attributes and no textual content. We've just seen an example of the empty value used above. The complete list of possible content model values is:

Type	Description
elementOnly	Can contain elements only
empty	Must contain no content
mixed	Can contain both text and elements
textOnly	Can only contain text

It is certainly possible that, in extreme cases, the nesting of complexTypes can get rather confusing. Types nested in types, each with attributes and facets, can be an exercise in mental gymnastics to decipher.

Consider the following example – for simplicity I've removed the patterns, enumeration and other complex facets (and changed the names to protect the innocent):

```
<element name='Data23'>
  <complexType content='mixed'>
    <element name='fromJohnFile'>
        <complexType content='mixed'>
          <element name='Item' type='string'/>
        </complexType>
    </element>
    <element name='Amount' type='positive-integer'/>
    <element name='Location' type='string'/>
    <element name='Fisker'>
    <complexType content="empty">
      <attribute name="units" type="string" />
      <attribute name="amount" type="decimal" />
    </complexType>
        </element>
        <element name='EnteredOn' type='xsd:date' minOccurs='0'/>
    </complexType>
</element>
```

Would result in this XML:

```
<Data23>
 <fromJohnFile>
   <Item> string content </Item>
 </fromJohnFile>
 <Amount> 34 </Amount>
 <Location> Here </Location>
 <Fisker units="lbs"  amount="24.4" />
 <EnteredOn />
</Data23>
```

Groups

As we have seen there may be, and usually are, many elements in a complex type. Until now, in all of our examples, every element that is listed in the schema has to exist in the instance document (unless minOccurs=0). This type of grouping is referred to as the sequence model. In the latest iteration of the schema definitions this is not the only option, just the default:

```
<complexType name='Data54'>
  <group order="sequence">
    <element name="firstname" type="string"
    <element name="lastname" type="string">
  </group>
</complexType>
```

When developing a complexType element it is possible to imagine scenario we would like to vary the required elements. An example of this would be in the case of internationalization. In one instance we might have a zip code that is represented in a string format, while in another country a numeric format might be more suitable. Why not offer a choice to the instance document? Another type of grouping, called the disjunction model addresses this:

```
<complexType name='Data54'>
  <group order="choice">
    <element name="zipcode" type="decimal"
    <element name="postalcode" type="string">
  </group>
</complexType>
```

In the above example either 'zipcode' *or* 'postalcode' is to appear in the instance document.

The second option (the conjunction model) for the group is that each element must appear in the instance document, but they can appear in any order. This would be a very useful option when attempting to use a common schema for two systems that use the same data files, but due to some design constraints of each of the systems, do not have the same layout:

```
<complexType name="TradeData">
  <group order="all">
    <element name="symbol" type="string">
    <element name="tradedate" type="date">
    <element name="price" type="decimal">
    <element name="amount" type="decimal">
  </group>
</complexType>
```

There are some constraints when using the `all` that you should bear in mind. First, is that only individual elements can be included in the `all`, no nested groups are allowed. Also, every item must have minOccurs=1 and maxOccurs=1 though this may change in the final specification.

Derivation

When we are creating a new data type we have to specify two attribute values: the base type that we are using for the new type, and its derivation. The base type must be one of the defined types that are listed earlier, or it may be a type that has been defined by the schema developer. The derivation of the new complex type can be either a `derivedBy` value of `extension` or `restriction`.

When deriving by `extension`, the new types declarations are added to the base type. This allows for adding elements or attributes that are not in the original base type.

In this example, we need to hold a shoe size along with units (US, UK, EUR) as an attribute. We could do this as follows:

```
<element name="shoeSize">
  <complexType base="decimal" derivedBy="extension">
    <attribute name="units" type="string" />
  </complexType>
</element>
```

The new element type shoeSize is created. A size 10 in the US would be:

```
<shoeSize Units="US">10</shoeSize>
```

In the other case, where the `derivedBy` attribute has the value `restriction`, we modify existing limitations of the base class. This is best illustrated using this schema code:

```
<schema targetNamespace="myURI" xmlns:myns="myURI"
        xmlns:xsd="http://www.w3.org/1999/XMLSchema/datatypes">

<complexType name="newsfeed" >
  <element name="headline" type="xsd:string" minOccurs="0"/>
  <element name="author" type="xsd:string" minOccurs="0"/>
  <element name="dateposted" type="xsd:date" />
  <element name="body" type="xsd:string" />
  <element name="artIncluded" type="xsd:boolean" />
  <!--Additional elements here -->
</complexType>

<complexType name="story" base="myns:newsfeed" derivedBy="restriction" >
  <restrictions>
    <element name="headline" type="xsd:string" minOccurs="1"/>
    <element name="author" type="xsd:string" minOccurs="1"/>
    <element name="dateposted" type="xsd:date" />
    <element name="body" type="xsd:string" />
    <element name="artIncluded" type="xsd:boolean" />
    <!--Additional elements here -->
  </restrictions>
</complexType>
</schema>
```

In this sample schema, the first type, newsfeed describes all of the various articles, and information feeds into a newsroom. Many of these are just quick bits if information that may not include all of the components of a final story that will be published. At this point, the data may not yet have a headline or an author. By the time the newsfeed is ready to be published as a story, the missing elements have been added to the instance document, and will need to be in compliance with the second type.

Programmatically, when additional data elements are added to the instance document the status can be modified from a newsfeed to a story. A simple process may be used later to extract all stories, and publish them.

Annotations

As described by the official documentation:

> "Annotation of schemas and schema components, with material for human or computer consumption, is provided for by allowing application information and human information at the beginning of most major schema elements, and anywhere at the top level of schemas."

The specification does not provide the rules for the processing of this information, and appears to leave it up the to schema parser to determine these.

When we looked at the snippet of the schema for the short (in the section on facets), we saw a real example using <appinfo> elements in the annotation. The <appinfo> elements are used by the parser to derive the new datatypes from the one identified in the base attribute.

The other use, that which provides documentation for the user, is implemented here:

```
<simpleType name="component" base:"xsd:uri-reference">
  <annotation>
    <documentation>
```

```
        Use this only in test conditions.
      </documentation>
    </annotation>
    <!-- Other declarations here -->
  </simpleType>
```

Though in both of these examples the `<annotation>` was in a `simpleType`, annotations can appear anywhere in the schema. Typically, a `<documentation>` note would be placed at the top of the schema and contain copyright data or other information to assist the reader.

DTD vs. Schemas (A Summary)

Though the goals of the schema and the DTD are about the same, we can see that the DTD technology falls short of the schema in many ways. For comparison purposes, here is the DTD approximation of the schema that appears at the beginning of this chapter:

```
<!DOCTYPE ARTICLE [
<!ELEMENT article (headline, ByLine, dateline, body, stats)>
<!ATTLIST article section CDATA "news">
<!ELEMENT headline (MainHead, SubHead)>
<!ELEMENT MainHead (#PCDATA)>
<!ELEMENT SubHead (#PCDATA)>
<!ELEMENT ByLine (Author, title?)>
<!ELEMENT Author (#PCDATA)>
<!ELEMENT title (#PCDATA)>
<!ELEMENT stats (submitted, wordCount, bureauID)>
<!ELEMENT submited (#PCDATA)>
<!ELEMENT wordCount (#PCDATA)>
<!ELEMENT bureauID (#PCDATA)>
<!ELEMENT body (#PCDATA)>
]>
```

As you can see, though it is shorter (a *very* slight benefit) it cannot contain as much information as in the schema. And, of course, schemas are written in XML, whereas DTDs are in a completely different language, which means more to learn for the budding XML programmer. Schemas are much more than just another way to describe the XML document. Looking back at each of the major drawbacks of the DTD it is easy to see why schemas are gaining in popularity, even though the W3C has not yet sanctioned them by issuing their recommendation.

Summary

In this chapter we learned about the basics of the new schema method for defining an XML instance document. Though this is a changing and (at this time of writing) unsanctioned technology, the state of the specification process is far enough along that we can learn about, and begin to implement, this technology now. We have reviewed many of the critical aspects of schemas, and how they can be used to describe the contents and semantics of the instance document.

One of the major issues missing from the DTD is the data-type. This has been handled so completely in the schema that the schema may be considered a type-centric description language. The fact that the schema is written using XML, and therefore uses the same parsers as XML, will assist in speeding its adoption once the final recommendation is in place. Of course, as one learns XML, it is also that little bit easier to learn how to develop schemas. Though the schema was developed to describe the XML instance document, as the nature of XML moves from document to data, we can certainly see that the XML schema definition language could be used to describe databases and other technologies beyond its original intent.

Before we move on, it is important to remember that this chapter was written based on the working draft documents, and as such, must be treated in the light that the information may be changed or modified at any time. It would not be a good idea for any production process be based on the information contained here. That said, there are no major changes anticipated at the time of writing and what we've learned about schemas will be very important in the near and long term. For up to date information about the status of schemas and other XML technologies, visit http:www.w3.org.

5

Document Object Model

Now that you know a bit about XML, you probably feel ready to begin working with XML documents in ASP. The easiest way to go about this in ASP is to use Microsoft's implementation of the World Wide Web Consortium's (W3C) Document Object Model (DOM). Similar to the HTML object model used by DHTML, the DOM is a set of interfaces that allows programmers to load XML documents into a tree structure and operate on them. Microsoft offers a high-performance COM component, MSXML, which exposes the DOM to scripted and compiled applications with some extensions. Since the focus of this book is XML in ASP applications, I will concentrate on the late bound interfaces suitable for scripting. If you are building compiled applications in C++ or Visual Basic, rest assured that detailed interfaces with strong type checking are available for early binding.

I'll begin with a quick sketch of how the XML DOM is used in actual ASP practice.

Knowing when to use the DOM interfaces and how to do so effectively is just as important as learning the interfaces themselves.

Next, I'll show you how to locate the right version of the component and even redistribute it with applications. Since the DOM is maintained by the DOM Working Group at the W3C (http://www.w3.org/DOM/), I'll give you a short look at the W3C's take on the core DOM, and contrast Microsoft's implementation with the Recommendation. The heart of this chapter, however, is a walk through the DOM as implemented in MSXML. I'll present a formal survey of the interfaces, enumerating the methods and properties of each. Using the DOM in ASP typically comes down to some common tasks, so I'll follow the survey with specific examples of how to perform these tasks in ASP script code. These tasks are:

❑ Document loading and validation

❑ Tree traversal

❑ Content creation

Those three tasks neatly cover all the ways you can manipulate XML from code. This sounds simple, doesn't it? Like XML itself, the DOM is a simple construct whose applications and ramifications are marvelous in their complexity. Before you can build grand edifices, though, you need to learn the tools of the trade. In the case of XML and ASP, that's the DOM. Later, in chapter 6, you'll see additional examples mixing ASP and the DOM. Let's get started.

As you go through this chapter, you may wish to refer to the documentation for the Microsoft DOM implementation. I also urge you to at least glance over the DOM Recommendation and preferably compare it to the details of the Microsoft implementation. Microsoft's documentation is found at http://msdn.microsoft.com/library/psdk/xmlsdk/xml_2rl1.htm, while the DOM Recommendation is found at http://www.w3.org/TR/REC-DOM-Level-1/.

Uses of the DOM

This is as much a question of how you can use XML in applications as it is one of using the DOM. Still, the DOM is not the only way to get at XML markup. Indeed, the DOM stands in the middle of the range between low-level APIs and high-level abstractions. The DOM's chief competitor, the Simple API for XML (SAX) is a very low-level, high-performance API. By contrast, the trend in e-commerce middleware projects is to shield application programmers from the DOM. Teams fluent in the DOM build business components that are used by the rest of the project staff. While it is certainly desirable for all programmers to know the DOM, it is unrealistic these days to count on staffing your entire team with programmers fluent in the DOM. It is important to know when to use the DOM, and where it belongs in your architecture. Some common trends can be identified in Web development practice today. These are:

❑ Publishing the same content in multiple forms

❑ Exchanging data between applications

❑ Capturing the data of business components

Multi-Use Content Publishing

HTML pages are a single source of content that can only be published in one form. They are, barring client-side DHTML code, static. Even with DHTML and ASP, Web pages usually expose only one view of the data contained within them. XML, by contrast, removes considerations of presentation from the data. Using the DOM and XSL, it becomes possible to publish the same data document in multiple views. An application would use the XML directly, while different subsets of the content and different presentation styles would be used to expose the data to different audiences. Without giving away too much about later chapters, we'll just say that XSL reads an XML document and produces another markup document – either XML or HTML – by applying certain rules to the original document. We say that the XSL processor **transforms** the XML document, or that an **XSL transformation** has been applied. The DOM is the appropriate API for this because the transformation acts on the document as a whole. The entire concept of an XSL transformation is something that is hard to encapsulate in a meaningful way as a business concept.

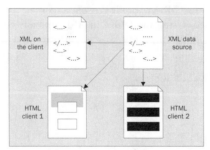

Platform Neutral Data Exchange

XML is structured text, and there is no data format more widely supported than text. As a consequence, XML is enjoying a great deal of popularity. XML bridges the incompatibilities between platforms. There is nothing to prevent you from using a low-level API like SAX (consult Appendix E for more information on SAX), but the DOM is appropriate for several reasons:

❑ Data exchanged tends to be relatively compact and well-defined.

❑ Structures are well-defined and tend to repeat, making template documents attractive.

❑ Validation of the document is often desirable when dealing with an external trading partner.

The last point is especially important if you are interested in the currently hot topic of business to business (B2B) e-commerce. Applications like Microsoft BizTalk Server and standardized frameworks like BizTalk Framework or RosettaNet exist to enable a company to communicate with their suppliers, partners, and customers using XML documents. We'll meet Biztalk again in Chapter 15.

Unlike transformations using XSL, though, the documents exchanged map very well to business concepts. It is becoming attractive to execute e-commerce solutions through the use of business objects that use XML for their implementation.

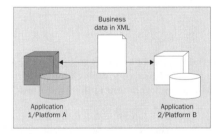

Business Components

Someone has to write the business objects that use XML. Application programmers may deal with the components – removing the need to deal with the DOM directly, but the component implementations require knowledge of the DOM. An intimate knowledge of the DOM is needed to create high-performance implementations. These components are the workhorses of an e-commerce or application integration solution, so performance is critical.

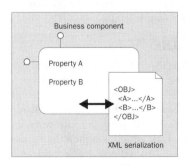

These business objects are the COM components familiar to Visual Basic and scripting developers. They expose business data as properties, and the rules and techniques of the business as methods. Rather than use DCOM across platform or security boundaries, though, objects are serialized as XML documents. Within such a component implementation, you use the DOM to read an XML document and initialize the component. When it becomes necessary to save the state of the component, you again use the DOM to write out an XML document. The benefit of this scheme is that it gains the advantages and portability of XML without requiring all developers to learn about XML and the DOM. If you want to build such components, though, you have to understand how to use the DOM efficiently. These components will be used and re-used, so there is much greater emphasis placed on writing effective code.

Getting the Right Parser

Happily for ASP developers, Microsoft is embracing XML as a core technology of the Windows DNA platform. Most Microsoft applications and servers are being rewritten to use or support XML in some way. This means you can almost always count on having MSXML available to you. The version of the parser that shipped with Internet Explorer 5.0 (MSXML 2.0) was the first version to support the W3C DOM interfaces. This is the version I'll be using throughout the rest of this chapter. A new version, MSXML 2.6, is on the verge of release with interesting new features (previews available at this time of writing). By the time you read this, it may well be the production version. I'll make mention of its new features, but I won't dwell on them. The DOM code in this chapter will continue to work with the new version of the parser. What is interesting about this component, though, is how Microsoft's view of XML evolved over time and how that is reflected in the distribution of the component.

Internet Explorer

Originally, XML was selected as the implementing technology for the Channel Definition Format (CDF) used to describe the organization and schedule of a Web Channel. This was implemented in Internet Explorer 4.0. There was no DOM Recommendation at that time, and MSXML was not intended for use by third-party programmers.

Shortly after that version shipped, however, XML came to public prominence. Windows developers wanted an XML parser, forcing Microsoft to go public with their hitherto internal tool. Developers quickly clamored for support for XML features that had not been included in that version of MSXML, prompting Microsoft to begin work on a new version. The DOM was standardized around this time, so the new version, which shipped with Internet Explorer 5.0, supported the new interfaces. This was still viewed largely as a Web tool though, so it was bundled with the browser. This was more than a casual decision; MSXML uses the WinInet libraries for some of its implementation. This made a good deal of sense – the parser needed to be able to load documents over the network, and the browser used WinInet for that capability, so why not do the same in the parser? Although, this still created an important dependency in the component, requiring that third-party developers make sure the proper version of Internet Explorer was available before installing their own software.

MSXML Redistributable

Many developers were interested in using MSXML, but worked for companies that had either standardized on Netscape or chosen not to use Internet Explorer for other reasons. They wanted to be able to distribute MSXML with their XML applications to ensure the component's availability. Some even saw the tying of MSXML to Internet Explorer in sinister terms. Owing to the WinInet dependency, Microsoft chose not to completely unbundle MSXML from their browser. They did, however, create a version that is compatible with Internet Explorer 4.01, which was then the version of the browser shipping with the various Windows operating systems. This redistributable package, available at http://msdn.microsoft.com/downloads/tools/xmlparser/xmlparser.asp, is almost identical to the original version of MSXML 2.0, lacking only some minor features.

The core XML and DOM features remain available in the redistributable component. Some features are unavailable because they are implemented in Internet Explorer 5.0, not MSXML. These include XML data islands and native browsing of XML files. Databinding to hierarchical files may be degraded. The XSL function formatNumber is not available unless you upgrade the DLL OLEAUT32.DLL with the version from Visual Studio 6.0. The most notable single feature lacking in the redistributable is the XMLHTTP interface (a nonstandard Microsoft extension) which is not available to users of the redistributable component.

Included with Windows

As the release of Windows 2000 drew near, XML had made its way into many Microsoft products. The Office 2000 productivity suite uses XML to preserve rich formatting taking a document through HTML and back to native Office formats. SQL Server was announcing plans to provide data as XML documents with the next version, while ADO 2.5 incorporated similar capabilities. It became obvious that MSXML would need to be updated more frequently than Internet Explorer. It had become so tied to a number of server products that it was desirable to ship a performance-enhanced version with Windows 2000. Such an upgrade was included with the release version. It offers no new interfaces, but does fix some bugs and improved performance in multiprocessor systems. The DLLs on which MSXML depends are part of the Windows 2000 release, thereby answering the dependency issue. It is Microsoft's stated intention to continue development and distribution of the parser on a schedule independent of Internet Explorer.

MSXML 2.6: A Preview

There are features other than simple performance enhancements that are needed to use MSXML in a scalable server environment. Although Windows 2000 is recently released as I write this, a significant upgrade to the parser is being made ready. It is in a beta release, technically a "technology preview", at this time, with a second release imminent. As of late April 2000, Microsoft has not announced a firm release schedule for the new parser, although they have committed to continued support for W3C standards. The technology preview may be obtained from http://msdn.microsoft.com/downloads/webtechnology/xml/msxml.asp, although you should check Microsoft's XML Center for the latest news. By the time you read this book, the parser may have moved into production status.

Again, this version adds nothing new to DOM support, but it does offer interesting new features. It is the first version to support the XSLT and XPath W3C Recommendations. These standards offer powerful tools for styling, transforming, and querying XML documents. The new parser offers the ability to cache XML schemas and XSL stylesheets. As you build more advanced XML applications in ASP, you will find these capabilities very important when considering scalability. For now, however, we will focus on MSXML 2.0 and its support for the DOM.

MSXML and the W3C XML DOM

MSXML abides closely to the interfaces set forth in the W3C Recommendation for Level 1 of the DOM. Like all practical implementations, however, it adds some extensions. Since we will be concentrating on programming with MSXML in ASP applications, I will not go into laborious detail on that Recommendation here. Whenever you are dealing with extensions or other deviations from some standard, you must know *when* you are deviating from the standard. In the survey section that follows, I will indicate extension properties and methods with italics. For now, though, let's consider the general structure of the DOM, Level 1, and how MSXML differs from it.

W3C Interfaces

The W3C's take on the DOM consists of two sets of interfaces: **core** and **flattened**. The core set of interfaces consists of a detailed hierarchy of interfaces collectively representing all the constructs in XML. The flattened set consists of a very minimal set of interfaces. Most notably, all the various sorts of XML constructs – elements, attributes, and so forth – are treated through the Node interface.

The two collections of interfaces exist due to the competing needs of two different sorts of applications. Objects in the core hierarchy require calls to QueryInterface (in COM) or casts (in Java and C++). These calls or casts give an application the most detailed and typed access to objects possible, but only at the expense of performance-consuming calls. The flattened interfaces introduce a measure of ambiguity – everything is a node – but are fast. In scripting environments such as ASP, programmers are used to ambiguity. After all, the single Variant type represents all data types supported in COM. Just as you are accustomed to examining the type of a variant, you will get used to checking the nodeType property of a node object. In circumstances where the program has implicit knowledge of the document's structure, the type of the node will be known from its context. In exchange for this flexibility, though, you give up some performance. Late binding in COM (the IDispatch interface, once known as OLE Automation), requires two trips through the COM layer for every request: once to locate a method within the interface given its name, and once to pass the parameters. Worse, the parameters are passed together with their types so that the COM infrastructure can check them. It is this information that allows a scripted application to make bad calls to nonexistent methods without crashing the entire application.

> *The full text of the W3C XML DOM Level 1 Recommendation is available from http://www.w3.org/TR/REC-DOM-Level-1/level-one-core.html. Level 1 is not the whole story, however. Level 2 of the DOM entered Candidate Recommendation status on 7 March 2000, promising important new features like events, extensions to the Level 1 interfaces, and extended tree traversal. Requirements for DOM Level 3 are currently being gathered.*

Core

Although every XML construct has an interface to represent it in the Core DOM collection of interfaces, everything is considered to derive from Node. Here are the core interfaces and their COM equivalents in Microsoft's implementation:

W3C DOM Interface	MSXML Interface
Document	IXMLDOMDocument
DocumentFragment	IXMLDOMDocumentFragment
DocumentType	IXMLDOMDocumentType
EntityReference	IXMLDOMEntityReference
Element	IXMLDOMElement
Attr	IXMLDOMAttribute
ProcessingInstruction	IXMLDOMProcessingInstruction
Comment	IXMLDOMComment
Text	IXMLDOMText
CDATASection	IXMLDOMCDATASection
Entity	IXMLDOMEntity
Notation	IXMLDOMNotation

Additionally, MSXML offers `IXMLDOMCharacterData`, which, though not corresponding to a particular node type, does provide methods used by `IXMLDOMText`, `IXMLDOMComment`, and `IXMLDOMCDATASection`.

> **The most important peculiarity of the Core is that it does not specify how a document comes into being. Consequently, every implementation *must* include proprietary extensions to load a document into memory.**

Flattened

As far as the W3C is concerned, the flattened interfaces reduce to the statement "everything is a Node". In practice, of course, a few more interfaces are necessary. The point, though, is that the DOM can treat every part of an XML document as a node, and the entire document consists of a hierarchically ordered tree of nodes. MSXML handles this with four interfaces: `Document`, `Node`, `NodeList`, `NamedNodeMap`, and an error handling interface.

Survey of MSXML Interfaces

The DOM in general, and MSXML in particular, exposes a view of the document consisting of a tree of nodes. The tree is rooted by the top-most element in the document. Every other construct in an XML document is represented as a node within the tree. When working with the DOM from ASP, you will be concerned with five principle interfaces:

❑ Documents

❑ Nodes

❑ Node lists

❑ Named node maps

❑ An error-handling interface

The illustration below depicts an idealized view of the DOM and its constituent parts.

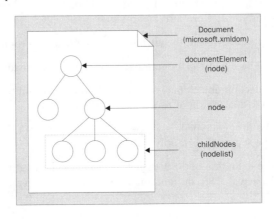

The `Document` object is what you get when you create a new instance of the parser. This object allows you to control the behavior of the parser and create new nodes. Its `documentElement` property is a specific instance of a node object. It represents the top-most element in the document. This is where you begin any traversal of the tree. Every other item – element, attribute, processing instruction, or what have you – in the document is a **node**. Nodes exist in a parent-child relationship throughout the document. Child nodes are exposed in one of two **node list** collections: attributes belong in the node list named `attributes`, while every other sort of node is collected in a node's `childNodes` collection. Later on, we'll see how we can use these facts to traverse the tree and what the two collections mean to ASP programmers.

Documents

The notion of a complete document is blended with the idea of a parser in Microsoft's implementation. MSXML actually provides two implementations, one rental-threaded for use by a single thread, and another that is free-threaded.

> *COM threading models are a difficult topic for beginning component programmers, albeit a very important one. Virtually all script code uses the rental threaded model, so we won't cover threading models here. For background information, please understand that the rental threading model allows the programmer to write code without worrying about concurrency issues that arise in multithreaded applications. Applications using rental threaded components do not scale as well as those using multi-threaded components, however.*

The `progID` for the first is `Microsoft.XMLDOM`, while the other is `Microsoft.FreeThreadedXMLDOM`. The former is what you will use most commonly in the body of an ASP page, although the latter is needed when you want to take advantage of some of the advanced scaling features of the new (i.e. technology preview) XML parser. Here are the properties of this interface:

> **Note: Extensions to the W3C interface are in italics:**

Property	Meaning
async	Indicates whether the document should be loaded synchronously (default – TRUE) or asynchronously (FALSE). If loaded asynchronously, check the `readyState` property; read-write
attributes	Collection object; the attributes of the document root; read-only
baseName	The base name of a namespace-qualified name; read-only
childNodes	Collection object; the immediate child elements of the document; typically, the XML declaration or root node; read-only
dataType	The strongly typed data type of the document root (Microsoft-specified data type support); read-only
definition	The definition of the root element in the associated DTD or schema (returns the actual XML declaration for an associated schema); read-only

Property	Meaning
doctype	Returns the document type node declaring the DTD, if any, for this document; read-only
documentElement	The root element (node) for the document; read-write
firstChild	References the first child of the document, typically the XML declaration, if any, or the document root element if that is the first node to appear; read-only
implementation	A reference to the DOM implementation; read-only
lastChild	References the last child of the document; if the document begins with a root element, firstChild and lastChild point to this node; read-only
namespaceURI	Returns the URI for a namespace qualified node; read-only
nextSibling	Returns the next sibling for this node; for a document object, this will be NULL; read-only
nodeName	String representation of the element name for this node; for a document, this will have the value #document; read-only
nodeType	The type of the node, in this case Document (9); read-only
nodeTypedValue	The node's value expressed in a strongly typed native data type; for a document, NULL; read-write
nodeTypeString	The type of the node in string form; for a document "document"; read-only
nodeValue	The text associated with a node; nominally read-write, MSXML will not permit an assignment operation on a document node
ownerDocument	Returns the root of the document containing this node; for a document object, this value will be NULL; read-only
parentNode	The parent node of a given node; for a document object, NULL; read-only
parsed	TRUE if all child elements have been parsed and instantiated, FALSE if parsing remains (will be TRUE following a synchronous load); read-only
parseError	An error-handling object reflecting any errors on the last load operation; read-only
prefix	Returns the namespace prefix; read-only
preserveWhiteSpace	TRUE if extra white space in the document is to be maintained, FALSE otherwise; read-write
previousSibling	Returns the left sibling for this node; NULL for document objects; read-only
readyState	Indicates the current state of the document; read-only

Table continued on following page

Property	Meaning
resolveExternals	TRUE if external definitions are to be resolved at load time irrespective of validation, FALSE otherwise; read-write
specified	Indicates whether the node is explicitly stated or derived from a default value; TRUE for document objects
text	The text content of the entire document; nominally read-write, an assignment is disallowed by MSXML for document objects
url	Canonical URL for the last document loaded; read-only
validateOnParse	TRUE if MSXML should try to validate the document upon loading (default), FALSE otherwise; read-write
xml	The markup content of the entire document; read-only

A detailed reference to the DOM as implemented in MSXML is also available in Appendix B.

You may have some confusion over nodeType, nodeTypedValue, and nodeTypeString. To start, nodeType is part of the DOM Level 1 Recommendation. It tells you whether a node is an element, attribute, processing instruction, or what have you. Its value is independent of the value contained in the node. The property nodeTypeString, though an extension, is similar in concept. It conveys the same information as a string rather than an enumerated value. Thus, the markup <Name>...</Name> would be represented in the DOM by a node. Calling nodeType on that node would return the value 1, i.e., NODE_ELEMENT, while nodeTypeString would return the value element. The property nodeTypedValue is quite different and is wholly a Microsoft extension. If we declared a particular attribute to be an integer (i.e., dt:int) we might write the following markup in the document:

```
<SomeElement count="14"/>
```

If you then navigated to the node representing the count attribute and called nodeTypedValue on it, you would receive the numeric value 14, not a string composed of the characters 1 and 4. This is convenient inasmuch as it lets the programmer rely on the parser for text to typed value conversions.

The readyState property is most useful when loading a document asynchronously, although you should get used to testing it whenever you load a document. The enumerated states for this property are as follows:

State	Value	Meaning
LOADING	1	Loading has begun, but parsing has not.
LOADED	2	Loading is complete, parsing has begun, but no objects are available in the DOM.
INTERACTIVE	3	Some objects in the DOM are available, but parsing is not complete. The document is read-only in this state.
COMPLETED	4	The document is loaded and parsed. Note this does not imply successful completion of parsing; you must check the parseError object.

Here are the methods of the document object:

Method	Meaning
abort	Aborts an in-progress asynchronous download.
appendChild(newChild)	Appends the newChild node to the end of the childNodes collection.
cloneNode(deep)	Creates an exact copy of this node; if deep is TRUE, then the node and its entire subtree is copied; if FALSE, only the node itself is copied. Returns the copy.
createAttribute(name)	Creates a new attribute with the name provided. Subsequently, the value of the new attribute's nodeName property will be equal to name; Returns an attribute node.
createCDATA Section(data)	Creates a new CDATA section whose nodeValue is data; returns the CDATA node.
createComment(data)	Creates a comment node with the string value provided in data; returns the comment node.
createDocument Fragment	Creates a new, empty document fragment; an alternative to calling createNode with the enumerated type NODE_DOCUMENT_FRAGMENT, this method returns a document fragment object that is associated with the document but not part of it. No namespace is associated with the fragment.
createElement(name)	Creates a new XML element whose nodeName is name; returns the element node.
createEntity Reference(name)	Creates and returns a node representing an entity reference with the name provided.
createNode (type, name, namespaceURI)	Creates a node of the enumerated type and name, qualified by the optional namespace; returns the newly created node (see the section on Nodes below for permissible values of type).
createProcessing Instruction (target, data)	Creates a PI node (target is the value immediately following the <?, data the remainder); the value of target is subsequently available as the nodeName property of the returned node.
createTextNode(text)	Creates and returns a text node, i.e., PCDATA content.
getElements ByTagName(name)	Returns a node list whose members have the specified element name; the wild card * returns all elements.
hasChildNodes	Returns TRUE if the node has children, FALSE otherwise.
insertBefore (newNode, refNode)	Inserts and returns newNode before refNode if newNode is permitted to be a child of the parent node. This operation will fail if the types are wrong, e.g. attempting to insert an element as a child of an attribute, or if the document's DTD or schema prohibits the parent-child relationship proposed. If successful, newNode becomes the left sibling of refNode.

Table continued on following page

Method	Meaning
load(URL)	Loads and parses the document referenced by the url parameter; on failure, the parseError property is set and documentElement is NULL; load may also take an object that supports the IStream interface in lieu of a URL. Examples include the ASP Request object and MSMQ message bodies; returns TRUE if the load succeeded, FALSE otherwise.
loadXML(stringDoc)	Attempts to load and parse stringDoc as an XML document; returns TRUE if the load succeeded, FALSE otherwise; upon failure, parseError is set and documentElement is NULL.
nodeFromID(idValue)	Returns the node bearing an attribute whose type is ID and whose value is idValue; if no such node is found, returns NULL.
removeChild (removeChild)	Removes and returns removeChild if found in the childNodes collection of the parent, NULL otherwise.
replaceChild (newChild, oldChild)	Replaces oldChild (if found) with newChild and returns oldChild, NULL otherwise; this operation will fail if newChild is not permitted to be a child of the parent.
save(obj)	Persists the document to the target object provided it supports IStream, IPersistStream, or IPersistStreamInit; examples include disk files (specified by a file name), the ASP Response object, MSMQ message bodies (SP4 and later), or other instances of MSXML.
selectNodes(pattern)	Returns the node list whose members match the XSL pattern specified (compatible with XPath paths in MSXML 2.6 if the selectLanguage property is set to XPath); returns NULL if no nodes in the document match the pattern.
selectSingleNode (pattern)	Returns the node matching the XSL pattern specified or NULL if no nodes match.
transformNode (stylesheetObj)	Transforms the document by applying the MSXML instance supplied in stylesheetObj provided it contains an XSL stylesheet document; the transformed document is returned as a string.
transformNodeToObject (stylesheet, outObj)	Transforms the document by applying the supplied stylesheet; the transformation is returned to the output object, which may be any object supporting IStream.

This interface also supports three events:

Event	Meaning
ondataavailable	Fired when data is available in the document.
onreadystatechange	Indicates a change in the value of the readyState property.
ontransformnode	Fires before a node if the stylesheet is applied to a node in the document (XSL/XSLT).

The extensions to the W3C Document interface fall chiefly into three areas: loading documents, namespaces, and data-typing. The W3C interfaces concern themselves only with access to the items of a loaded XML document. They do not provide for how that document gets into the DOM implementation. Consequently, methods like load and loadXML are added in Microsoft's implementation. Since loading a document involves state information and the possibility of failure, we have properties like readyState and parseError. Next, namespaces are not part of the XML 1.0 Recommendation, but MSXML supports the XML Namespaces Recommendation. That is why properties like baseName and namespaceURI are added to the standard DOM interface. Finally, data types are strictly a proprietary addition of Microsoft's, albeit one that answers a common need. Eventually, the XML Schema Working Group should address this topic in a standard way, at which time MSXML will probably conform to the W3C's view.

Nodes

Nodes are the workhorse objects of the DOM in ASP. They encompass all the various kinds of nodes a DOM tree can support: elements, attributes, PCDATA, processing instructions, and so forth. Here are the properties of this interface:

Property	Meaning
attributes	A named node map containing the attribute nodes for an element node; also valid with entities and notations, in which case it exposes the public and system IDs and NDATA; read-only.
baseName	The base name of a namespace-qualified name; read-only.
childNodes	Returns a node list of the immediate child nodes of this node; read-only.
dataType	For attributes, elements, and entity references, this returns the string representation of the data type specified in the schema or the document for this node; for text types, returns a string; read-write.
definition	For attributes and elements declared in an associated schema, returns the node in the schema declaring this node type; for unparsed entities, returns the NOTATION definition; for entity references, returns the node for the entity referenced; for all others, NULL; read-only.
firstChild	Returns the first (left-most) child for nodes that may have children, NULL otherwise; read-only.
lastChild	Returns the right-most child node for nodes that may have children, NULL otherwise; read-only.
namespaceURI	Returns the namespace URI for qualified names; read-only.
nextSibling	Returns the next child node (right sibling) in the childNodes collection if any, NULL otherwise; read-only.
nodeName	Returns a string (never NULL); for elements, attributes, and entities, this is the qualified name of the node; for other types, returns a fixed string, e.g. #document for NODE_DOCUMENT, or the name of the node, e.g. the name of the referenced entity for NODE_ENTITY_REFERENCE; read-only.
nodeType	Returns the enumerated type (see table below) of the node; read-only.
nodeTypedValue	Returns the strongly typed value of the node; read-write.

Table continued on following page

Property	Meaning
nodeTypeString	Returns a string representation of the enumerated node type; read-only.
nodeValue	For attributes, comments, CDATA sections, text nodes, and PIs, returns the textual content of the node; for all other types, notably elements, returns NULL; read-write.
ownerDocument	Returns the parent document object to which this node belongs; read-only.
parentNode	Returns the parent node for types that have parents; returns NULL for documents, document fragments, and attributes, or if a newly created node has not been inserted into a parent; read-only.
parsed	TRUE if the node and all its descendants are parsed, FALSE otherwise; read-only.
prefix	Returns the namespace prefix for a qualified name, or an empty string for unqualified names; read-only.
previousSibling	Returns the left sibling of the node or NULL if none exists; returns NULL for documents, document fragments, and attributes; read-only.
specified	Returns TRUE if an attribute node appears explicitly in a document, FALSE if it is specified by default in the DTD or schema; returns TRUE for all other node types; read-only.
text	Returns the text content for the node and all its descendants; read-write.
xml	Returns the markup for the node and all its descendants; read-only.

The properties attributes and childNodes are critical to the traversal of DOM trees, as we shall see later in this chapter. These properties are collections of nodes associated with the current node. Similarly, properties like firstChild, lastChild, and nextSibling refer to nodes related to the current node and are used to navigate the tree.

Other properties of the node interface tell us about the node we are currently examining. As we shall see later, it is imperative to check the value of the nodeType property when working with a node in an arbitrary document. This property will tell you the sort of node with which you are dealing, and hence the type of item in the XML document you are examining. The enumerated values for this property are as follows:

Node Type	Value	Meaning
NODE_ELEMENT	1	Element
NODE_ATTRIBUTE	2	Attribute
NODE_TEXT	3	Text content of an element
NODE_CDATA_SECTION	4	CDATA section
NODE_ENTITY_REFERENCE	5	Reference to any sort of XML entity in a document
NODE_ENTITY	6	Expanded entity
NODE_PROCESSING_INSTRUCTION	7	XML processing instruction

Node Type	Value	Meaning
NODE_COMMENT	8	Comment node
NODE_DOCUMENT	9	Document object; can only be returned from a document object
NODE_DOCUMENT_TYPE	10	Document type declaration
NODE_DOCUMENT_FRAGMENT	11	Document fragment (a node or subtree not actually contained within a document
NODE_NOTATION	12	A notation in the document type declaration

This interface supports a variety of methods used to manipulate the node's subtree. These involve selection, insertion and removal, and XSL transformation. In the version of MSXML we are discussing, selection uses XSL patterns. For version 2.6, XPath path strings may be used if the SelectLanguage property is set to XPath. The methods for this interface are as follows:

Method	Meaning
appendChild(newChild)	Appends newChild to the end of the childNodes collection and returns newChild
cloneNode(deep)	Creates and returns a copy of the node; if deep is TRUE, the entire subtree rooted by the node is copied; if FALSE, only the node itself is copied
hasChildNodes	Returns TRUE if the node has children, FALSE if it has no children or is a type that cannot have children
insertBefore(new, ref)	Inserts and returns new as the left sibling of ref; this operation will fail if invoked for nodes that cannot be children; an error is returned if ref is not a child of the parent node; if ref is NULL, new is inserted at the end of the childNodes collection
removeChild(child)	Removes and returns the specified child node
replaceChild(new, old)	Replaces old with new and returns old; if new is NULL, old is removed without replacement
selectNodes(pattern)	Returns a node list whose members match the XSL pattern provided; in version 2.6, this may be an XPath path if the document's selectionLanguage is set to Xpath
selectSingleNode(pattern)	Returns the node matching the pattern; if using v. 2.6, this may be an XPath path provided the document's selectionLanguage is set to XPath
transformNode(stylesheet)	Applies the XSL transformations specified in the provided stylesheet object to the node and its descendant subtree
transformNodeToObject* (stylesheet, outObj)	Transforms the document by applying the supplied stylesheet; the transformation is returned to the output object, which may be any object supporting IStream

Node Lists

The NodeList interface is used for any collection of nodes in an XML document. In practice, node lists are segregated into XML attributes (in the attributes collection) and everything else (in the childNodes collection). Node lists are also used to return the results of pattern-based selection. The NodeList interface has but one property:

Property	Meaning
length	Number of nodes in the NodeList collection

Node lists also have three methods:

Method	Meaning
item	Permits zero-based ordinal random access to the nodes in the collection
nextNode	Returns the next node in the collection when iterating through the NodeList
reset	Resets the iterator when using the nextNode method

Late binding COM interfaces have the notion of a default method, one which is invoked if the interface is called with no method explicitly named. The NodeList interface follows common practice for collections by making item the default for the interface. Consequently, the following two bits of code are equivalent:

```
for (var i = 0; i < node.childNodes.length; i++)
    Traverse(node.childNodes(i));
```

```
for (var i = 0; i < node.childNodes.length; i++)
    Traverse(node.childNodes.item(i));
```

Both fragments use the length property and the item collection to call the function Traverse on every child node of some selected node in a DOM tree. Node lists are the simplest way to traverse a given level of sibling nodes in a document, but it is not the most efficient given the way the DOM is implemented in MSXML. I will return to this topic and present two methods of traversing siblings when we get to the tree traversal section following the DOM survey.

Named Node Maps

This interface is similar to the NodeList, differing mainly in the fact that nodes are addressed by name instead of ordinal index. Another important distinction, however, is that this interface is used exclusively for attributes. This is because attribute names will be unique on any particular instance of an element, so named access is a natural method of addressing attributes. Such access is certainly more convenient than iterating through a collection checking the nodeName property of each member of the collection. The interface has a single property:

Property	Meaning
length	Number of nodes in the map

The methods for this interface are as follows:

Method	Meaning
getNamedItem(name)	Returns the named attribute.
getQualifiedItem (baseName, namespaceURI)	Retrieves a namespace-qualified attribute.
nextNode	Returns the next node in the collection, or NULL if the end of the collection has been reached.
removeNamedItem(name)	Removes and returns the named attribute if found; if not found, this method returns NULL.
removeQualifiedItem (baseName, namespaceURI)	Removes and returns the qualified attribute if found, otherwise returns NULL.
reset	Resets the iterator when traversing the collection using nextNode.
setNamedItem(newItem)	Sets the node supplied, replacing any attribute of the same name in the process. If newItem is not an attribute, an error is returned; otherwise, the newly set node is returned.

Note that the extensions made by this interface to the W3C model are chiefly for XML namespaces support and COM-style iteration (i.e., nextNode and reset).

Error Handling

MSXML supports the IXMLDOMParseError interface for handling errors generated during the parsing of an XML document. This interface is a critical part of the task of loading a document into the parser, as we shall see. All properties in this interface are read-only. Here they are:

Property	Meaning
errorCode	Error code, in decimal, of the last parse error
filepos	Absolute file position at which the parser detected the error
line	Number of the line containing the error
linepos	Character position within line where the error was detected
reason	Textual description of the reason for the error
srcText	The text of the line, including markup, containing the error
url	URL of the document containing the error

The errorCode property will have the value of zero when a document loads without error. When the validateOnParse property of the document object is set to TRUE, the document will be considered error-free only if it is both well-formed and valid. If the document is not being validated, i.e., validateOnParse is FALSE or no DTD or schema is associated with the document, then a well-formed document is all that is required to avoid an error condition. Since the errorCode property is the default property of this object, you may refer to parseError.errorCode as simply parseError. Here's an example of a very common bit of code used to check that a newly loaded document is valid and report the error if it is not:

```
if (doc.readyState == 4 && doc.parseError.errorCode == 0)
{
  // Do some processing here
}
else
  alert("Error: " + doc.parseError.reason);
```

The initial `if` statement checks to see if the parser has finished its work (`readyState` property) and the document has no errors (`parseError` interface's `errorCode` property). If these conditions do not apply, we use the `reason` property of the error handler interface to put a simple text explanation into a dialog box. If we were writing a debugging tool for developers, we could use the `filepos`, `line`, `linepos`, and `srcText` properties to locate the error for the developer.

Additions and Changes in the Technology Preview

The technology preview release of MSXML is unchanged from a strict DOM point of view. Nevertheless, ASP developers will be interested in it because this version adds a number of features, which, while not directly affecting the DOM, nevertheless alter the nature of XML applications that may be written in the ASP environment. These features include the ability to perform document validation on demand, caching features and interfaces for documents schemas and XSL stylesheets, and support for the new XSLT and XPath W3C Recommendations. The technology preview version of MSXML is currently (as at the time of writing) available for download at http://msdn.microsoft.com/downloads/webtechnology/xml/msxml.asp.

To support these new features, the technology preview release of MSXML adds five new interfaces:

Interface	Use
IXMLDOMDocument2	An extension of the DOM document interface that adds support for cached schema files and on-demand validation
IXMLDOMSchemaCollection	Allows frequently used schema files to be loaded and cached in memory for performance enhancement
IXMLDOMSelection	Enhanced interface representing the results of an XSL pattern or XPath query search, this interface offers more robust access to the results of the query
IXMLDOMXSLProcessor	A performance-related enhancement, this interface uses precompiled XSL stylesheets for transformation (see next interface)
IXMLDOMXSLTemplate	Allows precompiling of XSL stylesheets for performance gains

While it is inappropriate to dwell on the interfaces of a nonstandard technology preview in this chapter, it is worth looking at the changes to the basic document interface. You'll be using this core interface quite extensively later in the chapter. As you become familiar with the DOM, refer to the following table and see how the enhancements listed here address common problems.

Method	Meaning
getProperty	Retrieves values set by setProperty
namespaces	Returns the namespaces used in the document as a collection of schema objects

Method	Meaning
schemas	Sets the collection of cached schemas to be used with the document
selectNodes	Used to perform an XSL or XPath query similar to selectNodes in the core DOM; the node list returned has the IXMLDOMSelection interface rather than the node list returned by the DOM equivalent
setProperty	Sets default values; used in the technology preview to set whether XSL patterns or XPath syntax will be used as the query language
validate	Validates the document as it exists at the time the method is invoked using the specified DTD or schema collection (on-demand validation)

On-Demand Validation

Prior to this version, XML documents were validated only when they were loaded and parsed. This is perfectly adequate for static documents, but ASP developers frequently modify or create documents dynamically through script. The document interface adds a new method, validate, to the DOM that validates the document against the currently loaded DTD or schema collection. The latter is also new. It is an interface that allows a programmer to load a number of frequently used schemas and keep them in memory. They may be applied to subsequently loaded documents by passing the collection to a document through its schemas property, another addition and extension to the DOM.

Schema and Stylesheet Caching

We just noted that schemas can be loaded into an object that can be cached for future use. You create an instance of the XMLDOMSchemaCollection interface (MSXML2.XMLSchemaCache). This may be stored in session or application scope. The same is true for XSL stylesheets, although the process is a bit more complicated. You start by creating an instance of the XMLDOMXSLTemplate interface (MSXML2.XSLTemplate). Next, you create a free-threaded instance of an XML document and load the stylesheet into the template object by assigning the document object to the template's stylesheet property. The template is a free-threaded object suitable for caching in application scope, subject, of course, to the usual concerns regarding concurrent access. To make this easier, there is the XMLDOMXSLProcessor interface. You get one of these from the template object by calling its createProcessor method. A processor is rental-threaded, so you will want to obtain it, use it, and discard it within the scope of an ASP page. The two interfaces act together to allow us the ability to cache stylesheets without worrying unduly about concurrent access.

The typical use for templates is to cache an unchanging XSL stylesheet. Matters become more complicated if your application must modify the stylesheet dynamically. Obviously, a change to a cached template will be visible to everyone who needs to use the object. Such changes are not, however, reflected in existing processors created from the template. Processors are snapshots of the state of the template at the time createProcessor is called. If you want to make changes, use a non-cached stylesheet, or lock the cached template, make the changes, and create a new processor.

XSLT/XPath Support

The W3C promoted their XSLT and XPath drafts to Recommendation status on 16 November 1999. The documents, available at http://www.w3.org/TR/xslt and http://www.w3.org/TR/xpath, respectively, change the syntax for XSL transformations and patterns supported in MSXML. While similar in many regards, old stylesheets and patterns may not work. The new forms are standard, of course, and offer new features. Fortunately for our purposes, the two forms – old XSL and patterns and the newer XSLT and XPath syntax – are supported in MSXML's technology preview. The parser defaults to the old syntax for backward compatibility. To change the parser over to the new syntax, you call the document's setProperty method as follows:

```
document.setProperty("SelectionLangauge", "XPath")
```

To reset it, make a similar call with the second parameter set to XSLPattern. Documents also support the getProperty method for determining the current processing mode of the parser.

Tasks

Now that you've seen when you might want to use XML in ASP applications and surveyed the interfaces of MSXML, you are ready to begin learning how to perform the common tasks involved in manipulating XML in ASP. These are:

- ❑ Creating a suitable instance of the parser component
- ❑ Loading and validating documents
- ❑ Traversing the DOM tree
- ❑ Creating and modifying documents and content
- ❑ Transforming documents

Parser Creation

You can't do anything without an instance of MSXML. There are two types of instances, a single-threaded document and a free-threaded document. If you are working in a scripted environment like ASP, you will most typically use the first of these. Normally, you will use documents within the scope of a single ASP page. Unless you are using the specialized interfaces of MSXML 2.6, it is seldom worthwhile to cache an XML document in application or session scope due to the difficulties of concurrent access. Within an ASP page, it is impractical to perform asynchronous loads while working with a partially parsed document, so there is no real need for the overhead associated with the free-threaded version. You should, however, use the free-threaded version for cached documents.

To create an apartment-threaded document, use the following line:

```
doc = Server.CreateObject("microsoft.xmldom");
```

If there is a problem creating the object, the method will return NULL. If you need a free-threaded document, replace the progID in the call above with microsoft.FreeThreadedXMLDOM. In either case, be sure to set the document object to NULL when you are finished with it to ensure Windows is able to reclaim resources:

```
var doc, stylesheet;

doc = Server.CreateObject("microsoft.xmldom"); // create it

if (doc != null && stylesheet != null)
{
    doc.async = false;
    doc.load(Server.MapPath("some_file.xml"));

    if (doc.parseError == 0)
```

```
        // Some processing here
    else
        // Error processing here
    ...
    doc = null;                              // free the resource
}
else
    // more error handling here
```

Document Loading and Validation

A brand new instance of an XML document object is, of course, empty. Later on I'll cover creating a document through DOM calls, but first let's look at how you load an existing document and validate it against a DTD. For the next few examples I'll be using the XML document contained in the file team.xml:

> All sample files and source code for this chapter may be downloaded from our Web site at **http://www.wrox.com.**

Since we're going to be validating it, I've created a DTD and inserted the following DOCTYPE reference in the file:

```
<!DOCTYPE Team SYSTEM "team.dtd">
```

Now I'm ready to load the document from disk. This code is contained in the file basic.asp. Since I can't do anything until the entire document is loaded, I set the document's async property to FALSE, forcing a synchronous load, and call the document's load method:

```
doc.async = false;
doc.load(Server.MapPath("team.xml"));
```

Note this assumes that the file team.xml is located in the same directory as the ASP. When load returns, it should be fully loaded and parsed. Since I made a synchronous load, I don't really have to check the readyState property, but it's a good habit to get into. Most important, though, is checking the parseError property to see if an error has been detected. If the document is loaded, readyState will be 4 and the errorCode property of the error handler will be 0:

```
if (doc.readyState == 4 && doc.parseError.errorCode == 0)
{
    Response.Write("Doc is good");
}
else
    Response.Write("Error: " + doc.parseError.reason);
```

The errorCode property is the default property of the error handler interface, so the following shortcut is equivalent:

```
if (doc.readyState == 4 && doc.parseError == 0)
```

93

Once readyState reaches the fully loaded and parsed state (4), validation will have succeeded or failed. Consequently, if an error is detected, the reason property of the error handler can be checked to get a string description of the problem. If I need further diagnostics, linepos and srcText can help me locate the problem. However, they may not be entirely descriptive. Like a compiler's error message, they simply tell you where the parser detected the error. The real cause of the problem may lie elsewhere in the document.

Tree Traversal

Now I'm ready to do something with the document. The most important task is to be able to navigate through the document. I'll demonstrate this by showing you two ways to use the DOM to fully traverse the entire document and count all the nodes in the tree. First, here is the text of the sample file we're going to traverse. It is a very basic attempt to represent a team of people assigned to a project. This isn't a very rich representation; the intent is more to create a document with some nested content and a variety of elements and attributes so we can get some practice moving about in it.

```xml
<?xml version="1.0"?>
<!DOCTYPE Team SYSTEM "team.dtd">
<Team project="a134">
  <Manager person="a1"/>
  <Members people="b1 c2 c9"/>
  <Person sn="a1">
    <Name>
      <First>John</First>
      <Last>Doe</Last>
    </Name>
  </Person>
  <Person sn="b1">
    <Name>
      <First>Dudley</First>
      <Last>Doright</Last>
    </Name>
  </Person>
  <Person sn="c2">
    <Name>
      <First>Florence</First>
      <Last>Nightingale</Last>
    </Name>
  </Person>
  <Person sn="c9">
    <Name>ss
      <First>Giordano</First>
      <Last>Bruno</Last>
    </Name>
  </Person>
</Team>
```

NodeLists

Let's replace the alert call in the preceding code that advises us of a valid and loaded document with a call to a function that will traverse the tree:

```
if (doc.readyState == 4 && doc.parseError.errorCode == 0)
{
  Traverse(doc.documentElement);
  Response.Write("Nodes in the DOM for team.xml: " + nodes);
}
```

I'm going to recursively call `Traverse` to walk the tree, but I want it to start with the root `Team` element (conveniently skipping the XML and `DOCTYPE` declarations). `Traverse` takes a node and uses the `childNodes` property, a node list, to walk through the elements:

```
function Traverse(node)
{
  nodes += 1;
  if (node.attributes != null)
    nodes += node.attributes.length;

  for (var i = 0; i < node.childNodes.length; i++)
    Traverse(node.childNodes(i));
}
```

Recall that `length` gives us a one-based count of the number of child nodes, but attributes are not contained in this collection. If I want to count all the nodes, then I need to check the `length` property of the `attributes` collection. Every time I enter the function I increment the value of the variable `nodes` to reflect a new element, and I add `attributes.length` to that count to reflect the attributes belonging to the element. If my DTD provided default values for attributes, nodes would appear in the `attributes` collection even if the attribute did not explicitly appear. If you want to differentiate between nodes that are physically present in the document and attributes that are included by default, you need to walk through the collection and check each attribute's `specified` property.

I don't actually iterate through the `attributes` collection since `length` tells me what I want to know. If I needed to do so, I could perform the iteration the same way `Traverse` iterates through `childNodes`. If, however, I needed to get an attribute by name (say, to check or set a value) I don't need to walk the entire collection. I can use the `getNamedItem` method of the `attributes` collection (a named node map object) like this:

```
attr = node.attributes.getNamedItem("sn");
```

That call will retrieve the node representing the `sn` attribute if `node` represents a `Person` element in the document.

Getting at an Element's Text

If you've executed `basic.asp` and compared the results (a node count of 34) to the sample file, you might be surprised. The code doesn't count the XML declaration or the `DOCTYPE` declaration, but a quick count of the sample would suggest a node count of 26. That is, 19 elements and 7 attributes.

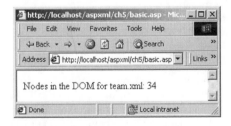

So, where are the other eight coming from? In XML, the markup fragment:

```
<First>John</First>
```

is a single element with PCDATA content. However, in the DOM, that's two nodes: one of type NODE_ELEMENT (1), and a child of type NODE_TEXT (3). Let's check this by expanding the code in basic.asp to look at the nodeType property while it is traversing the tree. Here is the version of Traverse found in the file typed.asp:

```
function Traverse(node)
{
  nodes += 1;

  switch (node.nodeType)
  {
    case 1: // elements
      elements += 1;
      if (node.attributes != null)
        attributes += node.attributes.length;
      for (var i = 0; i < node.childNodes.length; i++)
        Traverse(node.childNodes(i));
      break;

    case 2: // attributes
      // nothing to do -- attributes aren't picked up in childNodes
      break;

    case 3: // text nodes
      text_nodes += 1;
      break;
  }
}
```

Here, I'm switching on the value of the node's nodeType property to count the node in the property category. If you call this ASP, you see the numbers are what you expect – the extra eight nodes are text nodes. If you count the PCDATA in team.xml, you'll see this is the correct count.

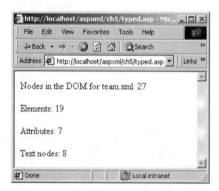

If you want to get at the textual content of an element, you need to do one of two things. If you implicitly know that the node contains nothing but text, you can avail yourself of the extension property text. Since there is only the text node below this one, you are safe in taking this shortcut. If, however, you are writing code that does not have implicit knowledge of the document structure, you must check the node's childNodes collection. Text-only nodes will have a single node, i.e., childNodes.length == 1, and its type will be NODE_TEXT, i.e., childNodes(0).nodeType == 3.

Siblings

There is another approach to traversing the DOM tree. Owing to the implementation of the `childNodes` collection in MSXML, this approach is also faster. It relies on the `firstChild` and `nextSibling` properties of the `Node` interface. These properties give us a linked list representation of the children of a particular node. We can use this to reproduce the behavior of `typed.asp` in a new ASP file, `linkedlist.asp`. There, I replace `Traverse` with `TraverseSibs`. It does everything that `Traverse` did, except when it comes to recursively calling itself. In `Traverse`, I called the function recursively for every member of a node's `childNodes` collection and I placed this loop within the case handling element nodes:

```
for (var i = 0; i < node.childNodes.length; i++)
  Traverse(node.childNodes(i));
```

In `TraverseSibs`, I have the following lines of code:

```
child = node.firstChild;
while (child != null)
{
  TraverseSibs(child);
  child = child.nextSibling;
}
```

These lines are outside the `switch` statement. They have the same effect as the prior traversal that iterated through `childNodes` and are slightly faster.

Path-Based Selection

There is one more method of tree traversal that is highly effective when you have some idea of the node or nodes for which you are looking. That is path-based selection using XSL patterns in MSXML 2.0 or their W3C successor, XPath expressions, in MSXML 2.6. Neither is, strictly speaking, part of the DOM. They are, however, techniques a working ASP programmer needs in his or her toolkit.

The idea is to pass an expression defining a path and, optionally, a filter expression to the `selectNodes` or `selectSingleNode` methods of the node and document interfaces. The parser is then responsible for traversing the tree and returning any nodes that match the conditions of the expression. This approach has two benefits. To begin with, once you master the expression syntax, your work is over. MSXML is responsible for the implementation, and you don't have to include the tree traversal code in your application. More importantly, you make a single call through COM – the real work occurs entirely within the parser, which, in MSXML's case, is written in highly optimized C++. The traversal and selection methods I've presented so far incur the overhead of a COM call every time they invoke a DOM method or property. This will make a great deal of difference in the performance of a high volume ASP application.

I'll briefly cover the XSL Pattern syntax supported in MSXML 2.0. This is an implementation of the XSL draft that was current when the component was released. Since then, XSL has progressed and the path selection language has been finalized in the XPath Recommendation (http://www.w3.org/TR/xpath). Microsoft is in the process of implementing XPath support in MSXML 2.6. As noted previously, the technology preview of this component has partial support right now. We'll go into more detail on XSL and patterns in a later chapter, but I want you to have some basic information at this stage so that we can use it in an example a little later in this chapter.

A pattern is a string consisting of element or attribute names, special operators, and collection functions. It specifies a path through the DOM tree that is read left (closest to the root) to right (deepest). Here are the special characters that are fundamental to XSL patterns:

XSL Pattern Character	Meaning
/	Immediate child operator; when a pattern begins with this character, it indicates that selection begins from the document root element
//	Recursive descent (selects the pattern that follows if it appears anywhere below the starting point); if the patterns begins with this, the remainder of the pattern may be matched anywhere within the document
.	Current context node
*	Wildcard operator selecting any element
@	Prefix indicating that the name immediately following refers to an attribute
@*	Attribute wildcard (selects all attributes)
:	Namespace separator
!	Applies an information method to the reference node
( )	Groups contents for precedence
[ ]	Applies a filter pattern
[ ]	Subscript operator for indexing into a collection

The pattern @sn invoked on a Person element returns the node representing the element's sn attribute. The pattern Person/Name invoked on a Team element selects all Name elements for Persons in that team. By contrast /Team/Person/Name selects all Name elements within the document. I can get the same effect with the pattern //Name (which selects any Name element occurring anywhere in the document), but it forces the parser to do much more searching.

> *Be judicious in your use of the recursive descent operator as it can have a major impact on performance. It is a convenient shorthand notation that squanders performance and should only be used when you cannot specify the path with greater precision.*

There are also some predefined collection methods for returning node lists of categories of nodes:

Collection	Meaning
ancestor(typeName)	Returns the parent node of type typeName that is nearest to the context pattern
attribute(nameStr)	Returns the attribute named nameStr; if the parameter is omitted, all attributes of the selected context are returned
comment	Returns all comment nodes

Collection	Meaning
element (nameStr)	Returns all elements of the type named; if the parameter is omitted, all elements within the selected context are returned
node	Returns all non-attribute nodes
pi	Returns all processing instruction nodes
textnode	Returns all text nodes

Thus, the pattern /Team/Person/attribute("sn") returns all the sn attributes in the document, while /Team/element() returns all child elements of the Team element in our sample. If you refine the last example to be /Team/element("Person"), only the Person child elements will be returned. The ancestor collection method is a bit different in that it takes an element name, not a string literal, e.g. ancestor(Team).

The XSL pattern syntax also includes some information methods which may be invoked on a node with the ! operator:

Information Method	Meaning
date	Casts values to the date format
end	Returns TRUE if the last node in a collection is selected
index	Returns the index number of the node within the parent
nodeName	Returns the qualified name of the node
nodeType	Returns a number indicating what type of node is selected
text	Returns the immediate text node of the selected element
value	Returns a type cast version of the value of an element

You may also establish filter expressions on patterns to limit the list of nodes returned. The XSL pattern syntax uses a set of keyword operators delimited by the $ character for conditional comparison. Shortcuts that will seem more natural to programmers are also defined for most operators:

Operator	Shortcut Form	Meaning
and	&&	Logical AND
or	||	Logical OR
not		Logical NOT
eq	=	Equals
ieq		Case insensitive equality
ne	!=	Not equal
ine		Case insensitive inequality

Table continued on following page

Operator	Shortcut Form	Meaning
lt	<	Less than
ilt		Case insensitive less than
le	<=	Less than or equal to
ile		Case insensitive less than or equal to
gt	>	Greater than
igt		Case insensitive greater than
ge	>=	Greater than or equal to
ige		Case insensitive greater than or equal to
all		Set operation returning TRUE if the condition is TRUE for all items in a collection
any		Set operation returning TRUE if the condition is TRUE for any item in a collection

We can combine the information methods and the conditional operators to make some interesting patterns. For example, suppose I have the vague idea that some element within one of the Person elements has the text content Dudley. I can find out that this is a First element by checking the nodeName property of the node returned by the pattern /Team/(Person//*)[./text() = "Dudley"].

ID and IDREF Relationships

XSL patterns (and their XPath successors in MSXML 2.6) allow us to implement the ability to trace relationships established using the XML attribute types ID, IDREF, and IDREFS. An IDREF must refer to a value of an attribute typed as ID, and that value must be unique throughout the document. An attribute typed as IDREFS, moreover, has a value consisting of one or more space-delimited ID values. Hence, ID and IDREF model a one-to-one relationship, and ID and IDREFS model a one-to-many relationship. The DOM doesn't tell us how to make use of this, and XML 1.0 only tells us the nature of these relationships. Let's go down this path, however, by taking a look at the DTD for our sample document:

```
<!ELEMENT Team    (Manager , Members , Person+ )>
<!ATTLIST Team    project ID #REQUIRED >
<!ELEMENT Manager EMPTY>
<!ATTLIST Manager  person IDREF  #REQUIRED >
<!ELEMENT Members EMPTY>
<!ATTLIST Members  people IDREFS  #REQUIRED >
<!ELEMENT Person   (Name )>
<!ATTLIST Person  sn ID  #REQUIRED >
<!ELEMENT Name    (First , Last )>

<!ELEMENT First   (#PCDATA )>

<!ELEMENT Last   (#PCDATA )>
```

We can get at the `Person` element pointed to by the `Manager` element with the following lines:

```
var selectPtn = "/Team/Person[@sn='" + node.attributes(0).nodeValue + "'";
node.selectSingleNode(selectPtn);
name = node.childNodes(0);
sFirst = name.childNodes(0).text;
sLast = name.childNodes(1).text;
alert("The person you seek is " + sFirst + " " + sLast);
```

These lines assume that `node` is the `Manager` element. When the first line is executed, `selectPtn` will have the value /Team/Person[@sn='a1']. In the syntax of XSL patterns, this means "`Person` elements that are children of `Team` elements and whose `sn` attribute's value is 'a1'". We've made a number of assumptions based on the known structure of the document. We know that the element we are looking for is a `Person` element, and such elements are the immediate children of the `Team` element. Moreover, we know that the first (and only) attribute of the `Manager` element is an `IDREF` referring to the `sn` attribute of `Person`. Given all that, `selectSingleNode` is an efficient way to retrieve the other end of the `Manager` – `Person` relationship. From the point of view of XML, however, this implementation isn't entirely satisfactory. It makes no use of the information in the DTD, placing the burden instead on the programmer. Worse, if we want to get at the team members via the `IDREFS` attribute on the `Members` element, we will have to do a lot of manipulation to come up with an expression that will work with `selectNodes`.

In XPath, we can do the same thing with the path expression `id("a1")`. This is more like it. It says, in effect, "return all nodes that have an `ID` whose value is a1". The parser, in this case MSXML 2.6, must get the information it needs from the DTD. Our code compresses to:

```
node.selectSingleNode("id('" + node.attributes(0).nodeValue + "'");
```

We can get all the members of the project with the path expression `id("b1 c2 c9")`. In that case, we would need to use `selectNodes` as we expect a node list containing multiple nodes. Rather than parse the individual `ID` tokens from the `IDREFS` value of the `people` attribute, you can just use the value of that attribute directly.

Content Creation

You can write some very interesting applications with what you've learned so far. Eventually, though, you will need to modify existing documents or create entire XML documents entirely in code. Fortunately, the DOM makes ample provision for this task. I'm going to leave `team.xml` behind now. In order to illustrate a variety of useful techniques in content creation, let's assume we need to transmit a restaurant menu as an XML document. Here's a brief sample of such a document. It's called `menu.xml` if you want to download it from the Wrox web site:

```
<?xml version="1.0"?>
<Menu effective="2000-04-01" expires="2000-06-30">
  <Appetizers>
    <Item>
      <Name>Deep Fried Mushrooms with Stuff in Them</Name>
      <Price>6.00</Price>
      <Description>All mushrooms look alike. Focus on the
             conversation</Description>
    </Item>
```

```
      </Appetizers>
      <Entrees>
        <Item>
          <Name>Hungry Texan Prime Rib</Name>
          <Price>29.95</Price>
          <Description>You can hear your arteries clog...</Description>
        </Item>
      </Entrees>
      <Desserts>
        <Item>
          <Name>Chilled Monkey Brain</Name>
          <Price>20.00</Price>
          <Description>Mmmm! A delicacy from exotic lands.</Description>
        </Item>
      </Desserts>
    </Menu>
```

There are various additions you might want to make in practice, not least of which is the addition of food you might actually want to eat. Fortunately, though, I am teaching programming and not restaurant management, so this document is perfectly adequate for our purpose. Let's write an ASP that generates this menu in script code. This file is called `MakeMenu.asp`, and is available at the Wrox web site at www.wrox.com.

Setting the MIME Type

Our ASP will differ from the kind you're used to creating. It will return pure XML, so we'll skip the static `<HTML>` and `<BODY>` tags and go right to the script portion. Since we will be returning XML and not HTML, we need to set the proper MIME type in the response header. That let's Internet Explorer know that it should use its default stylesheet for rendering XML as a tree structure. You do this with the following line:

```
Response.ContentType = "text/xml";
```

If your server is not configured for XML, you should also associate this MIME type with the file extension .xml so that you can serve up static documents properly. In the MMC, select the Web server and right click on it. Select Properties, then select the HTTP Headers tab. Click the File Types button and associate text/xml with the extension .xml. In Windows 2000 Server, the button is labelled Edit and is found in the Computer MIME Map group of the Properties dialog box.

New Documents

You've seen how to create an instance of MSXML. Once you've done that, you are faced with a blank document. How do you get started? You turn to your newly created document object and call the createElement method, passing it the name of your document root, in this case Menu. You still don't have a document root, however. The createElement method, like the other creation methods we shall see, creates a new node object but does not associate that node with the document. You have a free-floating node that is associated with the document for purposes of ownership but which has no position within the document. Here's what you need to do:

```
root = doc.createElement("Menu");
doc.documentElement = root;
```

The root variable is set to a new element node. The documentElement is the one node that always has a known location within a document, so assigning it the value of the new node gives us the start of our document. If we were to check the xml property of the document at this point, we would see the following markup:

```
<Menu/>
```

Still, it's a start. I'll show you how to add the attributes we need in a bit. For now, the important thing is that we have a starting point for our document. All the child elements we create can be added by beginning at this root.

Elements

Judging from our sample, every menu document will have three elements as children of the root: Appetizers, Entrees, and Desserts. Let's create an Appetizer element and attach it to the root element:

```
root.appendChild(doc.createElement("Appetizers"));
```

I've combined two method invocations in this line. I pass the results of the createElement call, a node, into the appendChild method of the document element. That method, you'll recall, appends the passed node to the end of the childNodes collection. If you use this method, order is important. I could add the nodes in any order if I used some combination of appendChild and insertBefore.

I use the same technique to create the other two nodes that must appear, Entrees and Desserts. Here's the start of a function that creates the shell of my document:

```
function MakeShell(doc)
{
  var root, attrNode, pi;

  root = doc.createElement("Menu");
  doc.documentElement = root;

  root.setAttribute("effective", "2000-04-01");
  root.setAttribute("expires", "2000-09-30");

  root.appendChild(doc.createElement("Appetizers"));
  root.appendChild(doc.createElement("Entrees"));
```

```
root.appendChild(doc.createElement("Desserts"));

// some lines I don't want you to see yet...

...
}
```

I've put all the remaining code into a function called AddItems. In a real menu-generating function, this is where I'd put the logic to do a SQL query and loop through the resulting recordset. Since this is a contrived document that focuses on the DOM, I'll hard-code the content instead. Let's begin by drilling down into the Appetizers element and add a menu item, i.e., an Item element, with all its children:

```
itemNode = doc.createElement("Item");
itemNode.appendChild(doc.createElement("Name"));
itemNode.appendChild(doc.createElement("Price"));
itemNode.appendChild(doc.createElement("Description"));
```

This is very similar to what you've seen previously. I still haven't plugged this node into the Appetizers element, nor have I created the PCDATA content. Now, given the cautionary warning I gave you about the difference between an element with PCDATA content and its text node, you might expect me to take the long way around and create the text nodes separately. In this case, however, I know about the content of my Name, Price, and Description elements, so I can take the shortcut of using the text property, which as you will recall is a proprietary extension to the DOM:

```
itemNode.childNodes(0).text = "Deep Fried Mushrooms with Stuff in Them";
itemNode.childNodes(1).text = "6.00";
itemNode.childNodes(2).text =
                    "All mushrooms look alike. Focus on the conversation";
```

Notice that I've used ordinal indices into the childNodes collection. This relies on knowing the order of the child elements with the Item element. Now that I have a fully formed subtree for Item, how do I attach it to the document? I know that Appetizer is the first child node of Menu, so the following line would serve:

```
root.childNodes(0).appendChild(itemNode);
```

This document has a known simple structure: the root always has three children, and all the variable content is appended to those children. In more general cases, though, you may need a more flexible approach. You can use selectSingleNode to perform a pattern-based selection of the child nodes:

```
appetizerNode = doc.selectSingleNode("/Menu/Appetizers");
if (appetizerNode != null)
{
    itemNode = doc.createElement("Item");
    itemNode.appendChild(doc.createElement("Name"));
    itemNode.appendChild(doc.createElement("Price"));
    itemNode.appendChild(doc.createElement("Description"));

    // set the values

    itemNode.childNodes(0).text = "Deep Fried Mushrooms with Stuff in Them";
    itemNode.childNodes(1).text = "6.00";
```

```
itemNode.childNodes(2).text =
                    "All mushrooms look alike. Focus on the conversation";

appetizerNode.appendChild(itemNode);
}
```

My knowledge that `Appetizer` is an immediate child of the root element, `Menu`, is encoded in the XSL pattern `/Menu/Appetizer`. This avoids worrying about the order in which the child nodes appear. Additionally, if I am mistaken and there is no `Appetizer` node, I can detect the problem and avoid adding the content.

Subtree Cloning

The subtree consisting of an `Item` element and its descendants will be repeated over and over throughout the document, albeit with different values for the textual content. Rather than continue to make repeated calls to expensive creation methods, I can use the subtree I just created as a template. The `cloneNode` method lets me make a deep copy of the `Item` node. After I have that, I change the values and attach the new node in its proper place:

```
entreeNode = doc.selectSingleNode("/Menu/Entrees");
if (entreeNode != null)
{
  cloneNode = itemNode.cloneNode(true);
  cloneNode.childNodes(0).text = "Hungry Texan Prime Rib";
  cloneNode.childNodes(1).text = "29.95";
  cloneNode.childNodes(2).text = "You can hear your arteries clog...";

  entreeNode.appendChild(cloneNode);
}
```

This pattern is particularly well suited for implementing a loop in which I iterate through a database recordset. In fact, if I were writing an ASP to implement menus for real, that's exactly what I would do. While this example clones a subtree consisting solely of element and text nodes, a deep clone using `cloneNode` will work for any content. If `Item` or its children had attributes, comments, or some other type of nodes, they would have been copied as well.

Attributes

Let's complement our knowledge of creating elements with a look at how to create and assign attributes. There are actually two ways to do this using the DOM. The first is similar to the methods needed to create an element. Let's use that approach to add the `effective` and `expires` attributes on the menu element:

```
attrNode = doc.createAttribute("effective");
attrNode.nodeValue = "2000-04-01";
root.attributes.setNamedItem(attrNode);
```

I create an attribute node using the document object, assign it a value, and then reach into the attributes collection to attach the new node to the property element. Recall that attributes has a named node map as its value, so the methods available to you are different than those in the `childNodes` collection.

There is, however, a much simpler technique. It relies on an interesting behavior of the node interface's `setAttribute` method. If the attribute you name in the first parameter corresponds to an existing attribute of the element in question, the method changes its value. If, however, no such named attribute exists, `setAttribute` will create it, then set the value. The three lines of code you just saw (which involve three COM calls) reduce to a single line that passes through the COM layer just once:

```
root.setAttribute("effective", "2000-04-01");
```

Other Constructs

Knowing how to create elements and attributes will take you pretty far in the ASP and XML world, but there are still other kinds of XML constructs you might need to create. The document I've built so far lacks the XML declaration, and it relies on the default stylesheet in Internet Explorer for rendering in the browser. Let's make it a little more interesting. In addition to the XML declaration, I want to create a link to a cascading stylesheet. Internet Explorer will use that stylesheet to make my menu look a bit better.

To do this, I need to call `createProcessingInstruction` and insert the resulting nodes prior to the document root.

> *According to the XML 1.0 Recommendation, the XML declaration isn't a processing instruction, but it acts like one in every respect other than name.*

In a processing instruction, the keyword immediately following the first ? character is the **target**, while everything that follows the target and precedes the final ? character is the **data**. Note this may involve whitespace. Here's the markup for a processing instruction that links an XML document to a cascading stylesheet:

```
<?xml-stylesheet type="text/css" href="menu.css" ?>
```

Here's the code that creates it and adds it to the document in the proper place:

```
pi = doc.createProcessingInstruction("xml-stylesheet",
                              "type='text/css' href='menu.css'");
doc.insertBefore(pi, doc.childNodes(0));
```

I've used the `insertBefore` method to position this new node prior to the first child of the document, which happens to be the document's root element.

The XML declaration needs to be the very first construct in an XML document; so after I've inserted the CSS processing instruction, a call to insertBefore will put the XML declaration in its proper place:

```
pi = doc.createProcessingInstruction("xml", "version='1.0'");
doc.insertBefore(pi, doc.childNodes(0));
```

With these two nodes in place, a request for `MakeMenu.asp` looks like this in Internet Explorer 5.0 or later:

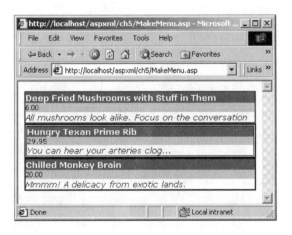

This isn't perfect, but it will look a lot better to prospective patrons than raw XML. Later on, in Chapter 8, you will be introduced to XSL. That XML application permits more powerful styling. Applied to the current application, for example, it would permit us to insert boilerplate headings like Menu, Appetizers, and so forth. It would also allow us to get at the attributes, convert them to a friendly, localized date format, and display them.

Most ASP-based XML applications don't bother with validation. After all, if you debug your code thoroughly, it should always generate valid documents, so why incur the overhead of validation at runtime? That may be a bit optimistic, but generally speaking, you won't bother with inserting DOCTYPE declarations.

If, however, you want to do that, you have a problem. The DOM specifies the document interface's DOCTYPE property to be read-only. We wouldn't want unscrupulous applications to swap DOCTYPE declarations, would we? MSXML honors this, so there is no way to create a document type declaration. The only way around this is to load a shell document containing the declaration into the parser and proceed with dynamic methods from there. The shell might look like this:

```
<?xml version="1.0"?>
<!DOCTYPE Aroot SYSTEM "tree.dtd">
<ARoot>
</ARoot>
```

Once this is loaded, you would navigate to the root and use the dynamic methods you have just seen to add child nodes and provide values.

> *This is not as bad as it seems. In fact, in some circumstances loading a shell document from a file can be more efficient than repeated COM calls to create needed nodes. This will be the case when the template nodes – those that are static – are large in relation to the nodes that require dynamic processing. In our example, the shell document is small enough to be hard-coded as a string and loaded using the document's loadXML method. This is the best of both worlds: we avoid both disk access and repeated createElement calls.*

Returning the Document

There's one very important task left. We've created a document, filled it with content, and added some useful processing instructions. The only problem is we never got around to returning it to the requesting client. There are two ways to do this. The string-oriented way to return the document is to use the document's xml property with ASP's Response object:

```
Response.Write(menuDoc.xml);
```

That causes the parser to blast the document into a string that is submitted to the Write method. That method, in turn, writes the parameter into the stream returned to the requesting client.

There is a slightly more elegant way to do this that takes advantage of the integration inherent in Windows DNA. MSXML can persist itself to an IStream interface via the save method of the document object, and Response supports just such an interface. Here's the approach I took:

```
menuDoc.save(Response);
```

The save method causes MSXML to query the Response object for its stream interface, then uses that interface to persist itself directly to the return stream.

Summary

We've had a look at the typical cases where an ASP programmer might use the API provided by the W3C's Document Object Model. Even though there is a trend toward encapsulating access to XML documents in business objects, there remains a demand for programmers who can code using the DOM. You've also seen that the DOM, by its nature, requires non-standard extension of any practical implementation. The DOM Recommendation has no provisions for loading or saving documents!

We moved quickly from there to a survey of Microsoft's XML parser as a commercial implementation of the DOM. You were inundated with the details of the principal scripting objects MSXML exposes through COM: `Document`, `Node`, `NodeList`, `NamedNodeMap`, and an error handler. The real work, however, began as we dug into the techniques needed to do practical ASP applications using the DOM. You learned how to do the following:

❑   Instantiate an appropriate instance of the parser component for your application

❑   Load and validate documents from files and strings

❑   Traverse the document tree and access node values

❑   Dynamically create and modify document contents and even entire documents

❑   Return XML documents to clients from an ASP

Along the way, I hinted at some performance implications. In particular, I presented three different ways to access nodes in a DOM tree. These techniques have different performance implications for your applications depending on how you need to access XML content. We even peeked at some of the forthcoming features and performance enhancements of the next release of MSXML. The Microsoft XML team has gone to great lengths to optimize their component for high performance, but the ultimate responsibility for scaling an ASP – XML application rests with you.

This chapter and the ones that preceded it have given you the basic tools for writing ASP applications that use XML. These tools alone give you what you need to build very sophisticated applications. That's the elegance of XML as a data format. It is simple, easily accessed, and extended. The DOM is similar. We are just getting started, however. The chapters to come will instruct in a variety of technologies and applications that have been built on top of XML and the DOM. They will greatly increase your productivity. Bear in mind, though, that all of these are built on the XML you know, and many are built on the DOM.

Integrating XML with ASP

So far, we have discussed XML in depth: its syntax, its validation using DTDs and schemas, and the DOM. However, whilst getting quickly up to speed with all this XML, we've put our ASP on hold. So it's about time we delved right back in there, now that we are becoming familiar with XML, and examine where and how ASP fits into this picture. This is the primary focus of the book, after all!

In this chapter we'll explore some of the simpler things that can be done with XML and Active Server Pages to whet your appetite and get your hands dirty once again with ASP coding. There's nothing fancy involved – we'll be progressing from here to more in-depth, integrated examples in the forthcoming chapters – but what you will be shown is a taster of the kinds of things that you can achieve with XML using ASP.

We'll start by actually looking at the ways in which we incorporate XML into ASP documents. We'll run through how we are able to create MSXML objects, and use them to load XML documents into the DOM. Then we'll move on to look at how we can insert XML into ASP code as a Server-Side Include, and finally, explore a third method, which uses the FileSystemObject to access XML documents via ASP.

Next we'll progress on to some extended examples. Starting off by sending XML data directly to the browser via ASP, we can then see how we can save the output as an HTML page. XSL is then worked into the equation as we can see how ASP can use it to modify data before the output is saved as an HTML file, giving us a taste for the chapter to come on styling with XSL.

Since we are not confined to simply storing textual data; the samples move on to demonstrate how XML can be an invaluable resource to your website with its ability to store more than just names and addresses, but links and settings too, for example. An XML document can capture information, which can be modified once and incorporated into your asp, instead of being hardcoded many times over. We'll also look at functions, which enable us to manipulate and make changes to the XML document itself, and finally we'll concentrate these various techniques into a more comprehensive, extended example.

So, we'll start by looking at the practicalities of accessing XML through ASP, by seeing exactly how we get them to function together.

How do ASP and XML Fit Together?

So the first thing that we need to do when incorporating XML data into ASP applications is to access the contents of the XML files. Technically speaking, there are three principal methods for reading and manipulating XML text in the ASP environment:

❑ Creating MSXML objects and loading XML documents into the DOM.

❑ Using Server-side Includes (SSI)

❑ Using the `FileSystemObject` to access XML documents as any other text file.

A fourth method is to create embedded data islands on the client, something which will be discussed further in Chapter 12.

Using the DOM

As we have seen earlier, this is probably the most common and, perhaps, most useful method from those in the list. A large proportion of the examples in this chapter, and indeed the book, will employ DOM functions and properties. In fact, you may find that you don't need to use any other method at all.

In order to use the DOM in your ASP code, you must create instances of the Microsoft XML parser, which is instantiated in the same way as any other COM component. As we saw in Chapter 5, several lines of standard code need to be written at the top of your page. These lines create an instance of the parser, load an XML document into the DOM, and set the root element (the `documentElement`) as the current node:

```
'Instantiate the XML Processor
Set objXML = Server.CreateObject("Microsoft.XMLDOM")

'Load the XML Document
objXML.load(Server.MapPath("mydata.xml"))

'Set the document element
Set objRootElement = objXML.documentElement
```

A fourth step that should occur before the XML document is loaded, is to set the `validateOnParse` property to `True`, which ensures it is a valid XML document that is loaded. This could save you a lot of trouble later on:

```
'Instantiate the XML Processor
Set objXML = Server.CreateObject("Microsoft.XMLDOM")

'The processor should validate the document
objXML.validateOnParse=True

'Load the XML Document
objXML.load(Server.MapPath("mydata.xml"))

'Set the document element
Set objRootElement = objXML.documentElement
```

Finally there is an optional step, also occurring before the load, which forces the file to load synchronously, i.e. all at once:

```
objXML.async = false
```

This does mean that the loading and parsing of very large files may take time. The alternative is to omit this step and allow asynchronous (or gradual) loading, which is the default. Once all these initialization steps are complete, the XML document is loaded and is ready to be manipulated; all of the considerable functionality of the DOM is at your disposal.

And as with any COM object, you must, of course, remember to destroy it after you have finished using it:

```
Set objXML = nothing
```

Server-Side Includes

The Server-Side Include (SSI) can be used to insert XML code into an ASP page just like any other text-based document. The only problem using this method is that the XML code is not parsed server-side, but is instead sent straight to the client as XML. Such behavior would be acceptable if you intended to create a client-side XML data island, but in most cases, the tags would be ignored by the browser and the result would be of little use.

The exception to this would be if the SSI code consisted of XML with HTML-type tags. Consider a medical application where notes from a doctor are saved in an XML document like this:

```
<?xml version="1.0"?>
<patient_notes patient="1823">
  <p>The patient reported with a slight fever this morning with swollen
  glands. Prescribed Trimox for 7 days.</p>
  <p>Patient reported that fever was gone in two days. Discontinued Trimox
  after third day.</p>
</patient_notes>
```

The <patient_notes> tag is a custom XML tag and would be unknown to the browser, so it will be ignored. However, the <p></p> tags are standard HTML and will be understood and hence will be processed. In the following ASP page (medicalhistory.asp), the above XML fragment is included as the john_doe.xml file:

```
<%@ Language=VBScript %>
<HTML>
<HEAD>
</HEAD>
  <BODY BGCOLOR=#FFFFFF>
    <H1>Medical History: John Doe</H1>
    <HR size=1>

    <!-- #INCLUDE file="john_doe.xml" -->

  </BODY>
</HTML>
```

And when the page is run, the inclusion is seamless:

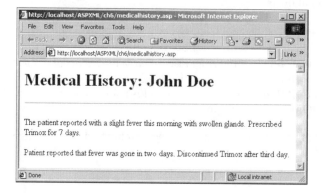

FileSystemObject

The `FileSystemObject` is the standard way to access text files from ASP pages, and since XML documents are text-based, it can be used to open them too. The MSXML processor that ships with IE5, however, has a `load` method for opening XML documents, thus making it unnecessary to resort to the `FileSystemObject` to do the same thing. However, there may be occasions when you would want to use the `FileSystemObject` to access an XML document, and carry out an action without actually loading it, such as checking the file's `Attributes` or `Date` properties, or deleting a temporary file at the end of a session.

Suppose you wanted to perform a simple text search using VBScript's `InStr` method. In such a situation, the XML processor is not required, as the `InStr` method is only interested in the text in the XML file, and not its structure. Let's look at an example page:

```
<%@ Language=VBScript %>
<HTML>
<HEAD>
</HEAD>
<BODY bgcolor=#FFFFFF>

<%
  Dim fso, file, XMLstring
  Set fso = CreateObject("Scripting.FileSystemObject")
  Set file = fso.OpenTextFile(Server.MapPath("/contacts.xml"), 1, False)
  XMLstring = file.ReadAll
  file.Close

  If InStr(XMLstring,"John Doe") > 0 Then
    Response.Write "Text was found!"
  Else
    Response.Write "Could not find the text."
  End If

  Set fso = nothing
%>
</BODY>
</HTML>
```

In this example, a `FileSystemObject` is created and is then used to open our XML document, `contacts.xml`. The contents of the XML file are read into the `XMLString` variable before the file is closed. The string "John Doe" is searched for, and a simple message is displayed, indicating whether the text is present or absent.

Examples of Processing XML using ASP Code

Now that we've seen that accessing XML data within the ASP environment is a relatively simple process, whichever method you select, we will now concentrate on using the DOM to access and use our XML data. We'll start off with some simple examples, then we'll gradually build up to some integrated applications later in the chapter.

Sending Data Directly to the Browser

This page (`displaycontacts.asp`) loads the XML file `contacts.xml`, parses it, and sends the resulting HTML straight to the browser:

```
<%@ Language=VBScript %>
<HTML>
<HEAD>
<TITLE> Displaying Contacts </TITLE>
</HEAD>
<BODY BGCOLOR=#FFFFFF>

<%
  Dim sourceFile, source, rootElement, HTMLCode

  ' Set the source of XML here
  sourceFile = Request.ServerVariables("APPL_PHYSICAL_PATH") + _
                                             "contacts.xml"

  ' Create an instance of the XML parser and load the XML into the DOM
  Set source = Server.CreateObject("Microsoft.XMLDOM")
  source.async = false
  source.load sourceFile
  Set rootElement = source.documentElement

  ' Build the string that will be sent to the browser
  HTMLCode = HTMLCode & "<FONT size=4 face=""verdana"">"
  HTMLCode = HTMLCode & rootElement.childNodes(0).text
  HTMLCode = HTMLCode & "</FONT><P></P><FONT size=3 face=""verdana""><I>"
  HTMLCode = HTMLCode & rootElement.childNodes(1).text
  HTMLCode = HTMLCode & "</I></FONT><P></P><FONT size=2 face=""verdana"">"
  HTMLCode = HTMLCode & rootElement.childNodes(2).text
  HTMLCode = HTMLCode & "</FONT><P></P>"

  Response.Write HTMLCode

  Set source = nothing
%>

</BODY>
</HTML>
```

The `contacts.xml` file just contains a few names and telephone numbers:

```xml
<?xml version="1.0"?>

<CONTACT_INFO>
  <CONTACT>
    <NAME>John Doe</NAME>
    <PHONE>555-5319</PHONE>
  </CONTACT>
  <CONTACT>
    <NAME>Mary Jones</NAME>
    <PHONE>555-9013</PHONE>
  </CONTACT>
  <CONTACT>
    <NAME>Mike Wilson</NAME>
    <PHONE>555-4138</PHONE>
  </CONTACT>
</CONTACT_INFO>
```

This is what is displayed in the browser when you load `displaycontacts.asp`:

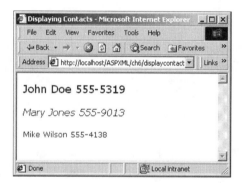

Saving Data as HTML

The above code can also be modified so that the output is saved as an HTML file. A
`FileSystemObject` object is used to achieve this. The complete file is called `savecontacts.asp`:

```
    ...

    ' Build the string that will be sent to the browser
    HTMLCode = HTMLCode & "<FONT size=4 face=""verdana"">"
    HTMLCode = HTMLCode & rootElement.childNodes(0).text
    HTMLCode = HTMLCode & "</FONT><P></P><FONT size=3 face=""verdana""><I>"
    HTMLCode = HTMLCode & rootElement.childNodes(1).text
    HTMLCode = HTMLCode & "</I></FONT><P></P><FONT size=2 face=""verdana"">"
    HTMLCode = HTMLCode & rootElement.childNodes(2).text
    HTMLCode = HTMLCode & "</FONT><P></P>"

    ' We use a FileSystemObject object to save the HTML to a file
    Set objFS = CreateObject("Scripting.FileSystemObject")
    Set objFile = _
      objFS.CreateTextFile(Request.ServerVariables("APPL_PHYSICAL_PATH") & _
                                            "\translation.htm")
```

```
    objFile.Write(HTMLcode)
    Response.Write "File Saved."

  Set objFS = nothing
  Set source = nothing
%>
...
```

Styling XML Data

Another variation of `displaycontacts.asp` uses Extensible Stylesheet Language (XSL) to modify the appearance of the data before it is saved as an HTML file.

In this example, which is available for download from the web site, we are working with three files: `stylecontacts.asp`, `contacts.xml`, and `contacts.xsl`. (We won't be discussing the code for `contacts.xsl` here, since we don't talk about XSL until chapters 8 and 9.) Using these three files, we can produce a file called `transformation.htm` which contains the same data as we saw before, but presented in a different style.

The `stylecontacts.asp` file looks like this:

```
<%@ Language=VBScript %>
<HTML>
<HEAD>
</HEAD>
<BODY BGCOLOR=#FFFFFF>

<%
  Dim sourceFile, source, styleFile, style, rootElement, HTMLCode, objFS, objFile

  ' Set the source and style sheet locations here. Note that two instances
  ' of the DOM are reuired for this operation.
  sourceFile = Request.ServerVariables("APPL_PHYSICAL_PATH") + _
                                            "\contacts.xml"

  styleFile = Request.ServerVariables("APPL_PHYSICAL_PATH") + _
                                            "\contacts.xsl"


  ' Load the XML
  Set source = Server.CreateObject("Microsoft.XMLDOM")
  source.async = false
  source.load(sourceFile)


  ' Load the XSL
  Set style = Server.CreateObject("Microsoft.XMLDOM")
  style.async = false
  style.load(styleFile)

  HTMLcode = source.transformNode(style)

  Set objFS = CreateObject("Scripting.FileSystemObject")
  Set objFile = _
      objFS.CreateTextFile(Request.ServerVariables("APPL_PHYSICAL_PATH") &_
                                        "\transformation.htm")

  objFile.Write(HTMLcode)
```

```
    Response.Write "File Saved."

    Set objFS = nothing
    Set style = nothing
    Set source = nothing
%>

</BODY>
</HTML>
```

The HTML that is produced looks like this when viewed in the browser:

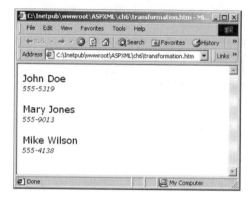

This is just a taste of what styling can achieve. The next four chapters are entirely devoted to this topic.

Using XML to Store Web Links and Property Settings

Having a single XML file containing all your contact information is very useful. Not only is the data in a single place that can be loaded and used by any XML-enabled application, and can be ported seamlessly between applications and platforms, but if any changes need to be made, then only one file needs to be updated.

The type of data that can be stored as XML is not restricted to names and telephone numbers. In fact, any data that can be stored in a hierarchical manner can be represented in an XML document in this way. The two examples in this section describe situations where an external XML document would provide a very useful resource for your web site.

❑ Storing web links – a single file where links to external or internal web pages are maintained

❑ Storing display settings – such as font styles and colors

Such files may be modified on a regular basis and would save a lot of time hard-coding the same information into many pages.

Web Links

The examples from the download consist of `navigate.asp` and `nav2html.asp`. The first sends the output straight to the browser and the second is a modified version of the first, which redirects the output to an HTML file. Both call the `links.xml` document, which is a very simple file containing just four example links, each contained in `<link>` tags:

```
<?xml version="1.0"?>

<relatedlinks>
  <link url="default.htm" target="_self">Front Page</link>
  <link url="news.htm" target="_self">News Section</link>
  <link url="sports.htm" target="_self">Sports Section</link>
  <link url="weather.htm" target="_self">Weather Page</link>
</relatedlinks>
```

Each `<link>` contains two attributes. The `url` attribute contains the destination URL, and the `target` attribute holds the calling page (in this case "_self", the current page, but it doesn't have to be). The text between the opening and closing tags will be the output that is displayed in the browser.

We can see how ASP uses this information by looking at `navigation.asp`:

```
<%@ Language=VBScript %>
<HTML>
<HEAD>
</HEAD>
<BODY BGCOLOR=#ffffff>

<%
  Dim objXML, objRootElement, strLinkName, strLinkURL, strLinkTarget, i

  'Instantiate the XML Processor
  Set objXML = Server.CreateObject("Microsoft.XMLDOM")

  'Load and validate the XML document
  objXML.validateOnParse=True
  objXML.load(Server.MapPath("links.xml"))

  Set objRootElement = objXML.documentElement

  'Loop through the XML <link> tags and get the information
  For i = 0 To objRootElement.childNodes.length - 1

    strLinkName = objRootElement.childNodes.item(i).text
    strLinkURL = objRootElement.childNodes.item(i).getAttribute("url")
    strLinkTarget = objRootElement.childNodes.item(i).getAttribute("target")

    ' Create the HTML <A> tags and send them to the browser
    Response.Write "<A HREF=""" & strLinkURL & """ target=""" & _
                          strLinkTarget & """>" & strLinkName & "</A><BR>"

  Next
  Set objXML = nothing
%>

</BODY>
</HTML>
```

After loading the XML, the `For...Next` loops gathers the information from each `<link>` tag in turn and creates an HTML `<A>` tag which is sent to the browser. The output looks like this:

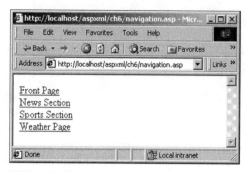

The `nav2html.asp` page works in a slightly different way:

```
...

    For i = 0 To objRootElement.childNodes.length - 1

        strLinkName = objRootElement.childNodes.item(i).text
        strLinkURL = objRootElement.childNodes.item(i).getAttribute("url")
        strLinkTarget = objRootElement.childNodes.item(i).getAttribute("target")

    ' Comment out the following lines to get formatted links
        strHTMLcode = strHTMLcode & "<A HREF=""" & strLinkURL & """ target=""" &_
                           strLinkTarget & """>" & strLinkName & "</A><BR>"

    ' Uncomment the following lines to get formatted links
    '       strHTMLcode = strHTMLcode & "<FONT FACE=""verdana"" size=2><LI>" & _
    '               "<A HREF=""" & strLinkURL & """ target=""" & strLinkTarget & _
    '                           """>" & strLinkName & "</A></LI></FONT><BR>"

    Next

    'Add the date
    strHTMLcode = strHTMLcode & "<BR><FONT FACE=""verdana"" size=1>" & _
                           "( LAST UPDATED: " &   Date() & ")</FONT>"

    Dim objFSO, objFile
    Set objFSO = CreateObject("Scripting.FileSystemObject")
    Set objFile = objFSO.CreateTextFile("C:\Inetpub\wwwroot\htmloutput.htm",True)
    objFile.Write(strHTMLcode)
    objFile.Close

    Response.Write "File Created: htmloutput.htm"
    Set objFSO = nothing

...
```

As it loops through the XML `<link>` tags, it builds up an HTML string containing a sequence of `<A>` tags, with optional formatting included as well, (just comment and uncomment the lines indicated to add the formatting code) and a "last updated" line is added for good measure. A `FileSystemObject` is instantiated to write the HTML string to a text file. The result, with extra formatting included, is this:

Display Settings

Finally, you can put all your font and style settings in an external file (`properties.xml`) and load it in to your ASP page. The XML document is very straightforward:

```
<?xml version="1.0"?>

<properties>
  <property name="Color_Primary">#0000AA</property>
  <property name="Color_Secondary">#FAEEDC</property>
  <property name="Color_Background">#FFFFFF</property>
  <property name="Color_BodyText">#222222</property>
  <property name="Color_Headlines">#555555</property>
  <property name="Font_Primary">Verdana</property>
  <property name="Font_Secondary">Arial</property>
</properties>
```

Six `<property>` elements each have a name attribute, which is used by ASP when selecting the property. The corresponding text for each property is contained between the opening and closing tags.

This is how the `propertiesdemo.asp` page handles this data:

```
<%@ Language=VBScript %>

<%
  Dim objXML, objRootElement, i

  'Instantiate the XML Processor
  Set objXML = Server.CreateObject("Microsoft.FreeThreadedXMLDOM")

  'Load and validate the XML Document
  objXML.validateOnParse=True
  objXML.load(Server.MapPath("properties.xml"))

  Set objRootElement = objXML.documentElement

  'Populate the array with the items
  For i = 0 To objRootElement.childNodes.length - 1
    Application(objRootElement.childNodes.item(i).getAttribute("name")) = _
                                objRootElement.childNodes.item(i).text

  Next
  Set objXMl = nothing
%>

<HTML>
<HEAD>
</HEAD>
<BODY BGCOLOR=<%=Application("Color_Background")%>>

  <!-- CODE INDENTED FOR EASIER READING -->
  <P>
    <FONT FACE=<%=Application("Font_Primary")%> SIZE=7
                COLOR=<%=Application("Color_Primary")%>>
                I'm easy to change!</FONT>
  </P>
```

```
<P>
  <FONT FACE=<%=Application("Font_Secondary")%> SIZE=4
                COLOR=<%=Application("Color_BodyText")%>>
                All you have to do is edit an XML file.</FONT>
</P>

</BODY>
</HTML>
```

The key code is the For...Next loop in the opening block of ASP:

```
For i = 0 To objRootElement.childNodes.length - 1
  Application(objRootElement.childNodes.item(i).getAttribute("name")) = _
     objRootElement.childNodes.item(i).text
Next
```

The code loops through the <property> tags, pulls out the name attributes and assigns it the corresponding text value. The property list is stored in the Application object for later use. (In fact this code could be included in the Application_OnStart subroutine in global.asa, and in a real-world example you would do this.)

The properties are then called in the second part of the page as follows:

```
<P>
  <FONT FACE=<%=Application("Font_Primary")%> SIZE=7
                COLOR=<%=Application("Color_Primary")%>>
                I'm easy to change!</FONT>
</P>
```

The output looks like this:

Using ASP to Manipulate XML Documents

So far we have discussed ways to read and process XML code using ASP before sending it to the browser or saving it as HTML. However, you can use ASP to modify the XML document itself. In this section, two ASP functions are described that do just that – adding a contact to an XML-formatted list, and deleting a contact.

Defining the Functions

The functions are contained in a file called scriptlibrary.asp, which contains two functions, AddContactXML and DeleteContactXML. Both files load the contacts2.xml file, which contains a longer contact list than the one we used earlier:

First the AddContactXML function:

```asp
<%
Option Explicit

Function AddContactXML(ContactType, LastName, FirstName, StreetInfo, City, State,
Zip, Phone)

   Dim XMLCode, sourceFile, xObj1, xObj2, rootNode, newNode, currentNode
   AddContactXML = 0

   'Build the XML content for the new contact node
   XMLcode = XMLcode & "<CONTACT><NAME><FIRST_NAME>" & FirstName & _
                                              "</FIRST_NAME>"
   XMLCode = XMLCode & "<LAST_NAME>" & LastName & "</LAST_NAME></NAME>"
   XMLCode = XMLCode & "<ADDRESS><STREET_INFO>" & StreetInfo & _
                                              "</STREET_INFO>"
   XMLCode = XMLCode & "<CITY>" & City & "</CITY><STATE>" & State & _
                                              "</STATE>"
   XMLCode = XMLCode & "<ZIP>" & Zip & "</ZIP></ADDRESS>"
   XMLCode = XMLCode & "<PHONE>" & Phone & "</PHONE></CONTACT>"

   'Set the source file location
   sourceFile = Request.ServerVariables("APPL_PHYSICAL_PATH") & _
                                              "\contacts2.xml"

   'Two instances of the XML DOM are required fro this operation, one for
   'the loaded XML file and another for the new contact.
   Set xObj1 = Server.CreateObject("Microsoft.XMLDOM")
   Set xObj2 = Server.CreateObject("Microsoft.XMLDOM")

   'Loads the contacts file
   xObj1.load(sourceFile)

   'Sets the document element as the current node
   Set rootNode = xObj1.documentElement

   'If no file loaded, then abort
   If Not IsObject(rootNode) Then
       Response.Write "No file loaded"
       Exit Function
   End If

   'Loads XMLCode string as XML into a new node
   xObj2.loadXML(XMLCode)
   Set newNode = xObj2.documentElement

   'Add the new node to the list
   Set currentNode =rootNode.appendChild(newNode)

   'Saves changes
   xObj1.save(sourceFile)

   Set xObj2 = nothing
   Set xObj1 = nothing
   AddContactXML = 1   ' When the code reaches this point, the Add has worked
End Function
%>
```

The code above isn't really as complicated as it may appear at first glance. After building the new contact's XML code, the function creates two instances of the DOM, one for the `contacts2.xml` file and a second one for the new node. The XML string is inserted into the second DOM object as a new node, which is then appended to the first DOM object as follows:

```
'Loads XMLCode string as XML into a new node
xObj2.loadXML(XMLCode)
Set newNode = xObj2.documentElement

'Add the new node to the list
Set currentNode =rootNode.appendChild(newNode)
```

The `DeleteContactXML` function searches the source file for a matching PHONE attribute and if it finds one, it deletes the corresponding contact. Note that this is just an example function and is not sophisticated enough to determine which contact to delete if more than one share the same telephone number – it deletes the first contact found with the matching number and then exits:

```
<%
Function DeleteContactXML(Phone)

   Dim sourceFile, xObj, xObj2, rootNode, i, oldItem
   DeleteContactXML = 0

   'Set the source file location
   sourceFile = Request.ServerVariables("APPL_PHYSICAL_PATH") & _
                                             "\contacts2.xml"

   Set xObj = Server.CreateObject("Microsoft.XMLDOM")
   xObj.load(sourceFile)
   Set rootNode = xObj.documentElement

   'Find the matching node
   For i = 0 To rootNode.ChildNodes.Length - 1

     If Phone = rootNode.ChildNodes(i).ChildNodes(2).text Then

        'Delete the matching node
        Set oldItem = rootNode.RemoveChild(rootNode.ChildNodes.item(i))

        xObj.save(sourceFile)

        ' When the code reaches this point, the Delete has worked
        DeleteContactXML = 1
        Set xObj = nothing
        Exit Function
     End If
   Next

   ' If the code reaches this point, the Delete has not worked
   Response.Write "No phone number found <BR>"
   Set xObj = nothing
End Function
%>
```

Testing the Functions

The above scripts can be tested using the following simple ASP page. The `testlibrary.asp` code, shown below, loads the script library through an SSI, before defining the text for the new contact and the telephone number for the contact to be deleted. Then the two functions are called in turn, and the XML file is modified accordingly. A brief note is sent to the browser to indicate success or failure of each operation:

```
<%@ Language=VBScript %>
<!-- #INCLUDE file="scriptlibrary.asp" -->

<HTML>
<HEAD>
</HEAD>
<BODY>

  <P>
<%
  Dim ContactType, FirstName, LastName, StreetInfo, City, State, Zip, Phone

  ContactType = "personal"
  LastName = "Stoopner"
  FirstName = "Jason"
  StreetInfo = "91B Perkins Lane"
  City = "Springfield"
  State = "LA"
  Zip = "70781"
  Phone = "555-0017"

  Response.Write "Was it added? " & AddContactXML(ContactType, LastName,
  FirstName, StreetInfo, City, State, Zip, Phone) & "<br>"

  Phone = "555-6666"
  Response.Write "Was it deleted? " & DeleteContactXML(Phone) & "<br>"
%>
  </P>

</BODY>
</HTML>
```

The "XML Brain"

Until now, the examples in this chapter have demonstrated one aspect of programming XML using ASP, either converting XML text into HTML for the browser, or manipulating the XML data itself. Now these techniques will be combined in a practical application.

The heart of this application involves a XML document called `settings.xml`. This file, reproduced below, contains two categories of settings, represented by the two child elements of the root `<site>` element: `<colors>` where various colors are defined for the display text and background etc., and `<navigation>` where details of web links are stored. Though we have only included two categories of settings here, this file could contain much, much more. Indeed all the settings of your web site can be stored here: font styles, font sizes, links to embedded graphics, server settings, input parameters and so on. The settings file could be the very nerve center for your web site, completely controlling its content and output, which is why I have called it the "XML Brain".

```
<?xml version="1.0"?>
<site>
  <colors>
    <Color_Primary>#004AA1</Color_Primary>
    <Color_Secondary>#002C6F</Color_Secondary>
    <Color_Highlight>#FFFF00</Color_Highlight>
    <Color_Background>#FFFFE6</Color_Background>
    <Color_HeaderText>#004E63</Color_HeaderText>
    <Color_BodyText>#555555</Color_BodyText>
  </colors>

  <navigation>
    <section URL="default.asp">
      <name>Home</name>
    </section>
    <section URL="showroom.asp">
      <name>Showroom</name>
    </section>
    <section URL="newcars.asp">
      <name>New Cars</name>
    </section>
    <section URL="preowned.asp">
      <name>Pre-Owned Cars</name>
    </section>
    <section URL="service.asp">
      <name>Service</name>
    </section>
  </navigation>

  <!--
  This file can be extended to store details on many other properties such
  as font style settings, font sizes, you name it
  -->

</site>
```

The node is worthy of further comment. Each <section> element contains a URL for a different page on the web site and the child <name> element contains the link's display text. This is not dissimilar to the relatedweblinks.xml file we saw earlier. However, for this example application, we will only use the part of the "brain" concerned with color settings. The <colors> node is very similar to the content of the properties.xml file, except the name of each property is an element name rather than an attribute of a common <property> element.

Editing the Settings File (or Brain...)

We now have a central XML "brain" containing the display settings for our web site, or specifically color settings and hyperlink information. These can be loaded into Application variables and are available to any page on your web site.

However, how do you go about changing your settings? One way would be to open settings.xml in Notepad and manually searching through the document to find the text that needs changing. We have already seen how to manipulate XML text using ASP functionality. Let's adapt this technique to change the color settings using an ASP page.

Because of its importance to the web site as a whole, `settings.xml` should be kept out of the way of other code, maybe in a folder all of its own. For our example we have put it in a subfolder called **admin**.

Here is the page, called `editsettings.asp`:

```asp
<%@ Language=VBScript %>
<% Option Explicit %>

<HTML>
<HEAD>
</HEAD>
<BODY bgcolor=#ffffff>
  <font face="verdana" size=2>
<%
  Dim sourceFile, xObj, rootSettings, rootColors, oldColors, newNode
  Dim currentNode

  'Set the source file location
  sourceFile = Request.ServerVariables("APPL_PHYSICAL_PATH") & _
                                              "\admin\settings.xml"

  'Loads the brain file
  Set xObj = Server.CreateObject("Microsoft.XMLDOM")
  xObj.load(sourceFile)
  Response.Write "XML brain file ""settings.xml"" loaded.<br>"

  'Sets the document element as the current node
  Set rootSettings = xObj.documentElement

  'Finds the node(element) "colors" and sets it as the current node
  Set rootColors = rootSettings.selectSingleNode("colors")
  Response.Write "Node ""colors"" is set to the current or active node.<br>"

  'Remembers what rootColors looks like before changes are made
  oldColors = rootColors.xml

  'Creates the new node "Color_Border
  Set newNode = xObj.createNode(1, "Color_Borders", "")
  Response.Write "New node ""Color_Borders"" is created in memory.<br>"

  'Add the new node "Color_Border to the "colors" family
  Set currentNode = rootColors.appendChild(newNode)
  Response.Write "New node ""Color_Borders"" is added as a child " & _
                                    "to ""colors"" node.<br>"

  'Gives new node "Color_Border" a value
  currentNode.text = "#090909"
  Response.Write "The value of ""#090909"" is assigned " & _
                                    "to ""Color_Borders"" node.<br>"

  'Deletes "Color_Highlight" node
  rootColors.removeChild(rootColors.childNodes.item(2))
  Response.Write "The old node ""Color_Highlight"" is deleted from " & _
                                    "the ""colors"" node.<br>"
```

```
'Saves changes
xObj.save(sourceFile)
Response.Write "XML brain file ""settings.xml"" is saved with changes.<P>"
Response.Write "</font><font face=""verdana"" size=3>"
Response.Write "OLD COLORS NODE:<br><pre>" & _
                              Server.HTMLEncode(oldColors) & "</pre>"
Response.Write "NEW COLORS NODE:<pre>" & _
                              Server.HTMLEncode(rootColors.xml) & "</pre>"
Set xObj = nothing
%>
</font>

</BODY>
</HTML>
```

The code starts by loading `settings.xml`. The entire file is loaded into the DOM even though we are only using a small part of it. The code then goes through the document making changes and reporting each one to the browser before displaying both the old and new settings on the screen. The code carries out a number of tasks: it creates a new property called `Color_Border` and assigns it a color, then deletes the `Color_Highlight` property:

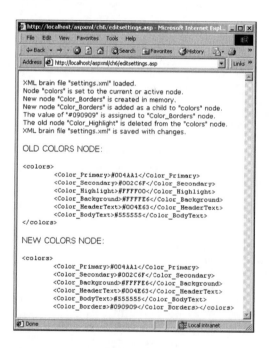

However, if you were a web administrator your job has not been made that much easier. Custom ASP pages, such as this, would be useful if you were going to make the same changes regularly – that is you would use the above code to change the settings and then have another page to change them back to the default values. If you want to make isolated or permanent changes, then it's pointless coding an ASP page for every single change. It would be better to go back to using Notepad and editing the XML by hand. A web administrator does not have the time (or the patience) to sift through code, whether it is ASP and XML, to change the odd word or character. A different approach is needed.

So now we come to the main application...

The Colorpicker Example

This web tool consists of just two ASP pages: `settings_colors.asp` and `colorpicker.asp`, which are included in the code download for this chapter. Together, they will allow you to use your mouse to select which part of your web page you would want to change the color settings for, change the color by modifying the RGB values, and save your settings afterwards. No code is presented to the user at all.

These two pages are rather long, and contain a lot of HTML for the user interfaces, so they are not reproduced here. As there is no XML-related code that has not been covered elsewhere in this chapter, we will only give the briefest overview of this useful tool.

settings_colors.asp

The code in this file loads the `settings.xml` file and displays a user interface, which allows you to choose the background colors of headers, highlights and body text. The user interface looks like this:

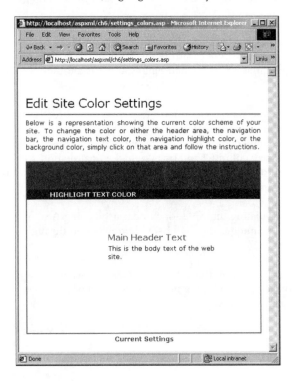

All the user has to do is click an area of the screen where a color change is required. Behind the scenes, the functionality of this page is governed by four subroutines:

- ❑ `Init()` – is called when the user first accesses the page and when a change is made. The `settings.xml` file is loaded and the color settings are passed to application variables.

- ❑ `ChangeColor()` – calls the colorpicker page (see below) and displays the current settings to match any changes made.

- ❑ `SaveChanges()` – saves the color settings if any changes have been made.

- ❑ `Reset()` – ignores any pending changes and restores the original color settings.

colorpicker.asp

This page is dedicated to providing a client user interface where a color property's setting can be changed with just a few clicks of the mouse. This is what the page looks like:

So there we have it. A user-friendly way of changing the color settings for a web site, which involves no sifting through web pages and no manual changes to code.

Summary

Okay so this chapter has let us dabble our toe in the ASP ocean after spending so long getting our XML up to scratch, and has allowed us to explore some of the possibilities that the ASP XML combination can offer.

We have examined the actual practicalities of incorporating XML into the ASP environment, using the DOM, server-side includes or in some cases the FileSystemObject. We also noted that a fourth option – accessing an XML document as an embedded data island – is another possibility which will be explored in Chapter 12.

We moved on to look at some simple examples of sending data directly to the browser and also how to make some basic alterations to the code in order to save the output as an HTML file. We had a taster of how the appearance of the data can be modified using XSL stylesheets before we saved the output; we'll be picking up XSL again in detail in Chapter 8. We had a neat demonstration of how XML documents don't have to be confined to storing straightforward text but can prove a useful external resource containing links and settings for your website, for example.

We then had a go at manipulating the XML document itself using ASP functions to add and delete data. Finally we combined the techniques that had been demonstrated throughout the chapter in the practical "XML Brain" application.

All this of course is just the tip of the iceberg. A mere taste of what's in store later on in the book and in the broader scope of your code developing now that you're starting to see what can be achieved when the power of XML is harnessed to ASP.

7

Using CSS with XML

So far, we have been looking at a lot of the background of XML. XML is a very flexible way to work with data, but most data ultimately needs to be presented on a client of some sort. In our case, that client is normally a web browser. The problem we need to solve is that XML is a data format, and as such has no intrinsic concept of style or presentation.

Currently, Microsoft Internet Explorer 5 (IE5) is the only major released browser that can display XML natively. The exception to this is XHTML, which, according to the W3C, is "a reformulation of HTML 4.0 as an XML 1.0 application". XHTML is basically well-formed HTML, and works in all reasonably modern browsers.

If you load an XML file directly into IE5, it will be displayed in a way that very clearly shows the different nodes and underlying data, but in a format that is rarely useful to anyone other than the programmer. To display the data in a presentable and useful format for the needs of your application, we need to look at technologies that can work together with XML to achieve this.

We can present this data with two main technologies – CSS and XSL. This chapter is mostly devoted to using Cascading Stylesheets (CSS) and XML in IE5. We will be comparing CSS with XSL later in the chapter, examining the pros and cons of each technology, and we'll also look at how they can be used together. In the next two chapters, we'll take a look at different ways XSL can present XML, and how XSL can also transform XML on both the client and server. We will also have a look at support for XML and CSS in the next generation browser from Netscape, Netscape 6.

We'll also be exploring some specific CSS features that are important when used with XML, and we'll take a quick refresher on using CSS with HTML, particularly some of the more common selectors. This section is not intended to get you up to speed with CSS – I am assuming you already have a working knowledge. Instead, it's focusing on particular aspects of CSS that take on a new level of importance when applied to XML, in contrast to the traditional use of CSS with HTML.

If you need to get up to speed on CSS, you should check out "Instant HTML Programmer's Reference" by Wrox Press (ISBN1-861001–56-8). For CSS syntax, there is also a CSS Reference in Appendix D.

The next section covers the main topic, using CSS with XML. This section will build up an example from a basic state, into a fairly sophisticated example of CSS with XML.

Following on from that is a quick look at Dynamic XML (DXML) – using script to modify XML styles dynamically. This provides you with different ways to present and modify your data at run time. We'll also run through a brief introduction to XSL and compare the differences between CSS and XSL.

Near the end of the chapter, we'll look at a couple of real applications for XML and CSS. First of these is an overview of CSS and XML support in Netscape Navigator 6. Netscape seem to be quite taken with this combination. We'll have a look at a specific XML application used in Netscape 6 XUL, which combined with CSS and some JavaScript, is used to build up the interface for the browser itself!

Last of all, we'll have a quick look a SVG – Structured Vector Graphics. SVG is an exciting new XML application being developed by the W3C. It's used for creating 2-dimensional graphics using XML together with CSS.

XML versus HTML

The first question to ask is "Why use XML on the client at all? What's wrong with HTML?"

There are many reasons for using XML across all the tiers of your application. In particular, we'll be looking at XML on the server later in the book. The single most compelling reason is one that excites so many web veterans – XML provides true separation of content from presentation. With HTML, the layout is intrinsically part of the content. This presents many problems when you want to change the client, change the way the application works, or simply change the presentation in a generic fashion.

Using XML on the client, particularly in conjunction with a standard DTD or Schema, can also provide external applications with the ability to browse, understand, and do useful things with your data. If you are already using XML on the server, why not use the same format on the client? Why go to all the trouble to reformat it as HTML, when there is no good reason to? Well, if you need to support older browsers, then this reformatting is still necessary. However, with the latest generation of browsers, we can send XML straight to the client. As we'll see throughout this chapter, there is a lot you can do to present your document in a way that is acceptable to users, without having to change or reformat the underlying data. The arguments for using XML on the client are many, and this isn't really the book to cover them in any depth. Rest assured, however, that XML on the client is here to stay, and as more and more external applications are developed which harness its power, your investment in XML will become more and more valuable.

Introducing Cascading Stylesheets

Cascading Stylesheets (CSS) is a way to control the presentation of documents. There are all sorts of different media and applications in which CSS can be used, but the most important of these is in web page presentation. CSS is a standard controlled by the W3C, the same group who controls the standard for XML, HTML, HTTP, etc. There are two recommendations for CSS: CSS1 and CSS2, as well as a third one (imaginatively called CSS3) which is under development at time of writing. IE5 supports a subset of both CSS1 and CSS2.

Different browsers support CSS with HTML to different levels. IE3 supports a subset of CSS1, IE4 supports a reasonably large subset of CSS1 and CSS2, IE5 even more so and IE5.5 even more again. Netscape 4 supports some CSS1, the forthcoming Netscape 6 will be the first browser to have complete support for CSS1, and will also partially support CSS2. Opera 3.6 does an excellent job of supporting much of CSS1 and CSS2. For details on which browsers support which CSS properties, I recommend you visit "The Master List" at http://style.webreview.com.

Some CSS Basics

Before we get too far into things, let's look at some basic concepts of CSS that are of particular interest when working with XML. This is not meant to be a reference guide or a complete CSS tutorial, but it should provide you with just enough information so you can learn from the examples later in the chapter, and can be in a position where if you choose to apply some of these examples to your own work, you'll have an understanding of what's going on.

CSS and HTML

Let's have a quick look at using CSS with HTML before we move on to XML.

```
<HTML>
  <HEAD>
    <STYLE TYPE="text/css">
      BODY {font-family: sans-serif;}
      text{font-size: 1.5em;}
    </STYLE>
  </HEAD>

  <BODY>
    <DIV CLASS="text">Underwater Basket Weaving</DIV>
      Covers the materials, equipment and latest techniques involved in
    <SPAN STYLE="font-style: italic;">Underwater Basket Weaving</SPAN>.
  </BODY>
</HTML>
```

When we embed CSS in HTML, it is defined inside the `<STYLE>` element, which is typically located in the head of the document. We'll look at different ways to associate CSS with XML later on. This example is a simple demonstration of a few of the ways we can select parts of the document using different selectors, and then alter their presentation.

Selectors

One of the more powerful features of CSS is the number of different ways in which you can select portions of your HTML/XML in order to apply styles to them. The use of selectors in HTML and XML is the same, so we'll continue on with the HTML example started above.

The CSS2 spec provides for some very powerful selectors, not all of which are implemented in IE5. The one I would really like to see, particularly for working with XML, is:

```
ELEMENT[attribute="value"] { …style… }
```

This allows you to select an element based on the value of its attribute, or on the existence of an attribute if you leave out the value. In IE5 selectors of this style are completely ignored. However, Netscape 6 DOES support this form of selection. It looks like cross browser compatibility problems are here to stay with us for a while yet!

Type Selectors

The first selector used is on the <BODY> element. This is called a **type selector**.

```
BODY {font-family: sans-serif;}
```

A type selector applies its style to every instance of that element. In this particular case, that's a bit redundant as there is only one <BODY> element in a well-formed HTML document. You would typically use a type selector to enhance, or effectively redefine an element by complementing or over-riding the default behavior for that element, as determined by the browser. Here, we are using this type selector to select the <BODY> tag, and simply specify that the font used is a sans-serif font. It's up to the browser to decide which font is actually used, as long as it is sans-serif.

Attribute Selectors

The next example is an **attribute selector**.

```
text {font-size: 1.5em;}
```

Attribute selectors are most commonly used with the HTML CLASS attribute. All HTML elements can have a CLASS attribute. Using the CLASS attribute allows you to apply a style definition to a group of elements that all share the same value for their CLASS attribute.

In this particular instance, we are applying the text class to this <DIV> element.

```
<DIV CLASS="text">Underwater Basket Weaving</DIV>
```

In this case, the text class sets the text to be larger than its default size. We'll have a look later in the chapter at what exactly the mysterious em unit is.

The last selector used in this example is a different type of attribute selector. This is using the STYLE attribute.

```
<SPAN STYLE="font-style: italic;">Underwater Basket Weaving</SPAN>
```

In this example, we are using the style inline, so it only applies to this specific instance of the element. It's generally best to avoid using the STYLE attribute selector where possible, as it goes against the principle of separating layout from content. It can also easily lead to code which is unmanageable as it allows style information to intermingle with data. Any changes to the data may then require changes to the style, which, when inline, can be a laborious task. This becomes particularly important when applying these techniques to XML, as XML should separate presentation from content as much as possible.

A different type of attribute selector not shown in the example above is the ability to select an element by its ID. If we had an element such as this:

```
<DIV ID="ubw04">Underwater Basket Weaving</DIV>
```

we could select this node using the following syntax:

```
#ubw04 { ...style... }
```

At this point in time, IDs don't get used much in XML. This may well change in time as Xlink and Xpointer become more widely used – your mileage may vary.

It's worth noting that when using CSS with XML, it can sometimes be very difficult to achieve true separation between code and content. In these examples, we potentially have to add a new attribute to the XML in order to determine style. Of course, in XML, a CLASS attribute might be used for a style, but it could also refer to what CLASS a student is currently in, or to a particular type of car, for instance you could use CLASS="classic", or anything else you want.

> **If you do end up using CLASS, STYLE, ID, etc, don't forget to allow for them in your DTD/Schema if you are using one.**

Combining Selectors

There are many different ways to combine selectors. We'll take a look at a few that are particularly relevant to working with XML.

If in the above example there were multiple DIV elements, and multiple elements with CLASS="text", we could select the combination of DIV elements with CLASS="text" by using this:

```
DIV.text { ...style... }
```

How about selecting a SPAN *only* when it's inside a DIV element? You can use this construct:

```
DIV SPAN { ...style... }
```

These are called **contextual selectors**. They can be nested multiple times; very useful when selecting XML nested deep inside a tree. Note that this example will select any SPAN element at *any* level beneath any DIV element. It doesn't necessarily have to be a child node.

These combinations can be combined further to create selectors such as:

```
DIV.text SPAN { ...style... }
```

Which, if read in English, would say:

> "Apply this style to all SPAN elements that are nested at any level beneath any DIV elements that have a CLASS value of text."

Another useful trick which we'll see used in examples later on is to combine multiple selectors which all require the same style. Borrowing from one of the examples we'll delve into in detail later on, we have an XML fragment like this:

```
<STREET>30 Ordain Street</STREET>
<CITY>London</CITY>
<POSTCODE>WC2H 8JB</POSTCODE>
<COUNTRY>United Kingdom</COUNTRY>
<PHONE>0207 123 4567</PHONE>
```

In this case, we want the same style applied to all of them. So, we combine our selectors in a comma-delimited list to produce something like this:

```
STREET, CITY, POSTCODE, COUNTRY, PHONE {
display: block;}
```

This is called **grouping**. As you can imagine, the possibilities of combinations are pretty impressive.

Boxes and the display Property

One of the most commonly used properties when using CSS with XML is the `display` property. In HTML, all elements have the `display` property predefined. For example, the sole difference between a HTML SPAN and DIV element is that DIV displays in a `block`, and SPAN is displayed `inline`. In XML, where there is no predefined `display` element and everything simply defaults to `inline`, we find ourselves changing this frequently. The `display` property determines what sort of container the content will live in. Listed below are the three possible values for the `display` property. The W3C standard has many more values such as `list-item`, `compact` and `table-cell` to name a few, but unfortunately IE5 doesn't implement them and there seems to be no plans to add them to IE6.

`block`	Elements start and end on a new line.
`inline`	Elements do not start and end on a new line. They will be displayed on the same line as the previous content. This is the default value.
`none`	Elements are hidden from view completely. No space is allocated for the element on the page.

*We're going to look at what **inheritance** is shortly. Until then, it's worth noting that* `block` *and* `inline` *are **not** inherited, but* `none` *is inherited.*

The `inline` and `none` values are self-explanatory. You'll see both of them used occasionally in the examples throughout this chapter. However, `block` needs a little more attention.

Padding, margin and border

Elements with a `display` value of `block` are surrounded by a boundary box. Around the boundary box are three separate belts, each having a collection of properties that can be set by using cascading stylesheets:

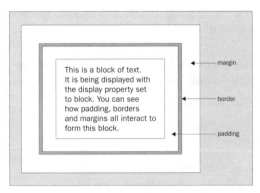

The three different belts all have a similar collection of possible properties for setting their size. Let's take padding for example. This has five properties:

- ❏ padding-top
- ❏ padding-right
- ❏ padding-bottom
- ❏ padding-left
- ❏ padding

The first four properties allow you to adjust the padding individually. The fifth, padding, is a short cut that applies its value to all four directions. These values are not cumulative, but rather follow the normal rule that the last definition is respected:

```
padding: 1em;
padding-top: 2em;
```

In this example, the padding would be 1em in all directions, except the top which would have a padding of 2em. Note that they must be listed in this order. If you used them in the reverse order, padding would be 1em in all directions. Don't worry about what an em is for now; we'll look at that next.

The margin belt follows the same rules as padding, with its properties being:

- ❏ margin-top
- ❏ margin-right
- ❏ margin-bottom
- ❏ margin-left
- ❏ margin

Border has all the same properties. However, each property takes three values in a space-delimited list. The format is:

```
border: width style color
```

For example:

```
Border-right: 2px solid black;
```

Possible values for the style portion of border that are currently supported in IE5 are:

- ❏ none
- ❏ solid
- ❏ double
- ❏ groove
- ❏ ridge
- ❏ outset
- ❏ inset

Note that some of these don't work if the `color` is set to `black`, as they rely on making parts of the border darker to achieve their effect.

It is also possible to access the individual `width`, `style` and `color` values using, for example, `border-left-color`, `border-top-style`, and `border-bottom-width`. Consult the CSS reference in Appendix D for more details.

Units, Em and You

There are various units that can be used to set CSS properties, for example, `font-size`, `padding` and `border-left` all need some sort of size value. In this section, we'll have a look at a few of the most common ones.

Relative units

The *em* is arguably the most powerful and least understood unit. In a nutshell, 1 em is equal to the default height of the font. This includes the ascender, the part of the letter "h" that sticks up, and the descender, the part of the letter "y" that hangs down. Note that traditionally an em is literally equal to the width of the letter m, although there are alternative definitions. However, CSS doesn't use this version of em.

The beauty of the em is that it deals with proportions, not sizes. The main concern when designing a web page is usually to make sure everything is in correct proportion to everything else. If you use em extensively in your stylesheet, then people viewing your page under different conditions are more likely to get a good experience. For example, if a user who has sight problems sets their font size in their browser to "large", the size of em changes. The text size will increase to reflect the new base of em, but all the other dimensions – padding and so forth, will still be in proportion because they'll change the same amount. If you specify your `font-size` using pixels, the end user will have no control over the font size, so some users may not be able to read your page.

Similar to the em is the *ex* unit. In theory, the ex unit is the height of the letter "x". In practice, most browsers seem to render it as half the height of em, so 0.5 em is equal to 1 ex. As a result, it's not especially useful in most situations.

Most properties also accept a percentage as a value. Exactly what the value is a percentage of, varies between properties. It is usually a percentage of the value that the property has in the `parent` element. Another interesting relative unit used for font-sizes are the `absolute-size` values. These are:

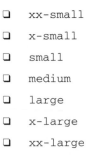

- ❑   xx-small
- ❑   x-small
- ❑   small
- ❑   medium
- ❑   large
- ❑   x-large
- ❑   xx-large

According to the W3C specification, each size should be 1.2 times bigger than the subsequent size. These allow scaling and are a good, simple solution for defining font sizes.

Absolute Units

The absolute units available in CSS, and their meanings, are listed below:

- ❑ mm (millimeter)
- ❑ cm (centimeter)
- ❑ in (inch)
- ❑ pt (point, 72 points = 1 inch)
- ❑ pc (pica, 1 pica = 12 points)

Unless you are certain of the output format being used, for example A4 paper, absolute units should generally be avoided. Unfortunately, as most designers still think in a printed paper mindset where you have absolute control over every aspect of the output, these units are still very commonly used and will probably be around for a while.

There are several units, less commonly used, that haven't been covered here. Please consult Appendix D for more information.

Inheritance and Cascading

Two of the great features that are fundamental to CSS are inheritance and cascading. These two combined give CSS the power, modularity, and reusability that it has become well-known for. Using them with a bit of thought can lead to much more compact and maintainable stylesheets. These two features are especially useful when using CSS with XML.

Inheritance

Inheritance (which we mentioned earlier) is the ability to have a style set on one part of the document tree (be it HTML or XML) to be transferred to a lower part of the tree. This is great when using CSS with XML, owing to its tree-like nature. Let's look at an XML fragment and consider the implications of inheritance.

```
<COURSE>
  <NAME>Underwater Basket Weaving</NAME>
  <ABSTRACT>
  Covers the materials, equipment and latest techniques involved in Underwater
Basket Weaving
  </ABSTRACT>
  <VENUE>
    <NAME>Bob's Training Co.</NAME>
    <STREET>30 Ordain Street</STREET>
    <CITY>London</CITY>
    <POSTCODE>WC2H 8JB</POSTCODE>
    <COUNTRY>United Kingdom</COUNTRY>
    <PHONE>0207 123 4567</PHONE>
  </VENUE>
</COURSE>
```

Let's say we wanted the entire fragment to use a sans-serif font. We could go and define a stylesheet something like this:

```
...
NAME {font-family: sans-serif;}
ABSTRACT {font-family: sans-serif;}
VENUE NAME {font-family: sans-serif;}
STREET {font-family: sans-serif;}
CITY {font-family: sans-serif;}
...
```

This seems a bit bloated and wasteful. We could go one step better and combine selectors like so:

```
NAME, ABSTRACT, VENUE NAME, STREET, CITY, POSTCODE, COUNTRY, PHONE {font-family:
sans-serif;}
```

Better, but still not ideal. However, using the power of inheritance we can do this instead:

```
COURSE {font-family: sans-serif;}
```

By defining the style on the root element of the fragment, all of its child nodes will inherit the style. The exception is when you override it using cascading (which is explained in the next section). If we only wanted the venue details to be in the sans-serif font, we could have just applied the style to the VENUE element. The VENUE element and all of its child nodes would have inherited the style, but none of the other elements in the fragment would.

Generally, CSS is pretty good and behaves as you expect it to without thinking about it. There are some CSS properties, however, that don't inherit from parent to child elements as described above. So, it's worth clarifying a few commonly used elements here specifically in regards to their inheritance.

When using CSS with XML, `display` is one of the most commonly used properties. The `display` property is not inherited, and so must be applied individually to each element. Some other commonly used properties that are not inherited are `clear`, `float`, `height`, `margin` and `padding`. According to the W3C, many properties, including `display`, have `inherit` as a possible value, which determines whether or not it should inherit its parent's properties. Unfortunately, IE5 doesn't support `inherit` for any style properties, and current documentation suggests IE5.5 will be the same. Netscape 6 in its current build (Preview Release 1 at time of writing) *does* support it. Netscape 6 promises full CSS1 support as per the W3C recommendation, which IE has yet to achieve in any version, and Netscape 6 will also have partial (but probably fairly comprehensive) CSS2 compatibility, so expect to see a future release of IE play catch up with Netscape on these specific features and others as well.

For a complete list of what is and isn't inherited, consult the CSS Reference in Appendix D.

Cascading

Cascading is the ability to have more than one style influence the presentation of a document or text. The concept of cascading is so simple, you often do it without realizing it. However it's worth a look at the rules behind cascading to understand what is going on behind the scenes – if you fully understand it, it will help you extract the maximum power from it. Let's look at an example of different types of cascading. We have three files here: cascade.xml, cascade1.css and cascade2.css:

cascade.xml

```
<?xml version="1.0" ?>
<?xml-stylesheet type="text/css" href="cascade1.css" ?>
<?xml-stylesheet type="text/css" href="cascade2.css" ?>
```

```
<NUMBERS xmlns:HTML="http://www.w3.org/TR/REC-html40">
  <HTML:STYLE>
    THREE {text-decoration: none;}
    FOUR  {text-decoration: line-through;}
  </HTML:STYLE>

  <ONE>First</ONE>
  <TWO>Second</TWO>
  <THREE>Third</THREE>
  <FOUR STYLE="font-weight:bold;">Fourth</FOUR>
</NUMBERS>
```

cascade1.css

```
ONE    {font-weight: bold;}
TWO    {font-size: .7em; font-style: italic;}
THREE  {text-decoration: underline !important;}
```

cascade2.css

```
TWO    {font-size: 1.3em;}
```

When you load `cascade.xml` into IE5, it renders like this:

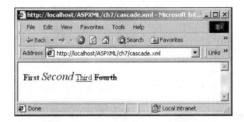

The general rule to determine which style gets used in stylesheets is that more specific rules get precedence over less specific rules, and that styles appearing later in the document get preference over those appearing earlier. In a typical document, that order from most to least preferred, by virtue of order would be:

❑ Inline

❑ Embedded

❑ Linked

As we'll see shortly, there is a chance to override this behavior.

Let's look at the ONE element. This gets its style from `cascade1.css`. Since there is no other definition for ONE, it gets applied.

For TWO, in `cascade1.css` we define `font-size: .7em;` and `font-style: italic;`, but in `cascade2.css` we then define it to be `font-size: 1.3em;`. Since there is no conflict in the `font-style` declaration, the text is correctly rendered in italic. However, there is a conflict in font size. When you use multiple stylesheets as we are here, later stylesheets are considered to be more specific than earlier stylesheets and so get precedence. In this case, the TWO element uses the `font-size: 1.3em;` from `cascade2.css`.

The THREE element is interesting. The `cascade1.css` file specifies the text to be underlined with `text-decoration: underline;`, but the embedded stylesheet has `text-decoration: none;` saying it shouldn't be underlined. Since this is more specific, the embedded stylesheet would normally win. In our particular case, if we have a closer look at the rule in `cascade1.css`, we'll notice something unusual.

```
THREE    {text-decoration: underline !important;}
```

This rule has been given the `!important;` flag, which means it has higher precedence than all other competing rules. Thus, this rule wins and the text is underlined.

Element FOUR has an embedded style and an inline style. The embedded style is `text-decoration: line-through;` and the inline style is `font-weight: bold;`. Since they are different properties there is no clash and the text is rendered in bold, and with a line through it.

Incidentally, the reason that all the text is rendered on the same line is that we haven't specified the CSS `display` property, and so they are using the default value of `inline`. If we had set `display` to `block`, they would have all been on separate lines.

As you can see from the examples above, the real power of inheritance and cascading comes when you combine the two. Learning how to use these features of CSS properly will enable you to create highly maintainable, flexible, and compact style sheets.

CSS and XML

By default, when you open an XML file in IE5, you are presented with something like this:

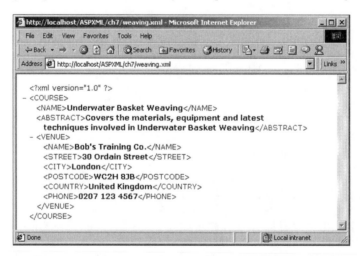

As we said at the beginning of the chapter, while this may be a very neat way to represent the data and the structure, it's probably not going to be of much use to most end users. We need to use CSS and/or XSL to make the data presentable to the end user. The default formatting as shown in the screenshot is actually using a default XSL stylesheet that comes with the browser. XSL is a very powerful language that can be used to transform XML on both the server and the client. We'll touch on XSL briefly later in this chapter, and in much more depth in later chapters. But now, on with CSS!

Associating CSS with XML Documents

The first thing before we start looking at the actual CSS, is to look at ways to associate stylesheets with XML documents. There are several different ways to do this.

Linking to External Stylesheets

The first method is to link an external stylesheet to the XML document using the special `xml-stylesheet` processing instruction.

```
<?xml-stylesheet type="text/css" href="training.css" ?>
```

This is equivalent to the `<LINK>` element in HTML.

```
<LINK type="text/css" href="training.css" rel="stylesheet">
```

> Note that the **xml-stylesheet** processing instruction is only valid in the prolog (before the top level element) of the XML document.

In much the same way as with HTML documents, linking external stylesheets to the XML document is usually the preferred method for the majority of cases. The main reason for this is that the stylesheet can then be shared amongst multiple XML documents, creating a centralized reusable collection of styles.

It is possible to have multiple stylesheets using multiple processing instructions. In the case where a style is defined in more than one stylesheet, the rules of inheritance are used as discussed previously. This allows great reusability of styles, as you can have a master stylesheet, which you can use for your entire application, and then override individual styles in subsections where the master style is inappropriate.

Embedded Stylesheets

It is also possible to embed stylesheets directly into an XML document. This should be reasonably familiar to those used to embedding styles in HTML.

```
<?xml version="1.0"?>
<?xml-stylesheet type="text/css"?>
<COURSE xmlns:HTML="http://www.w3.org/TR/REC-html40">
  <HTML:STYLE>
    COURSE{display: block;}
    TITLE{color:blue;font-size:150%;}
  </HTML:STYLE>

  <TITLE>Training Gophers for fun and for profit</TITLE>

</COURSE>
```

In this example, we define the HTML namespace in the root element:

```
<COURSE xmlns:HTML="http://www.w3.org/TR/REC-html40">
```

145

This is a special namespace that has a predefined meaning in the browser. It's an instruction to the browser to interpret any content in the HTML namespace as HTML, rather than XML, and to be rendered as such. We'll look at this a little more later on, but it opens up some interesting possibilities. For example, to insert an image to be displayed from an XML file we could do something like:

```
<HTML:IMG SRC="mypic.gif" />
```

in a document that had the HTML namespace defined as above.

In this case, we are using the HTML namespace to insert a STYLE element to house our stylesheet.

There is an alternative method which uses the following syntax:

```
<?xml version="1.0"?>
<?xml-stylesheet type="text/css" href="#style" ?>
<COURSE>
  <EXTRAS ID="style">
    COURSE{display: block;}
    TITLE{color:blue;font-size:150%;}
    EXTRAS{display: none;}
  </EXTRAS>
  <TITLE>Training Gophers for fun and for profit</TITLE>
</COURSE>
```

We can see here inside the processing instruction that we use an href of #style. This refers specifically to an element which has an ID of style. Note we set the style on the <EXTRAS> element housing the CSS to display:none. This is so the CSS itself doesn't get displayed. If you're using a DTD or Schema to validate your document, you would need to make sure the ID attribute is included.

In tests, I have found the behavior of this method of embedding styles to be unpredictable. As a result, at this point in time I wouldn't recommend you use this unless it is essential for your application.

Inline Styles

The last example is very similar to inline styles in HTML. You can simply place a style attribute inline in an XML element. As long as the xml-stylesheet processing instruction is in the XML document, it will render the style defined:

```
<?xml version="1.0" ?>
<?xml-stylesheet type="text/css" ?>
<COURSE>
  <TITLE style="font-size:150%;">Training Gophers for fun and for profit
  </TITLE>
</COURSE>
```

When using the xml-stylesheet processing instruction without specifying a file as we have done here, it acts as an instruction to the browser to follow any style instructions it finds embedded in the XML – effectively turning on the CSS parser.

The down side to this method is that it really removes the separation between content and presentation, and should be avoided in most situations. Note that you *must* have the xml-stylesheet processing instruction, the minimum instance being as shown above, in all cases in order for IE to make an attempt to interpret any CSS in the document.

Media-specific Styles

This is something we haven't looked into at all up to now. All the formatting work we've been doing has been focused entirely on output to the screen in a web browser. If you look at the W3C spec for CSS, you'll find that this is just one possible output medium. It does in fact support many different output types. This is a list of all the current output types:

- ❑ screen – the default, what we have been working with so far

- ❑ print – output to a printer on paper

- ❑ aural – speech synthesizers which read out web pages

- ❑ braille – for electronic braille readers which make tactile patterns

- ❑ embossed – for braille printers which emboss the braille onto paper

- ❑ handheld – for handheld devices, for example a Palm Pilot or Windows CE palmtop

- ❑ projection – projected presentations, either print to a transparency, or a computer hooked up to a projector

- ❑ tty – output to text based terminals, typically using fixed width fonts and with no graphics capabilities

- ❑ tv – output to television

- ❑ all – output to all devices

This is a very comprehensive list, and a great deal of thought has been put into it. The aural option is a particularly interesting one; there is an entire section of the CSS2 recommendation devoted to aural stylesheets, which includes some properties that seem quite bizarre when you are used to preparing stylesheets aimed solely at screen output:

```
H1 {
    voice-family: paul;
    stress: 15;
    richness: 100;
    cue-before: url("chimes.au");
    azimuth: center-left;
}
```

The aural stylesheet section of the CSS2 recommendation is quite comprehensive, and if you find it suitable for your application, you should consult the W3C web site at www.w3.org/Style/ for further information.

The bad news with all of this is that IE5 only supports three of these types: screen, print and all. Hopefully they'll add more to future versions of Internet Explorer to make it more accessible both to people with disabilities and as methods for browsing the net other than via desktop and laptop PCs becomes increasingly popular.

So, how do we use these different output media? There are two different ways to distinguish which styles are used for which media – in our case, effectively screen or print.

Linked Stylesheets

Here we'll take a look at how to attach external stylesheets targeted at different media:

```
<?xml version="1.0"?>
<?xml-stylesheet type="text/css" href="screen.css" media="screen" ?>
<?xml-stylesheet type="text/css" href="print.css" media="print" ?>

<COURSE>
  <TITLE>Training Gophers for fun and for profit</TITLE>
</COURSE>
```

As you can see, we've added a new media attribute to our xml-stylesheet processing instruction. We are now linking to two different stylesheets, one optimised for screen use and one optimised for printers. IE5 will select the appropriate stylesheet for the appropriate medium – the print styles will never be seen on screen and vice versa.

For example, it's quite common to use a sans-serif font for screen work, and a serif font for print work. So, for screen.css we can use:

```
TITLE {
font-size:2em;
font-family: sans-serif;
}
```

and then for print.css we can use:

```
TITLE {
font-size:2em;
font-family: serif;
}
```

That's all! The styles are optimized for the specific output media they are designed for. IE5 does all the selection work automatically, so the whole process is invisible to the user.

> *IE4 also supports output to different media types in the same way, although of course only in HTML documents, not XML documents.*

Mixed Media Styles

The other way to use media-specific styles is to mix and match them within the same stylesheets. Let's use the same example as before, but mix our styles this time.

Our XML, with particular attention being paid to the xml-stylesheet processing instruction, now looks like this:

```
<?xml version="1.0"?>
<?xml-stylesheet type="text/css" href="mixed.css" media="all" ?>

<COURSE>
  <TITLE>Training Gophers for fun and for profit</TITLE>
</COURSE>
```

And our new `mixed.css` file looks like this:

```
@media screen {
  TITLE {
  font-size:2em;
  font-family: sans-serif;
  }
}

@media print {
  TITLE {
  font-size:2em;
  font-family: serif;
  }
}
```

What we are doing here is grouping our styles into media types, which is done by using the `@media` keyword, and then appending the media type. Within the curly braces, we can then include as many styles as a normal stylesheet. An alternative version of `mixed.css` which harnesses the power of inheritance would be:

```
@media all {
  TITLE {
  font-size:2em;
  }
}

@media screen {
  TITLE {
  font-family: sans-serif;
  }
}

@media print {
  TITLE {
  font-family: serif;
  }
}
```

In this example, we define the font-size in a group suitable for *all* media types. We then specify the font desired for the specific media types.

You could use a similar concept with linked styles by using a generic stylesheet and then media-specific stylesheets, like this:

```
<?xml version="1.0"?>
<?xml-stylesheet type="text/css" href="generic.css" media="all" ?>
<?xml-stylesheet type="text/css" href="screen.css" media="screen" ?>
<?xml-stylesheet type="text/css" href="print.css" media="print" ?>

<COURSE>
  <TITLE>Training Gophers for fun and for profit</TITLE>
</COURSE>
```

The methods for combining styles, media types, and inheritance are quite powerful and provide the developer and designer with some powerful tools to create transparently optimized experiences for different users accessing your information in different ways.

Putting it all Together

Let's have a look at a complete example of formatting XML with CSS, and put into practice everything we've learnt so far. We'll have a look at the source code and analyze it in some detail before we move on to a more complex example. We'll take the example of a training company who wants to publish some information on their web site about some unusual courses they run:

```xml
<?xml version="1.0" ?>
<?xml-stylesheet type="text/css" href="training1.css" ?>

<COURSE>
  <NAME>Underwater Basket Weaving</NAME>
  <ABSTRACT>Covers the materials, equipment and latest techniques involved in
Underwater Basket Weaving</ABSTRACT>

  <VENUE>
    <NAME>Bob's Training Co.</NAME>
    <STREET>30 Ordain Street</STREET>
    <CITY>London</CITY>
    <POSTCODE>WC2H 8JB</POSTCODE>
    <COUNTRY>United Kingdom</COUNTRY>
    <PHONE>0207 123 4567</PHONE>
  </VENUE>
</COURSE>
```

As you can see, their information is pretty simple, but not for long – we'll expand on this in a later example. The xml-stylesheet processing instruction in the second line references an external file, training1.css. Here is training1.css in its entirety. As usual, this can be downloaded from http://www.wrox.com.

```css
COURSE {
font-family: sans-serif;}

NAME {
display: block;
font-size: 2em;
text-align: center;}

ABSTRACT {
display: block;
font-size: 1.1em;
padding: 0.5em;
text-align: center;}

VENUE NAME {
font-size: 1em;
display: block;
text-align: left;}

STREET, CITY, POSTCODE, COUNTRY, PHONE {
display: block;}
```

And when it's all loaded into a browser, we end up with something like this:

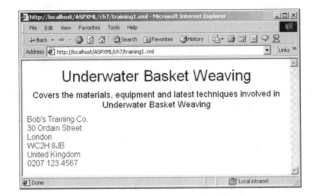

It's certainly not going to win any design awards!!!

Let's have a bit more of a detailed look at this sample to see how it works. Hopefully by this stage in the book you understand the XML so we won't go through that, apart from to point out the `xml-stylesheet` processing instruction which loads in the external stylesheet. As stated earlier, this is generally the preferred way of using stylesheets to enable maximum reusability and consistency of styles.

The first part of the stylesheet starts off by applying some formatting to the COURSE element.

```
COURSE {
font-family: sans-serif;}
```

Here we are using a type selector to select COURSE, the top-level element. As we want the default font for the document to be a sans-serif font, we choose to use `font-family: sans-serif` on this element. As `font-family` is an inherited property, applying it to the top level takes care of the whole document.

We have a look at the NAME element next. Once again, as with all the CSS in this example, we are using type selectors to apply our styles. As we have said before, whenever possible, you should use type selectors as they help maximize separation of data from presentation.

```
NAME {
display: block;
font-size: 2em;
text-align: center;}
```

The first thing we do is use `display: block` to have this displayed as a `block` element. This instructs the browser to display the text on its own line. We then set the font size to be twice the default size, and set the text to be center-aligned.

All the code in ABSTRACT has already been looked at, so we'll leave it except for a quick look at padding. This simply puts a small space between the abstract and the rest of the text.

```
ABSTRACT {
display: block;
font-size: 1.1em;
padding: 0.5em;
text-align: center;}
```

Now we come onto the venue's NAME.

```
VENUE NAME {
font-size: 1em;
display: block;
text-align: left;}
```

Here is an example of a contextual selector. We have already defined a value for NAME, but we only want to apply that definition to the context of the NAME of the course. So, we need to override this for the NAME element when it's in the context of the VENUE. We are deliberately setting the font size to 1em. Why do we do this when 1 em is the default size? Because it's inheriting the font-size: 2em from the course NAME element. Likewise, we explicitly define the text-align to left.

Finally, we specify that all the address nodes are displayed in a block format by grouping their selectors together. We've seen this section of code before:

```
STREET, CITY, POSTCODE, COUNTRY, PHONE {
display: block;}
```

You can see from this example that the whole idea is pretty simple, particularly if you are used to using CSS with HTML.

> *While developing some of the examples in this book, particularly the more advanced examples, I encountered a particularly annoying bug. This frustrating issue was white space sensitivity, particularly with carriage returns. In some cases*
>
> ```
> <ELEMENT>text</ELEMENT>
> ```
>
> *did not behave the same as*
>
> ```
> <ELEMENT>
>    text
> </ELEMENT>
> ```
>
> *I couldn't find clear reproducible steps, but it seemed most prevalent when the display property was set to block. Ironically, the main effect seemed to be adding additional space in the rendering when there was no space in the code such as the first example. It's one to watch out for.*

A More Advanced Example

We've had a look at the basics of how CSS is used to layout some simple XML. Now, let's go and have a look at a more advanced example which explores a few more ways we can use this technology. For those who are have spent some time working with DHTML, you'll find many of the ideas contained in this sample quite familiar.

Underwater what?

Here is the new expanded XML file for our slightly odd training company. You can download this file from the Wrox website at www.wrox.com. The file is called training2.xml:

```xml
<?xml version="1.0" ?>
<?xml-stylesheet type="text/css" href="training2.css" ?>

<COURSE xmlns:HTML="http://www.w3.org/TR/REC-html40" ID="course">

  <MENU>
    <LINK targetID="ABSTRACT">Abstract</LINK>
    <LINK targetID="DESCRIPTION">Description</LINK>
    <LINK targetID="DETAILS">Details</LINK>
    <LINK targetID="VENUE" position="0">London office</LINK>
    <LINK targetID="VENUE" position="1">Bolton office</LINK>
  </MENU>

  <NAME>Underwater Basket Weaving</NAME>
  <ABSTRACT>Covers the materials, equipment and latest techniques involved in
Underwater Basket Weaving. Available at 2 locations.</ABSTRACT>

  <DESCRIPTION>
  This course covers the following topics:
    <HTML:UL>
      <HTML:LI>Selecting the right diving equipment</HTML:LI>
      <HTML:LI>Selecting the right weaving equipment</HTML:LI>
      <HTML:LI>Different types of basket materials</HTML:LI>
      <HTML:LI>Weaving techniques</HTML:LI>
    </HTML:UL>
  </DESCRIPTION>

  <DETAILS>
    <HTML:HR />
    <LENGTH>Length: 4 days</LENGTH>
    <COST>Cost: £600 + VAT</COST>
    <HTML:HR />
  </DETAILS>

  <VENUE>
    <NAME>Bob's Training Co.</NAME>
    <STREET>30 Ordain Street</STREET>
    <CITY>London</CITY>
    <POSTCODE>WC2H 8JB</POSTCODE>
    <COUNTRY>United Kingdom</COUNTRY>
    <PHONE>
      0207 123 4567
    </PHONE>
  </VENUE>

  <VENUE>
    <NAME>Connie's Training Co.</NAME>
    <STREET>12 Treetop Street</STREET>
    <CITY>Bolton</CITY>
    <POSTCODE>BL7 TTG</POSTCODE>
    <COUNTRY>United Kingdom</COUNTRY>
    <PHONE>
      01204 123 4567
    </PHONE>
  </VENUE>
</COURSE>
```

The CSS that the XML links to in its stylesheet processing instruction is called `training2.css`, and can also be downloaded from the Wrox website. I've listed the text of the file here so you can consult it as we run through an explanantion of how it all works:

```css
COURSE {
display: block;
font-family: sans-serif;
width: 80%;
padding-left: 10em;}

/* start menu styles */
MENU {
width: 9em;
position: absolute;
top: 1em;
left: 1em;}

LINK {
display:block;
padding-bottom: 0.6em;
text-decoration: underline;
cursor: hand;
color: blue;
behavior:url(toggle.htc);}
/* end menu styles */

NAME {
display: block;
font-size: 2em;
text-align: center;}

ABSTRACT {
display: none;
font-size: 1.1em;
background-color: #E0E0E0;
padding: 0.5em;
text-align: center;}

DESCRIPTION {
display: none;
padding-top: 1em;}

HTML\:LI {
list-style-type: square;}

DETAILS {
display: none;}

LENGTH, COST {
display: block;}

VENUE {
display: none;
background-color: #E0E0E0;
border: 2px solid black;
padding: 1em;}
```

```
VENUE NAME {
font-size: 1em;
display: inline;
text-align: left;}

STREET, CITY, POSTCODE, COUNTRY, PHONE {
display: block;}
```

For those of you not familiar with it, we are using CSS comment syntax in this section, which use /* to open and */ to close.

> Note that for this example to work correctly, you will need to include the file `toggle.htc` in the same directory as `training2.xml` and `training2.css`, which is available for download from the Wrox site at **www.wrox.com**. The code for `toggle.htc` is discussed later in this chapter.

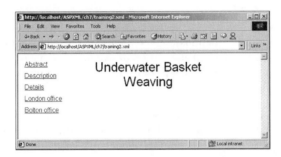

The first thing you'll notice about this is that we've now got a menu section. This menu allows us to select which section or sections of the course information we want to view at a given point in time. Clicking on the various links will reveal the appropriately labelled section, by toggling the display property of the particular node in the XML tree specified (NB: this will only happen if you included the `toggle.htc` file that was mentioned earlier, in the same directory as the `training2.xml` and `training2.css` files.) You'll also notice that there is no script or code of any type at all in the XML or in the CSS for that matter. So, how do we get this toggle effect? Using a feature that's new to IE5 called **behaviors**. We'll cover behaviors in more detail at the end of this section, as they really deserve a good mention since they lend themselves well to the sort of applications we are discussing. This is where we meet the mysterious `toggle.htc` file, and find out what it does.

Further down in the document, we are taking advantage of the HTML namespace again:

```
<DESCRIPTION>
This course covers the following topics:
  <HTML:UL>
    <HTML:LI>Selecting the right diving equipment</HTML:LI>
    <HTML:LI>Selecting the right weaving equipment</HTML:LI>
    <HTML:LI>Different types of basket materials</HTML:LI>
    <HTML:LI>Weaving techniques</HTML:LI>
  </HTML:UL>
</DESCRIPTION>
```

This enables us to display the description as an HTML list. In an ideal world, we would use CSS instead of resorting to HTML, and use `display: list-item` in order to set it to be a list. Unfortunately, IE5 doesn't support this part of CSS, and from my experiments with Netscape 6 (Preview Release 1) it seems to render `display: list-item` the same as `display: block`.

So, in order to overcome this, we can use the following method to set styles on the list:

```
HTML\:LI {
list-style-type: square;}
```

`HTML\:LI` refers to `LI` in the `HTML` namespace. The `\` is in there to distinguish between selecting from a namespace and using a pseudo-class. The `HTML` namespace also crops up briefly where we want to display a horizontal rule:

```
<HTML:HR />
```

All HTML is supported by simply defining the `HTML` namespace and making sure your HTML elements are included in that namespace.

Behaviors

In our example above, the toggle functionality is implemented using a behavior. So what is a behavior? Simply put, behaviors are components that are used to extend the functionality of a web page. Behaviors can respond to events fired by the page hosting the behavior, and can also expose their own methods and properties. And guess what – they are attached to a web page using our good friend CSS.

IE5 is the first mainstream browser to support behaviors. Microsoft has submitted their implementation of behaviors to the W3C to be made a standard; this process is still under way and it's not clear at this point whether or not they are likely to become an official W3C Recommendation.

> *Anyone who had a play with **scriptlets** in Internet Explorer 4 will be familiar with the general concept of behaviors, as scriptlets were quite similar. However, Microsoft no longer recommends the use of scriptlets and suggests behaviors instead.*

So why use behaviors? As I've already said, one of the biggest reasons for using XML is to completely abstract content away from both layout and code. Behaviors provide an excellent way to do this. They allow the author to encapsulate very powerful functionality into a completely reusable module that is kept separate from the content. Behaviors can be written with compiled languages or scripting languages. There are also several behaviors available to the developer which are installed by default with IE5. These are:

- ❑ `anchor (anchorClick)` – used to open a folder in Web Folder view
- ❑ `clientCaps` – provides information about the capabilities of the client browser
- ❑ `download` – can be used to download HTML pages and other files to the client
- ❑ `homePage` – allows you to query and change the user's Home Page setting
- ❑ `httpFolder` – used to open a folder in Web Folder, DAV or WEC view
- ❑ `saveFavorite` – allows the state of the page to be saved as a Favorites entry
- ❑ `saveHistory` – allows the state of the page and script variables to be saved as a History entry
- ❑ `saveSnapshot` – allows the state of the page and script variables to be saved
- ❑ `userData` – can be used to save values from controls between sessions

> For a much more detailed description of behaviors, and a default behavior reference guide, check out the Wrox Press Book "XML IE5 Programmers Reference" (ISBN 1-861001-57-6).

The Toggle Behavior

After that very brief introduction to behaviors, let's get on with having a look at how we've used behaviors specifically in this example.

If you look at the LINK selector in the CSS for the main example above, you'll see this line of code referencing a behavior:

```
behavior:url(toggle.htc);}
```

This associates the LINK tag with a particular behavior, toggle.htc in this case. Behaviors have a .htc extension (htc signifies HTML Components). And, yep, you associate behaviors with various parts of your document by using CSS. In this particular case, we are loading a behavior called toggle.htc. Behaviors can be compiled or written with script. We will only be looking at behaviors using script, so toggle.htc is just a text file, and is shown below. You can pass in any valid URL to load a behavior, such as:

```
behavior:url(toggle.htc);}
behavior:url(../behaviors/toggle.htc);}
behavior:url(http://www.wrox.com/code/toggle.htc);}
```

> Please note however that the Internet Explorer security model prevents behaviors from being loaded from a different domain or different protocol (such as HTTPS) from that of the calling document.

If you look at the source XML, you'll also notice that the LINK nodes have a new attribute called targetID:

```
<LINK targetID="ABSTRACT">Abstract</LINK>
```

The behavior picks up the value of this attribute, ABSTRACT in this particular instance, and uses it to determine which node's display property it should be toggling. The behavior also has an optional position attribute which isn't being used here; we'll look at that in a little while.

Let's have a look at the source code for the toggle.htc behavior, which is included with the code download, and see what makes it tick:

```
<COMPONENT>
  <PROPERTY NAME="targetID" />
  <PROPERTY NAME="position" />
  <ATTACH EVENT="onclick" HANDLER="toggle" />

  <SCRIPT LANGUAGE="JavaScript" TYPE="text/javascript">
```

```
    function toggle(){

      if(position==null){
        position=0
      } else {
        position = parseInt(position)
      }
      objDisplay = course.getElementsByTagName(targetID).item(position);

      if(objDisplay.style.display == "block"){
        objDisplay.style.display = "none";
      } else {
        objDisplay.style.display = "block";
      }
    }
  </SCRIPT>
</COMPONENT>
```

The first surprise looking inside the behavior is that it's written in a mixture of JavaScript and our favorite markup language, XML! It goes to shows how versatile XML is, and how many different people are using it in very diverse ways.

However, the behavior is not a true XML document, it just borrows some XML syntax. At this point in time, IE5 does not require that it should be well-formed; that is to say that the root tag, here called <COMPONENT>, is, in fact, currently optional. Of course, it is always good practice to produce well-formed XML even if it is not a requirement.

Next, we look at the attributes of the calling element in the behavior:

```
<PROPERTY NAME="targetID" />
<PROPERTY NAME="position" />
```

These take the targetID and position attributes of the element that fired the event to call the behavior (more on that in a minute) and expose them as variables within the behavior, making them accessible by script.

Next, we bind the onclick event to our one and only function:

```
<ATTACH EVENT="onclick" HANDLER="toggle" />
```

When the LINK element receives an onclick event in our XML document, it is passed to the behavior where it looks at the display property of the element specified in the calling element's targetID attribute, and toggles the property to turn the display on and off.

This is all fine, but the problem is that there are two VENUE elements. How does the script know which VENUE element to toggle? The behavior allows for an optional position attribute. Let me explain further.

The toggle() function finds the target element by using the getElementsByTagName method of the XML DOM. This will return all nodes in the document that have that element name. If we want to toggle an element apart from the first one in the document (in the 0 position), we can pass along an integer in the position attribute. If we don't use the position attribute, the behavior's position property returns null, and so we set it to a default of 0, the first node:

```
if(position==null){
  position=0
} else {
  position = parseInt(position)
}
```

For example this line of code:

```
<LINK targetID="VENUE" position="1">Bolton office</LINK>
```

would toggle the second element in the XML document, which in this case will display information about the Bolton office.

You could take this example further and include some error checking, and the ability to toggle multiple nodes, but it serves us well for this example. It's worth the investment spending some time playing around with behaviors, particularly if you work in an IE5 intranet environment. This is only a simple example, but you can take it a lot further by defining custom methods, encapsulating business logic, and so on. You could save a lot of development time and make your site more maintainable as well.

CSS and XSL: A Comparison

You've heard me mention XSL a few times. Why do we have two styling languages? When should you use one and when should you use the other?

Well, first of all, let's have a quick look at what XSL actually is. There's two chapters and a case study all about XSL later, so we won't cover it in great depth here. Borrowing from the W3C,

> **An XSL stylesheet specifies the presentation of a class of XML documents by describing how an instance of the class is transformed into an XML document that uses the formatting vocabulary.**

So, what does this really mean? At the most basic level, XSL is used to transform a piece of XML into a different format. This can mean all sorts of things. But in our application, it means HTML. Actually, it's really XHTML. XHTML is basically a reworking of HTML so that it's a well-formed XML application. For example, in HTML, you can quite happily use the <BR> element to your heart's content. But as you know, in XML, *all* elements *must* be closed. So, the XHTML equivalent is <BR/>.

> *XSL never became a W3C Recommendation, and instead has been superseded by XSLT and XPath. Oh dear, not ANOTHER language to learn, you all cry? No, not really. XSL was pretty much a combination of XSLT and XPath. It has changed in the separation, but most people find the most difficult part of learning XSL is getting their brains around the new mindset, and so an investment in learning XSL is not a wasted. Also, the XML parser that ships with IE5 only supports XSL, although an updated version with XSLT support is available from Microsoft. Updates to the MSXML Parser can be found at http://msdn.microsoft.com/downloads/webtechnology/xml /msxml.asp. Microsoft has also released a utility that will convert XSL files to XSLT files, taking the pain out of migration. This is available at http://msdn.microsoft.com/downloads /webtechnology/xml/xsltconv.asp.*

Here's a summary table of some of the key differences between XSL and CSS, based on a table on the W3C website:

	CSS	XSL
Can be used with HTML?	Yes	No
Can be used with XML?	Yes	Yes
Transformation language?	No	Yes
Syntax	CSS	XML
Client or Server	Client	Both
Support for media specific styles	Yes	No

With this summary behind us, let's look at these one point at a time to see what this means and where the real differences that affect your architecture decisions lie.

With HTML

As we know, CSS works well with HTML. How about XSL? Well, XSL is primarily a language to transform from XML into other formats, and so won't work on HTML. Strictly speaking, as XHTML is well-formed XML, we *could* transform XHTML into a different format, but in reality, this isn't practical. In HTML (and so in XHTML) the content is normally too heavily linked in with the layout to be able to extract any useful information from it. In most situations, CSS is the only practical choice for use with HTML.

With XML

We've been looking at XML and CSS extensively, so we should have a pretty good idea of how that works by now. XSL is designed from the ground up to work with XML. In fact, XSL is actually an XML application itself! So, both languages work very well with XML, just in quite radically different ways.

Transformation Language

This is where XSL really comes into its own. CSS is great, but has one major problem that XSL doesn't have – it has to work with the data that is already contained in the source XML document. It cannot change the content. With CSS, if you want something to appear in the final output, it has to be there in the original document. And if you don't want it there, the most you can do is specify `display: none`, which is useful but lacking a little in intelligence and flexibility. XSL can truly transform the document. Let's have a quick look.

In our main XML and CSS example, this node is used to store information about course length:

```
<LENGTH>Length: 4 days</LENGTH>
```

Now while this is great for our application, let's look at these two possible scenarios:

```
<LENGTH>Length: 2 hours</LENGTH>
```

```
<LENGTH>Length: 3 weeks</LENGTH>
```

If we want to put some rules in our application so that only courses that are less than one week in length get displayed, we *are* able to do it, but we would need to extract and parse the information manually to work it out, which would require a great deal of effort. How about this as an alternative:

```
<LENGTH TIME="4" UNIT="days" />
```

Now, we have a more clearly defined value which we can query. But how do we present this with CSS? Well, we can't! However, using XSL on that piece of XML (in the context of the complete file listed a few pages ago), we could do something like this in our XSL stylesheet:

```
<?xml version="1.0" ?>
<xsl:stylesheet xmlns:xsl="http://www.w3.org/TR/WD-xsl">

  <xsl:template match="/">
    <xsl:apply-templates select="/COURSE/DETAILS/LENGTH" />
  </xsl:template>

  <xsl:template match="LENGTH">
    Length:
    <xsl:value-of select="@TIME" />
    <xsl:value-of select="@UNIT" />
  </xsl:template>

</xsl:stylesheet>
```

Which, in this instance, would output **Length: 4 days** to the browser. However, with a small change to the XSL, it could just as easily output **This course runs for 4 days**. To do this with CSS, we would have to change the actual content, and worse than that, every single instance of the content. With XSL, you can just change the transformation rules in the XSL stylesheet once, and it's all done. We could also add a further layer of intelligence with the XSL, perhaps color coding courses that run for certain lengths. This sort of flexibility and logic is simply not possible with CSS.

XSL is also a great way to restructure your document for different clients. Let's say you are running a news web site. Of course, you want to display all your content in HTML so that the widest possible browser audience can view your content. But you also want to use the same content on your WAP site (WAP is the protocol used for mobile phones. In Europe, WAP phones use WML as their markup language, which is an XML 1.0 application). Then, there are all those feeds you are providing for your various partners. You *could* come up with a proprietary database-driven templating system. Or, you could store all your news feeds as XML. Then, you create three different XSL stylesheets. The first one transforms your XML into XHTML, and includes all your fancy menus, displays the image from the news item, etc. The second stylesheet gets the same piece of XML, but produces a lightweight version as a WML document suitable for browsing on WAP phones. Since the screen size is small, you decide to display only the headline and the abstract, and leave out the main body text. Also, you of course don't want the story image. So, you simply don't select the information in your XSL. Finally you use the last stylesheet to transform the story into the appropriate format for your content partner. One piece of content, three outputs. That is easy.

Client or Server

CSS, as used on the web, is purely a client-side technology, at least for the moment. CSS is always sent to the client and used to format a document – be it XML or HTML or whatever.

XSL, on the other hand, can be used on the client or server. The reason for this is XSL *transforms* XML into XHTML. This can be done on the client or the server, it doesn't matter which. The same XHTML is generated at the end of the day. In fact, if you load an XML document on the client, transform it with XSL, and then use script to manipulate the result, you'll find you'll be working with a well-formed HTML document, despite the fact that viewing the source of the document will show you the original pre-transformed XML.

Having the option to use XSL on the client or the server gives the developer a lot of flexibility. When working in an environment where the web client is unknown, such as the internet, transformations happen on the server. When you are working in an environment which is predictable, such as a corporate intranet, you can opt to transform the XML on the client. Why do this? Well, for one thing it can shift the burden on the server's processor to the client, making for a more scalable solution. Also, although the XML has been transformed into HTML on the client, it is still possible to get to the underlying XML and XSL and re-transform the document without doing an extra server hit. Less load for the server and faster response times for the client – a win-win situation!

Why Use CSS at All?

Right now, you might be thinking, "I just read half a chapter about CSS and XML, only to discover there's a better way!" It seems like, apart from media-specific outputs, XSL is always a better way to go. Well, the answer to this, to add to your confusion is, "yes and no". There is no doubt that XSL is a more powerful language. But it's not always as clear-cut as you might think – there is room for both. And as we'll see in a minute, they are not equivalent technologies and can work in conjunction really well.

The Benefits of CSS

So when and why does it become more advantageous to use CSS over XSL? We'll take a look now.

More Mature

CSS has been kicking around for quite some time – the W3C has been working with stylesheets since their inception in 1994. CSS is currently at version 2, with version 3 getting pretty close to being a Recommendation. Most major web sites use CSS to some degree or another, and every recent major browser has some level of support for CSS. Because of all of these factors, CSS is a tried and proven technology. XSL, and the W3C Recommendation of XSLT, are very new technologies. Not many people are using them yet, and only IE5 supports XSL on the client, with no major browser yet released supporting XSLT, although when finished Netscape 6 is likely to support this, and as mentioned earlier you can download an updated version of the Microsoft MSXML Parser which does support XSLT thus effectively upgrading IE5. IE 5.5 will ship with the new parser when that is released. With the maturity of CSS comes lots of high-quality-third-party documentation. There are literally dozens of books on the market and web sites that are either dedicated to stylesheets, or cover stylesheets in a significant way.

If stability and maturity are of concern in your environment, consider CSS.

Many Tools

As CSS has been around for so long, you can pretty much guarantee that every popular web-authoring tool on the market has some degree of CSS support. Latest versions (and in most cases, older versions) of popular programs such as Macromedia Dreamweaver, Microsoft Front Page, Microsoft Visual Interdev, Allaire's Homesite, Adobe GoLive and SoftQuad Hotmetal Pro, just to name a few, all have significant support for CSS.

Of course, the support for these tools has in most cases been written specifically for using HTML with CSS. Many of the tools are very flexible, and with little or no tweaking can produce CSS suitable for XML. It should be a relatively small job for many of the tools to make them fully designed to enable CSS to be used with XML, so I hope to see them modified over time.

XSL is a much more difficult language, both conceptually and in terms of syntax. While there are a few fledgling tools starting to appear, it will take time for these to reach maturity. Expect to use Notepad or your favorite text editor for a while yet.

Uses Existing Skills

One of the great things about using CSS with XML is that most web developers already know it! If you've had significant experience using CSS with HTML, and particularly if you use DHTML to manipulate CSS, you should have found most of this chapter very straightforward. XSL, on the other hand, is a completely new beast altogether. Despite using XML as its syntax, it's not quite like any other language commonly used by web developers, both in syntax and in mindset.

In many production houses, the client-side code is often carried out by graphic designers. People in these environments are probably going to prefer to use CSS rather than XSL on the client, at least until mature tools are in place.

Supports Media-specific Styles

As we saw several pages ago, cascading stylesheets can be used in some powerful ways to target the layout for either screen or print work. The problem is that this only works for CSS, and not for XSL. If you do want to be able to control the way users view your material on different media transparently, you have no choice but use CSS.

CSS and XSL Working Together

With all these pros and cons both ways, it might be hard to choose between the two technologies. The good news is that CSS and XSL are not mutually exclusive technologies, and in many cases, they can make great partners.

The main way to combine the two technologies is to use XSL first, and then apply CSS to the transformed output of the XSL. The XSL transform can be on the client or the server, it doesn't really matter from a CSS perspective as, at the end of the day, exactly the same output is produced.

The first variation is to transform the XML to HTML. With this combination, you can use CSS in the same way as it has traditionally been used in HTML. This is a great combination if you are working in an environment where the web browser is unknown and you need to maintain maximum compatibility. Of course, you'll also need to make sure the CSS stylesheet is compatible across all major browsers accessing your site, as well as allowing for users who have browsers that don't support CSS at all, such as Netscape 3. Particular attention needs to be paid if you have very old browsers visiting your site. Browsers such as Netscape 3 will simply ignore CSS, but older browsers aren't always so clever (Netscape 1 and IE 2 will actually display the CSS on screen). Make sure you test this thoroughly if support for very old browsers is a concern in your application.

The other main use is to transform the XML into a different XML, and then apply CSS to this new XML. At first glance, this sounds like it is a bit of a waste of time. After all, why transform an XML document into a different XML document and then apply a style to it? Why not just apply a style to the original XML? Although this seems quite obtuse at first, there are actual several scenarios where this could prove to be the best option.

One of the most obvious uses is when you need to provide for multiple media outputs. However, XSL simply doesn't support multiple output media at this point in time. So, you can use XSL to transform your XML into a more useful format, creating links in the HTML namespace and so forth, and then produce multiple CSS stylesheets, allowing you to tailor your formatting for the different media types that your application requires.

Another possible application would be in a situation where bandwidth is an issue. XSL is a rather verbose language, and the file sizes can get large. If you have customers accessing your application over a very slow application, perhaps using their laptops to connect to your application via their mobile phones, this is a consideration.

There is also talk of a future web dominated by personal agents that will find information for you by trawling through XML pages, and search engines that can understand the content on an XML formatted site, possibly via a set of standardized DTDs or schemas. Whether this turns out to be the case remains to be seen, but if you do have need to support technologies similar to these, you may need to transform your XML from your internal schema to a format more suitable for the agent. Since one transformation stage is being done, you can make use of it to further massage the XML in any way needed and then apply CSS for final presentation.

The last scenario we'll cover here is similar to the previous scenario, but simply massages the XML into a more palatable format because the staff taking care of the presentation layer coding do not have skills in XSL.

In summary, CSS is a very simple, easy to use formatting language which is widely accepted and widely used in the web today. However, it is *only* a formatting language and can't manipulate the underlying data in any significant way. On the other hand, XSL is a very new and very powerful language that is used to transform XML in powerful ways. There's no doubt that there are many jobs where CSS is simply not powerful enough to present XML without the help of XSL. Perhaps the most succinct description of whether or not to use CSS or XSL can be given as follows, again from the W3C web site:

> **Use CSS when you can, use XSL when you must.**

Mozilla & Netscape 6

So far in this chapter, we have been looking almost exclusively at using XML and CSS with Microsoft's Internet Explorer 5. Why? Because, at the time of writing, it's the only released mainstream browser available that natively supports these technologies. However, they won't have this space to themselves forever. A formidable competitor is on the horizon: Mozilla.

Mozilla, Gecko, Seamonkey - What's It All About?

Mozilla is a very interesting project, but it can be a little confusing. With lots of less-than-intuitive terms and code names like Mozilla, NGLayout, Seamonkey and Gecko being thrown around, it can be hard to penetrate the veneer to find out what the whole project is really all about. And aren't these all just fancy terms for Netscape 6 anyway? Let's have a quick look at the history of Mozilla to try and get a bit of a perspective on things.

In the beginning was Mosaic. In the early days of Netscape, when they were first developing Navigator, they were trying to create something move powerful, faster and generally better than Mosaic. Someone at the early Netscape coined the term "Mozilla" and an inside joke became a publicly known code name for Navigator, along with it's accompanying image of a fire-breathing lizard. Over the next few years, Netscape released 4 major versions of the Navigator browser, as well as their Communicator suite of tools. Then, in early 1998, Netscape announced that they were going to release the source code for their Communicator product to the public. They also announced that future versions of their browser would be released as open source.

So why would Netscape give away the source code for their browser? Straight from the lizard's mouth is this quote:

> "Netscape (and the world) benefits from giving away its source code in a number of different ways. First and foremost is from the expected explosion of creative input to the Communicator source code base. Netscape is confident that this will allow Communicator to retain its position as the pre-eminent communications software. Second, freeing the source code allows it to go places and into products that Netscape may never have had the resources or time to take it on its own, extending Internet accessibility to hardware platforms and software products far and wide."

Another quote from mozilla.org, which is an excellent summary of the philosophy behind the mozilla.org is "Mozilla is an open-source web browser, designed for standards compliance, performance and portability." The key point in this paragraph is *standards compliance*. A major drive behind the Mozilla project is to be completely standards compliant in every way possible. And guess what two key technologies are standards, and are being included in Mozilla? XML and CSS, of course!

And to answer the original question, hopefully you now know what Mozilla and mozilla.org is, Gecko is the core layout engine behind the Mozilla browser. NGLayout is a legacy term for Gecko, and Seamonkey the code name for the browser as whole, in much the same way as Mozilla was a code name for Navigator. Confused yet?

Standards Compliance

Some of the W3C standards planned to be included in the Gecko layout engine are:

- ❑ HTML 4.0 (except bi-directional text, used in Hebrew and Arabic languages)
- ❑ CSS1
- ❑ CSS2 – partial support to a level yet to be decided
- ❑ DOM Level 0, Level 1 Core and Level 1 HTML
- ❑ XML 1.0
- ❑ JavaScript 1.5, including ECMAScript compliance

There is also talk of support for XSLT and XPath now that they are W3C recommendations. Although I have not seen an official announcement to this effect, because of the open source nature of the project, anyone who feels strongly enough about it can simply write one. So, I think because of this, it's pretty likely it will be supported in the final release. However, there is no support for XSLT in the current version, and so the focus remains on XML and CSS.

XUL and Chrome

The Netscape 6.0 browser supports XML and CSS in a fairly similar way to IE5. Several of the examples in this chapter were smoke tested in Netscape 6 Preview Release 1, and mostly worked to some extent or another – some were fine, some had minor variations and a few were outright broken. Of course, things such as behaviors are not supported in Netscape 6, as the Mozilla group generally won't touch anything till it has a W3C recommendation, so for the time being, the support for behaviors is confined to Internet Explorer 5.

What Mozilla does have, is a very interesting application of XML and CSS. Chrome is the name for the user interface itself – the sum of all the windows, toolbars, menus, etc. The developers have such confidence in the power and speed of the Gecko engine that the actual interface to the Mozilla browser – chrome – is displayed entirely using Gecko! And you can guess what technology they used to do it – XML and CSS! They have developed a specific XML application which they have called **XUL**, which stands for **XML-Based User Interface Language**. It's pronounced "zool" and rhymes with "cool".

Why Bother with XUL at All?

The reasoning behind the development of XUL is a pretty sound one. They looked at the traditional way of creating interfaces where you would need to program the interface, typically using C++. Any necessary changes would require a developer, or possibly several developers – one for each supported platform – to get their hands dirty in the code and make the changes directly. This is hardly a very responsive or flexible way of working.

The reasoning at Netscape went on: W3C have got all these great standards for presentation, with a huge installed skill base, so why don't we make use of these technologies and skills, make the interface easier to develop and change, faster to update, and more accessible to the interface designers who are the most involved in the intricacies of designing the interface for the product?

They did, and XUL is the result of their endeavors.

An Introduction to XUL

In this section, we'll develop a simple interface for a multiple search provider aggregation service. The end result will be a fully developed interface, but we won't actually be making it functional. If you are interested in taking things further with making these interfaces fully functional, look up XPConnect at http://www.mozilla.org. XPConnect allows you to script the innards of Netscape 6 via JavaScript.

The first thing you'll need to do before having a play with XUL is, of course, to get the latest version of Mozilla. You can download the major releases from www.netscape.com, and the intermediate builds from www.mozilla.org. The examples below were developed using Netscape 6 Preview Release 1.

Directory and File Structure

The files that make up chrome are stored in a very well-defined structure, which makes it very easy to find exactly what you're looking for. It also has allowances for multiple skins (custom interfaces) and locales (region/language combinations), as we'll see shortly.

Let's assume you have installed Netscape 6 in c:\Netscape. The default chrome will by default be installed in c:\Netscape\Netscape 6\chrome. Each separate component of the interface has it own folder under here. Let's have a look at the structure of the bookmarks management window of the default components to see how this works.

The bookmarks top level folder is at c:\Netscape\Netscape 6\chrome\bookmarks. Under this, and every other folder, are three sub folders: content, locale and skin as follows:

The content and skin folders always contain a default folder, and possibly other folders as well. The default folder is for a feature of Mozilla planned for a later release, which is called skins. As with many popular consumer software packages these days, Mozilla is implementing skins functionality which will allow you to install you own customised interfaces, and switch between them at will. The different interfaces will be installed in folders other than default. We'll have a look at the repercussions of skins and file paths a bit later. The locale folder contains a folder for each locale you have installed; en-US is the default.

The different folders are used to store these different files:

Chrome/bookmarks/content/default	`.xul` and `.js`
Chrome/bookmarks/skin/default	`.css` and images
Chrome/bookmarks/locale/en-US	`.dtd`

Custom Search

Let's get into some actual code here, and build up an interface for a search box. The two code files that will build our customsearch user interface, sDialog.xul and sDialog.css, can be downloaded from www.wrox.com. You need to create a new directory, under the chrome directory, called customsearch, which has the same directory structure as, for example, the bookmarks directory. sDialog.xul needs to be saved within the chrome/customsearch/content/default directory. Here is sDialog.xul:

```
<?xml version="1.0"?>
<?xml-stylesheet href="chrome://global/skin/" type="text/css"?>
<?xml-stylesheet href="chrome://customsearch/skin/sDialog.css" type="text/css"?>

<window xmlns:html="http://www.w3.org/TR/REC-html40"
  xmlns="http://www.mozilla.org/keymaster/gatekeeper/there.is.only.xul"
  class="dialog"
  title="Custom Search">

  <box align="vertical" style="width: 100%; height: 100%">

    <box align="vertical" class="cSearchBox">
      <html:div>Search for:
      <html:input type="text" flex="1"/>
```

```
      </html:div>
    </box>

    <box align="vertical" class="cSearchBox">
      <html:div>Use these search engines</html:div>
      <html:div>
        <html:input type="checkbox" checked="true"/>Yahoo
      </html:div>
      <html:div>
        <html:input type="checkbox" checked="true"/>Altavista
      </html:div>
      <html:div>
        <html:input type="checkbox" checked="true"/>Looksmart
      </html:div>
      <html:div>
        <html:input type="checkbox" checked="true"/>Deja
      </html:div>
    </box>

    <box align="vertical" class="cSearchBox">
      <html:div>Search type</html:div>
      <html:div>
        <html:select style="margin-top:7px;">
          <html:option>Exact Phrase</html:option>
          <html:option>Boolean search</html:option>
          <html:option>All words</html:option>
          <html:option>Any words</html:option>
        </html:select>
      </html:div>
    </box>

    <spring flex="1"/>

    <box align="horizontal" style="margin: 7px;">
      <spring flex="1"/>
      <titledbutton id="search" class="dialog push" value="Search"/>
      <titledbutton id="reset" class="dialog push" value="Reset"/>
    </box>
  </box>
</window>
```

And our rather simple CSS file, sDialog.css, looks like:

```
.cSearchBox {
margin: 10px;
padding: 10px;
border: 2px groove white
}
```

sDialog.css doesn't actually need to be in the skin/default directory to work, but it's strongly recommended that you do put it there for both consistency and support for future features.

In order to launch the window so we can have a play around with it, let's just use a normal piece of JavaScript contained in a normal HTML file. I called mine default.html, and saved it within my chrome/customsearch/content/default directory.

```
<a href="#" onclick="window.openDialog('file:///C:/Netscape/Netscape
6/chrome/customsearch/content/default/sDialog.xul','demo','','');">Launch
search!</A>
```

When `default.html` is loaded into Mozilla, then the link is clicked, we get a window that looks like this:

As you can see from the code above, XUL is a normal, well-formed XML application – we can see this from the XML version declaration in the very first line. The part of the file of interest to note is that the CSS files are linked using special `chrome://` URLs.

```
<?xml-stylesheet href="chrome://global/skin/" type="text/css"?>
<?xml-stylesheet href="chrome://customsearch/skin/sDialog.css" type="text/css"?>
```

You can use `chrome://` URLs to reference files in much the same way as using the `http://` protocol. The reason for the chrome URLs is it allows Mozilla to work out the correct path, allowing for skin and locale settings. Notice that in the reference to the `sDialog.css` stylesheet, we don't include the **default** folder. Mozilla will pick up files from the correct folder for the currently selected skin. The functionality to change skins isn't implemented in the current version of Mozilla at this time of writing, so this couldn't be tested. You can also use `http://` URLs or normal paths such as `../images/icon.gif`.

The stylesheet referenced above, `chrome://global/skin/`, refers to a default stylesheet. This contains many generic styles, and is used to keep a consistent appearance between interface elements. It's worth having a look in the file as it contains some excellent examples of very advanced CSS selectors. Unfortunately, IE5 doesn't implement most of these advanced features.

You can also see the use of the HTML namespace throughout the document. There is great flexibility with XUL to mix and match XUL code with HTML. For example, you could display a button using the HTML input box (remembering to use the HTML namespace) or by using the XUL `<titledbutton>` element.

DTDs and Localisation

The code we have does have one major omission that has been made for the sake of simplicity. In order to create Mozilla as a truly globalised browser which can be rapidly localised into multiple languages, none of the XUL files should contain any display text. Instead, the approach the Mozilla team has taken is to define the text as entities in a DTD file instead. We could link to a DTD file like this:

```
<!DOCTYPE window SYSTEM "chrome://customsearch/locale/sDialog.dtd" >
```

and define an entity in the DTD like so:

```
<!ENTITY customSearch.title "Custom Search">
```

and then reference it in the XUL as you would a normal entity:

```
&customSearch.title;
```

Those who have been involved in large localisation projects will be able to appreciate the value of having the text clearly separated from the code in this way. DTD files should by default be placed in the `locale/en-us` directory.

There are some excellent and quite clear examples of using DTDs for localisation in the chrome directory of Netscape 6 for those who want to take this further.

Other Uses for XML and CSS

We've spent a bit of time looking at XUL, a specific XML application that relies heavily on CSS for its display. Let's have a brief look at another XML application that uses CSS.

SVG, **Scalable Vector Graphics**, is an exciting new XML application currently being developed by the W3C. It has a lot of weight behind it – some of the companies represented on the SVG committee are IBM, Microsoft, Apple, Xerox, Sun Microsystems, Hewlett-Packard, Netscape, Corel, Adobe, Quark, and Macromedia. With a collection of companies like that behind a standard, it's got a promising future indeed!

At its simplest level, SVG can produce vector graphics, in a similar way to Macromedia Flash. Vector graphics offer much flexibility in scaling and potentially very small file sizes leading to faster download times, as compared to bitmap image formats such as GIF and JPEG.

But where SVG takes the lead is that it uses completely open standards such as XML and CSS to define it. You'll see what I mean in a minute when we have a quick look at an example. Being based on XML, you can use the DOM to manipulate your SVG document as with any XML document. This is exciting – it means you can use JavaScript to script every aspect of your graphics – color, line width, shape; you name it, you can do it. Another great feature is that eventually the major search engines will start to crawl and index SVG documents – and why not, it's ultimately just a simple text file! This means that the current problem of text created as graphics being unsearchable is on its way to being solved.

I won't list all the companies planning to support SVG in some form, apart from that it is very extensive and growing rapidly. I will comment on a few of the most exciting plans though. First of all, both Microsoft and Netscape have announced they will support SVG in their browsers. To what level, isn't clear yet, but with both of them doing it, the competition should ensure a good implementation.

The other interesting product is a new program by Adobe called Live Motion. This is a vector graphics animation package that will produce files in many different formats, including the Macromedia Flash format (Macromedia are licensing their Flash player source code for free), and of course SVG. With a heavy-weight company like Adobe releasing a very promising authoring tool, this format has immense potential. You can find out more about Live Motion at www.adobe.com/livemotion/. JASC, the makers of Paint Shop Pro, have also got an early beta of a dedicated SVG authoring tool called Trajectory Pro. Check out www.jasc.com/trj.html for more information.

A Quick Look at SVG

I'm not going to get into SVG syntax at all here; instead I'll whet your appetite with a quick preview. If you are interested in finding out more about SVG, you can check out the W3C page at www.w3.org/Graphics/SVG/ or the SVG Central site at http://www.svgcentral.com.

Here is a quick sample of some SVG, just to get a taste of its power, and also so you can see for yourself that it really is based on XML and CSS!

This XML code is part of the source download and is called dashdemo.svg:

```
<?xml version="1.0" standalone="no"?>
<!DOCTYPE svg SYSTEM "svg-19991203.dtd" >

<svg width="600" height="500" >
  <style type="text/css">
    .demo{
    font-size:3em;
  }
  .dash{
    shape-rendering:default;
    stroke-width:14;
    stroke:#0000FF;
    fill:none
  }
  </style>
  <text x="15" y="35" class="demo">SVG Demo</text>
  <g class="dash">
    <path style="stroke-linecap:butt; stroke-dasharray:20 10" d="M20,100
    q50,150,100,0,50,-100,100,0,50,150,100,0,50,-100,100,0,50,150,100,0" />
  </g>
</svg>
```

SVG syntax is a whole book in itself. Here is a brief and partial explanation of the above just to get you thinking. The <text> tag is fairly self explanatory, and uses CSS in a fairly conventional way. The only thing to note on this element is the x and y attributes determine the absolute position within the SVG bounding box. The g element allows objects to be a *group*; they can be manipulated by CSS or the DOM as a whole. In the path element, the d attribute defines the path to be drawn. Various values will have different meanings, for example, <path d="M 50 50 L 250 50 L 250 150 L 50 150 z"/> will draw a rectangle, with M defining the starting point, L drawing lines to further points, and z closing the path back to the start.

171

If you display the above sample code in a browser with SVG support, it looks like this:

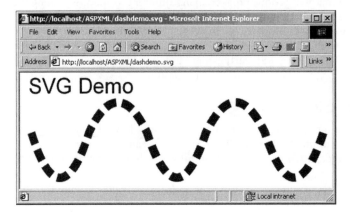

This was displayed in Internet Explorer 5 using the freely available plug-in from Adobe called svgview.exe, a self-extracting EXE of size 2.6 MB. Check out their SVG page at www.adobe.com/web/features/svg/main.html. There are some great samples there that include interactivity using JavaScript and the DOM.

Summary

The need to present XML to the user will become more common as programmers start to grasp the flexibility that XML offers them, and particularly as they see the benefits of using XML across all tiers of their application. We have seen that CSS is a simple way to display XML which re-uses existing skillsets and toolsets. There is clearly a limit to how far CSS can go, particularly when it comes to changing or restructuring the data, where XSL is the superior technology. However, for many applications, the simplicity of CSS makes it a clear choice for the rapid development of attractive and usable user interfaces.

We've also had a look at how two XML applications – XUL and SVG - use CSS. I hope that this has both whet your appetite for the CSS and XML combination, and also fired your imagination as to new and exciting ways to use them.

8

XSL – Extensible Stylesheet Language

Up to this point in time, we've mainly been concerned with dealing with data, rather than worrying too much about presentation. We've started looking at presentation using an ASP page to manually pluck data from the XML tree, and then format it accordingly using VBScript. Then, in the last chapter, we met Cascading Stylesheets (CSS), which took the issue of styling our data one step further.

In this chapter, however, you'll be introduced to the **Extensible Stylesheet Language** (**XSL**), an application of XML, which allows you to create special stylesheets for formatting XML files. Like Cascading Stylesheets (CSS), XSL is a data-driven means of modifying an XML document. Unlike CSS, which matches HTML presentation attributes to tags, XSL is a powerful transformation and styling language. CSS does not let you suppress content or change the order in which information is displayed. XSL uses pattern-matching to conditionally apply different formatting to different elements. You are able to use this to convert XML documents into any arbitrary markup vocabulary. We will be using it to conditionally transform XML documents into HTML documents. Later, in Chapter 9, you'll learn more advanced techniques for transforming content and changing the order of presentation.

There is another facet to XSL that is useful even if you do not perform document transformations. XSL includes constructs for specifying contents based on a path through the DOM tree. These constructs, called **XSL patterns**, can be used in MSXML even if you are not performing XSL-driven document transformations. They are similar in spirit, if not form, to regular expressions. Patterns are a powerful and high-performance means of locating nodes in a DOM tree. A single method call with a pattern can replace substantial amounts of DOM-related script. Patterns are an essential part of XSL stylesheets, as well. As you will see, each rule in a stylesheet includes a pattern. When the pattern matches the content in the source XML document, the rule is applied.

This chapter focuses on the basics of using XSL in web applications. In particular, you'll learn:

❑ How XSL and XML work together in transformations

❑ How to apply XSL stylesheets to XML in IE5

❑ The fundamentals of writing your own XSL stylesheets

❑ Locating content in an XML document using XSL patterns

❑ How to perform XSL transformations on the server in ASP

Using XSL Stylesheets

Do you remember IDC (Internet Data Connector) files from the earlier days of ASP? It was a very cumbersome and limiting way to retrieve data from a database. You provided a template that included a SQL query and received an HTML page containing the results. Once ADO hit the scene, there was no turning back. ADO brought a sense of freedom to ASP developers who had been tied to IDC for data retrieval. With ADO, it was much easier to bring data to almost any aspect of a web application. Using ASP and ADO, you could modify queries, refresh them, update the database, and work with the results in script.

Comparatively speaking, XSL provides the same breath of fresh air to the world of XML. Let's face it, climbing up and down an XML data tree for every little piece of data can be a coding headache. With XSL's unique template-based vocabulary, you can write a stylesheet with rich conditional logic that reacts to data content for total control over presentation. Right now, Internet Explorer 5.0 is the only mass-market browser that is able to apply an XSL stylesheet to an XML document. CSS is far more broadly supported in browsers than XSL is. In consequence, a common pattern for using XSL to present XML documents is to transform XML files on the server, thereby avoiding browser-specific issues.

How XSL Works

XSL is an application of XML; every stylesheet is a well-formed and valid XML document. It uses templates to shape the data into a more usable format. The XSL document is merely an instrument that transforms XML data into a specific presentation format for the receiving application. The basic pattern for transforming an XML document using XSL involves two input documents, which produce a single output document. The source XML document is loaded into one instance of the parser, while the XSL stylesheet is loaded into another. The stylesheet is then applied to the XML and the result is another document. In this chapter, that result will always be an HTML page, but that need not be the case in general.

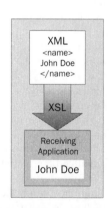

The receiving application can be a web browser but doesn't have to be. Indeed, many of the business-to-business e-commerce servers emerging right now use XSL to convert between XML vocabularies. In cases like that, the client is another program. For the purposes of this chapter, though, our ultimate target is a browser displaying HTML. Initially we'll be using the browser to effect the XSL transformation as well as display the results. Later, we'll use Active Server Pages to apply the XSL stylesheet, receive the output, and send it on to the browser. In that case, the browser client has no indication that the source document used XML. It requests a URL referencing an ASP and receives HTML content in reply.

Instead of sending the output to the browser, ASP can be used to create a number of different output formats, including text files, HTML files, XML files, XSL files and more. An ASP can detect the requesting client and conditionally generate the appropriate response document. For a browser, that would be HTML. A non-browser client, in turn, would receive XML. For now, we'll concentrate on creating output for the browser, both directly and via ASP.

XSL manipulates data using a set of elements and methods invoked using the **xsl namespace**. In the example that follows, the `xsl:template` element declares a namespace with the prefix `xsl` that refers to the W3C URI for the XSL effort. First consider an XML document that is representative of a vocabulary you wish to render as HTML:

```
<?xml version="1.0"?>

<CONTACT_INFO>
  <CONTACT>
    <NAME>John Doe</NAME>
    <PHONE>555-5319</PHONE>
  </CONTACT>
  <CONTACT>
    <NAME>Mary Jones</NAME>
    <PHONE>555-9013</PHONE>
  </CONTACT>
  <CONTACT>
    <NAME>Mike Wilson</NAME>
    <PHONE>555-4138</PHONE>
  </CONTACT>
</CONTACT_INFO>
```

This is a very simple contact list. The document element is CONTACT_INFO, and it contains CONTACT elements, each made up of two child elements, NAME and PHONE.

Assume you want to list your contacts and view the list in a browser. Consider the following XSL stylesheet that performs that very task:

```
<?xml version="1.0"?>

<xsl:template xmlns:xsl="http://www.w3.org/TR/WD-xsl">
  <HTML>
    <BODY>
      <xsl:for-each select="CONTACT_INFO/CONTACT">
        <DIV>
          <xsl:value-of select="NAME"/>
        </DIV>
      </xsl:for-each>
    </BODY>
  </HTML>
</xsl:template>
```

Notice that this document still has the familiar XML declaration and document element. It is a well-formed XML document, and it is valid according to the rules of the XSL DTD. The document element is used in connection with the `xsl` prefix, which invokes the `xsl` namespace. Although in this example the `xsl:template` is our document element, it doesn't have to be. In more complicated stylesheets, particularly when we are not transforming to an HTML document, the document element will be an `xsl:stylesheet` element.

The `template` element is just one of many XSL elements that perform various actions. As you may have guessed, the `for-each` element performs a looping action similar to what you might expect from the `For...Each` statement in VBScript. It is the construct by which XSL allows stylehseet designers to apply the same set of operations on multiple instances of an element. In the example above, we expect to find multiple CONTACT elements as children of CONTACT_INFO, so we need to iterate through them. In essence, when this stylesheet is applied, the shell of an HTML document is generated. Within the body, the `xsl:for-each` element generates a DIV for each CONTACT element that is an immediate child of CONTACT_INFO. The body of the DIV consists of the textual value of the CONTACT element's child NAME element. When the transformation is complete, we expect to have a list of all the names in the source XML document formatted as an HTML page. We'll explore these and other XSL elements throughout the remainder of the chapter.

If applied to this XML document, our XSL stylesheet would produce the following HTML output:

```
<HTML>
  <BODY>
    <DIV>John Doe</DIV>
    <DIV>Mary Jones</DIV>
    <DIV>Mike Wilson</DIV>
  </BODY>
</HTML>
```

This renders on-screen as:

Our XML document was transformed by the XSL document to produce what you see here – a simple HTML page. The only question is how was the transformation made? We learned in Chapter 1 that just opening our XML document in IE5 would produce this:

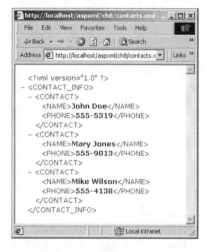

To transform the document with our XSL file, we must either link the stylesheet to the document by embedding an instruction within the XML document itself, or specifically tell the XML processor to do so from some other medium such as an ASP or HTML page. Since we're still learning the basics of XSL, for now we'll embed the instruction within the XML file.

Connecting XML to XSL

XML documents are never viewed directly in Internet Explorer 5. If an XML document arrives without explicit instructions, a default stylesheet is used. The problem for most of us is that the default styling is intended to highlight the raw XML form, not create a user-friendly rendition. If you want to over-ride the default, you can do so with a single line of code. Add the following declaration just after the XML declaration:

```
<?xml version="1.0"?>
<?xml-stylesheet type="text/xsl" href="stylecontacts.xsl" ?>
<CONTACT_INFO>
  <BUSINESS>
    ...
```

This is an excellent example of using an XML processing instruction to pass information to an XML application. The application in this case is the XSL processor. Other applications have no interest in XSL stylhseets, so embedding this information as an element or attribute would be inappropriate. Instead, XSL defines a PI that it will recognize and use to link to a stylesheet. The target of the href is the name of the stylesheet to use. This line directs the XML processor to request the stylesheet named, apply it to the document, and display the results.

As mentioned earlier, this is not the only way to transform XML documents with XSL stylesheets. Here are the three alternatives:

❑ Link the XML document to a stylesheet as shown above

❑ Use client-side script to select, obtain, and apply a stylesheet

❑ Apply the stylesheet from script on the server and return the results

The first two methods involve two roundtrips to the server: one for the document and one for the stylesheet. As you know, HTTP round-trips can be time consuming. The last two methods involve programming. These other methods will be discussed later in the chapter.

Applying an XSL transformation to a document results in some arbitrary output. In this chapter we are taking advantage of the fact that HTML output is easily created using XSL. As we proceed, bear in mind that we are producing HTML only because we choose to do so. Consider how we might generate other XML vocabularies, or even non-XML output. Before we can write any applications, however, you need to learn how to write an XSL stylesheet.

Programmatic XSL Transformations

The key to applying XSL transformations under programmatic control is the transformNode method that MSXML provides as an extension to the DOM, for both the DOM document and Node objects. This method takes an instance of MSXML, presumed to be loaded with an XSL stylesheet, and applies it to the XML document loaded in the instance on which the method is called. Here's an ASP, adv_style.asp, that returns the XML document if the client is Internet Explorer 5.0 or performs the XSL transformation on the server and returns HTML for all other clients:

```
<%@ Language="JavaScript" %>
<%
  var userAgent = new String(Request.ServerVariables("HTTP_USER_AGENT"));

  if (userAgent.indexOf("MSIE 5") >= 0)
```

```
      Response.Redirect("contacts.xml");
    else
      Response.Write(OnServer());

    function OnServer()
    {
      var doc, stylesheet;

      doc = Server.CreateObject("microsoft.xmldom");
      stylesheet = Server.CreateObject("microsoft.xmldom");

      if (doc != null && stylesheet != null)
      {
        doc.async = false;
        stylesheet.async = false;
        doc.load(Server.MapPath("contacts.xml"));
        stylesheet.load(Server.MapPath("stylecontacts.xsl"));

        if (doc.parseError == 0 && stylesheet.parseError == 0)
          return doc.transformNode(stylesheet);
        else
          return "<HTML><BODY>Error loading documents</BODY></HTML>";
      }
      else
        return "<HTML><BODY>Error creating server-side components</BODY></HTML>";
    }
%>
```

Note that this ASP code does not contain any of the usual boilerplate lines for the shell of an HTML page. I expect the ASP to do all the work. Most of this script is involved with preparing for the transformation and performing error checking. If the HTTP headers indicate that the client is Internet Explorer 5 or later, the raw XML file is redirected to the client and the user has to rely on the embedded link to the stylesheet transforming the document on the client. This is not the most efficient way of doing this – the redirect adds an additional round-trip on top of the two needed to fetch the XML document and the stylesheet, but it is quick and shows the technique in a few lines. Most importantly, it pushes the load of transforming the document down to the client whenever possible.

If some other browser is requesting the document (or, more importantly, if you comment out the other path so you can see this in IE 5), the server must perform the transformation as it cannot assume that the browser is XML and XSL-capable. Two instances of the XML parser are created, one for the XML document and one for the stylesheet. The two documents are loaded, and the script checks the parsers for errors:

```
doc.async = false;
stylesheet.async = false;
doc.load(Server.MapPath("contacts.xml"));
stylesheet.load(Server.MapPath("stylecontacts.xsl"));

if (doc.parseError == 0 && stylesheet.parseError == 0)
  ...
```

If none have been detected, transformNode is called on the document itself. This is the heart of the ASP and the only place where an XSL transformation is actually performed:

```
return doc.transformNode(stylesheet);
```

The same result would be obtained by calling `transformNode` on the node representing the document element, i.e. `doc.documentElement.transformNode(stylesheet)`. Since the return value from this method is a string, it can be passed through `Response.Write`. This results in the creation and return of an HTML document that is the result of applying the XSL transformation to the XML document.

XSL Stylesheets

An XSL stylesheet consists of one or more **templates**. As the name suggests, a template is a pattern for some part of the output document. Single-template stylesheets usually represent, or create, the entire HTML document that will be generated from the XML data. They are good for simple transformations that start at the top of a document and proceed downward in a regular fashion. It is easier to visualize what is happening in such a stylesheet as they force processing into a top-down, step-by-step pattern, just like a conventional programming language.

More complex transformations demand multiple templates. These are useful when processing is highly dependent on the context in which an element appears. For example, suppose the CONTACT elements in our sample contacts XML document could be children of either BUSINESS or PERSONAL elements. Instead of writing a single template with conditional branching, you could write two templates and direct that one is applied when CONTACT is a child of BUSINESS and the other when it is a child of PERSONAL. Extrapolate from this to a complex document that is more representative of what you will encounter in real-world applications, and you can begin to see how this might simplify your stylesheet.

Multiple-template stylesheets have a default template that instructs the XSL processor where to begin. The default template is executed first, and processing continues based on what happens in the body of each template. For the purposes of this chapter, we'll use the default to create the outer-most structure of the HTML page. From there, one or more secondary, or supporting, templates create islands of HTML that are called by the default template, for example:

```
<xsl:template match="/">
  <HTML>
    <BODY>
      <xsl:for-each select="CONTACT_INFO/CONTACT">
        <DIV>
          <xsl:value-of select="NAME"/>
        </DIV>
      </xsl:for-each>
    </BODY>
  </HTML>
</xsl:template>
```

We'll explain how this template works later. The important thing here is to realize that this template is executed when the root of the XML document is encountered (as indicated by the value of the `match` attribute), and the literal tags for the HTML and BODY elements are written into the output document. From there, some processing occurs. In this case, it ends there as we have a fairly simple example. We could, however, have directed the XSL processor to continue to apply other templates. If this instruction took the place of the `xsl:for-each` element, the results of that processing would be embedded in the body of the HTML output document. This is exactly the approach we will take in a slightly more advanced example later in this chapter.

181

The following illustration depicts the structure of an XSL stylesheet in the two forms. Both forms are similar – the action of an XSL transformation is implemented by templates. The difference is that the multiple-template form must involve some directives to pass control from one template to the rest.

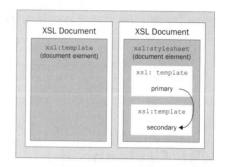

Although the second form shown in the illustration refers to a primary and a secondary template, there may be more than two templates. The point is that one template has control of processing and passes control off to another template based on some pattern in the XML document.

Whichever form suits your needs, you will be dealing with a stylesheet containing one or more templates. The template, then, is the common structure from which everything else in XSL hangs. Let's write a more advanced version of our stylesheet as a way to study XSL stylesheets and templates. Suppose that instead of simply dumping a list of contact names to the browser, we wanted to include their phone number, and suppose we added a parent element that divided our contacts document into business and personal contacts. For any given contact, we can add an attribute, relation, that lets us specify when a contact in the list is a family member. Here's the modified contacts document:

```xml
<?xml version="1.0"?>

<CONTACT_INFO>
  <BUSINESS>
    <CONTACT>
       <NAME>John Doe</NAME>
       <PHONE>555-5319</PHONE>
    </CONTACT>
  </BUSINESS>
  <PERSONAL>
    <CONTACT relation="family">
       <NAME>Mary Jones</NAME>
       <PHONE>555-9013</PHONE>
    </CONTACT>

    <CONTACT>
       <NAME>Mike Wilson</NAME>
       <PHONE>555-4138</PHONE>
    </CONTACT>
  </PERSONAL>
</CONTACT_INFO>
```

With the additional information in our document, we would like to do the following:

❑ Output a richly formatted banner to classify contacts as either business or personal

❑ Output each contact's name on one line, followed by their phone number on another in a smaller font

❑ When a contact is a family member, render his or her name in boldface

The results should look like this:

This can be implemented with inline styles like this:

```
<HTML>
  <BODY>
    <DIV STYLE="background-color:black; color:white;
            font-family:Verdana,arial,helvetica,sans-serif;
            font-size:12pt; padding:2px"> Business Contacts</DIV>
    <DIV>John Doe
      <DIV STYLE="font-size:10pt;left:.25cm;position:relative;">555-5319</DIV>
    </DIV>
    <P />
    <DIV STYLE="background-color:teal; color:white;
            font-family:Verdana,arial,helvetica,sans-serif;
            font-size:12pt; padding:2px"> Personal Contacts</DIV>
    <DIV STYLE="font-weight:bold">Mary Jones
      <DIV STYLE="font-size:10pt;left:.25cm;position:relative;">555-9013</DIV>
    </DIV>
    <DIV>Mike Wilson
      <DIV STYLE="font-size:10pt;left:.25cm;position:relative;">555-4138</DIV>
    </DIV>
    <P />
  </BODY>
</HTML>
```

Generating this will a bit more challenging. In fact, it will require a multi-template stylesheet using a few new XSL elements. We begin by moving the XSL namespace declaration from the first template element to the stylesheet element:

```
<?xml version="1.0"?>
<xsl:stylesheet xmlns:xsl="http://www.w3.org/TR/WD-xsl">

...

</xsl:stylesheet>
```

The stylesheet element becomes the document element of the stylesheet document as well as the parent element of all the XSL templates.

> Since the current production version of MSXML was produced, XSL has moved through the W3C process and achieved Recommendation status. In the process, the proper URI for the namespace declaration changed to http://www.w3.org/1999/XSL/Transform. This is supported by the beta version of MSXML 3.0. If you are using that version of the parser, you should use the updated URI.

In addition to the XSL namespace declaration, the `xsl:stylesheet` element supports four other attributes. These are:

❑ `default-space` – whether to preserve white space from the source document

❑ `indent-result` – whether to preserve white space originating in the stylesheet

❑ `language` – script language used within scripting elements in the stylesheet; defaults to JScript in MSXML

❑ `result-ns` – denotes the namespace of the output document resulting from the transformation defined in the stylesheet

These are defined by XSL. MSXML, however, has rather limited support for them. It only supports the value `default` for `default-space` and the value `yes` for `indent-result`, both of which mean white space from their respective sources is preserved. If you care about white space, you should get in the habit of using these attributes in case you try to use the stylesheet with another XSL processor. XML generally ignores white space, so it bad practice to write applications that count on the preservation of white space. If, however, you must worry about this, remember that MSXML will not honor any other value for these attributes.

If white space is an issue, you will have to control it either in the source XML document or in the stylesheet. All the examples in this chapter are indented and use line breaks for clarity. In practice, you may encounter some stylesheets that compress stylesheets so as not to introduce white space.

The `language` attribute is something you will be concerned about, although scripting elements are extensions to XSL introduced by MSXML.

XSLT introduces the concept of calling named templates and provides XSL elements for calling templates and defining parameters. This is the portable equivalent to MSXML 2.0's scripting extensions. Named templates are currently supported by the MSXML 3.0 beta release (March 2000).

Finally, MSXML 2.0 will ignore the value of `result-ns`. It treats the result of any XSL transformation as XML. You should use this attribute solely for your own information or for portability.

Templates

XSL is based entirely upon the concept of using templates to apply consistent formatting to repeated elements in an XML document. Templates are like rules to be applied under certain conditions. A template consists of a pattern that must be matched to the current context for the template body to be applied. For example, if processing has progressed to the point where the current node of the XML document is a CONTACT element, then CONTACT is the context, and a template whose pattern is CONTACT will match and the transformation specified in the template body will be applied.

How does the XSL processor know where to begin? In our single-template version, this was not a problem. For multi-template stylesheets, however, we have to give the processor a hint. XSL looks for a default template that applies to the root of the document:

```
<xsl:template match="/">
  <xsl:apply-templates />
</xsl:template>
```

In the next section, we'll discuss XSL patterns. For now, know that the single slash indicates the root of the document. The XSL processor starts there and continues as directed by the body of the template. In this case, the template tells the processor to apply any other templates for which a match can be made.

Finding Data with Patterns

In order to match templates, we have to be able to specify what nodes should be matched and under what circumstances. In its simplest form, we can provide the name of elements we want to match – CONTACT_INFO, CONTACT – but in our original example, we had the example of CONTACT_INFO/CONTACT. The implication there was that we wanted to match CONTACT elements that happened to be immediate child elements of CONTACT_INFO elements. This gave us some context with which to restrict the selection. Clearly, XSL patterns can be more complicated than simply specifying an element name. That example, moreover, came not in the match attribute of an xsl:template element, but in the select attribute of an xsl:for-each element.

The fact is, patterns are used whenever we need to specify some collection of nodes on which to act. Templates use them to specify what to match and act upon. Other elements use them as filters to refine what is acted upon or to act conditionally based on some test pattern. Before you can specify an action in the body of a template, you have to learn how to compose XSL patterns.

The following table lists the special characters used by XSL patterns:

XSL Pattern Character	Meaning
/	Immediate child operator; when a pattern begins with this character, it indicates that selection begins from the document root element
//	Recursive descent (selects the pattern that follows if it appears anywhere below the starting point); if the patterns begins with this, the remainder of the pattern may be matched anywhere within the document
.	Current context node
*	Wildcard operator selecting any element
@	Prefix indicating that the name immediately following refers to an attribute
@*	Attribute wildcard (selects all attributes)
:	Namespace separator
!	Applies an information method to the reference node
( )	Groups contents for precedence
[ ]	Applies a filter pattern
[ ]	Subscript operator for indexing into a collection

The topic of XSL patterns as understood by MSXML 2.0 split off from XSL proper during XSL's progression to Recommendation status. XSL became XSLT – XSL Transformations – while the pattern language split off to become XPath. XPath is similar to the pattern syntax you see here, but it adds a number of special characters, most notably the ability to choose a parent node with the double dot (..) pattern. XPath also introduces the topic of axes, which are pre-defined paths that are commonly used and referred to by keywords. Documentation for the XPath support in MSXML 3.0 is included with the SDK that may be downloaded from http://msdn.microsoft.com/ downloads/webtechnology/xml/msxml.asp. XPath is discussed in more detail in Appendix F.

Here are a few examples of patterns in the new stylesheet we will be building:

```
/CONTACT_INFO
CONTACT_INFO
CONTACT
```

These should be fairly clear to you. We're naming elements. What's the difference between the first two? Well, the first pattern requires that CONTACT_INFO be an immediate child of the document element, while the second merely says that element must be the current context of the processor. The first will be used if I want to write the HTML shell:

```
<xsl:template match="/CONTACT_INFO">
  <HTML>
    <BODY>
      <xsl:apply-templates />
    </BODY>
  </HTML>
</xsl:template>
```

The second will be used to provide the actual processing for the CONTACT_INFO element:

```
<xsl:template match="CONTACT_INFO">
  <xsl:for-each select="./*">
    <xsl:choose>
      <xsl:when test=".[.!nodeName()='PERSONAL']">
        <DIV STYLE="background-color:teal; color:white;
                font-family:Verdana,arial,helvetica,sans-serif;
                font-size:12pt; padding:2px">Personal Contacts</DIV>
      </xsl:when>
      <xsl:otherwise>
        <DIV STYLE="background-color:black; color:white;
                font-family:Verdana,arial,helvetica,sans-serif;
                font-size:12pt; padding:2px">Business Contacts</DIV>
      </xsl:otherwise>
    </xsl:choose>
    <xsl:apply-templates />
  <P/>
  </xsl:for-each>
</xsl:template>
```

Ignore the body of this template for the moment; we'll dive into what all the new elements mean in a few moments. If you glance over it though, you should get the sense that we are performing some processing to render the CONTACT_INFO element, whereas the first template simply wrote out the document's shell. The two could certainly have been combined, but this separation makes the two functions distinct and hopefully more readable. In addition, it allows the user to accommodate possible future changes to the document vocabulary that might permit CONTACT_INFO to occur elsewhere in the body of the document. Here's another pattern, this one found in the body of the template you just saw:

```
./*
```

Referring to the previous table, you should interpret this to mean "any element that is an immediate child of the current node". I use this in the xsl:for-each element to iterate through all the children of CONTACT_INFO. Here are two more patterns to give you some food for thought:

```
.[.!nodeName()='PERSONAL']
@relation[.!value()='family']
```

You can parse some of these expressions using the special characters listed previously, but there seem to be some functions embedded in the expressions. XSL provides some functions that provide information about the current node.

XSL Information Methods

If you are a really quick study, you'll have picked up on the use of the single dots, exclamation point, and filter brackets in the first example. However, what is nodeName()? The operator preceding it suggests that it is an information operator. If you thought that, you are right on target. XSL patterns provide a series of functions that return information about a particular node:

Information Method	Meaning
date	Casts values to the date format
end	Returns true if the last node in a collection is selected
index	Returns the index number of the node within the parent
nodeName	Returns the qualified name of the node
nodeType	Returns a number indicating what type of node is selected
text	Returns the immediate text node of the selected element
value	Returns a type cast version of the value of an element

In the first example above, then, I am interested in the current node only if its name is PERSONAL. This is used when I want to render the banner for personal contacts:

```
<xsl:when test=".[.!nodeName()='PERSONAL']">
  <DIV STYLE="background-color:teal; color:white;
          font-family:Verdana,arial,helvetica,sans-serif;
          font-size:12pt; padding:2px"> Personal Contacts</DIV>
</xsl:when>
```

When a PERSONAL element is encountered, an HTML DIV element is written out that has some inline styling that gives the solid colored banner with a distinctive font. In the second example above, the value method is used to see if the relation attribute's value is family. This lets such contacts be rendered in boldface:

```
<xsl:if test="@relation[.!value()='family']">
  <xsl:attribute name="STYLE">font-weight:bold</xsl:attribute>
</xsl:if>
```

XSL Operators

If you are writing filter conditions, you have to be able to compare two values. In addition to the information methods, XSL provides operators for this purpose:

Operator	Shortcut form	Meaning
and	&&	Logical AND
or	||	Logical OR

Table continued on following page

Operator	Shortcut form	Meaning
not		Logical NOT
eq	=	Equals
ieq		Case insensitive equality
ne	!=	Not equal
ine		Case insensitive inequality
lt	<	Less than
ilt		Case insensitive less than
le	<=	Less than or equal to
ile		Case insensitive less than or equal to
gt	>	Greater than
igt		Case insensitive greater than
ge	>=	Greater than or equal to
ige		Case insensitive greater than or equal to
all		Set operation returning TRUE if the condition is true for all items in a collection
any		Set operation returning TRUE if the condition is true for any item in a collection

You'll notice I've used the shortcut form exclusively. This is merely a preference on my part as I am coming from a background in conventional programming languages. The shortcut form is similar to the forms used in C++, Java, and JavaScript. There is no intrinsic benefit to either form, and you should use what is most comfortable for you and most readable for your fellow programmers.

Taking Action: Template Bodies

What makes templates so useful is that they perform the same action on groups of individual elements that match specific patterns such as we saw in the examples above. This pattern matching works differently depending on which XSL element uses it. The previous examples showed you a preview of a variety of other elements specified by XSL. These elements are what drive XSL and give you expressive capabilities similar to a programming language. Here is the list of XSL elements; the elements marked with an asterisk are non-standard extensions provided by the Microsoft XSL processor:

XSL element	Meaning
xsl:apply-templates	Guides the XSL processor in selecting the next template to match based on a pattern
xsl:attribute	Creates an attribute in the output document

XSL element	Meaning
xsl:choose	Provides multiple conditional testing similar to a JavaScript switch statement in conjunction with the xsl:when and xsl:otherwise elements
xsl:comment	Creates a comment node in the output
xsl:copy	Copies the current node or nodes to the output
xsl:element	Creates an element in the output document
xsl:eval*	Evaluates an in-line script to generate text output
xsl:for-each	Applies some processing iteratively to every node in a collection
xsl:if	Simple conditional processing
xsl:otherwise	Provides default processing for an xsl:choose element
xsl:pi	Creates a processing instruction in the output document
xsl:script*	Allows programmers to attach a body of script that may be called from elsewhere in the stylesheet
xsl:stylesheet	Document element for a multi-template stylesheet
xsl:template	Defines a processing rule for generating output when a specified pattern or context is encountered in the input document
xsl:value-of	Inserts the value of the selected node into the output document
xsl:when	Provides a single conditional test within an xsl:choose element

Let's look at a few of these in depth as we develop our stylesheet.

xsl:for-each

When we are working from a CONTACT_INFO element, we need to process each child element. These will be the BUSINESS and PERSONAL elements. When we encounter a CONTACT element, we need to iterate through each child – the NAME and PHONE elements. We need an iterator much like the for loop in JavaScript or C++, and xsl:for-each is that construct.

This element supports a select attribute that can be used to narrow down what we are iterating through. In the case of CONTACT_INFO, we want to iterate through every child element:

```
<xsl:template match="CONTACT_INFO">
  <xsl:for-each select="./*">
  . . .
  </xsl:for-each>
</xsl:template>
```

For CONTACT elements, we want to iterate through every CONTACT element:

```
<xsl:template match="CONTACT">
  <xsl:for-each select=".">
  . . .
  </xsl:for-each>
</xsl:template>
```

In both cases, the XSL processor will apply whatever processing – hard-coded text or XSL elements – appears within the body of the xsl:for-each element.

xsl:choose, xsl:when, xsl:otherwise

When we encounter a CONTACT_INFO element, we want to process each of its children. We know these will either be PERSONAL or BUSINESS elements. We want to set the styling so that each appears in a distinctive banner with a 12-point Verdana font. The xsl:choose element lets us perform multiple conditional tests like a switch statement. Each test is an xsl:when element whose test attribute's value is a pattern denoting the condition. When the condition evaluates to true, the body of the xsl:when element is applied. Just like a default branch in a switch statement, XSL provides the xsl:otherwise element. Here's how we apply these elements to in the CONTACT_INFO template:

```
<xsl:template match="CONTACT_INFO">
  <xsl:for-each select="./*">
    <xsl:choose>
      <xsl:when test=".[.!nodeName()='PERSONAL']">
        <DIV STYLE="background-color:teal; color:white;
                font-family:Verdana,arial,helvetica,sans-serif;
                font-size:12pt; padding:2px"> Personal Contacts</DIV>
      </xsl:when>
      <xsl:otherwise>
        <DIV STYLE="background-color:black; color:white;
                font-family:Verdana,arial,helvetica,sans-serif;
                font-size:12pt; padding:2px"> Business Contacts</DIV>
      </xsl:otherwise>
    </xsl:choose>
    <xsl:apply-templates />
  <P/>
  </xsl:for-each>
</xsl:template>
```

When the child node in question is a PERSONAL element, we write a DIV to the output document that places the text "Personal Contacts" in white Verdana characters on a teal (greenish blue) background. In every other case (here, that means BUSINESS elements), the default of white characters on a black background is applied:

```
<xsl:when test=".[.!nodeName()='PERSONAL']">
  <DIV ...>Personal Contacts</DIV>
</xsl:when>
<xsl:otherwise>
  <DIV ...>Business Contacts</DIV>
</xsl:otherwise>
```

We know that our document has additional structure below these elements, so we want to direct the XSL processor to continue working. Since we want to work within the context we have established, i.e. inherit the styling provided by the DIV elements by nesting the remaining content, we place an xsl:apply-templates element within the body of this template:

```
<xsl:for-each select="./*">
  <xsl:choose>
    . . .
  </xsl:choose>
```

```
        <xsl:apply-templates />
      <P/>
    </xsl:for-each>
```

This causes the XSL processor to continue chaining through to the rest of the templates before emerging from this one.

xsl:apply-templates

I've used the simplest form of apply-templates here. With no further qualification, `xsl:apply-templates` tells the processor to just keep going. That's appropriate here; I'll provide further qualification in the `match` attributes of the remaining templates, and our document isn't all that complicated. This element does allow for a `select` attribute, however. We could use this if we wanted to limit the scope of the processing. For example, if the XML document had elements besides CONTACT that I wanted to suppress, I could have written `<xsl:apply-templates select="./CONTACT"/>` which would have limited the processing to CONTACT elements.

xsl:if and xsl:attribute

Let's flesh out the CONTACT template now. Since these are nested within the DIV output by the CONTACT_INFO template, we have the font face and font size established. We need to change the font size when a telephone number is encountered and render the font in boldface when the `value` of the relation attribute of CONTACT elements is `family`. We need an `if` statement like those in conventional programming languages, and XSL has one in the aptly named `xsl:if` element:

```
<xsl:template match="CONTACT">
  <xsl:for-each select=".">
    <DIV>
    <xsl:if test="@relation[.!value()='family']">
      <xsl:attribute name="STYLE">font-weight:bold</xsl:attribute>
    </xsl:if>
    ...
    </DIV>
  </DIV>
  </xsl:for-each>
</xsl:template>
```

First, I look to see if the value of the relation attribute marks this as a family contact. If it is, the font is made bold. An in-line style could be written as in the CONTACT_INFO example, but then the DIV element would have to be substantially repeated in the default case. Besides, I need to introduce you to the `xsl:attribute` element. I always write the DIV element to the output document. If the condition evaluates `true`, an attribute is created. Since it occurs in the context of the DIV, the attribute will be attached to that element. The value of the attribute thus created is provided by the textual content of the `xsl:attribute` element, in this case `font-weight:bold`. Next, I need to write out the value of the NAME element, as well as the PHONE element with some additional styling. That brings us to the `xsl:value-of` element.

xsl:value-of

The `xsl:value-of` element writes the value of the current node to the output document. At this point in the CONTACT template, the current node is the CONTACT element itself. We want to select the NAME child element, then provide some styling and write the PHONE element:

```
    <xsl:value-of select="NAME"/>
      <DIV STYLE="font-size:10pt;left:.25cm;position:relative;">
    <xsl:value-of select="PHONE"/>
    </DIV>
```

The xsl:value-of element takes a select attribute that functions just as you have seen in the preceding elements. In this case, from the current node (CONTACT), I select the NAME element and write its value. Next, I write the DIV that changes the font and positioning for the PHONE content, and then I select that node (which is also a child of NAME and therefore within the context) and write its value.

The Complete Stylesheet

Here's how it all ties together:

```
<?xml version="1.0"?>
<xsl:stylesheet xmlns:xsl="http://www.w3.org/TR/WD-xsl">

<xsl:template match="/">
  <xsl:apply-templates />
</xsl:template>

<xsl:template match="/CONTACT_INFO">
  <HTML>
    <BODY>
      <xsl:apply-templates />
    </BODY>
  </HTML>
</xsl:template>

<xsl:template match="CONTACT_INFO">
  <xsl:for-each select="./*">
    <xsl:choose>
      <xsl:when test=".[.!nodeName()='PERSONAL']">
        <DIV STYLE="background-color:teal; color:white;
                font-family:Verdana,arial,helvetica,sans-serif;
                font-size:12pt; padding:2px"> Personal Contacts</DIV>
      </xsl:when>
      <xsl:otherwise>
        <DIV STYLE="background-color:black; color:white;
                font-family:Verdana,arial,helvetica,sans-serif;
                font-size:12pt; padding:2px"> Business Contacts</DIV>
      </xsl:otherwise>
    </xsl:choose>
    <xsl:apply-templates />
  <P/>
  </xsl:for-each>
</xsl:template>

<xsl:template match="CONTACT">
  <xsl:for-each select=".">
    <DIV>
```

```
    <xsl:if test="@relation[.!value()='family']">
      <xsl:attribute name="STYLE">font-weight:bold</xsl:attribute>
    </xsl:if>
    <xsl:value-of select="NAME"/>
    <DIV STYLE="font-size:10pt;left:.25cm;position:relative;">
      <xsl:value-of select="PHONE"/>
    </DIV>
  </DIV>
  </xsl:for-each>
</xsl:template>

</xsl:stylesheet>
```

The order of processing dictated by the various `xsl:apply-templates` elements is as follows:

❑   Start at the root

❑   Write the shell when the CONTACT_INFO child is found and dive into its subtree

❑   For every CONTACT_INFO node, process its child nodes after providing some conditional styling

❑   For each CONTACT, process its chilren

At the completion of the CONTACT template's execution, the XSL processor will unwind the call stack. In our case, the document consists of a single CONTACT_INFO element, so the processor is finished.

XSL Methods

In addition to the information methods and filter criteria you saw earlier, XSL provides several other methods that can be used to implement styling and presentation. These methods are invoked within `xsl:script` or `xsl:eval` elements. Here is the list of methods supported by MSXML:

Method	Meaning
absoluteChildNumber (oStartNode)	Returns the one-based index of the node in its parent's list of all child nodes
ancestorChildNumber (sNodeName, oStartNode)	Returns the one-based index of the nearest named ancestor of oStartNode in its parent's list of all child nodes, or null if no such ancestor exists
childNumber(oStartNode)	Returns the one-based index of the start node in its parent's list of child nodes of the same name
depth(oNode)	Returns the depth within the tree at which the specified node exists, where the document element occurs level 0
formatDate (varDate, sFormat, varLocale)	Formats the given variant date varDate according to specifications in the string sFormat, for the target local varLocale

Table continued on following page

Method	Meaning
`formatIndex` `(lIndex, sFormat)`	Formats an integer index using the supplied numbering system. Where `sFormat` is one of the following:
	1 standard integer numbering
	01 standard numbering with leading zeroes
	A A – Z, AA – ZZ ordering
	a a – z, aa – zz ordering
	I Uppercase Roman numeral ordering
	i lowercase Roman numeral ordering
`formatNumber` `(dNumber, sFormat)`	Formats a double-length real number using the supplied specification, `sFormat`
`formatTime` `(varTime, sFormat, varLocale)`	Formats a variant time using the supplied specification string `sFormat` for the target `varLocale`
`uniqueID(oNode)`	Returns the unique identifier for the supplied node

To demonstrate the utility of these methods, look at what we can do to our original XSL stylesheet to make it place capital letters in front of each contact's name:

```
<?xml version="1.0"?>
<xsl:stylesheet xmlns:xsl="uri:xsl">
  <xsl:template match="/">
    <HTML>
      <BODY>
        <xsl:for-each select="CONTACT_INFO/CONTACT">
          <xsl:apply-templates select="NAME"/>
          <xsl:apply-templates select="PHONE"/>
        </xsl:for-each>
      </BODY>
    </HTML>
  </xsl:template>

  <xsl:template match="NAME">
    <FONT size="4" face="verdana">

      <xsl:eval>
        formatIndex(ancestorChildNumber("CONTACT",this),"A")
      </xsl:eval>

      <xsl:value-of />
    </FONT>
    <BR/>
  </xsl:template>

  <xsl:template match="PHONE">
    <FONT size="2" face="verdana">
    <I>
```

```
        <xsl:value-of />
      </I>
    </FONT>
    <P></P>
  </xsl:template>

</xsl:stylesheet>
```

The `ancestorChildNumber` method has two parameters, the first of which asks for the specific ancestor element we're looking for, in this case `CONTACT`. The `this` parameter refers to the current context node. As each `NAME` element is transformed, this method will return the index of the `NAME` element's parent `CONTACT` element. This index is relative to the `CONTACT_INFO` element's list of child elements.

The `formatIndex` method converts those index numbers to an all-uppercase letter listing:

```
<HTML>
  <BODY>
    <FONT size="4" face="verdana">A John Doe</FONT>
    <BR />
    <FONT size="2" face="verdana"><I>555-5319</I></FONT>
    <P></P>
    <FONT size="4" face="verdana">B Mary Jones</FONT>
    <BR />
    <FONT size="2" face="verdana"><I>555-9013</I></FONT>
    <P></P>
    <FONT size="4" face="verdana">C Mike Wilson</FONT>
    <BR />
    <FONT size="2" face="verdana"><I>555-4138</I></FONT>
    <P></P>
  </BODY>
</HTML>
```

And this is what you get:

195

XSL Queries

XSL can also be used to perform queries in the midst of DOM code. This is a fast way to locate nodes you are after without resorting to tree-traversal methods. Internally, MSXML is performing a traversal, but you don't have to write the code. Equally important, all the traversal is occurring within an optimized C++ implementation without multiple calls through the COM layer, so performance is excellent. If you can specify a path to the node or nodes you want, or if you can specify a reasonable filter condition, XSL patterns are a useful way to locate nodes.

XSL queries can accomplish two tasks – filtering and sorting. This might sound a little daunting, but don't worry – you've already been using queries to a certain degree. The `match` and `select` attributes in XSL stylesheets are a form of querying.

> *XML queries are a persistent theme in the XML community. A note for a query language, XQL, was submitted to the W3C XSL Working Group in 1998. This work influenced XPath to some extent. The forthcoming version of Microsoft's parser, MSXML 3.0, provides some extensions to XPath that are derived from XQL. Work continues at the W3C, and draft requirements for an XML query language were made public on 31 January 2000 (http://www.w3.org/TR/xmlquery-rec).*

Based on Elements

Queries based on element values can deliver precision control over a template's output, allowing the author to display exactly the data he wants. Consider our original, basic XML document and its associated stylesheet. Let's modify it by filtering our data so that we only return contacts with the name Mary Jones. Edit the `for-each` line to look like the following:

```
<xsl:for-each select="CONTACT_INFO/CONTACT[NAME='Mary Jones']">
```

This tells the processor that under the CONTACT node, look for any NAME element matching the value **Mary Jones**. As you'd expect, the output to the browser is the same as a previous example, except that only one contact is returned:

This filtering method can be used not only with `for-each` elements, but also with the `template` element's `match` attribute. Also, other operators can be used in the query pattern. If we had wanted to return all contacts *except* Mary Jones, our line of code would have looked like this:

```
<xsl:for-each select="CONTACT_INFO/CONTACT[NAME!='Mary Jones']">
```

Of course, that isn't so very different from what we did in our expanded example, and I promised you a new technique to add to your DOM programming arsenal. The key is two methods MSXML adds to the DOM: `selectNodes` and `selectSingleNode`. Both take a string containing an XSL Pattern as their sole parameter. A node object is returned from `selectSingleNode`, while `selectNodes` returns a `NodeList` object. In both cases, the node or nodes returned are the results of applying the pattern to the subtree rooted by the node to which the method is applied. Thus, to search our document for Mary Jones, I might load the document into an instance of the parser named doc and make the following call:

```
maryNode =
doc.documentElement.selectSingleNode("CONTACT_INFO/CONTACT[NAME='Mary Jones']");
```

If you call `selectSingleNode` with a pattern that would return multiple matches if applied over the entire document or document subtree, the first match found by MSXML is returned:

> *MSXML 3.0, currently in beta, also supports XPath for queries. The default query language, however, is XSL Patterns for backward code compatibility. If you wish to take advantage of the new features provided by XPath, you must call the parser's* `setProperty` *method as follows:* `doc.setProperty("SelectionLanguage", "XPath").`

Based on Attributes

Queries based on the values of attributes work the same as they do for elements except that the names of attributes must be preceded by the @ symbol in the pattern. We saw this in our expanded stylesheet when we looked for contacts whose relation element indicated that the contact is a family member:

```
<xsl:if test="@relation[.!value()='family']">
```

The special character @ precedes the attribute name so that the parser understands that we mean to look for an attribute instead of an element. We can make queries on attributes within DOM-related code just as we did for elements. Be careful, however, when writing patterns. Consider the following two patterns applied to the expanded version of contacts.xml:

```
//@relation[.="family"]
CONTACT_INFO//CONTACT[./@relation="family"]
```

The first pattern returns the attribute node itself. In our example, that isn't very useful. We might use it in a case in which the `relation` attribute could take on many values if we wanted to see the range of values used. For example, we might use it to enumerate all the namespaces declared in an XML document. If we didn't care where they were used, this form would allow us to iterate through the node list and view the URIs.

The second form returns the CONTACT element or elements whose `relation` attribute marks it as a family member. This is the more typical usage. You will want to execute a query whose filter is some attribute-related condition, but you want to obtain the elements modified by the attribute condition.

> *A few programming notes are in order here. First, the first XSL pattern is a huge waste of processing as it uses the recursion operator. This forces the parser to traverse the entire tree to execute its search. Use this with caution! In the namespace enumeration example, it is a reasonable usage. Wherever possible, however, you should specify the path as closely as possible to restrict the scope the parser must traverse. This is what I do in the second pattern. Note, however, I still must resort to recursive descent because CONTACT is no longer an immediate child of CONTACT_INFO, since BUSINESS and PERSONAL elements intervene. Since this is further down on the tree, the waste of processing resources is mitigated somewhat, although the parser will still search the entire subtree rooted by the BUSINESS element without result.*

Sorting Data

Being able to sort the data being returned by the XSL stylesheet is the final piece of the query puzzle. Sorting is useful in relational databases to control the order of presentation, and it is even more useful here, particularly when you are generating HTML through an XSL transformation. While the results of a SQL query will have to go through additional processing to be visually presented to a human user, the results of an XSL transformation resulting in HTML goes directly to the user. If you can't control the order in which items appear in the original XML document, you must control it during the transformation.

Sorting is achieved by using the order-by attribute, which can be used with either the apply-templates or for-each element. Similar to the SQL language, this attribute specifies the criteria the processor is to use to order the data. The value of the order-by attribute is a list of sort criteria separated from one another by semicolons. Each criterion is an XSL pattern, just as you saw in the match and select attributes in the stylesheets developed for this chapter. The first non-whitespace character of each criterion specifies whether the sort is ascending or descending, with ascending being the default. An optional + denotes ascending order, while – denotes a descending sort. One facet of XSL sorting behavior that you might not expect is that MSXML does not automatically evaluate all the criteria in an order-by attribute. A criterion is applied only if the sort resulting from the preceding criteria results in two identical items. In that case, the criterion is applied in an effort to break the tie and change the sort order. Thus, if the first criterion results in a unique sorting, the remaining criteria will not be applied.

If you look carefully at our original XML file, you'll notice that the contact names appeared in alphabetical order. This was quite by accident, and the XSL stylesheet simply spits them out in the order of their occurrence in the source XML document. However, if we wanted to send them out in descending order instead, we could alter our for-each element to look like this:

```
<xsl:for-each select="CONTACT_INFO/CONTACT" order-by="- NAME">
  <xsl:apply-templates select="NAME"/>
  <xsl:apply-templates select="PHONE"/>
</xsl:for-each>
```

Sorting need not be static. Recall that a stylesheet is itself an XML document. If you load one into a DOM tree, you can access all its nodes, including the order-by attribute. If your application returns a web page with an HTML interface to an embedded XML document, you can do dynamic sorting. Suppose you wished to give the user the ability to sort the contacts list by name or phone number. You might wrap the NAME and PHONE entries with DIV elements containing event handlers:

```
<xsl:for-each select="CONTACT_INFO/CONTACT" order-by="- NAME">
  <DIV onclick="DoSort('NAME')">
  <xsl:apply-templates select="NAME"/>
  </DIV>
  <DIV onclick="DoSort('PHONE')">
  <xsl:apply-templates select="PHONE"/>
  </DIV>
</xsl:for-each>
```

The event handler DoSort would be script code inserted into the finished HTML page – not the stylesheet – that would retrieve the order-by attribute using an XSL pattern. Once the node is retrieved, its value would be set to the passed-in element name – NAME or PHONE – and the transformation would be called again to regenerate the contacts list with the desired sort order. This is a departure from what we have done so far. In this case, the HTML page returned by the ASP passes not finished HTML but an HTML shell including script, as well as the raw XML document and the stylesheet. It requires client-side scripting and access to MSXML, but it turns the returned document into an interactive page.

Summary

XSL is an XML vocabulary that defines a powerful alternative to CSS for rendering XML documents as HTML. In a later chapter, we'll see that it is also a powerful method of translating from one XML vocabulary to another, but in this chapter we focused on formatting XML documents for presentation. XSL operates by defining a series of templates which are applied when a pattern matches the current context in the document. We saw how to use Internet Explorer's native support for XSL stylesheet linking as well as using extensions to the DOM to perform XSL transformations from script. We used the latter feature to write an ASP that performs the transformation for browsers other than Internet Explorer 5.0.

We presented two forms: single template stylesheets that are little more than XSL instructions embedded in an HTML shell, and multi-template stylesheets permitting sophisticated XSL processing. You were introduced to the elements defined by XSL, and you saw how they work together to direct the flow of processing in a stylesheet. Together, we built several stylesheets that illustrated various techniques in XSL. An interesting offshoot of this was an introduction to using XSL patterns as a complement to the XML DOM. XSL patterns, and their W3C-approved successor, XPath expressions. This is an efficient method of retrieving collections of nodes given a path through the XML document or a filter expression.

MSXML implements a robust XSL processor in addition to its support for the DOM. The tool you have been using to build XML-driven ASP applications, therefore, becomes doubly useful now that you have learned the core techniques of XSL. You are free to choose the approach – DOM or XSL – that best suits the task at hand. You can use XSL to complement the DOM for node querying and retrieval, or use the DOM to modify an XSL stylesheet and make transformations interactive. Both operate on XML documents, yet XSL is an XML application. These two facets of XML show how versatile XML 1.0 really is. A relatively small set of rules allows us to build a more powerful application, that in turn acts on other instances of XML.

Advanced XSL Techniques

Now that we've become acquainted with what XSL has to offer, the next logical step is to find a way that makes transforming your XML data into a useful product easier. In the past, you would have had to create elaborate VBScript sections that not only read the data but also use it to build a navigation bar, or set the background and font colors of a website. Rather than use code scripts to do the work, we should be able to describe the task in data and have it carried out automatically. After all, what's the point of having self-describing XML content if you have to do all the work yourself?

XSL is just the tool for the job. As you saw in Chapter 8, it is an application of XML that understands how to transform XML data given a description of what you want to have happen in any particular context. We used it in Chapter 8 to visually render documents. That was helpful to prospective web masters in that it allows us to describe a style for our documents just once rather than having to manually markup each document in HTML. We'll continue to use this technique in this chapter.

Another use of XSL is to pre-render pages for our site. Most pages on a site only change slowly. In fact, it is not uncommon for a web master to hold the changes, and then re-stage the entire site periodically. In such cases it is unnecessary to perform the transformation for every page request. It would be much more efficient to perform the transform once for each page when the site is staged and let clients request HTML pages.

A third way XSL can help web masters, is to replace some tasks normally carried out in procedural code. I'm going to show you an example that creates a collapsible menu for our site. What is a menu, after all? It is mostly data – the menu items – with a limited set of behaviors. ASP programmers are familiar with writing procedural code to accomplish behavior, so the data takes second place to the code. When the time comes to change the content of the menus, you end up changing code even though it is the data that has changed. XSL will let us turn that around. The content of the menus will go in easily maintained XML documents, while the behavior of the menu will be implemented declaratively as a series of XSL templates.

Enhancing ASP with XSL

One of the best uses for XSL stylesheets in an ASP application is to format similarly structured data-sets as template HTML pages. The template is a design that can be implemented as a stylesheet. Online publications are using this methodology more and more as XML becomes a standard. Stories or articles in XML format must be formatted to have a consistent look and feel on the page no matter how long or how short they may be. The common structure of these stories can be directly translated into an XML vocabulary. An XSL stylesheet gives us the ability to create a visual presentation of any level of complexity. Since the styling is applied declaratively from the templates in the stylesheet, changing the visual theme of the site is reduced to the tasks of altering the stylesheet and performing the transformation. Since the transformation may be triggered from script, the only manual steps required are actually writing the new stylesheet and launching the script.

Consider a site that publishes a newspaper. The logical parts of a newspaper seldom change. Such a site accumulates a very large body of documents over time. Newspapers periodically alter their presentation style to keep the site looking fresh. If the content consists entirely of HTML, style changes become almost impossible to accomplish – each and every document must be changed. Cascading style sheets help somewhat – you can alter one stylesheet and change the presentation of all pages linked to it, but the nature of the styling changes that may be applied are limited. If the content is built entirely by ASP, say, by reading the text from a database and applying the styling programmatically, style changes become a matter of programming. Worse still, every page hit results in the execution of the ASP whether the content has changed or not.

The way we've used XSL and XML so far is similar to the ASP case. It is better, in that we don't have to modify an ASP's script-code to implement a styling change, but we still tax the server for every page hit. This is where the use of XSL as a batch process comes in. Since the logical structure of news stories will seldom change, content authors can work to an XML vocabulary without too much concern. When a style change is desired, all the XML content is run through an XSL transformation. This can take place on a machine separate from the web farm to avoid placing additional load on the site. When the batch transformation is complete, the new HTML pages take the place of the old ones and the site style change is complete. The result is a body of static HTML pages that may be served to browsers with very little load on the site.

The XML News site is dedicated to the development and promotion of an XML vocabulary for newspaper publishing. You can obtain details at www.xmlnews.org.

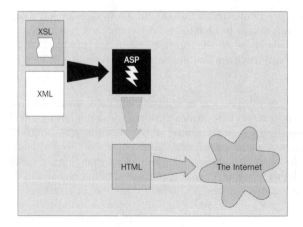

Transforming XML using XSL and ASP

Before we can do any of this, though, we must re-acquaint ourselves with the fundamental technique for transforming XML using XSL on the server. The process involves loading the XML document and the XSL stylesheet into instances of the MSXML parser, applying the transformation, and returning the result to the requesting browser. At no time does either document leave the server. The transformation is dynamic, involving a stylesheet-driven transformation within the MSXML component. So far as the receiving browser is concerned, XML and XSL are not involved. The code that follows may seem familiar to you from the stylecontacts.asp example in chapter 6:

```
<%
  ' Set the source and style sheet locations
  sourceFile = Request.ServerVariables ("APPL_PHYSICAL_PATH") + _
                                                   "\contacts.xml"
  styleFile = Request.ServerVariables("APPL_PHYSICAL_PATH") + _
                                                   "\contacts.xsl"

  ' Load the XML
  Set source = Server.CreateObject("Microsoft.XMLDOM")
  source.async = false
  source.load(sourceFile)

  ' Load the XSL
  Set style = Server.CreateObject("Microsoft.XMLDOM")
  style.async = false
  style.load(styleFile)

  Response.Write(source.transformNode(style))
%>
```

The transformNode method takes a parser instance (presuming it to contain an XSL stylesheet), and uses it to act on the document on which the method is invoked. The method is part of both the DOM document and node interfaces, so you can choose where to begin the transformation. For our purposes, it is simplest to apply it to the entire document. This pattern of loading two documents and applying one to the other will be at the heart of all the examples you will see in this chapter.

XSL Templates Revisited

The XSL template is exactly what its name implies: a section of code that is applied whenever a particular pattern is located in the source document. Let's start here with a standard contact list XML document:

```
<?xml version="1.0"?>
<CONTACT_INFO>
  <CONTACT TYPE="business">
    <NAME>
      <FIRST_NAME>John</FIRST_NAME>
      <LAST_NAME>Doe</LAST_NAME>
    </NAME>
    <ADDRESS>
      <STREET_INFO>103 Eastern Avenue</STREET_INFO>
      <CITY>Pleasantville</CITY>
      <STATE>Indiana</STATE>
      <ZIP>30113</ZIP>
    </ADDRESS>
```

```
    <PHONE>555-5555</PHONE>
  </CONTACT>
  <CONTACT TYPE="personal">
    <NAME>
      <FIRST_NAME>Alice</FIRST_NAME>
      <LAST_NAME>Smith</LAST_NAME>
    </NAME>
    <ADDRESS>
      <STREET_INFO>52B Wilkens Street</STREET_INFO>
      <CITY>Pleasantville</CITY>
      <STATE>Indiana</STATE>
      <ZIP>30113</ZIP>
    </ADDRESS>
    <PHONE>555-6666</PHONE>
  </CONTACT>
  <CONTACT TYPE="personal">
    <NAME>
      <FIRST_NAME>Bruce</FIRST_NAME>
      <LAST_NAME>Johnson</LAST_NAME>
    </NAME>
    <ADDRESS>
      <STREET_INFO>52B Wilkens Street</STREET_INFO>
      <CITY>Taylorton</CITY>
      <STATE>Texas</STATE>
      <ZIP>87713</ZIP>
    </ADDRESS>
    <PHONE>555-6981</PHONE>
  </CONTACT>
  <CONTACT TYPE="business">
    <NAME>
      <FIRST_NAME>William M.</FIRST_NAME>
      <LAST_NAME>Kropog</LAST_NAME>
    </NAME>
    <ADDRESS>
      <STREET_INFO>80698 Matthew Street</STREET_INFO>
      <CITY>Covington</CITY>
      <STATE>Louisiana</STATE>
      <ZIP>70433</ZIP>
    </ADDRESS>
    <PHONE>555-0713</PHONE>
  </CONTACT>
</CONTACT_INFO>
```

Now let's build an XSL file that will transform the XML into HTML that's a little more aesthetic than in previous chapters You saw a variety of XSL transformations applied to various versions of a `contacts.xml` file back in Chapter 8. Each sought to format the contact data with inline HTML styles to obtain a visually pleasing document. The stylesheet templates matched on specific XML elements and generated HTML in the final document. The HTML drew content from the source XML document but replaced the XML markup with generic HTML intended to provide visual styling. In that way, the stylesheet added styling without losing the data provided in the XML source. The stylesheet presented here consists of a single template that matches on the document element of the source XML document:

```
<?xml version="1.0"?>
<xsl:stylesheet xmlns:xsl="http://www.w3.org/TR/WD-xsl">
<xsl:template match="/">
  <HTML>
```

```
<BODY bgcolor="#FFFFFF">
<FONT face="verdana" size="6" color="#999999">Contacts</FONT>
<HR size="1" />
<BLOCKQUOTE>
<xsl:for-each select="CONTACT_INFO/CONTACT">
  <P>
    <FONT face="verdana" size="4" color="#777777">
      <xsl:value-of select="NAME/FIRST_NAME" />
      <xsl:value-of select="NAME/LAST_NAME" />
    </FONT>
    <FONT face="verdana" size="2" color="#000000">
      <BR/>
      <xsl:value-of select="ADDRESS/STREET_INFO" />
      <BR/>
      <xsl:value-of select="ADDRESS/CITY" />,
      <xsl:value-of select="ADDRESS/STATE" />
      <xsl:value-of select="ADDRESS/ZIP" />
      <BR/>
      <xsl:value-of select="PHONE" />
    </FONT>
  </P>
</xsl:for-each>
</BLOCKQUOTE>
<HR size="1" />
</BODY>
</HTML>
</xsl:template>

</xsl:stylesheet>
```

The first thing it does is to write the minimal elements of an HTML document, i.e., HTML and BODY. From there, it uses the xsl:for-each element to iterate through all the CONTACT children of CONTACT_INFO. HTML elements are hard-coded into the template and are used to wrap the values obtained from the XML document. The xsl:value-of element is used to extract those values from the source document and insert them into the result.

XSL Transforms XML

Although we have used XSL exclusively to write HTML, it is important not to fall into the trap of thinking that XML + XSL = HTML. In general, XSL can write any form of text as a result. The XSL implementation in MSXML takes a DOM tree representation of an XML document and generates textual output. This is almost always well-formed markup, though other kinds of output, e.g., comma-separated text, are possible. It just so happens that our HTML tags also function as well-formed XML tags. That's why we must close every tag, or at least use the truncated version you see above in the <HR> and <BR> elements.

The ASP code you saw a little while ago produces a text string and nothing more. We just happened to be writing it to the browser in the example, but we don't necessarily have to do so. In a moment you'll see an example that illustrates the batch processing of XML into HTML we discussed previously. Rather than write the XML to the Response stream, we'll need to be able to write the HTML to disk. In fact, MSXML does not require us to write the XML anywhere at all. MSXML offers another extension to the DOM interfaces for documents and nodes that returns a document interface: transformNodetoObject. It takes the same parameter as transformNode, but it returns an XML DOM object. This is useful when the results of the XSL transformation need further manipulation, such as when the transformation becomes a subtree of a larger document, or when the results need to be passed to a routine originally intended to act on documents.

Using the FileSystemObject Again

In Chapter 6, we saw how the `FileSystemObject` could be used to write XML-produced code to an HTML file, which reduces the load on the server because visitors are hitting a plain HTML file instead of a complicated ASP. This is a useful performance technique that can be employed by high-volume sites like newspapers. The same thing can be done just as easily with XSL stylesheets entered into the equation.

This procedure will by now be familiar to you. After the HTML code is produced, we save it to the disk. Look how this changes our example:

> *While our example shows an ASP page, it is performing a task best executed by a Webmaster, not a general visitor to the site. Any activity that writes files on a server should be carefully scrutinized for security concerns.*

```
<%
  ' Set the source and style sheet locations here
  sourceFile = Request.ServerVariables("APPL_PHYSICAL_PATH") + "\contacts.xml"
  styleFile = Request.ServerVariables("APPL_PHYSICAL_PATH") + "\contacts.xsl"

  ' Load the XML
  Set source = Server.CreateObject("Microsoft.XMLDOM")
  source.async = false
  source.load(sourceFile)

  ' Load the XSL
  Set style = Server.CreateObject("Microsoft.XMLDOM")
  style.async = false
  style.load(styleFile)

  HTMLcode = source.transformNode(style)

  Set objFS = CreateObject("Scripting.FileSystemObject")
  Set objFile = _
      objFS.CreateTextFile(Request.ServerVariables("APPL_PHYSICAL_PATH") & _
                                                     "\translation.htm")
  objFile.Write(HTMLcode)

  Response.Write("File Saved.")

  Set objFS = nothing
%>
```

Following the transformation, we use `FileSystemObject` to create a disk-based file named `translation.htm` in the same folder that contains the ASP. The results of the transformation are written into this file, resulting in an HTML page on disk ready to be served to browsers. A status line is written to the requesting browser to indicate that the transformation is complete.

As you can see, not a whole lot has changed, and the little that did change is almost identical to what we have done in previous chapters: create a trigger page to save an HTML file to the server. You might wonder why we are using an ASP instead of a script file loaded into the Windows Script Host (WSH). Indeed, in this sample, ASP doesn't add much to the experience, and using the WSH would do just fine. Imagine, though, how we might extend this example into the check-in facility for a distributed authoring system. A page might be created to elicit a file name from the author. The page would be POSTed to a page like this on the server, which would accept the XML, save it into an archive directory, apply the transformation, and write the resulting HTML into the publishing folder for the site. The point here is that XSL is a tool, just as ASP is. You should use whatever tools fit your application needs. ASP just happens to suit this situation.

The HTML produced by this script would look like this in the browser:

For comparison, here's a portion of the HTML source produced by the translation:

```
<HTML>
  <BODY bgcolor="#FFFFFF">
    <FONT face="verdana" size="6" color="#999999">Contacts</FONT>
    <HR size="1" />
    <BLOCKQUOTE>
      <P>
      <FONT face="verdana" size="4" color="#777777">John Doe</FONT>
      <FONT face="verdana" size="2" color="#000000">
        <BR />103 Eastern Avenue
        <BR />Pleasantville, Indiana 30113
        <BR />555-5555
      </FONT>
      </P>
      ...
    </BLOCKQUOTE>
    <HR size="1" />
  </BODY>
</HTML>
```

Using XSL stylesheets is much more convenient than writing scripting code using the XML DOM to achieve the desired results. For one thing, the templates are easier to write and maintain. The XSL approach will also yield better performance, whereas all the DOM calls to traverse the document involve late-binding calls through the COM layer. The single COM call to `transformNode`, however, causes similar actions to be taken within the parser. The calls are native to the component, however, so they avoid the overhead of multiple COM method invocations. MSXML also happens to be implemented with highly optimized C++ code. How often do you have the time to fully profile and tune your script code?

Logical XSL

It just so happens that our version of the sample contacts list already includes an attribute in each CONTACT element indicating whether the name is a personal contact or a business contact.

We can alter our stylesheet to make use of this data, thus displaying the contacts differently depending on what type they are. Here are the changes to the contacts.xsl document:

```
<?xml version="1.0"?>

<xsl:stylesheet xmlns:xsl="uri:xsl">

<xsl:template match="/">
  <HTML>
  <BODY bgcolor="#FFFFFF">
  <FONT face="verdana" size="6" color="#999999">Contacts</FONT>
  <HR size="1" />
  <BLOCKQUOTE>
  <xsl:for-each select="CONTACT_INFO/CONTACT">

      <xsl:choose>
        <xsl:when test =".[@TYPE='business']">
          <P>
            <FONT face="verdana" size="4" color="#000000"><B>
              <xsl:value-of select="NAME/FIRST_NAME" />
              <xsl:value-of select="NAME/LAST_NAME" />
              </B>
            </FONT>
            <FONT face="verdana" size="2" color="#000000">
              <BR/>
              <xsl:value-of select="PHONE" />
            </FONT>
          </P>
        </xsl:when>

        <xsl:otherwise>
          <P>
            <FONT face="verdana" size="2" color="#777777"><B>
              <xsl:value-of select="NAME/FIRST_NAME" />
              <xsl:value-of select="NAME/LAST_NAME" />
              </B>
            </FONT>
            <FONT face="verdana" size="2" color="#000000">
              <BR/>
              <xsl:value-of select="ADDRESS/STREET_INFO" />
              <BR/>
              <xsl:value-of select="ADDRESS/CITY" />,
              <xsl:value-of select="ADDRESS/STATE" />
              <xsl:value-of select="ADDRESS/ZIP" />
            </FONT>
          </P>
        </xsl:otherwise>
      </xsl:choose>

  </xsl:for-each>
```

```
        </BLOCKQUOTE>
        <HR size="1" />
        </BODY>
        </HTML>
    </xsl:template>

    </xsl:stylesheet>
```

The change takes place within the `xsl:for-each` block where we incorporate the `xsl:choose` statement and its two components, `xsl:when` and `xsl:otherwise`. Remember from Chapter 8 that the `xsl:choose` element acts like a `switch` statement. XSL doesn't offer anything analogous to the `if...then...else` construct available in most programming languages, so although we only have two choices for the value of the attribute we have to use `xsl:choose`. The test attribute's value – `.[@TYPE = 'business']` – means that the XSL processor must evaluate whether the current node's `TYPE` attribute has the value `business`. Since this is being evaluated within the `xsl:for-each` element that selects `CONTACT_INFO/CONTACT` elements, the current node is a `CONTACT` element that does, indeed, have such an attribute. If we run our ASP trigger page, it will again save the results to an HTML file, which should look like this in the browser:

None of this is really new stuff compared to what we did in earlier chapters, except this time we took it a bit further and saved it as an HTML file using ASP. Essentially this is a practical application of the XSL transformation concept as discussed in Chapter 8.

Incorporating Scripting and Logic into XSL

Let's leave our previous examples behind now and be creative for a moment. We know XSL can transform XML into well-formed HTML. That HTML can include inline styles and any other attribute that HTML can process. HTML spills over the line between presentation and behavior when client-side scripts and event handlers are used. This can be used to implement a user interface construct you see all the time on the Internet: expandable and collapsible navigation bars. We're going to create a new sample application now; an ASP, `menu.asp`, that uses XML and XSL to dynamically generate an HTML navigation bar such as you see in the illustration below. The XML (`links.xml` in our sample) contains the links and the structure of the navigation bar. The XSL (`links.xsl`) contains the rules to convert the XML data into HTML. We will also need a few GIFs for the navigational icons.

The files for this sample application, `menu.asp`, `links.xml`, and `links.xsl` can be downloaded from **www.wrox.com**.

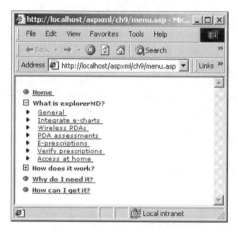

A complete list of HTML links is passed to the client. When the user clicks on a link that has child items, here denoted by links with the boxed plus sign icon, the items are made visible and the icon is changed to a boxed minus. Clicking on the link reverses the behavior. We know that items can be hidden and exposed by changing the display style property on a `DIV` that encloses them. Set it to `none` and the `DIV` is invisible. Change it to some other value and the HTML is rendered. This is complicated stuff at a low level, but DHTML exposes it to us as nothing more than a keyword. How can we capture the parent-child relationship in a manner acceptable to HTML, and how can we implement the code to show and hide items in a general way – one that doesn't depend on hard-coding the HTML?

Requirements for the Collapsing Navigation Tree

The first step in designing something of this nature is to decide on the specification, or exactly what you want the navigation tree to do and not do. We know it's a navigation bar, so we know that at the very least it has to provide a way to navigate the site. We also want, through the use of Dynamic HTML, to be able to save vertical space with the expanding and collapsing tree metaphor. And finally, we don't want the main section or group, titles that contain child elements, to be hyperlinks, only their children. In summary, our navigation bar should:

❑   Provide hyperlinked navigation

❑   Expand or collapse to expose or hide sub-links to save vertical space

❑   Main links or groups that have child links should not be links themselves

Let's take a moment and associate these functions with the various sections of code in the sample. The structure of the navigation bar (parent-child relationships) is encoded in the XML file together with the targets of the links. The XSL file takes care of converting this into HTML. The hyperlinks themselves will be standard HTML anchor tags generated by the XSL.

The second feature, expanding and contracting an item, relies on client-side DHTML script code. Since this must be embedded in the client page, and the ASP generates that page, the client side script is embedded in the ASP and is copied in its entirety to the client page when the ASP runs.

We know that XML is well-suited to capturing parent-child relationships, so it makes an ideal format for marking up the content of the menu. Individual links have a direct representation in the anchor element of HTML, so we know that this is what our XSL must produce when it transforms the XML for any particular link. I've already told you that `<DIV style="display:none">` takes care of collapsing a series of child links into their parent. How, though, do we tell HTML that an element has child items?

The key is in using the CLASS attribute. We can apply this to an anchor element to associate it with some arbitrary label of our choosing. Although this is most often used in conjunction with CSS styling, there is no restriction on the value this attribute can take on. We'll use it to denote the level of an item within the navigation bar hierarchy. Let's establish the convention of using LEVEL*x* to represent the hierarchy. Top-level links, then, should look like this:

```
<a CLASS="LEVEL1" href="somepage.asp">Some text</a>
```

If we then assign an event handler to the click event for any item on the page, we can check the identity of the clicked element and the value of its CLASS attribute. Using these two pieces of information, we can show and hide information as needed. Here is some pseudo-code to represent the page:

```
<HTML>
  <BODY>
    <SCRIPT>
      <!-- code associating onclick with the event handler -->
      <!-- event handler here -->
    </SCRIPT>

    <!-- HTML representing transformed XML menu items here -->
  </BODY>
</HTML>
```

Start with HTML

We'll start by examining what we want our final HTML document to look like, and then work towards that as we go along. Here is the HTML as it should appear when you view the source code of the display in the browser – the result of the XSL transformation:

```
<font face="verdana" size="1" style="cursor:hand; color:#AA0000;">
    <img src="images/icon_link.gif" WIDTH="9" HEIGHT="9" HSPACE="2"
      VSPACE="4" ALIGN="ABSMIDDLE">
    </img>
    <b>
        <a CLASS="LINK" href="default.asp">Home</a>
    </b>
    <br />
    <img src="images/icon_plus.gif" CLASS="LEVEL1" style="cursor:hand;"
        WIDTH="9" HEIGHT="9" HSPACE="2" VSPACE="4" ALIGN="ABSMIDDLE"
          id="OUT12i" />
    <b>
        <span CLASS="LEVEL1" id="OUT12t">What is explorerMD?</span>
    </b>
    <br />
    <div style="display:none" id="OUT12s">
      <img src="images/filler.gif" width="22" height="12" ALIGN="ABSMIDDLE" />
      <a CLASS="LEVEL2" id="OUT21t" href="whatis.asp">General</a>
```

```
   <br />
   <img src="images/filler.gif" width="22" height="12" ALIGN="ABSMIDDLE" />
   <a CLASS="LEVEL2" id="OUT22t" href="whatis.asp#mark1">Integrate e-charts
   </a>
   <br />
   <img src="images/filler.gif" width="22" height="12" ALIGN="ABSMIDDLE" />
   <a CLASS="LEVEL2" id="OUT23t" href="whatis.asp#mark2">Wireless PDAs</a>
   <br />
   <img src="images/filler.gif" width="22" height="12" ALIGN="ABSMIDDLE" />
   <a CLASS="LEVEL2" id="OUT24t" href="whatis.asp#mark3">
    PDA assessments</a>
   <br />
   <img src="images/filler.gif" width="22" height="12" ALIGN="ABSMIDDLE" />
   <a CLASS="LEVEL2" id="OUT25t" href="whatis.asp#mark4">
    E-prescriptions</a>
   <br />
   <img src="images/filler.gif" width="22" height="12" ALIGN="ABSMIDDLE" />
   <a CLASS="LEVEL2" id="OUT26t" href="whatis.asp#mark5">
    Verify prescriptions</a><br />
   <img src="images/filler.gif" width="22" height="12" ALIGN="ABSMIDDLE" />
   <a CLASS="LEVEL2" id="OUT27t" href="whatis.asp#mark6">Access at home</a>
   <br />
</div>
<img src="images/icon_plus.gif" CLASS="LEVEL1" style="cursor:hand;"
    WIDTH="9" HEIGHT="9" HSPACE="2" VSPACE="4" ALIGN="ABSMIDDLE"
       id="OUT13i" />
<b>
   <span CLASS="LEVEL1" id="OUT13t">How does it work?</span>
</b>
...
</font>
```

We use several 9 pixel by 9 pixel graphics to indicate if each node is expanded, collapsed, or just a link with no sub-menu. These are the boxed plus and boxed minus icons for expandable parents, two chain links for a single-level link with no child items, and bullets for the child links.

If desired, we could use a Cascading Style Sheet to dress up our HTML a bit using the included class names LEVEL1, LEVEL2 and so on. CSS is good for simple styling based on the class of an element. If we wanted to set the font or color of the top level items we could do so in CSS. XSL incorporates all the capabilities of CSS, although in somewhat different form. If we embedded the CSS inline, we would be in the strange position of asking XSL to output CSS instructions. It would be simpler to let XSL do the job directly. As an alternative, we could have the XSL write a link to an external CSS, but then we would be splitting our presentation rules in two files: the XSL stylesheet and the CSS.

Structure of the ASP

Since our application is going to combine server-side and client-side scripting, it is worth taking a look at the structure of the ASP that generates the menu, menu.asp:

```
<%@ Language="JavaScript" %>
<HTML>
<HEAD>
</HEAD>
```

```
<BODY>

<script LANGUAGE="JavaScript">
<!--
  // hard-coded client-side script to assign the click handler

  // hard-coded event handler function
//-->
</script>
<%
  // code to accomplish the XSL transformation and return HTML
  // for the menu
%>
</BODY>
</HTML>
```

We are able to hard-code the HTML shell elements. Since the client-side script is fixed, we can embed that as a literal script element as well. That script code does not execute on the server. So far as ASP is concerned, the client-side script is just HTML text.

The script code within the ASP script element executes on the server when the page is requested. This is code that you've seen before – the instructions needed to load the XML and XSL documents and perform the transformation:

```
<%
  var doc, stylesheet;

  doc = Server.CreateObject("microsoft.xmldom");
  stylesheet = Server.CreateObject("microsoft.xmldom");

  if (doc != null && stylesheet != null)
  {
    doc.async = false;
    stylesheet.async = false;

    doc.load(Server.MapPath("links.xml"));
    stylesheet.load(Server.MapPath("links.xsl"));

    if (doc.parseError == 0 && stylesheet.parseError == 0)
      Response.Write(doc.transformNode(stylesheet));
    else
      Response.Write("Could not generate menu content");
  }
  else
    Response.Write("Error: Unable to create server resources.");
%>
```

The XML containing the menu structure is found in links.xml, while the stylesheet, which we shall develop shortly, is in links.xsl.

Client-Side Script for DHMTL Effects

Let's go ahead and clear this hurdle right away since it has the least to do with ASP and XML technologies. Once rendered by our XSL stylesheet, our HTML code will rely on a client-side JavaScript function to actually perform the DHTML effects. When a user clicks on one of the LEVEL1 links with child menu items, this function will respond to the event by modifying the DHTML to reveal the child items.

The first thing we need to do, is associate the event-handler function with the `onclick` event. This happens in the main body of the script, together with the declaration of some global variables for pre-loading our icons:

```
<script LANGUAGE="JavaScript">
<!--
  var img1, img2;
  img1 = new Image();
  img1.src = "images/icon_plus.gif";
  img2 = new Image();
  img2.src = "images/icon_minus.gif";

  document.onclick = doOutline;
```

If you intend to run the sample code, be sure to create a folder named images and save the GIFs there. If you do not properly locate the images, the links will fail to render and you will be unable to expand and collapse the menu items.

When the browser receives the results of `menu.asp`, it executes this script. Thereafter, whenever any node in the page's document tree originates a click event, the function `doOutline` will be called. The event system for IE gives you global access to information regarding the identity of the originating node, and we will use this to determine what menu items to manipulate.

The event handler relies on a particular naming convention for parent menu items. The `img` tag will always have an ID whose value is `OUTxi`, where `x` is an integer used to differentiate different top-level items. The associated anchor will be named `OUTxs`, where `x` matches the integer in the image tag. All the sub-menu items are wrapped in a `DIV` tag whose ID is `OUTxt`.

The first thing to do when the event handler is called is to determine what node originated the event. The DHTML window object provides this information through its event property, which in turn exposes a `srcElement` property. From that, you can determine if it is a parent menu item by checking its `className` attribute value:

```
function doOutline()
{
  var targetId, srcElement, targetElement;
  srcElement = window.event.srcElement;

  if (srcElement.className == "LEVEL1")
  {
```

Any node that has a `className` other than `LEVEL1` can be ignored. Remember, this function will be called anytime the user clicks on the page, so it is possible for the function to be called for any mouse clicks that are unrelated to the menu. With the originating node's identity and our menu-item naming convention, you can construct the name of the `DIV` containing the child items:

```
srcElement = srcElement.id;
srcElement = srcElement.substr(0, srcElement.length-1);

targetId = srcElement + "s";
srcElement = srcElement + "i";
```

These are just names, though; you need the object that represents the DIV element:

```
srcElement = document.all(srcElement);
targetElement = document.all(targetId);
```

Now you have to make a choice. Is the menu item expanded or collapsed? You can get this information by looking at the value of the style.display property. If it has the value none, you know the item is collapsed. If the value is an empty string, it is open.

The fact that the value takes on an empty string value is purely an artifact of our code. The XSL transformation generates HTML this way when the page is created. The code you are about to see makes sure this value is set when opening the submenu. This property may take on any one of a number of different values according to HTML, so you must be careful when using this technique in other applications.

Once you know the state of the submenu (collapsed or extended), you change it to the opposite state by changing the display property and changing the target of the parent item's img tag:

```
if (targetElement.style.display == "none")
{
  targetElement.style.display = "";
  if (srcElement.className == "LEVEL1")
  {
    srcElement.src = "images/icon_minus.gif";
  }
}
else
{
  targetElement.style.display = "none";
  if (srcElement.className == "LEVEL1")
  {
    srcElement.src = "images/icon_plus.gif";
  }
}
```

That is all that is required. The native event-handling mechanism of DHTML gives you the tools to communicate between the page and your script. You use that information to determine which item originated the event and what state it is in.

A good introduction to the Internet Explorer event handler model is found online at http://msdn.microsoft.com/workshop/c-frame.htm?/workshop/author/html /reference/elements.asp.

DHTML also gives you the means to expand and collapse the menu. The hard work of smoothly revealing the child tags or collapsing them and redrawing the page is implemented in Internet Explorer. All you have to do is change some properties. Remember you can view the entire body of the client script that we've just discussed by downloading the sample code from www.wrox.com.

Remember, this script is not generated by the XSL transformation. Since it never changes, there is no reason to clutter the stylesheet with the script's source. As noted earlier, this is hard-coded into the body of the ASP.

Now it is time to turn our attention to the XML and XSL that work together to represent and render the menu. Without these, we would have to hard-code each and every menu.

XML Source

What is it that we must represent in our XML document? We need the menu items and the URLs associated with them, and we need to express the parent-child relationships. Our document element will be called `navigation`. It will have one or more `section` elements as its children. Each `section` will have a `name` element whose content will be the text that appears in the menu item. If the menu item represented by the `section` has no children, then the value of its `URL` attribute will be the value used for the link. Each `section` will also have a `NOSUBS` attribute whose value will indicate whether the item has child sub-items. Each sub-item will be represented by a `link` element:

```xml
<?xml version="1.0"?>

<navigation>
  <section NOSUBS="True" URL="default.asp">
    <name>Home</name>
    <description>Home</description>
  </section>
  <section NOSUBS="False">
    <name>What is explorerMD?</name>
    <link URL="whatis.asp">
      <urlname>General</urlname>
    </link>
    <link URL="whatis.asp#mark1">
      <urlname>Integrate e-charts</urlname>
    </link>
    <link URL="whatis.asp#mark2">
      <urlname>Wireless PDAs</urlname>
    </link>
    <link URL="whatis.asp#mark3">
      <urlname>PDA assessments</urlname>
    </link>
    <link URL="whatis.asp#mark4">
      <urlname>E-prescriptions</urlname>
    </link>
    <link URL="whatis.asp#mark5">
      <urlname>Verify prescriptions</urlname>
    </link>
    <link URL="whatis.asp#mark6">
      <urlname>Access at home</urlname>
    </link>
  </section>
  <section NOSUBS="False">
    <name>How does it work?</name>
    <link URL="service_info.asp">
      <urlname>Online Demo</urlname>
    </link>
    <link URL="service_coupons.asp">
      <urlname>Flow chart</urlname>
    </link>
    <link URL="service_reserve.asp">
      <urlname>e-Plates</urlname>
    </link>
```

```
      </section>
      <section NOSUBS="True" URL="specials.asp">
        <name>Why do I need it?</name>
      </section>
      <section NOSUBS="True" URL="creditapp.asp">
        <name>How can I get it?</name>
      </section>
  </navigation>
```

The link elements contain URL attributes, plus sub-elements describing the text name of the link. A section that has a NOSUBS attribute with the value, false, and will have one or more link elements. The XSL stylesheet, therefore, must transform the section-link construct into LEVEL1–LEVEL2 classes.

XSL Stylesheet

The one thing that we need to know right from the start, is that we have two kinds of nodes in our navigation bar: those that have sub-menus, and those that don't. This necessitates at least one main logical branch in our XSL document's structure. It makes sense to begin by iterating through the section elements since they form the bulk of the XML document and it is there that the menu structure is represented. Take a look at the structural shell:

```
<xsl:stylesheet xmlns:xsl="http://www.w3.org/TR/WD-xsl">
  <xsl:template match="/">
   <xsl:for-each select="/navigation/section">
    <xsl:choose>
      <xsl:when match=".[@NOSUBS='True']">
         <!-- NO SUB-MENU  -->
      </xsl:when>
      <xsl:otherwise>
         <!-- YES SUB-MENU  -->
      </xsl:otherwise>
    </xsl:choose>
   </xsl:for-each>
  </xsl:template>
</xsl:stylesheet>
```

Note the XSL pattern that tests the value of the NOSUBS attribute:

```
<xsl:when match=".[@NOSUBS='True']">
```

It uses a filter expression and the single dot operator denoting the current context node. This is the shell of our stylesheet. Now we need to fill in the two sections where we presently have comments as placeholders.

Plain Nodes

The non-sub-menu code (marked by <!--NO SUB-MENU -->) is straightforward. We just have to create an anchor tag, add the href attribute for it, and write the value of the URL attribute of our section element. Within the body of the anchor tag, we'll write the value of the section element's child name element for the text of the hyperlink. This is what it looks like with some formatting HTML added:

```
&#32;
<img src="images/icon_link.gif" WIDTH="9" HEIGHT="9" HSPACE="2" VSPACE="4"
     ALIGN="ABSMIDDLE">
```

```
</img>

&#32;
<b>
  <a CLASS="LINK">
    <xsl:attribute name="href">
      <xsl:value-of select="@URL"/>
    </xsl:attribute>
    <xsl:value-of select="name"/>
  </a>
</b>
<br/>
```

The initial entity --   -- is simply a space for formatting. Unlike HTML, which has many such entities pre-defined, XML has pre-defined only those characters used in markup, so we must use the hexadecimal form. We use xsl:attribute and xsl:value-of elements to make the hyperlink code. The xsl:attribute element encases the xsl:value-of element. This element, in turn, retrieves the URL attribute's value. In other words, the URL value is pulled from XML and then handed to the attribute method of XSL. That method inserts the value into the parent XML tag, which is creating an attribute on the HTML tag. As for the class attribute, since we do not have to retrieve its value from XML we can just write it directly into the HTML output document.

Menu-Containing Nodes

Those nodes that contain sub-menus require a bit more effort. First, we have to find a way to provide the incremental change in each <DIV> and <SPAN> element's id attributes. Then we have to get all the links for the sub-menu. The xsl:eval element lets us evaluate small pieces of script code, while two information methods, childNumber and formatNumber, are used to retrieve a node index and write it:

```
&#32;
<img src="images/icon_plus.gif" CLASS="LEVEL1" style="cursor:hand;" WIDTH="9"
HEIGHT="9" HSPACE="2" VSPACE="4" ALIGN="ABSMIDDLE">
  <xsl:attribute name="id">
<xsl:eval>"OUT" + formatIndex(childNumber(this), "1") + "i"</xsl:eval></xsl:attribute>
</img>

&#32;
<b>
  <span CLASS="LEVEL1">
    <xsl:attribute name="id">
      <xsl:eval>"OUT" + formatIndex(childNumber(this), "1") + "t"</xsl:eval>
    </xsl:attribute>

    <xsl:choose>
      <xsl:when match=".[@URL]">
        <a CLASS="LINK">
          <xsl:attribute name="href">
            <xsl:value-of select="@URL"/>
          </xsl:attribute>
        <xsl:value-of select="name"/></a>
      </xsl:when>
      <xsl:otherwise>
        <xsl:value-of select="name"/>
```

```
        </xsl:otherwise>
      </xsl:choose>
    </span>
  </b>
  <br/>

  <div style="display:none">
    <xsl:attribute name="id">
      <xsl:eval>"OUT" + formatIndex(childNumber(this), "1") + "s"</xsl:eval>
    </xsl:attribute>

    <xsl:for-each select="link">
      &#32;
      <img src="images/filler.gif" width="22" height="12" ALIGN="ABSMIDDLE"/>
      &#32;
      <a CLASS="LEVEL2">
        <xsl:attribute name="id">
          <xsl:eval>"OUT" + x + "t"</xsl:eval>
        </xsl:attribute>
        <xsl:attribute name="href">
          <xsl:value-of select="@URL"/>
        </xsl:attribute>
        <xsl:value-of select="urlname"/>
      </a>
      <br/>
    </xsl:for-each>
  </div>
```

The internal child number of the section node gives us a number we can use to create unique IDs for each element. This is because the three elements that need names – the img, <a>, and <div> elements – employ a naming convention (which we touched upon in our discussion of the client-side script) that uses the same ordinal index and a different letter at the end of the ID. We append the level of the menu item to the word OUT, i.e., OUT1, OUT2, to further distinguish the ID. The formatIndex method gives us a text representation that we need in order to compose the ID value through string concatenation.

You'll also notice that we have nested implementations of the xsl:for-each and xsl:choose elements within the xsl:otherwise element of the outermost xsl:choose element:

```
<xsl:choose>
    <xsl:when match=".[@NOSUBS='True']">
        ...
    </xsl:when>
    <xsl:otherwise>
        ...
        <xsl:choose>
            <xsl:when match=".[@URL]">
                <a CLASS="LINK">
                    <xsl:attribute name="href">
                        <xsl:value-of select="@URL"/>
                    </xsl:attribute>
                    <xsl:value-of select="name"/>
                </a>
            </xsl:when>
            <xsl:otherwise>
```

```
              <xsl:value-of select="name"/>
          </xsl:otherwise>
      </xsl:choose>
      ...
      <xsl:for-each select="link">
          &#32;
          <img src="images/filler.gif" width="22" height="12"
            ALIGN="ABSMIDDLE"/>
          &#32;
          <a CLASS="LEVEL2">
              <xsl:attribute name="id">
                  <xsl:eval>
                      "OUT2" + formatIndex(childNumber(this), "1") + "t"
                  </xsl:eval>
              </xsl:attribute>
              <xsl:attribute name="href">
                  <xsl:value-of select="@URL"/>
              </xsl:attribute>
              <xsl:value-of select="urlname"/>
          </a>
          <br/>
      </xsl:for-each>
      ...
  </xsl:otherwise>
</xsl:choose>
```

The `xsl:choose` block checks for the existence of the URL attribute. If it's there, it creates a hyperlink, if not, the text of the menu item is simply written. The `xsl:for-each` loop gets our sub-menu's links one at a time and formats them appropriately. It does this by writing an entity for a space character – `&#32;` – then the image tag, then another space, and finally the text hyperlink.

Putting The Complete Stylesheet Together

Our final product is somewhat lengthy, but now that you know how it is put together, you should recognize a few repeating patterns. It uses the `xsl:for-each` element to iterate through sections, and, later on, through `link` elements. It uses `xsl:eval` and two formatting methods to compose the unique IDs according to our naming convention. It uses `xsl:value-of` to extract values held in elements and attributes within the source XML document. Everything else is hard-coded HTML:

```
<?xml version="1.0"?>
<xsl:stylesheet xmlns:xsl="http://www.w3.org/TR/WD-xsl">
  <xsl:template match="/">
   <xsl:for-each select="navigation/section">
    <xsl:choose>
      <xsl:when match=".[@NOSUBS='True']">
        &#32;
        <img src="images/icon_link.gif"  WIDTH="9" HEIGHT="9" HSPACE="2"
          VSPACE="4" ALIGN="ABSMIDDLE">
        </img>
        &#32;
        <b>
         <a CLASS="LINK">
           <xsl:attribute name="href">
            <xsl:value-of select="@URL"/>
           </xsl:attribute>
```

```xsl
         <xsl:value-of select="name"/>
     </a>
   </b>
   <br/>
  </xsl:when>
  <xsl:otherwise>
  <xsl:script language="javascript">x=formatIndex(childNumber(this),"1")
  </xsl:script>
  &#32;
  <img src="images/icon_plus.gif" CLASS="LEVEL1" style="cursor:hand;"
      WIDTH="9" HEIGHT="9" HSPACE="2" VSPACE="4"
      ALIGN="ABSMIDDLE">
  <xsl:attribute name="id">
   <xsl:eval>
       "OUT" + formatIndex(childNumber(this), "1") + "i"
   </xsl:eval>
  </xsl:attribute>
  </img>
  &#32;
  <b>
  <span CLASS="LEVEL1">
   <xsl:attribute name="id">
    <xsl:eval>
       "OUT" + formatIndex(childNumber(this), "1") + "t"
    </xsl:eval>
   </xsl:attribute>
   <xsl:choose>
    <xsl:when match=".[@URL]">
      <a CLASS="LINK">
       <xsl:attribute name="href">
        <xsl:value-of select="@URL"/>
       </xsl:attribute>
       <xsl:value-of select="name"/>
      </a>
    </xsl:when>
    <xsl:otherwise>
      <xsl:value-of select="name"/>
    </xsl:otherwise>
   </xsl:choose>
  </span>
  </b>
<br/>

<div style="display:none">
  <xsl:attribute name="id">
   <xsl:eval>
       "OUT" + formatIndex(childNumber(this), "1") + "s"
   </xsl:eval>
  </xsl:attribute>

  <xsl:for-each select="link">
   &#32;
   <img src="images/filler.gif" width="22" height="12"
      ALIGN="ABSMIDDLE"/>
   &#32;
   <a CLASS="LEVEL2">
```

```
            <xsl:attribute name="id">
              <xsl:eval>"OUT" + x + "t"
              </xsl:eval>
            </xsl:attribute>
            <xsl:attribute name="href">
              <xsl:value-of select="@URL"/>
            </xsl:attribute>
            <xsl:value-of select="urlname"/>
            </a>
            <br/>
        </xsl:for-each>
      </div>
    </xsl:otherwise>
   </xsl:choose>
  </xsl:for-each>
 </xsl:template>
</xsl:stylesheet>
```

The Finished Product

By incorporating the XML source document shown earlier and the XSL stylesheet with the standard code used elsewhere to load the XML and stylesheet documents and transform the XML document, we got an ASP that dynamically generates the links for our collapsible navigation menu. By including a hard-coded event handler script that executes on the client, we created a dynamically generated menu that reacts to user actions. The hard part – actually executing the expansion and contraction of the menu in the final page – we received from DHTML for free. All we had to do was create a bit of XML to describe the link structure (links.xml), and then write a stylesheet (links.xsl) to transform our XML into HTML that the browser understands. Our ASP (menu.asp) then dynamically created a series of links in response to the client-side script.

Transforming other XML

XSL stylesheets can also be used to create XML documents. Suppose you had an XML document for storing contacts that used the following structure for each contact:

```
<CONTACT type="business" gender="male">
  <NAME>John Doe</NAME>
  <EMAIL>jdoe@something.com</EMAIL>
  <PHONE>555-5555</PHONE>
</CONTACT>
```

And let's say you needed to convert several hundred such contact lists into XML documents (or a single document) that had a different XML data structure like this:

```
<CONTACT>
  <TYPE>business</TYPE>
  <GENDER>male</GENDER>
  <NAME>John Doe</NAME>
  <EMAIL>jdoe@something.com</EMAIL>
  <PHONE>555-5555</PHONE>
</CONTACT>
```

By now you will hopefully realize that XSL is the best way to describe this transformation. It shouldn't take very long to come up with the following XSL stylesheet to do the job:

```xml
<?xml version="1.0"?>
<xsl:stylesheet xmlns:xsl="http://www.w3.org/TR/WD-xsl">
  <xsl:template match="/">
    <CONTACT_INFO>
      <xsl:for-each select="CONTACT_INFO/CONTACT">
        <TYPE>
          <xsl:value-of select="@TYPE" />
        </TYPE>
        <GENDER>
          <xsl:value-of select="@GENDER" />
        </GENDER>
        <NAME>
          <xsl:value-of select="NAME" />
        </NAME>
        <EMAIL>
          <xsl:value-of select="EMAIL" />
        </EMAIL>
        <PHONE>
          <xsl:value-of select="PHONE" />
        </PHONE>
      </xsl:for-each>
    </CONTACT_INFO>
  </xsl:template>
</xsl:stylesheet>
```

This stylesheet consists of a template that matches on the document element, writes out the CONTACT_INFO element, and then iterates through the CONTACT elements of the source document. The transposition of the TYPE and GENDER attributes of the source into similar elements in the output is accomplished through the use of the xsl:value-of element in the appropriate place. Remember that we need to tell the XSL processor that these are attribute names and not element names by prefacing them with the special character @.

Summary

In this chapter you saw how XSL could be used to provide data-driven transformations of XML documents. First, you saw how to use common scripting objects to automate the task of pre-compiling XML into HTML for efficient display on a web site. Using XSL in preference to CSS gives us more flexibility and control, and also lets us invoke the transformation from script. The latter feature is essential if we want to use a batch process to convert a busy site from XML documents to static HTML pages. Next, we used XML to represent a menu structure, then used XSL and DHTML to implement some programming behavior that results in an interactive user interface. Finally, we left HTML behind completely to prove that XSL could transform a document written according to one arbitrary XML vocabulary into a document written according to the rules of a second, arbitrary XML document.

The beauty of XSL is that it is a descriptive way of accomplishing a programming task. Usually, you tell the computer how to perform its task by specifying each step as one or more lines of script code. XSL provides a few powerful operations that let you specify a context and an operation. Instead of programming the entire flow of the task, you describe the structure the XSL processor will encounter and tell it what to write when it meets a particular pattern. XSL stylesheets allow you to easily describe a task that the XSL processor will labor to carry out.

You can write more involved tasks as a series of transformations. The final example in the chapter, in which we transformed one list of contacts into another, could have been combined with a stylesheet of the sort we saw earlier in the chapter as well as in chapter 8, where we turned XML into richly formatted HTML. With two stylesheets, we could go from one XML document to an HTML document in a very different form, rendered for viewing by a user with a browser.

The limits of XSL are largely those of your imagination. You are accustomed to writing procedural code. Experiment with XSL. See how many ordinary programming tasks can be replaced with XSL transformations. You will find that a few data documents will provide powerful content and interactivity on your site provided you write XSL stylesheets to transform your data into the form you need for the task at hand.

10

Case Study: Data-Driven XSL

Introduction

As business to business commerce and inter-enterprise communication via XML continues to explode, developers will continually be faced with situations where they must convert XML documents from an incoming structure to the structure they use internally. It is this translation requirement that we will use as the premise for this case study.

For an example situation where you might want to carry out such translations, consider converting an invoice sent by a field office into a format that is used by central office. The central office computer would have an application, or a web page, that could load the incoming invoice, extract only the information required by central office, and present it in a way that is relevant to the staff at central office, that is, with its data labels changed. Such a utility would save much time and trouble sifting through lots of data just to pick out the snippets of useful information.

In this case study we will show how to use ASP to create an XSL file dynamically, and we will data-drive the process using an XML file to define the contents of the XSL file. It is not the intent of this case-study to provide the ultimate translation tool. In fact, this is a simple translation tool that will only map elements to other elements, working within a fixed container/item structure. The mapping process that takes place could be achieved by a simple XSL transformation, which is effectively what we are doing, with the exception that the XSL is being generated on demand.

Meet the Puzzle Pieces

Our example consists of the following pieces:

File name	Description
incoming.xml	In-bound XML that needs to be translated
default.asp	Client-side test page that shows the translation at work
interpreter.asp	The ASP page that generates the XSL
interpreter.xml	The definition file for the translation. This is the data that defines the mapping between structures

The pieces are related to each other as shown below:

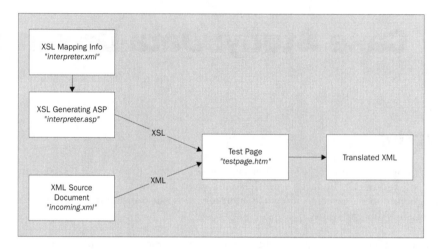

The Data

This case-study uses three XML files:

❏ The incoming data (input, aka: "incoming.xml")

❏ The translation definition file (process, aka: "interpreter.xml")

❏ The translated data (output, seen from the test page)

Let's look at the structure of each of these:

Input XML

```
<?xml version='1.0'?>
<shipments>
    <shipment>
        <waybill>123WXZ99</waybill>
```

```
        <carrier>Fedex</carrier>
        <shipDate>20000110</shipDate>
        <boxes>3</boxes>
    </shipment>
    <shipment>
        <waybill>79843A</waybill>
        <carrier>UPS</carrier>
        <shipDate>20000110</shipDate>
        <boxes>2</boxes>
    </shipment>
    <shipment>
        <waybill>XXX12A</waybill>
        <carrier>Fedex</carrier>
        <shipDate>20000110</shipDate>
        <boxes>8</boxes>
    </shipment>
</shipments>
```

Output XML

```xml
<?xml version='1.0'?>
<shipments>
    <shipment>
        <waybill>123WXZ99</waybill>
        <shippedby>Fedex</shippedby>
        <shipped>20000110</shipped>
        <numberOfBoxes>3</numberOfBoxes>
    </shipment>
    <shipment>
        <waybill>79843A</waybill>
        <shippedby>UPS</shippedby>
        <shipped>20000110</shipped>
        <numberOfBoxes>2</numberOfBoxes>
    </shipment>
    <shipment>
        <waybill>XXX12A</waybill>
        <shippedby>Fedex</shippedby>
        <shipped>20000110</shipped>
        <numberOfBoxes>8</numberOfBoxes>
    </shipment>
</shipments>
```

The Translation Process

As you can see, the input and desired output files have a similar structure, but there are three differences:

❑ "carrier" becomes "shippedby"

❑ "shipDate" becomes "shipped"

❑ "boxes" becomes "numberOfBoxes"

The required element mapping is defined in the following XML file:

```
<?xml version='1.0'?>
<shipments>
   <shipment>
      <xlat>
         <in name="waybill"/>
         <out name="waybill"/>
      </xlat>
      <xlat>
         <in name="carrier"/>
         <out name="shippedby"/>
      </xlat>
      <xlat>
         <in name="shipDate"/>
         <out name="shipped"/>
      </xlat>
      <xlat>
         <in name="boxes"/>
         <out name="numberOfBoxes"/>
      </xlat>
   </shipment>
</shipments>
```

As you can see, each <xlat> element contains an input element name and an output element name. This is the mapping we will use when we build our XSL. Note that the first of the <xlat> elements does something rather pointless – replacing "waybill" with "waybill". This has been included just to keep the code as simple as possible. You could put in some code to tell the interpreter not to process the <waybill> tags and only change the others.

> We could easily create similar translation documents for any number of input documents. This would allow us to translate all input documents with the same ASP page.

Generating the XSL

Now let's start looking at the process of generating the XSL file.

Normal XML rules apply. The XML generated by our ASP page must be well-formed, which means that case matters.

There are two approaches we could use in order to meet our goal of creating the XSL:

❑   We could build a string

❑   We could create an instance of the XML DOM, build a result tree and write out the XML as a string

Either approach is valid for our needs. The first is simpler, and may be faster, but it is a limited solution. Should we wish to revisit this application at some point in the future and extend its functionality, our options would very restricted. Furthermore, we would be limited to a linear building process, and it would be cumbersome to dynamically modify any part of the result string that had already been built. It would be difficult, for example, to add the capability of converting an attribute in the source document to an element in the result. By taking the XML DOM approach, all of the capabilities of the DOM are available to us, and we are not limited to a sequential result. Plus, it's more of an XML-purist approach to the problem.

So, we will need two instances of the XML DOM. The first will contain the result tree we will be building, whose XML source will ultimately become our return value, and the second instance will host the XML translation document that will drive the creation process.

As you're looking through the discussion of how this ASP page works, you may find it useful to refer to the end result, which is shown here as rendered in Internet Explorer 5, with the color coding and indentation provided by IE's default internal style sheet.

If you download the source code for this book and look at the `interpreter.asp` file in your browser, this is what you should see.

As is always the case when we use an ASP to generate XML, we need to set the response type:

```
<%
Response.ContentType = "text/xml"
Response.Expires = 0

dim result
dim interpreter
dim oNodes
```

Next we will create our required two instances of the XML DOM, and load in the `interpreter.xml` file (our mapping file):

```
Set result = Server.CreateObject("Microsoft.XMLDOM")

Set interpreter = Server.CreateObject("Microsoft.XMLDOM")
interpreter.async = false
```

```
'// load the definition file
sSource = Server.MapPath("interpreter.xml")
interpreter.load(sSource)

'// did the XML file load OK?
If interpreter.parseError.errorCode <> 0 Then
    msg = "<msg><gen>Error loading INTERPRETER data file.</gen>"
    msg = msg & "<br>Description: " & interpreter.parseError.reason &
            "</br>"
    msg = msg & "<br>Source text: " & interpreter.parseError.srcText &
            "</br></msg>"
    Response.Write msg
End If
...
```

Note that as this code is running server-side, we need to provide a physical path to the XML file that we are loading, which is done by using `Server.MapPath`. We set the `async` property of the interpreter file to `false`, as we cannot process anything until this file is completely loaded. The `async` property of the result tree is irrelevant.

Next we extract all of the `<xlat>` nodes from our definition tree:

```
Set oNodes = interpreter.documentElement.selectNodes("//xlat")
```

Now we are ready to start populating our result tree. The first step is to add the node that identifies this XML document as a style sheet:

```
'// add a node to the result tree for the stylesheet declaration
Set oNewNode = result.createNode("element","xsl:stylesheet", _
                                "http://www.w3.org/TR/WD-xsl")
result.appendChild(oNewNode)
```

Then we set the root element, the stylesheet declaration, as follows:

```
'// the stylesheet declaration is the outermost grouping tag. It is the root
'// element and parent to all other elements
Set root = result.documentElement
```

If you refer back to the IE5 view of the XSL shown in the previous figure, you'll see that the next entry is `<xsl:template match="/">`, which we create as follows:

```
'// create the XSL node
Set oTemp = result.createNode("element","xsl:template", _
                                "http://www.w3.org/TR/WD-xsl")
oTemp.setAttribute "match", "/"
root. appendChild(oTemp)
```

Rather than hard-coding the names of the root document and the item of the translation result (`<shipments>` and `<shipment>` in our example), we extract those tag names from the definition file. This is based on the assumption that the root element of the definition file will also be the root element of the translation result:

```
'// name of the container tag (eg: "shipments")
nodeName = interpreter.documentElement.firstChild.nodeName
Set oContainer = result.createNode("element", _
                                    interpreter.documentElement.nodeName,"")
oTemp.appendChild(oContainer)
```

Note that we have created the `oContainer` variable, which represents the root element (`shipments`) of the translated result.

Now we need to add a line to our XSL result tree that when processed will tell the XSL to iterate through all instances of the children (`shipment`) of that root. The following code will create an element containing `<xsl:for-each select="//shipment">` and append it to the result tree:

```
Set oLoop = result.createNode("element","xsl:for-each", _
                                "http://www.w3.org/TR/WD-xsl")
oLoop.setAttribute "select", "//" & nodeName
oContainer.appendChild(oLoop)
```

Next we create an entry for the contained item (that is `<shipment>`) and append it to the result tree:

```
Set oLoopParent = result.createNode("element",nodeName, "")
oLoop.appendChild(oLoopParent)
```

Now we get to the real work. In this section of the code, we iterate through each of the `<xlat>` mapping elements. For each one, we create an element using the `name` attribute of the `<out>` element, and an `<xsl:value-of>` from the `select` attribute from the `<in>` element. These items are added to the result tree.

An example of one of these would be:

```
<shippedby><xsl:value-of select="carrier"/></shippedby>
```

```
For Each oNode in oNodes
  Set oNewNode = result.createNode("element", _
                    oNode.selectSingleNode("out").getAttribute("name"), "")
  Set oSelect = result.createNode("element",_
                            "xsl:value-of","http://www.w3.org/TR/WD-xsl")
  oSelect.setAttribute "select",oNode.selectSingleNode("in").getAttribute("name")
  oNewNode.appendChild(oSelect)
  oLoopParent.appendChild(oNewNode)
Next
```

Finally, we need to add the `apply-templates` node:

```
Set oNode = result.createNode("element","xsl:apply-templates",
                                "http://www.w3.org/TR/WD-xsl")
oTemp.appendChild(oNode)
```

We have now completely built our result tree, and we return it to the calling application (which could be a browser, a script, an XML file, etc):

```
Response.Write result.xml
%>
```

> If you are considering adapting this procedure for your own project, then the first stage should be to create an XSL file that gets the data from the XML document. This way you can get the display right before you start writing your interpretation code.

The Test Page

Now let's see this all at work by looking at the test page, which is included in the source download as `default.asp`. We will use the JavaScript `alert()` function to display the XML because if we show it in the browser the tags will not be visible.

When it loads, the test page will invoke the `init()` function. It will create two instances of the XML DOM, one for the XML source document, and the second for the dynamic XSL file. The last thing it does is apply the XSL to the source XML, and saves the resulting string in the `"processed"` variable. This is our translated XML. The full code is shown here:

```
<html>
<head>
    <link REL="stylesheet" TYPE="text/css" HREF="list.css">
</head>
<body>
<hr color=red>

<button onclick='alert(source.xml);'>1. Show incoming.xml</button>
<button onclick='alert(dynstyle.xml);'>2. Show dynstyle.xsl</button>
<button onclick='alert(processed);' id=button1 name=button1>
    3. Show Translation
</button><br>
<hr color=red>
<script FOR="window" EVENT="onload">
  init();
</script>

<script>
var source;
var sourceName = "incoming.xml";
var dynstyle;
var dynstyleName = "interpreter.asp";
var processed = "";

function init(){
    // Do init stuff. Called by the parent frame.
    source = new ActiveXObject('Microsoft.XMLDOM');
    source.async = false;
    source.load(sourceName);
    // did the XML file load OK?
    if (source.parseError.errorCode != 0){
        msg = 'Error loading SOURCE file.'
        msg += '\nDescription: ' + source.parseError.reason
        msg += '\nSource text: ' + source.parseError.srcText
    }
```

```
        root = source.documentElement;

        dynstyle = new ActiveXObject('Microsoft.XMLDOM');
        dynstyle.async = false;
        dynstyle.load(dynstyleName)
        // did the XML file load OK?
        if (dynstyle.parseError.errorCode != 0){
            msg = 'Error loading DYNSTYLE file.'
            msg += '\nDescription: ' + dynstyle.parseError.reason
            msg += '\nSource text: ' + dynstyle.parseError.srcText
        }
        processed = source.transformNode(dynstyle)
    }
    </script>
    </body>
    </html>
```

I have provided three buttons on the test page that show the three entities that make up this example:

❑ Button 1 shows the original un-translated source document (incoming.xml)

❑ Button 2 shows the dynamically-generated XSL returned as a result from interpreter.asp

❑ Button 3 shows the translated version of the source document, after the style has been applied to it.

How it Works

The following screen shot shows the un-translated source document:

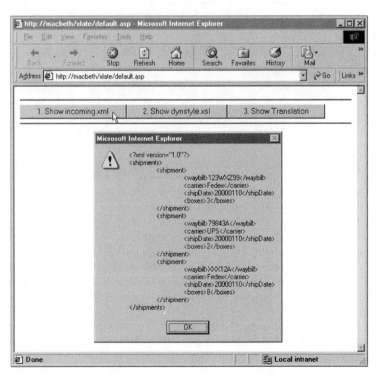

This screen shot shows our dynamically generated XSL:

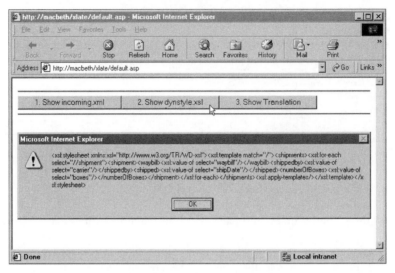

This final screen shot shows the result of the translation:

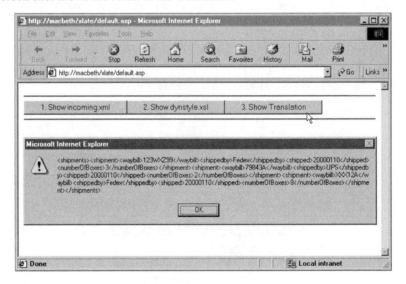

Summary

In this chapter, we have seen a way to use ASP to generate an XSL file dynamically. We did this by using an ASP page to create an instance of the XML DOM and employing DOM methods to build the result tree. The information needed to build the result tree came from the contents of an XML file. A test web page then used the dynamic XSL to translate from one XML structure to another.

So now we have finished our discussion on styling XML for our web browsers. We will use XSL frequently as we progress through this book. In the next chapter we shall move on to storing and retrieving XML data from databases using ActiveX Data Objects (ADO).

11

Integrating ADO and XML

Over the course of the preceding ten chapters we have covered XML topics such as syntax, data structure, structure-control mechanisms, and ways to alter XML for display. But we haven't yet looked at how XML can be used as a data-transport mechanism or data-retrieval methodology. In this chapter, we will look at:

❏ How XML relates to other technologies such as ADO

❏ When to use ADO and when to use XML

❏ How ADO and XML work together

❏ What the XML generated from ADO looks like

❏ Persistence with ADO and XML

ADO (**ActiveX Data Objects**) allows you to connect to just about any data source via OLE DB. It was originally designed by Microsoft to give universal access to data within a Web-based application. OLE DB providers under the ADO interface can be built to treat almost anything as a data source, from plain text files to business objects that expose information. It is also language independent, that is, you can easily write code in a variety of languages such as Visual Basic, Visual C++, or VBScript on an ASP page, to access data. Microsoft optimized ADO to provide performance and scalability. If you have used any of Microsoft's previous data objects (such as DAO or RDO), ADO is very easy to learn, and requires very little change in the code used for retrieving and processing your data.

So, with all these great features built into ADO, why would anyone want to use XML in the first place? Well, contrary to popular myth, not every system on the planet is built on Microsoft technology. Sure, ADO can read data from any format that has a provider written for it, but that doesn't mean that an ADO solution can be implemented on a non-Microsoft platform; for example, you cannot run ADO on a UNIX server. However, you can have a provider running on a Microsoft platform that accesses the information on the UNIX server. The ADO objects themselves run on the Microsoft platform but the data can be anywhere. Where ADO is able to provide universal *access* to data, XML provides universal *data*. XML is self-contained and doesn't require a third-party definition of the information.

However, now consider the same question phrased a little differently. If XML has such great potential, why would anyone choose to use ADO? Given the amount of hype that XML has received recently, this is a very good question. However, like most things that are subject to hyperbole, you have to look for the kernel of truth. XML is a pretty cool technology, but it has its place in the Web world. It will not solve all of your data problems, improve your love life, or clean the cat box!

Deciding on ADO, XML, or Both

It is rare today to be asked to develop a system where there are no pre-defined parameters. There is always some pre-existing condition that has to be incorporated, worked around, or planned for retirement. You may be asked to build a system on a UNIX platform that accesses mainframe data stored in DB2 format, or perhaps a traditional client/server application using a Windows NT server, and Windows 98 client. Now that the Y2K situation has passed, corporations may be looking to tie together their disparate systems into one cohesive whole, accessible through the Web or any web technology.

Knowing that you have to work with data in your application, the following question is bound to crop up some time or later. When should I use XML? There is no easy answer to this. Like any technology, you have to weigh the different options against the task at hand. Inter-operability, performance, ease of development, and size of datasets are all factors that need to be considered.

There really is no fixed limit on how large an XML dataset can be. However, because it is a newer technology there are practical limits. I was recently on a project where we decided to use XML to transmit directory and file information to the client. We were gathering the complete physical file list for a web site, and then building a DHTML tree-view. Because of the large nature of some of the client's web sites, it soon proved completely unusable. Storing the information in a database, and transmitting only small chunks of the data at a time proved much more effective.

Whenever I need to track information that is more hierarchical in nature, such as a file tree, I give XML a good look. If the amount of data is relatively small, and doesn't require extensive manipulation, XML is a possibility. When I need to move information from one platform to another (especially via the Web), XML is seriously considered for this task.

Another big advantage to XML is, as they say in the real estate business: Location, Location, Location. The chances are that users won't want to install a database just to view the content of your web site. While you might be able to impose that requirement for an intranet, this is rather demanding for the Internet. Generally speaking, however, no matter where your data comes from, it can be translated into XML. Once in XML, it can be sent to the client, where any number of different views can be generated. And best of all, the client is no longer tying up resources on your server. You can create **data islands** on the client, without the use of any external controls. We will talk more about the power of client-side XML in the next chapter.

XML is not the answer to every Web problem. ADO still has many uses and is not an endangered species. When dealing with a closed system on a Microsoft platform, I always look to ADO first, and if I need transactions, ADO is there. In fact, whenever there is an actual database involved (such as an RDBMS) ADO is your best choice for data access. To repeat what I stated earlier: When you need **universal access** to data you will find that ADO is just the ticket; however, if you need **universal data** then XML is the only choice.

ADO and ASP

Before venturing forth on the topic of universal data in your ASP pages, let's first look at universal access to data in your ASP pages. Since its inception, ADO has been touted at the cure-all for data access headaches. In version 2.5 we are truly starting to see some truth in that claim. The structure for Microsoft's Universal Data Access (UDA) strategy looks like the following:

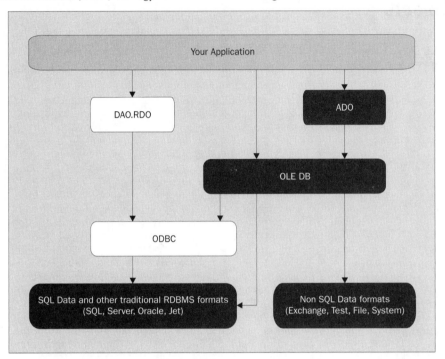

As we can see from the diagram, ADO and OLE DB are separate technologies, even though they are usually talked about interchangeably. OLE DB is the set of low-level COM interfaces that allows access to the data. There are many ways in which OLE DB differs from the older ODBC, but I will only mention a couple. First, ODBC was invented to work primarily with relational data. However, useful data does not always appear in, or conform to, a relational model; it often exists in plain old text files. OLE DB can use data in any format for which a provider exists, such as Microsoft Exchange, text files, DB2, or Windows Directory Services. ODBC just doesn't have this flexibility.

The way that OLE DB can utilize *other* forms of data, brings us to the other major difference from ODBC. OLE DB uses providers and ODBC uses drivers. You might be thinking that Microsoft created a new term to describe the same old thing, but they didn't. ODBC drivers operate using a set of API functions, which were designed to facilitate access to RDBMSs, but which were not tailored to any database in particular. Therefore you have one driver for every relational database system. On the other hand, the way OLE DB accesses data, based on the COM programming model, is through a common set of interfaces, which dictate the method of access and not the implementation of access. The same set of interface methods are used regardless of the data format. OLE DB providers currently exist for each type of data source, rather than for each and every database. For example, there is an OLE DB provider for ODBC drivers, a single program that allows access to a multitude of different ODBC-driven databases. Of course, OLE DB is flexible enough to allow one provider to exist for every database, and could, in time, render ODBC obsolete.

ADO sits on top of OLE DB. It provides similar functionality as RDO did for ODBC, that is, a simplified object model to hide the complexities underneath. ADO cannot actually do anything at all by itself. It requires an OLE DB provider. ADO then invokes methods on the common OLE DB interfaces to carry out the desired action. ASP programmers now have simplicity and consistency in their data access technology.

ADO Objects

OK, so what is ADO? It is a collection of COM objects that gives us access to an underlying data source via its OLE DB provider. In ADO 2.1, these are the `Connection`, `Command`, and `Recordset` objects. With ADO version 2.5 came the additional `Record` and `Stream` objects. The ADO object spaghetti looks like this:

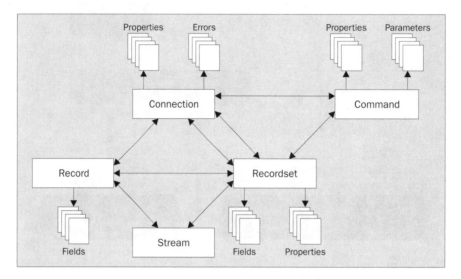

Although you need an `ActiveConnection` to communicate with your data source, it can be created before or after the `Recordset` object, and then attached when needed. Therefore there are several ways of accomplishing most tasks. Rowsets (that is, recordsets) can be retrieved via the `Recordset.Open`, `Connection.Execute`, or `Command.Execute methods`. The following ASP code demonstrates this point:

```
<%Option Explicit%>
<!-- #include file="adovbs.inc"  -->
<%
Dim connContacts      'Connection Object
Dim cmdContacts       'Command Object
Dim rsByConnection    'Recordset Object for Connection
Dim rsByCommand       'Recordset Object for Command
Dim rsByOpen          'Recordset Object for Recordset.Open
Dim szSQL             'SQL Command String

szSQL = "SELECT * FROM contacts"
Set connContacts = Server.CreateObject("ADODB.Connection")
connContacts.ConnectionString = _
                    "Provider=SQLOLEDB;Database=ASPXMLBook;uid=sa;pwd=;"
connContacts.Open     'Open the connection for use
```

Now that the connection to the datasource has been established we can just call the `Execute` method to get the recordset:

```
'Get Records by Connection
Set rsByConnection = connContacts.Execute(szSQL)
```

To use the `command` object, you have to create it, set the `CommandText`, give it an `ActiveConnection` and then call `Execute`:

```
Set cmdContacts = Server.CreateObject("ADODB.Command")
cmdContacts.CommandType = adCmdText
cmdContacts.CommandText = szSQL
Set cmdContacts.ActiveConnection = connContacts

'Get Records by Command
Set rsByCommand = cmdContacts.Execute
```

The last way to get the recordset is using the `Open` method. Don't forget to pass the connection object:

```
'Get Records by Open
Set rsByOpen = Server.CreateObject("ADODB.Recordset")
rsByOpen.Open szSQL, connContacts
...
%>
```

All of the returned recordsets will contain exactly the same data. In fact, the only difference between them is the method used to create them. Now that we have seen that we can use ADO to get data into our ASP pages, we can look at the XML features of ADO.

ADO Data in XML

Using ADO provides good performance, decent reliability, and far-reaching support. However, if you have to move information from a standard data source (SQL Server or Oracle) to a third-party or a non-standard platform, XML can easily provide the transport mechanism. With ADO you can have the best of both worlds. By exporting your data in XML format, consumers of your data do not have to comply with your choice of database server. You can provide universally viewable representations of your data. This functionality was included with ADO version 2.1 and is further enhanced in version 2.5.

Obtaining XML from ADO

You have determined that you want to retrieve XML from your ADO recordset. The next question is, how? Well, since ADO 2.1, we have had the ability to convert recordset data into XML. The process is fairly straightforward. In order to first obtain some data, you must have a connection. The following code creates a `Connection` object that points to a particular database (`ASPXMLBook`):

```
<!-- #include file="adoconst.asp"  -->
<%
Dim connContacts      'Connection Object
Dim cmdContacts       'Command Object
Dim rsContacts        'Recordset Object
Dim strmContacts      'Stream Object
Dim szXML             'The resulting XML text
Set connContacts = Server.CreateObject("ADODB.Connection")
```

```
connContacts.CursorLocation = adUseClient
connContacts.ConnectionString = _
                         "Provider=SQLOLEDB;Database=ASPXMLBook;uid=sa;pwd=;"
connContacts.Open        'Open the connection for use
```

Once you have a connection, there are a couple of different ways to retrieve data. One method is to execute a command directly on the connection; the other uses the `Command` object. For demonstration purposes, the `Command` object will be used, though in a real world scenario you might want to consider just calling `Connection.Execute` to reduce overhead and improve performance. The `Command` object is set up by the following code:

```
Set cmdContacts = Server.CreateObject("ADODB.Command")
cmdContacts.CommandText = "SELECT * FROM contacts"
cmdContacts.CommandType = adCmdText
Set cmdContacts.ActiveConnection = connContacts
```

Once the `Command` object is initialized with the desired parameters, the only thing left to do is get the data. The recordset is retrieved into a `Recordset` object with the following code:

```
Set rsContacts = Server.CreateObject("ADODB.Recordset")
rsContacts.CursorType = adOpenStatic
rsContacts.LockType = adLockReadOnly
rsContacts.Open cmdContacts

Set rsContacts.ActiveConnection = Nothing
connContacts.Close
Set cmdContacts = Nothing
Set connContacts = Nothing
```

Note, that the recordset's `ActiveConnection` property has been set equal to `Nothing`. This disconnects the recordset from the database `Connection` object. Now the connection can be safely closed and the `Connection` and `Command` objects cleaned up.

To actually retrieve the XML text, the `Stream` object is utilized – this is explained in more detail later on, when we discuss persistence:

```
Set strmContacts = Server.CreateObject("ADODB.Stream")
rsContacts.Save strmContacts, adPersistXML

szXML = strmContacts.ReadText
Set strmContacts = Nothing
Set rsContacts = Nothing

Response.Write(szXML)
%>
```

The recordset is temporarily stored into a `Stream` in XML format. Once it is in text form the `ReadText` method of the `Stream` object is used to store the information in a `Variant` string. Then the `Response` object can be used to send the XML data to the client. You might want to note that only ADO 2.5 can utilize the `Stream` object. In ADO 2.1, you can get the XML into a text file specifying a file name instead of a `Stream` object as follows:

```
rsContacts.Save "c:\myDirectory\myfile.XML", adPersistXML
```

The text file `myfile.XML` would reside on the server at the given location. It would be functionally the same as the XML returned earlier. This will be covered a little later when we look at persistence.

The ADO XML-Data Schema

The resulting format is a little different than what you might be expecting. Let's walk through XML the `Recordset` that is generated by the code we looked at previously. The first thing you might notice is the XML-Data schema is included in the text, followed by the data section. The included schema definition conforms to the XML-Data specification. For more information on this specification visit: http://www.w3.org/TR/1998/NOTE-XML-data/.

As we saw in Chapter 4, schemas are an alternative XML definition methodology to DTDs. The fact that schemas are written using XML for use with XML makes them easier to work with. All XML data generated from ADO will have the same general schema. Fields are defined in a consistent format, so once you figure out the basic structure, you're pretty much home and dry. The major benefit to this structure is portability back and forth to ADO. Not only can ADO write this XML, it can also read it back in. Let's look at the XML generated by the code above:

```xml
<xml xmlns:s='uuid:BDC6E3F0-6DA3-11d1-A2A3-00AA00C14882'
    xmlns:dt='uuid:C2F41010-65B3-11d1-A29F-00AA00C14882'
    xmlns:rs='urn:schemas-microsoft-com:rowset'
    xmlns:z='#RowsetSchema'>
<s:Schema id='RowsetSchema'>
    <s:ElementType name='row' content='eltOnly'>
        <s:AttributeType name='first_name' rs:number='1' rs:writeunknown='true'>
            <s:datatype dt:type='string' rs:dbtype='str' dt:maxLength='20'
            rs:maybenull='false'/>
        </s:AttributeType>
        <s:AttributeType name='last_name' rs:number='2' rs:writeunknown='true'>
            <s:datatype dt:type='string' rs:dbtype='str' dt:maxLength='25'
            rs:maybenull='false'/>
        </s:AttributeType>
        <s:AttributeType name='street_info' rs:number='3' rs:writeunknown='true'>
            <s:datatype dt:type='string' rs:dbtype='str' dt:maxLength='50'
            rs:maybenull='false'/>
        </s:AttributeType>
        <s:AttributeType name='city' rs:number='4' rs:writeunknown='true'>
            <s:datatype dt:type='string' rs:dbtype='str' dt:maxLength='50'
            rs:maybenull='false'/>
        </s:AttributeType>
        <s:AttributeType name='state' rs:number='5' rs:writeunknown='true'>
            <s:datatype dt:type='string' rs:dbtype='str' dt:maxLength='15'
            rs:maybenull='false'/>
        </s:AttributeType>
        <s:AttributeType name='zip' rs:number='6' rs:writeunknown='true'>
            <s:datatype dt:type='string' rs:dbtype='str' dt:maxLength='10'
            rs:maybenull='false'/>
        </s:AttributeType>
        <s:AttributeType name='phone' rs:number='7' rs:writeunknown='true'>
            <s:datatype dt:type='string' rs:dbtype='str' dt:maxLength='14'
            rs:maybenull='false'/>
        </s:AttributeType>
```

```
        <s:AttributeType name='type' rs:number='8' rs:writeunknown='true'>
            <s:datatype dt:type='string' rs:dbtype='str' dt:maxLength='10'
               rs:maybenull='false'/>
        </s:AttributeType>
        <s:extends type='rs:rowbase'/>
    </s:ElementType>
</s:Schema>
<rs:data>
    <z:row first_name='John' last_name='Doe' street_info='103 Easter Avenue'
        city='Pleasantville' state='Indiana' zip='30113' phone='555-5555'
        type='personal'/>
    <z:row first_name='Alice' last_name='Smith' street_info='52B Wilkens Street'
        city='Pleasantville' state='Indiana' zip='30113' phone='555-6666'
        type='personal'/>
    <z:row first_name='Richard' last_name='Blair'
        street_info='123 North Main Steet'
        city='Dearborn' state='Michigan' zip='48124' phone='555-4981'
        type='business'/>
    <z:row first_name='William M.' last_name='Kropog'
        street_info='80698 Matthew Street'
        city='Covington' state='Louisiana' zip='70533' phone='555-0713'
        type='business'/>
    <z:row first_name='Bill' last_name='Gates' street_info='1 Microsoft Way'
        city='Redmond' state='Washington' zip='97811' phone='555-1212'
        type='business'/>
</rs:data>
</xml>
```

You may have noticed the four defined namespaces. Each namespace contains a section of the XML document and is used for a specific purpose. For the round-trip communication between ADO and XML to function properly, everything must be explicitly defined. The four defined namespaces are: Schema, Data Types, RecordSet, and Rowset.

Schema (s:)

The following code defines the namespace for the schema information:

```
xmlns:s='uuid:BDC6E3F0-6DA3-11d1-A2A3-00AA00C14882'
```

```
<s:Schema id='RowsetSchema'>
```

Any tag you see preceded by s: pertains to the **definition** of the data or the schema. This includes element definitions, as well as field names (defined as attributes), and data type headers. The schema is also identified by the <... id='RowsetSchema'> tag. This allows the entire schema to be referenced by '#RowsetSchema' as we will see in just a bit, when I talk about the Rowset.

Data Types (dt:)

The Data Type namespace is defined by:

```
xmlns:dt='uuid:C2F41010-65B3-11d1-A29F-00AA00C14882'
```

This section contains information to define the type and limits of the data field. For example, `dt:type='string' dt:maxLength='25'` defines the data type as a string, with a maximum length of 25 characters. The actual definition of the field in the SQL Server table is `VarChar(25)`. So we can see the direct correlation between what is in the SQL Server table and what is defined in the schema. If you omit the `dt:type` attribute definition from the row definition, the column's type will default to a variable length string.

Recordset and Field Properties (rs:)

The following code defines the namespace for the `Recordset` and `Field` properties:

```
xmlns:rs='urn:schemas-microsoft-com:rowset'
```

The `Recordset` and `Field` properties namespace includes such information as the ordinal position of the fields, the `Field`'s data property, and whether or not it can contain null values. This information specifically pertains to the ADO `Recordset` properties and attributes.

Current Rowset (z:)

The `Rowset` namespace is defined:

```
xmlns:z='#RowsetSchema'>
```

Please note that this declaration references the schema's `id`, that was sent with the code: `<s:Schema id='RowsetSchema'>`. For ADO to properly handle this XML, the `id` must be `RowsetSchema` and the rowset schema must point to `#RowsetSchema`. This is where the schema is actually implemented to hold the data values. As a result of using the different namespaces, it is unlikely there will ever be ambiguity in the data definition. For example, your database might contain a user-defined data type called `phone`, and your table contains a field by the same name. Because each definition resides in a different namespace, they cannot conflict.

Once the schema is fully defined we see the start of the actual values. The schema ends with the tag `</s:Schema>`. The values begin with the `<rs:data>` tag. Each record is comprised of a `<z:row>` tag, with each of the fields defined as an attribute/value pair, which is just as the schema defined:

```
<rs:data>
    <z:row first_name='John' last_name='Doe' street_info='103 Easter Avenue'
        city='Pleasantville' state='Indiana' zip='30113' phone='555-5555'
        type='personal'/>
    <z:row first_name='Alice' last_name='Smith' street_info='52B Wilkens Street'
        city='Pleasantville' state='Indiana' zip='30113' phone='555-6666'
        type='personal'/>
    <z:row first_name='Richard' last_name='Blair'
        street_info='123 North Main Steet'
        city='Dearborn' state='Michigan' zip='48124' phone='555-4981'
        type='business'/>
    <z:row first_name='William M.' last_name='Kropog'
        street_info='80698 Matthew Street'
        city='Covington' state='Louisiana' zip='70533' phone='555-0713'
        type='business'/>
    <z:row first_name='Bill' last_name='Gates' street_info='1 Microsoft Way'
        city='Redmond' state='Washington' zip='97811' phone='555-1212'
        type='business'/>
</rs:data>
```

The rowset could be empty. Because all XML tags must have an end tag, an empty rowset could be identified with `<rs:data></rs:data>` or simply `<rs:data />`. Also, since the `rs` namespace is used by ADO, you should never create your own tags. However, the namespace labels are up to you. ADO uses `s, dt, rs, and z`, but you could define any label you wish as long as you use it consistently throughout the XML document.

Putting all of these sections together yields a complete XML document. Nothing is ambiguous; we know the field names, data types, maximum lengths, and values. ADO has information to process the XML back into a recordset. Viewing this document makes it easier to appreciate how powerful XML is. You can send this file anywhere and the data can be reproduced and understood. A little later, I will show you how to take this complex output and provide a simple view.

Persistence

The true power of XML becomes apparent when you need to publish your data in a way that does not diminish its usefulness as data. In other words, if you just want to list your data as a report, XML may not be your best answer. If you want to give your data consumers the ability to create, update and delete, XML can help. XML can also be used to pass parameters to disparate systems, or help maintain a component's state without having to keep the component around. The requirement for sending data out of your normal database format, and being able to do something with it when it comes back is called **persistence**.

One definition of persistence is *the method of retaining the values of objects after the source of that object has been removed*. When we talk about persistence, what we want is to take a snapshot of the data along with any useful meta-information. By doing that, the actual source of the data no longer has to be present. This means we can pass the data along to a function, web page, an application, or a customer and have it show up in a usable form. We have saved resources by disconnecting the source data from our image of it. Because we have also saved the meta-information (e.g.; column names, number of columns, data types) we can reconnect our recordset back to the source once we are finished, if we need to.

In today's distributed environments, this concept of persisted data is very important. Imagine a retail web site where users can peruse an on-line catalogue. Each page would require a connection to the database to retrieve the desired information. If each item for sale also had optional configurations, the servers could easily get bogged down just serving pages to a few users. Persistence allows us to get the data we want, close the connection, transfer the data to wherever we need it, manipulate the data, and then reconnect the data when finished. By doing this we have increased perceptible performance by storing the customer's desired information outside of the database system. We have also reduced the connection contention at the server, by only holding open connections for a brief time.

The true power of persistence comes from the ability to externalize the data. Persistence used in this way allows us to have remote data. Imagine a salesperson getting ready for a road trip. She can store her product data onto her laptop in XML format. Her browser-based application can read this data, show her customers brochures based on it, and help her create order records from it. In the evening, from her hotel room, she can dial up her main office and synchronize the data. New contacts are added to the corporate database, and new orders are placed into the production queue, and the proper credit checks are performed on new customers. She can also get updates to customer records for the following day's sales visits.

This example of remote data is probably not all that uncommon. You could have a database installed on the salesperson's laptop and just synchronize tables. However, what if the main office runs on DB2, the regional office she happens to dial into runs SQL Server, and she is partial to a Mac laptop? XML makes the data interchange easy and effective. ADO running at the server can create the proper XML structures and send them to her laptop. By keeping the data on the server and only storing what is immediately required on the client in XML format, performance can be enhanced, as well as reducing the system requirements on the client-side.

ADO Persistence

ADO goes about the business of persistence with the help of the Microsoft OLE DB Persistence Provider. Since version 2.0, ADO has allowed data persistence to and from files in the Advanced Data TableGram (ADTG) format. Recordsets could be saved to a disk file and at some later time re-opened from that saved file. The following diagrams show how data is stored and retrieved through the Persistence Provider:

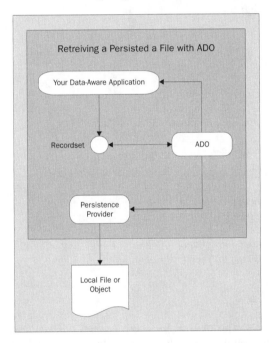

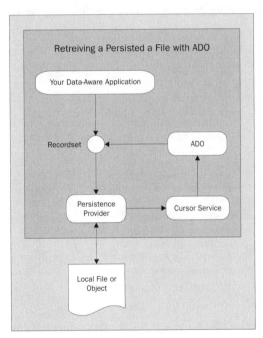

When you want to save or persist a recordset that your application has opened, the Save method of the Recordset object calls the Persistence Provider via ADO. The Persistence Provider then writes the rowset data and the required meta-information to recreate the recordset on the specified file. Once the file is written there is no need for the original data source and the connection can be closed.

When you want to retrieve a persisted recordset, the operation works in reverse. Your application creates a Recordset object. Then using the Open method, ADO can call the Persistence Provider to retrieve the data from the specified file. Once the data is retrieved by the Persistence Provider, it is transferred into a Cursor Service. The Cursor Service is a component of OLE DB that allows the loaded recordset to be manipulated. The recordset is then wrapped up into the Recordset object ready for use.

Microsoft added the XML format to recordset persistence with ADO 2.1. This version was limited in that it didn't support hierarchical Recordset objects nor the persistence of Recordset objects with pending changes. It did generate well-formed and valid XML from a Recordset, which lit the beacon for the future and allowed developers to become familiar with XML. As with version 2.0, the XML or ADTG formats had to be written to a file for persistence.

ADO 2.5 fixes some of these problems. With ADO 2.5, both XML and ADTG formats can be persisted to objects that support the IStream interface. These objects include the ADO Stream object, the ASP Response object, the ASP Request object, and the XML DOM Document object. The Response and Request objects provide the round-trip mechanism: XML can be saved to the Response object and read back in from the Request object. Let's look at how persistence can be implemented with ADO in XML format.

Persisting to a File

You can persist your data to a file by using the following:

```
<%
Dim rsTitles
Dim connNorthwind
Dim szFile

Set connNorthwind = Server.CreateObject("ADODB.Connection")
connNorthwind.open "provider=sqloledb; data source=Northwind; initial
catablog=pubs; user id=sa;password="
Set rsTitles = Server.CreateObject("ADODB.Recordset")
rsTitles.CursorLocation = adUseClient
rsTitles.Open "SELECT * FROM titles", connNorthwind
szFile = Server.MapPath("testfile.xml")
rsTitles.Save szFile, adPersistXML    'saves file in XML format
'rsTitles.Save szFile                 'saves file in ADTG (the default) format
rsTitles.Close
connNorthwind.Close
Set rsTitles = Nothing
Set connNorthwind = Nothing
...
%>
```

By specifying the adPersistXML constant (which has a value of 1) on the Save method call, we ensure the data is persisted in XML format. If this parameter is omitted or set to 0, that is the adPersistADTG constant is specified, then the file would be in the ADTG format. If we look on the server in the Virtual Directory's physical path we will find the testfile.xml file, which will have a similar structure to our example on schemas – the schema definition followed by the data itself. You can then open the persisted data using this code:

```
<%
...
'Reopen File
rsTitles.Open szFile,,,,adCmdFile
...
%>
```

The `Recordset` object will now contain exactly the same information as it did before it was persisted. Note that you don't have to re-open the persisted recordset straight after you save it – the reason for persistence is to be able to retrieve the data at any time. Note also, that although you can manipulate the XML file loaded from the server, such activity will be in vain, if the `Recordset` object was not originally declared as updatable. In this case, an error will be generated if you try to synchronize a modified recordset with the database.

Persisting to Streams

The addition of the `Stream` object to ADO 2.5 adds much greater flexibility to persistence. We are no longer tied to the file system as our only storage device.

Stream Object

The `Stream` object represents a stream of binary data or text. One context that may help you get to grips with this definition is the file system. In a directory tree, you can think of each file entry as a `record or row`. The `record` contains such column information as file name, date created, date last modified, access attributes, and size. Each `Record` object (or file) also has a `Stream` object associated with it – the contents of the file. In this example, we can see that the record doesn't mean a whole lot without the contents of the `Stream`. It would make little sense to know that a file named `MyXML.xml` was created on February 16, 2000 at 3:23PM and was 21,438 bytes long, if we could never access the actual contents. We can send XML from ADO to the `Stream` object with the following code:

```
<%
Dim rsTitles
Dim connNorthwind
Dim strmSaveXML

Set connNorthwind = Server.CreateObject("ADODB.Connection")
connNorthwind.open "provider=sqloledb; data source=Northwind; initial
catablog=pubs; user id=sa;password="

Set rsTitles = Server.CreateObject("ADODB.Recordset")
Set strmSaveXML = Server.CreateObject("ADODB.Stream")

rsTitles.CursorLocation = adUseClient
rsTitles.open "SELECT * FROM titles", connNorthwind
rsTitles.Save strmSaveXML, adPersistXML
rsTitles.Close
connNorthwind.Close
Set connNorthwind = Nothing

'ReOpen File
rs.Open strmSaveXML

...
%>
```

The `Stream` object used in the example above is included in ADO. However, it is just a wrapper around the generic `IStream` interface. ADO can persist to any COM object that exposes the `IStream` interface. An example that you are probably already familiar with (although you may not know it) is the `Response` object. The `Response` object sends a stream of data to the client browser for processing.

Persisting to the Response Object

Because the `Response` object exposes a stream, we can cut down on disk access when persisting our data and displaying it on the client. We can also save a step. We do not have to first persist the data to the `ADODB.Stream` and then get the text value and write it to the client. We can go to the client directly:

```
<%
Dim rsTitles
Dim connNorthwind

Response.ContentType = "text/xml"

Set connNorthwind = Server.CreateObject("ADODB.Connection")
connNorthwind.open "provider=sqloledb; data source=Northwind; initial
catablog=pubs; user id=sa;password="
Set rsTitles = Server.CreateObject("ADODB.Recordset")
rsTitles.CursorLocation = adUseClient
rsTitles.Open "SELECT * FROM titles", connNorthwind
Response.Write "<?xml version=""1.0"" encoding=""ISO-8869-1"" ?>" & vbCRLF
rsTitles.Save Response, adPersistXML
rsTitles.Close
connNorthwind.Close
Set rsTitles = Nothing
...
%>
```

The first thing we have to do is let the `Response` object know what kind of data we are sending down the wire. We do this with the line:

```
Response.ContentType = "text/xml"
```

After setting up the `Connection` and opening the `Recordset`, the next obvious difference is explictly sending the XML header to the browser:

```
Response.Write "<?xml version=""1.0"" encoding=""ISO-8869-1"" ?>" & vbCRLF
```

This lets the browser know that what follows is XML. We can then just save the `Recordset` to the `Response` object:

```
rsTitles.Save Response, adPersistXML
```

Because we have already sent the XML header down the wire, when the XML arrives it is processed by the browser, just like any other XML. As we will see in Chapter 12, this data could be written into a data island. The data could then have bound controls – all on the client side.

Persisting from the Request Object

Sending the data out into the world is a pretty neat feature. For some systems, that may be the only functionality you need. However, for most data-aware applications the phrase "it is better to give, than to receive" just has no place. Without worthwhile two-way communication, a lot of functionality is lost. Again, we have a solution involving `Streams`. The `Request` object is used to gather form fields and parameters passed on the URL, but we can also use it to retrieve XML from the client:

```
<%
...
Set rsNewTitles = Server.CreateObject("ADODB.Recordset")


'passed in the ADO XML-Data format
rsNewTitles.Open Request,,adOpenKeyset,adLockBatchOptimistic

rsNewTitles.ActiveConnection = connNorthwind
rsNewTitles.UpdateBatch adAffectAll


rsNewTitles.Filter = adFilterAffectedRecords
Response.Write "Record Synchronization Status"
Do While Not rsNewTitles.EOF
    Response.Write rsNewTitles!Title & " " & rsNewTitles.Status & "<BR>"
    rsNewTitles.MoveNext
Loop
rsNewTitles.Close
connNorthwind.Close
...
%>
```

The Open code looks very similar to the code used with the ADO Stream object. This isn't too surprising as the Request object exposes the IStream interface and therefore it functions the same way. After opening the Recordset, its ActiveConnection property is set and the synchronization is performed with UpdateBatch. The loop cycles through the records and displays the result of the synchronization effort. If a record has been modified since the recordset was persisted, an error will be generated and the record will not be updated in the database.

One important question at this point might be: how did the XML get into the request stream? There are a couple of ways to get the XML back to the server. The first method is to just pass the XML text in a hidden field or TextArea, which works well if the XML formatted text is not very large. The other method involves the XMLHTTP object. The following code shows an example (remember, we are on the client here, so the code is JavaScript):

```
...
var httpOb = new ActiveXObject("Microsoft.XMLHTTP");

//the page specified here is the ASP from the above example
httpOb.Open("POST","http://CodingCat/postContact.asp", false);

//Send the data to the server
httpOb.Send(xmlContacts.XMLDocument);
...
```

The first order of business is to create the XMLHTTP object, then call the Open method. This method takes the following five parameters: method, URL, asynchronous flag, user name and password. Only the method and URL are required. The method is the same as the typical <FORM METHOD="POST">. The URL is the page that will process the XML. The asynchronous flag tells the server whether to wait for the transfer to complete before continuing execution or not. Sending false for this parameter ensures the server will wait before continuing. The user name and password fields are only required if authentication is needed to access the given URL.

In order to utilize the XMLHTTP object, you have to have an XMLDOM object on the client. Once you populate the XMLDOM object with the desired data you call the Send method to transmit it to the server. In this example the data is coming from a data island named xmlContacts that was originally populated by the XML retreived from an ADO recordset. It may have been manipulated in some way and will now go back to the server to update the data source.

ADO with Style

As we saw in previous chapters, XSL allows us to format or transform XML into a user-friendly format. Since we can get XML out of ADO, we can take advantage of XSL for displaying results. Looking at the information generated by ADO, it is clear you would never want to display just raw data. Not only is it ugly, it is quite difficult to decipher. A much more pleasant view can easily be created and, with the data displayed in a table, the information is much easier to understand:

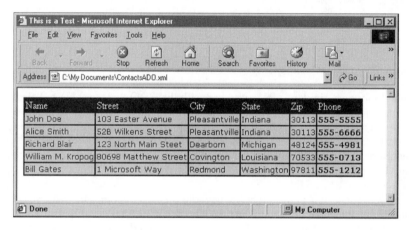

When you want to transform your XML using XSL there are several options. You could explicitly reference your XSL file in the XML source, such as:

```
<?xml version="1.0" ?>
<?xml-stylesheet type="text/xsl" href="contactsadolist.xsl" ?>
<Contacts>
        <Contact Name="John Doe" Street_Info="103 Easter Avenue"
          City="Pleasantville" State="Indiana" Zip="30113" Phone="555-5555"/>
...
</Contacts>
```

This directs an XML/XSL enabled browser (such as Microsoft Internet Explorer 5.0) to process the XML through your XSL file. Note that for this example ADO isn't used; an XML text file is being used. The XSL used to generate the view above looks like this:

```
<HTML>
  <HEAD>
    <TITLE>This is a Test</TITLE>
    <STYLE>
    .Table {background:black}
    .TableHead {font:bold; color:white; background:black}
    .TableColumnHead {font:normal 'Verdana' bold; color:white; background:#000000}
```

```
                .TableRow {font:x-small 'Verdana'; color:black; background:#CCCCCC}
         </STYLE>
     </HEAD>
     <BODY>

        <DIV xmlns:xsl="http://www.w3.org/TR/WD-xsl" >
          <TABLE CLASS="Table" ID="RecordTable">
            <THEAD>
              <TR CLASS="TableHead">
                <TD CLASS="TableColumnHead">Name</TD>
                <TD CLASS="TableColumnHead">Street</TD>
                <TD CLASS="TableColumnHead">City</TD>
                <TD CLASS="TableColumnHead">State</TD>
                <TD CLASS="TableColumnHead">Zip</TD>
                <TD CLASS="TableColumnHead">Phone</TD>
              </TR>
            </THEAD>

            <xsl:for-each select="xml/rs:data/z:row">
              <TR CLASS="TableRow">
                <TD>
        <xsl:value-of select="@first_name" /> <xsl:value-of select="@last_name" />
                </TD>
                <TD><xsl:value-of select="@street_info" /></TD>
                <TD><xsl:value-of select="@city" /></TD>
                <TD><xsl:value-of select="@state" /></TD>
                <TD><xsl:value-of select="@zip" /></TD>
                <TD><B><xsl:value-of select="@phone" /></B></TD>
              </TR>
            </xsl:for-each>
          </TABLE>
        </DIV>
     </BODY>
 </HTML>
```

The looping construct `<xsl:for-each...>` allows us to cycle through all of the data and format it accordingly. You will notice the `first_name` and `last_name` fields have been combined for the display (with a single space in between). Note that because ADO treats columns as attributes of the `Rowset`, each field is preceded by the attribute id character @.

This example also shows off the transformation capabilities of XSL. Since we are not concerned with the schema information when we want to display the data, XSL allows us to look at the rowset information (`xml/rs:data/z:row`). Try looking up the XML source code (called `ContactsADO.xml`, available for download free at www.wrox.com) in your browser. You might expect to see the HTML expanded with the actual data values, but what you see is the original XML structure, schema and all. Now uncomment the second line of code and Refresh the display, and see the tables appear! The XSL file has transformed the data into HTML and put the data in its correct place. Internet Explorer is doing the conversion internally. Even though both the XML and the XSL files will reside on the server, it is up to the client to apply the XSL to the data and display the results.

Server-Side Style

Another method is to do the transformation on the server. This is a more browser-neutral approach and probably more applicable to the modern distributed environment. To transform the XML data at the server and pass only the HTML down to the client, we can use the following code:

```
<%
...
Set xTitles = Server.CreateObject("Microsoft.XMLDOM")
xTitles.async = false      'load synchronously
xTitles.load(strmTitles)        'load the XML from the Stream

  'Set the style sheet location here
  styleFile = Server.MapPath("ContactsADOList.xsl")

  'Load the XSL
  xsStyle = Server.CreateObject("Microsoft.XMLDOM")
  xsStyle.async = False
  xsStyle.load(styleFile)         'load XSL file from server

  Response.Write(xTitles.transformNode(xsStyle))
...
%>
```

This approach takes advantage of the new `Stream` object support. By loading the XML into a `Stream` and then loading an XML DOM document from the `Stream`, we can take advantage of the `transformNode` method. This allows us to apply an XSL template to the data without explicitly having to define the link within the XML data. We can now fully separate the data from the display. In fact, we could have multiple XSL files and apply them to the same data to provide different views.

Summary

We have looked briefly at what ADO is and how it is used inside ASP. We saw three methods of returning a recordset using the `Connection` object, `Command` object, and the `Recordset` object. We looked at how you can use ADO and XML on the server to generate distributable data. We also looked at how persistence to either the file system or a `Stream` object, using the `Recordset` object's `Save` method, can help ease the burden of those distribution and integration headaches. We also touched briefly on how to transform the XML generated by ADO, and turn it into something informative and pleasant to look at. In the following chapter we will look at how to get even more power out of XML by using it on the client.

12

Client-side Data Binding with XML

The next two chapters look at how Microsoft Internet Explorer (version 4 and above) can be used with XML to create dynamic and network-friendly data-handling applications.

In this chapter, we look at the basics of **client-side data binding** in Internet Explorer, both the theory and the practice, and see how we can adapt it to work with XML data. Then in the following chapter, we'll move on to see some of the ways that we can use data binding, and some of the associated technologies that help us to make the most of it. The main topic areas for this chapter are:

❑ What is data binding?

❑ How do we display XML with data binding?

Before we start to look at XML data binding, we'll review what data binding actually is. Then we'll move on to see how we can use XML as a data source for data binding.

What is Data Binding?

Client-side data binding has long been the traditional way to build data-handling applications, even though many people think that the technique only arrived with Internet Explorer 4. In fact, programs like Microsoft Access have always provided data-binding in the form of data-bound **ActiveX** controls that can be placed on a form to allow the display, and updating of data, from a table or query.

In Visual Basic, and other programming languages like Borland Delphi, data-bound controls are available for use in your own applications. You define a connection and query that returns the data required for a form as a recordset, and drop suitable data-bound controls onto that form. They automatically reflect the matching field (or column) values of the current record, and usually allow these values to be updated (depending on the property settings for the controls), the query used to create the recordset, and the data source in use.

Data-Management Techniques on the Web

So data binding is nothing new, but the exciting aspect when IE4 was released was the ability to do native data binding client-side in a web browser. The traditional way of manipulating server-based data via a client-side browser is with custom CGI applications, Perl or IDC scripts, or (more recently) ASP. You send the user a page full of data extracted from the data source, displayed in a table or in HTML controls, and let them view it. If they want to, they can edit the contents of the HTML controls, or request a page with editing controls in it for a specific record. After editing the details, the form is posted back to the server where the `Request.Form` contents are used by the CGI application or ASP to update the data source.

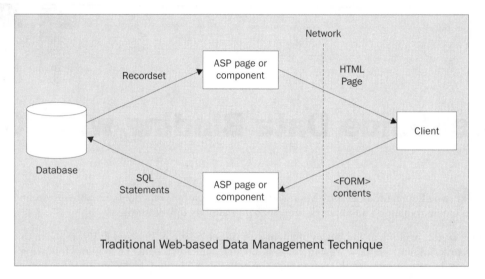

Traditional Web-based Data Management Technique

This is fine for simple data updates where the user can select a record that they want to update. However, it doesn't provide the same kind of working environment or user experience as, for example, a Microsoft Access application. Web-based applications are far less responsive (unless you have a very fast network), and often far less intuitive because the user has to navigate through many different pages selecting the records to edit, providing the new values, and then submitting them to the server.

In fact, the main reason that Access and similar applications are so much more responsive is that they don't have to keep going back to the server each time the user carries out an action, such as moving to another record or editing a value. Instead, they generally cache the results of the query that creates the recordset locally on the client. Hence, there is no communication delay reading the next record, and updates to the data are held locally until the source data is updated en-block when appropriate. This may be when the user closes the form, moves to another page, or issues an update request manually using the menu options.

Data-Binding Technology in Internet Explorer 4 and 5

Internet Explorer 4 and 5 can provide the same kind of features within a web page as Access and other similar applications do in their own environment. Client-side data binding removes the delays and concurrency problems that arise with pure server-side data management on the web. The delays are overcome by using the same technique as Access or a VB data-bound application – caching the recordset on the client.

This obvious solution needs a few web-specific wrinkles to be ironed out, of course. Amongst them:

❏ How do we get the data from the server to the client?

❏ How do we store it client-side, and how (i.e. with what) do we bind it to controls in a web page?

❏ How do we get the updates back to the server over HTTP?

❏ How do we use this information back on the server to update the original data source?

The answer is a set of ActiveX (COM) components that make up Microsoft's **Remote Data Service** (**RDS**).

The Microsoft Remote Data Service (RDS)

RDS is a way of providing a client-side data display and manipulation feature that works over the web, but provides a similar user experience to programs like Microsoft Access. To do this it uses a set of COM components that are part of the Microsoft ActiveX Data Objects library, and which are installed automatically with Internet Explorer 4 and above, and many other Microsoft client applications such as MS Office 97/2000 and Visual Studio 6.0. They are also part of Windows 2000.

The components consist of:

❏ The **Data Factory** component, which extracts the data from the data source. It uses special proxy and stub objects to communicate the recordset over HTTP from the server to the client. The recordset is encoded as a special MIME-type, and passed across the network in this format. The proxy then decodes it and makes it available to the other objects on the client as a normal recordset.

❏ The client-side **Data Source Object** (**DSO**) component collects the data from the data factory proxy object and handles the client-side caching. As a by-product, it makes the data available to script code running on the client, whether or not data-bound controls are used.

❏ The **Data-Binding Agent** component handles the connection between the DSO and the data-bound controls on the page, displaying the current values and passing updates back to the DSO so that it can update the cached recordset.

The next schematic shows the relationship between the various parts of the process, and the objects that implement it:

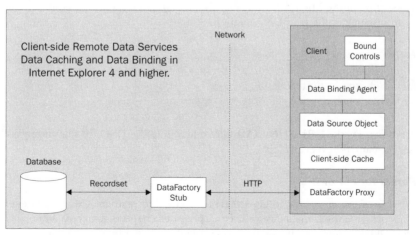

This combination of three objects (plus the client-side data cache) was originally called the Advanced Data Control (ADC) but in later releases has become closely integrated with ADO, and is now known as Remote Data Services (RDS). This is a typical definition for an instance of the RDS DSO:

```
<OBJECT CLASSID="clsid:BD96C556-65A3-11D0-983A-00C04FC29E33"
        ID="dsoData" HEIGHT=0 WIDTH=0>
  <PARAM NAME="Server" VALUE="http://www.yourserver.com">
  <PARAM NAME="Connect" VALUE="DSN=books;UID=anon;PWD=">
  <PARAM NAME="SQL" VALUE="SELECT * FROM BookList">
</OBJECT>
```

Creating the instance of the DSO on the client automatically instantiates the `DataFactory` and `Data Binding Agent` objects. Notice that the DSO takes parameters that define how to connect to the web server machine (the `Server` parameter) and the database itself, which could be on a separate machine from the web server. It also specifies the SQL statement that selects the data required from the database.

Data Source Objects for XML

If we want to display and manipulate XML data using data binding techniques, we can't provide the same kind of parameters as we do for connecting to a relational database (as in the previous code example). Instead, we need a data source object that can work with XML. There are several options available:

❑   The MS Java DSO Applet for IE4 or IE5

❑   The MSXML Parser for IE4 or IE5

❑   An XML Data Island using the `<XML>` element (IE5 only)

❑   The Latest RDS Components

The MS Java DSO Applet for IE4 or IE5

A Java applet is packaged with the latest Microsoft Java runtime installation, which you can download from the Java section of the Microsoft web site. It's also available separately from the same location. This is what an instance of the Java DSO might look like:

```
<APPLET CODE="com.ms.xml.dso.XMLDSO.class"
        ID="dsoBookList" WIDTH="0" HEIGHT="0" MAYSCRIPT="TRUE">
  <PARAM NAME="URL" VALUE="booklist.xml">
</APPLET>
```

The single parameter is the URL of the XML file to load into the DSO. In this case, we've specified a file on the server named `booklist.xml`.

The MSXML Parser for IE4 or IE5

Microsoft provides a parser written in C++ that can be used to read an XML document and cache it on the client. This parser is the same as we've used in previous chapters to access XML via the Document Object Model (DOM). However, it can also act as a DSO for data binding in exactly the same way as the other DSOs we describe here.

We usually instantiate the object using script code running on the client:

```
<SCRIPT LANGUAGE="JavaScript">
  var objXML = new ActiveXObject('microsoft.XMLDOM');
  objXML.load('booklist.xml');
...
</SCRIPT>
```

Note that this component is installed with Internet Explorer 5, Windows 2000 and some other client-side software such as MS Office 2000. It isn't installed with Windows 9x or Internet Explorer 4, but you can download and install it from the Microsoft XML site at http://msdn.microsoft.com/xml/default.asp.

An XML Data Island using the <XML> element (IE5 only)

If we can ditch the requirements for backward compatibility with IE4, we can use the new <XML> element that is supported in IE5 as our data source object. This is far easier and more efficient than using the Java applet or any other technique. It creates a **data island** within our HTML page, which acts as a DSO that we can reference and use with data binding or (as you'll see later) in client-side script.

We can create an inline XML data island by inserting the XML into the page directly, within the <XML> element. Here, we've set the ID attribute to "dsoBookList", and this magically becomes our DSO:

```
...
<XML ID="dsoBookList">
  <?xml version="1.0"?>
  <booklist>
    <book>
      <code>16-041</code>
      <category>HTML</category>
      <release_date>1999-10-07</release_date>
      <title>Instant XHTML</title>
      <sales>127853</sales>
    </book>
    <book>
      ...
    </book>
    ... etc ...
  </booklist>
</XML>
...
```

Rather than embedding the data directly into the HTML page, it generally makes a lot more sense to link to it. This makes it far easier to update the XML data without having to edit the HTML page, which could contain a lot of peripheral content such as presentation information and script code. To link to an XML file, we use the SRC attribute of the <XML> element:

```
<XML ID="dsoBookList" SRC="booklist.xml"></XML>
```

Note that <XML> is, in fact, an HTML element, and not an XML element. It is used in an HTML page to denote a section of the page that the browser should treat as being XML rather than HTML. It must have a proper closing tag as shown in the code above. The XML shorthand syntax will not work, so you cannot use:

```
<XML ID="dsoBookList" SRC="wontwork.xml" />
```

The Latest RDS Components

In the most recent version of ADO (version 2.5), the RDS DSO has been updated and now includes a new property named URL. This accepts the URL of an XML document, and the RDS DSO then exposes it in the same way as the other XML DSOs we've been discussing:

```
<!-- create an RDS DSO object -->
<OBJECT CLASSID="clsid:BD96C556-65A3-11D0-983A-00C04FC29E33"
        ID="dsoData" HEIGHT="0" WIDTH="0">
  <PARAM NAME="URL" VALUE="booklist.xml">
</OBJECT>
```

It might seem strange that this is the case, but it comes about because ADO now supports XML as a native persisted recordset format, as we saw in the previous chapter. So the DSO that the ADO team produces has to be able to handle their new XML-based data format.

Source Data Updates with XML

The various XML DSOs try to do for XML what the RDS DSO did for any ODBC-compliant data source. However, they all have one very large failing – they can only **read** data and display it. They can't automatically do server-side **updates** to the data as RDS does, because there is no server-located component to perform the action. With XML data binding, it's all done on the client.

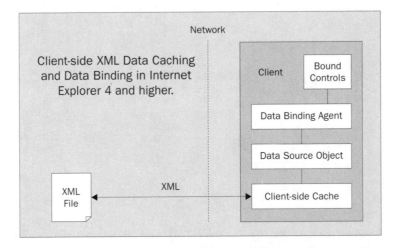

Besides, the XML source we've been using here is a text file on the server's disk, so all kinds of issues arise concerning concurrency when doing updates. The result is that, if we want to update the XML source data, we need to build a custom solution, or look for other technologies that can do it for us.

Displaying XML with Data Binding

In this section of the chapter, we'll look at how we bind our XML data to HTML controls and other elements in a web page. The technique is identical to that for traditional RDS data binding using recordsets extracted from relational databases. However, there are a few issues that arise due to the sometimes unstructured nature of XML documents. First, we'll summarize the basics of data binding.

Binding Elements to the Cached Data

All the DSOs expose the data that is cached on the client as a standard disconnected ADO recordset. Each field (or column) in the recordset can be bound to one or more of a selected range of elements in a web page. Thankfully, this is not some new custom set of elements that has been added to the browser, but the normal HTML controls that we use in our ordinary forms every day.

In IE4 and IE5, all HTML control elements – such as the INPUT TYPE="TEXT", INPUT TYPE="RADIO" and TEXTAREA – have attributes that are used to perform the connection between the data-binding agent and the control. Some other HTML elements, such as SPAN, DIV, IMG, PARAM, and others, also provide the same attributes and use the values to define the setting (i.e. the text content or the source of an image) that will be applied to that element.

The special attributes that these controls have are:

❑ DATASRC, which indicates which data source object the control is linked to (there can be more than one DSO on a page). In the special case of the TABLE element, all the records stored in the client-side data cache are displayed by the repetition of 'template' HTML code that defines how a row in the table corresponds to the data in the columns of each record

❑ DATAFLD is used in all elements (except generally the TABLE element) to define which column or field in the recordset this control should be bound to. The special case where this attribute is used with a TABLE element is for providing nested tables to display hierarchical and master/detail recordset data

❑ DATAFORMATAS is used with elements that provide a textual representation of the field or column value, and instructs the browser as to whether to parse the data (treat it as HTML) or just display it 'as is' (i.e. as text). The possible values for this attribute are "TEXT" and "HTML", with the default if omitted being "TEXT"

So, once our XML data has been retrieved and cached locally by a DSO, we can use it to populate HTML elements in the web page. This is the point where the actual binding goes on, where we connect fields in the recordset with appropriate controls or elements on the page. After the connection is complete and the data-binding agent has accomplished its task, they act just like bound controls in any other environment – such as Microsoft Access.

The HTML Elements Used in Data Binding

The full list of elements that can take part in data binding is shown in the following table. Note that the property of the element varies, depending on the element itself. For example, an <IMG> element uses the value in the bound field as the src property (i.e. the SRC attribute), so we would make sure that this field contains the URL of the image we want to display.

Some elements can be used to update the data in the cached recordset, and some can also display the value that they are bound to as HTML or text. Only the TABLE element can be used for tabular (i.e. repeated record) data binding. We'll look at this topic shortly:

HTML element	Bound property	Update data?	Tabular binding?	Display as HTML?
A	href	No	No	No
APPLET	param	Yes	No	No
BUTTON	innerText *and* innerHTML	No	No	Yes

Table continued on following page

HTML element	Bound property	Update data?	Tabular binding?	Display as HTML?
DIV	innerText *and* innerHTML	No	No	Yes
FRAME	src	No	No	No
IFRAME	src	No	No	No
IMG	src	No	No	No
INPUT TYPE="CHECKBOX"	checked	Yes	No	No
INPUT TYPE="HIDDEN"	value	Yes	No	No
INPUT TYPE="LABEL"	value	Yes	No	No
INPUT TYPE="PASSWORD"	value	Yes	No	No
INPUT TYPE="RADIO"	checked	Yes	No	No
INPUT TYPE="TEXT"	value	Yes	No	No
LABEL	innerText *and* innerHTML	No	No	Yes
MARQUEE	innerText *and* innerHTML	No	No	Yes
OBJECT	param	Yes	No	No
SELECT	text *of selected* option	Yes	No	No
SPAN	innerText *and* innerHTML	No	No	Yes
TABLE	*none*	No	Yes	No
TEXTAREA	value	Yes	No	No

So, given a simple XML document named booklist.xml, which looks like this:

```
<?xml version="1.0"?>
<booklist>
  <book>
    <code>16-041</code>
    <category>HTML</category>
    <release_date>1999-10-07</release_date>
    <title>Instant XHTML</title>
    <sales>127853</sales>
  </book>
  <book>
     ...
  </book>
  ... etc ...
</booklist>
```

We can bind a SPAN element to the value in the code element, which is in a recordset exposed by a DSO that has the ID of dsoBookList, using:

```
<SPAN DATASRC="#dsoBookList" DATAFLD="code"></SPAN>
```

The value of the code field in the current record in the recordset would then be displayed in the page within the SPAN element as plain text (the default). If the code field contains HTML formatting within the value, we can cause the browser to render it as such using:

```
<SPAN DATASRC="#dsoBookList" DATAFLD="code" DATAFORMATAS="HTML"></SPAN>
```

Including HTML in an XML Document

However, bear in mind that in our case, the data is coming from an XML document. HTML markup generally can't be included in XML in its native form, because some elements like <HR> don't conform to XML syntax requirements – they have no closing tag. And if the XML document contains a schema or data type definition (DTD) that specifies the structure, any HTML elements will probably void the definition. In this case, the HTML data must either be included in a CDATA section within the XML document:

```
<code><![CDATA[<B><I>Instant XHTML</I></B>]]></code>
```

Or else, the angled brackets can be escaped individually (i.e. the data must be 'HTML encoded'):

```
<code>&lt;B&gt;&lt;I&gt;Instant XHTML&lt;/I&gt;&lt;/B&gt;</code>
```

Types of Data Binding

The Data Binding Agent object can provide two types of data binding:

❑ **Tabular data binding** (sometimes referred to as table repetition agent binding)

❑ **Single record data binding** (often called current record data binding)

Tabular Data Binding

Tabular data binding depends on the ability of the <TABLE> element to repeat the contents of the <TBODY> section once for each record. The data source object is identified within the opening <TABLE> tag, and the column or field name for each bound control is identified within each table cell. Note that the <TD> element itself does not take part in the data binding process. Instead, a bound element is placed within each cell. This could be a <SPAN> or a <DIV> element, or one of the other HTML controls. For example:

```
...
<XML ID="dsoBookList" SRC="booklist.xml"></XML>
...
<TABLE DATASRC="#dsoBookList">
 <THEAD>
  <TR>
   <TH>Code</TH>
   <TH>Category</TH>
```

```
      <TH>Release Date</TH>
      <TH>Title</TH>
      <TH>Sales</TH>
    </TR>
  </THEAD>
  <TBODY>
    <TR>
      <TD><SPAN DATAFLD="code"></SPAN></TD>
      <TD><SPAN DATAFLD="category"></SPAN></TD>
      <TD><SPAN DATAFLD="release_date"></SPAN></TD>
      <TD><B><SPAN DATAFLD="title"></B></SPAN></TD>
      <TD><SPAN DATAFLD="sales"></SPAN></TD>
    </TR>
  </TBODY>
</TABLE>
...
```

Note that the use of a <TBODY> element is not mandatory when you want all the contents of the table to be repeated for each record, and in fact it is often omitted. IE will repeat all bound elements one for each record automatically even if there is no <TBODY> element.

Here's the result displayed in Internet Explorer 5.0 with the sample `booklist.xml` file we provide. This example page, named `tabular_binding.htm`, is included with the rest of the samples for this book, and can be downloaded from http:/www.wrox.com/:

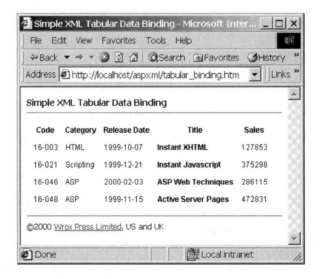

Table Paging with Tabular Data Binding

ADO recordsets support **paging**, which is useful if there are a lot of records to display. When tabular data binding is used, a <TABLE> is bound to the DSO that provides the source recordset and both the DSO properties and the properties of the underlying recordset are exposed through this element. The properties of the recordset include the `dataPageSize` property. This is mapped in HTML to the `DATAPAGESIZE` attribute of the table:

❑ `DATAPAGESIZE` – sets the maximum number of records that will be displayed within the body of a table

By setting this attribute in the opening HTML <TABLE> tag, we can create a table that displays only a specified number of records:

```
<TABLE DATASRC="#dsoBookList" DATAPAGESIZE="10">
```

Then, we can move through the recordset by using its nextPage and previousPage methods, as exposed by the DSO. In IE5, two new methods have been added, firstPage and lastPage, which allow us to go directly to the first or last page of records. The bound table also exposes the recordNumber property of the underlying data set for each element within the table.

Multiple Recordset (Nested Table) Data Binding

It's possible to use a DSO to embed data into a web page where that data doesn't fit neatly into a single table. This is the case with data that has repeating groups of records for each master record – generally referred to as master/detail recordsets. For example, given a list of books, each one might have more than one author. We can't express this relationship neatly within a single table, so we usually lift out the repeating group into a separate table, and link (or JOIN) it back to the master table:

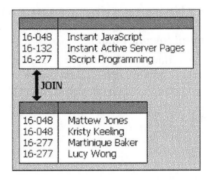

We can express this data as a hierarchical recordset and display it using nested tables. However, it's not all plain sailing when using XML data of this form, as the XML DSOs generally fail to expose it as a master/detail recordset successfully unless it follows a specific format. As an example, the following data file, named nonsym_books.xml, has repeating groups of <author> elements, each within an <authorlist> element. Because there could be zero, one or more authors for each book, the recordset is not 'symmetrical':

```xml
<?xml version="1.0" ?>
<booklist>
  <book>
    <code>16-048</code>
    <title>Instant Javascript</title>
    <sales>375298</sales>
    <authorlist>
      <author>
        <first_name>Martin</first_name>
        <last_name>Williams</last_name>
      </author>
      <author>
        <first_name>Cheryl</first_name>
        <last_name>Caprialdi</last_name>
      </author>
    </authorlist>
```

```
    </book>
    <book>
      <code>23-177</code>
      <title>Javascript Today</title>
      <sales>118524</sales>
      <authorlist>
        <author>
          <first_name>Angela</first_name>
          <last_name>Millania</last_name>
        </author>
      </authorlist>
    </book>
    ... etc ...
</booklist>
```

You can see that there are two authors for the first <book> element, but only one for the second. There may even be <book> elements in the data that have no authors (written by a ghost author perhaps?). In this form, the file won't display master/detail records correctly – in other words, the repeated author names will not appear unless we add some extra bits and pieces to force it to work.

XML File Structure for Master/Detail Record Binding

The reason is that the repeated data (the list of authors) is not directly within each <book> element. There is an <authorlist> element containing them, very much in the style of the 'tree' structure as is popular for XML files. Instead, we require a data file that contains the repeated elements directly within the parent 'record'. Look at the next extract to see how the <author> element is located and repeated directly within the <book> element:

```
    ...
    <book>
      <code>16-048</code>
      <title>Instant Javascript</title>
      <sales>375298</sales>
      <author>
        <first_name>Martin</first_name>
        <last_name>Williams</last_name>
      </author>
      <author>
        <first_name>Cheryl</first_name>
        <last_name>Caprialdi</last_name>
      </author>
    </book>
    ...
```

Master/Detail HTML Tables

To use this kind of master/detail data with our XML DSO for data binding, we have to use **nested** tables:

```
    ...
    <XML ID="dsoBookList" SRC="booklist.xml"></XML>
    ...
    <!-- outer table bound to master recordset, no DATAFLD attribute -->
    <TABLE DATASRC="#dsoBookList">
      <THEAD>
```

```
    <TR>
     <TH>Code</TH>
     <TH>Title</TH>
     <TH>Sales</TH>
     <TH>Author(s)</TH>
    </TR>
  </THEAD>
  <TBODY>
   <TR>
    <TD><SPAN DATAFLD="code"></SPAN></TD>
    <TD><B><SPAN DATAFLD="title"></B></SPAN></TD>
    <TD><SPAN DATAFLD="sales"></SPAN></TD>
    <TD>
     <!-- inner table bound to detail recordset via DATAFLD attribute-->
     <TABLE DATASRC="#dsoBookList" DATAFLD="author">
      <TR>
       <TD>
        <SPAN DATAFLD="first_name"></SPAN><SPAN DATAFLD="last_name"></SPAN>
       </TD>
      </TR>
     </TABLE>
    </TD>
   </TR>
  </TBODY>
 </TABLE>
 ...
```

This code contains a definition of a table that is bound to the DSO named `dsoBookList`. Within one of the table cells is a nested `<TABLE>` element that is also bound to `dsoBookList`. However, this table also has the `<author>` field specified in the binding, through the `DATAFLD` attribute. Within this nested table are the bindings to the `<first_name>` and `<last_name>` elements. The next screenshot shows the result. This sample page is named `nested_binding.htm`:

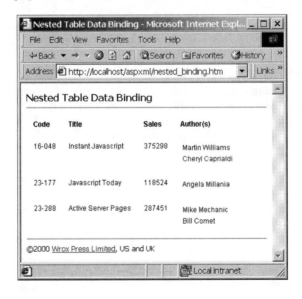

And if the data contained another level of 'nesting', i.e. another layer of repeated elements such as multiple first names, we would handle this in exactly the same way by adding another bound table within the existing one. So, this technique also provides us with a solution for the earlier XML document, where the author details are placed within an `<authorlist>` element. We can include a third level of table nesting, so that we have a table bound to the main (master) recordset, which holds a nested table bound to the `<authorlist>` field, which in turn holds another nested table bound to the `<author>` field.

Single Record Data Binding

Tabular display is fine for displaying data, but to edit it we really need to be able to display the values from one record at a time within HTML controls. As soon as a recordset is created by a DSO, the first record becomes the current record, exactly as it does when the recordset is created directly with ADO (if the recordset is empty, the `EOF` and `BOF` properties are both `True` at this point). We can display the values from the current record in any of the bindable HTML elements listed earlier by setting their `DATASRC` and `DATAFLD` properties. For example:

```
...
<XML ID="dsoBookList" SRC="booklist.xml"></XML>
...
Code:
<INPUT ID="Code" TYPE="TEXT" DATASRC="#dsoBookList" DATAFLD="code" SIZE="5">
<P>Title:
<INPUT ID="Title" TYPE="TEXT" DATASRC="#dsoBookList" DATAFLD="title" SIZE="30">
<P>Category:
<SELECT ID="Category" DATASRC="#dsoBookList" DATAFLD="CATEGORY" SIZE="1">
  <OPTION VALUE="HTML">HTML
  <OPTION VALUE="Scripting">Scripting
  <OPTION VALUE="ASP">ASP
</SELECT>
<P>Release date:
<SPAN ID="Release" DATASRC="#dsoBookList" DATAFLD="RELEASE_DATE"></SPAN>
<P>Sales to date:
<SPAN ID="Sales" DATASRC="#dsoBookList" DATAFLD="SALES"></SPAN><P>
...
```

Navigating the Recordset

If we are displaying only a single record at a time, we need to provide a way for users to move to another record. This is accomplished using the standard methods of the DSO that are exposed via ADO: `move`, `moveFirst`, `moveLast`, `moveNext` and `movePrevious`. So we can add some fancy controls to allow users to navigate through the records – here using the IE-specific `<BUTTON>` element:

```
...
<TABLE>
<TR><TD>
<BUTTON ONCLICK="dsoBookList.recordset.MoveFirst()">
     |&lt; 
</BUTTON >
<BUTTON ONCLICK="if (! dsoBookList.recordset.BOF)
                    dsoBookList.recordset.MovePrevious()">
   &lt; 
</BUTTON>
<BUTTON ONCLICK="if (! dsoBookList.recordset.EOF)
                    dsoBookList.recordset.MoveNext()">
```

```
      &gt; 
   </BUTTON >
   <BUTTON ONCLICK="dsoBookList.recordset.MoveLast()">
      &gt;| 
   </BUTTON >
   </TD></TR>
   </TABLE>
   ...
```

Note that we check the BOF property of the recordset before attempting to move backward, and the EOF property before attempting to move forward. This prevents errors being caused by moving beyond the limits of the recordset. The result looks something like this sample page named `current_binding.htm`:

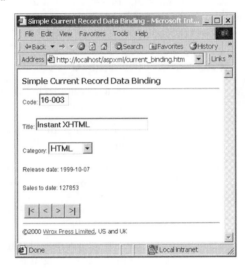

Data Binding Events

Both a DSO embedded within the page, and the browser itself, raise events that can be trapped and used in script on the client. We'll look at these events very briefly next. They can be divided into two groups: those raised by the browser or the controls on the page (when the user navigates to another page or edits the data in the HTML controls), and those raised by a DSO as the user edits the data it exposes. When a page containing a DSO is unloaded, or when the user edits the data in HTML controls that are bound to a DSO, various events are raised. Some can be cancelled by returning the value false from the event handler routine:

Event	Cancelable?	Description
onbeforeupdate	**Yes**	Occurs before the data in the control is passed to the DSO.
onafterupdate	No	Occurs after the data in the control has been passed to the DSO.
onerrorupdate	**Yes**	Occurs if an error prevents the data being passed to the DSO.
onbeforeunload	No	Occurs before the current page is unloaded.

The window object raises the onbeforeunload event, while the rest are raised by HTML controls on the page. With the exception of the onbeforeunload event, all events bubble up through the document hierarchy. So, we can display a message when the user changes the value in a control with:

```
<INPUT ID="txtTitle" DATASRC="#dsoBookList" DATAFLD="title">
...
<SCRIPT LANGUAGE="JScript">
function txtTitle.onbeforeupdate() {
  return confirm("Are you sure you want to change this value ?");
}
</SCRIPT>
```

The DSO itself raises events as various actions take place. The first four are concerned with indicating the current state of the DSO as it loads the data. The others are fired when the 'current record' changes as the user moves through the recordset, or when records are inserted, deleted or changed:

Event	Cancelable?	Description
ondataavailable	No	Occurs periodically while data is arriving from the data source
ondatasetcomplete	No	Occurs when all the data has arrived from the data source
ondatasetchanged	No	Occurs when the data set changes, such as when a filter is applied
onreadystatechange	No	Occurs when the readyState property of the DSO changes
onrowenter	No	Occurs for a record when it becomes the current one during navigating the recordset
onrowexit	**Yes**	Occurs for a record before another becomes the current record during navigation
onrowsdelete	No	New in IE5. Occurs when rows are about to be deleted from the current recordset
onrowsinserted	No	New in IE5. Occurs after rows are inserted into the current recordset
oncellchange	No	New in IE5. Occurs when the data in a bound control or table cell changes and the focus moves from that cell

Only the onrowexit event can be cancelled by returning false from the event handler routine. All events bubble up through the document hierarchy. It's usual to take advantage of the ondatasetcomplete event for any script that you want to run once the data has arrived. Here, we're using an <INPUT> element named txtStatus to display appropriate messages:

```
<INPUT ID="txtStatus" VALUE="Initializing, please wait ...">
...
<SCRIPT LANGUAGE="JavaScript">
```

```
    function dsoBookList.ondatasetcomplete() {
      txtStatus.value = "Data arrived OK";
    }
  </SCRIPT>
```

Accessing Data in a DSO with Script

We've already seen that data embedded in a web page through a Data Source Object is exposed as a recordset, and that this recordset can be used in data binding. However, the DSOs go further than this. Once data binding has been completed, the data in our source recordset or XML document is exposed as a standard ADO client-side (or disconnected) recordset, irrespective of the kind of DSO and data file we use. We can get a reference to this recordset from the DSO's `recordset` property:

```
  myRecordset = dsoMyDSO.recordset;        // JavaScript or JScript
  Set myRecordset = dsoMyDSO.recordset     ' same but in VBScript
```

Once we have a reference to the recordset, we can access the fields to get their values:

```
  theValue = myRecordset('field_name');    // JavaScript or JScript
  theValue = myRecordset("field_name")     ' same but in VBScript
```

And, of course, we can access all the other properties or methods of the recordset as well. However, as we've seen, this really only makes sense if the recordset is symmetrical; in other words if it looks like a set of normal database tables with the same number of fields in each record. The DSO will attempt to expose it as such, but with irregular XML-formatted data, this isn't always going to produce something useful. In particular, IE5 may create a recordset that bears no relation to what you expect if there are different numbers or types of child elements in each record.

In this case, we will usually access this kind of data using a different technique. This involves the Document Object Model (DOM), which exposes all the objects in the page as a tree and a series of collections. In particular, it exposes the XML content of the page (or a linked XML file) as a structure that we can access using special scripting techniques as you've seen in previous chapters. Of course, we can access any XML data using the DOM if we wish – it doesn't *have* to be in an 'irregular' format.

XML Data Binding in IE5 with Attributes

One issue that you will no doubt come across when you use data binding via the <XML> element in IE5 is that it all seems to fall apart if there are any attributes within the opening element tags. Unfortunately, the data-binding agent in IE5 does not parse the XML data in the same way as the RDS or Java parser components, and can fail to see or display the values of elements containing attributes.

The reason is due to the way that the latest versions of ADO can stream or persist data from a database table into XML automatically. But when they do, the field values are placed in attributes of an element rather than with each field as a separate element:

```
  <z:row fieldname='fieldvalue' fieldname='fieldvalue' fieldname='fieldvalue' />
```

rather than something more familiar like:

```
<record>
  <fieldname>fieldvalue</fieldname>
  <fieldname>fieldvalue</fieldname>
  <fieldname>fieldvalue</fieldname>
</record>
```

In this case, you can continue to use the parser component instead of a data island in IE5, but as data islands are more efficient and don't need a parser to be pre-installed by the user, it's worth looking at work-arounds that are possible to solve the problem. It arises because the IE5 data-binding agent treats an attribute in an element as a separate nested element, so:

```
<myElement myAttribute="attr_value">element_value</myElement>
```

is treated as though it were:

```
<myElement><myAttribute>attr_value</myAttribute>element_value</myElement>
```

To get round this, we have to use a data-bound table within the data-bound element to 'get at' the element's value rather than the attribute value. The text value of the element can be obtained by binding to the $TEXT property of the element:

```
<TABLE DATASRC="#dsoData" DATAFLD="myElement">
  <TR>
    <TD>
      <INPUT TYPE="TEXT" DATASRC="#dsoData" DATAFLD="$TEXT">
    </TD>
  </TR>
</TABLE>
```

If we are using tabular data binding, we already have a table to hold the element values. In this case, we place a nested table inside each existing table cell:

```
<TABLE DATASRC="#dsoData">
  <TR>
    <TD>
      <TABLE DATASRC="#dsoData" DATAFLD="firstColumnName">
        <TR><TD><SPAN DATAFLD="$TEXT"></SPAN></TD></TR>
      </TABLE>
    </TD>
  </TR>
  <TR>
    <TD>
      <TABLE DATASRC="#dsoData" DATAFLD="nextColumnName">
        <TR><TD><SPAN DATAFLD="$TEXT"></SPAN></TD></TR>
      </TABLE>
    </TD>
  </TR>
  ... etc ...
</TABLE>
```

This also means that if we need to access the values using script, via the recordset created by the data island, we have to refer to the $TEXT property of the nested element as well. For example, we would use:

```
var objDI = document.all('dsoData');
strValue = objDI.recordset.fields('column_name').value.fields('$TEXT');
```

instead of the more usual:

```
var objDI = document.all('dsoData');
strValue = objDI.recordset.fields('column_name').value;
```

Summary

In this chapter we looked at the basics of client-side data binding in Internet Explorer. We discussed the way that it works with ADO recordsets, and examined the differences that occur when we come to use XML data instead. As we found, moving to XML means losing many of the built-in features that make data binding with ADO so easy. However, there are ways to get round these issues, as we'll see in the next chapter.

In this chapter, we looked at:

- ❑ What is data binding?
- ❑ Displaying XML with data binding

So, having seen some theory and some practice of data binding with XML, we'll move on in the following chapter to consider the other issues, and see some real examples of it in use. This involves looking at how we can create XML documents for data binding, and update the source data store from an XML document.

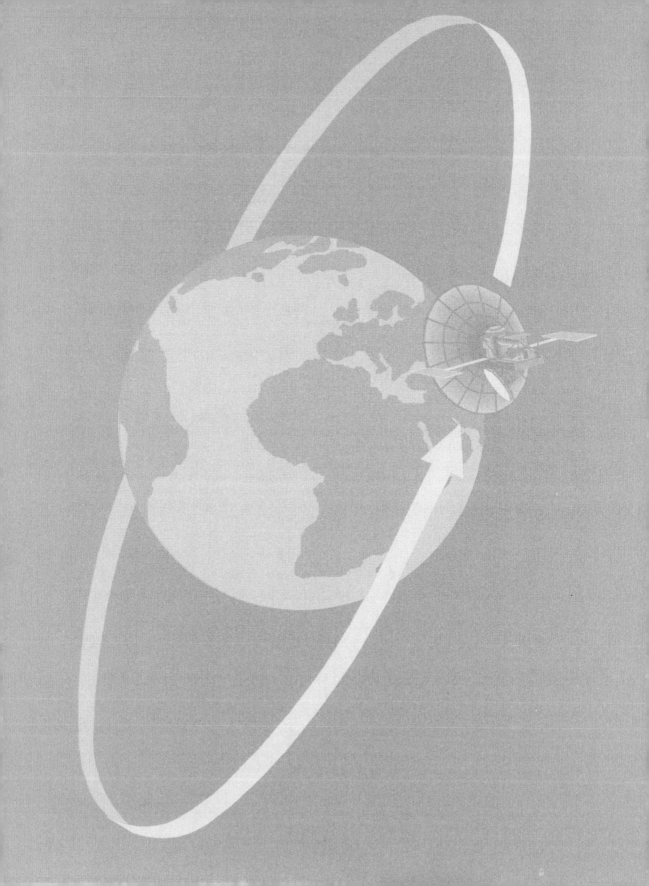

Working with XML Data Binding

In the previous chapter we looked at what data binding is, and how we can use it in Internet Explorer to create a richer, more responsive and more intuitive interface for working with data in a Web page. We saw how we can use an XML document as the source data for data binding, and discovered some of the problems that this introduces - in particular the loss of many of the features such as automatic management of updates that we get when binding to an ADO recordset.

So, in this chapter, we'll look at how we can get round some of the problems when we use XML documents with data binding. We'll see some of the techniques available for:

❑   Creating XML documents for data binding

❑   Updating the Source XML document on the server

We start with a look at some of the different ways that we can create XML documents from a data source.

Creating XML Documents Dynamically

The combination of XML and data binding on the client provides a very powerful and bandwidth-friendly way to provide data-management applications for users. The client behaves in a similar way to compiled applications written in languages like Visual Basic, C++, Delphi, or Office-style applications like Microsoft Access. In this section we move away from the client to look at the server side of the process, and explore how we can use ASP and other techniques to create XML documents dynamically.

Creating XML Documents from a Data Store

You'll have noticed that the XML DSOs we looked at in the previous section (with the exception of the in-line XML in an <XML> element) have a parameter for the XML source. In the Java DSO and the new RDS DSO, this is the URL parameter, set with a <PARAM> element:

```
<PARAM NAME="URL" VALUE="booklist.xml">
```

or as the `url` property at run-time. In an IE5 data island, the XML source is specified by an `SRC` attribute:

```
<XML ID="dsoBookList" SRC="booklist.xml"></XML>
```

These both assume that the source is an XML-format text file named `booklist.xml`. However, it could just as easily be `booklist.asp`, as long as the MIME-type of the file is `"text/xml"` so that the browser recognizes it as an XML file.

> *This also seems to work adequately without the MIME-type as `"text/xml"` in IE5; presumably the browser sees the opening `<?xml version="1.0"?>` element and behaves appropriately.*

So, we can get an ASP file to create our XML document as a stream rather than using a disk file. This can be done in at least four different ways:

❑ with ASP script

❑ with a custom component

❑ with the ADO Persistence methods

❑ with the SQLXML Technology Preview

Let's now take a very brief look at each one of these.

Creating XML with ASP Script

The simplest, but probably not the most efficient way of creating XML is to simply iterate through a set of data and write it out enclosed with the appropriate XML tags. Best of all, you get to create the XML in whatever format you like. This example creates an XML document from a database table containing information about famous Wrox authors, and streams it back to the browser:

```
<%@LANGUAGE="VBScript"%>
<%
Response.Buffer = False  'stream output to client as it is created
Response.ContentType="text/xml"  'tell the browser that it is XML
%>
<?xml version="1.0"?>
<authorlist>
<%
'-- select all the author details --
Set oConn = Server.CreateObject("ADODB.Connection")
oConn.Open "your_connection_string"
strSQL="SELECT * FROM Authors ORDER BY tLinkName"
Set oRs = oConn.Execute(strSQL)
strPhotoURL = ""
strInterview = ""
QUOT = Chr (34)
Do While Not oRs.EOF
  strLinkName = oRs("tLinkName")
  If oRS.Fields("bPhoto") <> 0 Then  'there is a photo on our server
    strPhotoURL = "http://webdev.wrox.co.uk/resources/authors/" _
                & strLinkName & ".gif"
```

```
      End If
      If oRS.Fields("bInterview") <> 0 Then   'there is an interview on our server
        strInterview = "http://webdev.wrox.co.uk/resources/authors/" _
                      & strLinkName & ".htm"
      End If
      Response.Write "  <authorinfo>" & vbCrlf
      Response.Write "    <author_name>" & oRs("tName") _
                      & "</author_name>" & vbCrlf
      Response.Write "    <SHORT_BIO>" & Server.HTMLEncode(oRs("tBio")) _
                      & "</SHORT_BIO>" & vbCrlf
      Response.Write "    <photo_url>" & strPhotoURL & "</photo_url>" & vbCrlf
      Response.Write "    <interview_url>" & strInterview _
                      & "</interview_url>" & vbCrlf

      Response.Write "  </authorinfo>" & vbCrlf
      oRs.MoveNext
Loop
oRs.Close
%>
</authorlist>
```

This creates an XML file that looks something like:

```
<?xml version="1.0"?>
<authorlist>
  <authorinfo>
    <author_name>Dave Sussman</author_name>
    <short_bio>David Sussman is a developer, trainer ...etc...</short_bio>
    <photo_url>http://webdev.wrox.co.uk/resources/authors/sussmand.gif</photo_url>
    <interview_url>
    http://webdev.wrox.co.uk/resources/authors/sussmand.htm
    </interview_url>
  </authorinfo>
  <authorinfo>
    <author_name>Chris Ullman</author_name>
    <short_bio>Chris is a computer science graduate ...etc...</short_bio>
    <photo_url>http://webdev.wrox.co.uk/resources/authors/ullmanc.gif</photo_url>
    <interview_url>
    http://webdev.wrox.co.uk/resources/authors/ullmanc.htm
    </interview_url>
  </authorinfo>
  <authorinfo>
    <author_name>Frank Boumphrey</author_name>
    <short_bio>Frank Boumphrey currently works for ...etc...</short_bio>
    <photo_url>
    http://webdev.wrox.co.uk/resources/authors/boumphreyf.gif
    </photo_url>
    <interview_url>
    http://webdev.wrox.co.uk/resources/authors/boumphreyf.htm
    </interview_url>
  </authorinfo>
  ...
  ...
</authorlist>
```

Notice how we include a full URL to the author's photo and interview page. This demonstrates one of the core reasons for using XML to distribute information. As the file structure is simple text, and in a standard format and structure, anyone can open this ASP page and get the XML data stream sent to them. They can then use it client-side in any way they like, and the URLs will still work because they point to the relevant resources on our server. The XML data could be used as the source to power an 'author info' search engine, combined with XML data from other sources, parsed or modified client-side to extract particular information, and displayed in any way that the recipient wishes.

Here, we're displaying it using client-side data binding. This sample page is named author_list.htm. Notice how the two URLs are used with HTML elements that use the DATASRC and DATAFLD attributes in place of the normal HTML attributes. The value of the current record in the recordset is used for the SRC of an <IMG> element when it is data bound, and for the HREF of an <A> element:

```
<XML ID="dsoBookList" SRC="authorlist_xml.asp"></XML>
...
<TABLE DATASRC="#dsoBookList" CELLSPACING="10">
  <TR>
    <TD ROWSPAN="2"><IMG HSPACE="15" DATAFLD="photo_url"></TD>
    <TD><SPAN CLASS="auth_name" DATAFLD="author_name"></SPAN></TD>
  </TR>
  <TR>
    <TD VALIGN="TOP">
      <SPAN DATAFLD="SHORT_BIO"></SPAN><P>
      Read an <B><A DATAFLD="interview_url">interview</A></B> with
      <SPAN DATAFLD="author_name"></SPAN>
    </TD>
  </TR>
</TABLE>
...
```

The result looks like this:

Creating XML with a Custom Component

Many suppliers provide components that can do the same job as ASP when creating XML documents, and we can of course build our own as well. The code used in the previous section can easily be converted to Visual Basic and wrapped up in an ActiveX DLL. This can provide suitable methods that return the XML document as a string, or stream it direct to the browser using `Response.Write`. And, like the all-ASP option described above, we can create the XML with whatever structure we like.

Some commercial components that are available for creating XML documents on various server platforms include:

ASP2XML - creates XML from an ODBC-compliant data source and can update the original data as well
See: http://www.stonebroom.com

DB2XML - a tool for transforming relational databases into XML documents
See: http://www.informatik.fh-wiesbaden.de/~turau/DB2XML/index.html

XML-DBMS - Java Packages for Transferring Data between XML Documents and Relational Databases
See: http://www.informatik.tu-darmstadt.de/DVS1/staff/bourret/xmldbms/readme.html

XMLServlet - A Java Servlet that uses XML instructions to combine XML or HTML templates with one another, and with live database values
See: http://www.beyond.com/PKSN102998/prod.htm

There is also a useful list of components and other XML resources at http://www.xmlsoftware.com/, which acts as a good starting point in a search for information and software of use to your XML-based applications.

Creating XML with the ADO Persistence Methods

In version 2.5 of ADO (as supplied with Windows 2000, or via an upgrade redistributable from the Microsoft Web site), new XML-based features have been added. These were discussed in detail in an earlier chapter. We'll briefly visit the **persistence** features that are directly useful for working with XML. ADO 2.5 fully implements the data persistence feature first introduced in ADO 2.1. This includes the ability to persist data from a recordset into XML format using the `Save` method of the `Recordset` object with the integral ADO constant value `adPersistXML` as the 'format' parameter:

```
objRS.Save "path_and_filename", adPersistXML
```

In this case, the first parameter specifies the full path and name of the XML file to be created. However, ADO 2.5 introduces the concept of a **stream** object, which allows data from recordsets to be passed directly from one application to another without being written to and read from disk. We can use this technique to stream the XML created from the recordset contents direct to the browser by simply replacing the path and filename with the ASP `Response` object:

```
objRS.Save Response, adPersistXML
```

Here's a simple page from the sample files, named `ado_persist_xml.asp`, which persists an ADO recordset as an XML stream to the `Response`:

```
<%@LANGUAGE="VBScript"%>
<!-- METADATA TYPE="typelib"
     FILE="C:\Program Files\Common Files\System\ADO\msado15.dll" -->
<%
Response.Buffer = False
Response.ContentType = "text/xml"
%>

<?xml version="1.0"?>

<%
'create an XML data island from an ADO recordset
strConnect = "connection_string"
strSQL = "SELECT * FROM BookList WHERE tTitle LIKE '%html%'"
Set objRS = Server.CreateObject("ADODB.Recordset")
objRS.Open strSQL, strConnect, adOpenDynamic, adLockOptimistic, adCmdText
objRS.Save Response, adPersistXML   'save it to the Response
objRS.Close
%>
```

Bear in mind that when using ADO like this, we have little control over the structure of the resulting XML document. The structure that is generated by ADO 2.5 includes an XML schema that describes the data structure, followed by a single XML <z:row> element for each record. The following example highlights the actual data in an example XML document:

```
<xml xmlns:s='uuid:BDC6E3F0-6DA3-11d1-A2A3-00AA00C14882'
  xmlns:dt='uuid:C2F41010-65B3-11d1-A29F-00AA00C14882'
  xmlns:rs='urn:schemas-microsoft-com:rowset'
  xmlns:z='#RowsetSchema'>
<s:Schema id='RowsetSchema'>
  <s:ElementType name='row' content='eltOnly' rs:updatable='true'>
    <s:AttributeType name='kBookCode' rs:number='1' rs:writeunknown='true'
                     rs:basecatalog='globalexample' rs:basetable='BookList'
                     rs:basecolumn='kBookCode' rs:keycolumn='true'>
      <s:datatype dt:type='string' dt:maxLength='50' rs:precision='0'
                     rs:maybenull='false'/>
    </s:AttributeType>
    <s:AttributeType name='dReleaseDate' rs:number='2' rs:nullable='true'
                     rs:writeunknown='true' rs:basecatalog='globalexample'
                     rs:basetable='BookList' rs:basecolumn='dReleaseDate'>
      <s:datatype dt:type='dateTime' rs:dbtype='timestamp' dt:maxLength='16'
                     rs:scale='3'rs:precision='23' rs:fixedlength='true'/>
    </s:AttributeType>
    <s:AttributeType name='tTitle' rs:number='3' rs:nullable='true'
                     rs:writeunknown='true' rs:basecatalog='globalexample'
                     rs:basetable='BookList' rs:basecolumn='tTitle'>
      <s:datatype dt:type='string' dt:maxLength='100' rs:precision='0'/>
    </s:AttributeType>
    <s:AttributeType name='tDescription' rs:number='4' rs:nullable='true'
                     rs:writeunknown='true' rs:basecatalog='globalexample'
                     rs:basetable='BookList' rs:basecolumn='tDescription'>
      <s:datatype dt:type='string' dt:maxLength='255' rs:precision='0'/>
    </s:AttributeType>
    <s:extends type='rs:rowbase'/>
  </s:ElementType>
</s:Schema>
```

```
<rs:data>
  <z:row kBookCode='1193' dReleaseDate='1998-01-12T00:00:00'
         tTitle='Instant Netscape DHTML' tDescription='... etc ...'/>
  <z:row kBookCode='1568' dReleaseDate='1998-03-13T00:00:00'
         tTitle='HTML Programmers Reference' tDescription='... etc ...'/>
  <z:row kBookCode='1746' dReleaseDate='1998-03-13T00:00:00'
         tTitle='IE5 Dynamic HTML' tDescription='... etc ...'/>
</rs:data>
</xml>
```

Dynamic Data Binding

Rather than specifying the data binding information as attributes when we create a page, we can use client-side script to set up or change the bindings once the page has loaded, by changing the `dataSrc`, `dataFld` and `dataFormatAs` properties of the appropriate elements. This is usually referred to as **dynamic data binding**. To remove the bindings, we just set the properties to an empty string. To change the binding of elements within a bound table, we must remove the binding of the table first (in the `<TABLE>` tag), change the bindings of the elements in the table, and then reset the binding of the table.

As an example, the following code uses the ADO page we saw earlier to create an XML data island, and then defines a series of three nested tables that will be bound to the data in this data island. Notice that none of the data binding attributes are set at the moment:

```
...
<XML ID="dsoData" SRC="ado_persist_xml.asp"></XML>
...
<!-- table to bind DATASRC="#dsoData" -->
<TABLE ID="tblMain">
  <TR><TD>
    <!-- table to bind DATASRC="#dsoData" DATAFLD="rs:data"-->
    <TABLE ID="tblSub">
      <TR><TD>
        <!-- table to bind DATASRC="#dsoData" DATAFLD="z:row"-->
        <TABLE ID="tblData" CELLPADDING="10">
            <THEAD><TR></TR></THEAD>
            <TBODY><TR></TR></TBODY>
        </TABLE>
      </TD></TR>
    </TABLE>
  </TD></TR>
</TABLE>
...
```

Notice that the innermost `<TABLE>` element defined in the HTML has no cells in the two rows. We'll be adding these to the table dynamically with script code later on. All the script in the page is executed in response to the `window_onload` event. It first gets a reference to the `<XML>` data island element, then accesses the nested recordset in the `<z:row>` section of the XML document, and assigns it to the variable `objRecs`:

```
<SCRIPT LANGUAGE="VBScript">
Sub window_onload()

  QUOT = Chr(34) 'double-quote character
```

```
    'get a reference to the <XML> data island element
    Set objXML = document.all("dsoData")

    'get a reference to the recordset in the data island
    Set objRecs = objXML.Recordset
    Set objRecs = objRecs("rs:data").value
    Set objRecs = objRecs("z:row").value
    ...
```

Now we can get a reference to the heading and body rows of the table, and loop through each of the records in the data section of our recordset. As long as the field name is not "$Text", we have a valid field containing data that we want to place into the page:

```
    ...
    'get a reference to the TR row of the innermost TABLE element
    Set objTableHead = document.all("tblData").rows(0)
    Set objTableRow = document.all("tblData").rows(1)

    'loop through the fields in the recordset
    intSpanID = 0
    For Each objField in objRecs.Fields

      strFieldName = objField.Name
      If strFieldName <> "$Text" Then   'this is a field containing data
        ...
```

However, recall that our table has no cells in the heading or body rows. Before we can fill in the field name or bind this field value to a cell in the table, we need to create the cells first. This is done with the `insertCell` method of the table row object (these methods were new in IE5). We put the field name in the new cell in the heading row, then create a new <SPAN> element with an appropriate DATAFLD attribute and insert it into the new cell in the body row:

```
        ...
        'create a new cell in the heading row of the table
        Set objTableCell = objTableHead.insertCell()
        objTableCell.innerHTML = "<B>" & strFieldName & "</B>"

        'create a new cell in the body row of the table
        Set objTableCell = objTableRow.insertCell()

        'create a SPAN element with appropriate DATAFLD attribute
        strNewSpanElem = "<SPAN DATAFLD=" & QUOT & strFieldName & QUOT & "></SPAN>"

        'insert the SPAN element into the cell
        objTableCell.innerHTML = strNewSpanElem

      End If
    Next
    ...
```

Now, having looped through all the records in the `<z:row>` section of the XML document and created a nested table structure with the correct DATAFLD attributes, we have to add the bindings to each of the tables to make the final connection between the data island and the elements in the page. This is simply a matter of assigning the appropriate `dataFld` and `dataSrc` attribute values to the tables:

```
...
document.all("tblData").dataFld="z:row"
document.all("tblData").dataSrc="#dsoData"
document.all("tblSub").dataFld="rs:data"
document.all("tblSub").dataSrc="#dsoData"
document.all("tblMain").dataSrc="#dsoData"

End Sub
</SCRIPT>
```

The result after all this effort is a data-bound table showing the values from the ADO-persisted XML. This page is available in the samples as `ado_dynamic.htm`:

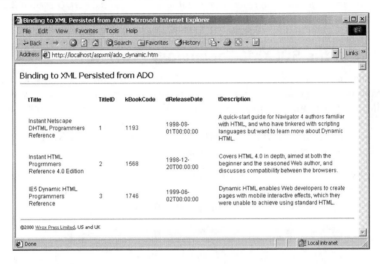

Using the RDS DSO with ADO Persisted Data

We mentioned in the previous chapter, when we discussed the various types of DSO that are available for use with XML, that the RDS DSO that is part of the ADO installation can be used with XML data. We've seen how data persisted as XML from within ADO is hard to access using the ordinary data island created by an `<XML>` element. However, the RDS DSO is designed to cope with this, and uses the schema that accompanies the data to figure out how to handle it.

This means that the DSO is able to expose the data we saw in the previous example data as a simple flat recordset. We no longer have to create multiple nested tables to get at the appropriate values in the XML. The next example, named `ado_xml_rds.htm,` uses the RDS DSO, and therefore needs only a simple table to perform the binding. The result, of course, is exactly the same as with the dynamic binding example we've just looked at:

```
<OBJECT CLASSID="clsid:BD96C556-65A3-11D0-983A-00C04FC29E33"
        ID="dsoData" HEIGHT="0" WIDTH="0">
  <PARAM NAME="URL" VALUE="ado_persist_xml.asp">
</OBJECT>
...
<TABLE ID="tblMain" DATASRC="#dsoData">
  <THEAD>
    <TR>
      <TH>kBookCode</TH>
      <TH>dReleaseDate</TH>
```

```
            <TH>tTitle</TH>
            <TH>tDescription</TH>
        </TR>
    </THEAD>
    <TBODY>
        <TR>
            <TD><SPAN DATAFLD="kBookCode"></SPAN></TD>
            <TD><SPAN DATAFLD="dReleaseDate"></SPAN></TD>
            <TD><SPAN DATAFLD="tTitle"></SPAN></TD>
            <TD><SPAN DATAFLD="tDescription"></SPAN></TD>
        </TR>
    </TBODY>
</TABLE>
```

Remember that this example will only work on client machines that have ADO version 2.5 installed.

Creating XML with the SQLXML Technology Preview

Microsoft has released a technology preview of **SQLXML**, a component that allows a relational database like SQL Server to read and present data in XML format. There is a very good chance that this technology will find its way into the next release of SQL Server, SQL Server 2000, due for release later this year. SQLXML is designed to allow you to access data in SQL Server using standard SQL statements, but have the result returned as XML. You can also use it with XML documents to edit, update, add and delete records in a database as well.

SQLXML works by associating (or **registering**) a virtual root on your Web site with a specific SQL Server database. You can create multiple registrations, each to a different database. The technology preview contains a graphical interface to set up these registrations:

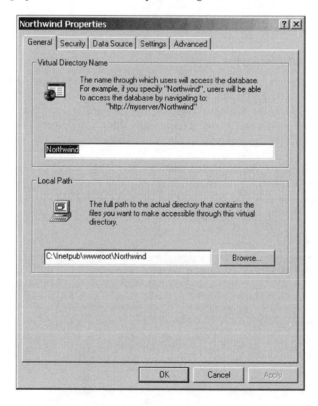

After registration, you simply reference a URL that specifies the virtual root for the database you want to access, and provide the SQL statement that retrieves the appropriate data. For example, providing we have created and registered a virtual root named `examples` pointing to the `GlobalExamples` database, we can get a list of books from our `BookList` table using:

```
http://yourserver/examples?sql=SELECT+*+FROM+BookList+FOR+XML+AUTO
```

This returns an XML document of the form:

```xml
<?xml version="1.0" encoding="UTF-8" ?>
<root>
  <BookList isbn="1-861002-88-2" title="Beginning Components for ASP"
            description="This book is about the broad flavors ... etc..." />
  <BookList isbn"1-861002-61-0" title="Professional Active Server Pages 3.0"
            description="ASP is the Microsoft technology for  ... etc..." />
  ... other books here ...
</root>
```

The format of the returned XML is dictated by the FOR clause at the end of the URL string. The example above uses FOR XML AUTO (the plus signs in the URL represent spaces). By adding the instruction DTD to the end of the FOR clause, we can instruct SQLXML to prefix the XML it returns with a Document Type Definition (DTD):

```
http://yourserver/examples?sql=SELECT+*+FROM+BookList+FOR+XML+AUTO,DTD
```

If we add the XMLDATA instruction, we get the resulting XML prefixed by a schema instead:

```
http://yourserver/examples?sql=SELECT+*+FROM+BookList+FOR+XML+AUTO,XMLDATA
```

The SQL statement can include multiple tables, joined on common key fields. In this case, the result is an XML document with the repeated child records nested within the parent records, exactly as we would expect. For example, the following URL and SQL statement accesses the sample `Northwind` database that comes with SQL Server:

```
http://yourserver/Northwind?sql=SELECT+Customers.CustomerID,OrderID,OrderDate+FROM
+Customers,+Orders+WHERE+Customers.CustomerID=Orders.CustomerID+Order+by+Customers
.CustomerID,OrderID+FOR+XML+AUTO
```

The result set is of the format:

```xml
<?xml version="1.0" encoding="UTF-8" ?>
<root>
  <Customers CustomerID="ALFKI">
    <Orders OrderID="10643" OrderDate="1997-08-25T00:00:00" />
    <Orders OrderID="10692" OrderDate="1997-10-03T00:00:00" />
  </Customers>
  <Customers CustomerID="ANATR">
    <Orders OrderID="10308" OrderDate="1996-09-18T00:00:00" />
  </Customers>
  ... other Customers records here
</root>
```

We can also execute stored procedures, and send parameters to them if required:

```
http://yourserver/Northwind?sql=execute+ProcedureName+@MyParam=12+FOR+XML+AUTO
```

*Appendix H includes more information about setup and configuration of the preview tool. For more information about the **SQL Server XML Technology Preview**, and to download an evaluation copy, check out http://msdn.microsoft.com/xml/articles/xmlsql/default.asp.*

Updating the Source XML Document

In all of the above, we still didn't answer one obvious question: How do we handle updates to the data back on the server? The client can cache the recordset we create, and edit the contents using data-bound controls or by executing script that modifies the contents of the DSOs recordset directly. What the XML DSOs can't do is arrange for that data to be automatically updated back on the server. However we can get round this in at least four ways:

- ❏ with ASP script and the MSXML (or another) parser component
- ❏ with a custom component designed to handle source data updating
- ❏ with the ADO Persistence methods
- ❏ with the SQLXML Technology Preview

Updating with ASP script and the MSXML Component

One of the components of Internet Explorer 5 and Windows 2000 is a C++ parser for XML. This is commonly known as the MSXML parser or MSXML component, though it has a class string (or ProgID) of "microsoft.XMLDOM" (the 'DOM' part, of course, stands for **Document Object Model** - a recommendation from the World Wide Web Consortium). This specifies details of the interfaces that an XML parser or application should provide for accessing any XML document that it hosts.

The MSXML component can load an XML document and present it to our code as a tree. It also provides a series of methods that we can use to traverse the tree, and read the values. Basically, MSXML does the hard work of breaking our XML document down into a manageable and navigable structure. You saw how we can use this component on the server in previous chapters, so we'll just overview the process here.

When working with the MSXML component, we can write the XML string sent from the browser to the server's disk using the `FileSystemObject` in our ASP page, and then open it into the component by specifying the file path and name in a call to the `load` method:

```
'create an instance of the MS XML Parser on the server and load the XML file
Set objXML = Server.CreateObject("microsoft.XMLDOM")
objXML.load "path_and_filename"
...
```

However, it's easier just to feed it directly to the component as a string, this time using the `loadXML` method:

```
'create an instance of MS XML Parser on the server and load XML file
Set objXML = Server.CreateObject("microsoft.XMLDOM")
objXML.loadXML Request.Form("txtXML")
...
```

Once the document has loaded, we can check to see if it was parsed OK – in other words if it is a well-formed document. If not, we display an error message and abort the page:

```
...
'see if it loaded OK, i.e. is a well-formed XML file
If objXML.parseError.errorCode <> 0 Then
   'error loading document so display error details
   strError = "<B>Invalid XML file !</B><BR>" _
            & "File URL: " & objXML.parseError.url & "<BR>" _
            & "Line No.: " & objXML.parseError.line & "<BR>" _
            & "Character: " & objXML.parseError.linepos & "<BR>" _
            & "File Position: " & objXML.parseError.filepos & "<BR>" _
            & "Source Text: " & objXML.parseError.srcText & "<BR>" _
            & "Error Code: " & objXML.parseError.errorCode & "<BR>" _
            & "Description: " & objXML.parseError.reason
   Response.Write strError & "</BODY></HTML>"
   Response.End
End If
...
```

If things went OK, and our XML document has been successfully parsed, we can then use the methods of the DOM to get at the contents. As we extract values from the XML, we use them to build up SQL statements that will update the original data source. Assuming that we have a relatively simple XML document such as:

```
<?xml version="1.0"?>
<booklist_update>
  <book>
    <!-- original book code number used to connect to the correct record -->
    <original_code>16-024</original_code>
    <!-- new values for this record -->
    <code>16-041</code>
    <category>HTML</category>
    <release_date>1998-03-07</release_date>
    <title>Instant HTML</title>
  </book>
  <book>
  ... etc ...
  </book>
</booklist_update>
```

This is the kind of code that we could use to update our data source:

```
...
'completed OK so can access the XML document

'connect to the data source ready to update it
Set objCon = Server.CreateObject("ADODB.Connection")
```

```
objCon.Open "your_connection_string"

'get a reference to the root element of the XML document booklist_update
Set objRoot = objXML.documentElement

'get a reference to the collection of ITEM child nodes
Set colItems = objRoot.childNodes

'loop through each <book> node and collect the values to update the database
For Each objItem in colItems

    'collect the values from the ITEM's child nodes
    Set objNode = objItem.selectSingleNode("original_code")
    strOriginalCode = objNode.text
    Set objNode = objItem.selectSingleNode("code")
    strNewBookCode = objNode.text
    Set objNode = objItem.selectSingleNode("category")
    strNewCategory = objNode.text
    Set objNode = objItem.selectSingleNode("release_date")
    strNewRelDate = objNode.text
    Set objNode = objItem.selectSingleNode("title")
    strNewTitle = objNode.text

    'build a SQL string to update the database
    strSQL = "UPDATE booklist SET kBookCode='" & strNewBookCode & "', " _
          & "tCategory='" & strNewCategory & "', " _
          & "tRelDate='" & strNewRelDate & "', " _
          & "tTitle='" & strNewTitle & "' " _
          & "WHERE kBookCode='" & strOriginalCode & "'"

    'execute this statement to update the data source
    objCon.Execute strSQL

Next
%>
```

The resulting SQL statement that this code creates from our sample XML document is:

```
UPDATE booklist SET kBookCode='16-041', tCategory='HTML', tRelDate='1998-03-07',
tTitle='Instant HTML' WHERE kBookCode='16-024'
```

However, notice that this will execute the SQL statement for every 'row' (i.e. every book) in the XML document. If some haven't been changed, you need to remove these from the XML document first to reduce both unnecessary server-side processing and bandwidth. We'll look into this issue in the next section.

Updating with a Custom Component

We mentioned earlier that you might consider buying or building your own custom components to access a database and return an XML document containing the data. You may also consider using such components to update the original data by feeding them a suitably formatted XML file – much like the ASP example we've just looked at.

However, there are a few issues to be aware of. Firstly, you need to keep a record of the original key value for the record(s) you want to update. This is necessary to be able to match the updated record to the original one in the table, especially if it's the key value that is being changed. That's why we included an extra field in the XML in our previous example, to store the original code number of the book:

```
...
<book>
 <!-- original book code number to use to connect to the correct record -->
 <original_code>16-024</original_code>
 <!-- new values for this record -->
 <code>16-041</code>
 <category>HTML</category>
 <release_date>1998-03-07</release_date>
 <title>Instant HTML</title>
</book>
...
```

Secondly, you'll probably find that you want to send several records to the client for data binding and viewing, but they may only elect to edit one or two of them. In this case, you only want to send back to the server the records that have changed, rather than sending back the whole document. This saves bandwidth and server processing, as only the changed records will be updated.

The easiest way to do this is to add another 'field' to the XML document when you create it, and use it to flag records that are to be updated when the client is editing the data. For example, you could include an element named `<update_action>` in each record, and set the initial value to 'NONE':

```
...
<book>
 <original_code>16-003</original_code>
 <code>16-003</code>
 <category>HTML</category>
 <release_date>1999-10-07</release_date>
 <title>Instant XHTML</title>
 <sales>127853</sales>
 <update_action>NONE</update_action>
</book>
...
```

The user can then change this value themselves (as shown in the next example), or you can set it using script code that runs in response to the data binding `onafterupdate` event of the controls in the page. We chose to display the value of the field in a data-bound drop-down list, allowing the user to change it when they want to update a record:

This sample page, named `send_updates.htm`, also contains a **Save** button. We use it to demonstrate how we can build up an XML document containing just the updated records to send back to our server. It runs a function in the page named `fnSaveChanges`. By iterating through the records, this function can check the value of each record's `<update_action>` element, and only marshal the changed records into the result string if it is not 'NONE':

```
<SCRIPT LANGUAGE="JScript">
function fnSaveChanges() {

  // move to last then first record to save current record values
  dsoBookList.recordset.MoveLast();
  dsoBookList.recordset.MoveFirst();

  // get a reference to the recordset in the data island
  var objRS = dsoBookList.recordset;
  // create string to hold updates XML document
  var strUpdates = '<?xml version="1.0"?>\n<booklist_update>\n';

  // loop through records collecting any with update_action
  // not set to NONE, and add to the string in strUpdates
  while (! objRS.EOF) {
    if (objRS('update_action') != 'NONE') {
      strUpdates += ' <book>\n'
          + '  <original_code>' + objRS('original_code') + '</original_code>\n'
          + '  <code>' + objRS('code') + '</code>\n'
          + '  <category>' + objRS('category') + '</category>\n'
          + '  <release_date>' + objRS('release_date') + '</release_date>\n'
          + '  <title>' + objRS('title') + '</title>\n'
          + ' </book>\n';
    }
    objRS.MoveNext();
  }
  strUpdates += '</booklist_update>\n';

  //put updates string into hidden control on form
  document.all('hidXML').value = strUpdates;

  alert('The XML updates document is:\n\n' + strUpdates)

  // submit form to the server where another
  // ASP page can update data source
  document.all('frmUpdate').submit();
}
</SCRIPT>
```

*This process is referred to as **marshalling**, and is done automatically by the RDS DSO when it is handling ordinary ADO-style recordsets via the `DataFactory` object and a relational database. Note that this is not 'marshalling' in the same sense as it is done at low-level within the COM runtime, although the concept is similar.*

The result when we edit the record for book code 16-003 (as shown earlier) is an `alert` dialog like that in the following screenshot. The XML updates document is then placed into a HIDDEN-type HTML control on a `<FORM>` in this page, and posted back to the server for processing by a component or ASP code like that we used with the MSXML parser earlier on.

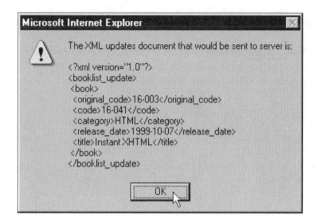

Managing Concurrent Updates

A third issue that is involved when we come to update data using XML is the thorny problem of concurrent updates. The RDS DSO hides much of the complexity from us when we use a relational database directly through the `DataFactory` object, but we have to face up to it ourselves when we use XML. The big issue is what happens in a multi-user environment, where several people could be updating the data source concurrently?

The RDS DSO normally manages this by keeping a copy of the original values in each of the records that it retrieves and sends to the client. Then, when the `SubmitChanges` method is called, it examines each one to see if the target record has been changed since the remote (client-cached) recordset was created. If so, it fails the update on these records and produces an error message. The user can then refresh the client-side recordset and examine the failed updates and decide what to do.

To do the same with XML is relatively simple, though it does require some extra work. The obvious technique is to include the original values of the data in the XML when it is created:

```
...
<book>
 <original_code>16-003</original_code>
 <code>16-003</code>
 <original_category>HTML</original_category>
 <category>HTML</category>
 <original_release_date>1999-10-07</original_release_date>
 <release_date>1999-10-07</release_date>
 <original_title>Instant XHTML</original_title>
 <title>Instant XHTML</title>
 <original_sales>127853</original_sales>
 <sales>127853</sales>
 <update_action>NONE</update_action>
</book>
...
```

You can see that all we've done is add another four 'original value' elements, the same as the one for the original book code. When an XML document in this format, with new values for the other fields, is submitted back to the server it can check to see if any of the original value in the fields have changed in the data source before performing the update. If so, it should fail the update and provide an error message.

Updating with the ADO Persistence Methods

ADO 2.5 provides us with an automated way to tackle source data updates, in much the same way as we do when using RDS with a relational database and `DataFactory` object. We can get the contents of an XML document into a normal ADO recordset with the `Open` method of the `Recordset` object. We have to specify the special 'persistence' OLE-DB provider, and the new integral 'format' constant `adCmdFile`:

```
objRS.Open "path_and_filename", "Provider=MSPersist;", , , adCmdFile
```

The source/destination parameter (here described as *path_and_filename*) can be a URL if required, or a relative path. However, it can also be a **stream**. By editing the XML on the client, we can create a recordset that contains updates to the data and then flush these changes back to the original data source. To do so, we use the same method as we would with RDS to update the original source data – we call the `UpdateBatch` method:

```
objRS.UpdateBatch
```

For this to work, we must have first opened a connection to the appropriate data source. Then we assign the connection to the recordset `ActiveConnection` property and call the `UpdateBatch` method:

```
Set objCon = Server.CreateObject("ADODB.Connection")
Set objRS = Server.CreateObject("ADODB.Recordset")
objCon.Open "connection_string"
objRS.Open "path_and_filename"
objRS.ActiveConnection = objCon
objRS.UpdateBatch
objRS.Close
objCon.Close
```

So, we can use script code or data binding (or any other method) to edit the XML on the client, then use this updated XML document on the server to update our original data source directly via ADO. This example opens an XML document into a recordset, changes a value in a field, and then updates the original data source:

```
Set objRS = Server.CreateObject("ADODB.Recordset")
objRS.Open "path_and_filename", "Provider=MSPersist;", , , adCmdFile
objRS.Find "field_name = 'value'"
If Not objRS.EOF Then    'found a matching record so update it
  objRS.("field_name") = 'new_value'"
  objRS.Update
  Set objCon = Server.CreateObject("ADODB.Connection")
  objCon.Open "connection_string"
  objRS.ActiveConnection = objCon
  objRS.UpdateBatch    'flush changes to original recordset
  objCon.Close
End If
objRS.Close
```

Note that this code loads an XML document file stored on the server's disk into the recordset. For this to be a feasible option, we have to have already sent the XML document back from the client to the server, and stored it on disk as a file. This is easy enough – we can use the technique we saw earlier of POSTing it from a form on the client and then collecting it from the ASP `Request` object as a string. We can then use the `FileSystemObject` in ASP to write the string to disk as a file, ready to be opened into an ADO recordset.

Posting XML Documents to a Stream

It's also possible to open an existing **stream** object that represents a recordset. This allows us to read data directly from the browser and into a recordset object on the server ready to use the `UpdateBatch` method. On the client, we use script code to do a direct HTTP post to the server using the new `XMLHTTP` component that is installed with IE5. Here's an example of the technique, using JScript:

```
<SCRIPT LANGUAGE="JScript">
function postXML() {
  // create an instance of the XMLHTTP component
  var xmlhttp = new ActiveXObject("Microsoft.XMLHTTP");
  // open a connection to your server ready to POST the data
  xmlhttp.open("POST", "http://yourserver.com/update_xml.asp", false);
  // send the complete XML document by referencing the root element
  xmlhttp.send(dsoBookList.XMLDocument);
  // display any response fom the server in the page
  document.write(xmlhttp.ResponseText);
}
</SCRIPT>
```

On the server, we can check if the request was a `POST`, and if so open the data stream directly into an ADO recordset by specifying the `Request` object as the data source. From there, we can update the source data in the same way as before with the `UpdateBatch` method:

```
If Request.ServerVariables("REQUEST_METHOD") = "POST" Then
   Set objCon = Server.CreateObject("ADODB.Connection")
   Set objRS = Server.CreateObject("ADODB.Recordset")
   objCon.Open "connection_string"
   objRS.Open Request, , , , adCmdFile
   objRS.ActiveConnection = objCon
   objRS.UpdateBatch
   objRS.Close
   objCon.Close
End If
```

Updating with the SQLXML Technology Preview

The SQLXML Technology Preview can also be used to update the data stored in SQL Server using an XML document of a suitable format. These documents are called **update grams**, and are specified as a string in the `template` parameter of the URL when referencing the registered virtual root. For example, the code:

```
strUG = "<root xmlns:sql='urn:schemas-microsoft-com:xmlsql'>" _
      & "<sql:sync><sql:after>" _
      & "<Orders OrderID='1' CustomerID='C1' EmpID='100'/>" _
      & "</sql:after></sql:sync>" _
      & "<sql:query>SELECT * FROM Orders FOR XML AUTO</sql:query>" _
      & "</root>"
strURL = "http://yourserver/examples?template=" & strUG
```

creates a URL containing the following update gram (the indenting and carriage returns are omitted in the code above as they are not required):

```
<root xmlns:sql='urn:schemas-microsoft-com:xmlsql'>
 <sql:sync>
  <sql:after>
   <Orders OrderID='1' CustomerID='C1' EmpID='100'/>
  </sql:after>
 </sql:sync>
 <sql:query>SELECT * FROM Orders FOR XML AUTO</sql:query>
</root>
```

The `<sql:query>` element specifies the recordset that is to be updated. SQLXML uses this to extract the records on the server and prepare them for updating. The `<sql:sync>` element contains the details of the update required. It can hold two different optional elements: `<sql:before>` and `<sql:after>`. In this example, we are only providing a `<sql:after>` element, because we want to insert this record into the recordset (and therefore into the database table).

We can include multiple new records in the `<sql:after>` element, and even specify that they are added to different tables by specifying more `<sql:query>` elements that create the appropriate recordsets. The documentation that is provided with the technology preview contains more details of how this is done.

If we provide a `<sql:before>` element, we are specifying the conditions that must exist before the contents of the `<sql:after>` element are processed. In other words, we can select an individual record to be updated by specifying the key that identifies it in the recordset:

```
<root xmlns:sql='urn:schemas-microsoft-com:xmlsql'>
 <sql:sync>
  <sql:before>
   <Customers ID="026534" Name="John Doe" />
  </sql:before>
  <sql:after>
   <Customers ID="026534" Name="Bill Doe" />
  </sql:after>
 </sql:sync>
 <sql:query>SELECT * FROM Customers FOR XML AUTO</sql:query>
</root>
```

There are also many other combinations of possibilities, including updating the key fields, and updating multiple records. To delete a record, we just specify a `<sql:before>` element and omit the `<sql:after>` element:

```
<root xmlns:sql='urn:schemas-microsoft-com:xmlsql'>
 <sql:sync>
  <sql:before>
   <Customers ID="026534" />
  </sql:before>
 </sql:sync>
 <sql:query>SELECT * FROM OrderDetails FOR XML AUTO</sql:query>
</root>
```

As you can see, this technology is incredibly powerful, and could well be useful if you intend to store data in SQL Server and then use it as XML documents.

Summary

In this and the previous chapter we've looked at topics that involve XML and client-side data binding. When you build XML-based applications, it's often necessary to implement much of the plumbing and data handling yourself, rather than relying on some clever built-in functions of the operating system or client application to do all the work. Data binding provides just one opportunity to provide a dynamic and usable client interface, and there are plenty of other ways you can do this. For example, you can use script code to manipulate XML documents via a client-based or server-based XML parser, such as the MSXML parser or the many others that are available both as free or commercial components.

However, this chapter was ostensibly just about working with XML data binding, so we have tried to steer a course through all the possibilities in order to concentrate on the topic in hand. As you have seen, however, we discovered that this does require us to 'wander off' the track a little. We also needed to consider some of the issues involved in creating the XML document in the first place, keeping the data up to date, transmitting it across the network, and managing updates to the original data back on the server.

So, in this chapter, we covered:

❑   Creating XML Documents for data binding

❑   Updating the Source XML document on the server

The next chapter introduces ASP-based Procedure Libraries that could help make working with XML on a day-to-day basis a little easier.

14

Creating XML Procedure Libraries

It's clear from the earlier chapters of this book that working with XML and the associated technologies often requires us to write a lot of peripheral code, even to achieve what seems at first like a simple task. This is due in part to the fact that XML is still a new and evolving language, and there are few tools and components available to make it easier to work with.

For example, we often have to create instances of one or more XML parser components in an ASP page, and load the appropriate documents. If we want to access XML files on disk, we often need to read and write them using the `FileSystemObject`. And even just getting the value of an element means many lines of code to load the XML document into a parser and then access it.

In this chapter, we'll look at how we might build some re-usable procedures that make these everyday tasks easier. We're going to build them as an ASP `#include` file, so that we can insert them into any ASP page with ease. But this doesn't mean that this is the way we'll always use them. Once you've built up a library of useful functions, you can use a language like Visual Basic to compile them into an ActiveX DLL so that they are easily available in any of your pages.

So, this chapter looks at:

- ❑   Why we might consider building a procedure library
- ❑   Some of the important issues involved in using it
- ❑   The functions we've chosen to implement in our sample library
- ❑   How the functions can be used in a sample page

We'll start with an overview of the library we're building, then move on to look at each function in detail.

The Contents of Our Procedure Library

We've provided a sample XML procedure library with the rest of the example code for this book. You can download it from our Web site at http://www.wrox/com/. Obviously, the procedures we've chosen may not suit your specific requirements exactly, but you can easily tailor them to match your needs or build extra ones.

To make it easier to use the procedures, and see what they do, we've also provided a sample page that allows you to execute each procedure with your own values. There are also a couple of sample XML and XSL documents that you can use to see the results of each procedure.

A Test Page for the Library Procedures

The next screenshot shows the sample 'test' page, named `default.asp`. Here, we've placed it in a directory named `4028proc` on our server named `wroxbox`:

This gives you an idea of the procedures that we have included. For each one, the parameters that you can set are displayed in HTML controls, so that you can enter your own values for each procedure. There is also a button that executes the procedures on demand. The values shown in the screenshot are the defaults that we set in the HTML code that creates the page.

The Structure of the Test Page

The test page consists of three distinct sections. After the `<HEAD>` section comes an SSI `#include` statement that inserts our procedure library file into the page. This file contains all the procedures we'll be using and describing in this chapter. After that is a server-side ASP code section, which is executed when any of the buttons on the test page is clicked. We'll look at the code that is here when we examine each of the library procedures:

```
<%@LANGUAGE="VBScript"%>
<HTML>
<HEAD><TITLE>XML Procedure Library</TITLE></HEAD>
<BODY BGCOLOR="#FFFFFF">
<SPAN>Using an XML Procedure Library</SPAN><HR>

<!-- #include file="xml_procedures.inc" -->

<%
  QUOT = Chr(34)      'double-quote character
  Dim strResult       'to hold result in function calls
  Dim strError        'to hold error message in function calls

  'look for a command sent from the FORM section buttons

    ... script code to see which button was clicked
    ... and call the appropriate method goes here
%>

<FORM ACTION="<%= Request.ServerVariables("SCRIPT_NAME") %>" METHOD="POST">

  ... HTML to create the controls required
  ... for the other library functions goes here

</FORM>
</HTML>
```

After the ASP code section comes the <FORM> that is used to submit the values to the server. As we use the name of the script in the ACTION attribute, the values will be submitted to this same page, and used in the ASP code in the upper section of the page. Again, we'll look at each of these sections of HTML as we examine the various library procedures later on in the chapter. But first, let's consider what procedures we might need, and which ones we've included in our sample library.

About the Procedure Library Include File

As we noted earlier, there are several tasks that we carry out regularly when working with XML and other associated technologies. XML files are plain text, often stored on the server's disk. Therefore, we can access them using the FileSystemObject that is part of the scripting runtime library for both VBScript and JScript (in this chapter we're using just VBScript, but you can convert it all to JScript if you wish).

Reading and Writing Text Files

So, the first procedures that we provide allow us to read from and write to a text file on disk without having to keep worrying about creating a FileSystemObject instance each time, and checking for errors at each stage of the process. These are the ReadFromFile and WriteToFile functions.

However, to make these functions work, we need to do some extra processing that is going to be repeated in many other procedures, so it makes sense to lift these out into separate functions. We obviously need to instantiate the FileSystemObject, and we'll be using this in most of our procedures. So we can create a separate function named CreateScriptingObject that does just this.

Getting an Absolute Path and File Name

A second issue is that of specifying the name of the file we want to read from or write to. It would be nice to allow the user to specify the name as either a virtual or physical path, and as a relative or absolute path. This would allow them to use any of the following forms:

```
c:\4028proc\test\myfile.xml      'absolute physical path
test\myfile.xml                  'relative physical path
/4028proc/test/myfile.xml        'absolute virtual path
test/myfile.xml                  'relative virtual path
myfile.xml                       'also a relative virtual path
```

To make this work reliably, we have to do some pre-processing of the file path and name that they provide. The obvious technique will be to map the value they provide to an absolute physical path every time, and for that we'll create a separate function called `GetAbsoluteFilePath`.

However, for some procedures, we'll also allow the user to provide the value as an XML string instead of a file path and name. This will be useful where the value has been captured from, say, the `Request.Form` collection by the ASP page. So our `GetAbsoluteFilePath` function will also cope with this option.

Reporting Status and Logging Errors

Obviously, there will be times when a call to one of our procedures will fail, maybe because the user provided invalid parameter values, or maybe because the environment is not what they expect. For example, the file they specify for reading may not exist, or the web server may not have the requisite permissions to write a file to a directory that they specify.

To cope with this, each procedure must be able to indicate the status of an operation, and perhaps also provide an error message that indicates what went wrong. However, the developer who is using our functions may not want to display these messages, so we can't just write them into the page we're creating. Instead, we'll arrange for error and status messages to be returned in a parameter of each function.

We'll also add the ability for each procedure to write out any error messages to a text log file on the server's disk. Some developers may prefer to use this to monitor operations, especially if they don't want to report errors to the user. So, we need a simple procedure that writes to a log file, which we can call from any other procedure (or directly from within our ASP code elsewhere in the page). This procedure is named `WriteToLogFile`.

Procedures for Working with XML Documents

Most of the functions we've described so far carry out the basic tasks that we know we'll need to accomplish on a regular basis. However, there are also tasks that are more specialized, but are still a regular requirement when working with XML documents. We've provided four in our sample library that we feel cover the most common tasks.

Building Document Prologs

All XML documents should contain an XML **prolog**, which describes the XML version, a stylesheet that is to be used with it, and perhaps a comment to describe the document. We'll create a function named `BuildXMLProlog` to do just this, allowing the user to specify the comment and the stylesheet to be included in the prolog.

Loading and Parsing XML Documents

Another of the most common tasks we carry out is loading an XML document into an XML parser component, such as Microsoft's MSXML component. This involves instantiating the parser component, choosing the correct 'load' method (depending on whether the document is held in a string variable or a file on disk), and then checking for any parsing errors. We'll create a simple function named `LoadAndParseXML` that does all this for us in one fell swoop.

Extracting Values from XML Documents

Obviously, one of the prime reasons for loading and parsing an XML document is to be able to get at the contents. We'll often want to be able to access specific elements and read their values. This is a hard procedure to build, because the requirements can vary widely. For example, you may want to extract the values of all matching elements, or just a specific one. You might want to extract the values of attributes, or whole sub-tree nodes.

We decided to create a function that, given an element name, will return an XML document containing only the elements with that name, but including all their content. In other words, the returned document will be a series of matching element nodes with all their descendants. This is accomplished by a function named `GetNodesFromXML`. Obviously, you can edit this or add other functions to meet your specific requirements.

Transforming XML Documents with an XSL Stylesheet

The final procedure we'll create meets another very common requirement. The transformation of an XML document into another output format (or into a different XML document) with an XSL stylesheet is reasonably simple. However, it does require the instantiation of two parser objects, a decision on which 'load' method to use for the specified disk file or XML document string, and all the associated error checking. It's also useful to be able to output the XML directly to a disk file, especially if we are transforming into HTML as a 'batch' process (i.e. only recreating the HTML page when the XML file is updated). For this, we'll create a function named `TransformXML`.

The Procedure Library File in Outline

The following code listing shows the outline of the procedure library file we provide – named `xml_procedures.inc`. Although it's quite a long listing, it demonstrates the structure and shows the parameters and a brief description of each function. We've omitted the code from each procedure for the time being, as we'll be examining each one in turn later.

Some points to note here are that most of the functions shown take a parameter named `strError` or `strResult`. This string variable (the value it contains is irrelevant) must be provided when the function is executed. On return, this parameter contains either the 'result' of the function or an error or status message. Most of the functions have a `Boolean` return value as their intrinsic value – either `True` if the process succeeds or `False` if not. The exceptions are the `BuildXMLProlog` function, which returns a reference to a parser object instance or `Nothing`, and the `LoadAndParseXML` method, which returns a `String` value.

Also notice the global variables we specify. The absolute physical path to the log file can be specified directly in the `gstrErrorLog` variable, instead of using the `Server.MapPath` method with a virtual path. This will be useful if you want to write the log file to a directory that does not have a virtual path. Make sure that it has the relevant permissions set up for the **IUSR_***machinename* and **IWAM_***machinename* accounts. If you don't want to create a log file, just set the value to an empty string instead.

*On a test server, you might like to give the IUSR and IWAM accounts or the Everyone group Full Control while you are setting up and testing the samples. However, **do not** do this on a production server or public server:*

```
<%
    'string to hold full path and name of error log file
    'if empty, no error log is created. Make sure IUSR
    'and IWAM accounts have write and modify permission
    'set for this file.
    VirtualPathToLogFile = "/4028proc/xml_procedures.log"

    'convert it to a full physical path and filename
    gstrErrorLog = Server.MapPath(VirtualPathToLogFile)

    'global variable used to hold instance of the
    'FileSystemObject that is used by most routines
    Set gobjFSO = Nothing


    '-------------------------------------------------
    Function CreateScriptingObject (strError)
        '-------------------------------------------------
        'Return value type: Boolean
        'Return value: True if the operation succeeds
        'Function Description:
        '   Creates a new instance of the scripting
        '   FileSystemObject if one is not already
        '   instantiated in global variable named gobjFSO.
        '   If it fails, places an error message in strError
        '-------------------------------------------------
        ...
        ... code goes here
        ...
    End Function


    '-------------------------------------------------
    Sub WriteToLogFile(strSource, strError)
        '-------------------------------------------------
        'Return value type: none
        'Routine Description:
        '   Takes two string parameters and appends a message
        '   containing them to the end of the log file if a
        '   full physical path is specified in the global
        '   variable gstrErrorLog.
        '-------------------------------------------------
        ...
        ... code goes here
        ...
    End Sub


    '-------------------------------------------------
    Function GetAbsoluteFilePath(strInput, blnMustExist, strResult)
        '-------------------------------------------------
        'Return value type: Boolean
        'Return value: True if the return value is valid
        'Function Description:
```

```
   '   Takes a string strInput and checks if it is an
   '   XML document or a file path/name. If it is a
   '   virtual file path/name, it returns the equivalent
   '   full physical path and name in strResult. If not,
   '   and the string contains a full physical path, it
   '   returns it unchanged. If it seems to be an XML
   '   document it returns it unchanged. If none of
   '   these, it returns an error message in strResult.
   '-----------------------------------------------------
   ...
   ... code goes here
   ...
End Function


'-------------------------------------------------------
Function WriteToFile(strFileName, strContent, strError)
   '-----------------------------------------------------
   'Return value type: Boolean
   'Return value: True if the operation succeeds
   'Function Description:
   '   Takes a full physical file path and name and
   '   writes the string in strContent to this file
   '   overwriting any existing file. If the process
   '   fails an error message is returned in strError
   '   and added to the log file if specified.
   '-----------------------------------------------------
   ...
   ... code goes here
   ...
End Function


'-------------------------------------------------------
Function ReadFromFile(strFileName, strResult)
   '-----------------------------------------------------
   'Return value type: Boolean
   'Return value: True if the operation succeeds
   'Function Description:
   '   Takes a full physical file path and name, reads
   '   entire content of the file and returns it in the
   '   string parameter strResult. If the process
   '   fails an error message is returned in strResult
   '   and added to the log file if specified.
   '-----------------------------------------------------
   ...
   ... code goes here
   ...
End Function


'-------------------------------------------------------
Function BuildXMLProlog(strComment, strStylesheet)
   '-----------------------------------------------------
   'Return value type: String
   'Return value: The complete XML document prolog
   'Function Description:
   '   Creates the prolog for an XML document given an
   '   optional comment or optional XSL stylesheet URL.
```

```
     '   Result includes <?xml version="1.0"?> and
     '   the comment and stylesheet instructions if values
     '   are provided for the parameters.
     '----------------------------------------------------
     ...
     ... code goes here
     ...
End Function


'----------------------------------------------------------
Function LoadAndParseXML(strInput, strError)
     '----------------------------------------------------
     'Return value type: Object or Nothing
     'Return value: MSXML Parser object on success
     '                 or Nothing on error or load failure
     'Function Description:
     '   Creates an instance of the MSXML parser and loads
     '   the document specified in strInput. This can be
     '   a virtual or physical path, or a string that
     '   contains a valid XML document. Returns any error
     '   in the strError parameter and adds it to log file.
     '----------------------------------------------------
     ...
     ... code goes here
     ...
End Function


'----------------------------------------------------------
Function GetNodesFromXML(strElementName, strXML, strResult)
     '----------------------------------------------------
     'Return value type: Boolean
     'Return value: True if process succeeds
     'Function Description:
     '   Takes the name of an element and an XML document,
     '   and returns the XML document for that element and
     '    all its contents in the strResult parameter.
     '   The parameter strXML can be virtual or physical file
     '   path and name, or an XML documents as a string.
     '   Returns any error in the strResult parameter and
     '   adds it to log file if previously specified.
     '----------------------------------------------------
     ...
     ... code goes here
     ...
End Function


'----------------------------------------------------------
Function TransformXML(strXML, strXSL, strOutFile, strResult)
     '----------------------------------------------------
     'Return value type: Boolean
     'Return value: True if transformation succeeds
     'Function Description:
     '   Takes an XML document and an XSL stylesheet and
     '   performs the transformation into a result document
     '   in the strResult parameter. The two parameters
     '   strXML and strXSL can be virtual or physical file
```

```
       '  paths and names, or XML documents as strings.
       '  If a virtual or physical path name is provided in
       '  strOutFile the result is written to this file.
       '  Returns any error in the strResult parameter and
       '  adds it to log file if previously specified.
       '--------------------------------------------------
       ...
       ... code goes here
       ...
    End Function
  %>
```

Include File Issues in ASP Pages

Obviously, the 'include' file we're building will be quite large. The sample file xml_procedures.inc runs to nearly 400 lines of code. You may read elsewhere that ASP is not an efficient technique for server-side processing when you have large or complex tasks to achieve. So, they would say, any ASP page that needs more that a few dozen lines of code should be classed as a dinosaur and immediately consigned to the Recycle Bin.

ASP Compiled Code Caching

While this may have been true in early versions of ASP, it's not always appropriate now. ASP interprets the page the first time it runs it, and compiles the ASP code in it. This compiled code is cached in memory on the server, and used for each request to that page until the page is edited. At this point, the next request causes it to be re-complied and cached again. So, the issue of loading, interpreting and compiling long pages is not really a problem. It also means that the comments you add to your code make no difference after the initial compilation stage, so there's no excuse for not including proper procedure definitions!

Of course, the execution speed of the compiled code might be an issue. If there are hugely complex and time-consuming actions to be carried out, you may be better off using a component written in C++ instead. However, building the library as an ASP 'include' file first does allow you to experiment with the concepts and techniques, and fine-tune the contents. After that you can always compile the code into a DLL, as we suggested earlier.

If you intend to compile the code into a DLL using C++, you might prefer to write the include file in JScript as the syntax is more like C++ that VBScript. However, if you intend to compile into a Visual Basic ActiveX DLL, you'll find that most of the VBScript code will be accepted directly by VB and you'll just need to add the data types and definitions, the interface code, and generally tidy up the rest.

Also, don't forget that you can insert an 'include' file into an ASP page using the <SCRIPT> element instead:

```
<SCRIPT RUNAT="SERVER" SRC="myincludefile.inc">
```

Using a Central Library Repository

Another technique that might be useful is to divide the procedures you use into separate 'include' files. You can insert one or more into your ASP pages, using only those that contain the set of procedures you require. Obviously some of the procedures will have to be in all or most of the 'include' files, such as the WriteToLog and CreateScriptingObject procedures.

It's also possible to create a central repository for your procedure library files. A directory that is off the root of the Web site can be used to hold all of them – perhaps in separate sub-directories if you have a great many library files. Then you can maintain a single central copy of each file, and insert them into any ASP page on the site by specifying the absolute virtual path to this directory:

```
<!-- #include virtual="/proc_library/xml/xml_procedures.inc" -->
```

The Procedure Functions in Detail

In this section of the chapter, we look at each of the functions we've been discussing in detail. We'll show you the code for the function and describe how it works. For the functions that are exposed through the 'test' page, we'll also look at the code in this page and see the function in action.

The CreateScriptingObject Function

We decided earlier that we will need to create an instance of the `FileSystemObject` for use in most of our procedures. However, we only need one, so it makes sense to create a single instance on demand and then reuse it as required while our page is executing. The global variable named `gobjFSO`, which is defined elsewhere in the 'include' file, will hold a reference to this object instance for use by any procedure.

This is the code for the `CreateScriptingObject` function. If the `gobjFSO` variable is `Nothing`, we know that there is no current instance of the object, so we create one using the `Server.CreateObject` method. If this fails, maybe because the object is not available, we return an error message by updating the value of the `strError` parameter and return `False` as the function value:

```
'-----------------------------------------------------
Function CreateScriptingObject(strError)
  '-----------------------------------------------------
  'Return value type: Boolean
  'Return value: True if the operation succeeds
  'Function Description:
  '  Creates a new instance of the scripting
  '  FileSystemObject if one is not already
  '  instantiated in global variable named gobjFSO.
  '  If it fails, places an error message in strError
  '-----------------------------------------------------
  On Error Resume Next
  If gobjFSO Is Nothing Then
    CreateScriptingObject = False
    Set gobjFSO = Server.CreateObject("Scripting.FileSystemObject")
    If Err.Number <> 0 Then
      strError = "Cannot create Scripting.FileSystemObject instance"
      Exit Function
    End If
  End If
  CreateScriptingObject = True
End Function
'-----------------------------------------------------
```

So, if the `gobjFSO` variable is not `Nothing`, we won't create a new instance. Providing that the object already exists, or that we successfully created a new instance, we set the function's return value to `True`. This function is not designed for use directly, only from within other functions in our 'include' file, so we haven't provided a feature to execute it specifically in the 'test' page. However, you can easily use it from your ASP code elsewhere in the page if required.

Notice that we don't attempt to write an error message to the log file if anything goes wrong, because if we can't create an instance of the `FileSystemObject` object, then our `WriteToLog` procedure (described next) won't work either!

The WriteToLogFile Subroutine

The next procedure is a simple subroutine that appends the values provided in the parameters to a log file, or creates a new log file if one doesn't already exist. We don't use our own `CreateScriptingObject` function here, because we can't handle errors properly if this routine fails. Instead, we just turn off error handling and go through the motions of opening the file, adding the new entry (including the date and time), and then closing the file. And if there is no value provided for the global `gstrErrorLog` variable, we don't even bother doing that, because this indicates that the user doesn't want to log errors:

```
'-----------------------------------------------------------
Sub WriteToLogFile(strSource, strError)
  '---------------------------------------------------------
  'Return value type: none
  'Routine Description:
  '  Takes two string parameters and appends a message
  '  containing them to the end of the log file if a
  '  full physical path is specified in the global
  '  variable gstrErrorLog.
  '---------------------------------------------------------
  If Len(gstrErrorLog) Then
    On Error Resume Next
    Dim strResult
    Set objFSO = Server.CreateObject("Scripting.FileSystemObject")
    Set objFile = objFSO.OpenTextFile(gstrErrorLog, 8, True)
    strToLog = FormatDateTime(Now, vbGeneralDate) _
      & " - " & strSource & vbCrlf & strError & vbCrlf
    objFile.WriteLine strToLog
    objFile.Close
  End If
End Sub
'-----------------------------------------------------------
```

The GetAbsoluteFilePath Function

The first of the 'public' functions is used to discover what type of file path the user has specified for a variable that can contain both a file path and name for an XML document as a string. This is used by several of the other procedures to open a text file on the server's disk, or load an XML document string into a parser. We previously indicated that we want to be able to handle absolute and relative paths, and both physical and virtual paths – as well as XML document strings.

First, we check to see if the value supplied in the strInput parameter looks like it is an XML document, and if so, we just return this as the result by updating the strResult parameter. If it's not an XML document, we next make sure that we've got a FileSystemObject available by calling our own CreateScriptingObject function. If this fails, we copy the error message to the strResult parameter of our function and exit:

```
'----------------------------------------------------
Function GetAbsoluteFilePath(strInput, blnMustExist, strResult)
   '----------------------------------------------------
   'Return value type: Boolean
   'Return value: True if the return value is valid
   'Function Description:
   '  Takes a string strInput and checks if it is an
   '  XML document or a file path/name. If it is a
   '  virtual file path/name, it returns the equivalent
   '  full physical path and name in strResult. If not,
   '  and the string contains a full physical path, it
   '  returns it unchanged. If it seems to be an XML
   '  document it returns it unchanged. If none of
   '  these, it returns an error message in strResult.
   '----------------------------------------------------
   On Error Resume Next
   GetAbsoluteFilePath = False
   Dim strError

   If InStr(strInput, "<") > 0 And InStr(strInput, ">") > 0 Then
     'probably an XML document string
     strResult = strInput
     GetAbsoluteFilePath = True
     Exit Function
   End If

   If Not CreateScriptingObject(strError) Then
     strResult = strError
     Exit Function
   End If
   ...
```

Now we can decide what type of file path and name the user supplied. If it contains a colon or double backslash, it's a full physical path and we can return it unchanged. If not, and it contains any single backslashes, it must be a relative physical path. In this case, we get the absolute virtual path and name of the current page from the Request.ServerVariables collection, strip off the file name, convert it to an absolute physical path using the Server.MapPath method, and then add on the value the user supplied. This is done with the BuildPath method of the FileSystemObject, which automatically ensures that the '\' path separator is properly included.

If neither of the above is true, we can assume that the value is an absolute or relative virtual path, in which case we can just use the Server.MapPath method to convert it to the appropriate absolute physical path:

```
   ...
   If InStr(strInput, ":") Or InStr(strInput, "\\") Then
     'a full physical path
     strPhysicalPath = strInput
```

```
    Else

      If InStr(strInput, "\") Then
        'a relative physical path
        strCurrentPath = Request.ServerVariables("SCRIPT_NAME")
        strCurrentPath = Left(strCurrentPath, InStrRev(strCurrentPath, "/"))
        strCurrentPath = Server.MapPath(strCurrentPath)
        strPhysicalPath = gobjFSO.BuildPath(strCurrentPath, strInput)
      Else

        'probably a virtual path
        strPhysicalPath = Server.MapPath(strInput)
      End If
    End If
    ...
```

Finally, we check the value of the `blnMustExist` parameter. If this is `True`, we need to confirm that the specified file actually exists. For this, we can use the `FileExists` method of the `FileSystemObject` and place an error message in the `strResult` parameter if it fails. Otherwise, we return the appropriate value for the `strResult` parameter and the function value:

```
    ...
    If blnMustExist Then
      'see if file exists
      blnExists = gobjFSO.FileExists(strPhysicalPath)

      If (Err.Number = 0) And (blnExists) Then
        strResult = strPhysicalPath
        GetAbsoluteFilePath = True
      Else

        strResult = "File '" & strPhysicalPath & "' does not exist"
        WriteToLogFile "Function:GetAbsoluteFilePath", strResult
        GetAbsoluteFilePath = False
      End If

    Else
      strResult = strPhysicalPath
      GetAbsoluteFilePath = True
    End If

  End Function
  '-----------------------------------------------------------
```

Notice also how we make a call to our `WriteToLog` subroutine if there is an error, specifying the current function name and the error string we've created. We'll take a look at the log file contents later in the chapter.

Using The GetAbsoluteFilePath Function

You can experiment with the `GetAbsoluteFilePath` function using the 'test' page. The page displays a set of HTML controls where you can enter the values you want to use:

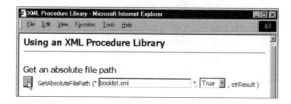

The HTML Controls to Test the GetAbsoluteFilePath Function

The HTML controls to create the part of the page seen above are shown next. We've provided a default value for the first parameter (the file path and name) of a file that is included in the samples:

```
...
<P>Get an absolute file path</P>
<INPUT TYPE="SUBMIT" NAME="cmdGetAbsolute" VALUE="   ">
  GetAbsoluteFilePath ("
<INPUT TYPE="TEXT" NAME="txtAbsoluteInput" SIZE="35" VALUE="booklist.xml"> ",
<SELECT NAME="selMustExist" SIZE="1">
<OPTION>True</OPTION>
<OPTION>False</OPTION>
</SELECT>, strResult )
...
```

The Script Code that Uses the GetAbsoluteFilePath Function

When the button is clicked to execute the GetAbsoluteFilePath function, the values in the <FORM> section are submitted back to this page again. Here, the ASP script code that resides in the page, before the <FORM> section, is executed. This section of code consists of a series of If...Then constructs, which check to see which of the SUBMIT buttons was clicked to submit the form.

If it was the button for our GetAbsoluteFilePath function, the name and the value (i.e. the caption) of this SUBMIT control are included in the Request.Form collection as "cmdGetAbsolute" and "   ". So, we can check to see if there is any value for a control named cmdGetAbsolute, and if so we know that our GetAbsoluteFilePath button was the one that was clicked to submit the form.

If this is the case, we collect the values sent from the HTML controls in this part of the page. If the current value of the selMustExist list control is the string "True", we set the variable blnMustExist to the Boolean value True, or False otherwise. Then we can execute our GetAbsoluteFilePath function and store the outcome in a variable named blnOK. The value of the result parameter (the path or an error message) is placed in the variable strResult by the function, and hence returned to the user:

```
...
'look for a command sent from the FORM section buttons
If Len(Request.Form("cmdGetAbsolute")) Then
  'get an absolute file path
  strFile = Request.Form("txtAbsoluteInput")
  blnMustExist = (Request.Form("selMustExist") = "True")
  blnOK = GetAbsoluteFilePath(strFile, blnMustExist, strResult)
  Response.Write "GetAbsoluteFilePath(" & QUOT _
    & Server.HTMLEncode(strFile) & QUOT _
    & ", " & blnMustExist & ", strResult) returned <B>" & blnOK _
    & "</B><BR>Value of strResult is " & QUOT & "<B>" _
    & Server.HTMLEncode(strResult) & "</B>" & QUOT & "<HR>"
End If
...
```

The rest of the code is concerned just with displaying the values we sent to the function, and the results. Notice that we have to use the `Server.HTMLEncode` method in case there are any non-legal characters in the strings, as will be the case if we provide an XML document as the input parameter. The next screenshot shows the result where our sample file does exist, and the `strResult` parameter returns the absolute physical path to it:

If we provide the name of a file that doesn't exist, the `GetAbsoluteFilePath` function still attempts to calculate the equivalent absolute physical path. As we've specified `True` for the `blnMustExist` parameter, it returns an error message indicating that the file does not exist, as shown in the next screenshot. However, we could specify `False` for this parameter instead, just to get the converted file path and name:

Finally, if we provide an XML document as a string for the input parameter, the `GetAbsoluteFilePath` function just returns the string as the result, and does not attempt to check if a file with this name exists:

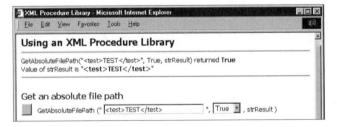

The WriteToFile Function

Our `WriteToFile` function is designed to create a new text file with the path and name specified in the `strFileName` parameter, and write the contents of the `strContent` parameter to the new file. First we create a `FileSystemObject` if one doesn't already exist, and then use it to create our text file. By specifying `True` for the second parameter of the `CreateTextFile` method, we force any existing file with the same path and name to be overwritten with the new file automatically.

Having checked that the file was created successfully, we write the specified content to it, and again check for any errors. Finally, we close the new file, and again check for any errors. If an error occurs anywhere in the process, we return a suitable message by assigning it to the `strError` parameter and write it to our log file with the `WriteToLog` function. We also return `False` as the value of the function in this case. However, if all goes well, we can return `True` as the value of the function:

```
'-------------------------------------------------------
Function WriteToFile(strFileName, strContent, strError)
  '---------------------------------------------------
  'Return value type: Boolean
  'Return value: True if the operation succeeds
  'Function Description:
  '  Takes a full physical file path and name and
  '  writes the string in strContent to this file
  '  overwriting any existing file. If the process
  '  fails an error message is returned in strError
  '  and added to the log file if specified.
  '---------------------------------------------------
  On Error Resume Next
  Dim strResult
  WriteToFile = False

  If Not CreateScriptingObject(strResult) Then
    strError = strResult
    Exit Function
  End If

  Set objFile = gobjFSO.CreateTextFile(strFileName, True)

  If Err.Number <> 0 Then
    strError = "Cannot create file '" & strFileName & "'"
    WriteToLogFile "Function:WriteToFile", strError
    Exit Function
  End If

  objFile.Write strContent

  If Err.Number <> 0 Then
    strError = "Cannot write to file '" & strFileName & "'"
    WriteToLogFile "Function:WriteToFile", strError
    objFile.Close
    Exit Function
  End If

  objFile.Close

  If Err.Number <> 0 Then
    strError = "Cannot close file '" & strFileName & "'"
    WriteToLogFile "Function:WriteToFile", strError
    Exit Function
  End If

  WriteToFile = True
End Function
'-------------------------------------------------------
```

Notice that we don't use the `GetAbsoluteFilePath` function to pre-process the file path and name. Instead, we allow the developer to call this function separately, before using the value it returns in this function. This allows them to use the `WriteToFile` function in exactly the way they need, without us imposing any constraints. This is demonstrated next in our 'test'page.

Using The WriteToFile Function

Our 'test' page provides a set of controls where you can experiment with the WriteToFile function. The default values specify a file in the current directory where the 'test' page resides. Remember that you will have to provide the IUSR and IWAM accounts with permission to write to and modify files in this directory for the function to work:

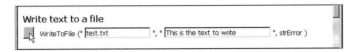

The HTML Controls to Test the WriteToFile Function

The HTML controls to create the part of the page seen above are shown next:

```
...
<P>Write text to a file</P>
<INPUT TYPE="SUBMIT" NAME="cmdWriteToFile" VALUE="   ">
  WriteToFile ("
<INPUT TYPE="TEXT" NAME="txtWriteFileName" SIZE="20" VALUE="test.txt"> ", "
<INPUT TYPE="TEXT" NAME="txtWriteContent" SIZE="35" VALUE="This is the text to
write">
", strError )

<P><DIV CLASS="subhead">Read from a text file</DIV>
<INPUT TYPE="SUBMIT" NAME="cmdReadFromFile" VALUE="   ">
  ReadFromFile ("
<INPUT TYPE="TEXT" NAME="txtReadFileName" SIZE="20" VALUE="test.txt">
", strResult )
...
```

The Script Code that Uses the WriteToFile Function

When we submit the page to the server using the WriteToFile function button, the ASP code that precedes the <FORM> section of the page first extracts the value for the file path and name. We then use this in a call to the GetAbsoluteFilePath function we described earlier to convert it to the equivalent absolute physical file path. Notice that we specify False for the blnMustExist parameter, as we aren't interested whether the file already exists. We are just going to overwrite it with the new file. Of course, we could set this parameter to True and then test the return value if we wanted to warn the user that they were about to overwrite an existing file:

```
...
'look for a command sent from the FORM section buttons

If Len(Request.Form("cmdWriteToFile")) Then
  'write text to a file
  strFile = Request.Form("txtWriteFileName")
  blnOK = GetAbsoluteFilePath(strFile, False, strResult)
  Response.Write "GetAbsoluteFilePath(" & QUOT _
    & Server.HTMLEncode(strFile) & QUOT _
    & ", False, strResult) returned <B>" & blnOK _
    & "</B><BR>Value of strResult is " & QUOT & "<B>" _
    & Server.HTMLEncode(strResult) & "</B>" & QUOT & "<BR>"
...
```

Then we display the results of the call to the `GetAbsoluteFilePath` function in the page. If this function call returned `True` (indicating that it returned the equivalent absolute physical path) we can go ahead and write the new file. To do this, we call the `WriteToFile` method we've just been describing:

```
...
   If blnOK Then
      strContent = Request.Form("txtWriteContent")
      blnOK = WriteToFile(strResult, strContent, strError)
      Response.Write "WriteToFile(" & QUOT _
         & Server.HTMLEncode(strResult) & QUOT _
         & ", " & QUOT & Server.HTMLEncode(strContent) & QUOT _
         & ", strError) returned <B>" & blnOK _
         & "</B><BR>Value of strError is " & QUOT & "<B>" _
         & Server.HTMLEncode(strError) & "</B>" & QUOT & "<HR>"
   Else
      Response.Write "Cannot write file.<HR>"
   End If
End If
...
```

Finally, we can display the results of the `WriteToFile` function in the page. This is what it looks like if it succeeds in writing the new file:

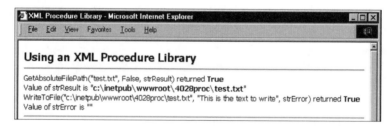

If we specify a directory that **does not** have the appropriate permissions set up, the `WriteToFile` method will fail. For example, if we provide the value `"/samples/test.txt"` for the `strFileName` parameter, we get this result:

The ReadFromFile Function

Our `ReadFromFile` function is similar in structure to the `WriteToFile` function. Again, it uses the `FileSystemObject` to access the specified file, but this time using the `OpenTextFile` method. Then it uses the `ReadAll` method to get the contents of the file into the string parameter variable `strResult`, and closes the file again. If any part of the process fails, an appropriate error message is returned in `strResult` instead:

```
'-------------------------------------------------------
Function ReadFromFile(strFileName, strResult)
  '---------------------------------------------------
  'Return value type: Boolean
  'Return value: True if the operation succeeds
  'Function Description:
  '  Takes a full physical file path and name, reads
  '  entire content of the file and returns it in the
  '  string parameter strResult. If the process
  '  fails an error message is returned in strResult
  '  and added to the log file if specified.
  '---------------------------------------------------

  On Error Resume Next
  Dim strError
  ReadFromFile = False

  If Not CreateScriptingObject(strError) Then
    strResult = strError
    Exit Function
  End If

  Set objFile = gobjFSO.OpenTextFile(strFileName)

  If Err.Number <> 0 Then
    strResult = "Cannot open file '" & strFileName & "'"
    WriteToLogFile "Function:ReadFromFile", strResult
    Exit Function
  End If

  strResult = objFile.ReadAll

  If Err.Number <> 0 Then
    strResult = "Cannot read from file '" & strFileName & "'"
    WriteToLogFile "Function:ReadFromFile", strResult
    objFile.Close
    Exit Function
  End If

  objFile.Close

  If Err.Number <> 0 Then
    strError = "Cannot close file '" & strFileName & "'"
    WriteToLogFile "Function:ReadFromFile", strError
    Exit Function
  End If

  ReadFromFile = True
End Function
'-------------------------------------------------------
```

Using The ReadFromFile Function

The sample 'test' page contains a set of controls that allow you to experiment with the ReadFromFile function. The default values we provide will read the contents of a file that has been created by the WriteToFile function that we've just been describing:

```
Read from a text file
   ReadFromFile (" test.txt              ", strResult )
```

The HTML Controls to Test the ReadFromFile Function

The HTML controls to create the part of the page seen above are shown next:

```
...
<P>Read from a text file</P>
<INPUT TYPE="SUBMIT" NAME="cmdReadFromFile" VALUE="   ">
  ReadFromFile ("
<INPUT TYPE="TEXT" NAME="txtReadFileName" SIZE="20" VALUE="test.txt">
", strResult )
...
```

The Script Code that Uses the ReadFromFile Function

When the SUBMIT button for the ReadFromFile function is clicked, the following section of ASP code, in the part of the page that precedes the <FORM> section, is executed. It is similar to the code we used to execute the WriteToFile function, calling the GetAbsoluteFilePath function we described earlier to convert it to the equivalent absolute physical file path. However, this time we specify True for the blnMustExist parameter, because we won't be able to open the file if it doesn't exist:

```
...
'look for a command sent from the FORM section buttons

If Len(Request.Form("cmdReadFromFile")) Then
  'read text from a file
  strFile = Request.Form("txtReadFileName")
  blnOK = GetAbsoluteFilePath(strFile, True, strResult)
  Response.Write "GetAbsoluteFilePath(" & QUOT _
    & Server.HTMLEncode(strFile) & QUOT _
    & ", True, strResult) returned <B>" & blnOK _
    & "</B><BR>Value of strResult is " & QUOT & "<B>" _
    & Server.HTMLEncode(strResult) & "</B>" & QUOT & "<BR>"

  If blnOK Then
    blnOK = ReadFromFile(strResult, strResult)
    Response.Write "ReadFromFile(" & QUOT _
      & Server.HTMLEncode(strResult) & QUOT _
      & ", strResult) returned <B>" & blnOK _
      & "</B><BR>Value of strResult is:<PRE>" _
      & Server.HTMLEncode(strResult) & "</PRE><HR>"
  Else
    Response.Write "Cannot read from file.<HR>"
  End If
End If
...
```

Once we're satisfied that the file exists, i.e. the blnOK variable is True, we can call our ReadFromFile function to get the content and display it in the page. If the ReadFromFile function fails, we simply display an error message. Here's the result when we open the file we created previously with the WriteToFile function:

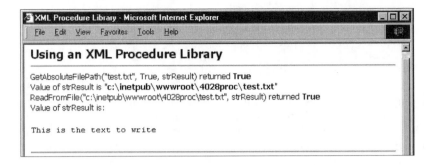

The BuildXMLProlog Function

The remaining functions in our sample procedure library are those that are directly related to XML activities. The first, BuildXMLProlog, takes a comment together with the (path and) name of a stylesheet and creates a suitable XML document prolog. This can save a lot of time when you are creating XML documents regularly.

The function is simple enough. It builds up a string in a local variable named strProlog, first adding the XML version processing instruction. If the user has provided a value for the strComment parameter of our function, this is added next within an XML comment element. Then the function creates a string containing the current date and time on the server, and adds it to the strProlog variable in a comment element. This is followed by another comment element containing the URL of the server's domain:

```
'-------------------------------------------------------
Function BuildXMLProlog(strComment, strStylesheet)
   '-------------------------------------------------------
   'Return value type: String
   'Return value: The complete XML document prolog
   'Function Description:
   '  Creates the prolog for an XML document given an
   '  optional comment or optional XSL stylesheet URL.
   '  Result includes <?xml version="1.0"?> and
   '  the comment and stylesheet instructions if values
   '  are provided for the parameters.
   '-------------------------------------------------------
   QUOT = Chr(34)  'double-quote character
   strProlog = "<?xml version=" & QUOT & "1.0" & QUOT _
      & " ?>" & vbCrlf

   If Len(strComment) Then
      strProlog = strProlog & "<!-- " & strComment _
         & " -->" & vbCrlf
   End If

   strDateTime = CStr(Year(Now)) & "-" _
      & Right("0" & CStr(Month(Now)), 2) & "-" _
      & Right("0" & CStr(Day(Now)), 2) & " at " _
      & Right("0" & CStr(Hour(Now)), 2) & ":" _
      & Right("0" & CStr(Minute(Now)), 2) & ":" _
      & Right("0" & CStr(Second(Now)), 2)
   strProlog = strProlog & "<!-- Created: " & strDateTime _
```

```
          & " -->" & vbCrlf
    strProlog = strProlog & "<!-- Server URL: http://" _
          & Request.ServerVariables("SERVER_NAME") _
          & "/ -->" & vbCrlf
 ...
```

Finally, we can see if the user provided a value for the `strStylesheet` parameter. If so, we examine this value to see what type of style sheet it is. If there is no file extension, we assume that it's an XSL stylesheet. We use the stylesheet type when creating the stylesheet processing instruction to provide the appropriate `type="text/xxx"` attribute value. Then we add the value they provided as the `href` attribute value, and return the complete prolog string by assigning it to the function name:

```
    ...
    If Len(strStylesheet) Then
      intPeriod = InStrRev(strStylesheet, ".")

      If intPeriod < Len(strStylesheet) Then
        strType = Mid(strStylesheet, intPeriod + 1)
      Else   'assume its an XSL stylesheet
        strType = "xsl"
      End If

      strProlog = strProlog & "<?xml-stylesheet type=" _
          & QUOT & "text/" & strType & QUOT & " href=" & QUOT _
          & strStylesheet & QUOT & " ?>" & vbCrlf
    End If
    BuildXMLProlog = strProlog
End Function
'--------------------------------------------------------
```

Using The BuildXMLProlog Function

The sample 'test' page contains a set of controls that allow you to experiment with the `BuildXMLProlog` function. The default values we provide create a prolog containing a comment and a stylesheet instruction:

The HTML Controls to Test the BuildXMLProlog Function

The HTML controls to create the part of the page seen above are shown next:

```
   ...
   <P>Create an XML document prolog</P>
   <INPUT TYPE="SUBMIT" NAME="cmdBuildProlog" VALUE="   ">
     BuildXMLProlog ("
   <INPUT TYPE="TEXT" NAME="txtComment" SIZE="30" VALUE="a sample document prolog">
   ", "
   <INPUT TYPE="TEXT" NAME="txtStylesheet" SIZE="30" VALUE="mystyle.xsl"> ")
   ...
```

The Script Code that Uses the BuildXMLProlog Function

When the SUBMIT button for the BuildXMLProlog function is clicked, the following section of ASP code, in the part of the page that precedes the <FORM> section, is executed. It simply extracts the values sent from the HTML controls from the Request.Form collection, and uses them in a call to our BuildXMLProlog function:

```
...
'look for a command sent from the FORM section buttons

If Len(Request.Form("cmdBuildProlog")) Then
  'create an XML document prolog
  strComment = Request.Form("txtComment")
  strStylesheet = Request.Form("txtStylesheet")
  strResult = BuildXMLProlog(strComment, strStylesheet)
  Response.Write "BuildXMLProlog(" & QUOT _
    & Server.HTMLEncode(strComment) & QUOT _
    & ", " & Server.HTMLEncode(strStylesheet) _
    & ") returned:<PRE>" _
    & Server.HTMLEncode(strResult) & "</PRE><HR>"
End If
...
```

The result is then displayed in the page as it reloads. Here's what it looks like with the default values we provide:

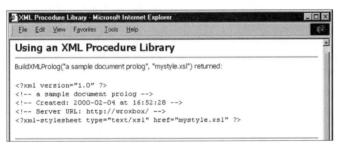

The LoadAndParseXML Function

One place where the GetAbsoluteFilePath function we created earlier proves to be really useful is when we come to load documents into a parser. The Microsoft MSXML parser has two different 'load' methods, one for disk files and one for XML documents held in string variables. The LoadAndParseXML function that we've provided in our procedure library takes this into account automatically. It also saves us from having to manually create an instance of the parser, and check for parser load errors.

Our LoadAndParseXML function starts by using the GetAbsoluteFilePath function to get the absolute physical path of the file (if it is a disk file) specified in the strInput parameter. It uses the value True for the blnMustExist parameter of the GetAbsoluteFilePath function, because if the file doesn't exist we won't be able to load and parse it.

Next, it sets a local variable named blnAsXMLString to True if the value returned from the GetAbsoluteFilePath function is an XML string. We can test for this by looking for any '<' character (remember that the GetAbsoluteFilePath function returns True if the file path specified that there is an XML string):

```
'-------------------------------------------------------
Function LoadAndParseXML(strInput, strError)
  '----------------------------------------------------
  'Return value type: Object or Nothing
  'Return value: MSXML Parser object on success
  '             or Nothing on error or load failure
  'Function Description:
  '  Creates an instance of the MSXML parser and loads
  '  the document specified in strInput. This can be
  '  a virtual or physical path, or a string that
  '  contains a valid XML document. Returns any error
  '  in the strError parameter and adds it to log file.
  '----------------------------------------------------
  On Error Resume Next
  Set LoadAndParseXML = Nothing
  Dim strResult

  If Not GetAbsoluteFilePath(strInput, True, strResult) Then
    strError = strResult
    Exit Function
  End If
  blnAsXMLString = False
  If InStr(strResult, "<") Then blnAsXMLString = True
  ...
```

Now we can instantiate our parser instance and check that this succeeded. If not, we set an error message in strError, write an entry to the log file, and exit. If we did create a parser instance successfully, we can continue by setting the async property to False so that the whole document will load before we check for errors. Then we can use our blnAsXMLString variable to decide which 'load' method to call to load the XML file or string:

```
  ...
  Set objDOM = Server.CreateObject("MSXML.DOMDocument")

  If Err.Number <> 0 Then
    strError = "Cannot create MSXML Parser object"

    If Not blnAsXMLString Then
      strError = strError & " for file '" & strResult & "'"
    End If

    WriteToLogFile "Function:LoadAndParseXML", strError
    Exit Function
  End If

  objDOM.async = False

  If blnAsXMLString Then
    objDOM.loadXML strResult
  Else
    objDOM.Load strResult
  End If
  ...
```

The final step is to check for any errors that occurred while loading and parsing the document. We can get the error details from the parser's `parseError` object properties, build up an error message, write it to the log file and return it in the `strError` parameter of our function. We also return `Nothing` for the function value. Otherwise, if all went well, we can return a reference to the parser object instance using the `Set` keyword:

```
   ...
  If objDOM.parseError.errorCode <> 0 Then
    strError = "Error loading document "
    If Not blnAsXMLString Then strError = strError & strResult & " "
    strError = strError & "- " & objDOM.parseError.reason _
            & " (line " & objDOM.parseError.Line & ")."
    WriteToLogFile "Function:LoadAndParseXML", strError
    Set LoadAndParseXML = Nothing
    Exit Function
  Else
    Set LoadAndParseXML = objDOM
  End If
End Function
'-------------------------------------------------------
```

Using The LoadAndParseXML Function

The sample 'test' page contains a set of controls that allow you to experiment with the `LoadAndParseXML` function. In this case, the default value we provide for the file name parameter is an XML document that contains an error. It isn't well formed, so it cannot be successfully parsed:

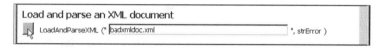

The HTML Controls to Test the LoadAndParseXML Function

The HTML controls to create the part of the page seen above are shown next:

```
...
<P>Load and parse an XML document</P>
<INPUT TYPE="SUBMIT" NAME="cmdLoadParse" VALUE="   ">
  LoadAndParseXML ("
<INPUT TYPE="TEXT" NAME="txtLoadInput" SIZE="60" VALUE="badxmldoc.xml">
", strError )
...
```

The Script Code that Uses the LoadAndParseXML Function

When the `SUBMIT` button for the `LoadAndParseXML` function is clicked, the following section of ASP code, in the part of the page that precedes the `<FORM>` section, is executed. It uses the value specified for the XML input and calls the `LoadAndParseXML` function:

```
...
'look for a command sent from the FORM section buttons

If Len(Request.Form("cmdLoadParse")) Then
  'load and parse an XML document
  strFile = Request.Form("txtLoadInput")
  Set objParser = LoadAndParseXML(strFile, strError)
```

```
      Response.Write "LoadAndParseXML(" & QUOT _
        & Server.HTMLEncode(strFile) & QUOT _
        & ", strError) returned <B>"

    If objParser Is Nothing Then
      Response.Write "Nothing</B>" _
        & "<BR>Value of strError is " & QUOT & "<B>" _
        & Server.HTMLEncode(strError) & "</B>" & QUOT & "<HR>"
    Else
      Response.Write "Valid MSXML Parser Instance</B><BR>" _
        & "Root element of XML document is <B>&lt;" _
        & objParser.documentElement.nodeName & "&gt;</B><HR>"
    End If

  End If
  ...
```

The remainder of the code is all concerned with displaying the parameter values we supplied to the function, and the result. If the load and parse process fails, as it will with the default value we provide, we display a suitable message as returned by the strError parameter:

However, if the function succeeds (it will if you specify booklist.xml for the input), we can prove this by extracting and displaying the root element name using the nodeName property of the documentElement node:

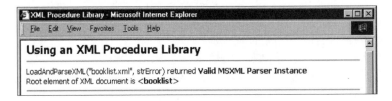

The GetNodesFromXML Function

The third of our sample XML-oriented procedures can be used to create an XML document that contains a set of nodes and their descendants, as extracted from another XML document. The code for this function, named GetNodesFromXML, is shown next.

The parameters for the function will specify the name of an element that we want to extract all instances of, and the path and name of a file or an XML document string to extract the elements from. So, the first step is to load the XML into a parser. We can use our own LoadAndParseXML function to do this, which will automatically cope with the fact that the strXML parameter value we provide could be a file path and name, or an XML document as a string. It also checks that the specified file exists, loads it, and returns a status or error message:

```
'-------------------------------------------------------
Function GetNodesFromXML(strElementName, strXML, strResult)
  '---------------------------------------------------
  'Return value type: Boolean
  'Return value: True if process succeeds
  'Function Description:
  '  Takes the name of an element and an XML document,
  '  and returns the XML document for that element and
  '  all its contents in the strResult parameter.
  '  The parameter strXML can be virtual or physical file
  '  path and name, or an XML documents as a string.
  '  Returns any error in the strResult parameter and
  '  adds it to log file if previously specified.
  '---------------------------------------------------
  On Error Resume Next
  Dim strError
  Set objXML = LoadAndParseXML(strXML, strError)

  If objXML Is Nothing Then
    strResult = strError
    GetNodesFromXML = False
    Exit Function
  End If
  ...
```

In our case, we're only interested in whether the document loaded OK. If it did, the return value of the `LoadAndParseXML` function will be `True`, and we can get on and extract the nodes we want. To do this, we chose to use the `selectNodes` method, which is a Microsoft-specific extension to the XML DOM `Node` object methods. We have to provide an XSL pattern-matching string as the parameter of the `selectNodes` method.

By using the element name specified by the user, preceded by double slashes, the method will return a `nodeList` collection containing all the nodes with that name. Once we've got the collection of nodes, we can create the result document. We use our own `BuildXMLProlog` function to create a document prolog, add an opening root tag named `<nodes_from_xml>`, and then iterate through the collection of nodes in our node list. For each one, we can extract the entire XML content from the `xml` property (another Microsoft extension to the XML DOM). Finally, we add the closing root tag, and return the XML string in the `strResult` parameter:

```
  ...
  Set objNodeList = objXML.documentElement.selectNodes("//" & strElementName)
  strComment = "Extracted on element name: '" & strElementName & "'"
  strResult = BuildXMLProlog(strComment, "") & vbCrlf _
            & "<nodes_from_xml>" & vbCrlf

  For Each objNode In objNodeList
    strResult = strResult & objNode.xml & vbCrlf
  Next

  strResult = strResult & "</nodes_from_xml>" & vbCrlf
  GetNodesFromXML = True
End Function
'-------------------------------------------------------
```

Using The GetNodesFromXML Function

The sample 'test' page contains a set of controls that allow you to experiment with the
GetNodesFromXML function. The default values indicate that we want to extract all the `title` elements
from the sample `booklist.xml` document:

The HTML Controls to Test the GetNodesFromXML Function

The HTML controls to create the part of the page seen above are shown next:

```
...
<P>Get elements by name from an XML document</P>
<INPUT TYPE="SUBMIT" NAME="cmdGetNode" VALUE="   ">
  GetNodesFromXML ("
<INPUT TYPE="TEXT" NAME="txtElementName" SIZE="12" VALUE="author"> ", "
<INPUT TYPE="TEXT" NAME="txtGetXML" SIZE="35" VALUE="booklist.xml">
", strResult )
...
```

The Script Code that Uses the GetNodesFromXML Function

When the SUBMIT button for the GetNodesFromXML function is clicked, the following section of ASP
code, in the part of the page that precedes the <FORM> section, is executed. We extract the value of the
element name, and the string that contains the file path and name or an XML document, and use them
in a call to our GetNodesFromXML function:

```
...
'look for a command sent from the FORM section buttons

If Len(Request.Form("cmdGetNode")) Then
  'get elements by name from an XML document
  strElemName = Request.Form("txtElementName")
  strFile = Request.Form("txtGetXML")
  blnOK = GetNodesFromXML(strElemName, strFile, strResult)
  Response.Write "GetNodesFromXML(" & QUOT _
    & strElemName & QUOT & ", " & QUOT _
    & Server.HTMLEncode(strFile) & QUOT _
    & ", strResult) returned <B>" & blnOK & "</B><BR>" _
    & "Value of strResult is"

  If blnOK Then
    Response.Write ":<PRE>" & Server.HTMLEncode(strResult) _
    & "</PRE><HR>"
  Else
    Response.Write " <B>" & Server.HTMLEncode(strResult) _
    & "</B><HR>"
  End If

End If
...
```

Again, the rest of the code is responsible for checking if the function succeeded, and displaying the input values and the result in the page. Here's the result using the default values specified in the 'test' page:

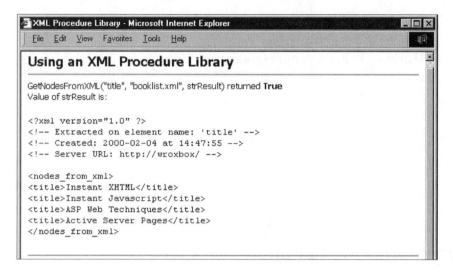

This creates an XML document containing just the `<title>` elements from the `boolist.xml` file. There are only `<title>` elements in this document because these elements have no descendents. However, if you repeat the process by specifying "`author`" as the element name, you get back an XML document that contains these elements and all their descendent elements as well:

```
<?xml version="1.0" ?>
<!-- Extracted on element name: 'author' -->
<!-- Created: 2000-02-04 at 16:57:56 -->
<!-- Server URL: http://wroxbox/ -->

<nodes_from_xml>
 <author>
  <first_name>Martin</first_name>
  <last_name>Williams</last_name>
 </author>
 <author>
  <first_name>Cheryl</first_name>
  <last_name>Caprialdi</last_name>
 </author>
 ...
 ... other author elements here
 ...
</nodes_from_xml>
```

To demonstrate the ability of our functions to accept an XML document as a string, rather than the name of a disk file, try entering some XML in the text box for the second parameter:

Get elements by name from an XML document

GetNodesFromXML (" test ", " `<test>A test XML string</test>` ", strResult)

This simple XML document contains only one element, and we are asking the function to return that element and its descendents. So, what we get back is this:

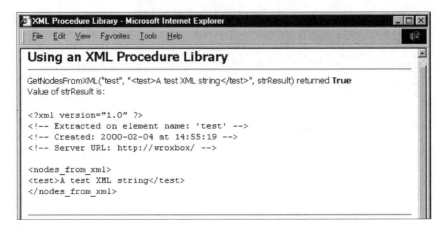

The TransformXML Function

The final function in our procedure library is designed to make the task of performing server-side XSL transformations easier, by encapsulating the whole process in one function. The `TransformXML` function takes two parameters that contain the source XML and source XSL documents, either as a string or as the appropriate file path and name. It also accepts a parameter that specifies a file to which the result will be written.

The code for the function is shown next. We first take advantage of our own `LoadAndParseXML` function to create two instances of the parser object, and load the XML and XSL documents into them. This automatically takes account of the type of value (file path and name or document string) for the `strXML` and `strXSL` parameter values, and performs the error checking. If either call to the `LoadAndParseXML` function fails, we return an error message and exit. Remember that the `LoadAndParseXML` function, and the functions that it uses, will look after writing their own error messages to the log file:

```
'-------------------------------------------------------
Function TransformXML(strXML, strXSL, strOutFile, strResult)
   '---------------------------------------------------
   'Return value type: Boolean
   'Return value: True if transformation succeeds
   'Function Description:
   '   Takes an XML document and an XSL stylesheet and
   '   performs the transformation into a result document
   '   in the strResult parameter. The two parameters
   '   strXML and strXSL can be virtual or physical file
   '   paths and names, or XML documents as strings.
   '   If a virtual or physical path name is provided in
   '   strOutFile the result is written to this file.
   '   Returns any error in the strResult parameter and
   '   adds it to log file if previously specified.
   '---------------------------------------------------
   On Error Resume Next
   TransformXML = False
```

```
      Dim strError
      Set objXML = LoadAndParseXML(strXML, strError)
      If objXML Is Nothing Then
        strResult = strError
        Exit Function
      End If

      Set objXSL = LoadAndParseXML(strXSL, strError)

      If objXSL Is Nothing Then
        strResult = strError
        Exit Function
      End If
      ...
```

Now we can perform the server-side transformation by calling the `transformNode` method of the parser object that is holding the XML document, specifying the other parser as the single parameter. If there is an error, we return a message, write it to the log file, and exit:

```
      ...
      strParseResult = objXML.transformNode(objXSL)

      If Err.Number <> 0 Then
        strResult = "Error while performing transformation"
        WriteToLogFile "Function:TransformXML", strError
        Exit Function
      End If
      ...
```

Now we can check to see if the user specified a value for the `strOutFile` parameter when they called our function. If so, we use our `GetAbsoluteFilePath` function to convert it to an absolute physical path. We specify `False` for the `blnMustExist` parameter because we don't care if the file already exists or not (again, you could use `True` for this parameter and add code here to warn the user before overwriting the existing file if required).

If our `GetAbsoluteFilePath` function returns `True`, we can then use our own `WriteToFile` function to write the transformed content to a disk file, and return a suitable status message. If the `WriteToFile` function fails, we return the error message it creates in our `strResult` parameter. Note that the variable named `strPath` will contain an error message if the call to the `GetAbsoluteFilePath` function returns `False`, so in this case we return the value of this variable:

```
      ...
      If Len(strOutFile) Then
        'write result to file
        Dim strPath

        If GetAbsoluteFilePath(strOutFile, False, strPath) Then

          If WriteToFile(strPath, strParseResult, strError) Then
            strResult = "Created file '" & strPath & "'"
          Else
            strResult = strError
            Exit Function
          End If
```

```
      Else
        strResult = strPath
        Exit Function
      End If

    Else
      'return the result
      strResult = strParseResult
    End If

    TransformXML = True
  End Function
  '-------------------------------------------------------
```

If the user provided an empty string for the `strOutFile` parameter when they called our function, we return the transformed XML, which we stored in the local variable `strParseResult` when we performed the transformation, to the user in the `strResult` parameter.

Using The TransformXML Function

The sample 'test' page contains a set of controls that allow you to experiment with the `TransformXML` function. The default values specify an XML and an XSL file that are provided with the samples. It also specifies `booklist.htm` as the output file name – as our sample XSL file performs a transformation into HTML:

The HTML Controls to Test the TransformXML Function

The HTML controls to create the part of the page seen above are shown next:

```
...
<P>Transform XML using an XSL stylesheet</P>
<INPUT TYPE="SUBMIT" NAME="cmdTransform" VALUE="   ">
  TransformXML ("
<INPUT TYPE="TEXT" NAME="txtTrnfmXML" SIZE="15" VALUE="booklist.xml"> ", "
<INPUT TYPE="TEXT" NAME="txtTrnfmXSL" SIZE="15" VALUE="booklist.xsl"> ", "
<INPUT TYPE="TEXT" NAME="txtTrnfmOut" SIZE="15" VALUE="booklist.htm">
", strResult )
...
```

The Script Code that Uses the TransformXML Function

When the `SUBMIT` button for the `TransformXML` function is clicked, the following section of ASP code, in the part of the page that precedes the `<FORM>` section, is executed. It extracts the values sent from the HTML controls from the `Request.Form` collection, and uses them in a call to our `TransformXML` function:

```
...
'look for a command sent from the FORM section buttons
If Len(Request.Form("cmdTransform")) Then
  'transform XML using an XSL stylesheet
  strXMLFile = Request.Form("txtTrnfmXML")
  strXSLFile = Request.Form("txtTrnfmXSL")
  strOutFile = Request.Form("txtTrnfmOut")
  blnOK = TransformXML(strXMLFile, strXSLFile, strOutFile, strResult)
  Response.Write "TransformXML(" & QUOT _
    & Server.HTMLEncode(strXMLFile) & QUOT & ", " & QUOT _
    & Server.HTMLEncode(strXSLFile) & QUOT & ", " & QUOT _
    & strOutFile & QUOT & ", strResult) returned <B>" _
    & blnOK & "</B><BR>Value of strResult is"

  If (blnOK) Then

    If Len(strOutFile) Then
      Response.Write " <B>" & Server.HTMLEncode(strResult) _
      & "</B><BR>Click to view the file </B><A HREF=" _
      & QUOT & strOutFile & QUOT & " TARGET=" & QUOT _
      & "_blank" & QUOT & ">" & strOutFile & "</A></B><HR>"
    Else
      Response.Write ":<BR><PRE>" _
      & Server.HTMLEncode(strResult) & "</PRE><HR>"
    End If

  Else
    Response.Write " <B>" & Server.HTMLEncode(strResult) _
      & "</B><HR>"
  End If

End If
%>
...
```

Again, the remainder of the code is concerned with displaying the result in an appropriate format. If the transformed result was written to a text file on disk, the page displays a hyperlink where you can view the result:

The next screenshot shows what our sample XML and XSL files create as `booklist.htm`. You can view the XML and XSL files (`booklist.xml` and `booklist.xsl`) to see what they contain:

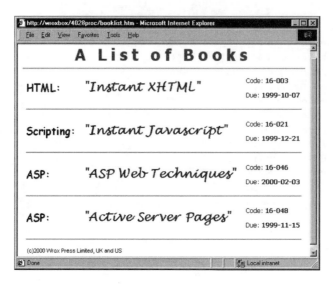

Because we're using our own custom functions in the TransformXML function, we don't have to worry about how they work and what happens if the parameter values or input files are invalid. As we discovered when we examined and experimented with these functions, they automatically look after these problems themselves. For example, if we specify the sample XML file that is **not** a well-formed document as the source XML, the result is an appropriate error message that is created by the LoadAndParseXML function and passed back to the TransformXML function:

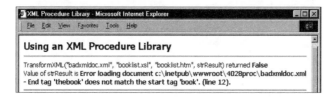

The Error Log File

Throughout most of the functions we've been describing, we make a call to the WriteToLogFile if we detect an error. Providing you've specified a path and name for the error log file, and granted that directory the appropriate permissions (as described earlier), the log file will be automatically collecting details of all these errors. This is what our log file looked like after a few experiments that caused errors to arise:

Summary

In this chapter, we've been looking at how we can build up a procedure library to make working with XML and the associated technologies much easier. While we didn't use the procedures we created in any major application, you can see from the 'test' page we provide that using them is a simple and efficient way to speed up development.

Of course, the procedures we've provided won't suit your needs in every case, and are only examples of what you might find useful. No doubt you will change, expand on and add new procedures to your own libraries as time goes on. The sample library, however, should provide a good starting point.

You also need to consider whether you are satisfied with using the functions as part of an ASP #include file, or whether you want to use a language like Visual Basic or C++ to compile them into an ActiveX DLL. It all comes down to the load you expect on your pages, i.e. the number of concurrent users.

In this chapter we looked at:

❑ Why we might consider building a procedure library

❑ Some of the important issues involved in using it

❑ The functions we've chosen to implement in our sample library

❑ How the functions can be used in a sample page

The next chapter introduces some XML-related technology that is still relatively new in the XML world.

Working with Emerging Standards in XML Technologies

Up to this point, we've been looking at quite a few facets of the XML world, and how they integrate with ASP. Now, we're going to take a step forward and take a look at emerging XML standards and technologies.

Almost everything related to XML is still in a very dynamic state of evolution, and as such, the material provided in this chapter may or may not be fully approved and recommended by the time you read this.

In this chapter we will look at:

❑ Schema repositories

❑ The BizTalk initiative

❑ The BizTalk framework specification

❑ Using `XMLHttpRequest` to transmit XML

❑ The SOAP protocol

❑ A sample distributed application using SOAP and `XMLHttpRequest`

Schema Repositories

As you have seen by now, an XML Schema (or a DTD) is a template that is used to define the grammar (structure) and vocabulary (elements) of an XML file.

From a conceptual standpoint, DTDs and schemas are intended to fulfill the same role, i.e. they are used to validate XML files. There are, however, significant differences in the details of implementation. DTDs are currently a W3C Recommendation, whereas schemas are not, although there is a working group for it at the W3C. DTDs have two significant shortcomings: they use a different and distinct syntax (with roots in SGML), and they offer no support for data typing. DTDs were an important early step in the evolution of XML, but are likely be superseded by the work being done today on schemas.

For the purpose of the discussion of schema repositories, you can think of schemas and DTDs as being functionally equivalent, as both are used to validate XML documents. Whatever form the standard eventually takes, there is a need for something that defines the structure of an XML file and can be used to validate the structure and vocabulary.

The Problem with "Roll Your Own" Tags

XML makes it easy for companies to create specialized markup languages that address their particular business needs. This is indeed a powerful capability. However, if everyone creates their own specialized schemas, the number of possible schemas permutations is great, and effortless inter-operability is jeopardized. There would be multiple ways to describe very similar data. Furthermore, there would be fragmentation and confusion in the marketplace, which would increase the cost of attaining inter-operability, and reduce the corporate desire to migrate to a world where XML-based inter-enterprise dataflow is easily achieved.

The cost of freedom in this scenario is very high: the very openness that makes XML so appealing would also stifle its own expansion and acceptance in the marketplace. So what's the solution? Well, a group of entities, "schema repositories", are emerging to address and hopefully correct this fragmentation and proliferation of "similar but not interchangeable" XML grammars and vocabularies.

What are Schema Repositories?

Schema repositories are virtual places where organizations can publish the schemas they have developed, with the goal of sharing data formats and even developing industry standards. Participation is voluntary, but there seems to be a groundswell building up where companies are eager to support such initiatives as they begin to recognize the significance of the problem.

From a real-world standpoint, your applications would not rely on retrieval of a schema from a repository on a just-in-time basis, as that would introduce an outside dependency to your systems, as well as a bottleneck that would impede scalability. You would more likely download a copy and maintain it locally. The just released (April 2000) XML parser technology preview from Microsoft goes one step further: it introduces support for in-memory schemas. This allows you to load a schema into memory once, and validate against it from there with no need for subsequent schema retrieval or disk access.

Why Do We Need Them?

We are at the very early stages of a business-to-business communications revolution that will change the way companies communicate forever. Without centralized repositories, the proliferation of schemas describing similar data and the ensuing fragmentation will continue unabated, slowing and needlessly complicating the acceptance of XML.

Benefits of Schema Repositories

Schema repositories offer numerous benefits:

- ❑ Accelerate adoption of B2B e-commerce by making schemas publicly available
- ❑ Provide collaboration venue for all interested parties (competitors, clients and suppliers)
- ❑ Provide a common, publicly or readily accessible storage point.

Business Resistance to Schema Repositories

A common opposition to publishing a schema is that it is a proprietary work. After all, a company has invested a large amount of developer and architect time to create the schema, why should they just give it away for free? Furthermore, are they giving a competitor inside information about how they work, or are they relinquishing a competitive advantage, by making their schemas freely available?

These are all very valid concerns, from a business point of view. Consider the dilemma of a fictitious web-based flower vendor: *Bloomtimes*. If Bloomtimes creates a COM object that a supplier uses to receive orders, and then publishes the schema of the XML message it receives, couldn't a competitor adopt their schema and start sending their orders to the same supplier? Yes, of course they could.

In this scenario, would Bloomtimes be hurt in any way? No. They would be revealing to the world the structure of their data, not the data itself. A lot of companies may feel that this is proprietary, but in the B2B world, when it really comes down to it, what's so special about the way a given company may choose to model an order in XML? There is a good chance that the business needs will be similar between close competitors, so it is follows that the solution will also be similar. Publishing schemas to the world effectively exposes the XML interfaces to your applications; you are not giving away the applications themselves.

Would the competitor benefit in the above scenario? Perhaps the competitor would save some development cost in adopting the schema. Or, if it was placed fully in the public domain with no intellectual property or other legal constraints, the competitor might extend and improve the schema and also publish it. Certainly the supplier would benefit if someone else starts using the same point of origin for incoming orders. Such are the benefits and risks of open source schemas.

But would Bloomtimes benefit in the above scenario? Maybe they wouldn't in a tangible sense. The supplier might become stronger financially as a result of the schema being published, which would indirectly benefit Bloomtimes. Or, they might just benefit by becoming widely known as the company that published the schema for flower order fulfillment. This fact could be publicized on the web site and other places, giving them increased visibility and recognition as being a forward-thinking industry leader.

Currently Existing Schema Repositories

There are many schema repositories in existence now, with more emerging all the time. These vary from loose inter-company collaborations to larger organized groups with significant corporate backing.

For our purposes we'll take a look at two of the main players in the world of schema repositories at the time of writing: **BizTalk** and **OASIS**.

BizTalk

BizTalk is a multi-faceted initiative by Microsoft to facilitate XML-based data exchange. Microsoft's BizTalk initiative consists of three parts:

❏ Schema Repository (BizTalk.org)

❏ Framework (the BizTalk specification)

❏ Enabling Tools (including the BizTalk server, schema mapper)

The BizTalk.org schema repository is intended to promote schema discovery, re-use and standardization. BizTalk.org is an independent body supported by numerous corporations including Microsoft, SAP, CommerceOne, Boeing, BP/Amoco and more.

The BizTalk framework is a specification that defines what the envelope of an XML message should look like. It provides a standard layout for information such as sender/recipient addresses and attachments, which can, in turn, be read and acted upon by BizTalk-aware tools and applications.

Lastly, there will be a suite of tools from Microsoft and other tool vendors that will be focused on facilitating the exchange of BizTalk messages. These will include the BizTalk server (a routing agent), the BizTalk mapper (used to define translation of XML documents from one schema to another) and BizDesk (manages trading relationships between supply chain partners). At the time of writing, these tools were all under development with expected ship dates beginning in the third quarter of 2000. Developers have, nevertheless, been able to become aquainted with BizTalk via the BizTalk JumpStart Kit, and then later with the BizTalk Technology Preview.

OASIS / XML.ORG

According to their web site:

> "OASIS, the Organization for the Advancement of Structured Information Standards, is a nonprofit, international consortium dedicated to accelerating the adoption of product-independent formats based on public standards. These standards include SGML, XML, HTML and CGM as well as others that are related to structured information processing. Members of OASIS are providers, users and specialists of the technologies that make these standards work in practice."

OASIS is member-supported and governed by an elected board. Sponsors include IBM, Sun, and CommerceOne.

As you can see, OASIS has a broader reach than just the world of XML. The OASIS-sponsored XML initiative is **XML.ORG**.

XML.ORG plans to be a repository for various DTDs, schemas, stylesheets, namespaces and more. Currently, they are not a central storage facility, but rather, are a listing of links to organizations creating schemas, such as NASA, FinXML, Microsoft. Motorola and many more. They are, however, planning to change that and actually host schemas and related documents in a future version of the site.

They are also striving to be more than just a central storage facility: they are attempting to provide a framework for metadata about schemas, DTDs and namespaces, thereby simplifying the task of indexing and searching them.

In addition to their ultimate goal of being a repository, XML.ORG publishes a specification for the creation of a repository. This means other interested parties would be able to establish their own "XML.ORG-compliant" repositories, and register themselves in a master index at the XML.ORG repository.

XML.ORG is working on an indexing strategy that will allow indexing of schemas and DTDs within their own repository, as well as in other "XML.ORG-compliant" repositories on the Internet. If this project fulfills its promises, it will yield a distributed schema repository searchable from a single point. BizTalk.org has indicated that once this specification is complete, they will participate in this indexing plan.

You can visit the OASIS home page at www.oasis-open.org, and XML.ORG at www.xml.org.

Do You Have to Choose?

There is some confusion about the relationship between OASIS and BizTalk. It is important to remember that BizTalk has three facets: the BizTalk.org website, the BizTalk framework and the commercial BizTalk server product for Windows 2000. OASIS and BizTalk share common purpose only with their attempts to make schema discovery easier.

BizTalk.ORG and XML.ORG are perhaps the two largest repositories on the Internet at the time of writing. There are more, and they will continue to proliferate as more and more businesses enter the world of XML-based structured document exchange. BizTalk and OASIS are not competitors. Microsoft is a member of OASIS, and has stated that BizTalk.org will support the OASIS metadata standard when it is available.

The benefits of some form of schema standardization are too compelling to be ignored. A comprehensive list of organizations developing schemas can be found at: www.xml.org/xmlorg_catalog.htm.

One of the beauties of XML is that it takes very little effort to convert data from one schema to another. That's the premise behind the XSLT (XSL Transformation) recommendation from the W3C. There are also third-party products available to meet this goal, and of course, you can write your own custom conversion tools. Despite the goals trying to attain some degree of conformity about schemas, some fragmentation will be inevitable, and there will be a strong need for conversion tools.

The BizTalk.org Schema Repository

The BizTalk schema repository can be accessed at www.biztalk.org.

Schemas are categorized by industry. There is no centralized index of all the schemas in the repository, but there is a search capability that lets you search for schemas based on keywords or industry. Schemas are also freely available for download.

Submissions are welcomed, but must conform to the BizTalk framework specification (see "The BizTalk Framework" later in this chapter) in order to be included, which means that XDR (XML Data Reduced) schemas must be provided, not DTDs.

Schema Registration

A nice feature of the BizTalk site is that you can register your interest in a schema. This serves two purposes – you get notified of any revisions to the schema, and it serves as an indication of the relative popularity of a given schema.

The registration, however, raises an interesting point. Just because someone has registered interest in a schema does not mean that they are actively using it. Perhaps they are an insurance company and have registered interest in all insurance-related schemas, even though they create their own enterprise-specific schemas. Perhaps an organization adopts a schema and twenty developers at the same company register their interest, thereby skewing the interest indicator.

BizTalk.org has taken the first step towards providing a mechanism to gauge the popularity of a schema, but it should not be used as a definitive measure. We can't assume that popularity equates to quality, comprehensiveness and relevance, although it could be an indicator of those attributes.

The BizTalk Framework

In this section we will take a closer look at the composition of a BizTalk document, as set forth by the BizTalk Framework specification. This discussion is based on the BizTalk 1.0a specification, which is the current release at the time of writing.

The BizTalk framework addresses the problem of data exchange (inter-application and inter-enterprise), an approach that sets it apart from schema efforts that strive for vocabulary and grammar standardization.

The BizTalk framework defines a structure to be used to host XML business data. The intention is that the framework specifies the "wrapper" or "envelope" that will be used to contain your XML message. The actual XML data you want to transfer becomes embedded in the BizTalk-compliant message, and the BizTalk specification does not impose any restrictions or guidelines on the structure or content of the embedded data.

By having a standard envelope, software vendors would then be able to write platform and language-independent "routers" that will be able to recognize a BizTalk message and, understanding the structure, be able to route the message to its designated recipient. This is analogous to the person in the mail room sorting through inbound mail and routing mail to the correct recipients, except in this case the mail is an XML message, and the recipient can be a person, process or application that is capable of understanding and acting on the message.

An example of this is the forthcoming (at the time of writing) BizTalk Server 2000 product from Microsoft. You can get the latest information about the product from http://www.microsoft.com/BizTalkServer (not to be confused with http://www.microsoft.com/BizTalk, which leads to information about the BizTalk initiative).

Anatomy of a BizTalk Document

As we saw in the earlier discussion of schema repositories, the BizTalk specification addresses the need for inter-application data transfer. The specification defines what the container will look like. The XML data you want to send gets embedded inside that container structure.

There are two key sections in a BizTalk-compliant message:

- ❑ Message header – `<header>`
- ❑ Message body – `<body>`

Before we go much further in our dissection of a BizTalk message, we should look at some terminology that will be used:

- ❑ A **BizTalk Message** is the data exchanged between servers. It contains the header and body.

- ❑ **BizTags** are the tags set forth in the BizTalk specification. They are the XML tags that constitute the envelope for the message, and all the delivery and manifest information that would go into the message header.

The following diagram shows the different parts of a BizTalk message and the containment relationships between them:

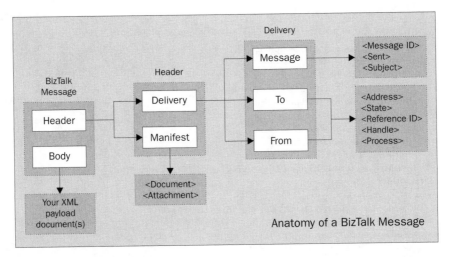

Anatomy of a BizTalk Message

A Sample BizTalk Message

The following is a sample BizTalk message:

```xml
<?xml version='1.0'?>
<biztalk_1 xmlns="urn:schemas-biztalk-org/biztalk_1.xml">
  <header>
    <delivery>
      <message>
        <messageID>8230948204820</messageID>
        <sent>1999-01-02T19:00:01+02:00</sent>
        <subject>New Purchase Order</subject>
      </message>
      <to>
        <address>http://www.flowerfarm.com/inbound.asp</address>
        <state>
          <referenceID></referenceID>
          <handle></handle>
          <process></process>
        </state>
      </to>
      <from>
        <address>mailto:purchasing@bloomtimes.com</address>
        <state>
```

```
            <referenceID>8790</referenceID>
            <handle>ORDER</handle>
            <process>PLACED</process>
          </state>
        </from>
      </delivery>
      <manifest>
        <document>
          <name>BloomTimes PO</name>
          <description>Purchase Order</description>
        </document>
      </manifest>
    </header>
    <body>
      <purchaseorder
        xmlns="x-schema:http://schemas.biztalk.org/BizTalk/madeitup8qx.xml">
        <header>
          <ponum>8790</ponum>
          <paymentby>invoice</paymentby>
          <shipby>Road</shipby>
        </header>
        <contact>
          <name>Sue Jones</name>
          <tel>(760) 967-1111</tel>
          <email>sjones@bloomtimes.com</email>
        </contact>
        <shipto>
          <address>321 Main Street</address>
          <city>Smalltown</city>
          <state>ca</state>
          <zip>12345</zip>
        <shipto>
        ...
      </purchaseorder>
    </body>
  </biztalk_1>
```

Before we get into any explanation, we'll break down the constituent parts of the delivery section of the BizTalk header.

Delivery Section

Element name	Description	Frequency	Mandatory?
<message>	Parent (grouping) element. Contains header information about this message	Once	Yes
<messageID>	Client-assigned unique identifier. See note below	Once	Yes
<sent>	Date message sent	Once	Yes
<subject>	Optional message subject	Zero or Once	No

Element name	Description	Frequency	Mandatory?
`<to>`	Parent (grouping) element. Contains message recipient information	Once	Yes
`<address>`	Logical address of recipient. If required, the application responsible for dispatching the BizTalk message would resolve this to a physical address	Once	Yes
`<state>`	Parent (grouping) element. Contains information about the state of a process	Zero or Once	No
`<referenceID>`	See note below	Zero or Once	Yes, if the parent `<state>` tag is present
`<handle>`	See note below	Zero or Once	No
`<process>`	See note below	Zero or Once	No
`<from>`	Parent (grouping) element. Contains message originator information	Once	Yes
`<address>`	Logical address of sender. If required, the application responsible for dispatching the BizTalk message would resolve this to a physical address	Once	Yes
`<state>`	Parent (grouping) Element. Contains information about the state of a process	Zero or Once	No
`<referenceID>`	See note below	Zero or Once	Yes, if the parent `<state>` tag is present
`<handle>`	See note below	Zero or Once	No
`<process>`	See note below	Zero or Once	No

You may have noticed that in the above layout there are three identifiers: a message ID in the `<message>` section and two reference IDs, one for each of the `<to>` and `<from>` sections. At first glance this may strike you as a redundancy, but this is not so.

The BizTalk framework was designed to accommodate long-running "conversations". In a scalable application, you would not send a message and keep your process alive waiting for a response. You would encode what you needed to identify the transaction, and the state would be persisted in some other fashion, likely as entries in a database. Once you received your response, the process state would be retrieved and processing would continue.

In order to retrieve process state in such a situation, you need a mechanism to associate the BizTalk message to the backend process state storage mechanism. This role is filled by the `<state>` tag and its three child tags: `<referenceID>`, `<handle>` and `<process>`. They are intended to be used in increasing order of refinement. For example, in a purchase transaction, the `<referenceID>` may contain the purchase order number, `<handle>` may contain a GUID or a process identifier such as "PlaceOrder", and `<process>` may contain a process identifier such as "ConfirmDelivery". The `<state>` tag itself is optional, but if present, at least the `<referenceID>` tag must be present as well. Note also that in the BizTalk schema, the `<state>` tag has an open content model, and as such, could be extended.

When a BizTalk message recipient receives a message and needs to send a response back to the message originator, the convention is that it would copy all the state information in the `<from>` tag of the message it received into the `<to>` tag of the response it is going to send, regardless of what's there. This way, the originating application will get back all the information it needs to identify positively that this is a continuation of an existing conversation, and if required, be able to restore state.

Manifest Section

The optional `<manifest>` section of the BizTalk document lists the XML documents that are contained in the `<body>` section:

```
<manifest>
    <document>
        <name>BloomTimes PO</name>
        <description>Purchase Order</description>
    </document>
</manifest>
```

Note that there could be one or more business documents included in a BizTalk document, but in most cases, it is likely that there would only be one (a purchase order, an invoice, etc.). The name is the same as the root tag in the body section. Document name references in the manifest should appear in the same order as the actual documents do in the body.

BizTalk documents can also carry attachments with them. Any attachments will be listed in the `<attachment>` section.

Element name	Description	Frequency	Mandatory?
`<document>`	Parent (grouping) element. Contains information about the XML document(s) included in this message	Once or More	Yes
`<name>`	Name of an XML business document included in the body of the message	Once	Yes
`<description>`	Description of an XML document included in the body of the message	Zero or Once	Yes
`<attachment>`	Parent (grouping) Element. Contains information about any files attached to this message	Zero or More	No

Element name	Description	Frequency	Mandatory?
`<index>`	Identifier for this attachment	Once	Yes
`<filename>`	Attachment file name	Once	Yes
`<description>`	Originator-defined text	Zero or Once	No
`<type>`	Implementation-defined file type, or "`biztalk`" if the attached file is another BizTalk message	Zero or Once	No

Body Section

The content of the `<body>` section is determined by the individual application. This is where the XML business document would be included, and the BizTalk framework does not impose any kind of structure or restrictions on the composition and structure of the document.

> **The only requirement is that if there are multiple documents contained in the body, then they must appear in the same order that they are declared in the manifest section.**

Extending the BizTalk Framework

Although the framework specification has been well thought out and is quite comprehensive, there will inevitably be cases where it needs to be extended to meet specific business requirements.

The best way to implement this extension would be to use namespaces to isolate the extensions, which would mean that the BizTalk message would still be compliant with the BizTalk schema it is based on, even though it contains additional information.

Consider the case where we want to add a version identifier:

```
<?xml version='1.0'?>
<biztalk_1 xmlns="urn:schemas-biztalk-org/biztalk_1.xml">
  <header>
    ...
    <manifest>
      <document>
        <name>BloomTimes PO</name>
        <description>Purchase Order</description>
        <bloomtimes:version
          xmlns:bloomtimes="urn=bloomtimes.com:purchaseOrder">
          1.2C
        </bloomtimes:version>
      </document>
    </manifest>
  </header>
  ...
</biztalk_1>
```

In this example, the BizTalk message would still be compliant with, and validate against, the BizTalk 1.0 schema. It would still validate properly because the `<version>` tag is prefixed with the `bloomtimes` namespace. If the namespace were missing, then the message would not be valid.

BizTalk Framework Summary

As the volume and demand for business-to-business e-commerce continues to explode, one of the biggest issues facing developers will be application inter-operability. The BizTalk framework addresses these issues, and when combined with a BizTalk-aware routing agent such as the BizTalk server, provides a solution. To learn more about the BizTalk framework, visit www.biztalk.org.

Transmitting XML over the Wire

In this section we will look at ways to send XML information from one point to another. We will examine client-to-server, bi-directional communication, as well as a purely server-based approach for server-to-server bi-directional communication.

We will use two new technologies to achieve this:

❑ The `XMLHttpRequest` object to transmit the data

❑ SOAP (Simple Object Access Protocol) to define the format of the message

We will start off by looking at the steps required to send an XML file, then discuss what SOAP is, and what changes are required in our application in order to conform to it.

Client Origination

At the time of writing, this approach is only something that can be done with Internet Explorer 5. The `XMLHttpRequest` object is one of the Microsoft XML DOM objects that perhaps may not get the attention some of the others do. It does, however, provide developers with a very powerful feature – the ability to send an XML document to a server, receive a result back from the server (in several different forms), and be able to parse that response with the XML DOM.

This is essentially the XML equivalent of POSTing an HTML form, with the exception that we are actually POSTing an XML document instead of form elements, and we can re-constitute that document at the receiving end.

As this is being written, `XMLHttpRequest` is not intended for use from a server-side ASP application. You cannot use it to load remote XML data or to transmit XML documents (not even to the same server). This is because HTTP requests are sent using the URLMON and WinInet components, which were intended for use only from a client machine in a regular user process. The IIS and ASP system runs in a protected server service, not in the regular user process, which impairs the functionality of the URLMON and WinInet components. The net effect of this is that server-side usage of `XMLHTTPRequest` from ASP or ISAPI is problematic and unreliable.

> *For complete details, please refer to the Microsoft Knowledgebase article http://support.microsoft.com/support/kb/articles/q237/9/06.asp.*

Hopefully this will change in the future, as XMLHttpRequest is very simple and easy to use, although it seems nobody expected it to be used as a conduit between servers. Note that in testing and limited deployment, we have used it server-side from inside a VB COM object, and in that environment we have not had any problems; but be forewarned, your experiences may differ. If you have a need for this kind of functionality from inside an ASP page, you may want to look at ASPHttp from serverobjects.com. There is also a strong possibility that a future version of XMLHttpRequest will eliminate these issues, and it may, in fact, be available by the time you read this.

Our sample application will be very simple and follows this sequence:

- ❑ On the client page, we press a "send order" button
- ❑ An XML order is sent from the client to the server. (This is where you'd normally do something meaningful with the order, but we won't in this example)
- ❑ The server builds an XML document and returns it
- ❑ The client takes the XML response and builds a confirmation message string
- ❑ The confirmation message is displayed

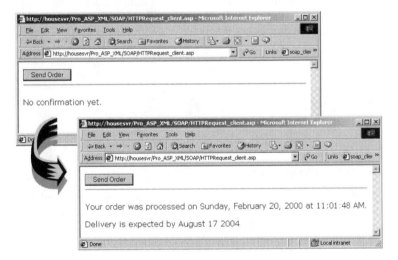

Note that our browser always stays on the same page throughout this entire process. We update the text by using DHTML to replace the innerHTML of a DIV element. There is no round-trip to the server to refresh the entire page.

Now lets look at how this was done. Two XML data islands are created: oOrder and oConfirm. oOrder includes the XML data that constitutes the order we will be posting. oConfirm exists to receive the XML file we will receive back from the server. The data islands are created on the client page using the <xml> tag:

```
<xml id="oOrder">
  <root>
    <item>1722</item>
    <description>Personal Stereo</description>
    <price>76.34</price>
  </root>
</xml>
```

```
<xml id="oConfirm">
</xml>

<button onclick="sendit()" id=button1>Send Order</button>
<hr color="salmon">
<p>
<div id="confmessage" style="font-family:verdana, arial; color:navy">
  No confirmation yet.
</div>
```

The recipient of the POST needs to be specified as a URL, which is built as shown in this server-side code:

```
<%
sPath = Request.ServerVariables("PATH_INFO")
sURL = "http://" & Request.ServerVariables("SERVER_NAME")& ":" &
Request.ServerVariables("SERVER_PORT") & _
    left(sPath, InstrRev(sPath,"/",-1,1)) & "receive_order.asp"
%>
```

The code that follows shows how simple it is to create, and send, an XML file using the
XMLHttpRequest object. When the open method is called, the action is specified, the destination that
the file is being sent to, and whether or not this is an asynchronous operation, which it isn't (false):

```
function sendit(){
  var oMsg = new ActiveXObject("Microsoft.XMLHTTP");
  var strMessage;

  oMsg.open("POST", "<%=sURL%>", false);
```

The send method is then called, passing through the XML document contained in the data island:

```
  oMsg.send(oOrder.XMLDocument);
```

Receiving and handling a response is just as easy. The responseText received is loaded into the XML
data island, oConfirm, and a test is made to ensure it parsed properly. An error message is displayed if
it didn't. A message string is then built for the end user by extracting the text of the processed and
delivery nodes. The message string is then displayed to the user by stuffing it into the innerHTML of
the <div>:

```
    oConfirm.loadXML(oMsg.responseText);
    if (oConfirm.parseError.errorCode != 0){
      strMessage = "XML Parse Error:" + oConfirm.parseError.reason +
                           " when attempting to get order confirmation.";
    }
    else
    {
      strMessage =
    oConfirm.documentElement.selectSingleNode("/orderconfirmation/processed").text;
      strMessage += "<br><br>";
      strMessage +=
     oConfirm.documentElement.selectSingleNode("/orderconfirmation/delivery").text;
    }
    confmessage.innerHTML = strMessage;
```

In this case we are using two XPath strings to explicitly extract what we need from the XML document, which pre-supposes some knowledge of what will be returned. In more complex situations, you could traverse the tree as required to achieve your goals.

That's all straightforward, but what about the missing piece? What went on in that ASP that we posted to? Surely that must have some complexity buried in it. Actually, it too is very straightforward. Let's take a look at what the ASP recipient of the POST is doing:

First, we need to set the response type to be XML:

```
Response.ContentType = "text/xml"
```

Those three lines are all that is required to take the XML document that was posted to this ASP and reconstitute in an XML DOM object:

```
Set xmldoc = Server.CreateObject("Microsoft.XML DOM")
xmldoc.async=false
xmldoc.load(Request)
```

First, we create an instance of the XML DOM. Next, we set its async property to false, meaning we do not want processing to continue until the entire document has been loaded and parsed. Then we call the load method of the XML DOM, which in this case does a binary read of the request string and parses it into the XML DOM document. So, after these three lines have executed, we have a fully loaded, parsed and ready to use XML document in our ASP, which contains the XML that was posted from the client.

This is the part where in a real-world situation you would do something with the order, but for our example all we'll do is dump it out to disk in an ASCII file:

```
Set fso = CreateObject ("Scripting.FileSystemObject")
Set logfile = fso.CreateTextFile(server.MapPath("receive_order_log.txt"), True)
logfile.WriteLine("***  Log Opened at " & now & "  ***"&vbLF)
logfile.WriteLine(xmldoc.documentElement.xml)
```

> Tip: Trying to debug the recipient of an **XMLHttpRequest** can be a challenge. One technique that makes this easier is to use the **FileSystemObject** to log activity. Be sure to grant the **IUSR_machinename** account Write privileges to the appropriate folder.

Lastly, we build our confirmation XML file and send it back to the calling script by doing a simple Response.Write:

```
strResult = "<orderconfirmation><processed>Your order was processed on " & _
     FormatDateTime(Now, vbLongDate) & " at "&time&".</processed>" & _
     "<delivery>Delivery is expected by August 17 2004</delivery>" & _
     "</orderconfirmation>"

Response.Write strResult
```

Summary of XMLHttpRequest

In this sample, we used XMLHttpRequest to send an XML file from a client to a server, and received an XML stream as a response from the server. We updated the client-side requesting page using DHTML, without refreshing the entire page. This sort of approach can form the basis of a much more appealing user interface and experience. We accomplished this without doing anything special on the server to enable remote scripting, DCOM or any other kind of remote procedure call mechanism. Lastly, as HTTP is being used as a transport mechanism, this would flow through a firewall without needing to make special arrangements or paying homage to the keepers of the network.

What is SOAP?

> **As we were about to go to press, the SOAP V1.1 Protocol was released. This chapter discusses the V1.0 protocol. There are semantic differences, but the overall concept and functionality remains the same. If you download the sample code for the sample application from the Wrox website, it will be Version 1.1 (at least) compliant. I apologize for any inconvenience this version shock may cause, but such is the price of life on the edge, and this chapter is, after all, about emerging standards.**

Every once in a while an idea comes along that on the surface appears very simple, yet has the power to affect the way applications are designed. SOAP (Simple Object Access Protocol) is such an idea. XML-based SOAP messages have the potential to transform the way we write distributed applications.

SOAP is a protocol for client-server communications across a network. At the time of writing it was not a standard, but had been submitted to the IETF (Internet Engineering Task Force) as an IETF Internet Draft.

> *The reason this is being done through the IETF instead of the W3C is because SOAP is a network protocol, and as such falls into the realm of the IETF.*

SOAP is not, however, a new technology. It is a protocol that combines two existing and widely accepted technologies: HTTP and XML. It makes use of our investments in those technologies by building upon them.

SOAP is yet another mechanism that permits remote procedure calls, or remote method invocation, just like DCOM (Distributed COM), IIOP (Internet Inter-ORB Protocol) and others. In fact, SOAP isn't as full featured as some of those. As stated in the SOAP IETF draft, it does not attempt to support:

❑ Distributed garbage collection

❑ Bi-directional HTTP communications

❑ Boxcarring or pipelining of messages (batching multiple method calls into a single message as an optimization and to reduce network traffic)

❑ Objects by reference

❑ Activation (creating components and establishing connections to components)

> It is perhaps because of its inherent simplicity that it stands a good chance of succeeding where the others have not made significant inroads. If it is accepted by the IETF, SOAP has the potential to standardize the way distributed applications communicate.

SOAP is platform-neutral, language-neutral and not dependent on any object model. Therefore, a SOAP-enabled distributed application could span multiple operating systems, consisting of objects from different vendors, written in different languages, and based on different object models.

SOAP and the BizTalk framework look similar on the surface: they both strive to set out what the envelope for an XML message should look like. They do, however, differ in their ultimate intended usages: BizTalk is transport-neutral focused on inter-operability and the exchange of XML documents within and between enterprises, whereas the current version 1.0 SOAP protocol is focused on remote method invocation and message exchanges via HTTP.

Conceptually, you can think of SOAP as being the XML version of DCOM. The SOAP specification defines what a remote object method call should look like. The fact that the method calls and data travel as plain text on the widely accepted and deployed HTTP port 80 means that SOAP-enabled distributed applications will be easier to deploy than DCOM-based distributed applications.

SOAP is a real-time communications protocol. It uses HTTP as a transport. There is no notion of persisting a message and sending it later. This raises a potential drawback: the system you are communicating with needs to be online when you send your message. The action to take if the recipient is not online is an implementation detail left to be resolved at an architectural level. You could keep retrying until you do get a response, or you could have some mechanism to provide a fail-over recipient, or perhaps you may want to serialize the message and queue it up to be sent once the recipient machine is reachable.

Conversation and Message Types

SOAP enables distributed applications through two types of web communication scenarios: request/response and fire-and-forget. In the fire-and-forget one-way communication scenario, the originator invokes a method call in a remote object, but doesn't require a return value. In the request/response scenario, objects can have a bi-directional communication, with the sender invoking a method call and receiving a return value. However, as stated above, there is no real-time bi-directional communication; method calls and return values are passed back and forth through HTTP.

A SOAP message will always fall into one, and only one, of the following categories:

- ❑ A method invocation, a Request
- ❑ The result of a method invocation, a Response
- ❑ A Fault

The method invocation originates on the SOAP client, and the result and fault are returned by the SOAP server. If a SOAP message is a fault, then, by definition, it cannot also contain a return value.

The Envelope Please

As with BizTalk, the SOAP protocol defines an envelope for a message, and a format for the XML payload container. The SOAP protocol includes custom HTTP headers, in addition to the XML of the message envelope and payload. Whereas BizTalk is not tied to a given transport, SOAP is, by definition, tied to HTTP.

The following is a graphical representation of a SOAP message:

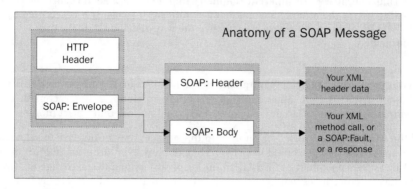

Here is a typical example of a method invocation:

This would go in the HTTP header:

```
POST /myserver HTTP/1.1
Host: www.mydomain.com
Content-Type: text/xml
Content-length:nnnn
SOAPMethodName: my-name-space#myMethod
```

This would go in the SOAP envelope:

```
<SOAP:Envelope xmlns:SOAP="urn:schemas-xmlsoap-org:soap:v1">
  <SOAP:Header>
    <t:transactionID xmlns:t="a-name-space" SOAP:mustUnderstand="1">
      19
    </t:transactionID>
  </SOAP:Header>
  <SOAP:Body>
    <m:myMethod xmlns:myMethod="my-name-space">
      <par1>foo</par1>
      <par2>bar</par2>
    </m:myMethod>
  </SOAP:Body>
</SOAP:Envelope>
```

A benefit of having the method name in the header is that it enables creation of routers that can grant or deny access to a SOAP call, and properly dispatch the SOAP calls just by reading the header, without requiring the ability to parse the XML in the message itself. A typical response could look something like this.

First the HTTP header:

```
HTTP/1.1 200 OK
Content-Type: text/xml
Content-length:nnnn
```

And now the contents of the SOAP envelope, or the payload:

```
<SOAP:Envelope xmlns:SOAP="urn:schemas-xmlsoap-org:soap:v1">
  <SOAP:Body>
    <m:myMethodResponse xmlns:m="my-name-space">
      <return>bonk</return>
    </m:myMethodResponse >
  </SOAP:Body>
</SOAP:Envelope>
```

The payload is a standard well-formed XML file. You could send binary data as part of the invocation or response, using Base64 encoding – the XML standard for encoded binaries. This would allow you to do things such as sending images with your SOAP request. Alternatively, rather than making binaries or resources part of the SOAP message, you can include a URI that points back at them.

The SOAP Header

The `<SOAP:Header>` element is optional. The intention behind the header is to send extended information along with the method call. `<SOAP:Header>` elements are used to pass implicit information. For example, a purchase transaction may consist of several individual messages that are part of a transaction. A `<SOAP:Header>` could be used to tie the related messages together. To enforce compatibility, elements contained inside a header can have a `mustUnderstand` attribute. If this attribute has a value of "1", it indicates to the receiving application that it must be able to understand and correctly process it. If the attribute has a value of "0", then it is functionally equivalent to it not being present.

Proper usage of this attribute will help in the creation of more robust applications that are extensible, but also able to raise errors if they receive messages containing data that is not fully understood.

If a SOAP server receives a message that includes a header element with a `mustUnderstand` value of "1", and it is not expecting it, then it should return a SOAP Fault with an error code of 200.

Whose Fault?

The SOAP protocol includes a way for the invoked method to return an error message to the requestor. This is achieved by having a `<SOAP:Fault>` tag as a child of the `<SOAP:Body>`. It is important to remember that there are only three types of SOAP messages: a request, a response, and an error condition. Any given SOAP message will fall into one and only one of those categories. As a result of this, the only items that will ever appear as children of the `<SOAP:Body>` tag are details of the error.

The Version 1 SOAP protocol defines four different error codes:

Code	Name	Description
100	Version mismatch	The request was made by an unsupported version of the SOAP protocol
200	Must understand	The request contained a `<SOAP:Header>` element that had a `mustUnderstand` attribute with a value of "1", and the application did not understand it
300	Invalid request	The request was not supported by the application
400	Application faulted	The application was able to understand the request, but an error occurred

The SOAP protocol dictates that a standard SOAP Fault message shall contain the following child elements:

Element	Contents
`<faultcode>`	One of the four numeric values presented above
`<faultstring>`	One of the strings listed above
`<runcode>`	An enumerated value that indicates whether or not the request was actually sent to the application. The three possible values are `Maybe`, `No` and `Yes`
`<detail>`	If present, contains application-specific error information

You may add additional sub-elements, provided they are namespace qualified. Any additional information you may wish to convey would, more than likely, be application-specific, and as such should be placed inside the `<detail>` element.

Serving It Up

The SOAP protocol defines what the message envelopes should consist of, and how error conditions should be communicated back to the requestor. Implementation details are completely up to the developer.

Whichever form the implementation takes, there will need to be some form of SOAP server that either acts upon, or acts as a routing agent for the SOAP message. This is the URI end point of the `POST`ed HTTP request.

Examples of this could include:

❑   An ASP that examines the message, instantiates a COM object and makes a method call (see our SOAP sample)

❑   A routing agent that looks at the HTTP header and routes the message on to another location

❑   An ASP that invokes a function within itself, using the XML payload as parameters

The above are only a few samples of SOAP end points. It is the fact that SOAP only defines a protocol, and that the entire implementation is left to the developer, that makes it so open and flexible.

Security

The good news is that you no longer have to pay homage to the keepers of the network, pleading with them to open a port. SOAP messages can be sent using the firewall-friendly and generally open port 80. The bad news is that any methods you expose will now be accessible to anyone that knows how to call them, so security is a concern.

However, this is not as serious a problem as many have envisaged. SOAP messages can be sent through normal secure mechanisms such as SSL or HTTPS, and use normal access control and authentication processes. Firewalls and other HTTP filters can be configured to block messages based on the content of the HTTP header, thereby determining which methods can be called, and even by whom. The fact that the method name is in the header (as well as in the body) means that messages can be blocked without needing to be able to understand the structure and content of the message itself.

In order for someone outside your firewall to wreak havoc, you would first need to give them the capability by exposing the objects and methods to do so when invoked, give them access privileges, and even then they would need to know what to call. In other words, if a little attention is paid to security during the architecture phase, security should not be problem. There is no inherent security breach created when you write a distributed application that uses SOAP messages. Good design practices coupled with an eye to security considerations will result in applications that can safely be exposed.

Encoding Data

The SOAP protocol defines a formal method for encoding data, and supports all simple and compound data types required by a modern application. It supports the passing of strings, integers, arrays (including multi-dimensional and partially transmitted arrays) and more.

When combined with transparent proxies (discussed later in this chapter), this formalization of the encoding of data is the key feature of SOAP that will enable cross-platform inter-operability of objects that are constructed using different object models.

Sample Application

In this section we will look at a sample application that uses the interoperability techniques we have presented so far.

The scenario is a three-computer architecture:

- ❏ An order entry point
- ❏ A "sales" server that accepts the order
- ❏ A "manufacturing" server that schedules the order for production

Note that this sample uses a direct SOAP communications path between pieces, as opposed to a proxied approach that makes it appear to the application that the remote object is in fact on the local machine. SOAP-based proxied approaches to remote object usage will likely become very popular in the future as the technology matures (please see the note at the end of this chapter concerning "transparent proxies").

The architecture and message flow will look like this:

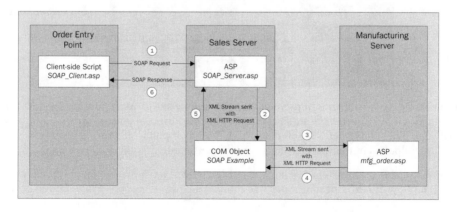

The usage scenario is as follows:

1. The order is entered and submitted

2. A "sales" server accepts the order

3. The "sales" server sends the order on to "manufacturing"

4. A "manufacturing" server accepts the order for production, and returns a confirmation

5. The "sales" server receives the confirmation and sends its own confirmation back to the client

6. The client displays confirmation details

Obviously this is the sort of application that will have many hidden complexities and nuances, which are beyond the scope of this sample. The purpose of this sample is solely to show how SOAP and `XMLHttpRequest` can be used as the messaging mechanism in a distributed application.

If you are curious about latency and how long it takes to complete this process, a cross-continent test of this sample application, through the Internet, yielded start-to-finish times ranging from sub-second up to 2 seconds. Considering the distances crossed, and the multiple layers involved, this kind of latency is well within bounds of an acceptable user experience.

Now let's look at each of these steps in a bit more detail, and see what's going on behind the scenes.

Layout of the Client-Side Page

This sample application includes a single client-side page that displays the request and response sides of this application:

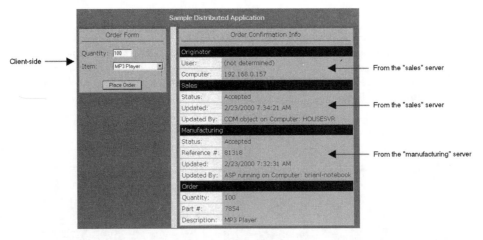

On the client, we have built an input screen that allows the user to specify which product is required and how many pieces. If you have three computers at your disposal and set up this sample, you'll find this input page quite convenient. If you don't have three computers at your disposal, you can modify the transmission endpoints in the source code to reflect your configuration.

On the left-hand side of the screen we have the order form. This is the origination point of the XML messages. The flow of XML messages starts as soon as the user clicks on "Place Order".

On the right-hand side are a series of named areas that we update using DHTML. This allows the screen to be updated as responses are received from the server, without needing to refresh the entire page. The information on the right is an aggregation of the information we get from the three different computers that participate in this exchange.

Drilling Into Code

As a first step in this process, when the user clicks the **Place Order** button on the `default.asp` client page, the client-side `sendIt` function is called. It is the controlling function that handles all the communications.

The first thing we need to do though, is construct a message based on the user selections, which is handled by the client-side `createOrder` function, also in `default.asp`:

```
function createOrder(){
  var oOrder = new ActiveXObject('Microsoft.XML DOM');
  var strXML;
  strXML =  '<?xml version="1.0"?>';
  strXML += '<SOAP:Envelope xmlns:SOAP="urn:schemas-xmlsoap-org:soap:v1"' +
                                        ' xmlns:m="my-name-space">';
  strXML += '  <SOAP:Body>';
  strXML += '    <m:order>';
  strXML += '      <quantity>' + quantity.value + '</quantity>';
  strXML += '      <item>' + selitem.options[selitem.selectedIndex].value +
                                                        '</item>';
  strXML += '      <description>' +
              selitem.options[selitem.selectedIndex].text + '</description>';
  strXML += '    </m:order>';
  strXML += '  </SOAP:Body>';
  strXML += '</SOAP:Envelope>';

  oOrder.loadXML(strXML);

  addOriginator(oOrder);

  // did the XML file load OK?
  if (oOrder.parseError.errorCode != 0){
    msg = 'Error loading SOURCE file.';
    msg += '\nDescription: ' + oOrder.parseError.reason;
    msg += '\nSource text: ' + oOrder.parseError.srcText;
    alert(msg);
  } else {
    return oOrder;
  }
}
```

This code builds a string that contains a valid XML structure representing a SOAP message. This string is then loaded into `oOrder`, which is an instance of the XML DOM. At this point, `oOrder` contains a fully parsed and ready-to-use XML DOM representation of our SOAP message.

The functionality contained in `addOriginator` is representative of the approach we have taken with our message handling – it accepts an existing SOAP message, and adds to it. At each step of the way ("client", "sales", "manufacturing") the computer handling the process will add its status to the message.

The functionality of addOriginator (which can be found in our client-side default.asp page) has been abstracted out into a separate function, as the originator information could conceivably be shared between several applications (for example, in an intranet or extranet) and be brought in via an include. A combination of client-side and server-side code is used to make this function work.

The function accepts an inbound oHost parameter, which is an XML document. Using XML DOM manipulation, we create a new element in the document called <originator>, and populate it with whatever identifying information we can determine about the client machine name and user:

```
function addOriginator(oHost){
  // add an "originator" element to the passed SOAP message
  var oParent, oChild;
  oParent = oHost.createElement("originator");
  <%
  ' note: using server-side code to add in computer identification info
  remote_user = Request.ServerVariables("REMOTE_USER")
  if remote_user = "" then
    user = "(not determined)"
    computer = request.servervariables("REMOTE_HOST")
    if computer = "" then
      computer = request.servervariables("REMOTE_ADDR")
    end if
  else
    pos = instr(remote_user,"\")
    computer = left(Request.ServerVariables("REMOTE_USER"),pos-1)
    user = mid(Request.ServerVariables("REMOTE_USER"),pos+1)
  end if
  %>

  oChild = oParent.appendChild(oHost.createElement("computer")).text =
      "<%=computer%>";
  oParent.appendChild(oHost.createElement("user")).text = "<%=user%>";
  oHost.selectSingleNode("//SOAP:Body").firstChild.appendChild(oParent);
}
```

The following is what our XML document would look like once this point has been reached:

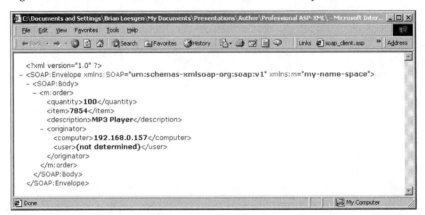

We have a server-side variable called sURL that is used to specify the SOAP server (recipient) which is the destination of this first SOAP message. We are doing this server-side so that the page can be run on a different server and sURL will still contain a fully-qualified URL (without any code changes).

Now that we have the XML portion of the SOAP message constructed, it's time to add the HTTP information and send the message on to the SOAP server we have specified in the sURL variable:

```
<%
sURL = "http://" & Request.ServerVariables("SERVER_NAME")& ":" & _
    Request.ServerVariables("SERVER_PORT") & _
    left(sPath, InstrRev(sPath,"/",-1,1)) & "SOAP_Server.asp"
%>

oMsg.open("POST", "<%=sURL%>", false);

// add the SOAP HTTP headers...
oMsg.setRequestHeader("SOAPMethodName", "order");
oMsg.setRequestHeader("MessageType", "Call");
oMsg.setRequestHeader("Content-Type", "text/xml-SOAP");

oMsg.send(oOrder.xml);
```

The SOAP message has now been sent on to the "sales server", where it is received by SOAP_Server.asp, which has the following responsibilities:

❑   It creates an instance of a class

❑   If the object *can* be instantiated, it invokes the method specified in the SOAP HTTP header and returns the result

❑   If the object *cannot* be instantiated, it responds to the SOAP message with a SOAP Fault

Note that the first thing that is done in the response type is set to text/xml. That's because when the response to this SOAP method invocation is received on the client, the XML stream will be loaded into an XML DOM object. We have hard-coded the class and destination, but these could also have been resolved dynamically. After the XML message has been parsed into an instance of the XML DOM, a string is built, based on the class name; the HTTP_SOAPMETHODNAME, which was in the HTTP header of the message received from the client, is appended, and then the string is evaluated:

```
<%
Response.ContentType = "text/xml"
Response.Expires = 0
Dim oObject, strMethodName
Dim oBody, oFault

strClass = "SOAPExample.AcceptOrder"
strMethodName = request("HTTP_SOAPMETHODNAME")

Set xmldoc = Server.CreateObject("Microsoft.XML DOM")
xmldoc.async=false
xmldoc.load(Request)

on error resume next
Set oObject = Server.CreateObject(strClass)

If IsObject(oObject) then
  strDestination = "http://your-server/soap/mfg_order.asp"
  strOut = eval("oObject." & strMethodName & "(xmldoc.xml, strDestination)")
...
```

For now, we will take an optimistic stance and assume that the message was constructed correctly and can be evaluated. We will follow the SOAP message on along the optimistic path to a COM object, which was written in Visual Basic. The COM object source code is included with the source code download for this sample application at the Wrox website, www.wrox.com.

The COM object's responsibilities are:

❑ Receive the XML message

❑ Send it to the manufacturing server

❑ Receive a confirmation from the manufacturing server

❑ Modify the message adding its own confirmation

Note that for brevity in this sample, we assume it's a perfect world where nothing ever goes wrong, so why even bother to trap for errors? If this existed in the real world, robust error-handling would need to be incorporated here, as well as at every other step in this process.

Following the message along this optimistic path, you can see the XML stream is received and sent on without change to the "manufacturing server" (as specified in the passed parameter):

```
Public Function order(strXML As Variant, strDestination As Variant)
    Dim oXMLdoc As MSXML.DOMDocument
    Dim oRequest As MSXML.XMLHTTPRequest
    Set oXMLdoc = New MSXML.DOMDocument
    Set oRequest = New MSXML.XMLHTTPRequest

    '// Specify an end-point. In this example it is a passed parameter
    '// from the calling ASP, but it could just as easily be dynamic
    '// based on the contents of the SOAP XML payload, a registry setting,
    '// a database field value, etc.
    oRequest.open "POST", strDestination, False

    '// Send the message
    oRequest.send (strXML)
```

The furthest point in the travels of our SOAP order is the `mfg_order.asp`. Its responsibilities are:

❑ Receive the SOAP order

❑ Add a "<manufacturing>" tag to hold the processing confirmation

❑ Return the modified XML stream

For the purpose of this sample application, we are not performing any actual database access. In the real world system, we would probably obtain our information from a database, or at least we would invoke local components to do this for us. Once a confirmation node is created (using a random number for the <mfgref> element value), it is inserted into the XML document and returned to the COM object:

```
<%@ Language=VBScript %>
<%
Response.ContentType = "text/xml"
```

```
Dim xmldoc

Set xmldoc = server.CreateObject("Microsoft.XML DOM")
xmldoc.load(request)

Set oNode = xmldoc.createElement("manufacturing")

Randomize
oNode.appendChild(xmldoc.createElement("mfgref")).text = int(rnd*100000)
oNode.appendChild(xmldoc.createElement("status")).text = "Accepted"
oNode.appendChild(xmldoc.createElement("updated")).text = now
oNode.appendChild(xmldoc.createElement("updatedBy")).text = _
  "ASP running on Computer: " & Request.ServerVariables("SERVER_NAME")

xmldoc.selectSingleNode("//SOAP:Body").firstChild.appendChild(oNode)

Response.Write xmldoc.xml
%>
```

After the manufacturing server has finished adding the `<manufacturing>` element, our XML message would look like this:

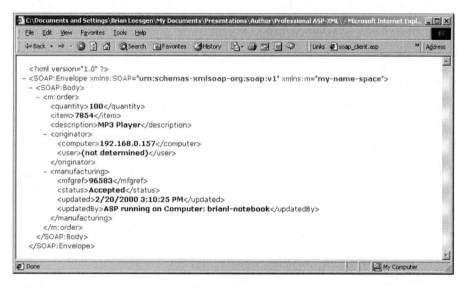

Once the COM object receives the response, it loads it into an XML DOM object. Just as on the production department's computer, a new node is created to hold confirmation information from the sales department. This new node is then appended to the existing message and returned. This addition to the XML document is done by the following DOM manipulation that occurs inside the COM object:

```
oXMLdoc.loadXML (oRequest.responseXML.xml)

'// Create an element to the message showing that we have
'// processed it
Set oNode = oXMLdoc.createElement("sales")
oNode.appendChild(oXMLdoc.createElement("status")).Text = "Accepted"
oNode.appendChild(oXMLdoc.createElement("updated")).Text = Now
```

```
oNode.appendChild(oXMLdoc.createElement("updatedBy")).Text = _
                              "COM object on Computer: " & whereami()

'// Append the element to the SOAP XML payload
oXMLdoc.selectSingleNode("//SOAP:Body").firstChild.appendChild (oNode)

'// Return the revised XML string
order = oXMLdoc.xml
```

Note that whereami() in the above code is a wrapper for a Windows API call to get the computer name:

```
Private Declare Function GetComputerName Lib "kernel32" Alias _
  "GetComputerNameA" (ByVal lpBuffer As String, lngSize As Long) As Long
...
Private Function whereami()
    Const BUFFER_SIZE = 255
    Dim lpBuffer As String 'buffer to receive machine name from API
    Dim lngErrorCode As Long

    'cause string to reserve buffer space by filling string with spaces
    lpBuffer = Space(BUFFER_SIZE)
    lngErrorCode = GetComputerName(lpBuffer, 255) 'Who am I?

    whereami = Trim(lpBuffer)
End Function
```

The last thing that the COM object does is to return the XML stream.

Back at the ASP page that invoked the COM object, the XML stream is received from the COM object and passed back to the client with a Response.Write.

After the <sales> element has been added, our XML message would look like this:

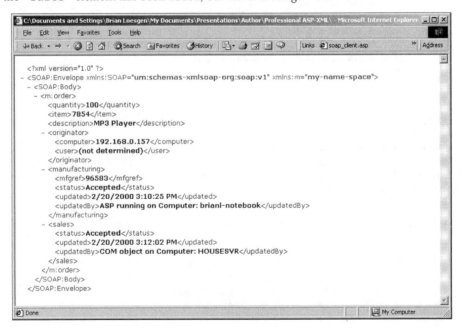

Talking About Problems – SOAP Style

As we have seen, the SOAP protocol includes a mechanism for communicating error conditions and details to the method invoker. Our sample application has an example of this. If the object instantiation fails in `SOAP_Server.asp`, we take the SOAP Message that was POSTed to us, and using XML DOM manipulation, strip out everything contained in the `<SOAP:Body>` and replace it with a `<SOAP:Fault>` message:

```
Sub LogErrorDetails(xmldoc, strError)
  '// This sub takes the passed xmldoc and replaces the
  '// elements below <SOAP:Body> with the <SOAP:Fault> message
  '// to tell the calling application about the problem
  Dim oFault, oBody
  Set oFault = xmldoc.createElement("SOAP:Fault")
  oFault.appendChild(xmldoc.createElement("faultcode")).text = "400"
  oFault.appendChild(xmldoc.createElement("faultstring")).text = _
      "Application Error"
  '// note, following line broken for formatting
  oFault.appendChild(xmldoc.createElement("detail")).
    appendChild(xmldoc.createElement("message")).text = strError
  Set oBody = xmldoc.selectSingleNode("//SOAP:Body")
  oBody.replaceChild oFault, oBody.firstChild
End Sub
```

Transparent Proxies

At the time of writing, pre-beta work was being done on products that would enable developers to make it appear that an object is running on a local server when it is, in fact, remote. Communications between the two machines would be done via SOAP messages. This means, for instance, that your ASP/VB COM application could invoke functionality that existed in a remote CORBA object. The proxy would determine what services the remote object could provide, and would present an interface to them for your local application to use.

This kind of re-use has a lot of appeal, but distributing the pieces of an application also increases the complexity of diagnosing and resolving problems. Your application becomes reliant on something that may or may not be under your control. Your application could fail because someone else's T1 line was severed. Fail-over, recovery techniques and appropriate levels of error trapping become even more important as your application begins to rely on web services provided by others.

Further, during development cycles, developers need to be able to adapt to a "what's running where" distributed mindset that can at times be perplexing. If you've ever made the common mistake of confusing client-side script code for server-side script or vice-versa, you can imagine how much easier it will be to make that kind of mistake when you have multiple servers involved in a solution.

Summary of SOAP Example

In this sample application, we have seen how SOAP messages and XML streams can be sent between computers using `XMLHttpRequest`. We have seen one approach to the handling of data that passes through several computers, the "trail of breadcrumbs" approach where every logical step adds data to the XML document to show it had been there and what the status is.

Learning More

In this section, you have been provided with an overview of the SOAP protocol.

It is still early in this game – remember that SOAP is not yet an accepted standard. However, if the degree of optimism and excitement shared among its proponents is any indication, the future looks very bright indeed for SOAP. The benefits are just too compelling to be ignored.

The SOAP V1.0 IETF draft is available at www.ietf.org/internet-drafts/draft-box-http-soap-01.txt.

Another excellent source for SOAP information can be found at www.develop.com/soap/.

Summary

This chapter has addressed emerging XML standards and technologies. We have looked at:

- ❑ Schema repositories
- ❑ The BizTalk initiative
- ❑ The BizTalk framework specification
- ❑ Using `XMLHttpRequest` to transmit XML
- ❑ The SOAP protocol
- ❑ A sample distributed application using SOAP and `XMLHttpRequest`

We have seen how these various technologies interact in order to achieve application inter-operability, and we have stepped through an example of a SOAP-enabled application, showing how the SOAP protocol can be used to package XML for inter-application exchange.

As I said at the beginning of the chapter, XML-related technologies are in a dynamic state of evolution, with new functionality and inter-operability emerging all the time. This may be the end of the chapter but it's certainly not the end of the story… watch this space!

Case Study – An On-Line Survey Tool

What are we doing here, anyway?

In the beginning, the Web was used simply as a way to provide information, a way to display pictures of my dog, Sarge, at play. Okay, maybe you didn't put pictures of my dog up, but back to the point, as more and more web pages were written, it became a natural need to ask the visitor to leave a comment, thus the "Feedback" page was born. This was usually done by writing a static HTML page containing a group of text boxes, coupled with some sort of script on the back-end, which would process the contents of these boxes. These pages were expanded, adding more and more fields, more types of fields (radio buttons, list boxes, check boxes, etc.) and, hey presto!, an online survey was born. With the advent of so-called "dot com" companies, many people jumped on the bandwagon, providing online survey services, replete with standard reports, web-based, user-friendly survey creation tools and a plethora of other gimmicks, hoping to snag the market.

At first glance, writing your own tool like this shouldn't be too difficult. After all, we simply need a way to ask questions and collect the answers. We can come up with a few pre-built reports, decide on a way for the user to generate these reports, and then we are done.

In this Case Study, we will do just that: build an online survey tool. As with most, if not all, case studies, it is not the intent of this study to develop a full-blown, production-ready system that you can spin onto your web server and begin to make a fortune, hoping for that IPO (Initial Public Offering) to make you a millionaire. Instead, we will be pushing to develop a basic system, which you can expand and enhance to satisfy the needs of your own project. Along with this, we will see a way to make use of this exciting new technology, XML, to create an extensible survey creation tool. At the end, once we have the basic tools for the survey system, we will spend some time discussing what improvements can be done to make this a true, production-ready system. Going with the idea of presenting only the major points, we will skim over some important issues: error handling, data validation, etc., returning to discuss them from a high-level.

Who is this Case Study for?

The technologies we use here are not always for the faint of heart. We won't be spending a lot of time on explanation here, instead focusing on a fairly code-heavy example. I'm expecting that you have an intermediate-level knowledge of VB, ASP, XML and XSL. Since the gist of this book was intended to bring you to this level, the tool we present here hopes to build on that introduction to show you an application of what you have learned.

So, let's get started!

Which technology will we use?

To develop the Online Survey Tool, we will be taking advantage of the following technologies:

XML

- ❏ Survey definition – create and define what questions are in the survey
- ❏ Survey results – retrieve the answers given to the questions in a survey
- ❏ Reporting – deliver a summary of the answers given to a survey

XSL

- ❏ Convert survey definition into a user interface
- ❏ Convert survey results into reports/reportable formats

ASP (VBScript)

- ❏ Deliver surveys to web browser clients
- ❏ Gather results for surveys
- ❏ Connect with database to retrieve surveys and save results

Visual Basic ActiveX In-Process Server (DLL)

- ❏ Encapsulate database access
- ❏ Encapsulate conversion from Recordset to XML
- ❏ Deliver XML to ASP page for display

Access Database

- ❏ Data store

Glossary of Terms

Whenever intending your development efforts to be seen by others, it is important to define some initial terminology. Nothing is worse than getting halfway through a system and realizing that the expectations are wrong due to a misunderstanding of a base term. Some of these may seem obvious, but usually the most obvious are the troublemakers.

❑   **Survey** – a list of questions.

❑   **Survey definition** – an XML document containing a list of questions, as well as general information about the survey.

❑   **Question** – a text string and a method to obtain an answer. Different methods for answering are provided, including, but not necessarily limited to, free-form and multiple-choice (single and multi-selection).

❑   **Surveyor** – a person who creates and defines a survey.

❑   **Surveyee** – a person who answers questions on a survey.

Design Considerations

As we all know, the most important part of the development process is the requirements definition and initial design. Without a solid foundation, our system is doomed to failure, doomed to spend its life going from one crash to the next, cursed by those who use it. As responsible designers, we will spend some time discussing our requirements and design. Some of these will seem self-evident, but we will write them down. Periodically, as we continue our system, we will refer back to these in an effort to keep on track.

Requirements and Parameters

Survey (general)

❑   A survey may consist of an unlimited number of questions.

❑   A survey does not contain branching. That is, the set and flow of the questions are always the same, regardless of the answers given. (Note: This is most definitely not true of all surveys, but we will take it as a requirement for our survey system.)

Survey (definition)

❑   Survey definition should be XML-based.

Survey (display)

❑   The minimum browser requirements will be Microsoft Internet Explorer 4.0 or Netscape 4.0.

❑   The survey should be delivered in a flavor of HTML that both browsers can read (i.e. so-called vanilla HTML, void of any browser-specific tag extensions).

❑   Any changes to formatting should be easy to implement.

❑   Survey questions will be displayed in an HTML table, the first column having the text of the question, the second column containing the answer.

Survey (creation)

❑   Survey creation should be web-based.

Reporting

❏ One pre-built report will be generated: a list of responses to the survey, which lists the answers given for each question. Naturally, more advanced reports will be needed for any robust system, particularly statistical reports. Since we are focusing on the system itself, rather than the reports, we will give enough information so you can add any other reports you like.

> With regard to our use of XML, some may view it as a bit extreme, perhaps using it in places where we don't really need to. To this, I simply say that we are building a working (and useable) example, intended to show the abilities and benefits of using XML. By handling the majority of our data in XML and transforming it with XSL into a displayable format (in our case, HTML), we are emphasizing the separation of data from formatting.

Site Overview

Sections

There are three major sections to our web site:

1. Survey Creation (defining a new or altering an existing survey).

2. Survey Delivery (displaying questions and saving answers).

3. Reporting (displaying answers for a survey in varying formats).

We will be discussing and building these systems in this order.

Survey Creation

When discussing survey creation, there are two major aspects that will need to be addressed: a standard XML-based format for survey definition and a web-based tool to generate a survey definition conforming to this XML schema. Before creating any tool, we will need to decide on what this tool will construct, so we will tackle that aspect first.

Our development of an XML schema for the survey will be rather lengthy, as, being the basis for our system, we will need to make it fairly complete. Since we will be displaying the survey on a web-browser, we can decide on user interface definitions at this time, as well. This will entail developing XSL transformations for each different way of displaying a question.

Entity Definition

Survey

The survey can be broken down into two sets of information, one survey-specific (Name, Title, etc.) the other question-specific (text, type, possible values). Since there can be multiple questions for a survey, it is natural to break the question off into its own entity. The following two tables show the data associated with these two items.

Survey	
id	Identifier for survey, unique
name	Short name of survey, used for easy identification
title	Title of survey
introduction	Introduction to survey, can include instructions, etc.
creationdate	Date survey was created

Question	
id	Unique identifier for question
surveyid	Which survey does this question belong to
sequence	Used for the ordering of questions when displaying survey
caption	Text of question
type	Type of question (Freeform or Multiple-choice)
attributes	Data-level attributes for question (maxsize, minsize, data type, etc.)
options	List of possible values for multiple-choice questions
format	XSL transformation to format this question (in our case, into HTML)
creationdate	Date question was created

> It should be noted that we are writing a web-specific tool, so I have chosen to place the XSL inside the question definition or itself. In order to fully satisfy a possible requirement to allow this to be totally UI-independent, we would need to create a list of transformations for each question, one for each UI type.

Our next step will be to take this list of information and turn it into an XML Schema, in order to have a basis for working with the data. Here is the schema:

```
<Schema xmlns="urn:schemas-microsoft-com:xml-data">
<AttributeType name='surveyID' required='yes' />
<ElementType name='name' content='textOnly' />
<ElementType name='title' content='textOnly' />
<ElementType name='intro' content='textOnly' />
<ElementType name='survey' content='eltOnly' order='many'>
  <attribute type='surveyID' />
  <element type='name' minOccurs='1' maxOccurs='1' />
  <element type='title' minOccurs='1' maxOccurs='1' />
  <element type='intro' minOccurs='1' maxOccurs='1' />
</ElementType>
</Schema>
```

The application of this schema can be seen best through an example, a sample survey, which we will use in this case study to build a survey for our web site.

```
<survey id="1">
  <name>Test 1</name>
  <title>Test Survey 1</title>
  <intro>This is a test survey for the ProXMLASP book</intro>
</survey>
```

We have a top-level element (<survey>), which has one required attribute (id) and three children, all of them required (<name>, <title>, and <intro>).

The question schema will be a bit more complicated, as we have several options with regard to questions. Before constructing the schema, we need to take a look at what we mean by a question.

What is a Question?

At the simplest level, a question consists of two things: a caption and an answer. There are two types of questions, one allowing any answer to be given (free-form) and one which restricts you to a choice from a pre-defined set (multiple-choice). The first type, free-form, is fairly simple; we simply need to collect a string from the user. This can be done with one of two HTML elements: the textbox (for single line) and the textarea (for multi-line). In the case of multiple-choice questions, we have a slightly more complicated situation, but definitely not an insurmountable one; a multiple-choice question can be single-selection or multi-selection. In the case of the single-selection, we can use either a drop-down combobox, a list box or a set of radio buttons (radio buttons are handy for creating Likert scale rating questions, for example 'strongly disagree', 'disagree', 'agree', 'strongly agree'). For multi-selection questions, we can use either a multi-select list box or a set of check boxes. When defining a multiple-choice question, we will also need a way to list the set of choices. Along with all this, we will want a way to order these questions, so we know in what sequence to present them.

Here is the question schema, followed by two examples and a bit more explanation:

```
<Schema xmlns="urn:schemas-microsoft-com:xml-data">
<AttributeType name='questionID' required='yes' />
<AttributeType name='sequence' required='yes' />
<AttributeType name='type' required='yes' />
<AttributeType name='attname' required='yes' />
<AttributeType name='attvalue' required='yes' />
<ElementType name='att' content='empty'>
  <attribute type='attname' />
  <attribute type='attvalue' />
</ElementType>
<ElementType name='atts' content='eltOnly' order='many'>
  <element type='att' minOccurs='1' maxOccurs='*' />
</ElementType>
<ElementType name='optcaption' content='textOnly' />
<ElementType name='optvalue' content='textOnly' />
<ElementType name='opt' content='eltOnly' order='many'>
  <element type='optcaption' minOccurs='1' maxOccurs='1' />
  <element type='optvalue' minOccurs='1' maxOccurs='1' />
</ElementType>
<ElementType name='opts' content='eltOnly' order='many'>
  <element type='opt' minOccurs='1' maxOccurs='*' />
```

```
    </ElementType>
    <ElementType name='caption' content='textOnly' />
    <ElementType name='question' content='eltOnly' order='many'>
      <attribute type='questionID' />
      <attribute type='sequence' />
      <attribute type='type' />
      <element type='caption' minOccurs='1' maxOccurs='1' />
      <element type='atts' minOccurs='0' maxOccurs='1' />
      <element type='opts' minOccurs='0' maxOccurs='1' />
    </ElementType>
  </Schema>
```

The simplest question will look something like:

```
<q id='3' seq='1' type='1'>
  <caption>Please enter your name</caption>
</q>
```

A complicated one might look like:

```
<q id='7' seq='4' type='2'>
  <caption>What do you think of this book?</caption>
  <atts>
    <att name='default' value='1' />
  </atts>
  <opts>
    <opt>
      <caption>Good</caption>
      <value>0</value>
    </opt>
    <opt>
      <caption>Superb</caption>
      <value>1</value>
    </opt>
    <opt>
      <caption>Spectacular</caption>
      <value>2</value>
    </opt>
  </opts>
</q>
```

The `seq` attribute allows us to order the questions and the `type` attribute allows us to keep track of what type of question we are dealing with.

The `<atts>` tag allows us to define attributes for a question, for example a default value. As can be seen in the schema and the example, the format for an attribute is very simple.

```
<att name='attribute_name' value='attribute_value'>
```

The `<opts>` tag allows us to define the set of possible values for a multiple-choice question. The format for an individual option looks as follows:

```
<opt>
  <caption>caption for the option</caption>
  <value>value of the option, this will be stored in the response</value>
</opt>
```

We've mentioned the possible types of question; here is a table outlining them and their respective type IDs:

Question Types			
ID	**Typename**	**Description**	**HTML Equivalent(s)**
1	free-form	Allow any entry	`<textarea></textarea>` or `<input type='text'>`
2	multiple-choice single-select	Choose one item from a list	`<select>` or `<input type='radio'>`
3	multiple-choice multi-select	Choose multiple items from a list	`<select>` or `<input type='checkbox'>`

We could have separated the different HTML elements into their own types, but that goes against our idea of maintaining a distinction between the question and the format. The HTML will be placed into our transformation.

For each question in a survey, we will have an associated XSL transformation to convert it to a displayable format. The formatting (size, number of items visible, horizontal versus vertical display of radio buttons and check boxes, etc.) will be specific to the individual questions, but we can create some templates for the transformations that will simply need to be adjusted for the formatting. We will deal indepth with the actual customization of these templates when we discuss the survey creation tool. For now, we will assume that we have a method for customizing the templates.

Since we will be displaying the surveys in an HTML table, each question will have a `<tr></tr>` pair and two `<td></td>` pairs. These have several properties that can be customized; the following two tables outline them (we will deal with these more extensively when we develop the survey creation tool):

Customizable attributes for `<TR></TR>` pair		
Attribute Name	**Possible Values**	**Description**
`align`	`left, center, right`	Horizontal alignment for cells
`valign`	`bottom, middle, top`	Vertical alignment for cells
`bgcolor`	Predefined color or RGB value	Background color for row

Customizable attributes for <TD></TD> pair		
Attribute name	**Possible Values**	**Description**
align	left, center, right	Horizontal alignment for cells
valign	bottom, middle, top	Vertical alignment for cells
width	value or percent	Width or fraction of total table that this cell takes up
bgcolor	Predefined color or RGB value	Background color for cell

Needless to say, there are many more attributes, some Internet Explorer-specific and some Netscape-specific. We will constrain ourselves to this small subset, though. To find out more information about browser-specific tags and attributes, you can visit their respective sites at Microsoft and Netscape.

When transforming into HTML, we will use the name attribute of each type to keep track of the question ID, prefacing it with "_q" (for example, `<input type='text' name='_q1'>` for question 1) as a means to identify which form elements contain answers to questions. The underscore will give us a reasonable confidence that the name will be unique and specific to our survey tool.

Free-Form Questions

In HTML, there are two types of free-form questions: single line and multiple line. Since this is a display issue and not a data one, we will take care of this in the transformation itself.

Single Line

This is the easiest of all the questions, as it simply needs to be transformed into `<input type='text'>`. We would like this code:

```
<q id='1' type='1' seq='1'>
  <caption>Please enter your first name</caption>
</q>
```

to become this, by way of our transformation:

```
<tr>
  <td>Please enter your name</td>
  <td><input value='' type='text' name='_q1' /></td>
</tr>
```

The following XSL fragment will accomplish this:

```
<tr>
  <td><xsl:value-of select='q/caption' /></td>
  <td>
    <input value=''>
      <xsl:attribute name='type'>text</xsl:attribute>
      <xsl:attribute name='name'>_q<xsl:value-of select='q/@id' />
      </xsl:attribute>
    </input>
  </td>
</tr>
```

Multiple Line

This is also fairly easy, transforming something like this:

```
<q id='2' type='1' seq='1'>
  <caption>Please leave a message</caption>
</q>
```

into this:

```
<tr>
  <td>Please leave a message</td>
  <td><textarea name='_q2'> </textarea></td>
</tr>
```

A slight variation on the XSL for a textbox will accomplish this transformation:

```
<tr align='left' valign='top'>
  <td><xsl:value-of select='q/caption' /></td>
  <td>
    <textarea>
      <xsl:attribute name='name'>_q<xsl:value-of select='q/@id' />
      </xsl:attribute>
      <![CDATA[]]>
    </textarea>
  </td>
</tr>
```

The `<![CDATA[]]>` element is included because if we do not put some sort of value between the `<textarea>` and the `</textarea>`, the XSL transformation will yield `<textarea />`, which, while valid XML, isn't recognized as valid HTML by our web browsers.

Attributes for Free-Form Questions

By using the `<atts>` tag, we can define some question-specific attributes for the data. The following is a list of attributes that a free-form question can have:

Attributes for free-form questions			
Name	Possible values	Effect	Single-line or Multi-line
maxsize	number	Set the maximum number of characters that can be accepted as a response	single-line
default	string	Value that will be accepted if nothing else is accepted. In HTML, this will be the value originally shown.	both

To handle these, our XSL transformations will need to be altered slightly.

Single Line

Once again, here is some example XML:

```
<q id='1' type='1' seq='1'>
  <caption>Please enter your first name</caption>
```

```
   <atts>
     <att name='maxsize' value='5' />
     <att name='default' value='Corey Haines' />
   </atts>
 </q>
```

The following XSL fragment:

```
<tr>
  <td><xsl:value-of select='q/caption' /></td>
  <td>
    <input>
       <xsl:attribute name='type'>text</xsl:attribute>
       <xsl:attribute name='name'>_q<xsl:value-of select='q/@id' />
       </xsl:attribute>
       <xsl:if test='q/atts/att[@name = "maxsize"]'>
         <xsl:attribute name='maxsize'>
           <xsl:value-of select='q/atts/att[@name="maxsize"]/@value' />
         </xsl:attribute>
       </xsl:if>
       <xsl:choose>
         <xsl:when test='q/atts/att[@name = "default"]'>
           <xsl:attribute name='value'>
             <xsl:value-of select='q/atts/att[@name="default"]/@value' />
           </xsl:attribute>
         </xsl:when>
         <xsl:otherwise>
           <xsl:attribute name='value'></xsl:attribute>
         </xsl:otherwise>
       </xsl:choose>
    </input>
  </td>
</tr>
```

will result in the following HTML:

```
<tr>
  <td>Please enter your first name</td>
  <td>
    <input type="text" name="_q1" maxsize="5" value="Corey Haines" />
  </td>
</tr>
```

This XSL deserves a few remarks, specifically about the `<xsl:if>` and the `<xsl:choose>` elements.

The the following lines test to see if there is an attribute with the name of maxsize and, if there is, add a maxsize attribute to the input box:

```
<xsl:if test='q/atts/att[@name = "maxsize"]'>
  <xsl:attribute name='maxsize'>
    <xsl:value-of select='q/atts/att[@name="maxsize"]/@value' />
  </xsl:attribute>
</xsl:if>
```

The following lines look for an attribute with a name of "default" value, and, if it is there, add that as the `value` attribute of the input box, otherwise they simply place an empty string:

```
<xsl:choose>
  <xsl:when test='q/atts/att[@name = "default"]'>
    <xsl:attribute name='value'>
      <xsl:value-of select='q/atts/att[@name="default"]/@value' />
    </xsl:attribute>
  </xsl:when>
  <xsl:otherwise>
    <xsl:attribute name='value'></xsl:attribute>
  </xsl:otherwise>
</xsl:choose>
```

Multiple Line

A multiple line, free-form question has only one attribute, the default value. We can add this to the XML:

```
<q id='2' type='1' seq='1'>
  <caption>Please leave a message</caption>
  <atts>
    <att name='default' value='This is fun' />
  </atts>
</q>
```

The attribute-aware XSL transformation looks like this:

```
<tr>
  <td><xsl:value-of select='q/caption' /></td>
  <td>
    <textarea>
      <xsl:attribute name='name'>_q<xsl:value-of select='q/@id' />
      </xsl:attribute>
      <xsl:choose>
        <xsl:when test='q/atts/att[@name = "default"]'>
          <xsl:value-of select='q/atts/att[@name="default"]/@value' />
        </xsl:when>
        <xsl:otherwise><![CDATA[]]></xsl:otherwise>
      </xsl:choose>
    </textarea>
  </td>
</tr>
```

This results in the following HTML:

```
<tr>
  <td>Please leave a message</td>
  <td>
    <textarea name="_q2">This is fun</textarea>
  </td>
</tr>
```

Again, the `<xsl:choose>` element simply decides whether or not to place a default value. In the case of the `<textarea>` element, though, the default value is not placed as an attribute, but, rather, as a value in-between the opening and the closing tag. The formatting (where we put the closing `</xsl:when>` and `</xsl:otherwise>` tags) is so that the `</textarea>` follows the text immediately.

If we take out the default value attribute from the XML, we are left with the following HTML:

```
<tr>
  <td>Please leave a message</td>
  <td><textarea name="_q2"></textarea></td>
</tr>
```

Multiple-Choice Questions

Needless to say, because of the many different ways to display a multiple-choice question, the list of possible transformations will be much longer than in the case of the free-form question. There are two styles, single-select and multi-select, which we will be addressing.

Single Select

A single-select, multiple-choice question can be displayed in three different ways: a listbox, a drop-down combobox or a set of radio buttons.

The XML definition of the question looks as follows (yes, I know this is a very biased and leading question, but, since I wrote part of this book, I'd hate for you to rate it poorly):

```
<q id='3' seq='3' type='2'>
  <caption>What do you think of this book?</caption>
  <opts>
    <opt>
      <caption>Good</caption>
      <value>0</value>
    </opt>
    <opt>
      <caption>Superb</caption>
      <value>1</value>
    </opt>
    <opt>
      <caption>Spectacular</caption>
      <value>2</value>
    </opt>
  </opts>
</q>
```

Display as a List Box

In order to display this as a list box, we will need to transform it into the following HTML (the number of items listed should be configurable at survey creation):

```
<tr>
  <td>What do you think of this book?</td>
  <td>
    <select size='3' name='_q3'>
```

```
            <option value='0'>Good</option>
            <option value='1'>Superb</option>
            <option value='2'>Spectacular</option>
          </select>
        </td>
      </tr>
```

To reach this HTML fragment, we can apply the following XSL transformation:

```
<tr>
  <td><xsl:value-of select='q/caption' /></td>
  <td>
    <select size='3'>
      <xsl:attribute name='name'>_q<xsl:value-of select='q/@id' />
      </xsl:attribute>
      <xsl:for-each select='q/opts/opt'>
        <option>
          <xsl:attribute name='value'><xsl:value-of select='value' />
          </xsl:attribute>
          <xsl:value-of select='caption' />
        </option>
      </xsl:for-each>
    </select>
  </td>
</tr>
```

Display as a Combo Box

Displaying as a combobox is basically the same as displaying as a listbox, except that the size attribute of the <select> tag should be set at 1:

```
<tr>
  <td>What do you think of this book?</td>
  <td>
    <select size='1' name='_q3'>
      <option value='0'>Good</option>
      <option value='1'>Superb</option>
      <option value='2'>Spectacular</option>
    </select>
  </td>
</tr>
```

Thus, the XSL should be the same, with the small change in the size attribute:

```
<tr>
  <td><xsl:value-of select='q/caption' /></td>
  <td>
    <select size='1'>
      <xsl:attribute name='name'>_q<xsl:value-of select='q/@id' />
      </xsl:attribute>
      <xsl:for-each select='q/opts/opt'>
        <option>
          <xsl:attribute name='value'><xsl:value-of select='value' />
          </xsl:attribute>
```

```
            <xsl:value-of select='caption' />
          </option>
        </xsl:for-each>
      </select>
    </td>
  </tr>
```

Display as Radio Buttons

Displaying as radio buttons gives us a slightly more interesting transformation, as there are two ways to list the options, either horizontally or vertically. Of course, we will provide both capabilities.

Horizontal Displaying

This is a common setup when you have a scale. The captions for the buttons are listed across the top with the radio buttons directly underneath them, as in the following illustration:

The desired HTML is also a bit more complicated:

```
<tr>
  <td>What do you think of this book?</td>
  <td>
    <table width="100%">
      <tr align="center" valign="bottom">
        <td>Good</td>
        <td>Superb</td>
        <td>Spectacular</td>
      </tr><tr align="center" valign="top">
        <td><input type="radio" name="_q3" value="0" /></td>
        <td><input type="radio" name="_q3" value="1" /></td>
        <td><input type="radio" name="_q3" value="2" /></td>
      </tr>
    </table>
  </td>
</tr>
```

This can achieved with the following bit of XSL:

```
<tr>
  <td><xsl:value-of select='q/caption' /></td>
  <td>
    <table width='100%'>
      <tr align='center' valign='bottom'>
        <xsl:for-each select='q/opts/opt'>
          <td><xsl:value-of select='caption' /></td>
        </xsl:for-each>
      </tr><tr align='center' valign='top'>
        <xsl:for-each select='q/opts/opt'>
          <td><input type='radio'>
            <xsl:attribute name='name'>_q<xsl:value-of select="../../@id" />
            </xsl:attribute>
```

```
               <xsl:attribute name='value'><xsl:value-of select="value" />
               </xsl:attribute>
           </input></td>
         </xsl:for-each>
      </tr>
    </table>
  </td>
</tr>
```

Vertical Displaying

This is a common setup when you have many items to choose from, too many to put side-by-side. The radio buttons are listed in a line running down the left with the captions beside them, as in the following illustration:

The desired HTML is much less complicated than the horizontal display (no nested table):

```
<tr>
  <td>What do you think of this book?</td>
  <td nowrap='1'>
    <input type='radio' name='q4' value='0' /> Good<br />
    <input type='radio' name='q4' value='1' /> Superb<br />
    <input type='radio' name='q4' value='2' /> Spectacular<br />
  </td>
</tr>
```

and it can be obtained with the following XSL (within whitespace differences):

```
<tr>
  <td><xsl:value-of select='q/caption' /></td>
  <td nowrap='1'>
    <xsl:for-each select='q/opts/opt'>
      <input type='radio'>
        <xsl:attribute name='name'>_q<xsl:value-of select="../../@id" />
        </xsl:attribute>
        <xsl:attribute name='value'><xsl:value-of select="value" />
        </xsl:attribute>
      </input>
      <xsl:value-of select='caption' /><br />
    </xsl:for-each>
  </td>
</tr>
```

Multi Select

A multi-select, multiple-choice question can be displayed in two different ways: a listbox or a set of checkboxes.

The XML definition of our example question addresses the question of your favorite vegetable:

```
<q id='4' seq='4' type='3'>
  <caption>Which are your favorite vegetables? (Choose as many as you like)
  </caption>
  <opts>
    <opt>
      <caption>Carrots</caption>
      <value>0</value>
    </opt>
    <opt>
      <caption>Broccoli</caption>
      <value>1</value>
    </opt>
    <opt>
      <caption>Spinach</caption>
      <value>2</value>
    </opt>
    <opt>
      <caption>Squash</caption>
      <value>3</value>
    </opt>
    <opt>
      <caption>Peas</caption>
      <value>4</value>
    </opt>
  </opts>
</q>
```

Displaying this question is incredibly similar to the single-select version, so I will refrain from listing all the HTML; instead I shall make two comments and display the necessary XML:

❑ Displaying as a multi-select listbox is exactly the same as a single-select listbox with the exception that another attribute must be added to the `<select>` tag: multiple='1'

❑ Displaying as a set of checkboxes is exactly the same as radio buttons, including the vertical and horizontal displaying, with the exception that the type attribute of the `<input>` tag is set to checkbox rather than radio.

Here is the XSL for displaying as a multi-select listbox:

```
<tr>
  <td><xsl:value-of select='q/caption' /></td>
  <td>
    <select size='3' multiple='1'>
      <xsl:attribute name='name'>_q<xsl:value-of select='q/@id' />
      </xsl:attribute>
      <xsl:for-each select='q/opts/opt'>
        <option>
          <xsl:attribute name='value'><xsl:value-of select='value' />
          </xsl:attribute>
          <xsl:value-of select='caption' />
        </option>
      </xsl:for-each>
    </select>
  </td>
</tr>
```

And for displaying as checkboxes, displayed horizontally:

```
<tr>
  <td><xsl:value-of select='q/caption' /></td>
  <td>
    <table width='100%'>
      <tr align='center' valign='bottom'>
        <xsl:for-each select='q/opts/opt'>
          <td><xsl:value-of select='caption' /></td>
        </xsl:for-each>
      </tr><tr align='center' valign='top'>
        <xsl:for-each select='q/opts/opt'>
          <td><input type='checkbox'>
            <xsl:attribute name='name'>_q<xsl:value-of select="../../@id" />
            </xsl:attribute>
            <xsl:attribute name='value'><xsl:value-of select="value" />
            </xsl:attribute>
          </input></td>
        </xsl:for-each>
      </tr>
    </table>
  </td>
</tr>
```

And for displaying as checkboxes, displayed vertically:

```
<tr>
  <td><xsl:value-of select='q/caption' /></td>
  <td nowrap='1'>
    <xsl:for-each select='q/opts/opt'>
      <input type='checkbox'>
        <xsl:attribute name='name'>_q<xsl:value-of select="../../@id" />
        </xsl:attribute>
        <xsl:attribute name='value'><xsl:value-of select="value" />
        </xsl:attribute>
      </input>
      <xsl:value-of select='caption' /><br />
    </xsl:for-each>
  </td>
</tr>
```

Attributes for Multiple-Choice Questions

By using the `<atts>` tag, we can define some question-specific attributes for the data. The following is a list of attributes that a multiple-choice question can have:

Attributes for multiple-choice questions			
Name	**Possible values**	**Effect**	**Single-select or Multi-select**
default	string	Value(s) that will be selected if no others are selected. In HTML, these will be selected upon opening the page.	both

To handle these, our XSL transformations will need to be altered slightly.

Single Select

Because we have two different display methods (listbox/combobox or radio button), we will have two slightly different ways to initially select a default value, based on the following XML question definition:

```
<q id='3' seq='3' type='2'>
  <caption>What do you think of this book?</caption>
  <atts>
    <att name='default' value='1' />
  </atts>
  <opts>
    <opt>
      <caption>Good</caption>
      <value>0</value>
    </opt>
    <opt>
      <caption>Superb</caption>
      <value>1</value>
    </opt>
    <opt>
      <caption>Spectacular</caption>
      <value>2</value>
    </opt>
  </opts>
</q>
```

Listbox/Combobox

To initially select an item in a listbox or a combobox, you must set `selected='1'` as an attribute of the associated `<option>` tag. Here is the XSL for a listbox, as mentioned above; the combobox can be achieved by simply changing the `size` attribute of the `<select>` tag, since this attribute controls how many items are shown: a value of 1 will give us a drop-down and anything greater than 1 will give us a listbox with that many rows visible.

```
<tr>
  <td><xsl:value-of select='q/caption' /></td>
  <td>
    <select size='3'>
      <xsl:attribute name='name'>_q<xsl:value-of select='q/@id' />
      </xsl:attribute>
      <xsl:for-each select='q/opts/opt'>
        <option>
          <xsl:attribute name='value'><xsl:value-of select='value' />
          </xsl:attribute>
          <xsl:if test='//atts/att[@name="default" and
                                   @value = context()/value]'>
            <xsl:attribute name='selected'>1</xsl:attribute>
          </xsl:if>
          <xsl:value-of select='caption' />
        </option>
      </xsl:for-each>
    </select>
  </td>
</tr>
```

Radio Buttons

To select a radio button initially, you must set checked='1' as an attribute of the associated <input> tag. Here is the XSL for the radio buttons:

Horizontal displaying

```
<tr>
  <td><xsl:value-of select='q/caption' /></td>
  <td>
    <table width='100%'>
      <tr align='center' valign='bottom'>
        <xsl:for-each select='q/opts/opt'>
          <td><xsl:value-of select='caption' /></td>
        </xsl:for-each>
      </tr><tr align='center' valign='top'>
        <xsl:for-each select='q/opts/opt'>
          <td><input type='radio'>
            <xsl:attribute name='name'>_q<xsl:value-of select="../../@id" />
            </xsl:attribute>
            <xsl:attribute name='value'><xsl:value-of select="value" />
            </xsl:attribute>
            <xsl:if test='//atts/att[@name="default" and
                                     @value = context()/value]'>
              <xsl:attribute name='checked'>1</xsl:attribute>
            </xsl:if>
          </input></td>
        </xsl:for-each>
      </tr>
    </table>
  </td>
</tr>
```

Vertical Displaying

```
<tr>
  <td><xsl:value-of select='q/caption' /></td>
  <td nowrap='1'>
    <xsl:for-each select='q/opts/opt'>
      <input type='radio'>
        <xsl:attribute name='name'>_q<xsl:value-of select="../../@id" />
        </xsl:attribute>
        <xsl:attribute name='value'><xsl:value-of select="value" />
        </xsl:attribute>
        <xsl:if test='//atts/att[@name="default" and
                                 @value = context()/value]'>
          <xsl:attribute name='checked'>1</xsl:attribute>
        </xsl:if>
      </input>
      <xsl:value-of select='caption' /><br />
    </xsl:for-each>
  </td>
</tr>
```

Multi Select

Multi-select, multiple-choice questions have two different formats: listbox and checkboxes. Here is the XML for the example multi-select question with defaults (my favorite vegetables from this list):

```
<q id='4' seq='4' type='3'>
  <caption>Which are your favorite vegetables? (Choose as many as you like)
  </caption>
  <atts>
    <att name='default' value='1' />
    <att name='default' value='2' />
    <att name='default' value='3' />
  </atts>
  <opts>
    <opt>
      <caption>Carrots</caption>
      <value>0</value>
    </opt>
    <opt>
      <caption>Broccoli</caption>
      <value>1</value>
    </opt>
    <opt>
      <caption>Spinach</caption>
      <value>2</value>
    </opt>
    <opt>
      <caption>Squash</caption>
      <value>3</value>
    </opt>
    <opt>
      <caption>Pees</caption>
      <value>4</value>
    </opt>
  </opts>
</q>
```

Because of the way we structured the `<xsl:if>` (searching for the existence of a default attribute) clauses in the XSL for the single-select questions, we can reuse it here, as well. Here are the XSL transformations for multiple-select listbox and checkboxes with default values:

Listbox/Combobox

```
<tr>
  <td><xsl:value-of select='q/caption' /></td>
  <td>
    <select size='3' multiple='1'>
      <xsl:attribute name='name'>_q<xsl:value-of select='q/@id' />
      </xsl:attribute>
      <xsl:for-each select='q/opts/opt'>
        <option>
          <xsl:attribute name='value'><xsl:value-of select='value' />
          </xsl:attribute>
          <xsl:if test='//atts/att[@name="default" and
                                            @value = context()/value]'>
            <xsl:attribute name='selected'>1</xsl:attribute>
```

```
        </xsl:if>
        <xsl:value-of select='caption' />
      </option>
    </xsl:for-each>
  </select>
  </td>
</tr>
```

Checkboxes – *Horizontal Displaying*

```
<tr>
  <td><xsl:value-of select='q/caption' /></td>
  <td>
    <table width='100%'>
      <tr align='center' valign='bottom'>
        <xsl:for-each select='q/opts/opt'>
          <td><xsl:value-of select='caption' /></td>
        </xsl:for-each>
      </tr><tr align='center' valign='top'>
        <xsl:for-each select='q/opts/opt'>
          <td><input type='checkbox'>
            <xsl:attribute name='name'>_q<xsl:value-of select="../../@id" />
            </xsl:attribute>
            <xsl:attribute name='value'><xsl:value-of select="value" />
            </xsl:attribute>
            <xsl:if test='//atts/att[@name="default" and
                                            @value = context()/value]'>
              <xsl:attribute name='checked'>1</xsl:attribute>
            </xsl:if>
          </input></td>
        </xsl:for-each>
      </tr>
    </table>
  </td>
</tr>
```

Checkboxes – *Vertical Displaying*

```
<tr>
  <td><xsl:value-of select='q/caption' /></td>
  <td nowrap='1'>
    <xsl:for-each select='q/opts/opt'>
      <input type='checkbox'>
        <xsl:attribute name='name'>_q<xsl:value-of select="../../@id" />
        </xsl:attribute>
        <xsl:attribute name='value'><xsl:value-of select="value" />
        </xsl:attribute>
        <xsl:if test='//atts/att[@name="default" and @value =
                                            context()/value]'>
          <xsl:attribute name='checked'>1</xsl:attribute>
        </xsl:if>
      </input>
      <xsl:value-of select='caption' /><br />
    </xsl:for-each>
  </td>
</tr>
```

Let's Start Coding!

Technologies

Before we start discussing the tools that we will build to support our survey system, we should take a look at the technologies that we will be using. For delivery to the Web, we will be making use of Active Server Pages; for database access, we will be writing an ActiveX DLL in Visual Basic 6.0, hosted in Microsoft Transaction Server; for data storage, we will be using Access 2000. For a production system, it isn't recommended to use Access, due to scalability issues, but for our example, it will more than suffice. Later, we will be discussing methods for porting our database to either SQL Server or Oracle. In order to make the move to an enterprise-level database, we will strive to make our system as database-type-independent as possible.

Our first step in creating an actual system is to create the directories on the web server and create any support files that we need.

Directory structure

For this application, we will use the following directory structure:

```
ProXMLASP
    images
    bin
        scripts
        includes
        xsl
```

- ❑ The ProXMLASP (root) directory contains static HTML pages (in our case, index.html, the main menu). This directory is configured in IIS for read-only, no directory browsing, and no script execution.

- ❑ The images directory contains images that are used in the site. This directory is set for read-only, no directory browsing, and no script execution.

- ❑ The bin directory contains any binary files; our DLL will go there, along with our database file. It is set for execute access only, no read/write, no directory browsing.

- ❑ The scripts directory stores our ASP pages. It is set for script execution only, no read/write or directory browsing.

- ❑ The includes directory is where our include files are stored. These are included into our ASP pages on the server, so we can remove all access (i.e. Permissions = None).

- ❑ The xsl directory is where our XSL files are contained. Since all our transformations will be on the server, this can be set to no access at all.

By separating our files out into logical groups (given by the directories), we make it easier to maintain and administer, and users are only given as much access as is absolutely needed.

Support Files

There are a couple of support files that we will use to make coding easier, the specifics of which we will talk about in a bit. These will be included into our ASP files as needed. This way, we can centralize some commonly used routines and information. Whenever you are dealing with include files, there are a few issues which need to be addressed:

❑ Naming conflicts – Often, you will create a variable with a certain name (Title, for example), and you may run into problems with these names conflicting with other variables in either your main ASP or other included files.

❑ Dependencies – If an included file itself includes another file, you may run into a conflict if you include the same file, in effect including the file twice.

❑ Output – If a function in an include file contains calls to Response.Write, you may run into trouble if you want to use the function, but don't want output or want to change where the output is placed on the screen.

To get around these issues, we will state few guidelines:

❑ Include files must contain only functions, and those functions' names will be prefaced with the include filename (example: paths_getWebRoot()).

This will help alleviate the naming conflicts in two ways. First, by not allowing "naked" code (code not in a function), you are narrowing the possibility that a variable defined in an include file will conflict with a variable or function in the main page or another include file. Second, prefacing your function name with the name of the file will narrow the possibility of your function names conflicting with variables and functions defined in the main page or another include file.

❑ Include files cannot, themselves, include other files. That is, no nested includes.

This will cut down on the chance that, inadvertently, a file will be included twice.

❑ Functions in an include file which produce HTML output will return that output as a string. The main page will then do a Response.Write of that string.

This will allow the main page to control where all user interface elements are placed.

❑ Include files will contain no raw HTML; all HTML will be generated and returned from a function.

This adds to the idea that the main page should control placement of user interface elements.

One other thing is worth note when dealing with include files: many times, include files are given the extension of .inc. Unfortunately, if an external user somehow accesses the include file itself, they are shown the ASP code (try it!). Naturally, we don't want our code exposed to the outside world, so we will get around this by naming our include files with an ASP extension. This way, if a user accesses the page, the code will be parsed by the ASP engine, and an empty page will be sent to the browser.

There are two main include files that we will use across our system: paths.asp and dbconnstr.asp.

paths.asp

paths.asp is an include file that contains methods to retrieve paths to other files in our system. This allows us to keep from hard-coding paths into our individual files, allowing us the ability to change our directory structure, if needed.

The base functions in this file are as follows:

`paths_getWebRoot()`	Returns path to the root of the application
`paths_getScripts()`	Returns path to the scripts directory
`paths_getImages()`	Returns path to the images directory
`paths_getDefaultDocument()`	Returns path to the default document

For example, if you wanted to generate a "return to home" link, you would put code like this into your page:

```
<p>return to <a href='<%= paths_getDefaultDocument()%>'>home</a></p>
```

If, for some reason, you changed the name or location of the default document, you would simply need to make a change in the include file, rather than in all your files.

In our case study, the file looks like:

```
<%
Function paths_getWebRoot()
  paths_getWebRoot = "http:/localhost/proxmlasp/"
End Function

Function paths_getScripts()
  paths_getScripts = paths_getWebRoot () & "scripts/"
End Function

Function paths_getImages()
  paths_getImages = paths_getWebRoot() & "images/"
End Function

Function paths_getDefaultDocument()
  paths_getDefaultDocument = paths_getWebRoot() & "index.HTML"
End Function
%>
```

Naturally, in your system, at least the `getWebRoot()` function would return a different value.

dbconnstr.asp

`dbconnStr.asp` contains one base function:

`DBConnStr_getConnStr()`	This returns the connection string used to connect to the database

```
<%
Function DBConnStr_getConnStr()
  DBConnStr_getConnStr = "Provider=Microsoft.Jet.OLEDB.4.0;Data Source=" & _
                         Server.MapPath("/proxmlasp/bin/survey3.mdb")
End Function
%>
```

All of our ASP pages will begin with the following code, setting our language of choice (VBScript) and including the two files:

```
<%@LANGUAGE="VBSCRIPT" ENABLESESSIONSTATE="FALSE" %>
<%option explicit %>
<!--#include file="includes/paths.asp" -->
<!--#include file="includes/dbconnstr.asp" -->
```

Notice the command ENABLESESSIONSTATE="FALSE" that we have placed inside the first line. Since we are not making use of any session functionality in our system, we can instruct IIS to not bother setting up a session when a web page is requested. This can increase the performance of our system, since the web server can skip the steps required to initiate a session.

Of course, no mention needs to be made of option explicit, since it is just good practice to force the declaration of variables.

Survey Creation Tool (createsurvey.asp)

The diagram below shows the activity diagram for our system. Our first step will be to gather the survey-specific information, followed by looping through the questions, and gathering the necessary information for each one. When we have retrieved the information for all the questions, we save the survey into the database.

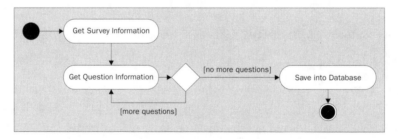

Looking at this diagram, we can see that our ASP page will basically be a simple state machine (a program that executes different functionality based on some parameter) with three possible states: Get Survey Information, Get Question Information, Save Into Database. In order to implement this, we will need two things: a way to keep track of what state we are in and a way to navigate between states. The first can be solved with a parameter on our URL; we will call it step and it will take on 3 different values:

❑   "" (empty string) or 1 – Get survey information (the default state)

❑   2 – Get question information

❑   3 – Save into database

While in state 2, we will need a way to decide which question we are requesting information about. The easiest way to do this is to use another URL parameter, this time called curq, and it will simply take an integer as a value, depending on what question we are on. When it reaches the max number of questions, we will move on to step 3.

The second issue, movement between states, almost screams for a select case statement. We will use the following code:

```
dim lStep

lStep = Trim(Request("step"))
select case lStep
case "", "1"
  ShowSurveyInfoForm
case "2"
  ProcessQuestions
case "3"
  SaveSurvey
case else
  ShowSurveyInfoForm
end select
```

Now, we simply need to implement each function that corresponds to a specific state.

ShowSurveyInfoForm()

At the survey level, we need to gather the following information:

❑ Survey name

❑ Survey title

❑ Survey introduction

In order to loop through our questions, we will also ask the user at this point how many questions there will be in the survey.

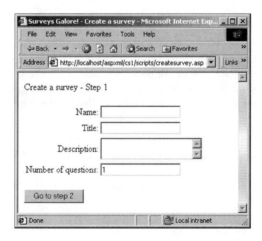

Here is the HTML for this page:

```
<HTML>
<head>
  <title>Surveys Galore! - Create a survey</title>
</head>
<body>
```

```
    <form action='http://localhost/proxmlasp/createsurvey.asp?step=2&curq=1'
        method='post'>
    <table>
      <tr><td align='right'>Name:</td>
        <td><input type='text' name='_survname' value=''></td></tr>
      <tr><td align='right'>Title:</td>
        <td><input type='text' name='_survtitle' value=''></td></tr>
      <tr><td align='right'>Description:</td>
        <td><textarea name='_survintro'></textarea></td></tr>
      <tr><td align='right'>Number of questions:</td>
        <td><input type='text' name='_qcnt' value='1'></td></tr>
    </table>
    <p><input type='submit' name='submit' value='Go to step 2' /></p>
    </form>
  </body>
</HTML>
```

This is pretty easy to implement in ASP, as we don't have any real parameterized HTML. We can simply wrap the above code in a function (with one exception):

```
Sub ShowSurveyInfoForm()
%>
   ' HTML listed above
<%
End Sub
```

The exception is on the path to the `createsurvey.asp` given for the action of the form. The ASP code actually looks like:

```
<form action='<%=paths_getScripts() %>createsurvey.asp?step=2&curq=1'
    method='post'>
```

This makes use of our `paths.asp` function `paths_getScripts()` to get the path for the `createsurvey.asp`. Admittedly, this might be a bit of overkill, since we are redirecting to the same page, so it will, of course, be in the same directory as itself. However, I prefer to use it across the board, whether we are going to the same page or a different one; this keeps some sort of consistency in our code.

ProcessQuestions()

For a question, we will need to gather the following information:

❑ Caption

❑ Type

❑ (If multiple-choice) Possible values

❑ (If multiple-choice) Display type (listbox, combobox, radio buttons, check boxes)

❑ (If radio or check) Layout (horizontal or vertical)

A simple page to gather this information would look like the following:

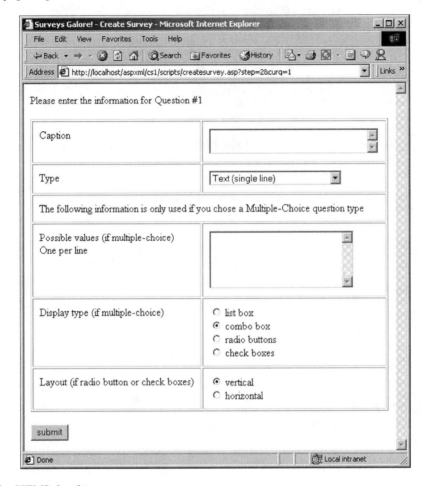

Here is the HTML for this page:

```
<HTML>
<head>
  <title>Surveys Galore! - Create Survey</title>
</head>
<body>
<p>Please enter the information for Question #1</p>
  <form action='createsurvey.asp?step=2&curq=2' method='post'>
    <table border='1' cellpadding='10'>
      <tr align='left' valign='top'>
        <td>Caption</td>
        <td><textarea rows='2' cols='30' name='_q1cap'></textarea></td>
      </tr><tr align='left' valign='top'>
        <td>Type</td>
        <td>
          <select name='_q1type'>
            <option value='1'>Text (single line)</option>
```

```
                    <option value='2'>Text (multi-line)</option>
                    <option value='3'>Multiple-Choice (single select)</option>
                    <option value='4'>Multiple-Choice (multi-select)</option>
                </select></td>
            </tr><tr align='left' valign='top'>
                <td colspan='2'>The following information is only used
                    if you chose a Multiple-Choice question type</td>
            </tr><tr align='left' valign='top'>
                <td>Possible values (if multiple-choice)<br/>One per line</td>
                <td><textarea rows='5' cols='25' name='_q1opts'></textarea></td>
            </tr><tr align='left' valign='top'>
                <td>Display type (if multiple-choice)</td>
                <td>
                    <input type='radio' onclick='checkdisplaytype(1);
                                'name='_q1disptype' value='1'/> list box<br/>
                    <input type='radio' onclick='checkdisplaytype(2);
                        'name='_q1disptype' value='2' checked='1'/> combo box<br/>
                    <input type='radio' onclick='checkdisplaytype(3);
                                'name='_q1disptype' value='3'/> radio buttons<br/>
                    <input type='radio' onclick='checkdisplaytype(4);
                                'name='_q1disptype' value='4'/> check boxes<br/>
                </td>
            </tr><tr align='left' valign='top'>
                <td>Layout (if radio button or check boxes)</td>
                <td>
                    <input type='radio' name='_q1layout'
                                        value='1' checked='1'> vertical<br/>
                    <input type='radio' name='_q1layout' value='2'> horizontal
                </td>
            </tr>
        </table>
        <input type='hidden' name='_survname' value='test'/>
        <input type='hidden' name='_survtitle' value='test'/>
        <input type='hidden' name='_survintro' value='test'/>
        <input type='hidden' name='_qcnt' value='1'/>
        <p><input type='submit' name='submit' value='submit'/></p>
    </form>
</body>
</HTML>
```

It is worth noting that the names of the input fields are of the form _q<question number><name of data>, for example _q1cap for question 1's caption, _q1type for question 1's type, etc.

As we move through the question pages, gathering the information for the specific pages, we will be storing all the question data as hidden fields in the HTML, the names of the fields conforming to our _q<question number><name of data> format. This way, when we reach the point of saving the questions into the database, we simply loop through all the hidden fields, gathering the information for each question.

Once we collect all the information, we will display it to the user for preview before we save it to the database. This has the added benefit of allowing us a smooth transition to the next state in our state machine.

Here is what the final page will look like (ignore the sample data):

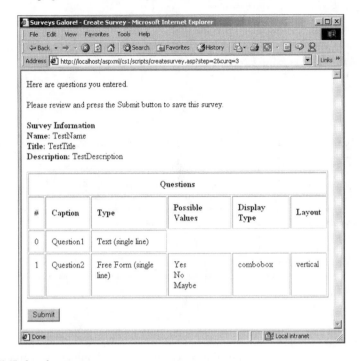

Here is the HTML for this page:

```
<HTML>
<head>
  <title>Surveys Galore! - Create Survey</title>
</head>
<body>
  <p>Here are questions you entered.</p>
  <p>Please review and press the Submit button to save this survey.</p>
  <p><b>Survey Information</b>
  <br/><b>Name:</b> testname
  <br/><b>Title:</b> testtitle
  <br/><b>Description:</b>testdesc</p>
  <table cellpadding='10' border='1'>
    <tr>
      <td align='center' colspan='6'><b>Questions</b></td>
    </tr><tr>
      <td><b>#</b></td>
      <td><b>Caption</b></td>
      <td><b>Type</b></td>
      <td><b>Possible Values</b></td>
      <td><b>Display Type</b></td>
      <td><b>Layout</b></td>
    </tr><tr valign='top'>
      <td>0</td>
      <td>q1</td>
      <td>Text (single line)</td>
      <td></td>
```

```
               <td></td>
               <td></td>
          </tr><tr valign='top'>
               <td>1</td>
               <td>q2</td>
               <td>Text (multi-line)</td>
               <td></td>
               <td></td>
               <td></td>
          </tr>
     </table>
     <form action='http://localhost/proxmlasp/scripts/createsurvey.asp?step=3'
          method='post'>
     <input type='hidden' name='_survname' value='testname'/>
     <input type='hidden' name='_survtitle' value='testtitle'/>
     <input type='hidden' name='_survintro' value='testdesc'/>
     <input type='hidden' name='_q1cap' value='q1'/>
     <input type='hidden' name='_q1type' value='1'/>
     <input type='hidden' name='_q2cap' value='q2'/>
     <input type='hidden' name='_q2type' value='2'/>
     <input type='hidden' name='_qcnt' value='2'/>
     <p><input type='submit' name='submit' value='submit'/></p>
     </form>
  </body>
  </HTML>
```

Notice that we have hid the information in hidden fields of the same format as when we are stepping through the questions. This will make it possible to use the same techniques for stripping the data from the submitted information when we submit to the database as when we are looping through the questions.

Our ASP for this function will be a bit more complicated than when we were simply displaying the survey information form, as, for each question's information, we will need to gather the information for the survey and the previous questions, then store those in hidden fields before outputting the form for gathering the current question's information. The flow will look like the following diagram:

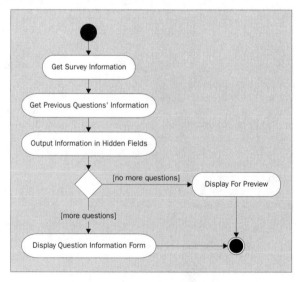

The task of collecting the information for the first two steps can be placed into functions in our ASP page:

```
Function GetSurveyInfo()
  dim asSurvInfo(2)

  asSurvInfo(0) = Trim(Request("_survname"))
  asSurvInfo(1) = Trim(Request("_survtitle"))
  asSurvInfo(2) = Trim(Request("_survintro"))

  GetSurveyInfo = asSurvInfo
End Function

Function GetQs(lCurQ)
  dim asQs()
  dim sOpts
  dim lIndex

  redim asQs(4, CInt(lCurQ)-1)
  if lCurQ >= 1 then
    for lIndex = 1 to Cint(lCurQ)
      asQs(0, lIndex-1) = Trim(Request("_q" & lIndex & "cap"))
      asQs(1, lIndex-1) = Trim(Request("_q" & lIndex & "type"))
      select case asQs(1, lIndex-1)
      case "3", "4"
        sOpts = replace(Trim(Request("_q" _
          & lIndex & "opts")), chr(13) & chr(10), ":")
        asQs(2, lIndex-1) = sOpts
        asQs(3, lIndex-1) = Trim(Request("_q" _
          & lIndex & "disptype"))
        asQs(4, lIndex-1) = Trim(Request("_q" _
          & lIndex & "layout"))
      end select
    next
  end if
  GetQs = asQs
End Function
```

These functions then can be called from `ProcessQuestions()` each time that we loop into it. We can also use them to gather the information to display to the user and finally to be placed into the database. With these two functions, the actual code for `ProcessQuestions()` is fairly simple. We need to simply output the information returned from these functions as hidden fields, and then display the form for the current question.

We will create two more functions, `QArrayToHiddenFields()` and `SurvInfoToHiddenFields()`, to convert the arrays into hidden HTML form fields. Here is the code for these two functions:

```
Function QArrayToHiddenFields(asQs)
  dim sHidFlds
  dim lIndex

  for lIndex = 1 to ubound(asQs, 2)
    sHidFlds = sHidFlds & "<input type='hidden' name='_q" & lIndex & _
```

```
                "cap' value='" & asQs(0, lIndex-1) & "' />" & _
                "<input type='hidden' name='_q" & lIndex & _
                "type' value='" & asQs(1, lIndex-1) & "' />"
           select case asQs(1, lIndex-1)
           case "3", "4"
              sHidFlds = sHidFlds & "<input type='hidden' name='_q" & lIndex & _
                 "opts' value='" & asQs(2, lIndex-1) & "' />" & _
                 "<input type='hidden' name='_q" & lIndex & _
                 "disptype' value='" & asQs(3, lIndex-1) & "' />"
              select case asQs(3, lIndex-1)
              case "3", "4"
                 sHidFlds = sHidFlds & "<input type='hidden' name='_q" & lIndex & _
                     "layout' value='" & asQs(4, lIndex-1) & "' />"
              end select
           end select
      next
      QArrayToHiddenFields = sHidFlds
   End Function

   Function SurvInfoToHiddenFields(asSurvInfo)
      dim sHidflds
      sHidFlds = "<input type='hidden' name='_survname' value='" & _
                 asSurvInfo(0) & "' />"
      sHidFlds = sHidFlds & "<input type='hidden' name='_survtitle' value='" & _
                 asSurvInfo(1) & "' />"
      sHidFlds = sHidFlds & "<input type='hidden' name='_survintro' value='" & _
                 asSurvInfo(2) & "' />"
      SurvInfoToHiddenFields = sHidflds
   End Function
```

Inside `ProcessQuestions()`, we will need to first get the current question from the URL (curq parameter). By comparing this to the number of questions in the survey (_qcnt form variable), we can tell whether we need to gather information about another question or go to the preview screen.

Here is the ASP code for `ProcessQuestions()`:

```
Sub ProcessQuestions()
   dim lCurQ
   dim lQCnt
   dim asQs
   dim asSurvInfo
   dim lIndex
   dim sToWrite

   lQCnt = Trim(Request("_qcnt"))
   if IsNumeric(lQCnt) then
      lQCnt = CInt(lQCnt)
      if lQCnt > 0 then
         lCurQ = Trim(Request("curq"))
         if IsNumeric(lCurQ) then
            lCurQ = CInt(lCurQ)
            asQs = GetQs(lCurQ)
            asSurvInfo = GetSurveyInfo()
            Response.Write "<HTML><head>" & _
                    "<title>Surveys Galore! - Create Survey</title></head><body>"
```

```
    if lCurQ <= lQCnt then
    Response.Write "<p>Please enter the information for Question #" & _
            lCurQ & "</p>" & _
        "<form action='" & paths_getScripts() & _
            "createsurvey.asp?step=2&curq=" & _
        lCurQ + 1 & "' method='post'>" & _
        "<table border='1' cellpadding='10'>" & _
        "<tr align='left' valign='top'><td>Caption</td>" & _
        "<td><textarea rows='2' cols='30' name='_q" & lCurQ & _
            "cap'></textarea></td>" & _
        "</tr><tr align='left' valign='top'><td>Type</td>" & _
        "<td><select name='_q" & lCurQ & "type'>" & _
        "<option value='1'>Text (single line)</option>" & _
        "<option value='2'>Text (multi-line)</option>" & _
        "<option value='3'>Multiple-Choice (single select)</option>" & _
        "<option value='4'>Multiple-Choice (multi-select)</option>" & _
        "</select></td>" & _
        "</tr><tr align='left' valign='top'>" & _
        "<td colspan='2'>The following information is only used if " & _
            "you chose a Multiple-Choice question type</td>" & _
        "</tr><tr align='left' valign='top'>" & _
        "<td>Possible values (if multiple-choice)<br />One per line" & _
            "</td><td><textarea rows='5' cols='25' name='_q" & lCurQ & _
        "opts'></textarea></td></tr><tr align='left' valign='top'>" & _
        "<td>Display type (if multiple-choice)</td>" & _
        "<td><input type='radio' onclick='checkDisplayType(1);'name='_q" &_
            lCurQ & _
        "disptype' value='1' /> list box<br />" & _
        "<input type='radio' onclick='checkDisplayType(2);'name='_q" & _
            lCurQ & _
        "disptype' value='2' checked='1' /> combo box<br />" & _
        "<input type='radio' onclick='checkDisplayType(3);'name='_q" & _
            lCurQ & _
        "disptype' value='3' /> radio buttons<br />" & _
        "<input type='radio' onclick='checkDisplayType(4);'name='_q" & _
            lCurQ & _
        "disptype' value='4' /> check boxes<br />" & _
        "</td></tr><tr align='left' valign='top'>" & _
        "<td>Layout (if radio button or check boxes)</td>" & _
        "<td><input type='radio' name='_q" & lCurQ & _
            "layout' value='1' checked='1'> vertical<br />" & _
        "<input type='radio' name='_q" & lCurQ & _
            "layout' value='2'> horizontal</td>" & _
        "</tr></table><input type='hidden' name='_qcnt' value='" & _
            lQCnt & "' />"
    sToWrite = SurvInfoToHiddenFields(asSurvInfo)
    sToWrite = sToWrite & QArrayToHiddenFields(asQs)
    Response.Write sToWrite & _
"<p><input type='submit' name='submit' value='submit' /></p></form>"
    else
    Response.Write "<p>Here are questions you entered.</p>" & _
        "<p>Please review and press the Submit button to save this " & _
            "survey.</p>" & _
        "<p><b>Survey Information</b>" & _
        "<br /><b>Name:</b> " & asSurvInfo(0) & _
        "<br /><b>Title:</b> " & asSurvInfo(1) & _
```

```
              "<br /><b>Description:</b> " & asSurvInfo(2) & "</p>" & _
              "<table cellpadding='10' border='1'>" & _
      "<tr><td align='center' colspan='6'><b>Questions</b></td></tr>" & _
          "<tr><td><b>#</b></td><td><b>Caption</b></td>" & _
          "<td><b>Type</b></td>" & _
          "<td><b>Possible Values</b></td><td><b>Display Type</b></td> & _
          "<td><b>Layout</b></td></tr>"
        sToWrite = ""
        for lIndex = 0 to lQCnt-1
          sToWrite = sToWrite & "<tr valign='top'><td>" & lIndex & _
                 "</td><td>" & asQs(0, lIndex) & "</td><td>"
          select case asQs(1, lIndex)
          case "1"
            sToWrite = sToWrite & "Text (single line)"
          case "2"
            sToWrite = sToWrite & "Text (multi-line)"
          case "3"
            sToWrite = sToWrite & "Free Form (single line)"
          case "4"
            sToWrite = sToWrite & "Free Form (single line)"
          case else
            sToWrite = sToWrite & "Unknown Type"
          end select
          sToWrite = sToWrite & "</td><td>" & _
                     replace(asQs(2, lIndex), ":", "<br />") & "</td><td>"
          select case asQs(3, lIndex)
          case "1"
            sToWrite = sToWrite & "listbox"
          case "2"
            sToWrite = sToWrite & "combobox"
          case "3"
            sToWrite = sToWrite & "radio buttons"
          case "4"
            sToWrite = sToWrite & "checkboxes"
          end select
          sToWrite = sToWrite & "</td><td>"
          select case asQs(4, lIndex)
          case "1"
            sToWrite = sToWrite & "vertical"
          case "2"
            sToWrite = sToWrite & "horizontal"
          end select
          sToWrite = stoWrite & "</td></tr>"
        next
        Response.Write sToWrite & "</table>" & _
          "<form action='" & paths_getScripts() & _
                              "createsurvey.asp?step=3' method='post'>"
        sToWrite = SurvInfoToHiddenFields(asSurvInfo)
        sToWrite = sToWrite & QArrayToHiddenFields(asQs)
        Response.Write sToWrite & _
          "<input type='hidden' name='_qcnt' value='" & lQCnt & "' />" & _
         "<p><input type='submit' name='submit' value='Submit' /></p>" & _
              "</form>"
      end if
      Response.Write "</body></HTML>"
    end if
```

```
        end if
      end if
   End Sub
```

It is rather long, due to the fact that we are constructing the HTML pages in here. Walk through it, and you will see that it basically just does what we outlined: check to see if we need to gather information about more questions. If the answer is yes (lCurQ<=lQCnt), then display the question form and output the hidden fields (making use of our pre-built functions). If we don't have any more questions (lCurQ>lQCnt), then we will display the preview page, as well as place the hidden fields into a form to be submitted to the next step.

Again, notice that we are using our paths.asp functions to get the path for our form action.

SaveSurvey()

At this point, all we have left to do is construct the function for saving our survey into the database, SaveSurvey(). We can use our previous functions, GetSurveyInfo() and GetQs() to strip the information from the submitted form, then convert it into the format that the database needs and start inserting it.

At this point, we will need to decide on exactly what is meant by "the format that the database needs".

Database

The database schema can be drawn from the tables previously created regarding the data for a survey and a question; I'll reprint them here for reference:

Survey		
id	number	Identifier for survey, unique
name	char(15)	Short name of survey, used for easy identification
title	char(50)	Title of survey
introduction	memo	Introduction to survey, can include instructions, etc.
creationdate	date	Date survey was created

Question		
id	number	Unique identifier for question
surveyid	number	Which survey does this question belong to
sequence	number	Used for ordering of questions when displaying
caption	char(50)	Text of question
type	number	Type of question (Freeform or Multiple-choice)
attributes	memo	Data-level attributes for question (maxsize, minsize, data type, etc.)

Table continued on following page

Question		
options	memo	List of possible values for multiple-choice questions
format	memo	XSL transformation to format this question (in our case, into HTML)
creationdate	date	Date question was created

Database access, itself, will be done through an ActiveX DLL, written in Visual Basic. We will name our component SurveyUtils, and it will have a single class, Surveys. As we continue through the case study, more methods will be added to the interface for this class, but, for now, we will have need for only one: SaveSurvey(). This method will accept the survey information and the information on the question, save it in the database, and return the survey ID for the newly created survey. This survey ID will then be displayed to the user. Making use of this component, the ASP code for SaveSurvey() will be very simple:

```
Sub SaveSurvey()
  dim asSurvInfo
  dim asQs
  dim lQCnt

  dim oSurvUtils
  dim lSurvID

  lQCnt = Trim(Request("_qcnt"))
  asQs = GetQs(lQCnt)
  asSurvInfo = GetSurveyInfo()

  on error resume next
  set oSurvUtils = Server.CreateObject("SurveyUtils.Surveys")
  lSurvID = oSurvUtils.SaveSurvey(asSurvInfo, asQs, DBConnStr_getConnStr())
  set oSurvUtils = Nothing

  Response.Write "<HTML><head><title>Surveys Galore! - " & _
                              "Create Survey</title></head><body>"
  if (lSurvID > 0) or (Err.Number <> 0) then
    Response.Write "<p>Survey was successfully saved. It's ID is " & _
                              lSurvID & ".</p>"
  else
    Response.Write "<p>Could not save survey.</p>" & )
      "<p>Error Number: " & err.number & _
      "Error Description: " & err.description
  end if
End Sub
```

We are making use of the two functions for stripping the survey and question data from the form, then passing these two arrays into the component.

> **Where to store the connection string?**
>
> When designing a database access component, the question of where to put the connection string is always a large design issue. We have several options, including hardcoding it into the component; saving it in the registry; passing it in on each function call; and so forth. Hardcoding is not really an option, as migrating to a new database requires a recompile of the DLL. Saving it into the registry is an option, but then all the machines running this system will have to have that registry setting, creating a little more maintenance. When migrating to a new platform, if one machine is forgotten, then we will have a nice little debugging issue on our hands. Personally, I prefer to pass the connection string into the method, relying on an include file to contain this connection string. Since this file is included in all our pages, we can safely assume that it will be consistent across all pages, and, if we move this file to a new machine, we are guaranteed that it will be the same across machines. This is always a controversial issue, but I feel it is one of personal preference. You have to weigh the advantages and disadvantages, and then decide which one is best for your application.

SurveyUtils.Surveys.SaveSurvey()

The interface for our method will be:

```
Public Function SaveSurvey(ByVal SurveyInfo As Variant, _
    ByVal Questions As Variant, _
    ByVal ConnStr As Variant) As Variant
```

SurveyInfo is a one-dimensional array that contains the survey information. Questions is a two-dimensional array that contains the information about all the questions. ConnStr is the database connection string.

Notice the use of variants as our parameter types. Since VBScript, a typeless language, will be the language that is touching this function, it makes sense to treat all incoming and outgoing parameters as variants.

When talking about database access, it is very important to take into account that we are going to be running on the Web, where the number of concurrent users could be very great. We will be using ADO as our method of database access, relying on the ability to disconnect a recordset from the database and then reconnect it to do any updates. The goal is to minimize the time that a connection is open to the database. To achieve this goal, we will develop two general purpose methods in our component for working with recordsets, OpenRS() and UpdateRS(). Since these will be internally used in our component, we can strongly type our parameters.

```
Private Function OpenRS(SQL As String, ConnStr As String) _
    As ADODB.RecordSet

Private Sub UpdateRS(ByRef RS As ADODB.Recordset, ByVal ConnStr As String)
```

Our error trapping will use a rippling idea; each method will raise an error to the calling method, appending the method to the description of the error, in effect building a call stack as it climbs the chain to whoever chooses to handle the error. In code, it looks like the following:

```
Err_Hand:
  Err.Raise Err.Number, ERR_SOURCE, _
    ERR_SOURCE & ".UpdateRS" & vbCrLf & Err.Description
```

ERR_SOURCE is a module-scope constant defined as:

```
Private Const ERR_SOURCE = "Surveys"
```

Here is the code for OpenRS():

```
Private Function OpenRS(ByVal SQL As String, ByVal ConnStr As String) _
          As ADODB.Recordset
  On Error GoTo Err_Hand

  Dim oRS As ADODB.Recordset

  Set oRS = CreateObject("ADODB.Recordset")
  oRS.CursorLocation = adUseClient
  oRS.Open SQL, ConnStr, ADODB.CursorTypeEnum.adOpenForwardOnly, _
    ADODB.LockTypeEnum.adLockBatchOptimistic, _
    ADODB.CommandTypeEnum.adCmdText

  Set oRS.ActiveConnection = Nothing
  Set OpenRS = oRS
  Set oRS = Nothing

  Exit Function
Err_Hand:
  Err.Raise Err.Number, ERR_SOURCE, _
    ERR_SOURCE & ".OpenRS" & vbCrLf & Err.Description
End Function
```

We first create the recordset, execute the SQL statement, and then disconnect the recordset from the database. Here is the code for UpdateRS():

```
Private Sub UpdateRS(ByRef RS As ADODB.Recordset, ByVal ConnStr As String)
  On Error GoTo Err_Hand

  RS.ActiveConnection = ConnStr
  RS.UpdateBatch ADODB.AffectEnum.adAffectAll
  Set RS.ActiveConnection = Nothing

  Exit Sub
Err_Hand:
  Err.Raise Err.Number, ERR_SOURCE, _
    ERR_SOURCE & ".UpdateRS" & vbCrLf & Err.Description
End Sub
```

To insert into the database using these two methods, we will first open an empty recordset containing the necessary fields. We can do this by using a WHERE id=null clause in a SELECT statement. Since our id fields are our primary keys, we will be guaranteed that id is never null, thus the recordset will be empty. We will loop through the records to insert, executing an AddNew on the empty recordset. When done, we will send it to UpdateRS() for insertion.

To create the empty recordset for inserting the survey information, we will execute:

```
SELECT id, name, title, introduction FROM survey WHERE id=null
```

Which we can fill from the `SurveyInfo` array passed into `Surveys.SaveSurvey()` as our first parameter. When we update this recordset, the autonumber functionality (`id` uses this) will automatically fill the `id` item. This can be used as a reference when adding the questions.

To create the empty recordset for inserting the individual questions, we will execute:

```
SELECT id, surveyid, sequence, caption, type, attributes, options, format
   FROM question WHERE id=null
```

We can loop through the `Questions` array that is passed into our method adding new elements to the recordset, finally passing the recordset to `UpdateRS()`.

Here is the code for `Surveys.SaveSurvey()`. Notice that we are formatting the options array into XML.

```
Public Function SaveSurvey(ByVal SurveyInfo As Variant, ByVal Questions As
Variant, ByVal ConnStr As Variant) As Variant
On Error GoTo Err_Hand

    Dim rsSurvey As ADODB.Recordset
    Dim rsQuestions As ADODB.Recordset

    Dim asOpts() As String
    Dim sOpts As String
    Dim lOptIndex As Long

    Dim lSurvID As Long
    Dim lSeq As Long
    Dim lQIndex As Long

    Set rsSurvey =
 OpenRS("SELECT id,name,title,introduction FROM survey WHERE id=null",ConnStr)
    rsSurvey.AddNew
    rsSurvey("name") = SurveyInfo(0)
    rsSurvey("title") = SurveyInfo(1)
    rsSurvey("introduction") = SurveyInfo(2)
    UpdateRS rsSurvey, ConnStr
    lSurvID = rsSurvey("id")
    rsSurvey.Close
    Set rsSurvey = Nothing

    Set rsQuestions =
 OpenRS("SELECT id,surveyid,sequence,caption,type,attributes,options,format FROM
 question WHERE id=null", ConnStr)
    lSeq = 0
    For lQIndex = LBound(Questions, 2) To UBound(Questions, 2)
        rsQuestions.AddNew
        lSeq = lSeq + 1
        rsQuestions("surveyid") = lSurvID
```

```
                rsQuestions("sequence") = lSeq
                rsQuestions("caption") = Questions(0, lQIndex)
                Select Case Questions(1, lQIndex)
                Case 1
                    rsQuestions("type") = 1
                    rsQuestions("format") = GetFormatXSL(1)
                Case 2
                    rsQuestions("type") = 1
                    rsQuestions("format") = GetFormatXSL(2)
                Case 3
                    rsQuestions("type") = 2
                    asOpts = Split(Questions(2, lQIndex), ":")
                    sOpts = ""
                    For lOptIndex = 0 To UBound(asOpts)
                        sOpts = sOpts & "<opt><caption>" & _
                        asOpts(lOptIndex) & "</caption><value>" & _
                        lOptIndex & "</value></opt>"
                    Next lOptIndex
                    rsQuestions("options") = sOpts
                    rsQuestions("format") = GetFormatXSL(3, _
                        CLng("0" & Questions(3, lQIndex)), _
                        CLng("0" & Questions(4, lQIndex)))
                Case 4
                    rsQuestions("type") = 3
                    asOpts = Split(Questions(2, lQIndex), ":")
                    For lOptIndex = 0 To UBound(asOpts)
                        sOpts = sOpts & "<opt><caption>" & _
                        asOpts(lOptIndex) & "</caption><value>" & _
                        lOptIndex & "</value></opt>"
                    Next lOptIndex
                    rsQuestions("options") = sOpts
                    rsQuestions("format") = GetFormatXSL(4, _
                        CLng("0" & Questions(3, lQIndex)), _
                        CLng("0" & Questions(4, lQIndex)))
                End Select
            Next lQIndex
        If rsQuestions.RecordCount > 0 Then
            UpdateRS rsQuestions, ConnStr
        End If
        rsQuestions.Close
        Set rsQuestions = Nothing

        SaveSurvey = lSurvID

    Exit Function
Err_Hand:
    Err.Raise Err.Number, ERR_SOURCE, ERR_SOURCE & ".SaveSurvey" & vbCrLf & _
        Err.Description
End Function
```

GetFormatXSL() is a helper function which returns the XSL for formatting each question type into HTML. The method definition is:

```
Private Function GetFormatXSL(ByVal QType As Long, _
        Optional ByVal DType As Long, Optional ByVal Orient As Long) As String
```

This XSL was defined in our analysis and definition of the survey XML, so I won't include the function here, other than to note that it consists of several `select case` statements, based on the question type (`QType`), the display type (`DType`) and the layout (`Orient`, either horizontal or vertical).

Let's Create a Survey!

Now that we have the necessary code to create and save a survey into the database, it is time to use our tool to create a sample survey. We will then use this survey as a basis for developing our survey display tool and our reporting tool. Our example survey will contain a question for each question type to illustrate each.

Here is the information for our example survey:

Survey	
name	Example Survey
title	Corey's Example Survey 1
introduction	This is a sample survey illustrating the different question types
number of questions	9

Question #1	
caption	Please enter your name:
type	Text (single line)
possible values	n/a
display type	n/a
layout	n/a

Question #2	
caption	What is your favorite animal?
type	Multiple-choice (single select)
possible values	dog, cat, horse, other
display type	combobox
layout	n/a

Question #3	
caption	What is your favorite color?
type	Multiple-choice (single select)
possible values	red, blue, green, black, other
display type	listbox
layout	n/a

Question #4	
caption	What do you think of this book?
type	Multiple-choice (single select)
possible values	Good, Superb, Spectacular, Outstanding
display type	radio buttons
layout	vertical

Question #5	
caption	On a scale of 1 to 5, how would you rate your knowledge of XML?
type	Multiple-choice (single select)
possible values	1, 2, 3, 4, 5
display type	radio buttons
layout	horizontal

Question #6	
caption	Which technologies do you use? (Choose as many as you like)
type	Multiple-choice (multi-select)
possible values	XML, XSL, ASP, Visual Basic, MTS (COM+)
display type	listbox
layout	n/a

Question #7	
caption	Pick the two highest numbers:
type	Multiple-choice (multi-select)
possible values	5, 3, 8, 10, 20
display type	checkboxes
layout	horizontal

Question #8	
caption	Pick the two lowest numbers:
type	Multiple-choice (multi-select)
possible values	20, 10, 5, 4, 100
display type	checkboxes
layout	vertical

Question #9	
caption	Please add any additional comments:
type	Text (multi-line)
possible values	n/a
display type	n/a
layout	n/a

After typing this information into the web page and clicking submit on the preview page, we are greeted with:

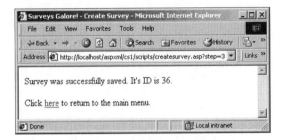

Which is exactly what we were expecting. We now have the information successfully saved into the database, so we can continue on to the next step: taking a survey!

Taking a Survey (takesurvey.asp)

The meat of our system is the displaying of a survey and processing of the responses. The basic process can be outlined as follows:

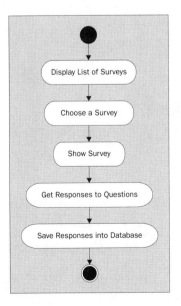

From this, we can discern that there are three basic functions that our Survey Delivery system will have to perform: Show a list of surveys; show a specific survey; and process responses for a survey.

Following the method we used before, we will create an ASP page called `takesurvey.asp` and implement a simple state machine. We will have a URL parameter called `step` which will be either 1, 2 or 3. If the parameter doesn't exist at all, the default value is 1.

```
dim lStep

lStep = trim(Request("step"))
select case lStep
case "", "1"
  ShowSurveySelect()
case "2"
  ShowSurvey()
case "3"
  SaveResponses()
case else
  ShowSurveySelect()
end select
```

ShowSurveySelect()

This method will have to do two things: Get a list of surveys from the database and display them in a listbox for selection. This is a fairly simply operation. We will need a method on our component `SurveyUtils.Surveys` that will return a list of all the surveys in the database (in XML, of course). We will then format this using an XSL transformation into a listbox. We would like to end up with something like:

Here is the HTML for this page:

```
<HTML>
<head>
  <title>Surveys Galore! - Take a Survey</title>
</head>
<body>
  <p>Please choose a survey to take.</p>
  <form action='http://localhost/proxmlasp/scripts/takesurvey.asp?step=2'
      method='post'>
```

```
      <select name="_survid" size="5">
        <option value="36">Example Survey</option>
      </select>
    <p><input type='submit' value='take survey'/></p>
    </form>
  </body>
</HTML>
```

The XML that we would like to be returned from our component is of the following format:

```
<surveys>
  <survey id='36'>
    <name>Example Survey</name>
  </survey>
</surveys>
```

There is a separate <survey> node for each survey in the database. Notice that we are only returning the ID and the name of the survey. The ID will be used in the HTML to choose which survey will be displayed, and the name is shown in the listbox. In order to turn this into a listbox, we can use the following XSL transformation:

```
<xsl:stylesheet xmlns:xsl="http://www.w3.org/TR/WD-xsl">
<xsl:template match="/">
  <select name='_survid' size='5'>
  <xsl:for-each select="surveys/survey">
    <option>
      <xsl:attribute name='value'><xsl:value-of select="@id" />
      </xsl:attribute>
      <xsl:value-of select='name' />
    </option>
  </xsl:for-each>
  </select>
</xsl:template>
</xsl:stylesheet>
```

Thus, our ASP page will simply need to make a call to our component to get the survey list, then transform it using this XSL and display the result (wrapped in the appropriate HTML for the form, of course). Here is the code to accomplish this task:

```
Sub ShowSurveySelect()
  dim sSurvList
  dim domSurvs
  dim domXSL

  dim sToWrite
  dim sTransformed

  on error resume next
  sSurvList = GetSurveyHeaders()
  if err.number <> 0 then
    sToWrite = "<p>Could not get list of surveys.<br />Error: " & _
                    err.description & "</p>"
  else
    set domSurvs = Server.CreateObject("MSXML.DOMDocument")
```

```
        if not domSurvs.loadxml(sSurvList) then
          sToWrite = "<p>Could not load survey list.<br />Error: " & _
            domSurvs.parseerror.reason & "</p>"
        else
          set domXSL = Server.CreateObject("MSXML.DOMDocument")
          if not domXSL.load(Server.MapPath("xsl/surveylisttohtml.xsl")) then
           sToWrite = "<p>Could not load survey list conversion.<br />Error: "&_
             domXSL.parseerror.reason & "</p>"
          else
            on error resume next
            sTransformed =  domSurvs.transformnode(domXSL)
            if err.number <> 0 then
              sToWrite = "<p>Could not convert survey list to HTML.<br />" & _
                         "Error: " & err.description & "</p>"
            else
              sToWrite = "<p>Please choose a survey to take.</p>" & _
                "<form action='" & paths_getScripts() & _
                "takesurvey.asp?step=2' method='post'>" & _
                sTransformed & "<p><input type='submit' value='Take Survey' />&_
                         "</p></form>"
            end if
          end if
        end if
      end if
  Response.Write "<HTML><head><title>Surveys Galore! - Take a
Survey</title></head><body>"
  Response.Write sToWrite
  Response.Write "</body></HTML>"
End Sub
```

The XSL document is stored in the XSL subdirectory from the includes directory.

Notice the call to GetSurveyHeaders(). This is another function in our ASP page which simply makes a call to our component, returning the list of survey headers:

```
Function GetSurveyHeaders()
    dim oSurvUtils
    dim sSurveyList

    set oSurvUtils = Server.CreateObject("SurveyUtils.Surveys")
    sSurveyList = oSurvUtils.GetSurveyHeaders(DBConnStr_getConnStr())
    set oSurvUtils = Nothing

    GetSurveyHeaders = sSurveyList
End Function
```

If the call to our component raises an error for some reason, this error will propogate back out to ShowSurveySelect() and it will be displayed.

SurveyUtils.Surveys.GetSurveyHeaders()

True to the nature of this step, the method in our component will be very simple. It simply needs to get the list of surveys from the database, convert them to XML and return them. Here is the code, so you can see for yourself:

```
Public Function GetSurveyHeaders(ByVal ConnStr As Variant) As Variant
On Error GoTo Err_Hand

    Dim sSQL As String
    Dim rsSurvs As ADODB.Recordset
    Dim sSurvs As String

    sSQL = "SELECT id, name FROM survey"
    Set rsSurvs = OpenRS(sSQL, ConnStr)

    sSurvs = "<surveys>"
    Do Until rsSurvs.EOF
        sSurvs = sSurvs & "<survey id='" & rsSurvs("id") & _
                "'><name>" & rsSurvs("name") & "</name></survey>"
        rsSurvs.MoveNext
    Loop
    rsSurvs.Close
    Set rsSurvs = Nothing
    sSurvs = sSurvs & "</surveys>"
    GetSurveyHeaders = sSurvs
    Exit Function
Err_Hand:
    Err.Raise Err.Number, ERR_SOURCE, _
            ERR_SOURCE & ".GetSurveyHeaders" & vbCrLf & Err.Description
End Function
```

Notice that we reusing the `OpenRS()` function that we created when we developed the survey creation tool.

Showing a Survey

Taking a survey is a bit more complicated, as we need to draw the information back out of the database and present it to the user in a nice format. We have chosen to display our survey's questions as rows in an HTML table; that is what the saved XSL transformation will do for us. The steps for displaying a survey boil down to the following diagram:

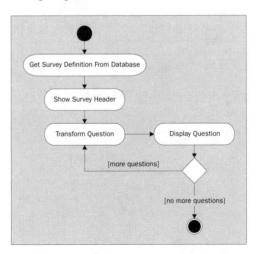

The meat of `ShowSurvey()` will be two main functions: one living in our Visual Basic component to extract the survey information from the database and format it into XML; the other a function in our ASP which will go through the extracted survey definition and convert it into HTML, applying the necessary XSL transformations. We would very much like to use our previous survey definition XML schema here, but unfortunately, we are doing a slightly different process here – the questions need to be separated out with their respective XSL transformations.

SurveyUtils.Surveys.GetSurvey()

Our Visual Basic component's method will return a two element array: the first item will be our survey header (formatted in XML for easy transformation), the second element will be another array, this time two-dimensional. This sub-array will contain the questions and their XSL transformations. Here is the code, followed by some explanation:

```
Public Function GetSurvey(ByVal SurveyID As Variant, ByVal ConnStr As Variant) As
Variant()
On Error GoTo Err_Hand

    Dim sSQL As String
    Dim rsSurvey As ADODB.Recordset

    Dim rsQuestions As ADODB.Recordset
    Dim asQuestions() As Variant
    Dim lQIndex As Long

    Dim avRetVal (0 To 1) As Variant

    sSQL = "SELECT name, title, introduction FROM survey WHERE id=" & _
                                                        SurveyID
    Set rsSurvey = OpenRS(sSQL, ConnStr)

    If Not rsSurvey.EOF Then
        avRetVal(0) = "<survey id='" & SurveyID & "'><name>" & _
        rsSurvey("name") & "</name><title>" & _
        rsSurvey("title") & "</title><intro>" & _
        rsSurvey("introduction") & "</intro></survey>"
    End If


    sSQL = "SELECT id, sequence, caption, type, attributes, " & _
                "options, format FROM question " & _
                "WHERE surveyid=" & SurveyID & " ORDER BY sequence"
    Set rsQuestions = OpenRS(sSQL, ConnStr)

    ReDim asQuestions(0 To rsQuestions.RecordCount - 1, 0 To 1) As Variant
    lQIndex = 0
    Do Until rsQuestions.EOF
        asQuestions(lQIndex, 0) = "<q id='" & rsQuestions("id") & "' " & _
                "seq='" & rsQuestions("sequence") & "' " & _
                "type='" & rsQuestions("type") & "'>" & _
                "<caption>" & rsQuestions("caption") & "</caption>"
        If Len(rsQuestions("attributes")) > 0 Then
            asQuestions(lQIndex, 0) = asQuestions(lQIndex, 0) & _
                "<atts>" & rsQuestions("attributes") & "</atts>"
        End If
        If Len(rsQuestions("options")) > 0 Then
            asQuestions(lQIndex, 0) = asQuestions(lQIndex, 0) & _
```

```
                   "<opts>" & rsQuestions("options") & "</opts>"
        End If
        asQuestions(lQIndex, 0) = asQuestions(lQIndex, 0) & "</q>"
        asQuestions(lQIndex, 1) = rsQuestions("format")
        rsQuestions.MoveNext
        lQIndex = lQIndex + 1
    Loop
    avRetVal(1) = asQuestions
    GetSurvey = avRetVal

    Exit Function
Err_Hand:
    Err.Raise Err.Number, ERR_SOURCE, ERR_SOURCE & _
                 ".GetSurvey" & vbCrLf & Err.Description
End Function
```

The survey header (the first element of the returned array) for our example survey looks like this:

```
<survey id='36'>
  <name>Example Survey</name>
  <title>Corey's Example Survey 1</title>
  <intro> This is a sample survey illustrating the different question types
  </intro>
</survey>
```

We will provide a fairly simply XSL transformation for this, placing the title and the intro as `<h1>` and `<h2>` tags, respectively. We will store this transformation in the file system, in our **xsl** directory. Here is the text for the document.

```
<xsl:stylesheet xmlns:xsl="http://www.w3.org/TR/WD-xsl">
<xsl:template match="/">
  <h1><xsl:value-of select="survey/title" /></h1>
  <h2><xsl:value-of select="survey/intro" /></h2>
</xsl:template>
</xsl:stylesheet>
```

The questions are a little more complicated, but not much more; we simply wrap the columns of the database in XML tags (`<opts>` for options and `<atts>` for attributes). For example, our question number 6 would look like this:

```
<q id="49" seq="7" type="3">
  <caption>Pick the two highest numbers:</caption>
  <opts>
    <opt>
      <caption>5</caption>
      <value>0</value>
    </opt>
    <opt>
      <caption>3</caption>
      <value>1</value>
    </opt>
    <opt>
      <caption>8</caption>
      <value>2</value>
    </opt>
    <opt>
```

```
          <caption>10</caption>
          <value>3</value>
        </opt>
        <opt>
          <caption>20</caption>
          <value>4</value>
        </opt>
      </opts>
    </q>
```

The second element of the array is simply the XSL that is stored in the database under the format column for that question. To review the XSL that is saved, re-read the section entitled "What Is A Question?", where we developed the XML Schema and XSL transformation for each question type.

Armed with this knowledge, we can tackle our next ASP function.

ShowSurvey()

Here is the code for the ShowSurvey():

```
Sub ShowSurvey()
  dim lSurvID

  dim asSurveyDef

  dim sHeaderHTML
  dim sQuestionsHTML

  lSurvID = Trim(Request("_survid"))
  if not IsNumeric(lSurvID) then
    Response.Write "<p>Invalid survey selection.</p><p>Click <a href='" & _
      paths_getScripts() & "takesurvey.asp?step=1'>here</a>" & _
              " to choose another survey."
  else
    lSurvID = CInt(lSurvID)
    on error resume next
    asSurveyDef = GetSurveyDef(lSurvID)
    if err.number <> 0 then
     Response.Write "<p>Invalid survey selection.</p><p>Click <a href='" & _
              paths_getScripts() & "takesurvey.asp?step=1'>here</a>" & _
              " to choose another survey.</p>"
    else
      on error goto 0
      sHeaderHTML = ConvertSurveyHeader(asSurveyDef(0))
      sQuestionsHTML = ConvertSurveyQuestions(asSurveyDef(1))
      Response.Write "<HTML><head><title>Survey's Galore</title>" & _
              "</head><body>" & sHeaderHTML & "<form action='" & _
              paths_getScripts() & _
              "/takesurvey.asp?step=3' method='post'>" & sQuestionsHTML & _
              "<input type='hidden' name='_survid' value='" & lSurvID & _
              "' /><p><input type='submit' name='submit' " & _
              "value='Save Responses' /></p></form></body></HTML>"
    end if
  end if
End Sub
```

We start the function with our standard check for a valid survey ID. If it is a number, then we make a call to `GetSurveyDef()` (another ASP function), which will call the Visual Basic component. This returns the array described above, which we will then pass the elements of to two other ASP functions: `ConvertSurveyHeader()` and `ConvertSurveyQuestions()`, which return the transformed HTML. Our last task is to write our HTML to the browser. Note that we also add a hidden field in the form to save our survey ID.

`ConvertSurveyHeader()` simply takes the survey header XML and applies the transformation. Here is the code:

```
Function ConvertSurveyHeader(sSurveyHeader)
  dim domHeader
  dim domXSL
  dim sHeader

  set domHeader = Server.CreateObject("MSXML.DOMDocument")
  if not domHeader.loadxml(sSurveyHeader) then
    sHeader = "<p>Could not load survey header.<br />Error: " & _
                    domHeader.parseerror.reason & "</p>"
  else
    set domXSL = Server.CreateObject("MSXML.DOMDocument")
    if not domXSL.load(Server.MapPath("xsl/surveyheader.xsl")) then
      sHeader = "<p>Could not load survey header transformation.<br />" & _
                    "Error: " domXSL.parseerror.reason & "</p>"
    else
      sHeader = domHeader.transformnode(domXSL)
    end if
    set domXSL = Nothing
  end if
  set domHeader = Nothing

  ConvertSurveyHeader = sHeader
End Function
```

This is, indeed, a fairly straightforward method, so we will move on to `ConvertSurveyQuestions()`, which is slightly more complicated:

```
Function ConvertSurveyQuestions(asQuestions)
  dim lQIndex
  dim sQHTML
  dim sQsHTML
  dim sXSL
  dim domQ
  dim domXSL

  set domQ = Server.CreateObject("MSXML.DOMDocument")
  set domXSL = Server.CreateObject("MSXML.DOMDocument")
  for lQIndex = 0 to ubound(asQuestions, 1)
    if not domQ.loadxml(asQuestions(lQIndex, 0)) then
      sQHTML = "<tr><td>Could not load question #" & lQIndex+1 & _
                    "</td><td>" & domQ.parseerror.reason & "</td></tr>"
    else
      sXSL = "<xsl:stylesheet xmlns:xsl='http://www.w3.org/TR/WD-xsl'>" & _
                    "<xsl:template match='/'>" & asQuestions(lQIndex,1) & _
                                    "</xsl:template></xsl:stylesheet>"
      if not domXSL.loadxml(sXSL) then
```

```
        sQHTML = "<tr><td>Could not transformation for question #" & _
          lQIndex+1 & "</td><td>" & domXSL.parseerror.reason & "</td></tr>"
      else
        on error resume next
        sQHTML = domQ.transformnode(domXSL)
        if err.number <> 0 then
          sQHTML = "<tr><td>Could not transform question #" & lQIndex+1 & _
                          "</td><td>" & err.description & "</td></tr>"
        end if
        on error goto 0
      end if
    end if
    sQsHTML = sQsHTML & sQHTML
  next
  set domQ = Nothing
  set domXSL = Nothing
  sQsHTML = "<table border='1'>" & sQsHTML & "</table>" & _
    "<input type='hidden' name='qcnt' value='" & lQIndex & "' />"

  ConvertSurveyQuestions = sQsHTML
End Function
```

This is a bit longer, but the majority of the code is simply error handling. The main part is the for-next loop we set up to step through the array. For each element of the array, we load up a DOM with the question definition (the first element of the array), then load up a DOM with the associated XSL (the second element of the array) and, finally, apply the transformation. Doing this, we build up a string that describes our question table. At the end of the function, we wrap the questions in a `<table>` tag, add a hidden field with the question count (for ease of processing when we need to grab the submitted responses), and we have our HTML to return to the `ShowSurvey()`.

Here is what our survey looks like in the browser:

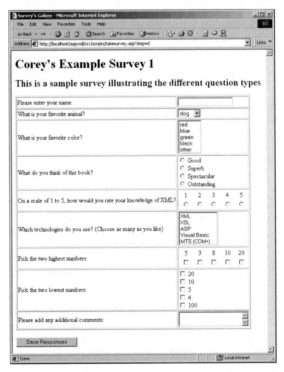

We will fill in the form with the following information, then press Submit and look to saving the data into the database:

Please enter your name:	Corey Haines
What is your favorite animal?	dog
What is your favorite color?	green
What do you think of this book?	spectacular
On a scale of 1 to 5, how would you rate your knowledge of XML?	4
Which technologies do you use? (Choose as many as you like)	XML, XSL, ASP
Pick the two highest numbers:	10,20
Pick the two lowest numbers:	4,5
Please add any additional comments:	This is a fun tool

SaveResponses()

To store responses, we are going to need to briefly step back and decide exactly how we want to save the answers in the database.

When speaking about responses, there are two concepts: a set of answers and the answers themselves. We will be creating two tables in our database, `Response` and `ResponseItem`. The `Response` table will include information that is common to all the answers given to a specific time taking the survey; the `ResponseItem` will basically just include the answer given to a specific question.

Response		
id	number	Identifier for response, unique
surveyid	number	Which survey is this response for
creationdate	date/time (default to current date)	Date response was given
creationtime	date/time (default to current time)	Time response was given

ResponseItem		
id	number	Identifier for individual answer, unique
responseid	number	Which response does this answer belong to
questionid	number	Which question is this an answer to
value	memo	Text of the answer

When passing our responses to the component, we will use the following XML schema:

```
<Schema xmlns="urn:schemas-microsoft-com:xml-data">
<AttributeType name='surveyid' required='yes' />
```

```
<AttributeType name='qid' required='yes' />
<ElementType name='r' content='textOnly'>
  <attribute type='surveyid' />
</ElementType>
<ElementType name='rs' content='eltOnly' order='many'>
  <attribute type='qid' />
  <element type='r' minOccurs='1' maxOccurs='*' />
</ElementType>
</Schema>
```

To show a concrete XML fragment, let's answer the questions in our example survey:

```
<rs surveyid="36">
  <r qid="47">3</r>
  <r qid="43">Corey Haines</r>
  <r qid="44">0</r>
  <r qid="45">2</r>
  <r qid="46">2</r>
  <r qid="48">0</r>
  <r qid="48">1</r>
  <r qid="48">2</r>
  <r qid="49">3</r>
  <r qid="49">4</r>
  <r qid="50">2</r>
  <r qid="50">3</r>
  <r qid="51">This is a fun tool!</r>
</rs>
```

A couple of items to note in this XML:

❑   On multiple-choice questions, we are listing the answers as separate response items.

❑   The value is actually the value in our <opts> list under the question. Using this technique, we will look up the actual text of the answer at report time.

The main task of the ASP code for saving the responses is to find the answers, convert them to this XML document, and then send them to a method of our Visual Basic component for saving into the database.

Here is the code for SaveResponses(), followed by a bit of explanation:

```
Sub SaveResponses()
  dim lSurvID

  dim lQCnt
  dim sResp
  dim sResponses
  dim frm
  dim lRespCnt
  dim lIndex

  dim lSaveCnt
  lSurvID = Trim(Request("_survid"))
  Response.Write "<HTML><head><title>Surveys Galore! - " & _
                               "Save Responses</title></head><body>"
  if not isnumeric(lSurvID) then
```

```
                  Response.write "<p>Invalid survey.</p>"
         else
            lSurvID = CInt(lSurvID)
            lQCnt = Request.Form("qcnt") - 1
            if lQCnt >= 0 then
               redim asResponses(lQCnt)
               lIndex = 0
               sResponses = "<rs surveyid='" & lSurvID & "'>"
               for each frm in Request.Form
                 if left(frm, 2) = "_q" then
                    for lRespCnt = 1 to Request.Form(frm).Count
                       sResp = "<r qid='" & _
                          right(frm, len(frm)-2) & "'>" & _
                          Request.Form(frm)(lRespCnt) & "</r>"
                       sResponses = sResponses & sResp
                       lIndex = lIndex + 1
                    next
                 end if
               next
               sResponses = sResponses & "</rs>"
            end if
            on error resume next
            lSaveCnt = SaveResponsesToDB(sResponses)
            if err.number <> 0 then
               Response.Write "<p>Could not save responses.</p><p>Error: " & _
                                                  err.description & "</p>"
            else
               Response.Write "<p>Saved " & lSaveCnt & _
                  " of " & lIndex & " responses.</p>"
            end if
         end if
         Response.Write "<p>Click <a href='" & paths_getDefaultDocument & _
            "'>here</a> to return to main menu.</p></body></HTML>"
   End Sub
```

This, of course, begins with our standard check of the survey ID, make sure it is there and that it is a valid integer. We then get the number of questions and start looping through the form variables. This loop is an interesting one, so we will take a bit of time to look at its inner workings.

First of all, the line for each frm in Request.Form will give us a string containing the names of all the form elements. This is a handy way to process a form. We check to make sure that the form element starts with "_q" to insure that it is a question for our survey. The line after that deserves special note:

```
for lRespCnt = 1 to Request.Form(frm).Count
```

When you have multi-select listboxes or checkboxes, then the data is returned as pairs of values. The Count method of an individual form item (in our case, accessed by Request.Form(frm)) returns the number of name-value pairs for the given name (frm). We can then loop through them all using:

```
Request.Form(frm)(lRespCnt)
```

Once we have built up our XML document containing the responses, we make a call to another ASP function, SaveResponsesToDB(), which simply makes the call to our Visual Basic component, passing in the responses.

```
Function SaveResponsesToDB(sResponses)
   dim oSurvUtils

   dim lSaveCnt

   set oSurvUtils = Server.CreateObject("SurveyUtils.Surveys")
   lSaveCnt = oSurvUtils.SaveResponses(sResponses, DBConnStr_getConnStr())
   set oSurvUtils = Nothing

   SaveResponsesToDB = lSaveCnt
End Function
```

It looks like almost all of the other ASP functions access our Visual Basic component. Remember that `DBConnStr_getConnStr()` is contained in our `dbconnstr.asp` include file; we know this, of course, because the function name is prefaced with the filename and an underscore.

After filling in our sample survey, hitting submit, and running through `SaveResponses()`, we can cast our eyes towards the last section of our tool: the report.

Reporting (showreport.asp)

Displaying the survey results is where we will be able to make full use of the advantages inherent in our choice of employing XML and XSL in our application. We will be developing one basic report format: a list of responses per surveyee. After that, we will discuss some possible improvements and methods to display more advanced reporting. Since a survey may receive many responses, we will give an option for the user to view the results for a data range.

In order to allow survey-level customization of the reports, we will construct a general template for each report type, but keep a separate copy of the XSL script for each survey, similar to how we allowed question-level customization for survey displaying. We will approach the solution in the following manner:

❑ Define an XML schema for receiving response list

❑ Define XSL transformations for reports

❑ Define a database schema for storing report definitions

❑ Add functions to the VB component to retrieve responses

❑ Create ASP pages for reporting sections

XML Schema for Responses

When deciding on a schema, we need to address the issue of what information we will need when displaying a survey. Naturally, we will need the actual responses themselves; the big question is what other information will we need? In most reports, we will probably want the text of the questions themselves, as well as the text for the optional answers for multiple-choice questions. You might want to include the header information for the survey. Since this basically amounts to the entire survey with the responses appended to it, we will reuse our schema for the survey definition, wrapping it together with the responses. A response is basically a list of answers, so we can use something like the following for the list of all responses:

```
<AttributeType name='qID' required='yes' />
<ElementType name='q' content='textOnly'>
  <attribute type='qID' />
</ElementType>
<AttributeType name='rID' required='yes' />
<ElementType name='response' content='eltOnly' order='many'>
  <attribute type='rID' />
  <element type='q' minOccurs='0' maxOccurs='*' />
</ElementType>
<ElementType name='responses' content='eltOnly' order='many'>
  <element type='response' minOccurs='0' maxOccurs='*' />
</ElementType>
```

We will couple this with the definition for a survey, wrapping everything as a top-level tag, called
<survres>. Here is the complete schema:

```
<Schema xmlns="urn:schemas-microsoft-com:xml-data">

<AttributeType name='questionID' required='yes' />
<AttributeType name='sequence' required='yes' />
<AttributeType name='type' required='yes' />
<AttributeType name='attname' required='yes' />
<AttributeType name='attvalue' required='yes' />
<ElementType name='att' content='empty'>
  <attribute type='attname' />
  <attribute type='attvalue' />
</ElementType>
<ElementType name='atts' content='eltOnly' order='many'>
  <element type='att' minOccurs='1' maxOccurs='*' />
</ElementType>
<ElementType name='optcaption' content='textOnly' />
<ElementType name='optvalue' content='textOnly' />
<ElementType name='opt' content='eltOnly' order='many'>
  <element type='optcaption' minOccurs='1' maxOccurs='1' />
  <element type='optvalue' minOccurs='1' maxOccurs='1' />
</ElementType>
<ElementType name='opts' content='eltOnly' order='many'>
  <element type='opt' minOccurs='1' maxOccurs='*' />
</ElementType>
<ElementType name='caption' content='textOnly' />
<ElementType name='q' content='eltOnly' order='many'>
  <attribute type='questionID' />
  <attribute type='sequence' />
  <attribute type='type' />
  <element type='caption' minOccurs='1' maxOccurs='1' />
  <element type='atts' minOccurs='0' maxOccurs='1' />
  <element type='opts' minOccurs='0' maxOccurs='1' />
</ElementType>
<ElementType name='qs' content='eltOnly' order='many'>
  <element type='q' minOccurs='1' maxOccurs='*' />
</ElementType>

<AttributeType name='surveyID' required='yes' />
<ElementType name='name' content='textOnly' />
<ElementType name='title' content='textOnly' />
```

```
<ElementType name='intro' content='textOnly' />
<ElementType name='survey' content='eltOnly' order='many'>
  <attribute type='surveyID' />
  <element type='name' minOccurs='1' maxOccurs='1' />
  <element type='title' minOccurs='1' maxOccurs='1' />
  <element type='intro' minOccurs='1' maxOccurs='1' />
  <element type='qs' minOccurs='1' maxOccurs='1' />
</ElementType>

<AttributeType name='qID' required='yes' />
<ElementType name='q' content='textOnly'>
  <attribute type='qID' />
</ElementType>
<AttributeType name='rID' required='yes' />
<ElementType name='response' content='eltOnly' order='many'>
  <attribute type='rID' />
  <element type='q' minOccurs='0' maxOccurs='*' />
</ElementType>
<ElementType name='responses' content='eltOnly' order='many'>
  <element type='response' minOccurs='0' maxOccurs='*' />
</ElementType>

<ElementType name='survres' content='eltOnly'>
  <element name='survey' minOccurs='1' maxOccurs='1' />
  <element name='responses' minOccurs='1' maxOccurs='1' />
</ElementType>

</Schema>
```

After taking our survey, the XML for our survey and the responses that we will get back from our
Visual Basic component is listed here:

```
<?xml version="1.0"?>
<survres>
  <survey id="36">
    <name>Example Survey</name>
    <title>Corey's Example Survey 1</title>
    <intro>This is a sample survey illustrating the different question types
    </intro>
  </survey>
  <qs>
    <q id="43" seq="1" type="1">
      <caption>Please enter your name:</caption>
    </q>
    <q id="44" seq="2" type="2">
      <caption>What is your favorite animal?</caption>
      <opts>
        <opt>
          <caption>dog</caption>
          <value>0</value>
        </opt>
        <opt>
          <caption>cat</caption>
          <value>1</value>
        </opt>
```

```
        <opt>
          <caption>horse</caption>
          <value>2</value>
        </opt>
        <opt>
          <caption>other</caption>
          <value>3</value>
        </opt>
      </opts>
    </q>
    <q id="45" seq="3" type="2">
      <caption>What is your favorite color?</caption>
      <opts>
        <opt>
          <caption>red</caption>
          <value>0</value>
        </opt>
        <opt>
          <caption>blue</caption>
          <value>1</value>
        </opt>
        <opt>
          <caption>green</caption>
          <value>2</value>
        </opt>
        <opt>
          <caption>black</caption>
          <value>3</value>
        </opt>
        <opt>
          <caption>other</caption>
          <value>4</value>
        </opt>
      </opts>
    </q>
    <q id="46" seq="4" type="2">
      <caption>What do you think of this book?</caption>
      <opts>
        <opt>
          <caption>Good</caption>
          <value>0</value>
        </opt>
        <opt>
          <caption>Superb</caption>
          <value>1</value>
        </opt>
        <opt>
          <caption>Spectacular</caption>
          <value>2</value>
        </opt>
        <opt>
          <caption>Outstanding</caption>
          <value>3</value>
        </opt>
      </opts>
    </q>
```

```
<q id="47" seq="5" type="2">
<caption>On a scale of 1 to 5, how would you rate your knowledge of XML?
</caption>
  <opts>
    <opt>
      <caption>1</caption>
      <value>0</value>
    </opt>
    <opt>
      <caption>2</caption>
      <value>1</value>
    </opt>
    <opt>
      <caption>3</caption>
      <value>2</value>
    </opt>
    <opt>
      <caption>4</caption>
      <value>3</value>
    </opt>
    <opt>
      <caption>5</caption>
      <value>4</value>
    </opt>
  </opts>
</q>
<q id="48" seq="6" type="3">
  <caption>Which technologies do you use? (Choose as many as you like)
  </caption>
  <opts>
    <opt>
      <caption>XML</caption>
      <value>0</value>
    </opt>
    <opt>
      <caption>XSL</caption>
      <value>1</value>
    </opt>
    <opt>
      <caption>ASP</caption>
      <value>2</value>
    </opt>
    <opt>
      <caption>Visual Basic</caption>
      <value>3</value>
    </opt>
    <opt>
      <caption>Microsoft Transaction Server</caption>
      <value>4</value>
    </opt>
  </opts>
</q>
<q id="49" seq="7" type="3">
  <caption>Pick the two highest numbers:</caption>
  <opts>
    <opt>
```

```
          <caption>5</caption>
          <value>0</value>
        </opt>
        <opt>
          <caption>3</caption>
          <value>1</value>
        </opt>
        <opt>
          <caption>8</caption>
          <value>2</value>
        </opt>
        <opt>
          <caption>10</caption>
          <value>3</value>
        </opt>
        <opt>
          <caption>20</caption>
          <value>4</value>
        </opt>
      </opts>
    </q>
    <q id="50" seq="8" type="3">
      <caption>Pick the two lowest numbers:</caption>
      <opts>
        <opt>
          <caption>20</caption>
          <value>0</value>
        </opt>
        <opt>
          <caption>10</caption>
          <value>1</value>
        </opt>
        <opt>
          <caption>5</caption>
          <value>2</value>
        </opt>
        <opt>
          <caption>4</caption>
          <value>3</value>
        </opt>
        <opt>
          <caption>100</caption>
          <value>4</value>
        </opt>
      </opts>
    </q>
    <q id="51" seq="9" type="1">
      <caption>Please add any additional comments:</caption>
    </q>
  </qs>
  <responses>
    <response id="16">
      <date>3/23/00</date>
      <q id="43">Corey Haines</q>
      <q id="44">0</q>
      <q id="45">2</q>
```

```
        <q id="46">2</q>
        <q id="47">3</q>
        <q id="48">2</q>
        <q id="48">1</q>
        <q id="48">0</q>
        <q id="49">4</q>
        <q id="49">3</q>
        <q id="50">3</q>
        <q id="50">2</q>
        <q id="51">This is a fun tool!</q>
      </response>
    </responses>
  </survres>
```

Using this as a basis, we can develop the XSL for our basic report. This report will simply list all the answers given, separated by actual surveyee.

XSL Transformation for a Basic Report

Our report will basically have two sections: the report header, containing the report name and description, and HTML tables containing the answers for a given question. Here is a screenshot of how we want our report to look:

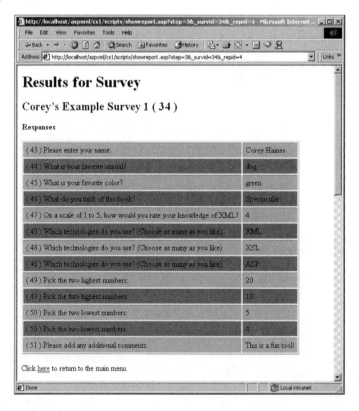

Since we have only taken the survey once, it only lists one group; any more responses would be placed in their own tables.

To get this effect, we can use the following XSL transformation:

```
<xsl:stylesheet xmlns:xsl="http://www.w3.org/TR/WD-xsl">
<xsl:template match="/">
  <xsl:apply-templates select="survres/survey" />
  <xsl:apply-templates select="survres/responses" />
</xsl:template>

<xsl:template match="responses">
  <p><b>Responses</b></p>
  <xsl:for-each select="response">
    <p><table border='1' cellpadding='5'>
      <xsl:for-each select="q">
        <xsl:apply-templates select="." />
      </xsl:for-each>
    </table></p>
  </xsl:for-each>
</xsl:template>

<xsl:template match="q">
  <tr>
    <xsl:choose>
      <xsl:when expr='childNumber(this) % 2 == 0'>
        <xsl:attribute name='bgcolor'>GRAY</xsl:attribute>
      </xsl:when>
      <xsl:when expr='childNumber(this) % 2 == 1'>
        <xsl:attribute name='bgcolor'>SILVER</xsl:attribute>
      </xsl:when>
    </xsl:choose>
    <td>(<xsl:value-of select="@id" />) 
      <xsl:value-of select="/survres/qs/q[@id = context()/@id]/caption" />
    </td>
    <td>
      <xsl:choose>
        <xsl:when test="/survres/qs/q[@id=context()/@id and @type != '1']">
          <xsl:value-of select=
    "/survres/qs/q[@id=context()/@id]/opts/opt[value=context()]/caption" />
        </xsl:when>
        <xsl:otherwise>
          <xsl:value-of select="." />
        </xsl:otherwise>
      </xsl:choose>
    </td>
  </tr>
</xsl:template>

<xsl:template match="survey">
  <h1>Results for Survey</h1>
  <h2><xsl:value-of select="title" /> (<xsl:value-of select="@id" />)</h2>
</xsl:template>
</xsl:stylesheet>
```

At its root, this transformation simply loops through all the responses, then loops through each question for each response. There are two items worth mentioning in this transformation: the two `<xsl:choose>` elements. The first one simply grabs the caption (i.e. the text) of the question with the same id as the current response question:

```
(<xsl:value-of select="@id" />) 
        <xsl:value-of select="/survres/qs/q[@id = context()/@id]/caption" />
```

The second grabs the caption of the option that was chosen as the answer to the question:

```
<xsl:value-of select=
        "/survres/qs/q[@id=context()/@id]/opts/opt[value=context()]/caption" />
```

Database Schema for Storing Report Definitions

The XSL transformation given above was simply a template; many aspects of it can be customized (background of the page, colors in the HTML tables, fonts, etc.), so we will be storing a separate XSL document for each survey, rather than sharing the transformation.

The following table shows the data we will be saving for each report:

Report		
id	number	Identifier for report, unique
surveyid	number	Which survey is this report for
name	text	Name of this report
description	memo	Description of this report
transformation	memo	XSL transformation for report
creationdate	date/time (default to current date)	Date report was created

showreport.asp

Similar to our other pages, we will be setting up the showreport.asp page as a simple state machine, allowing the step to be given by a URL parameter, step. Here is the activity diagram for showing a report:

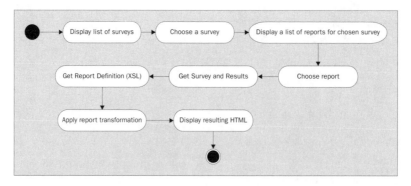

From this we can see that there are basically three steps – display list of surveys, display list of reports for chosen survey, and show the chosen report. As in the other pages, we will implement this state machine with a select case statement.

```
dim lStep

lStep = trim(Request("step"))
select case lStep
case "", "1"
  ShowSurveySelect()
case "2"
  ShowReportSelect()
case "3"
  ShowReport()
case else
  ShowSurveySelect()
end select
```

ShowSurveySelect()

This function is exactly the same as the one from `takesurvey.asp` with one exception, so we will simply copy it here.

```
Sub ShowSurveySelect()
  dim sSurvList
  dim domSurvs
  dim domXSL

  dim sToWrite
  dim sTransformed

  on error resume next
  sSurvList = GetSurveyHeaders()
  if err.number <> 0 then
    sToWrite = "<p>Could not get list of surveys.<br />Error: " & _
                          err.description & "</p>"
  else
    set domSurvs = Server.CreateObject("MSXML.DOMDocument")
    if not domSurvs.loadxml(sSurvList) then
      sToWrite = "<p>Could not load survey list.<br />Error: " & _
                          domSurvs.parseerror.reason & "</p>"
    else
      set domXSL = Server.CreateObject("MSXML.DOMDocument")
      if not domXSL.load(Server.MapPath("xsl/surveylisttohtml.xsl")) then
        sToWrite = "<p>Could not load survey list conversion.<br />Error: "&_
                          domXSL.parseerror.reason & "</p>"
      else
        on error resume next
        sTransformed =  domSurvs.transformnode(domXSL)
        if err.number <> 0 then
          sToWrite = "<p>Could not convert survey list to HTML.<br />"& _
                          "Error: " & err.description & "</p>"
        else
          sToWrite = "<p>Please choose a survey to report on.</p>" & _
              "<form action='" & paths_getScripts() & _
              "showreport.asp?step=2' method='post'>" & _
            sTransformed & "<p><input type='submit' value='Take Survey' />"&_
                          "</p></form>"
        end if
```

```
      end if
    end if
  end if
  Response.Write "<HTML><head><title>Surveys Galore! - Show a
report</title></head><body>"
  Response.Write sToWrite
  Response.Write "</body></HTML>"
End Sub
```

I won't put a screen shot here, since the only differences lie in the titles that we show: the page title is "Show a report," and the instruction line for the list is "**Please choose a survey to report on**". And, of course, the form's action is `showreport.asp?step=2`.

ShowReportSelect()

The idea behind this page is similar to `ShowSurveySelect()`, except we will list the reports as links, rather than in a listbox. Here is how we would like our page to look (having included the basic report defined above):

The HTML for this page is as follows (notice the format of the link itself):

```
<HTML>
<head>
  <title>Surveys Galore!</title>
</head>
<body>
  <h2>Please choose a report for the survey</h2>
  <p>
    <a href='viewreport.asp?step=3&surveyid=34&reportid=4'>Basic Report</a>
    - This report lists all the responses for a given survey</p>
</body>
</HTML>
```

The ASP code is a little more complex, because we are doing some DOM searches, rather than using an XSL document:

```
Sub ShowReportSelect()
  dim lSurvID
  dim sRepDefs
  dim domRepDefs
  dim nlRepDefs
  dim nodRepDef
```

```
            dim lRepIndex
            dim sLink
            dim sRepLink

            lSurvID = Trim(Request("_survid"))
            Response.Write "<HTML><head><title>Surveys Galore! - " & _
                            "Choose a Report</title></head><body>"
            if not IsNumeric(lSurvID) then
              Response.Write "<p>Invalid survey.</p>"
            else
              lSurvID = CInt(lSurvID)
              sRepDefs = GetReportDefinitionHeaders(lSurvID)
              set domRepDefs = Server.CreateObject("MSXML.DOMDocument")
              if not domRepDefs.loadxml(sRepDefs) then
                Response.Write "<p>Could not load report list.<br />Error: " _
                                & domRepDefs.parseerror.reason & "</p>"
              else
                set nlRepDefs = domRepDefs.selectnodes("reports/report")
                for lRepIndex = 0 to nlRepDefs.length-1
                  set nodRepDef = nlRepDefs.item(lRepIndex)
                  sLink = paths_getScripts() & _
                              "showreport.asp?step=3&_survid=" & lSurvID & _
                              "&_repid=" & _
                    nodRepDef.attributes.getnameditem("id").text
                  sRepLink = sRepLink &  "<p><a href='" & sLink & _
                              "'>" & nodRepDef.selectsinglenode("name").text & _
                              "</a> - " & _
                    nodRepDef.selectsinglenode("description").text & "</p>"
                next
                Response.Write "<h1>Please select a report to view</h1>"
                Response.Write sRepLink
              end if
            end if
            Response.Write"</body></HTML>"
      End Sub
```

In this method, we chose a more brute-force approach to creating the list, getting all the `<report>` nodes of the document and looping through them, grabbing the name and the description, setting up hyperlinks for them. `GetReportDefinitionHeaders()` makes a call to our Visual Basic component to return a list of our report definitions for the chosen survey. Here is the code (located in our ASP page) for `GetReportDefinitionHeaders()`:

```
Function GetReportDefinitionHeaders (lSurveyID)
  dim oSurvUtils
  dim sSurRes

  set oSurvUtils = Server.CreateObject("SurveyUtils.Surveys")
  sSurRes = oSurvUtils.GetReportDefinitionHeaders(lSurveyID, _
                      DBConnStr_getConnstr())
  set oSurvUtils = Nothing

  GetReportDefinitionHeaders = sSurRes
End Function
```

SurveyUtils.Surveys.GetReportDefinitionHeaders()

The Visual Basic function returns a list of report headers, formatted in XML, of course, which looks like the following example with one report node for each report definition:

```
<reports surveyid='36'>
  <report id='4'>
    <name>Basic Report</name>
    <description>This report lists all the responses for a given survey
    </description>
  </report>
</reports>
```

Here is the Visual Basic code for our method:

```
Public Function GetReportDefinitionHeaders(ByVal SurveyID As Variant, _
    ByVal ConnStr As Variant) As Variant
On Error GoTo Err_Hand

    Dim sSQL As String
    Dim rsRep As ADODB.Recordset
    Dim sRetVal As String

    sSQL = "SELECT id, name, description FROM report WHERE surveyid=" & _
                    SurveyID

    Set rsRep = OpenRS(sSQL, ConnStr)

    sRetVal = "<reports surveyid='" & SurveyID & "'>"
    Do Until rsRep.EOF
        sRetVal = sRetVal & "<report id='" & rsRep("id") & "'><name>" & _
                    rsRep("name") & "</name><description>" & _
                    rsRep("description") & "</description></report>"
        rsRep.MoveNext
    Loop
    sRetVal = sRetVal & "</reports>"

    GetReportDefinitionHeaders = sRetVal
    Exit Function
Err_Hand:
    Err.Raise Err.Number, ERR_SOURCE, _
        ERR_SOURCE & ".GetReportDefinitionHeaders" & vbCrLf & Err.Description
End Function
```

These methods together will produce the HTML output that we require.

ShowReport()

Our last ASP function, ShowReport(), takes a surveyid and a reportid and produces HTML output. We have already defined the format for the XML we receive when requesting a survey's results, so we simply need to code around that. Here is the activity diagram for ShowReport():

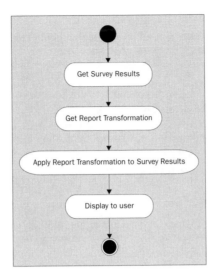

Here is the base code for `ShowReport()`, followed by the supporting functions (including the Visual Basic function) that it uses:

```
Sub ShowReport()
  dim lSurvID
  dim lRepID

  dim sSurvRes
  dim sRepDef

  lSurvID = Trim(Request("_survid"))
  lRepID = Trim(Request("_repid"))

  if not IsNumeric(lSurvID) then
    Response.Write "<p>Invalid survey id.</p>"
  else
    if not IsNumeric(lRepID) then
      Response.Write "<p>Invalid report id.</p>"
    else
      lSurvID = CInt(lSurvID)
      lRepID = CInt(lRepID)
      on error resume next
      sSurvRes = GetSurveyAndResults(lSurvID)
      if err.number <> 0 then
        Response.Write "<p>Could not get survey and results.<br />Error: "&_
                        err.description & "</p>"
      else
        sRepDef = GetReportDefinition(lRepID)
        if err.number <> 0 then
          Response.Write "<p>Could not get report definition.<br />Error: "&_
                          err.description & "</p>"
        else
          ShowReportHTML sSurvRes, sRepDef
        end if
      end if
    end if
  end if
```

```
      end if
      Response.Write "<p>Click <a href='" & paths_getDefaultDocument() & _
         "'>here</a> to return to the main menu.</p>"
   End Sub
```

There are three support functions listed here: `GetSurveyAndResults()`,
`GetReportDefinition()`, and `ShowReportHTML()`.

The first two are simply access methods to our component; they look like all the others:

```
Function GetSurveyAndResults(lSurveyID)
   dim oSurvUtils
   dim sSurRes

   set oSurvUtils = Server.CreateObject("SurveyUtils.Surveys")
   sSurRes = oSurvUtils.GetSurveyAndResults(lSurveyID, DBConnStr_getConnStr())

   set oSurvUtils = Nothing

   GetSurveyAndResults = sSurRes
End Function

Function GetReportDefinition(lReportID)
   dim oSurvUtils
   dim sRepDef

   set oSurvUtils = Server.CreateObject("SurveyUtils.Surveys")
   sRepDef = oSurvUtils.GetReportDefinition(lReportID, DBConnStr_getConnStr())

   set oSurvUtils = Nothing

   GetReportDefinition = sRepDef
End Function
```

The last helper function, `ShowReportHTML()`, takes the survey results and applies the report definition
transformation to it, displaying the resulting HTML. We drew this into another function, as
transforming XML with an XSL stylesheet, as we've seen, needs to have a bit of error checking, so, to
keep our main function less cluttered, we moved this into its own method.

```
Sub ShowReportHTML(sSurvRes, sRepDef)
   dim domSurv
   dim domRepDef
   dim sRepHTML

   set domSurv = Server.CreateObject("MSXML.DOMDocument")
   if not domSurv.loadxml(sSurvRes) then
      Response.Write "<p>Cannot load survey and results.<br />Error: " & _
                        domSurv.parseerror.reason & "</p>"
   else
      set domRepDef = Server.CreateObject("MSXML.DOMDocument")
      if not domRepDef.loadxml(sRepDef) then
         Response.Write "<p>Cannot load report definition.<br />Error: " & _
                        domRep.parseerror.reason & "</p>"
      else
```

```
         on error resume next
         sRepHTML = domSurv.transformnode(domRepDef)
         if err.number <> 0 then
            Response.Write "<p>Cannot transform report.<br />Error: " & _
                           err.description & "</p>"
         else
            Response.Write sRepHTML
         end if
      end if
      set domRep = Nothing
   end if
   set domSurv = Nothing
End Sub
```

This function looks very similar to the other methods that transform our XML documents. One possible enhancement to the system would be to create a generic `TransformXML()` method and put it into an include file. That can, of course, be left as an exercise to the reader.

The last methods exist in our Visual Basic component, and we will look at them in order that they are accessed in our ASP.

SurveyUtils.Surveys.GetSurveyAndResults()

```
Public Function GetSurveyAndResults(ByVal SurveyID As Variant, _
                                    ByVal ConnStr As Variant) As Variant

    On Error GoTo Err_Hand

    Dim avSurvey() As Variant
    Dim avQs() As Variant
    Dim avRetVal As Variant
    Dim lIndex As Long

    avSurvey = GetSurvey(SurveyID, ConnStr)
    avRetVal = avSurvey(0)
    avQs = avSurvey(1)

    avRetVal = avRetVal & "<qs>"
    For lIndex = LBound(avQs, 1) To UBound(avQs, 1)
        avRetVal = avRetVal & avQs(lIndex, 0)
    Next lIndex
    avRetVal = avRetVal & "</qs>"

    avRetVal = avRetVal & GetResults(SurveyID, ConnStr)
    GetSurveyAndResults = "<survres>" & avRetVal & "</survres>"
    Exit Function
Err_Hand:
    Err.Raise Err.Number, ERR_SOURCE, _
            ERR_SOURCE & ".GetSurveyAndResults" & vbCrLf & Err.Description
End Function
```

Here, `GetSurvey()` is the same method we used when displaying a survey, so we won't cover it again. This is the benefit of reusing the XML Schema from before: we can reuse the methods used to work with it, as well. `GetResults()` is a new function that we use to access the database and return the results formatted in the required XML. Here is the code:

```
Public Function GetResults(ByVal SurveyID As Variant, _
                                    ByVal ConnStr As Variant) As Variant
    On Error GoTo Err_Hand

    Dim sSQL As String
    Dim sRetVal As String
    Dim sTemp As String
    Dim lCurRespID As Long
    Dim rsResp As ADODB.Recordset

    sSQL = "SELECT rv.responseid, rv.questionid, rv.value, r.creationdate "&_
                    "FROM responseitem rv, response r" & _
                    " WHERE rv.responseid = r.id AND r.surveyid = " & _
                    SurveyID & " ORDER BY r.id, rv.questionid"

    Set rsResp = OpenRS(sSQL, ConnStr)

    sRetVal = "<responses>"
    If rsResp.RecordCount > 0 Then
        lCurRespID = rsResp("responseid")
        sRetVal = sRetVal & "<response id='" & lCurRespID & "'>"
        sRetVal = sRetVal & "<date>" & rsResp("creationdate") & "</date>"
        Do Until rsResp.EOF
            If lCurRespID <> rsResp("responseid") Then
                sRetVal = sRetVal & "</response><response id='" & _
                            rsResp("responseid") & "'>"
                sRetVal = sRetVal & "<date>" & _
                            rsResp("creationdate") & "</date>"
                lCurRespID = rsResp("responseid")
            End If
            sRetVal = sRetVal & "<q id='" & rsResp("questionid") & _
                        "'>" & rsResp("value") & "</q>"
        rsResp.MoveNext
        Loop
    sRetVal = sRetVal & "</response>"
    End If
    rsResp.Close
    Set rsResp = Nothing

    sRetVal = sRetVal & "</responses>"
    GetResults = sRetVal

    Exit Function
Err_Hand:
    Err.Raise Err.Number, ERR_SOURCE, _
                    ERR_SOURCE & ".GetResults" & vbCrLf & Err.Description
End Function
```

This might look complicated, but it really is just transforming the recordset into the required XML structure that was outlined before.

SurveyUtils.Surveys.GetReportDefinition()

GetReportDefinition() is significantly simpler than the other function, since it really just goes out to the database and grabs a column (the XSL transformation for the report). Let's take a look at the code:

```
Public Function GetReportDefinition(ByVal ReportID As Variant, _
                               ByVal ConnStr As Variant) As Variant

    On Error GoTo Err_Hand

    Dim sSQL As String
    Dim rsDef As ADODB.Recordset
    Dim sRetVal As String

    sSQL = "SELECT transformation FROM report WHERE id=" & ReportID

    Set rsDef = OpenRS(sSQL, ConnStr)
    If Not rsDef.EOF Then
        sRetVal = rsDef("transformation")
    End If
    rsDef.Close
    Set rsDef = Nothing

    GetReportDefinition = sRetVal
    Exit Function
Err_Hand:
    Err.Raise Err.Number, ERR_SOURCE, _
                ERR_SOURCE & ".GetReportDefinition" & vbCrLf & Err.Description
End Function
```

This method truly is simple, hardly worth a mention, especially thanks to our handy helper function, `OpenRS()`.

Gluing all this discussion together, we arrive at the complete `showreport.asp` page. Running through the steps, we arrive at the HTML page that lists all the responses to a given survey, just like magic.

Where to now?

Well, as promised in the introduction, we have developed a fairly bare-bones, but functional, online survey system. Looking back, we covered a lot of ground; we did some analysis of our problem, finally ending with some XML schemas, XSL transformations and Visual Basic code to support access to our database. There are definitely parts of this system which will need to be refined before placing it on a production survey, and this is what we will address in this last section. These were parts which were left out either due to space considerations or because they weren't really inside the scope of this book. We will first go through the different sections of the system, discussing what was left out, what could be added and what enhancements and additional functionality we could provide to make this a really useful system for you to use.

Survey Creation

The first part of our system, survey creation, definitely has some features that could be added or improved:

❑ First of all, as in all the web pages we developed here, the user interface itself leaves something to be desired. We have focused entirely on functionality, rather than form, which is a definite no-no when developing a system that the world will be using. Some sort of menu should be provided, which would allow the user to return to previous steps, return to the main menu, etc. Perhaps you could display the survey itself, while building it, so the survey creators could decide whether they wanted to make changes without having to re-enter the entire thing.

❑ Another aspect missing is the lack of support for question attributes, namely the default value that our XSL transformations support. This is a necessary part of any question-based system, including our survey tool. The delivery system supports it; you will simply need to add it to the survey creation section.

❑ There is no tool for updating an existing survey, something that will definitely need to be added, since a user would not want to redo a survey simply to change the text on one of the questions. This could be realized fairly easily; simply grab the XML for the survey, display it for the user to make changes, then resave it using the existing functionality.

❑ Customization of the survey delivery is not supported: background colors, row-level customizations, and logos. All these would be welcome additions to any industrial-strength surveying system.

❑ There is no support for more than one user. Admittedly, this is major flaw, since we will want to keep track of our "surveyors". A slight change to the database (adding a surveyor table and linking it to the survey table) would make this possible.

Survey Delivery

The second part of our system, survey delivery, also has some parts which were left out:

❑ Our XSL transformations need to be adjusted to support display customizations (background colors, logos, etc.).

❑ No support for stop-and-continue-later. Basically, our system supports one-shot attempts at taking the survey. To make this possible, you would need to develop a method for an individual response to be linked to a surveyee. This might be accomplished in a similar way to the solution for adding "surveyor" functionality.

❑ Seamless integration into alternative delivery mechanisms, that is, true user interface independence, is definitely closer with this system, although a few slight modifications would need to be made. Because we did separate the definition from the display, you can add XSL transformations for different user interfaces. Admittedly, this is not totally possible with ours, since the XSL transformations are stored in the same database table as the questions themselves. If you were to pull them into another table, linked to the question table, you could support different transformations for different user interfaces. The wrapper tags for the questions would need to be abstracted out to support alternative methods, for example WAPs use of decks and cards, rather than the Web's reliance on pages and tables.

Reporting

Our reporting system is fairly robust from the point of view that all you need to do to support a new report type is to add an XSL transformation. Naturally, though, there are a few more enhancements that need to be added:

❑ First, of course, we could definitely do with more reports. The single report we developed is sufficient for small lists of responses, but we definitely could add some more summary reports.

❑ Adding reports is not too easy right now, so it would help to have a method to choose which reports you want for a survey, and, perhaps, a method to generate some *ad hoc* reports.

❑ Some form of security should be developed for accessing the reports. This could, of course, go along with the concept of "surveyors" that will need to be developed for the survey creation.

And Finally...

Well, after looking back at the system and possible enhancements to it, it is up to you to take what you have seen and learned in both this book and this case study and put it to good use.

Good luck!

Case Study – An On-line Documentation System

When looking at many of the case studies that we programmers have read over the years, one thing seems to stand out – for the most part, while they are interesting, the topics usually do not apply to the business that we are in. We've read about, and used code from, real estate offices, travel agencies and, of course, coffee importers, even though most us of know nothing about these businesses. This case study, hopefully, plays in an arena that is closer to home for most programmers.

One of the major trends in computing, for some time now, has been the development of re-usable components. With the advent of COM+ and DCOM, and the ease of component development using languages such as Visual Basic, this trend can only increase. For reusability to succeed, however, we need to provide programmers with details of what components have been developed, and how to use them. And that means documentation – the bane of the programming community. Many development environments have had edicts come down from above and requests come up from below to provide documentation for everything. All goes well for a while, and then someone requests an emergency programming job. All attention is then focused on the task at hand; the edicts break down, and we know the rest of the story.

The motivation behind this case study is an effort to take a new look at the problem of programmer documentation. Our department was growing, and it became impossible to rely on the visit to the coffee bar to keep up-to-date with all of the new developments. Components for data access, business data transformations etc., were being developed, sometimes with duplicated efforts. Programmers did not know what components were available on the server for use, much less their methods and properties.

This case study will walk through the process of creating an on-line documentation system. The information that the user of a particular component needs is stored in the XML data file. We decided to use XML primarily as a proof of concept. We could have done the project with SQL server or MS Access, but we figured we'd give this a try. The ASP/XSL code that is described fulfills all of the requirements for a complete system:

❑ Input, Update and Delete of multi-level XML data – using ASP

❑ Viewing the XML data with element-level sorting – using XSL

❑ Viewing a particular XML node and its children – using ASP

❑ Viewing a selected or filtered list from a collection – using ASP

> **For reasons of clarity (and the fact that we are a fully IE 5.0-compliant Intranet and development shop), browser detection has been left out of this code. As a result, while the code will *run* on pre IE 5.0 browsers, it may fail to give the results that you would like.**

Architectural Overview

There are two main sides to our Component Management system. As a rather arbitrary designation (it's how I first drew it on the white board – no politics were involved) one section was called the Left system, while the other was (obviously) referred to as the Right. As designed, each system could stand on it own as a viable tool in the effort to document and understand the components utilized in our environment. When used together, however, we hoped that the result would be greater than the simple sum of the parts. This is how my drawing looked:

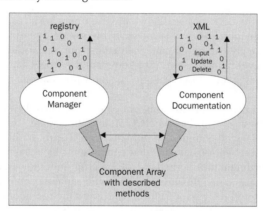

The Left / Middle Systems – Overview

The Left System is used to gather the basic information about what components are available for programmer use. It relies on several truisms:

❑ For a component to be available, it must reside on a server.

❑ For a component to be available, its details must be in the registry.

❑ For a component to be useful, it must have at least one public property and / or method.

Since the actual programs that are used in the Left System do not lie within the scope of this book, I will not be describing them to you in the same depth as the Right System. The specifications, however, will give you a good running start if you decide to build the thing yourself.

The source code for this chapter is available for download from www.wrox.com. The files included in the download form the framework of a system that can be built upon.

There are two parts to this system, the ASP code and the `isComponentMgr` component. The left side ASP scripts are used exclusively as the reporting layer for the system, with all of the work done in the component.

A note on the component names: All of our component names have defined prefixes. Each area of the IS department had a designation (e.g. `isComponent` is used by the main development team, whereas `finComponent` is used by the Financial Services group, etc.) This scheme:

1) Helps identify the authoring team.

2) Keeps all the components together in an alpha listing such as the registry.

Because all of our prefixes use a starting letter from the beginning of the alphabet, we do not have to scroll through too much to get to our stuff.

The Middle System, while in the original design specification, has not been needed to date, and therefore not built. This was designed to be a collection of scripts to periodically review the registered components, and verify that the associated XML documentation was written. The discussion of the possible features of this code included: checking the time stamp or the version number of the DLL and comparing that to the XML modification date. (We would have needed some additional audit elements). This was to make sure that the documentation was verified whenever the DLL was modified. This 'big-brother' concept was not adopted, and we've not had a problem yet.

The Right System – Overview

The Right System is used to maintain the actual programmer documentation. When we were discussing the possibilities of this system, we reviewed the various methods of documentation that we've encountered in the past.

- ❏ **In-the-code Flower Boxes** – the concept of keeping the Docs with the code, set off by stars or slashes or whatever the comment symbol of the language happens to be. The downside is that the documentation is inaccessible and never kept current.

- ❏ **Near-line Word documents** – put in some common location a word-processed document that "must follow" some template. This method is even less likely to be current.

- ❏ **A database of component docs** – this had some potential. The documentation could be available to programmers that are at the office as well as those that work from home. As we drew the data structure, we realized that quite a number of tables would be required. And the data, for the most part, formed a tree type layout.

❏ **An XML data document** – this fits our data, as well as having the information accessible via a web interface. The real deciding factor, of course, was that we all wanted to get more involved in XML technology. Due to the size of our shop, we decided not to worry about scalability as it relates to performance or multi-user contention.

The basic idea was that the `isComponentMgr` would search the registry for installed components and make a list of them. Using this list, the programmer would then be able to find the XML based documentation about the component and its methods and properties. If, for example, the documentation for a method was not found (or was inaccurate), the original author could be contacted to fix the situation. The merging of what the `isComponentMgr` reported with what the programmer has written is at the crux of these systems.

The Systems

The isComponentMgr System

As mentioned above, the `isComponentMgr` component forms the basis for this system. It is written in VC++ and is installed on the target servers that host other shared components. Its task is to inquire and report information about any component listed in the registry. A brief description of the component's methods follows:

Public Methods

GetComponents	
Syntax:	`Array = isComponentMgr.GetComponents(strMask)`
Parameters:	StrMask – this is used to selectively retrieve components. A '*' at the end of a partial string will wildcard the search.
Returns:	The method returns an array of registered component names.

Once we have the component list, we are able to derive a great deal of information about what is available to the programmer:

GetDllInfoAddress	
Syntax:	`Str = isComponentMgr.GetDllInfoAddress(strComponent)`
Parameters:	strComponent – this is a known component name.
Returns:	The base address of the installed component.

GetDllInfoVersion	
Syntax:	`Str = isComponentMgr.GetDllInfoVersion(strComponent)`
Parameters:	strComponent – this is a known component name.
Returns:	The version number of the installed component.

GetDllInfoDescription	
Syntax:	`Str = isComponentMgr.GetDllInfoDescription(strComponent)`
Parameters:	`strComponent` – this is a known component name.
Returns:	The DLL description from the type library.

GetDllInfoPath	
Syntax:	`Str = isComponentMgr.GetDllInfoPath(strComponent)`
Parameters:	`strComponent` – this is a known component name.
Returns:	The true disk location of the installed component.

Because several programmers have access to the test servers, we find that checking the DLL path is useful in making sure that everything is in its proper place.

GetMethods	
Syntax:	`Array = isComponentMgr.GetMethods(strComponent)`
Parameters:	`strComponent` – this is a known component name.
Returns:	The method returns an array of the public methods exposed by the component.

GetMethodType	
Syntax:	`Str = isComponentMgr.getMethodType(strComponent, strMethod)`
Parameters:	`strComponent` – this is a known component name.
	`strMethod` – the name of a known method.
Returns:	This reports the return type of the method.

GetMethodParams	
Syntax:	`Array = isComponentMgr.getMethodParams(strComponent, strMethod)`
Parameters:	`strComponent` – this is a known component name.
	`strMethod` – the name of a known method.
Returns:	This method returns an array of the parameter types.

GetProperties	
Syntax:	`Array = isComponentMgr.GetProperties(strComponent)`
Parameters:	`strComponent` – this is a known component name.
Returns:	Returns an array of the public properties exposed by the component.

GetPropertyType	
Syntax:	Str = isComponentMgr.GetPropertyType(strComponent, strProperty)
Parameters:	strComponent – this is a known component name.
	strProperty – the name of a known property.
Returns:	This method returns the data type of the property.

GetPropertyDefaultValue	
Syntax:	Variant = isComponentMgr.GetPropertyDefaultValue(strComponent, strProperty)
Parameters:	strComponent – this is a known component name.
	strProperty – the name of a known property.
Returns:	This method returns the default value of the property.

The associated ASP scripts generate simple pages to view the output of these methods.

The XML Data File

The structure of the XML file that we will be using is relatively simple, yet contains most of the basic elements that are needed in most organizations. The DTD that we use to define the XML structure is called components.dtd, and it looks like this:

```
<?xml version="1.0"?>

    <!ELEMENT components   (component*)>
    <!ELEMENT component    (name, author, overview, methods, properties)>
    <!ELEMENT name         (#PCDATA)>
    <!ELEMENT author       (#PCDATA)>
    <!ELEMENT overview     (#PCDATA)>
    <!ELEMENT methods      (method*)>
    <!ELEMENT properties   (property*)>
    <!ELEMENT method       (syntax, description, example)>
      <!ATTLIST method name CDATA #REQUIRED>
    <!ELEMENT property     (description, example)>
      <!ATTLIST property name CDATA #REQUIRED>
    <!ELEMENT syntax       (#PCDATA)>
    <!ELEMENT description  (#PCDATA)>
    <!ELEMENT example      (#PCDATA)>
```

We see from the DTD that the component element will be repeating, and that within each component there are two 'collections' – methods and properties. The result is an XML file (components.xml) that (though empty) might look something like this:

```
<?xml version="1.0"?>
<!DOCTYPE components SYSTEM "components.dtd">
<components>
  <component>
  <name />
  <author />
```

```
    <overview />
    <methods>
      <method name="">
        <syntax />
        <description />
        <example />
      </method>
    </methods>
    <properties>
      <property name="">
        <description />
        <example />
      </property>
    </properties>
    </component>
  </components>
```

Like pseudo-code, this file makes it easy to see from the outset the structure of the XML document that we will be using.

In a production environment, of course, additional elements would be required. We would want to track multiple authors (last name, first name, phone extension, e-mail address), version history, a URI (or URL) of on-line documents such as the UML design files and documents or perhaps the sign-off forms required to expense the software effort and other pertinent information.

The Right System

The core of this study is in this section. Before we begin with the code, I would like to offer several caveats. The code that is presented here is, by necessity, not the same that would be used in our production environment. There are two major reasons for this.

❑   The production code contains our menu systems, which would be inappropriate for this book.

❑   The production code contains many more elements. Including these elements would add nothing to the learning experience, and require a lot more typing on everyone's part.

In addition to the above, external stylesheets and some edit checking, error handling, and other code were removed from these ASPs or modified to improve clarity.

That said, the code that is presented here can be used in a production environment, and is, I hope, modifiable enough so that you can use it for your own projects. I have tried to keep the use of graphics to an absolute minimum so that you will be able to create fully working code with just your favorite text editor.

Each of the ASP scripts that are used in this system is included here. Because scripts will be 'interrupted' with commentary, I will include the name of the scripts at both the beginning and ending of each listing to make it easier to know the beginning and ending of the code.

The ASP Files

The following ASP map shows the various files used in the system and how they relate to each other. IIS prefers to handle security on the directory level. Though we are not utilizing it in this code, a user login requirement for the administration would enable auditing, and such features as component ownership (only the user or group that added a component can modify it). This would be easily accomplished by isolating the Admin code in its own directory structure. As a design consideration, therefore, none of the ASPs that are used by the administrative functions are shared by the reporting system.

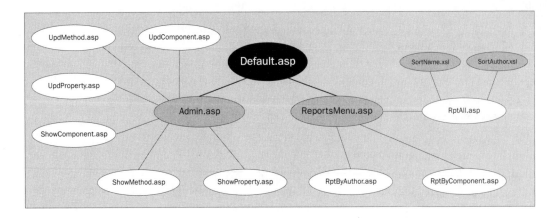

The Home Page

The ASP file `default.asp` is the starting point of our journey. The simple example presented here provides a short description of the application, along with some explanation of how to use the other two options.

default.asp

```
<html>
<head>
  <Title> Component Manager </Title>
</head>

<style type="text/css">
  body {font-family:verdana,helvetica;font-size:8pt}
  table {font-family:verdana,helvetica;font-size:8pt}
</style>
```

These are the only two styles used on this page.

While styles should be in their own CSS file, thereby ensuring multi-script consistency, these were included here for ease of readability.

This system (as presented here) uses a simple navigation scheme that is not very elegant or sophisticated. Other than the fact that it works, the best that can be said is that it is easy to remove – so that you can add your own navigation system. The 'whole page table' with the `<tr>` top row menu will be repeated on the other pages of this project.

```
<body>

<table border="0" cellspacing="0" cellpadding="20" height="200" width="95%">
  <tr><td> </td>
    <td width="40" bgcolor="LIGHTYELLOW"><a href="default.asp"> Home </a>
    </td>
    <td width="40" bgcolor="#B0C4DE"><a href="admin.asp"> Admin </a></td>
    <td width="40" bgcolor="LIGHTGREEN"><a href="ReportMenu.asp">Reports</a>
    </td>
    <td> </td>
  </tr>
```

The next bit sets up and fills the `<tr>` for the 'body' area of the pages. Typical information on the application home page would be the usage, the number of the corporate help desk, and maybe some flashy graphic element.

```
    <tr>
       <td colspan="5" height="175" bgcolor="LIGHTYELLOW" valign="TOP">
         <font face="Arial" SIZE="2">
           <P><B>System Description</B>:<BR>These pages describe the components
             that are available for programmers' use. This project is for
             demonstration purposes only, and does not necessarily refect the
             current state of the system.</P>
           <B>System Usage:</B>
           <LI><U>The Admin Section:</U>All XML edits take place in this area.
             On the first screen the user can add, delete or modify the basic
             component information. Once a component is created, go to the
             <I>Edit</I> area to administer the methods and properties.
           <LI><U>The Reports Section:</U> This page gates into three reports:
           <OL>
             <LI>The first lists all components in the XML file, with the
               assiciated methods and properties.
             <LI>The second reports the details for a selected component.
             <LI>The third shows all of the components written by the selected
               author.
           </OL>
           </P>
         </font>

       </td>
     </tr>
   </table>
 </body>
 </html>
```
(end) default.asp

The `global.asa` file is being used to initialize the session variable containing the disk name of the XML document that we will be using necessarily.

global.asa
```
<SCRIPT LANGUAGE=VBScript RUNAT=Server>

Sub Session_OnStart
  session("xmlFileName")="components.xml"
End Sub

'Session_OnEnd            Runs when a user's session times out or quits
'                         your application
'Application_OnStart      Runs once when the first page of your application
'                         is run for the first time by any user
'Application_OnEnd        Runs once when the web server shuts down

</SCRIPT>
```
(end) global.asa

If everything is in working order, you should see a `default.asp` looking something like this:

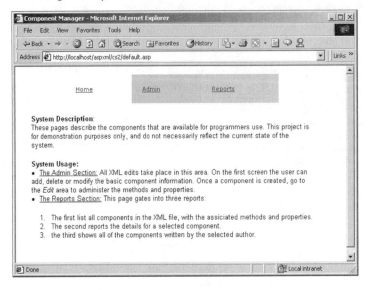

The Admin Page

It is in the Administration page that things start to get interesting. As we've seen in the ASP map this section consists of the master script `admin.asp` and six 'helper' scripts. It's fairly long, so let's just jump right in.

Before we start, here is a screen shot of the Admin page with several components already added. We can see the request buttons that are, I hope, self-explanatory. The **Add** and **Edit** buttons will open a new browser window for the input / edit form. While opening multiple browser windows is not our preferred user interface, we will be using it here. This is because it is hoped that this example will be used and expanded upon. Because you may be adding many different elements to your XML schema, the vehicle of the separate "form window" can be expanded accordingly without overly modifying or confusing the code.

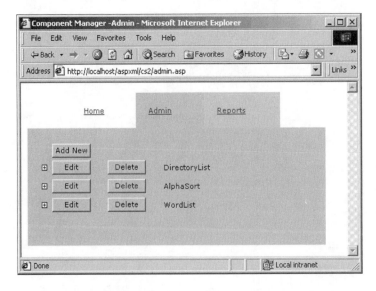

The first section of the code is not all that interesting, and does not really require much commentary. We set up several styles for later use, and open the page table that contains the navigation elements. Also, you will notice a `dummydiv` following the body tag. Its use will be described when we get to the functions section of the code.

admin.asp

```
<%
Option Explicit
Response.Expires = -1
%>

<html>
<head>
  <Title> Component Manager -Admin </Title>
</head>

<style type="text/css">
  body {font-family:verdana,helvetica;font-size:8pt}
  table {font-family:verdana,helvetica;font-size:8pt}
  button {background-color:#FFCC00;font-family:verdana,helvetica;
          font-size:8pt;width:60}
  input {font-family:verdana,helvetica;font-size:8pt}
  select {font-family:verdana,helvetica;font-size:8pt; valign:top;}
</style>
```

The `dummydiv` can appear anywhere in the body section. I usually place it at the top.

```
<body>
<div id="dummydiv"></div>
<table border="0" cellspacing="0" cellpadding="20" height="200" width="95%">
  <tr>
    <td width="15%">
       
    </td>
    <td bgcolor="LIGHTYELLOW">
      <a href="default.asp"> Home </a>
    </td>
    <td bgcolor="#B0C4DE">
      <a href="admin.asp"> Admin </a>
    </td>
    <td bgcolor="LIGHTGREEN">
      <a href="ReportMenu.asp"> Reports </a>
    </td>
    <td width="15%">
       
    </td>
  </tr>
  <tr>
    <td colspan="5" height="175" bgcolor="#B0C4DE" valign="TOP">
      <font face="Arial" SIZE="2">
```

We'll declare our variables and load up the XML document. The first row of the Admin table is the **Add New** button, which simply calls the `addComponent` function. We'll be looking at that later in the script.

```
    <%
      Dim objXML, objRootElement, objRootComponent,
      Dim counter, i, detailCounter,
      Dim imgid, divid, idmenu
```

```
        Set objXML = Server.CreateObject ("Microsoft.XMLDOM")
        objXML.load(Server.MapPath(session("xmlFileName")))
    %>
    <form method="post" name="component_form">
      <table border="0" width="70%"  bgcolor="#B0C4DE">
        <tr><td> </td>
          <td colspan="3">
            <button id="addNew" onclick="addComponent()">Add New</button>
          </td>
        </tr>
```

This sets up the visible section of the opening page. We begin by collecting the elements by name so that we'll easily be able to loop through each component.

The first cell contains the plus/minus GIFs that are used to expand the view. The next two cells trigger the editComponent and deleteComponent functions, while the last displays the text of the element name.

```
    <%
       counter=1
       detailCounter=1
       Set objRootComponent = _
                   objXML.documentElement.getElementsByTagName("name")
       For i = 0 to objRootComponent.Length - 1
         Imgid = "img" & counter
         divid = "div" & counter
    %>
    <tr>
      <td>
        <img id="<%=imgid%>" src="images/plus.gif"
            onclick="imgidclick('<%=imgid%>', '<%=divid%>');"
            onmouseover="this.style.cursor='hand';" WIDTH="9"
            HEIGHT="9"></td>
      <td>
        <button id="edit" onclick="editComponent('<%=i%>')">Edit
        </button>
      </td>
      <td>
        <button id="delete" onclick="deleteComponent('<%=i%>')">Delete
        </button>
      </td>
      <td><%=objRootComponent.Item(i).text %> </td>
    </tr>
```

In the following row we will be displaying the **Add New Method** button.

```
    <tr>
      <td colspan="4">
        <%
          Set objRootElement=objXML.documentElement
        %>
        <div id="<%=divid%>"
             style="display:None;background-color:#B0C4DE">
          <table border="0" width="100%">
            <tr><td> </td>
              <td colspan="3" align="left">
```

```
                        <span id="addNew" style="background-color:#000033;
                                color:White"
                            onmouseover="this.style.cursor='hand';"
                            onclick=
"addMethod('<%=i%>','<%=objRootComponent.Item(i).text %>')">
                            Add New Method</span>
                    </td>
                </tr>
```

In this section we loop through the methods of the component, but first we'll set up `objSubElement` to point to the methods of the 'i'th element. In this section we will be using five `<span>` tags.

1. Displays the name of the method using `getAttribute`.

2. Encloses the next three, and is used to show and hide the **Edit** or **Delete** buttons.

3. Supplies the `onClick` and `onMouseOver` for the **Edit** button.

4. Gives the bar a clean area.

5. Supplies the `onClick` and `onMouseOver` for the **Delete** button.

The `detailCounter` variable is used to create unique span IDs.

```
<%
    Set objSubElement = _
objRootElement.childNodes.Item(i).childNodes.Item(3).getElementsByTagName("method")
    For j = 0 to objSubElement.Length - 1
        idmenu="idmenu" & detailCounter
        popdiv="popdiv" & detailCounter
%>
<tr><td> </td>
    <td colspan="3">
        <span ID="<%=idmenu%>"
            onmouseover = "this.style.cursor='hand';"
            onclick="showPopup('<%=idmenu%>','<%=popdiv%>')">
            <%=objSubElement.Item(j).getAttribute("name") %>
        </span>
        <span id="<%=popdiv%>" style="display:'None'">
        <font color="#990000">-
            <span style="background-color:#CCCCCC;color=Black"
            onclick="editMethod('<%=i%>','<%=j%>','<%=objRootComponent.Item(i).text %>')"
            onmouseover="this.style.cursor='hand'"
            style="font-family:Verdana,sans-serif;font-size:7pt;font-weight:bold">Edit
            </span>
            <span bgcolor="#CCCCCC">|</span>
            <span style="background-color:#CCCCCC;color=Black"
            onclick="deleteMethod('<%=i%>','<%=j%>')"
            onmouseover="this.style.cursor='hand';"
            style="font-family:Verdana,sans-serif;font-size:7pt;font-weight:bold">Delete
            </span>
        </span>
    </td>
</tr>
<%
    detailCounter = detailCounter + 1

    next
%>
```

All of the work that we did for our methods is repeated here for the properties. Note that the `detailCounter` variable is not re-initialized but continues to increment. This creates unique IDs throughout the page.

```
        <!-- for the properties-->
        <tr><td> </td>
          <td colspan="3" align="left">
            <span id="addNew" style="background-color:#000033;color:White"
            onmouseover="this.style.cursor='hand';"
onclick="addProperty('<%=i%>','<%=objRootComponent.Item(i).text %>')">
              Add New Property
            </span>
          </td>
        </tr>
        <%
          Set objSubElement = _
objRootElement.childNodes.Item(i).childNodes.Item(4).getElementsByTagName("property")
          For j = 0 to objSubElement.Length - 1
            idmenu="idmenu" & detailCounter
            popdiv="popdiv" & detailCounter
        %>
        <tr><td> </td>
          <td colspan="3">
            <span ID="<%=idmenu%>" onmouseover="this.style.cursor='hand';"
              onclick="showPopup('<%=idmenu%>','<%=popdiv%>')">
              <%=objSubElement.Item(j).getAttribute("name") %></span>
            <span id="<%=popdiv%>" style="display:'None'">
            <font COLOR="#990000">-
              <span style="background-color:#CCCCCC;color=Black"
onclick="editProperty('<%=i%>','<%=j%>','<%=objRootComponent.Item(i).text %>')"
              onmouseover="this.style.cursor='hand'"
              style="font-family:Verdana,sans-serif;font-size:7pt;font-weight:bold">
              Edit</span>
              <span bgcolor="#CCCCCC">|</span>
              <span style="background-color:#CCCCCC;color=Black"
                onclick="deleteProperty('<%=i%>','<%=j%>')"
                onmouseover="this.style.cursor='hand';"
style="font-family:Verdana,sans-serif;font-size:7pt;font-weight:bold">
              Delete</span>
            </span>
          </td>
        </tr>
        <%
            detailCounter=detailCounter + 1
          next
        %>
      </table>
    </div>
  </td>
</tr>
<%
    counter=counter+1
  Next
%>
</table>
```

We close the detail table, and like the good programmers that we are, we clean up the object that we've created. Since we're done displaying data, we might as well close up the main table and also the <body> element.

```
<%set objXML=nothing%>

</td>
</tr>
</table>
</body>
```

The function section starts with a toggle for the '+' and '-' buttons. Each click will flip the switch – and show or hide the component details. Note that the display value of none is case sensitive.

Also, we initialize the prevdiv to the dummydiv that we've created at the top of the page. This avoids a 'first time through' problem in the showPopup function.

```
<script language="Javascript">

var mywin
var prevdiv="dummydiv"

function imgidclick(imgID,divID)
{
  if (document.all(divID).style.display == "none")
  {
    document.all(divID).style.display="";
    document.all(imgID).src="images/minus.gif";
  }
  else
  {
    document.all(divID).style.display="None";
    document.all(imgID).src="images/plus.gif";
  }
  window.event.cancelBubble=true;
}
```

When the user clicks to delete a component, we just go ahead and do it. Some organizations may like to add a "please verify" dialog box at some point.

Both the addComponent and the editComponent open a new window with the showComponent.asp file. We will be using the action to determine the header and processing path in the target script.

```
function deleteComponent(i)
{
  location.href="updComponent.asp?functionname=delete&selComponent=" + i
}

function addComponent()
{
var str;
  str="showComponent.asp?action=add";
  if (mywin!=null)
  {
```

```
      if (!mywin.closed)
      {
        mywin.close();
        mywin=null;
      }
    }

    mywin=window.open(str,null,
        "directories=no,location=no,menubar=no,status,toolbar=no,resizable,scrollbars");
    window.event.cancelBubble=true;
}

function editComponent(i)
{
var str;
    str="showComponent.asp?action=edit&ComponentID=" + i;
    if (mywin!=null)
    {
      if (!mywin.closed)
      {
        mywin.close();
        mywin=null;
      }
    }

    mywin=window.open(str,null,
        "directories=no,location=no,menubar=no,status,toolbar=no,resizable,scrollbars");
    window.event.cancelBubble=true;
}
```

This short little function is responsible for showing the **Edit** or **Delete** menu for the methods and properties. It is here that we use the `dummydiv` as a target to set `display` to `none` the first time this function is called. (Remember that we initialized `prevdiv="dummydiv"` earlier in the code.) This simple technique lets us avoid excessive logic at the beginning of this function.

```
function showPopup(MenuID,popupID)
{
  document.all(prevdiv).style.display="None";
  document.all(popupID).style.display="";
  prevdiv=popupID;
  window.event.cancelBubble=true;
}
```

The six `add`, `edit`, and `delete` functions for the methods and properties are essentially the same as the component functions above, so no additional commentary is necessary.

```
function addMethod(i,ComponentName)
{
var str;
    str = "showMethod.asp?action=add&elementID=" + i + "&ComponentName=" +
              ComponentName;

    if (mywin!=null)
    {
```

```
      if (!mywin.closed)
      {
        mywin.close();
        mywin=null;
      }
    }
    mywin=window.open(str, null, "directories=no, location=no,
                      menubar=no, status, toolbar=no, resizable, scrollbars");
    window.event.cancelBubble=true;
}

function editMethod(i,j,ComponentName)
{
var str;
    str = "showMethod.asp?action=edit&elementID=" + i + "&detailID=" + j +
            "&ComponentName=" + ComponentName;
    if (mywin!=null)
    {
      if (!mywin.closed)
      {
        mywin.close();
        mywin=null;
      }
    }
    mywin=window.open(str,null,
        "directories=no,location=no,menubar=no,status,toolbar=no,resizable,scrollbars");
    window.event.cancelBubble=true;
}

function deleteMethod(i,j)
{
    location.href = "updMethod.asp?functionname=delete&elementID=" + i +
        "&detailID=" + j
}

function addProperty(i,ComponentName)
{
    var str;
    str = "showProperty.asp?action=add&elementID=" + i + "&ComponentName=" +
    ComponentName;

    if (mywin!=null)
    {
    if (!mywin.closed)
    {
     mywin.close();
    mywin=null;
    }
  }
    mywin = window.open(str, null,
      "directories=no,location=no,menubar=no,status,toolbar=no, resizable, scrollbars");
    window.event.cancelBubble=true;
}

function editProperty(i,j,ComponentName)
{
```

```
        var str;
        str="showProperty.asp?action=edit&elementID=" + i + "&detailID=" + j +
            "&ComponentName=" + ComponentName;
        if (mywin!=null)
        {
            if (!mywin.closed)
            {
                mywin.close();
                mywin=null;
            }
        }
        mywin=window.open(str,null,
                "directories=no,location=no,menubar=no,status,toolbar=no,
resizable,scrollbars");
        window.event.cancelBubble=true;
    }

    function deleteProperty(i,j)
    {
      location.href="updProperty.asp?functionname=delete&elementID=" + i +
    "&detailID=" + j
    }

    </script>
    </html>
```

(end) Admin.asp

Before we continue, let's take a look at the Admin page with the components expanded:

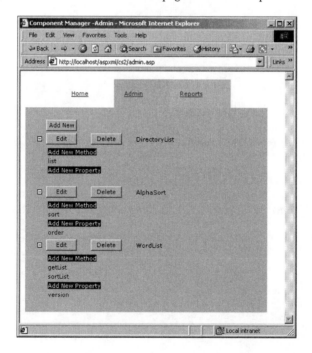

The showComponent.asp is called when we need to add or modify an entry node. It is opened in its own window from the admin.asp script. We start out in a pretty standard way, setting up the styles and declaring our variables. As mentioned, the use of this separate window lets anyone revising this code add many more elements to the schema.

showComponent.asp

```
<%@ Language=VBScript %>
<%
Option Explicit
Response.Expires = -1
%>
<html>

<style type="text/css">
   body {font-family:verdana,helvetica;font-size:8pt}
   table {font-family:verdana,helvetica;font-size:8pt}
   button {background-color:#FFCC00;font-family:verdana,helvetica;font-
size:8pt;width:130}
   input {font-family:verdana,helvetica;font-size:8pt}
   select {font-family:verdana,helvetica;font-size:8pt; valign:top;}
</style>
```

This script handles two different actions, Add and Edit. Each path requires the appropriate header on the screen and a different URL into the update script. In addition, on Edit, we need to open the XML document to display the current data.

```
<%
  Dim objXML, objRootElement
  Dim action, headerString, processFile, selComponent
  action=Request.QueryString("action")

  if action="add" then
    headerString="Add a New Component"
    processFile="updComponent.asp?functionname=addNew"
  else
    selComponent = Request.QueryString("ComponentID")
    headerString = "Edit a Component"
    processFile  = "updComponent.asp?functionname=saveEdit&selComponent=" &_
                   selComponent
    Set objXML = Server.CreateObject ("Microsoft.XMLDOM")
    objXML.load(Server.MapPath(session("xmlFileName")))
    Set objRootElement = objXML.documentElement
  end if
%>

<body>
<center>
<h2 Align=center><%=headerString%></h2>
<form name="thisform" method="post">
<table border="0">
```

Inside the display table, we create the input and text areas for user input. If we're editing, we load the element data from the objRootElement.

```
   <tr>
     <td width=60>Name:</td>
     <td><input type="text"  name="Name" size="60"
       <%if action="edit" then %>
   value="<%=objRootElement.childNodes.Item(selComponent).childNodes.Item(0).text%>"
       <%end if%>>
     </td>
   </tr>
   <tr>
     <td width=60>Author:</td>
     <td><input type="text"  name="Author" size="60"
       <%if action="edit" then %>
      value="<%=objRootElement.childNodes.Item(selComponent).childNodes.Item(1).text%>"
       <%end if%>></td>
   </tr>
   <tr>
     <td width=60>Overview:</td>
     <td><textarea name="Overview" rows=5 cols=50>
       <%if action="edit" then
Response.write(objRootElement.childNodes.Item(selComponent).childNodes.Item(2).text)
       end if%></textarea></td>
   </tr>
   <tr>
     <td colspan=2 align=center>
       <button onclick="saveThis()">Save</button> 
       <button onclick="window.close()">Cancel</button></td>
   </tr>
</table>
</form>
</center>
<%set objXML=nothing%>
</body>

<script language="javascript">
function saveThis()
{
  thisform.action="<%=processFile%>"
  thisform.submit();
}
</script>
</html>
```

(end) showComponent.asp

We'll leave it to the reader, and their design group to add the appropriate colors and logos to the showComponent screen.

The workhorse of the administration section is the update script. For reasons of clarity, there are three scripts, each one handling its own level of the XML document. The first one that we encounter is the `updComponent.asp`. This script does not actually display anything in the client browser – it just quietly does its job and returns control to `admin.asp`.

We begin the script by branching to the appropriate function that we need to execute.

updComponent.asp

```
<%@ Language=VBScript %>
<%
Option Explicit
Response.Expires = -1
%>

<html>
<%
  Dim xmlName, xmlAuthor, xmlOverview
  Dim functionname, elementID
  functionname=Request.QueryString("functionname")

  select case functionname
    case "addNew"
        call addNew
    case "delete"
        call delete
    case "saveEdit"
        call saveEdit
  end select
```

In the `addNew` function we gather the data from the form on the previous page, and create a node string compliant with our XML schema. At this point we do not have any methods or properties defined, so we'll just add placeholder tags. I'm partial to using the `insertBefore` method so that the new node is at the top of the XML document. If you then look at the XML (with IE5, for example), it's not necessary to scroll down to see the addition.

```
sub addNew

  Dim objXML, objRootElement
  Dim strNewNode

  xmlName     = trim(Request.form("Name"))
  xmlAuthor   = trim(Request.form("Author"))
  xmlOverview = trim(Request.form("Overview"))

  Set objXML = Server.CreateObject ("Microsoft.XMLDOM")

  strNewNode = "<component>"
  strNewNode = strNewNode & "<name>"     & xmlName     & "</name>"
  strNewNode = strNewNode & "<author>"   & xmlAuthor   & "</author>"
  strNewNode = strNewNode & "<overview>" & xmlOverview & "</overview>"
  strNewNode = strNewNode & "<methods /> <properties />"
  strNewNode = strNewNode & "</component>"

  objXML.LoadXML(strNewNode)
  set objNewNode = objXML.DocumentElement
```

```
objXML.Load(Server.MapPath(session("xmlFileName")))
set objRootElement = objXML.DocumentElement

Set objMyFinal = objRootElement.insertBefore(objNewNode,
    objRootElement.childNodes.item(0))
objXML.Save(Server.MapPath("components.xml"))
set objXML=nothing
end sub
```

The `delete` function simply finds the appropriate node and removes it from the XML document.

```
sub delete
  Dim objXML, objRootElement
  Set objXML = Server.CreateObject ("Microsoft.XMLDOM")

  objXML.load(Server.MapPath(session("xmlFileName")))
  Set objRootElement = objXML.documentElement

  elementID   = Request("selComponent")

  Set objMyFinal = _
      objRootElement.removeChild(objRootElement.childNodes.Item(elementID))
  objXML.Save(Server.MapPath("components.xml"))
  set objXML=nothing
end sub
```

This simple function replaces the `Item(x).text` data in the selected node:

```
' This function updates the selected Element
sub saveEdit
  Dim objXML, objRootElement
  Set objXML = Server.CreateObject ("Microsoft.XMLDOM")

  objXML.load(Server.MapPath(session("xmlFileName")))
  Set objRootElement = objXML.documentElement

  elementID   = Request("selComponent")
  xmlName     = trim(Request.form("Name"))
  xmlAuthor   = trim(Request.form("Author"))
  xmlOverview = trim(Request.form("Overview"))

  objRootElement.childNodes.Item(elementID).childNodes.Item(0).text = xmlName
  objRootElement.childNodes.Item(elementID).childNodes.Item(1).text = xmlAuthor
  objRootElement.childNodes.Item(elementID).childNodes.Item(2).text = xmlOverview

  objXML.Save(Server.MapPath("components.xml"))
  set objXML=nothing
end sub
%>
<script language="Javascript">
<%if functionname="delete" then%>
  location.href="admin.asp"
<%else%>
  window.close()
  window.opener.location.href="admin.asp"
```

```
<%end if%>
</script>
</html>
```

(end) updComponent.asp

To administer the methods we use code that is (almost) identical to the scripts that we've used for the component level elements.

showMethod.asp

```
<%@ Language=VBScript %>
<%
Option Explicit
Response.Expires = -1
%>

<html>
<style type="text/css">
  body {font-family:verdana,helvetica;font-size:8pt}
  table {font-family:verdana,helvetica;font-size:8pt}
  button {background-color:#FFCC00;font-family:verdana,helvetica;font-
size:8pt;width:130}
  input {font-family:verdana,helvetica;font-size:8pt}
  select {font-family:verdana,helvetica;font-size:8pt; valign:top;}
</style>

<%
  dim objXML, objRootElement,objSubElement
  dim action, headerString, processFile, selComponent
  dim elementID, detailID, ComponentName

  action=Request.QueryString("action")
  elementID = Request.querystring("elementID")
  detailID  = Request.querystring("detailID")
  ComponentName=Request.querystring("ComponentName")

  if action="add" then
    headerString="Component : " & ComponentName & " - Add a Method"
    processFile="updMethod.asp?functionname=addNew&elementID=" & _
                elementID & "&detailID=" & detailID
  else
    Set objXML = Server.CreateObject ("Microsoft.XMLDOM")
    objXML.load(Server.MapPath(session("xmlFileName")))
    Set objRootElement = objXML.documentElement
    set objSubElement = _
objRootElement.childNodes.Item(elementID).childNodes.Item(3).getElementsByTagName("method")
    headerString="Component : " & ComponentName & " - Edit a Method"
    processFile="updMethod.asp?functionname=saveEdit&elementID=" & _
                elementID & "&detailID=" & detailID
  end if
%>

<body>
<center>
<h2 Align=center><%=headerString%></h2>
<form name="thisform" method="post">
```

```
    <table border="0">
      <tr>
        <td width=60>Name:</td>
        <td><input type="text"  name="Name" size="60"
          <%if action="edit" then %>
          value="<%=objSubElement.Item(detailID).getAttribute("name")%>"
          <%end if%>></td>
      </tr>
      <tr>
        <td width=60>Syntax:</td>
        <td><input type="text"  name="syntax" size="60"
          <%if action="edit" then %>
          value="<%=objSubElement.Item(detailID).childNodes.Item(0).text%>"
          <%end if%>></td>
      </tr>
      <tr>
        <td width=60>Description:</td>
        <td><textarea  name="Description" rows=5 cols=50>
            <%if action="edit" then
            Response.write(objSubElement.Item(detailID).childNodes.Item(1).text)
              end if%>
          </textarea></td>
      </tr>
      <tr>
        <td width=60>Example:</td>
        <td><textarea  name="Example" rows=5 cols=50>
            <%if action="edit" then
            Response.write(objSubElement.Item(detailID).childNodes.Item(2).text)
            end if%>
          </textarea></td>
      </tr>
      <tr>
        <td colspan=2 align=center>
          <button onclick="saveThis()" id=button1 name=button1>Save
          </button> 
          <button onclick="window.close()" id=button2 name=button2>Cancel
          </button></td>
      </tr>
    </table>
  </form>
  </center>
<%set objXML=nothing%>
</body>
<script language="javascript">
function saveThis()
{
  thisform.action="<%=processFile%>";
  thisform.submit();
}
</script>
</HTML>
```

(end) showMethod.asp

The associated update file for the methods is also basically the same as the one that we've seen:

updMethod.asp

```
<%@ Language=VBScript %>
<%
Option Explicit
Response.Expires = -1
%>


<%
  Dim objXML, objRootElement, objSubElement
  Dim xmlName, xmlCallSeq, xmlDesc, xmlExample
  Dim elementID, detailID

  functionname=Request.QueryString("functionname")
  elementID = Request.QueryString("elementID")
  detailID  = Request.QueryString("detailID")

  select case functionname
    case "addNew"
        call addNew
    case "delete"
        call delete
    case "saveEdit"
        call saveEdit
  end select

sub addNew

  Dim strNewNode
  xmlName    = trim(Request.form("name"))
  xmlCallSeq = trim(Request.form("syntax"))
  xmlDesc    = trim(Request.form("description"))
  xmlExample = trim(Request.form("example"))

  Set objXML = Server.CreateObject ("Microsoft.XMLDOM")

  strNewNode = "<method name=""" & xmlName & """>"
  strNewNode = strNewNode & "<syntax>" & xmlCallSeq & "</syntax>"
  strNewNode = strNewNode & "<description>"  & xmlDesc    & "</description>"
  strNewNode = strNewNode & "<example>"       & xmlExample & "</example>"
  strNewNode = strNewNode & "</method>"

  objXML.LoadXML(strNewNode)
  set objNewNode = objXML.DocumentElement

  objXML.Load(Server.MapPath(session("xmlFileName")))
  set objRootElement = objXML.DocumentElement
  objRootElement.childNodes.Item(elementID).childNodes.Item(3).appendChild(objNewNode)


  objXML.Save(Server.MapPath("components.xml"))
  set objXML=nothing

end sub
```

The `delete` function is different than the one used for the component. First we find the child method that we wish to delete, and then we call the `removeChild` method from its parent node.

```
sub delete

  Set objXML = Server.CreateObject ("Microsoft.XMLDOM")

  objXML.load(Server.MapPath(session("xmlFileName")))
  Set objRootElement = objXML.documentElement

'   create a NodeList of all methods
  set objSubElement =
objRootElement.childNodes.Item(elementID).childNodes.Item(3).getElementsByTagName("method")

  '   Find the Node to delete
  set objNode = objSubElement.Item(detailID)

  '   Delete the node from the parent Item
  objNode.parentNode.removeChild(objNode)

  objXML.Save(Server.MapPath("components.xml"))
  set objXML=nothing
end sub

' This function updates the selected Element
sub saveEdit

  xmlName     = trim(Request.form("Name"))
  xmlCallSeq = trim(Request.form("syntax"))
  xmlDesc     = trim(Request.form("Description"))
  xmlExample = trim(Request.form("Example"))

  Set objXML = Server.CreateObject ("Microsoft.XMLDOM")

  objXML.load(Server.MapPath(session("xmlFileName")))
  Set objRootElement = objXML.documentElement

  set objSubElement = _
objRootElement.childNodes.Item(elementID).childNodes.Item(3).getElementsByTagName("method")

  objSubElement.Item(detailID).attributes(0).value = xmlName
  objSubElement.Item(detailID).childNodes.Item(0).text = xmlCallSeq
  objSubElement.Item(detailID).childNodes.Item(1).text = xmlDesc
  objSubElement.Item(detailID).childNodes.Item(2).text = xmlExample

  objXML.save(Server.MapPath("components.xml"))
  set objXML=nothing
end sub
%>

<script language="Javascript">
<%if functionname="delete" then%>
  location.href="admin.asp"
<%else%>
  window.close()
  window.opener.location.href="admin.asp"
```

```
    <%end if%>
    </script>
    </html>
```

(end) updMethod.asp

The 'properties' section is the final piece of the administrative section. Like the method code, it operates on a subElement.

showProperty.asp

```
    <%@ Language=VBScript %>
    <%
    Option Explicit
    Response.Expires = -1
    %>

    <HTML>
    <head>
      <title> component manager </title>
    </head>

    <style type="text/css">
      body {font-family:verdana,helvetica;font-size:8pt}
      table {font-family:verdana,helvetica;font-size:8pt}
      button {background-color:#FFCC00;font-family:verdana,helvetica;font-
    size:8pt;width:130}
      input {font-family:verdana,helvetica;font-size:8pt}
      select {font-family:verdana,helvetica;font-size:8pt; valign:top;}
    </style>

    <%
      Dim objXML, objRootElement,objSubElement
      dim action, headerString, processFile, selComponent
      dim elementID, detailID, ComponentName

      action=Request.QueryString("action")
      elementID = Request.querystring("elementID")
      detailID  = Request.querystring("detailID")
      ComponentName=Request.querystring("ComponentName")

      if action="add" then
        headerString="Component : " & ComponentName & " - Add a Property"
        processFile="updProperty.asp?functionname=addNew&elementID=" & _
                    elementID & "&detailID=" & detailID
      else
        Set objXML = Server.CreateObject ("Microsoft.XMLDOM")
        objXML.load(Server.MapPath(session("xmlFileName")))
        Set objRootElement = objXML.documentElement
        set objSubElement = _
    objRootElement.childNodes.Item(elementID).childNodes.Item(4).getElementsByTagName("property")
        headerString="Component : " & ComponentName & " - Edit a Property"
        processFile="updProperty.asp?functionname=saveEdit&elementID=" & _
                    elementID & "&detailID=" & detailID
      end if
    %>
    <body>
```

```
<center>
<h2 Align=center><%=headerString%></h2>
<form name="thisform" method="post">
<table border="0">
  <tr>
    <td width=60>Name:</td>
    <td><input type="text"  name="Name" size="60"
      <%if action="edit" then %>
        value="<%=objSubElement.Item(detailID).getAttribute("name")%>"
      <%end if%>></td>
  </tr>
  <tr>
    <td width=60>Description:</td>
    <td><textarea  name="Description" rows=5 cols=50>
      <%if action="edit" then
        Response.write(objSubElement.Item(detailID).childNodes.Item(0).text)
        end if%>
      </textarea></td>
  </tr>
  <tr>
    <td width=60>Example:</td>
    <td><textarea name="Example" rows=5 cols=50>
      <%if action="edit" then
        Response.write(objSubElement.Item(detailID).childNodes.Item(1).text)
      end if%>
      </textarea></td>
  </tr>
  <tr>
    <td colspan=2 align=center>
      <button onclick="saveThis()" id=button1 name=button1>Save
      </button> 
      <button onclick="window.close()" id=button2 name=button2>Cancel
      </button></td>
  </tr>
</table>
</form>
</center>
<%set objXML=nothing%>
</body>

<script language="javascript">
function saveThis()
{
  thisform.action="<%=processFile%>"
  thisform.submit();
}
</script>
</html>
```

(end) showProperty.asp

updProperty.asp

```
<%@ Language=VBScript %>
<%
Option Explicit
Response.Expires = -1
%>
```

```asp
<%
  Dim objXML, objRootElement, objSubElement
  Dim xmlName, xmlCallSeq, xmlDesc, xmlExample
  Dim elementID, detailID

  functionname=Request.QueryString("functionname")
  elementID = Request.QueryString("elementID")
  detailID  = Request.QueryString("detailID")

  select case functionname
    case "addNew"
        call addNew
    case "delete"
        call delete
    case "saveEdit"
        call saveEdit
  end select

sub addNew
  Dim strNewNode

  xmlName    = trim(Request.form("name"))
  xmlDesc    = trim(Request.form("description"))
  xmlExample = trim(Request.form("example"))

  Set objXML = Server.CreateObject ("Microsoft.XMLDOM")

  strNewNode = "<property name=""" & xmlName & """>"
  strNewNode = strNewNode & "<description>" & xmlDesc    & "</description>"
  strNewNode = strNewNode & "<example>"     & xmlExample & "</example>"
  strNewNode = strNewNode & "</property>"

  objXML.LoadXML(strNewNode)
  set objNewNode = objXML.DocumentElement

  objXML.Load(Server.MapPath(session("xmlFileName")))
  set objRootElement = objXML.DocumentElement

  objRootElement.childNodes.Item(elementID).childNodes.Item(4).appendChild(objNewNode)
  objXML.Save(Server.MapPath("components.xml"))
  set objXML=nothing
end sub

sub delete

  Set objXML = Server.CreateObject ("Microsoft.XMLDOM")

  objXML.load(Server.MapPath(session("xmlFileName")))
  Set objRootElement = objXML.documentElement

'  create a NodeList of all methods
  set objSubElement = _
objRootElement.childNodes.Item(elementID).childNodes.Item(4).getElementsByTagName("property")
  ' Find the Node to delete
  set objNode = objSubElement.Item(detailID)
  ' Delete the node from the parent Item
```

```
    objNode.parentNode.removeChild(objNode)

    objXML.Save(Server.MapPath("components.xml"))
    set objXML=nothing
end sub

' This function updates the selected Element
sub saveEdit
  xmlName    = trim(Request.form("Name"))
  xmlDesc    = trim(Request.form("Description"))
  xmlExample = trim(Request.form("Example"))

  Set objXML = Server.CreateObject ("Microsoft.XMLDOM")

  objXML.load(Server.MapPath(session("xmlFileName")))
  Set objRootElement = objXML.documentElement
  set objSubElement = _
objRootElement.childNodes.Item(elementID).childNodes.Item(4).getElementsByTagName("property")

  objSubElement.Item(detailID).attributes(0).value = xmlName
  objSubElement.Item(detailID).childNodes.Item(0).text = xmlDesc
  objSubElement.Item(detailID).childNodes.Item(1).text = xmlExample

  objXML.save(Server.MapPath("components.xml"))
  set objXML=nothing
end sub
%>

<script language="Javascript">
<%if functionname="delete" then%>
  location.href="admin.asp"
<%else%>
  window.close()
  window.opener.location.href="admin.asp"
<%end if%>
</script>
</html>
```

(end) updProperty.asp

The Reports Page

The reporting section of this project displays three different types of reports. The first is a full listing of all the known components, the second displays a specific component, and the third lists all of the components with a selected author. As each of these reports uses a different path to the final page, we can examine different technologies as we go.

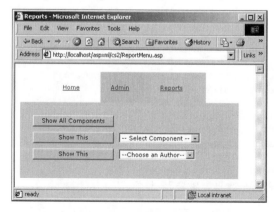

The top part of `reportMenu.asp` script starts out like the scripts that we've seen except notice that the body tag has an `onload` function – `waitTillLoaded()`. This function appears at the beginning of the script section. It's used to wait until the full XML document is read before the author selection is created.

ReportMenu.asp

```
<html>
<head>
  <Title> Reports </Title>
</head>

<style type="text/css">
  body {font-family:verdana,helvetica;font-size:8pt}
  table {font-family:verdana,helvetica;font-size:8pt}
  button {background-color:#FFCC00;font-family:verdana,helvetica;font-
size:8pt;width:160}
  select {font-family:verdana,helvetica;font-size:8pt; valign:top;}
</style>

<body onload="waitTillLoaded()">
<%
  Dim objXML, objRootElement

  Set objXML = Server.CreateObject ("Microsoft.XMLDOM")
  objXML.load(Server.MapPath(session("xmlFileName")))
%>

<table border="0" cellspacing="0" cellpadding="20" height="200" width="95%">
  <tr>
    <td width="15%"> </td>
    <td bgcolor="LIGHTYELLOW">
      <a href="default.asp"> Home </a>
    </td>
    <td bgcolor="#B0C4DE">
      <a href="admin.asp"> Admin </a>
    </td>
    <td bgcolor="LIGHTGREEN">
      <a href="ReportMenu.asp"> Reports </a>
    </td>
    <td width="15%"> </td>
  </tr>
```

We've used this technique for the buttons on prior pages. The select box for the component list is a simple extract from the XML document of all 'name' elements.

```
<tr>
  <td colspan="5" bgcolor="LIGHTGREEN" valign="TOP">
    <table border="0" cellspacing="0" cellpadding="5">
      <form method="post" name="show_form">
        <tr>
          <td bgcolor="LIGHTGREEN" valign="TOP">
            <button onclick="buttonClicked('showAll')">Show All Components
            </button>
          </td>
        </tr>
        <tr>
```

```
            <td><button onclick="buttonClicked('showComponent')">Show This
            </button></td>
            <td>
              <div id="select_div">
                <select id="selComponent" name="selComponent">
                  <option value="-1">-- Select Component --</option>
                  <%
                    Set objRootElement = _
objXML.documentElement.getElementsByTagName("name")
                    For i = 0 to objRootElement.Length - 1 %>
                    <option value="<%= i %>"><%=objRootElement.Item(i).text %>
                    </option>
                  <%Next%>
                </select>
              </div>
            </td>
          </tr>
```

This row contains an empty `<div>` that will be filled by a list of unique authors.

```
          <tr>
            <td><button onclick="buttonClicked('showAuthor')"
                    id=button1 name=button1>Show This</button></td>
            <td><div id="selectAuthor_div"></div></td>
          </tr>
        </form>
      </table>
    </td>
  </tr>
</table>
<% set objXML=nothing %>
</body>
```

The `buttonClicked` function routes the process to the appropriate page.

```
<script language="javascript">

function buttonClicked(s)
{
  switch(s)
  {
    case "showAll" :
      show_form.action="rptAll.asp";
      show_form.submit();
      break;
    case "showComponent" :
      if (document.all("selComponent").selectedIndex ==0 )
        return;
      show_form.action="rptByComponent.asp";
      show_form.submit();
      break;
    case "showAuthor" :
      if (document.all("selAuthor").selectedIndex == 0)
        return;
      show_form.action="rptByAuthor.asp";
      show_form.submit();
      break;
  }
}
```

The `waitTillLoaded` function is called when the script first loads. Notice way down at the bottom of this script is the `<xml>` tag. This triggers the loading of the XML documents we will identify as `Authors`. This 'wait' function will call itself until the document is completely loaded. (Note, however, that a `readyState` of `complete` does not necessarily mean that the load was successful.) When the load is done, we call `fillBoxes` – which contains only a call directly into `makeBox`.

Why don't we just go right into the `makeBox` function? In a full production system, we would perhaps have several select boxes, or other processes that we'd like to handle. Several function calls would therefore typically be in the `fillBoxes` function.

```
//Calls fillboxes() only after the entire XML document has been loaded
function waitTillLoaded(){
  window.status = "loading XML data...";
  if (Authors.readyState != "complete")
    window.setTimeout("waitTillLoaded()",100);

  window.status = "ready" ;
  fillBoxes();
}

function fillBoxes(){
    makeBox("author", "selAuthor");
}
```

This function creates the node list of unique authors. While this technique works fine with small XML documents, if the scope of the list is hundreds of entries scalability will become a factor. The function works by creating a node list of unique nodes. At each read, the text is compared to each item in `holderNode`. When we've finished with the XML document, we build the select.

```
function makeBox(elementName, boxName){

  var srchPattern = "//" + elementName;
  var selNodes = Authors.documentElement.selectNodes(srchPattern);
  var holderNode = Authors.createNode(1, "holder","");
  holderNode.insertBefore(selNodes.item(0).cloneNode(true), null);

  for (var j=1;j< selNodes.length;j++){
    counter = 0;
    for (var k=0; k< holderNode.childNodes.length;k++){
      if (selNodes.item(j).text == holderNode.childNodes.item(k).text ||
          selNodes.item(j).text == ""){
        counter=1;
        break;
        }
      else counter = 0;
      }
    if (counter == 0){
      holderNode.insertBefore(selNodes.item(j).cloneNode(true), null);
      }
    }
  buildSelect(boxName,holderNode.childNodes);
}
```

These two functions work together to build the select boxes. Input and select boxes don't take kindly to quotes.

```
// This function replaces a apostrophe with a /.
// The reverse is carried out in rptDetailsAuthor
function escapeQuote(str)
{
  var i,tempstr ;
  tempstr="" ;
  i=str.indexOf("'",0)
  while (i > -1)
   {
     tempstr=tempstr.concat(str.substring(0,i))
     tempstr=tempstr.concat("/")
     str=str.substring(i+1,str.length)
     i=str.indexOf("'",0)
   }
  tempstr=tempstr.concat(str)
  return tempstr
}

 //build the select boxes using the nodelist built in makeBox
function buildSelect(boxName, selNodes){
  var str = "<SELECT NAME='" + boxName + "' SIZE=1><OPTION VALUE='-1'>
           --Choose an Author--";
  for (var i=0; i < selNodes.length; i++){
     str += "<OPTION VALUE='" + escapeQuote(selNodes.item(i).text) + "'>" +
        selNodes.item(i).text;
  }
  str += "</SELECT>";
  //   load the str into the page div
  selectAuthor_div.innerHTML=str;
}

</script>
<xml ID="Authors" SRC="<%=session("xmlFileName")%>"></xml>
</html>
```

(end) reportMenu.asp

The Reports

The simplest of the three reports is the individual component script: `rptByComponent.asp`. We come into this script with a selected component, and find the appropriate node of the XML document to display.

rptByComponent.asp

```
<%@ Language=VBScript %>
<%
Option Explicit
Response.Expires = -1
%>

<html>
<head>
  <Title> Reports </Title>
```

```
</head>

<style type="text/css">
  body {font-family:verdana,helvetica;font-size:8pt}
  table {font-family:verdana,helvetica;font-size:8pt}
  button {background-color:#FFCC00;font-family:verdana,helvetica;font-
size:8pt;width:80}
  select {font-family:verdana,helvetica;font-size:8pt; valign:top;}
</style>

<body>
<%
  Dim objXML, objRootElement, objSubElement
  Dim elementID, i

  elementID=Request.Form("selComponent")
  Set objXML = Server.CreateObject ("Microsoft.XMLDOM")

  objXML.load(Server.MapPath(session("xmlFileName")))
  Set objRootElement = objXML.documentElement
%>

<table border="0" cellspacing="0" cellpadding="20" height="200" width="95%">
  <tr><td> </td>
    <td width="40" bgcolor="LIGHTYELLOW"><a href="default.asp">Home</a></td>
    <td width="40" bgcolor="#B0C4DE"><a href="admin.asp">Admin</a></td>
    <td width="40" bgcolor="LIGHTGREEN">a href="ReportMenu.asp">Reports</a>
    </td><td> </td>
  </tr>
```

As in our other scripts, the top portion is dedicated to loading the XML document and some navigational code.

```
    <tr>
      <td colspan="5" bgcolor="LIGHTGREEN" valign="TOP">
        <table border="0" cellspacing="0" cellpadding="5" width="100%">
        <tr>
          <td valign="TOP" align="LEFT">Name: <b>
            <%= objRootElement.childNodes.Item(elementID).childNodes.Item(0).text %>
          </b></td>
          <td align="right">Author: 
            <%= objRootElement.childNodes.Item(elementID).childNodes.Item(1).text %>
          </td>
        </tr>
        <tr>
          <td colspan="2">
            <table>
              <tr>
                <td valign="top">Description:</td><td>
<%=objRootElement.childNodes.Item(elementID).childNodes.Item(2).text %>
                </td>
              </tr>
            </table>
          <td>
        </tr>
```

Above, we display the component header information.

In the methods section below, we first set the `objSubElement` to the node list of the component's methods. We can then use the `for...next` to display all of the methods.

```
<%Set objSubElement = _
objRootElement.childNodes.Item(elementID).childNodes.Item(3).getElementsByTagName("method")
    If objSubElement.Length > 0 then%>
    <tr>
      <td valign="TOP" align="LEFT" colspan="2"><b>Methods</b></td>
    </tr>
    <tr>
      <td colspan="2">
        <table width="100%" border="0" cellspacing="0" cellpadding="0">
          <%For i = 0 to objSubElement.Length -1%>
          <tr>
            <td colspan="2"><i>
              <%= objSubElement.Item(i).getAttribute("name")%></i>
            </td>
            <td>Syntax: 
              <%= objSubElement.Item(i).childNodes.Item(0).text %>
            </td>
          </tr>
          <tr><td> </td>
            <td valign="top">Description: </td>
            <td><%= objSubElement.Item(i).childNodes.Item(1).text %></td>
          </tr>
          <tr><td> </td>
            <td valign="top">Example: </td>
            <td><%= objSubElement.Item(i).childNodes.Item(2).text %></td>
          </tr>
          <tr><td colspan="3"> </td></tr>
          <%Next%>
        </table>
      </td>
    </tr>
    <%Else%>
    <tr><td valign="TOP" align="LEFT" colspan="2">
      No described methods</td>
    </tr>
    <%End If%>
```

The code from above is (mostly) repeated for the properties section.

```
<%Set objSubElement =
objRootElement.childNodes.Item(elementID).childNodes.Item(4).getElementsByTagName("property")
    If objSubElement.Length > 0 then%>
    <tr>
      <td valign="TOP" align="LEFT" colspan="2"><b>Properties</b></td>
    </tr>
    <tr>
      <td colsp n="2">
        <table width="100%" border="0" cellspacing="0" cellpadding="0">
          <%For i = 0 to objSubElement.Length -1 %>
          <tr>
```

```
                <td colspan="2"><i>
                  <%= objSubElement.Item(i).getAttribute("name") %></i></td>
              </tr>
              <tr><td> </td>
                <td valign="top">Description: </td>
                <td><%= objSubElement.Item(i).childNodes.Item(0).text %></td>
              </tr>
              <tr><td> </td>
                <td valign="top">Example: </td>
                <td><%= objSubElement.Item(i).childNodes.Item(1).text %></td>
              </tr>
              <tr><td colspan="3"> </td></tr>
              <%Next%>
            </table>
          </td>
        </tr>
        <%Else%>
        <tr>
          <td valign="TOP" align="LEFT" colspan="2">  No described
                                                    properties</td>
        </tr>
        <%End If%>
        </table>
      </td>
    </tr>
  </table><%set objXML=nothing%>
</body>
</html>
```

(end) rptByComponent.asp

An example of the component report is:

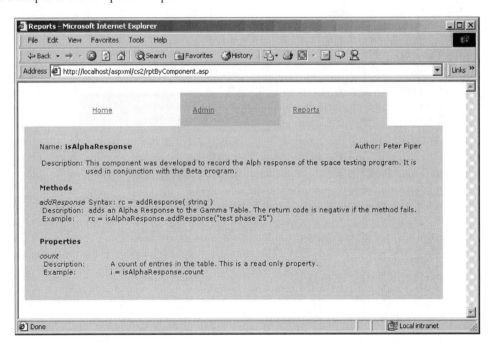

The `rptByAuthor` script is similar to the code that we've just examined. Looking at the beginning of the script, we see one of the first differences – we are handling the quote / apostrophe issues that arise when using a web form. The other major difference is that we will be dealing with a node list rather than a single node.

rptByAuthor.asp

```
<%@ Language=VBScript %>
<%
Option Explicit
Response.Expires = -1
%>

<html>
<head>
  <Title> Reports </Title>
</head>

<style type="text/css">
  body {font-family:verdana,helvetica;font-size:8pt}
  table {font-family:verdana,helvetica;font-size:8pt}
  button {background-color:#FFCC00;font-family:verdana,helvetica;font-
size:8pt;width:80}
  select {font-family:verdana,helvetica;font-size:8pt; valign:top;}
</style>

<body>
<%
  Dim objXML, objRootElement, objSubElement, objNodeList
  Dim authorName, i

  authorName=trim(Request.Form("selAuthor"))
  'replace the / with apostrophes
  authorName=replace(authorName,"/","'")
  'replace the apostrophes with a \' to escape the apostrophe
  authorName=replace(authorName,"'","\'")

  'Pattern indicates find all nodes from the root which match the authorname
  patternString="component/author[. = '" & authorName & "' ]"
  'patternString="component/author[. = 'Mr O\'Brien' ]"
  Set objXML = Server.CreateObject ("Microsoft.XMLDOM")

  objXML.load(Server.MapPath(session("xmlFileName")))

  Set objRootElement = objXML.documentElement ' returns a node object
```

We create the node list selected using a particular pattern – the 'escaped' author name.

```
  Set objNodeList=objRootElement.selectNodes(patternString)
' returns a nodelist
%>
<table border="0" cellspacing="0" cellpadding="20" height="200" width="95%">
  <tr>
    <td> </td>
    <td width="40" bgcolor="LIGHTYELLOW"><a href="default.asp"> Home
    </a></td>
```

```
    <td width="40" bgcolor="#B0C4DE"><a href="admin.asp"> Admin
  </a></td>
    <td width="40" bgcolor="LIGHTGREEN"><a href="ReportMenu.asp"> Reports
  </a></td>
    <td> </td>
</tr>
```

The main body of this page is a loop through the node list created above.

```
<tr>
  <td colspan="5" bgcolor="LIGHTGREEN" valign="TOP">
    <table border="0" cellspacing="0" cellpadding="5" width="100%">
      <%for index=0 to objNodeList.length -1
        Set objNode=objNodeList.item(index) 'gives the author node
      %>
      <tr>
        <td valign="TOP" align="LEFT">
          Name: <b>
          <%= objNode.parentNode.childNodes.Item(0).text %></b>
        </td>
        <td align="right">
          Author: <%= objNode.parentNode.childNodes.Item(1).text %>
        </td>
      </tr>
      <tr>
        <td colspan="2">
          <table>
            <tr>
              <td valign="top">Description:</td>
              <td><%= objNode.parentNode.childNodes.Item(2).text %></td>
            </tr>
          </table>
        </td>
      </tr>

      <%
        Set objSubElement = _
      objNode.parentNode.childNodes.Item(3).getElementsByTagName("method")
        If objSubElement.Length > 0 then
      %>
      <tr>
        <td valign="TOP" align="LEFT" colspan="2"><b>Methods</b></td>
      </tr>
      <tr>
        <td colspan="2">
          <table width="100%" border="0" cellspacing="0" cellpadding="0">
            <%For i = 0 to objSubElement.Length -1%>
            <tr><td colspan="2"><i>
              <%= objSubElement.Item(i).getAttribute("name") %></i>
              </td>
              <td>Syntax: 
              <%= objSubElement.Item(i).childNodes.Item(0).text %></td>
            </tr>
            <tr><td> </td>
              <td valign="top">Description: </td>
```

485

```
        <td>
          <%= objSubElement.Item(i).childNodes.Item(1).text %>
        </td>
      </tr>
      <tr><td> </td>
        <td valign="top">Example: </td>
        <td>
          <%= objSubElement.Item(i).childNodes.Item(2).text %>
        </td>
      </tr>
      <td colspan="3"> </td></tr>
      <%Next%>
    </table>
  </td>
</tr>
<%Else%>
<tr>
  <td valign="TOP" align="LEFT" colspan="2">
  No described methods</td>
</tr>
<% End If %>
```

And now for the properties:

```
    <%
      Set objSubElement = _
objNode.parentNode.childNodes.Item(4).getElementsByTagName("property")
      If objSubElement.Length > 0 then
    %>
    <tr>
      <td valign="TOP" align="LEFT" colspan="2"><b>Properties</b></td>
    </tr>
    <tr>
      <td colspan="2">
        <table width="100%" border="0" cellspacing="0" cellpadding="0">
          <%For i = 0 to objSubElement.Length -1%>
          <tr>
            <td colspan="2"><i>
              <%= objSubElement.Item(i).getAttribute("name")%></i></td>
          </tr>
          <tr><td> </td>
            <td valign="top">Description: </td>
            <td>
              <%= objSubElement.Item(i).childNodes.Item(0).text %></td>
          </tr>
          <tr><td> </td>
            <td valign="top">Example: </td>
            <td>
              <%= objSubElement.Item(i).childNodes.Item(1).text %></td>
          </tr>
          <tr><td colspan="3"> </td></tr>
          <%Next%>
        </table>
      </td>
    </tr>
    <%Else%>
```

```
        <tr>
          <td valign="TOP" align="LEFT" colspan="2">
            No described properties</td>
        </tr>
        <% End If %>
```

Let's throw in a `<hr>` tag between components.

```
        <tr height="3"><td colspan="2"><HR> </HR></td></tr>
        <%next %>
      </table>
    </td>
  </tr>
</table>

<%set objXML=nothing%>
</body>
</html>
```
(end) rptByAuthor.asp

The Show All Components report uses a different technology. In this script we will be using XSL and DSO to collect and order the data. We will still be using the ASP script to format the output.

Within the `<head>` tag, we script an `event=onload`, so that when we first view this page, the data is presented in a defined sort order. The down side of this procedure is that the data is loaded twice, and there is a perceptible delay in the rendering of the display, especially for larger XML documents.

rptAll.asp

```
<%@ Language=VBScript %>
<%
Option Explicit
Response.Expires = -1
%>

<html>
<head>
  <title> Show All Components </title>
  <script for=window event=onload>
    // This set the starting Sort Order
    sort(sortName.XMLDocument)
  </script>
</head>

<style type="text/css">
  body {font-family:verdana,helvetica;font-size:8pt}
  table {font-family:verdana,helvetica;font-size:8pt}
</style>
<body>
```

Here are the three basic XML tags. The first refers to the XML document itself, and the two XSL documents.

```
<XML id=xmldso></XML>
<XML id=sortName src="sortName.xsl"></XML>
<XML id=sortAuthor src="sortAuthor.xsl"></XML>
```

The work of this script is done here. The `transformNodeToObject` method will process the full document according to the XSL specifications.

```
<script>
xmldso.async = false;
xmldso.load("<%=session("xmlFileName")%>");
var xmldoc = xmldso.cloneNode(true);

function sort(xsldoc){
  xmldoc.documentElement.transformNodeToObject(xsldoc.documentElement,
  xmldso.XMLDocument);
}
</script>

<table border="0" cellspacing="0" cellpadding="20" height="200" width="95%">
  <tr><td> </td>
    <td width="40" bgcolor="LIGHTYELLOW"><a href="default.asp">
    Home </a></td>
    <td width="40" bgcolor="#B0C4DE"><a href="admin.asp"> Admin </a></td>
    <td width="40" bgcolor="LIGHTGREEN"><a href="ReportMenu.asp">
    Reports </a></td>
    <td> </td>
  </tr>
```

The whole data table is from the `DATSRC` `xmldso`. On the inner repeats, we'll need to have additional tables with the `DATSRC` re-defined. Note the `onclick` in the header tags.

```
  <tr><td colspan="5" height="175" bgcolor="LIGHTGREEN" valign="TOP">
    <table DATASRC='#xmldso' border="0" cellpadding="0" cellspacing="0"
                                                        width="100%">
      <thead>
        <th Title="Click to sort Acending">
          <span onclick="sort(sortName.XMLDocument);"
            onmouseover = "this.style.cursor='hand'"><U>Name</U></span>
        </th>
        <th Title="Click to sort Acending">
          <span onclick="sort(sortAuthor.XMLDocument);"
            onmouseover = "this.style.cursor='hand'"><U><B>
            Author</B></U></span>
        </th>
      </thead>
      <tr>
        <td valign="TOP" align="LEFT"><B>
        <span DATAFLD="NAME">/<B></span></td>
        <td align="right"><span DATAFLD="author"></span></td>
      </tr>
      <tr>
        <td colspan="2">
          <table>
            <tr>
              <td valign="top">Description:</td><td>
              <span DATAFLD="overview"></span></td>
            </tr>
          </table>
        </td>
      </tr>
```

We need to handle the inner loop for the methods as a separate table with its own `DATASRC` value.

```
        <tr>
          <td valign="TOP" align="LEFT" colspan="2"><b>Methods</b></td>
        </tr>
        <tr>
          <td colspan="2">
            <table DATASRC="#xmldso" DATAFLD="method" width="100%" border="0"
                                                      cellpadding="0">
              <tr>
                <td colspan="2" width="15%"><I>
                <span DATAFLD="name"></span></I></td>
                <td>Syntax: <span DATAFLD="syntax"></span></td>
              </tr>
              <tr><td> </td>
                <td valign="top">Description: </td>
                <td><span DATAFLD="description"></span></td>
              </tr>
              <tr><td> </td>
                <td valign="top">Example: </td><td>
                <span DATAFLD="example"></span></td>
              </tr>
            </table>
          </td>
        </tr>
```

Now, the inner loop for the properties:

```
        <tr>
          <td colspan="2"><B>Properties</B></td>
        </tr>
        <tr>
          <td colspan="2">
            <table DATASRC="#xmldso" DATAFLD="property" width="100%" border="0"
                                                        cellpadding="0">
              <tr>
                <td colspan=2 width="15%"><i>
                <span DATAFLD="name"></span></i></td>
                <td> </td>
              </tr>
              <tr><td> </td>
                <td valign="top">Description: </td>
                <td><span DATAFLD="description"></span></td>
              </tr>
              <tr><td> </td>
                <td valign="top">Example: </td>
                <td><span DATAFLD="example"></span></td>
              </tr>
            </table>
          </td>
        </tr>
        <tr height="3"><td colspan="2"><HR> </HR></td></tr>
      </table>
    </td></tr>
  </table>
  </body>
  </html>
```

(end) rtpAll.asp

The two XSL files are identical except for the 'order-by' clause. When coding sortAuthor use the following code as the first level xsl:for-each directive:

```
<xsl:for-each order-by="+ author" select="component"
                        xmlns:xsl="http://www.w3.org/TR/WD-xsl">
```

The complete code for sortName.xsl follows:

sortName.xsl / sortAuthor.xsl

```
<?xml version="1.0" ?>
<components>
  <xsl:for-each order-by="+ name" select="component"
                        xmlns:xsl="http://www.w3.org/TR/WD-xsl">
    <component>
      <name><xsl:value-of select="name"/></name>
      <author><xsl:value-of select="author"/></author>
      <overview><xsl:value-of select="overview"/></overview>

      <xsl:for-each select="methods/method">
        <method>
          <xsl:attribute name="name">
            <xsl:value-of select="@name" />
          </xsl:attribute>
          <syntax><xsl:value-of select="syntax" /></syntax>
          <description><xsl:value-of select="description" /></description>
          <example><xsl:value-of select="example" /></example>
        </method>
      </xsl:for-each>

      <xsl:for-each select="properties/property">
        <property>
          <xsl:attribute name="name">
            <xsl:value-of select="@name" />
          </xsl:attribute>
          <description><xsl:value-of select="description" /></description>
          <example><xsl:value-of select="example" /></example>
        </property>
      </xsl:for-each>
    </component>
  </xsl:for-each>
</components>
```
(end) sortName.xsl / sortAuthor.xsl

Summary

In this case study we've looked at a simple mechanism for creating and maintaining an on-line documentation system. We've seen how, in a very practical sense, we can input, update and delete multi-level XML data. This basic technology is transferable to an infinite number of applications. We've also seen how we can develop ASP pages that will view a filtered list from the instance document, and zoom in on a particular node and its children.

While all of the parts of the system are in place, and we found this project to be an excellent learning tool for XML, this case study definitely would not measure up to 'production code' in several respects:

❑ It is browser specific and there is no browser detection code in place.

❑ We would need to track additional information to be completely useful.

❑ We'll have an issue with scalability if we start to get too much data (though moving it to a database with XML access would not be too much of a headache).

❑ We definitely need to improve the GUI.

But it's a start. I hope that this code will be useful as the basis for many XML data store projects that you may encounter.

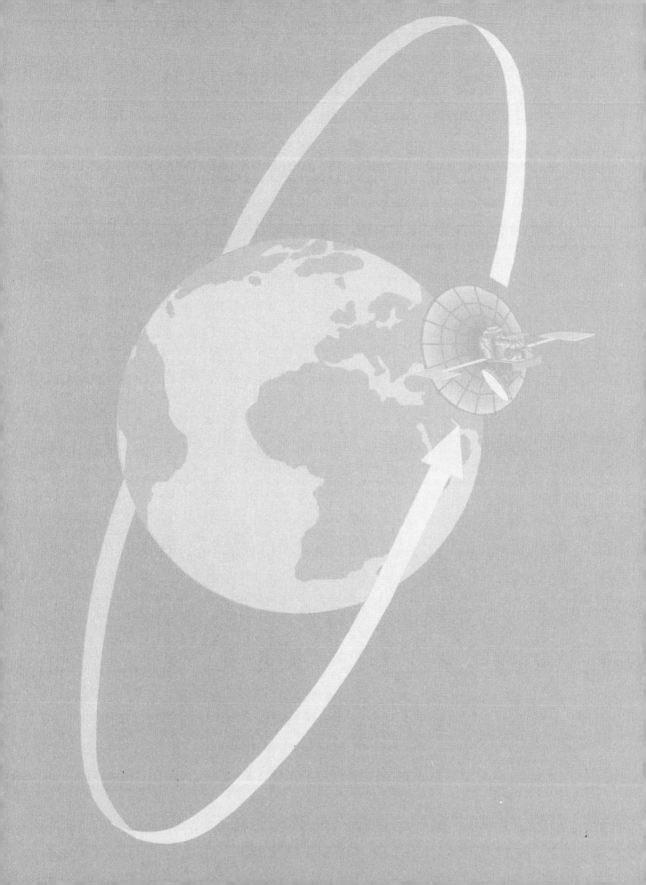

Case Study – An Online Shopping Cart

In the beginning, the World Wide Web was primarily a means of distributing free information to anyone who had the right software to receive it. As time has progressed, the variety of applications that can read and utilize web information has grown, and with it the range of possible users. Among those who were exploiting these new web technologies, was the business community who identified the Web as a way of promoting their products to the expanding Internet-enabled public. The Internet, therefore, began to revolutionize the very nature of marketing and the relationship between business and consumer across industries. The Internet enables the promotion of brands, products and services to a far wider cross-section of consumers (potentially millions) at relatively little cost. With the Internet currently becoming *the* main means of rapid communication, the marketing possibilities seem endless.

When HTML forms were added to the HTML specification and CGI began to be used for server-side applications, it enabled the user at home to communicate with the server and obtain information. The Internet became a two-way communicating medium. The business community exploited this capability and over time applications were developed to enable financial transactions over the wire and with them the ability to order and purchase products over the Internet. So, the concept of the on-line store was born. And, e-commerce, as we know it today, remains in an ever-evolving state of technological advancement.

In this case study, I will present to you one essential feature of an on-line store, a shopping cart, which is the electronic equivalent of the ubiquitous shopping basket. A shopping cart is a small application that maintains a list of the on-line consumer's shopping selections in such a way that they can be viewed and modified by the consumer at any time. In isolation, the shopping cart is a relatively simple tool, but when combined with an inventory, an order processing system, and a database, it becomes very powerful indeed, and XML combined with the power of ASP ties these elements of the application together.

Over the course of this case study, we will be designing and building a shopping cart application for a sample on-line bookstore. The application will harness the functionality of ASP and XML to transfer data from our on-line store's primary product and customer database to the waiting consumer requesting information at the client browser. Product data translates very easily to the hierarchical format of XML, and using XML as an intermediate data format in this type of application, where product data needs to be accessed quickly, avoids having to make multiple database calls across a network. We can trigger an XSL transformation of our XML product data from an ASP script environment, and then send the newly formatted data to the client's browser for display in a user-friendly or *consumer-friendly* format.

Our case study is written entirely in ASP, XML and XSL. A lot of the functionality that is currently in the ASP code could be encapsulated into a VB component, if you prefer, but since this is a book about ASP and XML, I thought I'd stick to these areas.

So, let's get started. First, let's consider what the requirements of our shopping cart will be and what capabilities it needs to have.

Shopping Cart Design

So, what are the typical requirements of our shopping cart design? A shopping cart for any half-decent on-line store would need to fulfill the following criteria:

- ❏ Persist across web pages
- ❏ Store selected items in an easily retrievable form
- ❏ Be easily modified by the user
- ❏ Be browser independent

Data Persistence

First and foremost, it has to persist from web page to web page. So, some sort of technique needs to be used to associate an identifier with the shopping cart, and then to persist that identifier between web pages. The items contained in the cart do not need to be accessible from all pages, but the cart identifier does. Owing to this necessary functionality, shopping carts are usually dependent on web client cookies to maintain the link between the cart and the shopper.

There *are* other techniques that can be used to persist information about the cart between pages. Some developers use hidden form fields (containing the shopping cart identifier or possibly a string of the cart's items), or add shopping cart information to the end of the URL of the new page that is being accessed as a querystring. Both of these techniques make the cart information available in the new page. To use these techniques in an ASP shopping cart, you would access the hidden form fields from the Forms collection of the Request object; or the appended URL information from the QueryString collection that is also part of the Request object.

If a store chooses to support a shopping cart for a session only (carrying information from the user's initial store access until they log out, close their browser, or disconnect from the Internet), then either hidden form fields or the query string method will work fine. However, if store wishes the user's cart to persist beyond the session, then you have to use cookies.

Using cookies alone, the shopping cart and its contents are maintained solely on the client machine, so the cart's contents can be accessed quickly. There is, unfortunately, a major limitation with this approach – cookies can usually hold a maximum of 50 to 75 items. If the cart needs to hold more than this, then cookie technology by itself simply isn't a feasible approach, because the cookie string can become too large. Even a few items can create a large cookie string.

For the purpose of this case study, however, we are able to use client-side cookies.

Our Shopping Cart Application

We stated in our general criteria for the shopping cart, just a moment ago, that it needs to be able to store selected items in an easily retrievable form and also be easily modified by the user. So, in terms of specific functionality, which will make our shopping cart application as user-friendly as possible for customers at our on-line store, we want to construct it with the following capabilities:

❑　The ability to add items to the cart at the touch of a button.

❑　The ability to persist items for more than one session (as long as cookies are still present on the machine) so that the customer can return to the Web at a later time and continue their shopping experience.

❑　The ability for web shoppers to view the contents of their shopping cart at any time.

❑　The ability for shoppers to remove one, a few, or all of the items from the cart before they proceed with any transaction.

❑　The display of a current total for the items in the shopping cart.

❑　The ability to follow the client (again using cookies, which are created for the user on whatever client he or she happens to be using) giving the customer the flexibility to log on to the store from any client machine.

These are the issues that we will need to address during the construction of our application, which we'll move on to shortly.

The Technology Set-Up

Earlier on, we briefly touched upon how we'll be using ASP and XML in this case study. Before we actually get started on the building of our shopping cart, let's just see how we're going to use ASP and XML alongside other technologies to pull together the functionality we need for the application.

Take a look at the diagram below:

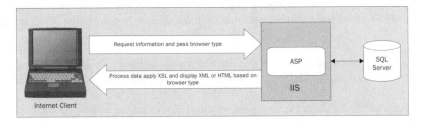

So how does each technology feature in the shopping cart construction?

❑ **ASP** – We'll use ASP to control the processing flow of the entire application. ASP scripts will be responsible for detecting the client browser when the user requests information. ASP will also execute the XSL transformations, implement transaction logic when the user proceeds with an order, and control the connection to the primary product database. To improve on this case study, you could incorporate the heavy duty work, like the transaction logic, into a Visual Basic DLL, and host this on MTS (or COM+ if you are running Windows 2000).

❑ **XML and XSL** – We will use XML as our intermediate data format to house product data in an ASP environment between the primary product database and the XSL transformation that creates the final formatted data for display in the client browser.

❑ **SQL Server 7.0** – This will act as our primary datebase storing all our shopping cart information, which is accessed from ASP.

Other Technical Requirements

In addition, there are some requirements for your system that you need to consider before building the shopping cart application. The cart will operate on Windows NT 4.0 or Windows 2000 and requires Internet Information Server and SQL Server to create the primary product database.

We also mentioned in our general criteria for a good shopping cart, that the application should be browser independent. So our shopping cart will support Internet Explorer 4.0 (with the MSXML parser Installed) or later and it will also support Netscape Navigator 4.0 or later. In this case study I will be using Netscape Navigator 4.72.

> *You will already be equipped with a fairly comprehensive understanding of ASP and, by now, we hope that you will have grasped the fundamentals of XML that we've covered in this book. For the purposes of the application, we will also be touching upon a little bit of SQL for our database; don't worry about this – it will be explained. However, if you would like more information, try the following book:*
>
> *Professional SQL Server 7 Programming published by Wrox Press, ISBN 1861002-31-9.*

So, now that we have established some goals for our application, let's start building the shopping cart.

> The source code is available from **www.wrox.com** with an accompanying Word document, which explains how to set up the application.

Setting up the Cart Environment

As we said previously, we are not going to try to implement all the aspects of the shopping cart within ASP script. We're going to use stored procedures to access the primary database. We already know that we're using XML as an intermediary datastore, and that we'll use XSL to transform the XML into a final format for display.

> *The format will depend upon the browser that our ASP detects the client to be using. If it is running IE, the display format will be XML; if it is running Netscape, the data will be displayed as HTML.*

Before we delve into the details of the shopping cart itself, let us take a look at the product and customer database setup.

The Product & Customer DataBase – ShopCart

You will get the complete database in the source code, so you need not worry how to create the procedures and the database.

The primary database for our on-line store holds all information relating to products, orders and customers in five relational tables.

❑ **Product** – We store product information in this table.

❑ **Customer** – We store the customer's user name, password and name in this table.

❑ **Customer_Address** – This table is used to store the address for our customer. This table has one-to-many relationship with the `Customer` table.

❑ **Orders** – We store information like the order ID and date in this table, which has a one-to-many relationship with the Order_Item_Detail table.

❑ **Order_Item_Detail** – We store the details of the order in this table, such as product ID and quantity.

We can see how the tables link together in the diagram below:

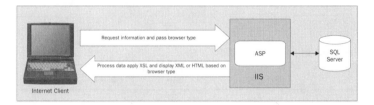

Database Definition

The following tables will allow you to understand in more detail how the database is constructed, before we move on to using it in our application.

The Product Table

Name	Data Type	Length	Precision	Scale	Default Value
Product_Id	Numeric	9	18	0	
Product_Name	VarChar	50	0	0	
Product_Description	VarChar	50	0	0	
Price	Money	8	19	4	1
Discount	Currency	8	19	4	
Add_Date	Date/Time	8	0	0	(GetDate())
Add_User_Id	Char	10	0	0	(User_Name())
Modification_Date	Date/Time	8	0	0	(GetDate())
Modification_User_Id	Char	10	0	0	(User_Name())

The Customer Table

Name	Data Type	Length	Precision	Scale	Default Value
Customer_Id	Numeric	9	18	0	
User_Name	Char	10	0	0	
Password	Char	10	0	0	
Last_Name	Varchar	50	0	0	
First_Name	Varchar	50	0	0	
Middle_Init	Char	1	0	0	
Email	Varchar	50	0	0	
Preferences	Varchar	50	0	0	
Register_Date	Date/Time	8	0	0	
Add_Date	Date/Time	8	0	0	(GetDate())
Add_User_Id	Char	10	0	0	(User_Name())
Modification_Date	Date/Time	8	0	0	(GetDate())
Modification_User_Id	Char	10	0	0	(User_Name())

The Customer_Address Table

Name	Data Type	Length	Precision	Scale	Default Value
Customer_Address_Id	Numeric	9	18	0	
Customer_Id	Numeric	9	18	0	
Address_Type_Code	Char	5	0	0	
Company	Varchar	30	0	0	
Day_Phone	Char	10	0	0	
Evening_Phone	Char	10	0	0	
Fax	Char	10	0	0	
Email	Varchar	50	0	0	
Street1	Varchar	50	0	0	
Street2	Varchar	50	0	0	
City	Varchar	50	0	0	
State	Varchar	50	0	0	
Zip	Char	10	0	0	
Attention	Varchar	50	0	0	
Add_Date	Date/Time	8	0	0	(GetDate())
Add_User_Id	Char	10	0	0	(User_Name())

Name	Data Type	Length	Precision	Scale	Default Value
Modification_Date	Date/Time	8	0	0	(GetDate())
Modification_User_Id	Char	10	0	0	(User_Name())
Ship_Bill_Check	Char	1	0	0	

The Orders Table

Name	Data Type	Length	Precision	Scale	Default Value
Order_Id	Numeric	9	18	0	
Customer_Id	Numeric	9	18	0	
Order_Date	Date/Time	8	0	0	
Order_Status	Varchar	50	0	0	
Add_Date	Date/Time	8	0	0	(GetDate())
Add_User_Id	Char	10	0	0	(User_Name())
Modification_Date	Date/Time	8	0	0	(GetDate())
Modification_User_Id	Char	10	0	0	(User_Name())

The Order_Item_Detail Table

Name	Data Type	Length	Precision	Scale	Default Value
Order_Item_Id	Numeric	9	18	0	
Order_Id	Numeric	9	18	0	
Product_Id	Numeric	9	18	0	
Quantity	Numeric	9	18	0	
Order_Item_Status	Char	10	0	0	
Add_Date	Date/Time	8	0	0	(GetDate())
Add_User_Id	Char	10	0	0	(User_Name())
Modification_Date	Date/Time	8	0	0	(GetDate())
Modification_User_Id	Char	10	0	0	(User_Name())

We manage the data within these tables via several stored procedures that we will call from our ASP script.

- ❑ Proc_AddingItem
- ❑ Proc_CreateNewCart
- ❑ Proc_UpdateCustID
- ❑ Proc_DeleteCart
- ❑ Proc_GetCustID
- ❑ Proc_GetCustInfo

- ❏ Proc_GetItems
- ❏ Proc_GetItemsTotal
- ❏ Proc_UpdateQuantity
- ❏ Proc_CartID

We'll also be using SQL to query the database and return records, but we'll look at that later on as we examine the code.

Creating a New Cart and Adding Items to a Cart

Proc_CreateNewCart

The first requirement of the shopping cart is that users can add items to it, and implicitly, the ability to create a cart. We'll implement both of these requirements as methods. A cart can be created either when a shopper first accesses a site, or when the shopper makes an initial move to add an item to the cart. The cart we are going to build here will only be created if none already exists. If one exists, we will ask the shopper to log in and retrieve the cart.

You can add a new cart through a stored procedure called Proc_CreateNewCart, which adds a new record to the Orders table, and returns a unique cart identifier:

```
CREATE PROCEDURE [Proc_CreateNewCart]
AS
BEGIN
Insert Into Orders(order_date)
Values (getdate())
SELECT @@IDENTITY  As 'OrderId'

END
```

This procedure is called as necessary via Cart.asp.

Proc_AddingItem

We've implemented the functionality to add a new cart, but of course this isn't very useful unless we can add items to it. We call the stored procedure called Proc_AddingItem to handle the addition of a new cart item. Within this procedure, the Orders table is checked to see if a record already exists for the specific cart and product item. If the record is found then the quantity passed to the stored procedure is added to the quantity for the cart item in the database. If a record is not found, a new entry to Order_Item_Detail is made for the specific cart and product:

```
CREATE PROCEDURE [Proc_AddingItem]
(@cartid int, @itemid int, @qty int)
AS
BEGIN
IF (Select Count(*) From Order_Item_Detail Where Order_ID =@cartid And
        Product_ID = @itemid) > 0
    Update Order_Item_Detail
    Set Quantity = Quantity + @qty Where Order_ID = @cartid And Product_Id =
        @itemid
ELSE
    Insert Into Order_Item_Detail Values (@cartid, @itemid, @qty,'Pending',
        GetDate(),User_Name(),GetDate(),User_Name())
END
```

This procedure is also called via `Cart.asp` as necessary.

So, at this point we've created a cart and added an item to it. The next logical step to take in developing the shopping cart component and application is to provide a technique for displaying the cart contents.

Displaying the Cart's Contents

The shopping cart display is the most visual aspect of a shopping cart application, and it is also one of the easiest to implement. We will be using XML to achieve this, which we'll look at in detail later in the case study. First of all let's look at the code which gets the contents information for us that we can later display.

Proc_GetItems

A new stored procedure is created, `Proc_GetItems`, which obtains information from the `Order_Item_Detail` and the `Product` tables. The items that the cart contains are located in `Order_Item_Detail`, but the information about each item, such as product name, price, and quantity per unit are found in `Product`. Additionally, a total price is calculated from the quantity of items ordered and the price per item, and this total is added as a "column" to the record being returned.

```
CREATE PROCEDURE [Proc_GetItems]
(@cartid int)
AS
BEGIN
Select   Product.Product_ID,
         Product_Name,
     Product_Description,
     Product.Price,
     Product_Name,
         Quantity,
         Price * Quantity total
     From Order_Item_Detail, Product Where Order_Id = @cartid And
     Product.Product_ID = Order_Item_Detail.Product_ID
END
```

Again, `Cart.asp` calls this function as necessary.

Deleting Items and Updating Shopping Cart Contents

Proc_UpdateQuantity

Modifying cart items includes being able to change the quantity of an item in the cart and to remove an item from the cart altogether – this only requires one stored procedure, `Proc_UpdateQuantity`. The quantity being passed is checked within the stored procedure: if the value is 0, the cart item is deleted from `Order_Item_Detail`; otherwise the value is updated. In addition, the stored procedure checks to see if a row exists for the cart and for the item in `Order_Item_Detail`. If it does, the value is updated; otherwise the stored procedure `Proc_UpdateQuantity` is called to create a new cart item with the new quantity.

```
CREATE PROCEDURE [Proc_UpdateQuantity]
(@cartid int, @itemid int, @qty int)
AS
BEGIN
IF @qty = 0
    Delete From Order_Item_Detail Where Order_Id = @cartid And Product_Id =
        @itemid
ELSE IF (Select Count(*) From Order_Item_Detail Where Order_Id =
```

```
            @cartid And Product_Id = @itemid) > 0
        Update Order_Item_Detail
            Set Quantity =  @qty Where Order_Id = @cartid And Product_Id = @itemid
    ELSE
        Exec Proc_AddingItem @cartid, @itemid, @qty
    END
```

This procedure is also called from `Cart.asp`

Emptying the Cart

Proc_DeleteCart

This stored procedure is called when the contents of the cart are to be deleted.

```
CREATE PROCEDURE [Proc_DeleteCart]
(@cartid int)
AS
BEGIN
    Delete From Order_Item_Detail Where Order_ID = @cartid
    Delete From Orders Where Order_Id = @cartid
END
```

The ASP Code

The ASP in this case study provides a large amount of functionality. It has to liaise with our SQL Server database, find the data that's required, work with our intermediate XML data store, and control the formatting of the data, which appears in the shopper's browser. The ASP files in this chapter rely on `DataConnect.asp` to establish a connection to our database. Also included in this file, is another include file, which is the `ADOVBS.inc` constants library. `DataConnect.asp` is used in all the pages that require a connection to the database as an include file:

```
<!-- #Include File="ADOVBS.INC" -->
<%
Dim rs ,con, ConnectionString,Cmd

ConnectionString = "dsn=shopcart;server=myservername;database=shopcart;_
                                            uid=shopuser;pwd=shop"
Set Con=Server.CreateObject ("ADODB.Connection")
Set Rs=Server.CreateObject("ADOBD.Recordset")
Con.Open ConnectionString
Rs.ActiveConnection = Con
Rs.CursorLocation = adUseClient
Set Cmd= Server.CreateObject("ADODB.Command")
Cmd.ActiveConnection =ConnectionString
%>
```

This file is available, along with all the other code for this case study, for download from the Wrox website at www.wrox.com. All you need to do to connect to your database is alter this file accordingly.

So, let's start looking at the application. The first interface that the user sees when they browse to the on-line store, is the shop front of our Sample Bookstore, `storefront.asp`. We'll look at this page next.

The Store Front

Our shopping cart will have a main entry screen where we will check the client cookies and get the shopper profile from the customer table in our database. This is how the main screen looks:

If we have an existing customer, we retrieve their existing order using the code, which we've just been examining, and then display it (which we'll see how to do shortly). The ASP pages that perform this logic are `login.asp`, which contains the form for the user to enter their username and password, and `loginCheck.asp`.

This is the screen produced by `login.asp`, which is displayed once we click the link at the top of the page:

For the purposes of this example, if you have downloaded the code for this chapter, you can log in with **Username: Dinar, Password: Dinar**. This will display some sample datas which you can look at.

The `loginCheck.asp` file will display information about previous orders after the returning customer logs in the system:

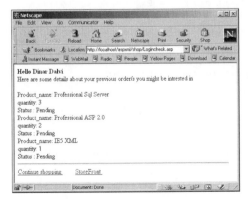

So how do we retrieve the user's details and arrive at this screen shot? First, the script captures the shopper's username and password from the form on the login page, `login.asp`, and verifies the information entered in `logincheck.asp`:

```
<%@ LANGUAGE="VBSCRIPT" %>
<% Response.AddHeader "pragma","no-cache" %>
<% Response.Expires =0 %>
<!-- #Include File="DataConnect.ASP" -->
...
UserName= Request.Form ("UserName")
Password=Request.form("Password")
```

Our include file, `DataConnect.asp` instantiates the connection object and the recordset object. It opens a database connection to the `shopcart` database with our connection string, and creates an active connection to the recordset.

We then use a lengthy SQL statement to extract the product and order information we require from the database. *If* the criteria are met where `Customer_Ids` match, `Order_Ids` match, and `Product_Ids` also match in the specified database tables, and the username and password that the shopper logs in with match the ones stored in the Customer table, the customer's details and order history are returned:

```
Sql=" Select o.ORDER_id, prod.product_name,o.customer_id, c.last_name, " & _
        " c.first_name, c.customer_id, ord.product_id, ord.quantity," & _
        " ord.order_item_status FROM orders o, customer c, " & _
        " order_item_detail ord, product prod" & _
        " WHERE c.customer_id = o.customer_id AND " & _
        " ord.product_id = prod.product_id AND " & _
        " ord.order_id = o.order_id AND " & _
        " UPPER(LTRIM(RTRIM(c.user_name))) = " & "'" & ucase(username)& _
        "'" & " AND UPPER(LTRIM(RTRIM(c.password))) =" & "'" & _
        " ucase(password) & "'"
Rs.Open Sql,Con,adOpenDynamic
```

Once all the data is retrieved, the customer's cookie is updated:

```
If Not (Rs.BOF or Rs.EOF ) Then
  CustomerID= Rs("customer_id")
  Response.Cookies("cartid" = Rs("order_id"))
  Response.Cookies("customerid" = Rs("customer_id"))
  Response.Cookies("customerid".Expires = "December 31, 2005")
  Response.Write "<B>Hello " & Rs("first_name") & " " & Rs("last_name") &_
                    "</B><BR>"
```

A personalized message is then written to the browser:

```
Response.Write "Here are some details about your previous order/s you " & _
                    "might be intrested in  <BR> <BR>"
```

And the code loops through and displays the product and order information until it reaches the end of the returned recordset:

```
Do While Not Rs.EOF
    Response.Write "Product_name:" & "   " & Rs("product_name") & "<BR>"
    Response.Write "Quantity:" & "   " & Rs("quantity") & "<BR>"
    Response.Write "Status :" & "   " & Rs("order_item_status") & "<BR>"
    Rs.MoveNext
  Loop
Rs.close
```

So that's the result if the customer's input matches the contents of a shopping cart stored in the database. If there is no customer order history in the database, however, the code still searches for an existing `customer_Id` by using SQL, again to match the username and password that the customer enters, with a username and password stored in the database:

```
Else

  Sql=" Select customer_Id from customer c Where " & _
    " UPPER(LTRIM(RTRIM(c.user_name))) = " & "'" & ucase(username) & "'" & _
    " And UPPER(LTRIM(RTRIM(c.password))) =" & "'" & ucase(password) & "'"
```

If a match is made and a recordset is returned, the data is used to up-date the customer's cookie:

```
Rs.Open Sql,Con,adOpenDynamic
  If Not (Rs.BOF Or Rs.EOF ) Then
    customerid= Rs("customer_id")
    Response.Cookies("customerid") =customerid
    Response.Cookies("customerid").Expires = "December 31, 2005"
```

The customer is then sent to the store's main page, `storefront.asp`:

```
Response.Redirect "storefront.asp"
```

If no match is made with the database, a message is written to the browser:

```
Else
    Response.Write "<H2> We could not find your records please " & _
              "re-register or contact your sales representative </h2><BR>"
    Response.Write "<H4> Or go to the store front to continue shopping " & _
              "</h4> <BR>"
  End If
End If
```

Finally, the script writes some HTML anchor tags containing links to the products page and the store front page so that the user can click on them to continue their on-line shopping experience.

```
Response.Write "<hr>"
Response.Write "<a href = products.asp> Continue shopping </A>"
Response.Write "        "
Response.Write "<a href = storefront.asp> StoreFront </A> "
%>
```

The display of the storefront will have changed once a user has logged in, to show details of any orders that are currently in their cart:

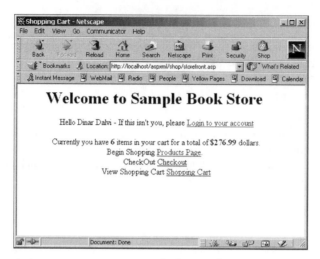

Next, we'll step through the `storefront.asp` code that produces the screen above. Firstly, we use `DataConnect.asp` to connect to our database once more. Then we check to see if there is a cookie entry for `cartID` and `CustomerID`.

```
CartID = Request.Cookies("CartID")
CustomerID = Request.Cookies("CustomerID")
```

The code then tries to find the customer record for the present cookie (`"CustomerID"`). If the customer ID variable isn't empty, then we use a SQL query to match the content of the variable housing the cookie to the `customer_id` field in the `Customer` table, and return the first and last names of that customer.

```
If CustomerID <> "" Then
  Ssql= "Select first_name, last_name from Customer Where Customer_id = " &_
          CustomerID
Rs.Open Ssql,conn,adOpenKeyset
```

If the returned recordset contains data, then the script writes a personalized greeting to the customer for display in the browser:

```
If Rs.RecordCount > 0 Then
  Response.Write ("<center>Hello " & rs("first_name") & " " & _
                                        rs("Last_Name"))
  Response.Write (" - If this isn't you, please <a href='login.asp'>login"&_
                                " to your account</a></center>" )
  Rs.close
```

The code then calls the `Proc_CartID` stored procedure, and opens a recordset that holds the records returned by the procedure. If the customer referred to by the `customerID` is found in the database, then the stored procedure returns the contents of the related `Order_Id` by reading the first order in the recordset, and assigns it to the ASP variable `CartID`.

```
Rs.ActiveConnection = Con
Rs.CursorLocation = adUseClient
Rs.Source = "Proc_CartID " & customerID
Rs.Open
```

```
   If Rs.RecordCount > 0 Then
     Rs.MoveFirst
     CartID = Rs(0)
   Else
     CartID = 0
   End If

   Rs.close
```

If the value of `Order_Id` is zero, then the variable `CartID` remains empty.

If the cookies, `CartID` and `CustomerID`, were empty, the code would write a message telling the returning customer to log in to their account to retrieve their shopping cart:

```
ElseIf CartID = "" AND Customer_ID = "" Then
  Response.Write("<br> <Center><a href='login.asp'>Returning customers " &_
          "login to your Account to retrieve an existing cart</a></Center>")
  Response.Write("<BR>")
End If
```

If the `CartID` variable is empty, the code writes a message to inform the shopper:

```
If CartID = "" Then
  Response.Write "<br><center> Currently, your shopping cart is empty" &_
                                              " </center>"

Else
```

If the `getCartID` function did return some data to the variable, however, we re-establish a connection to the database, then our ASP code writes the order details on the page.

```
   Rs.ActiveConnection = Con
   Rs.CursorLocation = adUseClient
   Rs.Source = "Proc_GetItemTotals " & CartID
   Rs.Open

   If Rs.RecordCount > 0 Then
     Rs.MoveFirst
     Response.Write("<br><center> Currently you have <strong>" & Rs(0) & _
                                   "</strong> items in your cart ")
     Response.Write("for a total of <strong>$" & Rs(1) & "</strong> " & _
                                   "dollars.</center> ")

     Rrs.close
   End If
End If

Response.Write "<center>Begin Shopping <a href='products.asp'>" & _
                                   "Products Page</a>. <br>"
Response.Write " CheckOut <a href='order.asp'>Checkout</A> <br>"
Response.Write "View Shopping Cart <a href='cart.asp'>" & _
                                   " Shopping Cart</a></center> <br>"

%>
```

Inside the Shopping Cart

The shopper can move from the store front page to the products page, which looks something like this:

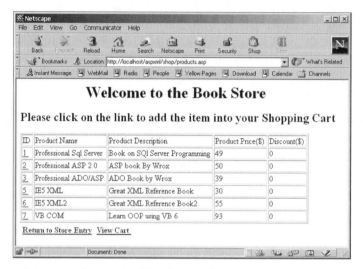

The customer can click on numbers in the ID column, which are actually hyperlinks, that enable them to select an item for purchase, and add it to their shopping cart.

We need to look at no less than three files to discover how this page is generated. First the `products.asp` page itself. Its primary purpose is to create our intermediate data store as XML, thereby allowing clients running browsers other than IE5 to display the product data. Building an XML string also makes life easier for the client because it is able to cache locally the XML and the XSL document that will transform it, minimizing trips to the server.

First we determine which browser the client is running:

```
<%@ Language=VBScript %>
<% Response.AddHeader "pragma","no-cache" %>
<% Response.Expires =0 %>
<!-- #Include File="DataConnect.ASP" -->
<%
Dim Client, ClientVer, fs, XMLDoc, XSLDoc

Client= Request.ServerVariables("HTTP_USER_AGENT")
ClientVer=Split(Client,";")
```

Before requesting all the records from the Product table.

```
Rs.Open("select * from product"), con, adOpenKeyset
```

We then build an XML string from the data by looping through each record, extracting the product information and placing it within the string between relevant XML tags:

```
xmlstr = "<?xml:stylesheet type=""Text/xsl"" href=""products.xsl""?>"
xmlstr = xmlstr & vbCrLf & "<Stores>" & vbCrLf

Do While Not rs.EOF
  xmlstr = xmlstr & vbtab & "<Product>" & vbcrlf & vbtab & vbtab
```

```
    xmlstr = xmlstr & "<Name>" & Trim(rs("Product_Name")) & "</Name>"
    xmlstr = xmlstr & vbcrlf & vbtab & vbtab & "<ID>" & Trim(rs("product_id"))
    xmlstr = xmlstr & "</ID>" & vbcrlf & vbtab & vbtab &"<product_Description>"
    xmlstr = xmlstr & Trim(rs("product_description"))& "</product_Description>"
    xmlstr = xmlstr & vbcrlf & vbtab & vbtab & "<Price>" & clng(rs("price"))
    xmlstr = xmlstr & "</Price>" & vbcrlf & vbtab & vbtab & "<Discount>"
    xmlstr = xmlstr & Trim(rs("discount")) & "</Discount>" & vbcrlf  & vbtab
    xmlstr = xmlstr & vbtab & "<Action>AddItem </Action>" & vbCrLf
    xmlstr = xmlstr & vbtab &  "</Product>" & vbCrLf
    rs.MoveNext
Loop
xmlstr = xmlstr & vbtab & "</Stores>" & vbcrlf
```

We open a FileScripting object and generate an XML file:

```
Set fs=server.CreateObject("scripting.FilesystemObject")
Set MyFile=FS.CreateTextFile("c:\inetpub\wwwroot\aspxml\shop\products.xml",true)
```

The XML string is written to the XML file that was created, and then the file stream is closed.

```
MyFile.write(xmlstr)
MyFile.close
```

Next we'll apply XSL to render the XML file we've just created, but before we can do that, we need to check which browser the code detected earlier. If the client is running IE5 then this code is run:

```
If instr(1,ClientVer(1),"MSIE 5.") > 0 Then
   Set XmlDoc= Server.CreateObject("MSXML.DOMDocument")
   Set xsldoc= Server.CreateObject("MSXML.DOMDocument")
   xmldoc.async=false
   xmldoc.load ("c:\inetpub\wwwroot\aspxml\shop\products.xml")
   xsldoc.async=false
   xsldoc.load ("c:\inetpub\wwwroot\aspxml\shop\products.xsl")
   Response.Write xmldoc.transformnode(xsldoc)
```

If a browser other than IE5 is running, however, the code executes the `Else` condition of the statement:

```
Else
  Set XmlDoc = Server.CreateObject("MSXML.DOMDocument")
  Set xsldoc = Server.CreateObject ("MSXML.DOMDocument")
  XMLDoc.Async = false
  XMLDoc.Load ("c:\inetpub\wwwroot\aspxml\shop\products.xml")
  XSLDoc.Async=false
  XSLDoc.Load ("c:\inetpub\wwwroot\aspxml\shop\products.xsl")
  Response.Write XmlDoc.documentElement.transformNode(XslDoc.documentElement)
  Response.Write XmlDoc.transformNode(XslDoc)
End If
%>
```

Let's look at the XML code for `products.xml`, which was generated by the code that we've just seen. It has been indented to make it easier for you to read:

```xml
<?xml:stylesheet type="Text/xsl" href="products.xsl"?>
<Stores>
  <Product>
    <Name>Professional Sql Server</Name>
    <ID>1</ID>
    <product_Description>Book on SQl Server Programming
    </product_Description>
    <Price>49</Price>
    <Discount>0</Discount>
    <Action>AddItem</Action>
  </Product>
  <Product>
    <Name>Professional ASP 2.0</Name>
    <ID>2</ID>
    <product_Description>ASP book By Wrox</product_Description>
    <Price>50</Price>
    <Discount>0</Discount>
    <Action>AddItem</Action>
  </Product>
  <Product>
    <Name>Professional ADO/ASP</Name>
    <ID>3</ID>
    <product_Description>ADO Book by Wrox</product_Description>
    <Price>39</Price>
    <Discount>0</Discount>
    <Action>AddItem</Action>
  </Product>
  <Product>
    <Name>IE5 XML</Name>
    <ID>5</ID>
    <product_Description>Great XML Reference Book</product_Description>
    <Price>30</Price>
    <Discount>0</Discount>
    <Action>AddItem</Action>
  </Product>
  <Product>
    <Name>IE5 XML2</Name>
    <ID>6</ID>
    <product_Description>Great XML Reference Book2</product_Description>
    <Price>55</Price>
    <Discount>0</Discount>
    <Action>AddItem</Action>
  </Product>
  <Product>
    <Name>VB COM</Name>
    <ID>7</ID>
    <product_Description>Learn OOP using VB 6</product_Description>
    <Price>93</Price>
    <Discount>0</Discount>
    <Action>AddItem</Action>
  </Product>
</Stores>
```

Now here's the stylesheet `products.xsl`, which will render the above XML into the format shown in the screenshot. We won't show the whole file, just the parts that do the transformation. The code loops through the elements and assigns the data values to the columns in the table:

```
<xsl:for-each select="Stores/Product">
  <tr>
    <td>
      <xsl:element name="a">
        <xsl:attribute name="href">cart.asp?additem;
          <xsl:value-of select="ID"/>
        </xsl:attribute>
      </xsl:element>
      <xsl:value-of select="ID"/>
    </td>
    <td>
      <xsl:value-of select="Name"/>
    </td>
    <td>
      <xsl:value-of select="Product_Description"/>
    </td>
    <td>
      <xsl:value-of select="Price"/>
    </td>
    <td>
      <xsl:value-of select="Discount"/>
    </td>
  </tr>
</xsl:for-each>
```

Notice how the hyperlink is added to each element listed in the first column, ID, of the table:

```
<td>
  <xsl:element name="a">
    <xsl:attribute name="href">cart.asp?additem;
      <xsl:value-of select="ID"/>
    </xsl:attribute>
  </xsl:element>
  <xsl:value-of select="ID"/>
</td>
```

Now, let's look at how to add a product to the shopping cart. It is accessed when the user clicks on that hyperlink in the ID column on the products page.

Cart Contents Screen

This is the cart contents page:

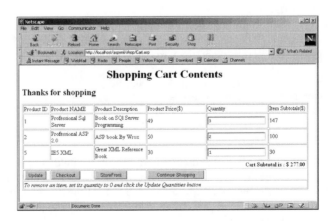

511

Let's take a look at the code for `cart.asp` to see how we add the product to our shopping cart and display the cart in the browser. This ASP file is quite hefty, since there's a lot for it to look after. Let's get started.

We connect to the database via our include file in the usual way, and then retrieve the value of the shopping cart cookie, to see if there is an existing cart. If the cookie is empty, we set the value of `cartid` to 0.

```
<%@ Language=VBScript %>
<% Response.AddHeader "pragma","no-cache" %>
<% Response.Expires =0 %>
<!-- #Include File="DataConnect.ASP" -->
<%
Dim cartID, itemID, temp, customerID

CartID = Request.Cookies("cartID")
If cartID = "" Then
   cartID =0
End If
```

We then check the cookie called `customerID`. As long as it isn't empty, we get any existing orders from the customer's shopping cart.

```
If customerID <> "" Then
  Rs.Source = "Proc_CartID " & customerID
  Rs.Open

  If Rs.RecordCount > 0 Then
    Rs.MoveFirst
    CartID = Rs(0)
  Else
    CartID = 0
  End If

  Rs.Close
End If

Temp = split(Request.QueryString,";")
If ubound(temp) > -1 Then
  action = temp(0)
End If
```

So if the customer's shopping cart is currently empty (i.e. they don't have any existing orders), but the `action` variable contains the action `additem`, passed in a querystring from the previous page, then a new shopping cart is created and the variable is given the value 0.

```
If cartID = 0 AND action <> "" Then
   cartID = SCart.creatNewCart()
   If isnull(cartID) then
     cartID = 0
   End If
```

The next section of the page handles procedure calls to the database. Firstly, if the user hasn't yet got a cart, the `Proc_CreateNewCart` procedure is called, which creates one for them, ready for the customer to fill. The Stored Procedure returns a new `cartID`. If the Stored Procedure returns a null we take care if it by assigning `cartID=0`, to prevent an error. This rarely happens, but we need to trap these potential problems as early as possible:

```
If cint(cartID) = 0 AND action  <> "" Then
   Rs.CursorLocation = adUseClient
   Rs.Source = "Proc_CreateNewCart"
   Rs.Open
   cartID  = Rs(0)
   Rs.Close
   If isnull(cartID) then
      cartID=0
   End If
```

We then create a cookie for the user so that it points to the cart that is currently in use:

```
Response.Cookies("cartID") = cartID
Response.Cookies("cartID").Expires = "December 31, 2031"
```

Next, we try to catch any users that have orders on file, left over from a previous visit, but who haven't registered with the database. This will occur if the user isn't registered, has a shop, then closes the browser and goes away. At a later time if they try to access their cart, they won't have a cart ID, but they will still have records in the actual cart. So, how do we retrieve this information? We still have their CustomerID stored in cookie. If we are fortunate, and the cookie is present, we try to retrieve the records back from the database, based on the customerID read from the cookie:

```
If customerID <> "" Then
   Rs.CursorLocation = adUseClient
   Rs.Source = "Proc_CartID " & customerID
   Rs.Open
   If Rs.RecordCount > 0 Then
     Rs.MoveFirst
     lcart = Rs(0)
   Else
     lcart = 0
   End If
   Rs.close
```

If the customer is recognised, the variable lcart will have a value other than "0". We can then go ahead and call the Proc_GetItems procedure, and retrieve the details of the order:

```
If lcart > 0 Then     ' We have an existing customer
   Rs.Source = "Proc_GetItems " & cartID
   Rs.Open
   Set Rs.ActiveConnection = Nothing
   Set Rs1 = Rs.Clone
   Rs.Close
```

We're now working with a new recordset, that will deal specifically with the quantities of the products that we're working with.

So, next we check that the quantities of products are valid – for example, we have to check that the customer doesn't order a negative quantity of books! This comes into use when we update the quantities on the page, since when we first arrive at this page, it's unlikely that the quantities will be negative:

```
                    For i = 1 To Rs1.RecordCount
                      If Rs1(4)< 0 Then
                        Response.Write "Quantity cannot be less than 0 <BR>"
                        Response.Write "<a Href='Cart.asp'> Go Back </A>"
                        Response.End
                      End If
```

This next section of code calls the `Proc_UpdateQuantity` procedure, which does three things. Firstly, if the quantity of an item is set to zero, when the update button is pressed, it will delete this item from the order. Secondly, if the quantity has been changed, when the update button is pressed, it updates the quantity field in our database. Finally, if we arrive at this page having clicked on a product on the products page, the procedure calls a procedure itself – the `Proc_AddingItem` procedure.

This procedure is itself in two sections. Firstly, if the user wishes to add a product that they haven't added to their cart before, then the cart is updated with the item information. Secondly, if the user has clicked on a product that they already have a quantity of in their cart, the quantity that is currently stored is updated.

```
                    Ssql = "Proc_UpdateQuantity " & lCartID & "," & Rs1(0) & "," & Rs1(4)
                    Con.Execute Ssql
                    Next
```

We then close down this second recordset, having updated any changes to the database.

```
                    Rs1.Close
                    Set Rs1= Nothing
```

At this point, we have a `cartID` from the cookie, and we have a `customerID` from the cookie. We now try to retrieve the actual `cartID` from the database, and compare the value with the `cartID` from the cookie. If they don't match, then there is a problem, and we clear the cart corresponding to the `cartID` we got from the cookie.

```
                    If lcart <> CartID Then
                        Con.Execute ("Proc_DeleteCart " & CartID)
                    End If
```

If the above stored procedure, which returns the `cartID` from the database, returns a 0, then we create a customer record using the `cartID` and the `customerID` read from the cookie.

```
                    ElseIf lcart = 0 Then    ' We do not have the customer
                        lcart = CartID
                        Ssql = "Proc_UpdateCustId " & CartID & "," & CustomerID 'create a cust
                        Con.Execute Ssql
                    End If
```

Next, the variable `StoreAction` is created, and the customer is transferred to different pages based on the value of the earlier variable `action`.

```
                  StoreAction= Request.Form("action")

                  If Ucase(action) = Ucase("additem") Then
                    itemid= temp(1)
```

```
        If itemid <> "" Then
          Ssql = "Proc_AddingItem " & CartID & "," & ItemID & ",1"
          Con.Execute Ssql
        End If
```

The next bit of code validates the form when the user clicks the **update** button:

```
ElseIf ucase(StoreAction) = ucase("update") Then
  For i = 1 to Request.Form("quantity").Count

    If Request.Form("quantity")(i) < 0 Then
      Response.Write "Quantity Cannot be Less than 0 <BR>"
      Response.Write "<a Href='Cart.asp'> Go Back </A>"
      Response.End
    End If

    Ssql = "Proc_UpdateQuantity " & cartid & "," & _
           Request.Form("itemid")(i) & "," & Request.Form("quantity")(i)
    Con.Execute Ssql
    Request.Form("quantity")(i)
  Next
End If
```

Or, depending on which buttons they click on the page (Checkout, Storefront, Continue Shopping), the values of which are stored in the variable StoreAction, the shopper may be transferred to new pages:

```
If ucase(StoreAction) = ucase("storefront") Then
  Server.Transfer "/aspxml/shop/storefront.asp"
End If
If ucase(StoreAction) = ucase("checkout") Then
  Server.Transfer "/aspxml/shop/order.asp"
End If
If ucase(StoreAction) = ucase("continue shopping") Then
  Server.Transfer "/aspxml/shop/products.asp"
End If
```

In the final section of the page, we loop through the contents of the getItems recordset retrieved from the shopping cart and find the subtotal of the customer's orders. An XML string is then assembled containing the product information. This is then written to a file and rendered in the same way as we did in the previous page.

```
' show shopping cart items
If cartid = "" Then
  cartid = 0
End If

Set Rs1 = Rs.Clone

If Rs1.recordcount > 0 Then
  Dim SubTotal
  xmlstr = "<?xml:stylesheet type=""Text/xsl"" href=""cart.xsl""?>" & vbCrLf
  xmlstr = xmlstr & "<Cart>" & vbCrLf

  ' Create the XML string for the cart
```

```
Do While Not Rs1.EOF
   SubTotal = cint(FormatNumber(SubTotal,2)) + _
                             cint(FormatNumber(Rs1("Total"),2))
  xmlstr = xmlstr & vbtab & "<Product>" & vbcrlf & vbtab & vbtab
  xmlstr = xmlstr & "<ItemId> " & Trim(Rs1(0)) & " </ItemId>" & vbcrlf
  xmlstr = xmlstr & vbtab & vbtab & "<Name> " & Trim(Rs1(1)) & " </Name>"
  xmlstr = xmlstr & vbcrlf & vbtab & vbtab & "<product_Description> "
  xmlstr = xmlstr & Trim(Rs1(2)) & " </product_Description>"
  xmlstr = xmlstr & vbcrlf & vbtab & vbtab & "<Price> " & clng(Rs1(3))
  xmlstr = xmlstr & " </Price>" & vbcrlf & vbtab & vbtab & "<Quantity> "
  xmlstr = xmlstr & Rs1(5) & " </Quantity>" & vbcrlf & vbtab & vbtab
  xmlstr = xmlstr & "<ItemSubTotal> " & clng(Rs1(5)) * clng(Rs1(3))
  xmlstr = xmlstr & " </ItemSubTotal>" & vbCrLf & "</Product>" & vbcrlf

   Rs1.MoveNext
Loop
xmlstr= xmlstr & "<Subtotal> "  & FormatNumber(SubTotal,2)
xmlstr= xmlstr & " </Subtotal>" & vbcrlf & "<Action> Update </Action>"
xmlstr= xmlstr & vbcrlf & "</Cart>" & vbcrlf

Client= Request.ServerVariables("HTTP_USER_AGENT")
ClientVer=Split(Client,";")

Dim FS
Set FS = Server.CreateObject("Scripting.FileSystemObject")
Set MyFile=
 FS.CreateTextFile("c:\inetpub\wwwroot\aspxml\shop\cart" & Cartid & _
                                          ".xml" ,true)
MyFile.Write (xmlstr)
MyFile.Close

' Here we apply ourXSL to render the XML file the code just created

If instr(1,ClientVer(1),"MSIE 5.") > 0 then
  Set XMLDoc= server.createObject("MSXML.DOMDocument")
  Set XSLDoc= server.CreateObject("MSXML.DOMDocument")
  XMLDoc.async=false
  XMLDoc.load ("c:\inetpub\wwwroot\aspxml\shop\cart" & Cartid & ".xml")
  XSLDoc.async=false
  XSLDoc.load ("c:\inetpub\wwwroot\aspxml\shop\cart.xsl")
  Response.Write (XMLDoc.transformnode(XSLDoc))
Else
  set XMLDoc= server.createObject("MSXML.DOMDocument")
  set XSLDoc= server.CreateObject ("MSXML.DOMDocument")
  XMLDoc.async=false
  XMLDoc.load ("c:\inetpub\wwwroot\aspxml\shop\cart" & Cartid & ".xml")
  XSLDoc.async=false
  XSLDoc.load ("c:\inetpub\wwwroot\aspxml\shop\cart.xsl")
Response.Write XMLDoc.documentElement.transformNode(XSLDoc.documentElement)
  Response.Write XMLDoc.transformnode(XSLDoc)
  End If
Else
  Response.write "Shopping Cart Empty <BR>"
  Response.write "<A HREF='/aspxml/shop/Products.asp'>" & _
                                    " Please Shop for Items </a>"
End If
```

```
Rs1.Close
Rs.Close
Set Rs1 = Nothing
Set Rs = Nothing
%>
```

Here is the XML code created by the above ASP code. Every time the shopping cart is either updated or modified, the code does the necessary modifications to the cart's XML data file; in other words as we add items to or delete items from our cart, the XML file keeps on changing. The code has been indented for easy reading:

```
<?xml:stylesheet type="Text/xsl" href="cart.xsl"?>
<Cart>
  <Product>
    <ItemId> 1 </ItemId>
    <Name> Professional Sql Server </Name>
    <product_Description> Book on SQl Server Programming
    </product_Description>
    <Price> 49 </Price>
    <Quantity> 1 </Quantity>
    <ItemSubTotal> 49 </ItemSubTotal>
  </Product>
  <Product>
    <ItemId> 2 </ItemId>
    <Name> Professional ASP 2.0 </Name>
    <product_Description> ASP book By Wrox </product_Description>
    <Price> 50 </Price>
    <Quantity> 1 </Quantity>
    <ItemSubTotal> 50 </ItemSubTotal>
  </Product>
  <Product>
    <ItemId> 7 </ItemId>
    <Name> VB COM </Name>
    <product_Description> Learn OOP using VB 6 </product_Description>
    <Price> 93 </Price>
    <Quantity> 1 </Quantity>
    <ItemSubTotal> 93 </ItemSubTotal>
  </Product>
  <Subtotal> 192.00 </Subtotal>
  <Action> Update </Action>
</Cart>
```

The cart.xsl file, which transforms the above XML to what is viewed in the browser, is shown below. Once again, only the code that does the transformation is presented:

```
<xsl:for-each select="Cart/Product">
  <tr>
    <td>
      <input type='hidden' name='ItemId'>
      <xsl:attribute name="Value"><xsl:value-of select="ItemId"/>
      </xsl:attribute>
      </input>
      <xsl:value-of select="ItemId"/>
    </td>
```

```
      <td>
        <xsl:value-of select="Name"/>
      </td>
      <td>
        <xsl:value-of select="product_Description"/>
      </td>
      <td>
        <xsl:value-of select="Price"/>
      </td>
      <td>
        <input type='text' name='Quantity'>
        <xsl:attribute name="Value"><xsl:value-of select="Quantity"/>
        </xsl:attribute>
        </input>
      </td>
      <td>
        <xsl:value-of select="ItemSubTotal"/>
      </td>
    </tr>
  </xsl:for-each>
  <xsl:for-each select="Cart/Subtotal">
    <tr>
      <td align='right' colspan='6'>
        <strong>
          Cart Subtotal is : $ <xsl:value-of />
        </strong>
      </td>
    </tr>
  </xsl:for-each>
```

Checkout Screen

This is the final ASP page of this project, which we shall look at in detail. It is called `order.asp` and this is how it looks in the browser:

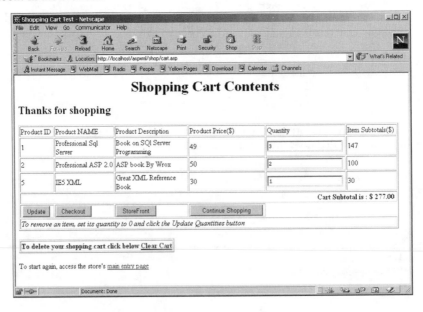

Here is the ASP code that created the page. As before, we include our `DataConnect.asp` to establish our connection to the database, then we retrieve our cookie:

```
<%@ LANGUAGE="VBSCRIPT" %>
<% Response.AddHeader "pragma","no-cache" %>
<% Response.Expires =0 %>
<!-- #Include File="DataConnect.asp" -->
<%
  Dim cartID
  cartid = Request.Cookies("cartID")
```

If the `cartid cookie` isn't empty, the order details are retrieved from the database, using the Proc_GetItems procedure.

```
If cartid <> "" Then
  Rs.Source = "Proc_GetItems " & cartID
  Rs.Open
```

If there are no records to return, a message is written to the browser containing a hyperlink back to the Products Page:

```
If Rs.recordcount = 0  Then
  Response.Write " <H1><CENTER> Check Out</H1> </CENTER>"
  Response.Write "<HR><BR><CENTER>"
  Response.Write "Shopping cart is empty why not fill it with items " &_
                                       "and then check out.</P>"
  Response.Write "<A HREF = Products.asp > Go to Products Page </A>"
  Response.Write "</CENTER>"
  Rs.Close
```

Alternatively, as you will see, if the recordset contains records, a different message is written and the contents are displayed in a table, the format being decided upon by detecting the browser type:

```
  Else
    Client = Request.ServerVariables("HTTP_USER_AGENT")
    ClientVer=Split(Client,";")
    If instr(1,ClientVer(1),"MSIE 5.") > 0 then
     set XmlDoc= Server.CreateObject("MSXML.DOMDocument")
     set XslDoc= Server.CreateObject("MSXML.DOMDocument")
     XmlDoc.async=false
     XmlDoc.load ("c:\inetpub\wwwroot\aspxml\shop\cart" & Cartid & ".xml")
     XslDoc.async=false
     XslDoc.load  ("c:\inetpub\wwwroot\aspxml\shop\cart.xsl")
     Response.Write (xmldoc.transformnode(xsldoc))
    Else
     Set XmlDoc= Server.CreateObject("MSXML.DOMDocument")
     Set XslDoc= Server.CreateObject ("MSXML.DOMDocument")
     xmldoc.async=false
     XmlDoc.load ("c:\inetpub\wwwroot\aspxml\shop\cart" & Cartid & ".xml")
     XslDoc.async=false
     XslDoc.load ("c:\inetpub\wwwroot\aspxml\shop\cart.xsl")
Response.Write XmlDoc.documentElement.transformNode(XslDoc.documentElement)
     Response.Write XmlDoc.transformnode(XslDoc)
    End If
```

A variable is then declared to store the customer ID which matches the shopping cart.

```
Dim lcust
If cartid <> "" Then
  Rs.Source = "Proc_GetCustID " & CartID
  Rs.Open

   ' get cartID
  If Rs.RecordCount > 0 Then
    If IsNull(Rs(0)) Then
      lcust = 0
    Else
      lcust = Rs(0)
    End If
  Else
    lcust = 0
  End If
```

If no match is made, you can add some code to provide a link to a registration page, so this system will become a multi-user system. For the purposes of this case study, we have provided a fully working case study for a single user. Since a multi-user system presentation wouldn't be much different from the point of view of the XML code, and how it relates to ASP code, we haven't included code to add users here.

```
If CINT(lcust)=0  then
  ' code to link to a registration page
  Response.Write "<td>" ' align='center' colspan='1'>" & vbcrlf
  Response.Write "<strong>To delete your shopping cart, click here"&_
                                        "</strong>"
  Response.Write "<strong><a href='clearcart.asp'>Clear Cart" & _
                                        </a></strong>"
  Response.Write "</tr>" & vbcrlf & "</table>"

Else
  Response.Write("<p><strong><a href='clearcart.asp'>" & _
                              "Clear Cart</a></strong></p>")
  End if
End If
End if
Else
  Response.Write "<H1><center> Order Processing </H1> </center>"
  Response.Write "<HR>"
  Response.Write "<BR>"
  Response.Write "<center>"
  Response.Write "Shopping cart is empty why not fill it with items" & _
                                        and then check out.</p>"
  Response.Write "<a href = products.asp > Go to Products Page </A>"
  Response.Write "</center>"
End If

Response.Write "<P>To start again, access the store's " & _
                    "<a href= storefront.asp >main entry page</a></p>"
Response.Write "</BODY> </HTML>"%>
```

Summary

In this case study, we took a look at one specific application of an on-line store, the shopping cart, and demonstrated how a cart can be implemented without large chunks of complicated code. We used the combined power of ASP and XML, which meant that lengthy calls back and forth across a network were reduced because data could be cached client-side. It also allowed us to make our on-line store available to all potential customers regardless of the browser their client machine was running, making our real-world example as consumer-friendly as possible.

In particular we have looked at:

❑ Using XML as an intermediate datastore

❑ Using XSL to transform XML into HTML depending on the browser type

❑ Making an XML application browser independent using server-side XSL

Case Study – Workflow Application

This is a case study that illustrates an application of ASP and XML technologies. I will introduce a particular type of application – workflow, provide some background on workflow and how it can be used, define an approach to doing workflow on the Web, and, finally, take you through the process of designing and implementing a web-based workflow framework. I will incorporate some other common web development technologies along the way. Chief among them is COM+ Component Services serving as a middle tier transaction management mechanism and object broker.

I have a few goals in mind that I'd like to achieve by the time we get done. First, I want to showcase Active Server Pages and XML working together on the Web. That shouldn't be too hard, as that's what ASP was designed for, after all. Second, I want to illustrate the use of XML as a marshaling technique between our ASP scripts and middle tier components running in COM+. Third, I want to present this entire case study in a way that closely follows the organization of any typical software project – product requirements, design, and implementation. (Testing is an obviously important phase of any project, but is beyond our scope in this case.) Lastly, I want to present a workflow framework that is reusable and flexible enough to be extended to include features I haven't covered in this chapter.

The technologies I'll feature and their roles are as follows:

❑ **XML** – We'll use XML for intra-component communication. Primarily between ASP scripts and Visual Basic components running in COM+ on Windows 2000 or MTS in Windows NT 4.0. We will develop an XML schema and talk about its member attributes and elements.

❑ **XSL** – Any XML encoded data destined for a user will be transformed using XSL stylesheets. We will discuss the process of creating XSL, apply it to our XML schema and view the results we get from that transformation.

❏ **Active Server Pages** – We'll use ASP to control the processing flow of the entire application. These scripts will be responsible for executing our XSL transformations, and instantiating and working with the VB components in COM+.

❏ **VB and COM+** – We'll have some VB server components running under Component Services (or MTS) that do some heavy processing for us. They will be responsible for XML generation and all database access.

I anticipate the typical reader of this case study will have a decent level of understanding of ASP and XML fundamentals. We have just finished a book on ASP and XML applications, after all. It will also be helpful if you have some familiarity with Visual Basic since our middle tier components are written in VB. If you haven't worked with VB, you'll find its structure very similar to ASP, since we are using VBScript to write the code. I plan to cover some MTS/COM+ basics where appropriate since many of us may have not yet worked with a COM+ application.

OK, let's get going. We'll start with some background on workflow – what it is, where we might find workflow applications, and some common workflow scenarios. Then we'll discuss the requirements of the Workflow Framework project. That includes the definition of an application framework and the functional and technical requirements necessary to deliver that framework. Then we'll create a design based on those requirements. Once we've discussed the design, we'll start writing code.

What is Workflow?

Bear with me as I explain workflow in some detail. Even if you are not interested in workflow per se, an understanding of some common concepts and terms will help when we get to looking at design and coding issues.

Workflow is the collection of tasks or procedural steps, people, and tools necessary to complete a business process. For our purposes, a workflow application is software that automates a business process by enabling better communication and collaboration between workflow participants. Workflow processes must be well defined and repeatable.

An easy method of describing a workflow application is one that requires **rules** for controlling workflow progress, **roles** that identify users to which specific tasks are assigned, and a **routing** – the defined path of a particular process from one step to another.

As an example, consider a loan approval process at a bank. The workflow process starts when an applicant sits down with a Loan Representative and completes an application. Once complete, that application could be sent to a Loan Administrator for review and preliminary approval or disqualification. The Loan Administrator could manually review the application data or use some software to help him or her make a decision. If that application gets a preliminary approval, bank rules might dictate that a Vice President then reviews the application to double check the Loan Administrator. If the VP gives approval then the loan is officially approved and sent to a Loan Clerk to produce some paperwork. Once the paperwork is completed, the entire package is routed back to the originating Loan Representative who calls the happy applicant in to sign away their car or house or whatever they put up as collateral.

In this example we can clearly see our workflow rules. For example, take the following:

If an application is given a preliminary approval by the Loan Administrator, the application is routed to a Vice President for approval. If the VP approves a loan then the loan application is routed to a Loan Clerk to prepare the paperwork that eventually gets signed by the applicant.

We can see some user roles emerging:

❑ Loan Representative

❑ Loan Clerk

❑ Loan Administrator

❑ Vice President

Notice a workflow is designed around roles, not specific users. Users are assigned roles and those roles are then associated with specific workflow steps. We'll get into why a little later on, but you can probably figure it out.

This example also has a clearly defined routing. The Loan Rep starts the process, and then sends an application to a Loan Administrator, who then forwards the application to a Vice President. The VP decides whether to accept the application or not. If you can picture a flowchart in you head, then you've got it.

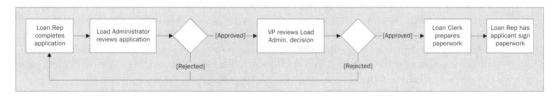

Workflow Application Structure

Most workflow applications have a similar structure. They typically have the following components:

❑ **Workflow Engine**: The workflow engine is a centralized component responsible for keeping track of workflows in progress, controlling the execution of individual workflow steps, and sending and receiving workflow procedure requests to and from users.

Although the workflow engine itself is not immediately evident in our Loan Processing example, the results of its execution are. For instance, when a loan application is preliminarily approved by a Loan Administrator, it automatically gets routed to a Vice President for review. It is the workflow engine that receives the approval message from the Administrator and determines whether sending the application to the Vice President is the next appropriate action.

❑ **Messaging Mechanism**: The workflow engine needs a way to communicate with workflow users. It will send requests asking for a response from a user like an approval or rejection. For every request it sends, there must be a method for receiving responses. In most commercial workflow applications, vendors rely on applications like Microsoft Exchange or Lotus Notes, since those products already provide a strong messaging and collaboration framework. We will take a different approach to communicating with users, as you'll see shortly, but we will still have a messaging component in our application.

❑ **Workflow Client**: When a user receives workflow requests and returns their responses to the workflow engine they typically use custom software to manage that process. Client software is responsible for knowing where to find workflow requests sent by the workflow engine, how to interpret those requests into some meaningful interface for the user, and returning the user response to the workflow engine.

525

Our Loan Processing example could have a relatively simple workflow client application installed in each user's computer. A user could see loan approval tasks or requests in an Inbox structure similar to most e-mail applications. When a particular request is selected, a form is presented giving the details of that loan application – personal information on the applicant, a history of the processing for that particular loan, and maybe a link to an image of the application itself. The user is also given a list of all the possible responses that could be made for this request.

❑ **Administrative Tools**: Someone has to have the capability to build new workflows, make changes to existing workflows, define workflow steps, manage users, etc. Generally this is done with a separate administration module that accompanies the workflow engine.

Taking our Loan Processing example again, a workflow administrator would use an administrative application to create the routing we discussed by building the individual steps of an application, a Loan Administrator review and Vice President approval, and then linking them together.

❑ **Workflow Database**: We need a place to store our workflows, their component steps or procedures, the rules that link them all together, and the users associated with each step. We also need a place to store details about all the workflows we have in process at any one time – which stage a particular workflow is on, what response was given at a particular step, and so on. So, think of the workflow database as having two distinct parts. The first stores workflow metadata, that is the structure of a workflow – rules, roles and routing. The other part stores production details – responses from users, status, etc.

Storing data collected at each step in a Loan Processing workflow could be useful. For example, a Senior Vice President may want statistics describing how long a typical loan approval takes. They would run a report on the production detail side of the workflow database that calculates the number of days between the Application and Approval steps.

❑ **Predefined Steps**: Any workflow consists of one or more steps. At design time, an Administrator selects specific steps from a predefined list. They will be prompted for specific parameters depending on step type. For instance if they have added a user response step to a workflow they will be asked for a list of possible responses. The Workflow Engine will detect the "step type" to determine what type of processing is required when it receives a response from a workflow user.

The most common workflow steps include:

❑ **Start**: This step indicates to the workflow engine a new workflow should be started. In our example, a Loan Representative would execute a Start step while working with the application filling out paperwork.

❑ **User Response**: This step sends a message to a user that asks for a specific response, usually chosen from a list of responses. Most workflow steps are User Responses. In the loan example, any time a Loan Administrator or Vice President receives an application to approve or deny, that is a User Response.

❑ **Notification (FYI)**: this step sends a one-way message to a workflow recipient – an interested observer of the workflow but with no rights to control the workflow process. For example, if an approved loan is sent to a Loan Clerk to produce the formal paperwork, that individual's manager may want to be notified as well to make sure the job is done properly and in a timely manner.

❑ **Stop**: This step is the normal end of a workflow.

Now that you understand what workflow is, let's take a minute to talk about how we are approaching workflow for this case study. We will construct a framework that consists of all the standard workflow components with the exception of the administrative tools. Those tools are typically single user, graphical desktop applications that have little need for ASP or XML. I don't discount their importance, but their design and implementation are beyond the scope of this study.

Our focus will be on designing the workflow engine component, both parts of the workflow database, a workflow client component, and the method that our components use to talk to each other. If you are thinking ahead you can probably figure out we'll be using COM+ for the workflow engine components, ASP for our client functions, and XML as the glue that brings it all together. You would be correct, but since I've already mentioned that this Case Study is organized to follow the major steps in a development project, we need to clearly define what our application has to do before we consider anything else.

Project Description – A Workflow Framework

OK, we are ready to build a workflow application. Since we already know a little bit about workflow, we have some idea of what this product will to do. But that's not enough. Any good application developer already knows that delivering an effective product is difficult without a clear definition of what that product is supposed to do. So our first step is to define the purpose of our workflow framework.

At the very least a "good requirements" document will clearly define a product vision, functional requirements as seen by users, any technical requirements placed on the application by a particular environment or the need to integrate with existing software, and any assumptions we've made along the way. From a project management standpoint, it is also a good idea to clearly state any risks or other issues associated with developing the product, but I'll leave that for an enterprising project management case study author.

Project Vision

My vision of this project is developing a product that delivers the following key functions:

❑ **Workflow Execution (Server)**: Whenever a workflow is started, or users respond to steps in a particular workflow, a process must be executed that checks if the rules associated with that step have been met, finds the next step in the workflow, and sends a request to the user associated with that next step.

❑ **Workflow Request Management (Client)**: When a user receive a workflow request, he or she will have the ability to view the details of that request, and deliver an appropriate response back to the workflow engine running on the server.

Functional Requirements

I happen to like using **use cases** to help elicit functional requirements. By sitting with users and talking about their business processes and then documenting those processes in a standard format, you'll have a better chance at getting your requirements right the first time. So let's walk through a couple of workflow use cases, starting with defining what types of users our application will have.

Use Cases

- ❑ **Workflow Administrator**: A workflow administrator is allowed to create, modify, and delete workflow templates. This includes working with the individual steps that comprise an entire workflow and the rules that link them together.

- ❑ **Workflow User**: A workflow user can take any role assigned to a workflow step. These users will receive workflow requests when that step is executed. Workflow users have the ability to respond to specific requests, and in some cases, delegate those requests to other users. They cannot change workflow templates.

- ❑ **Workflow Recipient**: A workflow recipient is a user who receives messages from the workflow, but is not asked to respond to those messages. Typically a Workflow Recipient will be identified in a particular type of step that asks the workflow engine to send a one-way message or a copy of a document to a user for their information only.

Now that we know the types of users we'll encounter we can start defining the tasks that they perform. For this purpose, use cases are employed. There are many ways to format your use cases. I like the format Jake Sturm presented in the Wrox publication, VB6 UML Design and Development, (ISBN 1-861002-51-3). Consider the following example that helps describe what a user will do when they respond to a workflow request.

Use Case A: Respond to Workflow Request Item

Overview:	The purpose of this use case is to respond to a workflow request item.
Primary Actor:	Any workflow user.
Secondary Actor:	None.
Starting Point:	The actor must have the details of a workflow request item displayed.
Ending Point:	The actor has submitted a response to the system for a particular request.
Measurable Result:	The response for a request has been updated.
Flow of Events:	This use case starts when the actor views request item details. The actor reviews the contents of a particular item including special notes or comments, attachments supplied by other users, and a list of possible responses. The actor selects a particular response, sends that response to the system for processing, and receives notification of the status of that processing in the form of a message returned from the system.
Alternative Flow of Events:	An error will result if the actor's username and password are not properly authenticated when the response is processed. An error will also result if the actor does not select a response from the list of possible responses, or if the response is not found in the list. In this case the system will return a message along with the workflow item and require the actor to re-submit the item with a new response.
Use Case Extensions:	None.

Let's spend a little time discussing the structure of this use case. First, the Primary Actor is the main actor who will execute the use case. The Secondary Actor is any other actor or actors who can execute the use case. The Starting Point defines the first step in the use case, and the Ending Point is the last step. The Measurable Result is the result we expect from the use case. The Flow of Events is a narrative of everything that occurs between the Starting Point and the Ending Point. Alternative Flow of Events is anything that can occur in the use case not included in the Flow of Events, which typically includes error conditions. And finally, Use Case Extensions describe any use cases used by this one – it is possible to break your use cases into pieces to make them easier to work with.

Notice that our Primary Actor in Use Case A is any workflow user. The flow of events described in this use case will serve as the basis of our design for our client software.

Now, here's an interesting twist. The following use case describes the process the workflow engine takes when it processes a particular type of workflow step. The primary actor in this case is an application component – our workflow engine. Actors don't have to be people.

Use Case B: Execute 'Start' Workflow Step

Overview:	The purpose of this workflow is to execute a standard Start workflow step.
Primary Actor:	The workflow engine.
Secondary Actor:	None.
Starting Point:	The actor has received a Start workflow step request.
Ending Point:	The Start workflow step has been executed and any subsequent step has been started.
Measurable Result:	The results of executing a Start step have been written to the database.
Flow of Events:	This use case starts when the actor receives a request from a workflow user to execute a particular Start step. The actor evaluates the description step data received from the user and determines if it has enough information to proceed. In the case of the Start workflow step, the requirements to execute the step are very simple; if the step has been received and a workflow template has been properly identified then the Start is executed.
	Upon deciding that it is proper to start a new workflow, the actor finds the workflow template identified in the Start message. It creates a new Workflow Process and updates it with the originator's name, the start date and other general information. The actor then creates a Procedure Process with a type of Start and immediately sets its complete time to the current date and time. Then the actor determines which step immediately precedes this particular Start step using the workflow template, sends a start message to that workflow step, and stops its own processing, giving up control to the next step to continue the workflow.
Alternative Flow of Events:	An error will result if the actor receives a Start step request and there is no workflow to which that particular step belongs. An error will also result if the requesting user sends an improper username or password to the actor.
Use Case Extensions:	None.

I haven't seen too many examples of non-user primary actors in use cases, but hopefully you'll agree this use case describes what the workflow engine has to do to complete its job in this case.

Functional Requirements

Using our use cases as guidelines, I like to state functional requirements in terms of direct statements. If we look at our workflow product in terms of major system features, these are the main functional requirements:

Workflow Request Management (Client)

❑ The product will display lists of active workflow items for a particular user.

❑ The product will send to the user detailed information about a particular workflow item including receive date, sender, description, status, required date, notes or comments from the workflow originator or other users, attachments, and a list of possible responses.

❑ The product will capture the user's response to a workflow and return that response to the workflow server.

❑ The product will display workflow status including step detail to any user participating in that workflow.

Workflow Execution (Server Side)

Upon receiving a response the product will determine the step type, perform step specific logic to determine state of completeness, and determine the next step. When the next step has been found, the product will execute any preconditions (rules) assigned to that step. If those rules are satisfied the product will start the next step. To start a step, the product will make appropriate database changes and send enough information to a particular user for that user to respond to that step.

The product will know how to execute the following types of workflow steps:

❑ **Start Step** – to start a workflow.

❑ **End Step** – to end a workflow.

❑ **Abort Step** – to terminate a workflow abnormally.

❑ **User Response Step** – this step sends a list of responses to a user and expects the user to return one of those responses.

❑ **FYI (Notification) Step** – this step sends a one-way message to a workflow recipient.

The product will support the following preconditions (rules). Each of these preconditions can be assigned to any of the workflow steps defined above.

❑ **Is Done** – checks to make sure a particular step has been completed successfully.

❑ **Is Response** – checks to make sure a particular response has been given to a previously completed User Response.

The product will maintain in-process information about every active workflow. This includes user responses and start and complete dates for each step in the workflow.

Technical Requirements

We also have some technical requirements we need to implement:

❑ The product's workflow engine will operate on Windows NT 4.0 or Windows 2000 and requires Internet Information Server.

❑ The product will support Internet Explorer 4.0 or better or Netscape Navigator 4.0 or better.

Application Design

Now that we understand what we have to do, let's get started designing the application. Our first step is to describe our design in a few sentences, and call it a solution statement. That gives us a clear idea of the big picture, so when we get into the details, we'll have something to refer back to. Once we touch on the high points of the design, we'll start looking at code.

Solution Statement

We will deliver the requirements outlined in the previous section by implementing our workflow application using Active Server Pages to control user interaction with the workflow engine. That includes communicating user commands to the workflow engine, waiting for results, and returning those results to individual users. The workflow engine will be implemented as VB components running in COM+. It will be responsible for all system database activity, sending requests to users as new steps, receiving responses from users as steps are completed, and otherwise managing the workflow process. Our ASP scripts and the workflow engine will communicate using XML. Workflows and their associated steps will be stored in an Access database as well as details about any workflow that's currently active.

XML Design

Let's consider our use of XML first. Seems like a logical place to start, since we will rely on XML as the glue to hold the system together.

Role of XML

As I keep mentioning, the job we are using XML to perform is integrating our ASP scripts and the workflow engine. It's a marshaling device for moving data from one logical tier to another. If you've worked with ASP for a while, you know there are several alternatives to marshaling – ADO recordsets, for example. I don't discount those other techniques, but there are several reasons I think XML is a better technique for moving data between components or applications. They include:

❑ **XML is platform and language independent**. All you need is a parser; and XML parsers have been written for just about every major platform already, and most are freely available. As long as two systems can exchange XML based messages, they can probably work together.

❑ **XML is extensible**. Hopefully you agree with me that the best application designs are extensible and building such applications is always a design consideration. XML was designed with extensibility in mind, after all. Unlike other formats like EDI (Electronic Data Interchange) that require a specific order to their documents, we can add elements to our XML designs without breaking systems already in production.

❑ **XML is easy to read**. Really all you need is Notepad or some other simple text editor to look at an XML document. Because it's self describing it makes sense to us humans almost immediately.

Contents

OK, enough of that stuff. We are going to use XML to talk back and forth between ASP and COM+ components. So what exactly should we include in the XML? To answer that, we need to look at what our components expect in terms of input. We haven't gotten there yet, but you'll soon discover that our workflow engine really only works on one workflow step at a time. In other words it processes the workflow one step at a time and doesn't really care too much what occurred one or two steps ago, or even what will happen three steps from now.

That makes our job easier. We need to describe a workflow step at any one point in time. That means we have to list data items like step name, description, start date, user information, etc. If we keep those items in mind then our XML design starts taking shape. Consider the following schema:

```
<Schema name='workflowSchema'
  xmlns='urn:schemas-microsoft.com:xml-data'
  xmlns:dt='urn:schemas-microsoft-com:datatypes'

<ElementType name='Description' content='textOnly' model='closed'
      dt:type='string'>
  <Description>Contains the description of a workflow Procedure
  </Description>
</ElementType>

<ElementType name='Status' content='textOnly' model='closed'
      dt:type='enumeration'
      dt:values= 'Open Complete Error Cancelled'>
  <Description>Indicates the state of this workflow procedure
  </Description>
</ElementType>

<ElementType name='Type' content='textOnly' model='closed'
      dt:type='enumeration'
      dt:values= 'Start Stop Response FYI'>
  <Description>Indicates type of workflow procedure</Description>
</ElementType>

<ElementType name='Notes' content='textOnly' model='closed'
      dt:type='string'>
  <Description>User notes.</Description>
</ElementType>

<ElementType name='FullName' content='textOnly' model='closed'
      dt:type='string'>
  <Description>A user full name</Description>
</ElementType>

<ElementType name='UserName' content='textOnly' model='closed'
      dt:type='string'>
  <Description>The login username for a workflow user</Description>
</ElementType>

<ElementType name='Password' content='textOnly' model='closed'
      dt:type='string'>
  <Description>The login password for a workflow user</Description>
```

```
</ElementType>

<ElementType name='User' content='eltOnly' model='closed'>
  <Description>Indicates type of workflow procedure</Description>
  <element type='FullName' />
  <element type='UserName' />
  <element type='Password' />
</ElementType>

<ElementType name='ResponseID' content='textOnly' model='closed'
      dt:type='string'>
  <Description>ID used to identify a specific Response</Description>
</ElementType>

<ElementType name='ResponseBody' content='textOnly' model='closed'
      dt:type='string'>
  <Description>The text body of a response</Description>
</ElementType>

<ElementType name='Response' content='eltOnly' model='closed'>
  <Description>A response to a workflow request</Description>
  <element type='ResponseID' />
  <element type='ResponseText' />
</ElementType>

<ElementType name='ResponseLIST' content='eltOnly' model='closed'
    minOccurs='1' maxOccurs='*'>
  <Description>List of all possible responses</Description>
  <element type='Response' />
</ElementType>

<ElementType name='UserResponse' content='eltOnly' model='closed'
    minOccurs='1' maxOccurs='1'>
  <Description>List of all possible responses</Description>
  <element type='Response' />
</ElementType>

<ElementType name='StartDate' content='textOnly' model='closed'
      dt:type='date'>
  <Description>The start date of this workflow procedure</Description>
</ElementType>

<ElementType name='CompleteDate' content='textOnly' model='closed'
       dt:type='date'>
  <Description>The completion date of this workflow procedure</Description>
</ElementType>

<ElementType name='ExpirationDate' content='textOnly' model='closed'
      dt:type='date'>
  <Description>The expiration date of this workflow procedure</Description>
</ElementType>

<ElementType name='Priority' content='textOnly' model='closed'
      dt:type='enumeration'
      dt:values= 'High Standard Low'>
  <Description>Indicates the three states of request priority</Description>
```

```
    </ElementType>

    <ElementType name='MessageBody' content='textOnly' model='closed'
    dt:type='string'>
      <Description>Textual Body of a message.</Description>
    </ElementType>

    <ElementType name='MessageType' content='textOnly' model='closed'
          dt:type='enumeration'
          dt:values= 'Info Warning Error'>
      <Description>Indicates the three types of messages sent to users
      </Description>
    </ElementType>

    <ElementType name='Message' content='eltOnly' model='closed'>
      <Description>A response to a workflow request</Description>
      <element type='MessageType' />
      <element type='MessageBody' />
    </ElementType>

    <ElementType name='AttachName' content='textOnly' model='closed'
          dt:type='string'>
      <Description>Name or description given to an attachment.</Description>
    </ElementType>

    <ElementType name='AttachPath' content='textOnly' model='closed'
          dt:type='string'>
      <Description>Full Server path of attachment location</Description>
    </ElementType>

    <ElementType name='Attachment' content='eltOnly' model='closed'>
      <Description>A response to a workflow request</Description>
      <element type='AttachName' />
      <element type='AttachPath' />
    </ElementType>

    <AttributeType name='ProcedureID' dt:type='string' />
    <AttributeType name='WORKFLOWID' dt:type='string' />

    <ElementType name='Procedure' content='eltOnly' model='closed'>
      <Description>A workflow procedure</Description>
      <attribute type='ProcedureID' />
      <attribute type='WORKFLOWID' />

      <element type='Description' />
      <element type='Status' />
      <element type='Type' />
      <element type='Notes' />
      <element type='User' />
      <element type='ResponseLIST' />
      <element type='UserResponse' />
      <element type='StartDate' />
      <element type='CompleteDate' />
      <element type='ExpirationDate' />
      <element type='Priority' />
      <element type='Attachment' />
```

```
  </ElementType>

<ElementType name='ProcedureList' content='eltOnly' model='closed'>
  <Description>A list of workflow requests, usually destined for one user
  </Description>
  <element type='Procedure' />
<ElementType>
```

Is all of that needed just to describe one workflow step? You got it! Now in practice, a real XML document, even full of data, is generally much easier to read than its schema. Take this example:

```
<Procedure ID="003" WorkflowID="002">
  <Name="Request for Approval"</NAME>
  <Description>This is a sample XML document</Description>
  <Status>Open</Status>
  <Type>Response</Type>
  <User>
    <FullName>John Slater</FullName>
    <UserName>jslater</UserName>
    <Password>password</Password>
  </User>
  <ResponseList>
    <Response>
      <ResponseID>001</ResponseID>
      <ResponseText>Accept</ResponseText>
    </Response>
  </ResponseList>
  <UserResponse>
    <Response>
      <ResponseID>001</ResponseID>
      <ResponseText>Accept</ResponseText>
    </Response>
  </UserResponse>
  <StartDate>03/19/2000</StartDate>
  <CompleteDate>03/19/2000</CompleteDate>
  <Priority>1</Priority>
  <ExpirationDate/>
  <Message>
    <Body>Please select a response.</Body>
    <Type>Info</Type>
  </Message>
  <Attachment>
    <Name>Loan Application</Name>
    <FilePath>/attachments/app102.doc</FilePath>
  </Attachment>
</Procedure>
```

Now if we encountered the source XML document without its schema we'd have a good idea what was happening in the document. Nonetheless, understanding the schema is important so let's take a minute to point out some of the more interesting parts.

First, notice that I introduced a new word – Procedure. A procedure is a step. There is no difference between the two as far as I am concerned, but Step just didn't look good once I had the document designed. In some development languages, 'Step' is a reserved word. I doubt we'll have problems with it, but I switched to Procedure anyway. Second, notice I like enumerators. An enumerator in the following fragment defines the third element, Status:

```
<ElementType name='Status' content='textOnly' model='closed'
    dt:type='enumeration'
    dt:values= 'Open Complete Error Cancelled'>
  <Description>Indicates the state of this workflow procedure</Description>
</ElementType>
```

This forces the XML parser to only accept one of four values for Status – Open, Complete, Error, or Cancelled. In some ways I like that restriction. If I can comfortably state that any value for Status other than those four values should throw an error and halt processing, then this is a good design decision. If I thought I would routinely encounter all sorts of variation in this element, then I wouldn't use an enumeration type. I would simply state it this way:

```
<ElementType name='Status' content='textOnly' model='closed'
    dt:type='string'>
  <Description>Indicates the state of this workflow procedure</Description>
</ElementType>
```

One last point about our schema and then we'll move on. One of the jobs I am assigning to XML is to send to the client as much information as it needs to process one workflow request – basically one step. Part of the data we have to send to the client is a list of responses to choose from. (The response list is first built by our Workflow Administrator user class, which I do not plan to cover in any detail. In case you were wondering where the response list comes from, now you know.) We also need to be able to bring back the chosen response.

Here's how I planned for that need in the schema:

```
<ElementType name='ResponseID' content='textOnly' model='closed'
    dt:type='string'>
  <Description>ID used to identify a specific Response</Description>
</ElementType>

<ElementType name='ResponseBody' content='textOnly' model='closed'
    dt:type='string'>
  <Description>The text body of a response</Description>
</ElementType>

<ElementType name='Response' content='eltOnly' model='closed'>
  <Description>A response to a workflow request</Description>
  <element type='ResponseID' />
  <element type='ResponseBody' />
</ElementType>

<ElementType name='ResponseList' content='eltOnly' model='closed'
    minOccurs='1' maxOccurs='*'>
  <Description>List of all possible responses</Description>
  <element type='Response' />
</ElementType>

<ElementType name='UserResponse' content='eltOnly' model='closed'
    minOccurs='1' maxOccurs='1'>
  <Description>List of all possible responses</Description>
  <element type='Response' />
</ElementType>
```

I define a `Response` element to consist of two child elements – `ResponseID` and `ResponseBody`, both of which are strings. I then define a `ResponseList`, a list of possible responses, in terms of the generic `Response` element. The `ResponseList` attributes of `minOccurs` and `maxOccurs` are set to force at least one possible response to be present in the document. The `UserResponse` element is constructed identically except its `maxOccurs` is set to `1` to ensure we only ever get one `UserResponse`.

XSL Design

Since we are talking about XML, let's talk about how we'll use XSL. Because we'll be using ASP to render HTML and send it to the browser, that's the perfect place to do simple XML to HTML transformations.

There are several places we will employ XSL transformations:

❏   Sending a list of workflow requests to the user. One of our requirements states that the application needs to display all active workflow requests in a nicely formatted manner.

❏   Displaying the details about a particular request. Remember, our XML design ensures we have all the data necessary to work with a workflow request. In this case our XSL will create an HTML form and populate the form controls.

❏   Displaying results when a user submits a response. This is very similar to the last item, except we will not use HTML form controls that accept user input; they will be display only.

We'll look at the XSL code snippets when we get to our ASP code.

ASP Design

Now that we have our communication mechanism designed, let's design one side of the conversation – the ASP side. I'll take the major pieces one at a time.

View Workflow List

Once a user is logged into the workflow system, they are presented with a list of active workflow requests. The list will look like an e-mail program inbox, but with some workflow specific pieces of information. The process is relatively straightforward – after the user logs in, send a request to the workflow engine for their list of requests, transform the workflow engine's XML response using an XSL stylesheet and return HTML to the browser.

The following activity diagram may make it clearer:

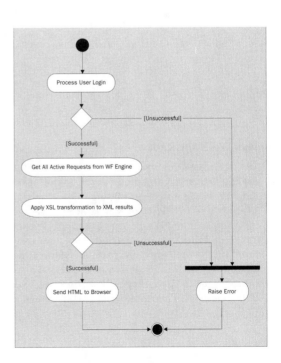

View Workflow Item

Now that we have a list of active workflow requests sitting in the user's browser, we can ask the workflow engine for details on one request in the list. We'll do this by creating another ASP script that sends the workflow engine some of the details it got from the View Workflow List process. The workflow engine will return a single procedure formatted in XML. We will take another XSL script and transform that XML into HTML that contains form controls – text boxes and radio buttons to present step details, including all the possible responses our user is given.

The real workhorse in this step is the XSL. This activity diagram is relatively simple:

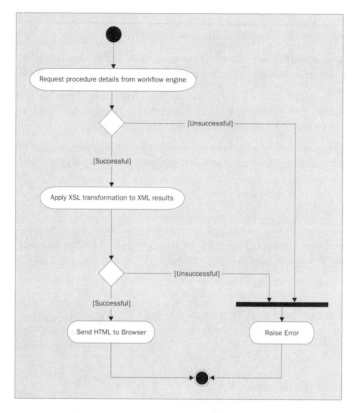

Process Workflow Item

Now we are getting into a slightly more complicated part of the application. Remember that we've already delivered formatted HTML to our user's browser. Say they have reviewed the details of a step and have made a decision. Using their browser they make a selection and press the **Reply** button. The `ProcessItem` ASP script will gather the values of HTML form controls and reformat that data using our XML schema. If no errors are produced, the script will create an instance of the workflow engine and send it the XML that includes our user response. When the engine gets that data it makes decisions based on the user's response and the state of the workflow as it finds it in the database. The engine then sends the XML with included information to indicate processing success or failure and any appropriate messages for the user. The ASP script takes over again by transforming that XML using yet another XSL stylesheet. The resulting HTML is returned to the user as notification of the processing status of their reply.

538

Proving that a picture is worth a thousand words, particularly a thousand of my words, here we go:

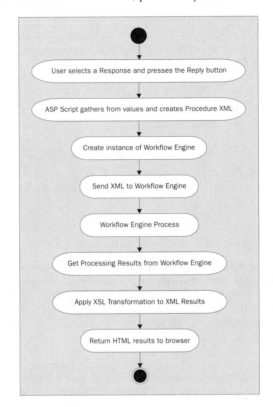

Workflow Engine Design

Now let's take a look at our workflow engine design. Remember we've already stated that it will run in Component Services and will be implemented using Visual Basic. VB makes the construction job a little easier than building the engine in something like C++, but our design should still be decently robust with little regard to a specific development environment.

To deliver those requirements that we stipulated earlier on, the workflow engine needs to know how to process a variety of workflow steps. It also needs to be able to handle the addition of new workflow steps. Remember we are only dealing with four types – Start, Stop, Response, and FYI. What happens when some hot-shot programmer comes along and says "Why can't I implement parallel workflows that branch at some point and come back together later?" or "Can your workflow conditionally launch a second workflow?" So, our design must support our existing rules and make it easy to add new ones.

The workflow engine doesn't just process workflow steps, it also makes sure users are logged in properly, returns lists of active workflow items to users and helps display workflow items' details.

So, with all that in mind, we can start seeing some workflow engine components taking shape. For one thing we need something to manage the whole process – basically, to serve as the public interface to the workflow engine. We'll ask that workflow manager to do a few specific things. First it needs to return a list of open workflow items when a user requests it. It also needs to return an individual procedure whenever a user requests it. Remember the workflow engine thinks of its users as ASP scripts and doesn't care what happens with the XML it produces once the ASP script gets it.

The Workflow Manager Class

The workflow manager class has this definition:

```
clsWorkflowManager

StepManager As clsStepManager

getWorkflowList(in UID As String, in PWD As String) As String

getWorkflowItem(in UID As String, in PWD As String, in workflowID As String,
in ProcedureID As String) As String

executeWorkflow(procedureXML As String) As String
```

getWorkflowList is a public method that returns an XML string containing a list of all active workflow requests for a particular user identified by UID and authenticated with their password coming in as PWD.

getWorkflowItem is another public method that takes a ProcedureID and the workflowID as input parameters. It will return an XML string containing one procedure. Notice, it also requires the UID and PWD.

executeWorkflow is our main working method in this class. It expects an XML-formatted procedure to be passed in. It will pull apart the procedure and process it, looking to see if proper responses have been given, etc. Once processing is done, it will return an XML representation of that same procedure, except this time the status of the procedure may have changed from Open to Complete or Error and there may be text messages in the Message element.

The Step Manager

Because one of our stated design needs is to make this workflow framework extensible to include new types of steps, we need a mechanism to process steps individually that is separate from the Workflow Manager. It is called the Step Manager. The role of this component is to take individual procedures as input, determine the type of procedure, and use the tools it has at its disposal to process that procedure. As long as it knows what tools it has to work with and what procedure types require what tools, then we have some built in flexibility to add new procedures and new procedure-working tools.

We will do this by creating classes for each procedure type (remember steps are procedures). The Step Manager will interrogate a procedure, find its type, and instantiate a proper procedure worker class to do all the work necessary to determine if that procedure is complete and if its rules have been met.

So here is what Step Manager looks like:

```
clsStepManager
#processStep(sProcedureXML As String) As String
```

Sort of disappointing, huh? Well, if you think about how we are relying on individual procedure worker classes to do all the work necessary to process a procedure, then we only need clsStepManager to manage the process.

processStep takes an XML string containing a procedure as input and returns an XML string containing the processed procedure with messages and a change in procedure status. The logic it uses is relatively simple – get the procedure XML as input, parse it, and find the procedure type. When the procedure type is known, a procedure worker class is instantiated to do the work. Once the work is done the results are returned to clsWorkflowManager.

If we added new procedure or step types in the future this is one place we'd have to make a change. Our change would require telling `clsStepManager` that a new procedure type exists and which worker class to use to work on it.

So what does this worker class look like? Regardless of the procedure type they are destined to work on, all of the procedure classes will have some things in common because `clsStepManager` needs a consistent way to talk to them. In fact the only way to ensure our procedure classes will always work with `clsStepManager` is to force them to have a consistent interface. To do this we create the following interface that defines three methods:

```
Interface IProcedureItem

startItem() As Boolean

stopItem() As Boolean

getNextItem()
```

Using this interface `clsStepManager.processStep` can always assume whatever procedure worker class it is working on will have three methods – `startItem`, `stopItem`, and `getNextItem`.

How we implement the logic for stopping a particular item – checking to make sure we've gotten the correct responses, etc. is of no concern to `clsStepManager`. It only cares that we have implemented `IProcedureItem`.

We'll look at this a little closer when we get to the code. The class diagram for our workflow engine looks like this:

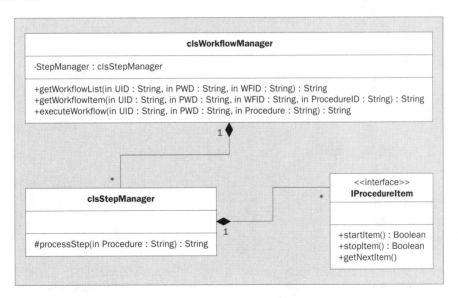

Application Messaging

One last thought before we get into implementing this design. I like to use interaction diagrams to show message passing between components. There are two types of UML interaction diagrams – collaboration and sequence. I chose sequence for no other reason than I think it made sense.

Implementation

Database Model

Let's first look at our database layout. We've basically ignored it until last, which is not by design. It just happened that way. By now you are familiar with workflow and workflow components, so I'll just jump right into the table structure.

Recall we have two parts to our database – workflow metadata and workflow process tracking. The first, metadata, is responsible for keeping our workflow templates and their component steps and rules. The process tracking part is responsible for keeping an updated status of every workflow in process. That means storing the responses users have given to completed steps, start and end dates, etc.

Here's the table layout:

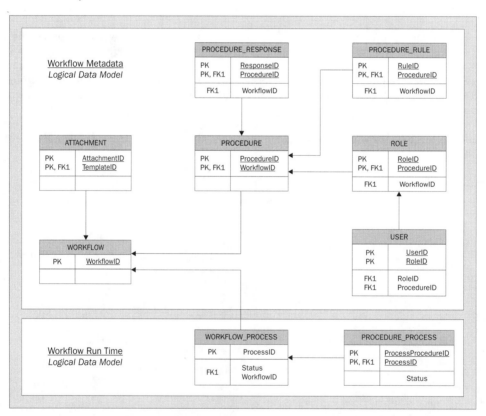

Notice we have a metadata parent table named `Workflow` that has a single child – `Procedure`. Each `Procedure` can have zero or more rules and responses. Each `Procedure` must have a `Role`. And each `Role` must have a `User`.

As far as our run time process tracking is concerned the table structure is relatively simple. `Workflow_Process` tracks open workflows in process. It has a foreign key back to `Workflow`. `Procedure_Process` tracks in process procedure details. It has a foreign key back to `Procedure`.

Here's what our `Workflow` table looks like:

Field	Type	Description	Primary Key
WorkflowID	Integer	Unique sequential workflow ID.	Yes
Name	String	A short name for a workflow.	
Description	String	A longer description of the workflow, its purpose and maybe the routing it will take.	
Originator	String	User name of the person who started the workflow.	
EffectiveDate	Date	Date at which this workflow becomes effective.	
ExpirationDate	Date	Date at which the workflow expires.	
ParentWorkflowID	Integer	WorkflowID of a parent workflow. It is possible to have one workflow start or launch another workflow.	
Status	String	Status of the workflow: Complete, Open, Cancelled, or Error.	

The workflow table basically describes itself. We have fields for storing workflow level details including an effective date for controlling when a workflow becomes available for users to start and an expiration date that controls when workflows can be taken out of production.

Now the `Procedure` table:

Field	Type	Description	Primary Key
ProcedureID	Integer	Unique sequential Procedure ID.	Yes
WorkflowID	Integer	Foreign key back to Workflow Table.	Yes
Name	String	A short display name for this procedure.	
Description	String	A textual description that explains this procedure and its role in the workflow.	
Type	String	Describes the type of procedure – Start, Stop, Response, FYI.	
Priority	String	Assigns the priority of procedure.	
RoleID	Integer	Role assigned to this procedure.	

Our `Procedure` table consists of a foreign key back to the `Workflow` table, `WorkflowID`, so we identify to what workflow a particular procedure belongs. Its `Type` field is used to indicate what type of procedure we are describing. The workflow engine uses this field to determine what type of procedure worker class to instantiate to process a procedure.

In my first data model I included the following two fields in the `Procedure` table:

Field	Type	Description	Primary Key
PreviousProcedureID	Integer	Link to the most immediate procedure. This is used in the execution of some rules.	
NextProcedureID	Integer	Link to the next procedure. This is used in the execution of some rules.	

Their purpose was to link any procedure with its immediate predecessor, `PreviousProcedureID`, and its most immediate successor. I had an image of a linked list in my head. But as I got further into the design, I realized the mechanism that links procedures in a workflow are not direct links between the procedures themselves but virtual links created by the rules we assign to each procedure. As you'll see we will let the `Rule` table create our workflow routing, in effect a virtual path between procedures.

The `Response` table has this design:

Field	Type	Description	Primary Key
ResponseID	Integer	Unique sequential ResponseID.	Yes
ProcedureID	Integer	Foreign key back to the Procedure table.	Yes
ResponseText	String	The response text displayed to the user in a list.	

`Response` has a many to one relationship with our `Procedure` table, enabled by the `ProcedureID` foreign key. The table exists only to store our list of possible responses for any user response procedure type.

Next, the `Rule` table:

Field	Type	Description	Primary Key
RuleID	Integer	Unique sequential Rule ID.	Yes
ProcedureID	Integer	Foreign key back to Procedure Table.	Yes
Type	String	Type of Rule – IsDone or IsResponse.	
IsDoneProcedureID	Integer	ProcedureID to check for completeness if rule type equals IsDone.	
IsResponseProcedureID	Integer	ProcedureID to check is rule type equals IsResponse.	
IsResponseTarget	String	Target response to check for if rule type is IsResponse.	

`Rule` is our first de-normalized database table, because any single record in `Rule` can describe more than one rule type – an `IsDone` rule or an `IsResponse` rule. It has a many-to-one relationship with `Procedure` and is responsible for describing any rules or preconditions we assign to a procedure. In our case we have drastically limited the types of rules we can apply to this workflow. Since we have so few rules, I took the liberty to lump them all into one table. Notice we have a `Type` field that can contain `IsDone` or `IsResponse`. Based on that value we pay attention to other fields in the table.

If the value of `Type` is `IsDone`, then the workflow engine will know it has to check another procedure's status before it will allow this procedure to start. Since `IsDoneProcedureID` stores another `ProcedureID`, it's a simple matter to go and check that `ProcedureID` and get its `Status`. If the value of `Status` is `Complete`, then the rule condition is met and we can continue.

If the value of `Type` is `IsResponse`, then we have to check another `ProcedureID` and determine its response value. We find the `ProcedureID` in the `Rule` field `IsResponseProcedureID`. We also find the target string value the rule is looking for in the `IsResponseTarget` field. If the `IsResponseProcedureID` is found and the value of `Status` is `Complete`, and the response given for that procedure equals `IsResponseTarget`, then our rule condition is met and we continue.

Now let's take the `Role` and `User` tables together:

First the `Role` table:

Field	Type	Description	Primary Key
RoleID	Integer	Unique sequential role ID.	Yes
Name	String	Role name.	
Description	String	Description of the role, its duties, etc.	

Now the `User` table:

Field	Type	Description	Primary Key
UserID	Integer	Unique sequential user ID.	Yes
RoleID	RoleID	Foreign key back to `Role` table.	Yes
FullName	String	User full name.	
UserName	String	Username used to log into the workflow system.	
Password	String	User password.	

This is a relatively simple arrangement. We create roles and link them to procedures by including `RoleID` in the `Procedure` table. For every role, we assign a user. This assignment gives the workflow engine a name and a face to work with, so to speak. When a procedure starts, the workflow engine will find the associated role and work down the database tree to the `User` table. Once it finds the `UserID` associated with the `RoleID` it retrieved from the `Procedure` table, it can continue by assigning that workflow procedure to the `UserName` it found.

One thing to note here is that we can have multiple users assigned to any one role. That makes sense in a way; roles are abstractions of users, giving us the ability to conveniently work with groups of users represented by a particular type of role. However, for our purposes here, we will be assigning one user to one role and leaving it at that. If we assigned multiple users per role, we would have to implement logic that determines which of the user group gets a particular request, and if more than one user gets that request, etc.

Now let's take a look at our Workflow Run Time data model. Remember this is where we'll be tracking active workflows once they've been started.

The `Workflow_Process` table has this structure:

Field	Type	Description	Primary Key
WorkflowProcessID	Integer	Unique sequential workflow process ID.	Yes
WorkflowID	Integer	Foreign key back to Workflow table.	Yes
Status	String	Status of the workflow: Complete, Open, Cancelled or Error.	
StartDateTime	Date	Date the workflow was started.	
CompleteDateTime	Date	Date the workflow was completed either successfully or unsuccessfully.	

`Workflow_Process` is where the workflow engine keeps track of workflow state – its current status, the date and time when the workflow was started, and the date and time when it was completed. While a status is active and being processed normally, its state is said to be Open. If there is a processing error at any point its `Status` is set to `Error`. If a workflow administrator cancels the workflow once it has been started then the `Status` is set to `Cancelled`. Of course, normal termination of a workflow results in a status set to `Complete`.

Notice we have a relationship with the `Workflow` table in our foreign key `WorkflowID`. That is our run time link to the metadata world.

Finally, the `Procedure_Process` table:

Field	Type	Description	Primary Key
ProcedureProcessID	Integer	Unique sequential procedure process ID.	Yes
WorkflowProcessID	Integer	Foreign key back to Workflow_process table.	Yes
ProcedureID	Integer	Foreign key back to Procedure table.	Yes
Status	String	Status of the procedure: Complete, Open, Cancelled, or Error.	

Field	Type	Description	Primary Key
Response	String	Response received from the user: `Accept` or `Reject`.	
UserName	String	The name of the user who is assigned this request.	
StartDateTime	Date	Date the procedure was started.	
CompleteDateTime	Date	Date the procedure was completed.	

`Procedure_Process` is relatively similar to `Workflow_Process`, except it is concerned with procedure level status and responses. Notice we have a `Response` field that contains any response given by the user, if one was requested. We also have a `UserName` field that contains the `UserName` of the workflow user who sent the response back to the workflow engine.

ASP Code

Let's tackle an easy one first – getting the list of active workflow items for a particular user. The following snippet of ASP is part of a script that executes immediately following a successful login, `WorkflowList.asp`:

```
<%@LANGUAGE="VBSCRIPT" %>
<%option explicit %>

<%
  Const XSLPATH = "/XSL/"

  Dim sUID
  Dim sPWD
  dim sWFID
  Dim oWFE
  Dim sProcedureXML
  Dim domProcedures
  Dim domXSL

  sUID = Session("UID")
  sPWD = Session("PWD")

  Set oWFE = Server.CreateObject("WorkFlowEngine.clsWorkflowManager")

  If Not oWFE is Nothing Then
    sProcedureXML = oWFE.getWorkflowList(CStr(sUID), CStr(sPWD))

    If sProcedureXML <> "" Then

      Set domProcedures = Server.CreateObject("MSXML.DOMDocument")
      domProcedures.loadxml sProcedureXML
      Set domXSL = Server.CreateObject("MSXML.DOMDocument")
      domXSL.load Server.MapPath(XSLPATH & "procedurelist.xsl")

      Response.Write domProcedures.transformnode(domXSL)
```

```
      End If
    End If

    Set oWFE = Nothing
    Set domProcedures = Nothing
    Set domXSL = Nothing
 %>
```

Looking at the code you can see I set the path of our XSL stylesheets in a constant. There are better methods of managing your web projects (see the Survey Tool case study in this book), but this technique will work for our purposes.

I get the user's `UserID` and password from previously written session variables. The `Login.asp` script writes those session variables, which I won't present here as it is relatively simple. Then I create a new workflow engine instance using `Server.CreateObject`.

If the `oWFE` instance is properly created I send the `UID` and `PWD` to `getWorkflowList`. In this one line we wrap a lot of processing. That's a nice thing about using components – the details of implementation are hidden. At this point, our ASP pages are just consumers that really don't care how a component is implemented as long as we get expected results.

If a string is returned from `getWorkflowList` then it is passed to the XML parser. A second instance of the XML parser is created for the XSL stylesheet, which is used to transform the XML data into HTML that looks something like this in our web browser:

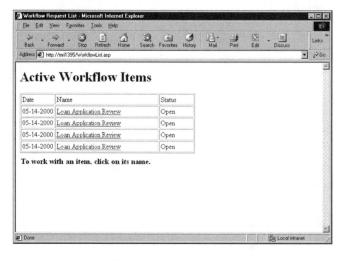

The HTML behind the browser looks like this:

```
<HTML>
<head>
  <title>Workflow Request List</title>
</head>
<body>
  <h1>Active Workflow Items</h1>
  <table cellspacing="2" cellpadding="2" border="1">
    <tr>
```

```
        <td width="20%">Date</td>
        <td width="60%">Name</td>
        <td width="20%">Status</td>
      </tr>
      <tr>
        <td>05-14-2000</td>
        <td>
          <a href="getworkflowitem.ASP?UID=jslater&amp;
            PWD=password&amp;WFID=2&amp;PROCID=41">
            Loan Application Review
          </a>
        </td>
        <td>Open</td>
      </tr>
      <tr>
        <td>05-14-2000</td>
        <td>
          <a href="getworkflowitem.ASP?UID=jslater&amp;
            PWD=password&amp;WFID=2&amp;PROCID=43">
            Loan Application Review
          </a>
        </td>
        <td>Open</td>
      </tr>
      <tr>
        <td>05-14-2000</td>
        <td>
          <a href="getworkflowitem.ASP?UID=jslater&amp;
            PWD=password&amp;WFID=2&amp;PROCID=45">
            Loan Application Review
          </a>
        </td>
        <td>Open</td>
      </tr>
      <tr>
        <td>05-14-2000</td>
        <td>
          <a href="getworkflowitem.ASP?UID=jslater&amp;
            PWD=password&amp;WFID=2&amp;PROCID=46">
            Loan Application Review
          </a>
        </td>
        <td>Open</td>
      </tr>
    </table>
    <table>
      <tr></tr>
      <tr></tr>
      <tr>
        <td><h3>To work with an item, click on its name.</h3></td>
      </tr>
    </table>
  </body>
</HTML>
```

The XSL used to make the table above looks like the following:

```
<xsl:stylesheet xmlns:xsl="http://www.w3.org/TR/WD-xsl">
<xsl:template match="/">
<HTML>
<head>
  <title>Workflow Request List</title>
</head>

<body>
<h1>Active Workflow Items</h1>
<table cellspacing="2" cellpadding="2" border="1">
  <tr>
    <td width='20%'>Date</td>
    <td width='60%'>Name</td>
    <td width='20%'>Status</td>
  </tr>

  <xsl:for-each select='ProcedureList/Procedure'>
    <tr>
      <td><xsl:value-of select="StartDate"/></td>
      <td>
        <a>
          <xsl:attribute name='href'>getWorkflowItem.asp?UID=
            <xsl:value-of select='User/UserName'/>&amp;PWD=
            <xsl:value-of select='User/Password'/>&amp;WFID=
            <xsl:value-of select='@WFID' />&amp;PROCID=
            <xsl:value-of select='@ID' />
          </xsl:attribute>
          <xsl:value-of select='@Name'/>
        </a>
      </td>
      <td><xsl:value-of select="Status"/></td>
    </tr>
  </xsl:for-each>
</table>
<table>
  <tr></tr>
  <tr></tr>
  <tr>
    <td><h3>To work with an item, click on its name.</h3></td>
  </tr>
</table>
</body>
</HTML>
</xsl:template>
</xsl:stylesheet>
```

There are a couple of XSL items worth noting here. First, I use an `<xsl:for-each>` to iterate through the collection of Procedure elements within the ProcedureList root element. I don't know how many Procedure elements I could have, so this list will grow and shrink with request activity.

You might also notice a rather complicated looking value in the middle cell of our little HTML table. This section of code:

```
<td>
  <a>
    <xsl:attribute name='href'>getworkflowitem.ASP?UID=
      <xsl:value-of select='User/UserName'/>&amp;PWD=
      <xsl:value-of select='User/Password'/>&amp;WFID=
      <xsl:value-of select='@WFID' />&amp;PROCID=
      <xsl:value-of select='@ID' />
    </xsl:attribute>
    <xsl:value-of select='@Name'/>
  </a>
</td>
```

Creates this HTML:

```
<td>
  <a href="getWorkflowItem.asp?UID=jslater&amp;
    PWD=password&amp;WFID=2&amp;PROCID=43">
    Loan Application Review
  </a>
</td>
```

What it's actually doing is creating an `<A href>` tag using XSL to provide some of the ASP parameters and the displayed text in the hyperlink. Take a closer look and you'll notice the anchor tag stands alone in the XSL. The `href` attribute actually is defined in a `<xsl:attribute name='href'>` tag. The `WFID=<xsl:value-of select='@ID' />` sequence returns the value stored in the procedure attribute named `ID`, and that gets wrapped into the reference to our next ASP script so it looks like `getWorkflowItem.asp?UID=jslater&PWD=password&WFID=2&PROCID=41` in HTML.

In a browser it all looks like the following:

| 05-14-2000 | Loan Application Review | Open |

Now let's turn our attention to returning a single request item to a user. Remember when we look at a single request, we'll be displaying details about that request including a list of possible responses, if it's a user response step.

The `getWorkFlowItem.asp` ASP page creates a new instance of `clsWorkflowManager` and calls `getWorkflowItem`, expecting to receive an XML string. The code snippet that achieves this is the following:

```
set oWFE = Server.CreateObject("WorkFlowEngine.clsWorkflowManager")

sProcedureXML = oWFE.getWorkflowItem(CStr(sUID), CStr(sPWD), _
                                     CStr(sWFID),CStr(sProcID))
```

When it gets the XML back from the workflow engine, it follows a nearly identical process for transforming the XML into HTML as we did with the request list ASP code. With the exception of the XSL file name, the code is identical. In fact, I copied it from one script to the other. Take a look:

```
Set domProcedures = Server.CreateObject("MSXML.DOMDocument")
domProcedures.loadxml sProcedureXML
```

```
    Set domXSL = Server.CreateObject("MSXML.DOMDocument")
    if domXSL.load(Server.MapPath(XSLPATH & "proceduredetail.xsl")) then
      Response.Write domProcedures.transformnode(domXSL)
    else
      Response.Write domXSL.parseError.reason
    end if
```

Notice we are using `proceduredetail.xsl` in this case to transform our procedure XML instead of `procedurelist.xsl` as in our previous example.

For sake of completeness here is the entire file:

```
<%@LANGUAGE="VBSCRIPT" %>
<%option explicit %>

<%
  Const XSLPATH = "/XSL/"

  Dim sUID
  Dim sPWD
  dim sWFID
  dim sProcID
  Dim oWFE
  Dim sProcedureXML
  Dim domProcedures
  Dim domXSL

  sUID = Request.QueryString("UID")
  sPWD = Request.QueryString("PWD")
  sWFID = Request.QueryString("WFID")
  sProcID = Request.QueryString("PROCID")

  Set oWFE = Server.CreateObject("WorkFlowEngine.clsWorkflowManager")

  If Not oWFE is Nothing Then
    sProcedureXML = oWFE.getWorkflowItem(CStr(sUID), CStr(sPWD), _
                                         CStr(sWFID), CStr(sProcID))

    If sProcedureXML <>"" Then

      Session("ProcedureXML") = sProcedureXML

      Set domProcedures = Server.CreateObject("MSXML.DOMDocument")
      domProcedures.loadxml sProcedureXML
      Set domXSL = Server.CreateObject("MSXML.DOMDocument")
      if domXSL.load(Server.MapPath(XSLPATH & "proceduredetail.xsl")) then
        Response.Write domProcedures.transformnode(domXSL)
      else
        Response.Write domXSL.parseError.reason
      end if
    End If
  End If

  Set oWFE = Nothing
  Set domProcedures = Nothing
  Set domXSL = Nothing
%>
```

The HTML generated by the `proceduredetail.xsl` transformation is a very simple HTML table that looks like the following in our web browser:

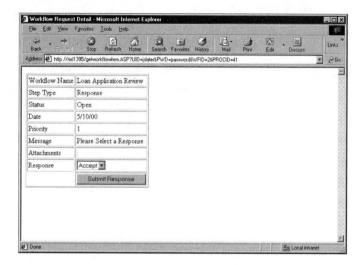

As you can see, it is a rather uninteresting table of two columns. The HTML behind the browser looks like this:

```
<html>
<head>
  <title>Workflow Request Detail</title>
</head>
<body>
  <form action="processitem.asp" method="post">
    <table cellspacing="2" cellpadding="2" border="1">
      <tr>
        <td>workflow name</td>
        <td>Loan application review</td></tr>
      <tr>
        <td>Step Type</td>
        <td>Response</td></tr>
      <tr>
        <td>Status</td>
        <td>Open</td></tr>
      <tr>
        <td>Date</td>
        <td>5/10/00</td></tr>
      <tr>
        <td>Priority</td>
        <td>1</td></tr>
      <tr>
        <td>Message</td>
        <td>Please select a response</td></tr>
      <tr>
        <td>Attachments</td>
        <td>:</td></tr>
      <tr>
        <td>Response</td>
```

```
              <td>
                <select name="cboResponse">
                  <option>Accept</option>
                  <option>Reject</option>
                </select></td></tr>
           <tr>
              <td></td>
              <td>
                <input value="Submit Response" type="submit" name="btnResponse" />
              </td>
           </tr>
         </table>
         <input type="hidden" name="txtUID" value="jslater" />
         <input type="hidden" name="txtPWD" value="password" />
         <input type="hidden" name="txtWFID" value="2" />
         <input type="hidden" name="txtProcID" value="41" />
      </form>
   </body>
   </html>
```

To create the HTML, we use the following XSL:

```
<xsl:stylesheet xmlns:xsl="http://www.w3.org/TR/WD-xsl">
<xsl:template match="/">
<html>
<head>
  <title>Workflow Request Detail</title>
</head>

<body>
<form action="processitem.asp" method="post">
<table cellspacing="2" cellpadding="2" border="1">
  <tr>
     <td>Workflow Name</td>
     <td><xsl:value-of select="Procedure/@name" /></td></tr>
  <tr>
     <td>Step Type</td>
     <td><xsl:value-of select="Procedure/Type" /></td></tr>
  <tr>
     <td>Status</td>
     <td><xsl:value-of select="Procedure/Status" /></td></tr>
  <tr>
     <td>Date</td>
     <td><xsl:value-of select="Procedure/Startdate" /></td></tr>
  <tr>
     <td>Priority</td>
     <td><xsl:value-of select="Procedure/Priority" /></td></tr>
  <tr>
     <td>Message</td>
     <td><xsl:value-of select="Procedure/Message" /></td></tr>
  <tr>
     <td>Attachments</td>
     <td>
       <xsl:value-of select="Procedure/Attachment/Name" />:
       <xsl:value-of select="Procedure/Attachment/Path" /></td></tr>
```

```
      <tr>
        <td>response</td>
        <td>
          <select>
            <xsl:attribute name='name'>cboResponse</xsl:attribute>
            <xsl:for-each select="Procedure/ResponsePool/Response">
              <option>
                <xsl:value-of select="ResponseText" />
              </option>
            </xsl:for-each>
          </select></td></tr>
      <tr>
        <td></td>
        <td>
          <input value='submit response'>
            <xsl:attribute name='type'>submit</xsl:attribute>
            <xsl:attribute name='name'>btnResponse</xsl:attribute>
          </input>
        </td>
      </tr>
    </table>

    <input>
      <xsl:attribute name='type'>hidden</xsl:attribute>
      <xsl:attribute name='name'>txtUID</xsl:attribute>
      <xsl:attribute name='value'>
        <xsl:value-of select='Procedure/User/UserName'/></xsl:attribute>
    </input>
    <input>
      <xsl:attribute name='type'>hidden</xsl:attribute>
      <xsl:attribute name='name'>txtPWD</xsl:attribute>
      <xsl:attribute name='value'>
        <xsl:value-of select='Procedure/User/Password'/></xsl:attribute>
    </input>
    <input>
      <xsl:attribute name='type'>hidden</xsl:attribute>
      <xsl:attribute name='name'>txtWFID</xsl:attribute>
      <xsl:attribute name='value'>
        <xsl:value-of select='Procedure/@WFID' /></xsl:attribute>
    </input>
    <input>
      <xsl:attribute name='type'>hidden</xsl:attribute>
      <xsl:attribute name='name'>txtProcID</xsl:attribute>
      <xsl:attribute name='value'>
        <xsl:value-of select='Procedure/@ID' /></xsl:attribute>
    </input>
    </form>
    </body>
    </html>

  </xsl:template>
  </xsl:stylesheet>
```

The most interesting feature of the `proceduredetail.xsl` stylesheet is the structure that creates the combo box that contains our response texts. That is the following snippet:

```
<tr>
  <td>response</td>
  <td>
    <select>
      <xsl:attribute name='name'>cboResponse</xsl:attribute>
      <xsl:for-each select="Procedure/ResponsePool/Response">
        <option>
          <xsl:value-of select="ResponseText" />
        </option>
      </xsl:for-each>
    </select></td></tr>
```

Let's take a little closer look. The table cell that contains the SELECT control has to have this HTML to have the look and function we want:

```
<tr>
  <td>
    <select name="cboResponse">
      <option>Accept</option>
      <option>Reject</option>
    </select>
  </td>
</tr>
```

It's implemented in XSL as another <xsl:for-each> but this time we are iterating through a potentially limitless number of response elements called ResponsePool. If you refer back to the ResponsePool definition in the schema, every child element will be of type Response and every Response element consists of a ResponseID and ResponseText.

Recall this schema fragment:

```
<ElementType name='ResponseID' content='textOnly' model='closed'
      dt:type='string'>
  <Description>ID used to identify a specific Response</Description>
</ElementType>

<ElementType name='ResponseBody' content='textOnly' model='closed'
      dt:type='string'>
  <Description>The text body of a response</Description>
</ElementType>

<ElementType name='Response' content='eltOnly' model='closed'>
  <Description>A response to a workflow request</Description>
  <element type='ResponseID' />
  <element type='ResponseBody' />
</ElementType>

<ElementType name='ResponseList' content='eltOnly' model='closed'
      minOccurs='1' maxOccurs='*'>
  <Description>List of all possible responses</Description>
  <element type='Response' />
</ElementType>
```

We iterate through every response and create a new OPTION item in the SELECT control. That's done in XSL as follows:

```
<option>
  <xsl:value-of select="ResponseText" />
</option>
```

Notice that we can directly refer to ResponseText without naming parent elements. That is because we are working within a `<xsl:for-each>` loop that takes every Response element one at a time.

When a user has responded to a request item with a valid response, we need to show some confirmation that a process has started, done its work and completed successfully or failed to do its work. We do this by writing XSL to work on our procedure XML, that is similar to proceduredetail.xsl, but will not transform the XML to HTML that takes any kind of user input.

Take the following example. It is almost identical to the proceduredetail.xsl stylesheet, except we've gotten rid of the SELECT control and replaced it with a simple label.

```
<xsl:stylesheet xmlns:xsl="http://www.w3.org/TR/WD-xsl">
<xsl:template match="/">
<html>
<head>
  <title>Workflow Request Detail</title>
</head>

<body>
<h2>Workflow Execution Results</h2>
<form action="workflowlist.asp" method="post">
<table cellspacing="2" cellpadding="2" border="1">
  <tr>
    <td>workflow name</td>
    <td><xsl:value-of select="Procedure/@name" /></td></tr>
  <tr>
    <td>step type</td>
    <td><xsl:value-of select="Procedure/Type" /></td></tr>
  <tr>
    <td>status</td>
    <td><xsl:value-of select="Procedure/Status" /></td></tr>
  <tr>
    <td>date</td>
    <td><xsl:value-of select="Procedure/StartDate" /></td></tr>
  <tr>
    <td>priority</td>
    <td><xsl:value-of select="Procedure/Priority" /></td></tr>
  <tr>
    <td>message</td>
    <td><xsl:value-of select="Procedure/Message/MessageBody" /></td></tr>
  <tr>
    <td>attachments</td>
    <td><xsl:value-of select="Procedure/Attachment/Name" />:
        <xsl:value-of select="Procedure/Attachment/Path" /></td></tr>
  <tr>
    <td>response</td>
    <td>
```

```
            <xsl:value-of select="Procedure/UserResponse/ResponseText" />
      </td></tr>
</table>
<a>
   <xsl:attribute name='href'>WorkflowList.asp </xsl:attribute>
   <h3>Return to your open item list</h3></a>
</form>
</body>
</html>


</xsl:template>
</xsl:stylesheet>
```

Now instead of listing all possible responses for this request, we simply display the response the user gives. The assumption we've made here is that the workflow engine will indicate success or failure using a combination of the Status and Message elements in our Procedure XML. In fact, a successfully completed executeWorkflow will result in something like the following XML:

```
<Procedure ID="003" WorkflowID="002">
   <Name="Request for Approval"</NAME>
   <Description>Loan Application - Sherman Potter</Description>
   <Status>Open</Status>
   <Type>Response</Type>
   <User>
      <FullName>John Slater</FullName>
      <UserName>jslater</UserName>
      <Password>password</Password>
   </User>
   <ResponseList>
      <Response>
         <ResponseID>001</ResponseID>
         <ResponseText>Accept</ResponseText>
      </Response>
      <Response>
         <ResponseID>001</ResponseID>
         <ResponseText>Reject</ResponseText>
      </Response>
   </ResponseList>
   <UserResponse>
      <Response>
         <ResponseID>001</ResponseID>
         <ResponseText>Accept</ResponseText>
      </Response>
   </UserResponse>
   <StartDate>03/19/2000</StartDate>
   <CompleteDate>03/19/2000</CompleteDate>
   <Priority>1</Priority>
   <ExpirationDate/>
   <Message>
      <Body>Your response has been processed successfully. Thank you.</Body>
      <Type>Info</Type>
   </Message>
   <Attactment>
      <Name>Loan Application</Name>
      <FilePath>/Attachments/App102.doc</FilePath>
   </Attactment>
</Procedure>
```

This sure is a nice workflow engine. Check out how polite its message to the user is:

```
<Message>
  <Body>Your response has been processed successfully. Thank you.</Body>
  <Type>Info</Type>
</Message>
```

After being transformed by our procedure execution results stylesheet, the browser displays something like the following:

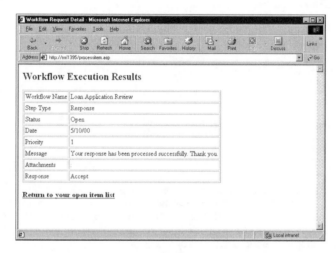

There is nothing too exciting about this, but it is important to always notify users of a process status – whether it succeeded or not. It's frustrating to sit there and wait for an expected notification and never get it.

COM+ Components

When we first talked about our COM+ components we said we'd have a class called clsWorkflowManager that was in charge of the workflow engine. Our ASP scripts instantiate this class and ask it to do work for them. There are three main functions of this class:

❑   Return a list of workflow requests for a particular user.

❑   Return details about a particular workflow request, including possible responses.

❑   Execute a reply to a workflow request.

This is what the class looked like at design time:

```
clsWorkflowManager

StepManager As clsStepManager

getWorkflowList(in UID As String, in PWD As String) As String

getWorkflowItem(in UID As String, in PWD As String, in WFID As String,
in ProcedureID As String) As String

executeWorkflow(procedureXML As String) As String
```

Here is how it looks in VB Code. We'll take each method one at a time.

Let's look at `getWorkflowList` first. It takes a `UID` and finds all open requests for that username from the `Procedure_Process` table. The resulting recordset is converted to XML and returned.

```vb
Public Function getWorkflowList(sUID As String, sPWD As String) As String

On Error GoTo Error_Handler:

  Dim conWF As ADODB.Connection
  Dim rsProcedure As ADODB.Recordset
  Dim sSQL As String
  Dim sProcedureXML As String

  Set conWF = New ADODB.Connection

  With conWF
    .ConnectionTimeout = 10
    .ConnectionString = "DSN=workflow"
    .Open
  End With


  sSQL = "SELECT Procedure_Process.*, Procedure.*, User.* " & _
      "FROM (Role INNER JOIN [User] ON Role.RoleID = User.RoleID) " & _
      "INNER JOIN ([Procedure] INNER JOIN Procedure_Process ON " & _
      "Procedure.ProcedureID = Procedure_Process.ProcedureID) ON " & _
      "Role.RoleID = Procedure.RoleID " & _
      "WHERE (((User.UserName)='" & sUID & "') AND & _
      Procedure_Process.CompleteDate is null)"

  Set rsProcedure = New ADODB.Recordset
  rsProcedure.Open sSQL, conWF, adOpenForwardOnly, adLockReadOnly

  sProcedureXML = "<ProcedureList>"

  While Not rsProcedure.EOF

    sProcedureXML = sProcedureXML & _
      "<Procedure ID='" & rsProcedure("ProcedureProcessID") & "'WFID='" & _
      rsProcedure("WorkflowID") & "' Name='" & rsProcedure("Name") & "'>" &_
      "<Description>" & rsProcedure("Description") & "</Description>" & _
      "<Status>" & rsProcedure("Status") & "</Status>" & _
      "<Type>" & rsProcedure("Type") & "</Type>" & _
      "<User>" & _
      "<FullName>" & rsProcedure("FullName") & "</FullName>" & _
      "<UserName>" & rsProcedure("UserName") & "</UserName>" & _
      "<Password>" & rsProcedure("Password") & "</Password>" & _
      "</User>" & _
      "<ResponsePool></ResponsePool>" & _
      "<UserResponse></UserResponse>" & _
      "<StartDate>" & Format$(Now, "mm-dd-yyyy") & "</StartDate>" & _
      "<CompleteDate></CompleteDate>" & _
      "<Priority>" & rsProcedure("Priority") & "</Priority>" & _
      "<ExpirationDate/><Message/><Attachment/></Procedure>"
```

```
        rsProcedure.MoveNext

    Wend

    sProcedureXML = sProcedureXML & "</ProcedureList>"

    rsProcedure.Close
    conWF.Close

    getWorkflowList = sProcedureXML

    Set rsProcedure = Nothing
    Set conWF = Nothing

    Exit Function
Error_Handler:

    m_objContext.SetAbort
    Err.Raise vbObjectError, ERROR_SOURCE, Err.Description
    Exit Function

End Function
```

I don't think you'll find anything unusual here. An ADO recordset is created that contains data from `Procedure`, `Procedure_Process`, `Role`, and `User` tables. That recordset describes all open requests for a particular user.

The next step is to generate an XML document that matches our schema. There are two ways to do this – create an XML string manually or use the parser in MSXML to build the document one element at a time. I chose the easy way out with the following code snippet:

```
    sProcedureXML = sProcedureXML & _
      "<Procedure ID='" & rsProcedure("ProcedureProcessID") & "'WFID='" & _
      rsProcedure("WorkflowID") & "' Name='" & rsProcedure("Name") & "'>" &_
      "<Description>" & rsProcedure("Description") & "</Description>" & _
      "<Status>" & rsProcedure("Status") & "</Status>" & _
      "<Type>" & rsProcedure("Type") & "</Type>" & _
      "<User>" & _
      "<FullName>" & rsProcedure("FullName") & "</FullName>" & _
      "<UserName>" & rsProcedure("UserName") & "</UserName>" & _
      "<Password>" & rsProcedure("Password") & "</Password>" & _
      "</User>" & _
      "<ResponsePool></ResponsePool>" & _
      "<UserResponse></UserResponse>" & _
      "<StartDate>" & Format$(Now, "mm-dd-yyyy") & "</StartDate>" & _
      "<CompleteDate></CompleteDate>" & _
      "<Priority>" & rsProcedure("Priority") & "</Priority>" & _
      "<ExpirationDate/><Message/><Attachment/></Procedure>"
```

I happen to think this technique is faster and easier than building an XML document one element at a time using `MSXML.DOMDocument.createElement`.

Here is the code for the function that returns the XML for one procedure. Notice we have some extra processing for the `ResponseList` element.

```
Public Function getWorkflowItem(sUID As String, sPWD As String, sWFID As String,
sProcID As String) As String

  Dim conWF As ADODB.Connection
  Dim rsProcedure As ADODB.Recordset
  Dim rsResponse As ADODB.Recordset
  Dim rsAttachment As ADODB.Recordset
  Dim sSQL As String
  Dim sResponseXML As String
  Dim sProcedureXML As String

  Set conWF = New ADODB.Connection

  With conWF
    .ConnectionTimeout = 10
    .ConnectionString = "DSN=workflow"
    .Open
  End With

  sSQL = "SELECT Response.*, Procedure_Process.ProcedureProcessID " & _
         "FROM ([Procedure] INNER JOIN Procedure_Process ON " & _
         "Procedure.ProcedureID = Procedure_Process.ProcedureID) " & _
         "INNER JOIN Response ON Procedure.ProcedureID = & _
         Response.ProcedureID " & _
         "WHERE (((Procedure_Process.ProcedureProcessID)=" & sProcID & "))"

  Set rsResponse = New ADODB.Recordset
  rsResponse.Open sSQL, conWF, adOpenForwardOnly, adLockReadOnly

  While Not rsResponse.EOF
    sResponseXML = sResponseXML & _
      "<Response>" & _
      "<ResponseID>" & rsResponse("ResponseID") & "</ResponseID>" & _
      "<ResponseText>" & rsResponse("ResponseText") & "</ResponseText>" & _
      "</Response>"
    rsResponse.MoveNext
  Wend

  rsResponse.Close
  Set rsResponse = Nothing

  sSQL = "SELECT Procedure.*, Procedure_Process.*, User.*, " & _
         "Procedure_Process.ProcedureProcessID " & _
         "FROM (Role INNER JOIN ([Procedure] INNER JOIN " & _
         "Procedure_Process ON Procedure.ProcedureID = " & _
         "Procedure_Process.ProcedureID) ON Role.RoleID = " & _
         "Procedure.RoleID) INNER JOIN [User] ON Role.RoleID = " & _
         "User.RoleID WHERE (((Procedure_Process.ProcedureProcessID)=" & _
         sProcID & "))"

  Set rsProcedure = New ADODB.Recordset
  rsProcedure.Open sSQL, conWF, adOpenForwardOnly, adLockReadOnly

  sProcedureXML = sProcedureXML & _
    "<Procedure ID='" & rsProcedure("ProcedureProcessID") & "' WFID='" & _
```

```
    rsProcedure("WorkflowID") & _
    "' Name='" & rsProcedure("Name") & "'>" & _
    "<Description>" & rsProcedure("Description") & "</Description>" & _
    "<Status>" & rsProcedure("Status") & "</Status>" & _
    "<Type>" & rsProcedure("Type") & "</Type>" & _
    "<User>" & _
    "<FullName>" & rsProcedure("FullName") & "</FullName>" & _
    "<UserName>" & rsProcedure("UserName") & "</UserName>" & _
    "<Password>" & rsProcedure("Password") & "</Password>" & _
    "</User>" & _
    "<ResponsePool>" & sResponseXML & "</ResponsePool>" & _
    "<UserResponse><ResponseID></ResponseID>" & _
    "<ResponseText></ResponseText></UserResponse>" & _
    "<StartDate>" & rsProcedure("StartDate") & "</StartDate>" & _
    "<CompleteDate></CompleteDate>" & _
    "<Priority>" & rsProcedure("Priority") & "</Priority>" & _
    "<ExpirationDate>" & rsProcedure("CompleteDate") & _
    "</ExpirationDate><Message><MessageID></MessageID>" & _
    "<MessageBody>Please Select a Response</MessageBody>" & _
    "</Message><Attachment> </Attachment></Procedure>"

    rsProcedure.Close
    conWF.Close

    getWorkflowItem = sProcedureXML

    Set rsProcedure = Nothing
    Set conWF = Nothing

    Exit Function
Error_Handler:

    m_objContext.SetAbort
    Err.Raise vbObjectError, ERROR_SOURCE, Err.Description
    Exit Function

End Function
```

To create the `ResponseList` XML source, I simply create another recordset that finds all the Responses our Administrator might have created and assigned to this procedure. It simply loops through the recordset and creates the following XML structure:

```
<ResponseList>
  <Response>
    <ResponseID></ResponseID>
    <ResponseText></ResponseText>
  </Response>
</ResponseList>"
```

There is one last method in `clsWorkflowManager` – `executeWorkflow`. Since this is the key method of the workflow engine let's spend a little time here. You will find that explaining how `executeWorkflow` works will require an understanding of `IProcedureItem` and our procedure rule classes.

First, here's the code for executeWorkFlow:

```
Public Function executeWorkflow(ProcedureXML As String) As String

    Dim oStepManager As clsStepManager
    Set oStepManager = New clsStepManager

    executeWorkflow = oStepManager.processStep(ProcedureXML)

End Function
```

All the code does is create an instance of the clsStepmanager class and call its one and only method, processStep:

```
Public Function processStep(sProcedureXML As String) As String

    Dim xmlDoc As MSXML.DOMDocument
    Dim xmlStartNode As MSXML.IXMLDOMNode
    Dim xmlNewNode As MSXML.IXMLDOMNode
    Dim sType As String
    Dim oProcWorker As IProcedureItem
    Dim oNextProc As IProcedureItem

    processStep = "Error"

    Set xmlDoc = New DOMDocument
    If xmlDoc.loadXML(sProcedureXML) Then
      Set xmlStartNode = xmlDoc.documentElement
      sType = xmlStartNode.selectSingleNode("Type").Text

      Select Case xmlStartNode.selectSingleNode("Type").Text
        Case "Response"
          Set oProcWorker = New clsResponseProcedure
        Case "Start"
          Set oProcWorker = New clsStartProcedure
        Case "Stop"
          Set oProcWorker = New clsStopProcedure
        Case "FYI"
          Set oProcWorker = New clsFYIProcedure
      End Select

      oProcWorker.Populate xmlDoc

      If oProcWorker.IsProcedureComplete Then
        oProcWorker.procedureStop

        Set oNextProc = oProcWorker.getNextProcedure

        If Not oNextProc Is Nothing Then
          oNextProc.procedureStart
        End If
        xmlDoc.documentElement.selectSingleNode("Message").childNodes.Item(1).Text = _
          "Your response has been processed successfully. Thank you."
```

```
          Else
   xmlDoc.documentElement.selectSingleNode("Message").childNodes.Item(1).Text = _
          "A required procedure was not completed."
      End If

   Else
      Dim strErrText As String
      Dim xmlPE As MSXML.IXMLDOMParseError

      Set xmlPE = xmlDoc.parseError
       With xmlPE
        strErrText = "Your XML Document failed to load" & _
            "due the following error." & vbCrLf & _
            "Error #: " & .errorCode & ": " & xmlPE.reason & _
            "Line #: " & .Line & vbCrLf & _
            "Line Position: " & .linepos & vbCrLf & _
            "Position In File: " & .filepos & vbCrLf & _
            "Source Text: " & .srcText & vbCrLf & _
            "Document URL: " & .url
       End With
   End If

   Set xmlPE = Nothing

   processStep = xmlDoc.xml

   End Function
```

The function uses an instance of MSXML.DOMDocument to load the procedure XML as the input parameter. If no errors result, it will find the childElement named Type. Using the value stored in that Type element it applies the following case statement, which results in an instantiated procedure worker class.

```
      Select Case xmlStartNode.selectSingleNode("Type").Text
        Case "Response"
           Set oProcWorker = New clsResponseProcedure
        Case "Start"
           Set oProcWorker = New clsStartProcedure
        Case "Stop"
           Set oProcWorker = New clsStopProcedure
        Case "FYI"
           Set oProcWorker = New clsFYIProcedure
      End Select
```

processStep then tells the worker class to populate itself using the procedure XML passed into the function. Once that is done, we ask oProcWorker if it is done working as a procedure. If it is, we tell it to stop itself and ask it for its next procedure. Once we get an instance of the next procedure, we ask that procedure to start itself.

Notice the code that manages the procedures doesn't really care what type of procedure it is working on. It knows to expect certain methods regardless of procedure worker class type. To get this type of behavior we created an interface called IProcedureItem that lists those methods clsStepManager can always expect from the procedure worker classes.

So when VB sees this code:

```
Dim oProcWorker As IProcedureItem
Dim oNextProc As IProcedureItem
```

it can make some assumptions about what to expect to find in `oProcWorker` and `oNextProc`, our working procedure class and the instance that gets returned from `oProcWorker.getNextProcedure()`.

In the case statement we can instantiate any new class and assign it to `oProcWorker` or `oNextProc`, as long as those instantiated classes implement `IProcedureItem`.

We then leave it up to our procedure worker classes to implement the methods in the interface however they want. `clsStepManager` doesn't really care as long as it gets a response back that it expects.

Here's what `clsResponseProcedure` looks like without code. Notice the only methods in the class come from `IProcedureItem`:

```
Option Explicit

Implements IProcedureItem

Private Function IProcedureItem_getNextProcedure() As IProcedureItem
  'Implementation here
End Function

Private Function IProcedureItem_IsProcedureComplete() As Boolean
  'Implementation here
End Function

Private Function IProcedureItem_procedureStart() As Boolean
  'Implementation here
End Function

Private Function IProcedureItem_procedureStop() As Boolean
  'Implementation here
End Function

Public Sub Populate(domProcedure As MSXML.DOMDocument)
  'Implementation here
End Sub
```

So, our `IProcedureItem` interface gives us some built-in flexibility. When we go to add another procedure type – say a branch or join procedure, we simply create a new class and implement `IProcedureItem`. Then, when we add it to the `Case` statement in `clsStepManager.executeWorkflow()` the code there still works.

Summary

We've covered quite a bit in this case study. Let's briefly review what we covered and some of the things we learned.

I tried to structure this chapter in a form most projects would have. We started by discussing what workflow was and what core components any workflow application should have. From there we developed a Product Vision that led to specific functional requirements that we developed with the help of use cases.

The functional requirements led us to an application architecture that included a core workflow engine implemented as Visual Basic components, Active Server Pages as the method to manage user interaction with the workflow engine, and XML as the method of passing data between ASP pages and VB components. We took advantage of even more XML technology by writing XSL transformations that rendered HTML from our XML data sets.

The application framework we were left with at the end serves as an example of how well ASP and XML work together. It illustrates how ASP can communicate with other applications using XML as a data exchange technique. Our ASP pages were able to communicate with a workflow engine implemented as VB components in XML. Similarly our ASP pages were able to return properly formatted content to browsers using XSL transformations.

In conclusion, I think this case study serves as an example of applications that are becoming more commonplace. It is web based, it relies on seamless interfaces to other applications or components, and it requires a large amount of flexibility. Using ASP and XML together is a combination that you may find useful as you are asked to develop these types of application.

Case Study – Using XML and TIP for Distributed Web Transactions

In these Internet times, information is everything. It flows around with no barriers at all. Or, at least it should do. Reality is different; you expose services using a single technology and the data carried by these services can be read only by components that use the same technology. XML is trying to tackle this problem. If you expose your services using XML, everyone out there can use them. You can bring back to life old procedures lying idle on mainframes, mix different distributed technologies and make heterogeneous operating systems communicate with each other.

Few technologies have gained so much attention in recent years as XML. Nowadays, all the major companies are planning to integrate XML into the database layer, as a publishing technology, as a document model, as an add-in to their products, and so on.

XML by itself, though, is not enough. After all, it is only a standard to delimit text data. We need rich infrastructures based upon it to be able to fulfill the requirements of modern distributed systems. What we want to do here is present an example of XML being used as a communication protocol not only to exchange data, but also to call methods on remote components.

But methods cannot exist in isolation. They can, however, be bound in transactions. As soon as you start to use your chosen protocol in a real project to execute function calls on distributed components, you suddenly need some form of transaction. If you choose an XML based protocol like **XML-RPC**, which will be described later on, or **SOAP** (Simple Object Access Protocol) for that matter, then you really also need a transaction protocol that is as "Internet friendly" as XML; a transaction protocol that spans operating systems and component models. What you need, is **TIP** which stands for **Transaction Internet Protocol.** We shall also be explaining this relatively new protocol later on in this case study.

Transaction Internet Protocol is described in RFC 2371 and 2372.

There are many explications of the term XML and a number of proposed uses for this technology. In this case study we will be discussing XML as a protocol to connect different applications and systems.

This discussion is actually an extension of case studies presented in "Professional XML" published by Wrox Press (ISBN 1-861003-11-0). This case study adds heterogeneous distributed transactions to the mix.

Business Needs

The sample business that we'll be using concerns motor vehicles. The company's name is **LUMA** and it is basically a reseller of cars and other road vehicles. No need to guess what the significance of the name is (Luca and Mario, obviously!).

With the ongoing growth of the Internet, LUMA decides not to miss out on the commercial opportunities that the Web offers, and adds a web site dimension to the business. From this case study perspective, the primary purpose of the site is essentially to present the client with a list of vehicles and let the client order what he or she needs. At the same time, the site should be able to save time and resources by automating the various tasks involved in processing an order.

The Application Domain

However, the reality of the situation is that LUMA is not at the center of the world. It can't instruct its business partners, at the click of a finger, to prepare their systems to process orders in this new LUMA format. Each single company has its own way of doing this kind of thing, and LUMA has no authority to make them change.

So, one solution would be to integrate heterogeneous systems. But then there are other issues to address. This set up must take into account security, scalability, graphical appeal, and all the usual challenges of modern web-based applications. To keep our case as simple as possible, we won't dwell too much on these matters. Instead, we'll be concentrating largely on the primary considerations: integration and transactions.

Let's take a look at a possible working scenario for the LUMA Company:

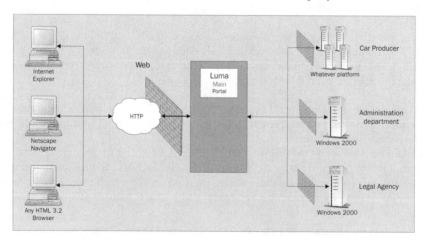

Here we have:

1. The LUMA main portal – this is the place every client points his browser to. It must coordinate the operations among the heterogeneous systems and present the user with a list of motor vehicles.

2. One sample vehicle producer server – this is where LUMA wants to place orders.

3. LUMA administration department server – it must be notified of every order placed.

4. A legal agency server – it must be notified of every order placed to prepare the needed documents.

5. Firewalls at various levels between the servers and the clients. Though firewalls are an essential part of a real-world distributed architecture, for the sake of simplicity we will not be impelementing them in this case study.

LUMA can take control maybe of the administration department server, but all the others systems roll their own software and hardware configurations. Let's suppose it has no control over the administration server too.

Constraints

So, what does LUMA require from each of its partners?

❑ A computer

❑ A TCP port for HTTP transactions

❑ A second TCP port to enable communication via the TIP protocol

Please note that these are very loose requirements. You can expect a web server to be available on almost every platform; it is probably the weakest assumption to make about a communication protocol.

Solution Analysis

In this case study, we use a lightweight approach to analysis. We basically formalize as much as we need to incorporate in the design. We present use cases and sequence diagrams to describe the system we are building (the to-be domain).

Use Cases

Use cases are a very useful tool to describe the expected behavior of a software system. They are part of Unified Modeling Language (UML), and nowadays form the starting point of modern object-oriented methodologies. So the external behavior of the system is described in terms of one use case diagram.

For a full description of use cases, please refer to the Wrox book "Instant UML" (ISBN 1-861000-87-1).

There were many use cases involved in the process of putting the LUMA Company on the Web – too many for all to be described here. We will concentrate on the two main ones. This first example represents the core of the LUMA business, which is to sell vehicles. In this diagram we have two very simple use cases representing the typical interaction with the LUMA Cars portal:

❑ The first one concerns browsing the catalog

❑ The second one is about purchasing the chosen vehicle

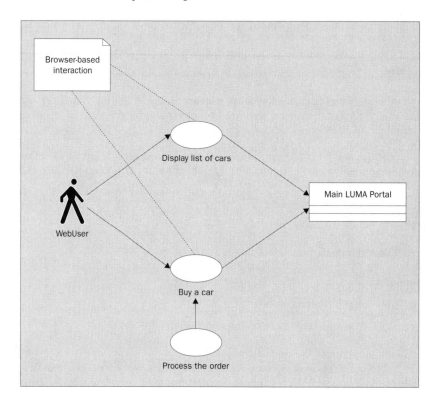

Sequence Diagrams

Sequence diagrams are an important part of UML too. They are very well suited to represent the dynamic interactions among various pieces of a system. They are used as an aid in understanding the message flow among the components of the LUMA distributed application.

Here we use them to describe the previous two cases.

Presenting a Vehicle List

This is the user interface as seen by the client:

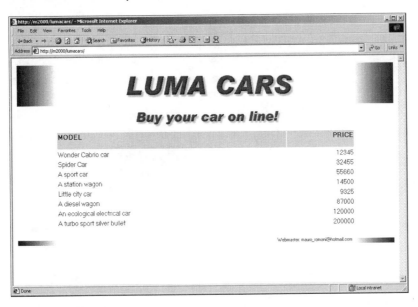

The first use case is probably the easiest to understand. There is not that much to say about it except that it covers the process of going to the car models database, and presenting the client with a list of models to choose from. As far as the code is concerned, this is a classic case of using ASP to talk to a COM component to generate the output.

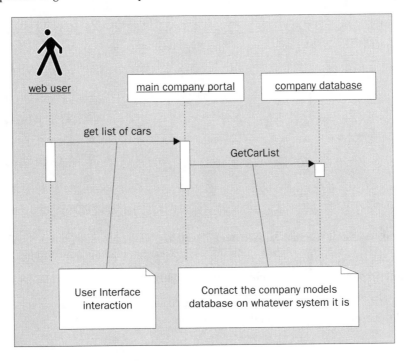

Registering the Client Order

When the client comes to make an order, this is the interface that he or she is presented with:

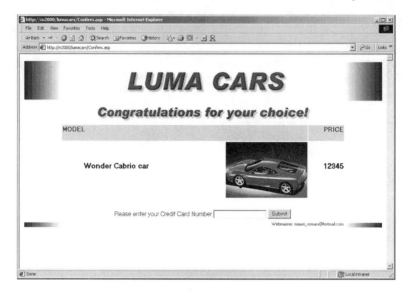

This action is a little more complex than the previous one. Take a look at the sequence diagram below:

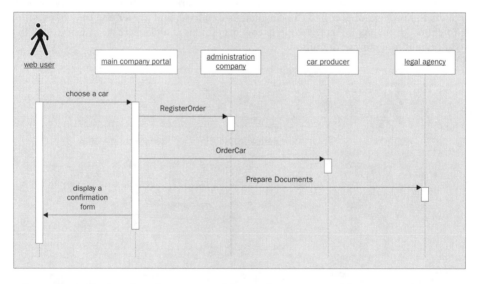

It basically consists of a distributed transaction among three heterogeneous systems. When the client chooses a car model to buy, the LUMA main portal application must do three things:

- ❑ Register the order with the Administration Department
- ❑ Order the car from the appropriate car producer
- ❑ Send the details of the order to the legal agency

These steps must be done in an all-or-nothing fashion. There must never be a case where only part of the whole procedure is carried out. To ensure that all three steps are completed satisfactorily, we will employ transactions. There is nothing inherently difficult about transactions. We use them all the time in our applications, whether we are aware of it or not. However, it is the distributed environment that can sometimes make transactions seem more complex.

What makes transactions a little less simple is the fact that we potentially have firewalls between the web server and all the other applications involved in the transaction, and we cannot presume they are on the same machine or even on the same network. Such a scenario is common in the real world. A company doesn't have to manage all its business by itself; it can delegate certain specialized tasks to third parties. Alternatively, a company could be so big that the machines that host the administration system would be on a completely different network from that of the web server. Maybe LUMA will be the next NASDAQ champion in the book case study area! So let's get ready for the big time and make the Administration Department an external entity.

Solution Design

Our solution is not tied to this particular problem. However, it is meant to be a kind of framework solution. We have tried to maintain a clear separation between business logic for this particular case study and any applications that can be used in other situations.

The COM+ based implementation of the framework requires Windows 2000. This is due to the fact that the Distributed Transaction Coordinator that is shipped with Windows 2000 supports the TIP protocol and we used the interfaces to bring up a TIP transaction offered by COM+ Services. Otherwise you can easily figure out that the framework is really independent of the technology so long as you have a machine with a web server and a TIP-enabled transaction manager.

Infrastructure Design

It is better to start with a picture of our solution just to present some context for the rest of the discussion. Here is a schematic view encompassing all the pieces of the puzzle:

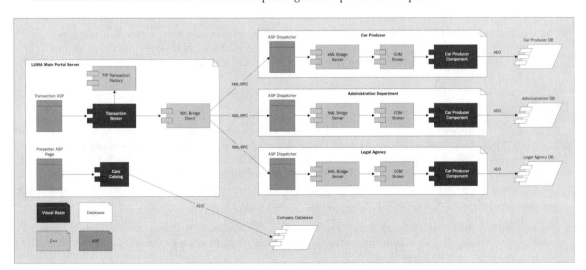

We tried to make a strong distinction between the infrastructure pieces and the business logic components. At the same time we separated the normal ASP/COM+ duties in the first use case from the more advanced requirements of the distributed transaction in the second one. You can see this in the picture: components in the lower part encompass the first use case, components in the upper part encompass the second one.

Now we'll look at the various pieces of our solution and the role each one plays in the overall design. There is a more detailed description, with code fragments for all of them, in a later section.

Some of these parts are ASP pages; others are components written in VB. However, we've also used C++ components, created using ATL (Active Template Library). We used ATL essentially for speed and flexibility, and to create a framework that can be easily ported to different platforms. For this purpose, the Xerces XML parser (created by the Apache group) was used, which is a freely available C++ implementation of XML-RPC.

Don't worry if you're not a C++ programmer – these components are available to download from the Wrox web site at www.wrox.com. However, if you are a C++ guru interested in looking at how they work, and want to see the code for these components, it is included and discussed later in the study.

The Presenter, the Confirm, and the Submit ASP Pages

These are standard ASP pages. The Presenter page just takes the list of vehicles from a COM+ component and presents it to the user. The user can then click on a model to buy it.

We have compiled the sample in Windows 2000 using Visual Studio 6 service pack 3.

When the user clicks on a model, the presenter page calls the Confirm page. This asks the user for a Credit Card ID. The data is then posted to the Submit page that calls the Transaction Broker COM+ component to start the distributed transactions.

OK folks, there's nothing esoteric going on here!

The Cars Catalog

This is a standard MTS/COM+ configured component. It is called from the main ASP page to present a detailed list of the car models available in the LUMA Company site. It receives the list from the company database, and sends it to the Presenter page. This component and the Presenter ASP page encompass the first use case.

The Transaction Broker

This is the component that takes care of starting the TIP transaction and gets it back to the user. It could be placed in a dedicated server on its own. Once again, it is a simple MTS/COM+ configured component. As this is not part of the infrastructure, but really business logic, it is coded in Visual Basic. The Transaction Broker component acts as a wrapper over all our business logic, masking all the implementation details. It gives us a very simple interface over the company business rules, enabling us to change everything if, for example, our company has a growth spurt.

So how does it fulfill such a complex operation using a distributed heterogeneous transaction? It is really quite simple; it uses two infrastructure components – one to manage the TIP, and the other one to call methods on remote servers.

We'll treat each of these in turn.

The TIP Transaction Factory

This is a very simple ATL COM+ component. It must be configured as "Requires new transaction".

Its only purpose is to start a local transaction and return the TIP ID to the client for that transaction. This TIP ID can then be sent by the caller to the remote servers, to enable them to enlist the distributed transaction that it identifies.

The XML Bridge Client

This is an ATL COM component that implements the client part of the XML-RPC protocol. It can be called very easily from Visual Basic. It automatically translates VB function calls in XML-RPC calls, sends them to a remote HTTP server, and gets back the result as a native VB type or a COM object where there is no suitable VB type (for structures and arrays). If there is an error in the remote server it translates the error XML stream to a Visual Basic style exception. These last components are two parts of the reusable components of the framework.

We can now move to the "transaction participants" side. We will describe only one remote server design because the three of them are quite similar. Let's take the Car Producer server as an example.

The ASP Dispatcher

This is a super-simple ASP page, but it plays a very important role in the framework. It is the page called by the XML Bridge Client, and therefore is the first piece of software that has a grasp on the function call.

The page simply creates an instance of the XML Bridge Server, and assigns it the task of managing the request. It calls a function of the XML Bridge Server, passes the ASP Request object and then returns the result of the function call in the Response object.

This framework is used in real projects, and it's constantly evolving, so we will implement this procedure as an IIS ISAPI. Check out http://www.genoavalley.org/xmlrpc to see how we did it. Anyway this way is simpler and more didactic.

The XML Bridge Server

This is one of the cooler components in the entire framework. It is an ATL COM component and its duties are to:

❑ Take the Request object and extract the XML-RPC request string

❑ Extract the name of the function to call from the XML stream

❑ Convert the parameters of the call to an array of Variants

❑ Create the COM Broker and call it with the function name and the given parameters

❑ Return the result converted in XML-RPC to the ASP page

Wow! What a busy component it is!

Actually to use it, you don't have to do anything at all. You just write standard Visual Basic COM+ components, and the framework will call your code if a request arrives for them.

The COM Broker

This is actually the component that really creates your particular Business Component and calls its functions. It is an ATL COM+ component and it exposes only one function. You call it passing a string as the first parameter, and an array of variant as the second.

The format of the first parameter is:

```
[TIP:]ProgID.FunctionName
```

If the whole string starts with "TIP:", then the first parameter of the array of variants must be the TIP ID to enlist the component into. If the string doesn't start with "TIP:" then the component is created and the function is called in its normal context.

This component is never actually called by the ASP page or by any business entity. Only the XML Bridge Server uses it. It is documented here only to expose part of the inner working for a C++ user to understand.

The single function of the IBroker interface is Execute. In our implementation, this function parses the string passed as a parameter to see:

❑ The ProgID of the component

❑ The function name to be invoked

❑ If the component is part of an Internet Transaction

If the component is to be part of an Internet Transaction, specified by the parameter TIP, this function brings up the "Byot.ByotServerEx" component and queries for the ICreateWithTipTransactionEx interface. An instance of the required component is then created using the method CreateInstance of the ICreateWithTipTransactionEx interface passing it the TIP URL.

When we have an instance of our actual component, we can query the IDispatch interface, find the method required using GetIDsOfNames and then invoke the method passing it the parameters.

The Car Producer Business Component

This is an ordinary COM+ configured component that accesses data from a database. It can be written in whatever language you like. We wrote it in Visual Basic for clarity.

This component is marked "Transaction Required" because it must participate in the TIP transaction. This participation is totally transparent. There is no point in the code at which you can guess it is running in a TIP transaction. You can totally reuse whichever component you previously kept on the server without modifying it. It is the infrastructure that places it in the transaction. It is a simple VB application that updates the Car Producer local database with the order from the LUMA Company. We have a few other components implementing the business rules; for example, the Administration department and Legal Agency, but in this simple example they are very similar so we'll leave it to you to view the implementation details.

In our test environment, we created a distinct COM+ application for every business component. So we have an application called Administration with the Administration.Prepare component and so on. We can, however, figure out a more complex scenario in which every department has a different location, even external to the organization. In such a case, all the departments would have their own implementation of the framework, even on their own proprietary systems. But for the sake of simplicity you can reproduce the entire environment on your single machine.

Moreover, we have a COM+ application containing the three components used by the ASP page: LUMACars.Catalog, LUMATTFactory, and Transaction.Submit.

> **Just a tip on the installation: all the business components have to be marked as Require Transaction.**

Encapsulation All Around

What is encapsulation and why it is so important? The concept behind this term is very simple. Encapsulation is just a way to hide the inner workings of something behind some sort of interface.

There are many kinds of encapsulation around with different pros and cons. They go from code encapsulation, like functions in a procedural language or classes in an object oriented one, to binary encapsulation. In our opinion, the latter is a superior form because it hides even the implementation details such as the programming language, or the calling convention, and the other technical stuff.

The ability to change the behavior of one component at runtime without invalidating the others referring to it, is one of the big benefits of Component Based Design (CBD). Our framework is component-based in that, the units of granularity are components, not classes or functions. More than that, it is a COM component framework.

One of the typical patterns in a COM component framework is the division between C++ and VB code. Usually this kind of system is comprised of complex C++ based infrastructure components and simple Visual Basic business logic components. The normal user will only need to understand how to use the high-level business components, whereas the "power user" can modify the low-level infrastructure to better suit his or her needs.

Exposing Business Logic Through XML

The fact that the business logic layer is all encapsulated behind an XML curtain is one of the most obvious benefits of this approach. It is very important that there is no modification to do to a component to expose it as an XML service to the world.

> *Here we describe the exposition of a business layer based on COM+, but we have other implementations too. You can check out the site www.genoavalley.org/xmlrpc to download our Enterprise JavaBeans based framework. It exposes all your EJB components through XML-RPC.*

One of the important things to keep in mind in the case study is that our XML Bridge Client can talk with a server running on any operating system because it communicates in XML. You are not restricted to using ASP on Windows 2000.

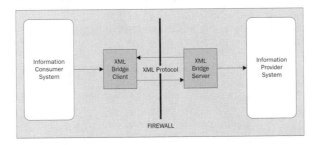

Wire Protocol

XML-RPC is a very useful protocol. It's very simple to understand and implement. This is probably its best quality (for a full discussion of XML-RPC consult **www.xmlrpc.com**). But it is not the only protocol around.

Our framework uses it, but it is really only encapsulated in two of our components: the XML Bridge Client and the XML Bridge Server. It should be no problem at all to use the alternative protocol, SOAP, as a wire protocol (for more information about SOAP you can go to Chapter 15). You would just have to substitute the previous two components with SOAP-enabled ones.

If you decide to use SOAP, you will only have to replace the two components shown below in a darker shade:

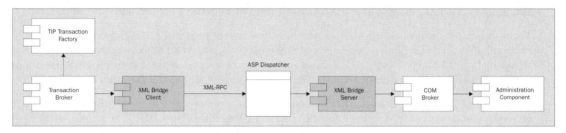

Transaction Protocol

We tried to encapsulate the notion of transactions, and we succeeded in part. If you look at all the server side infrastructures, you will see that you don't have to do anything special to expose your COM+ components. The notion of TIP transaction is totally hidden inside the COM Broker implementation. To modify it, you just have to modify or substitute this component.

On the client side, the whole notion of a TIP transaction is implemented inside the TIP Transaction Factory, so you have a single point to refer to. The use of this component is quite obvious. You call `BeginTransaction`, `Commit`, and `Rollback` to delimitate your transaction. It is a very common programming model; we are all used to it, but it is not perfect.

What we'd like to have is a hook to the declarative transaction management of COM+, something like "Require TIP transaction", so we could start and propagate a TIP transaction in a declarative way as usual in the MTS/COM+ environment.

One of the primary goals of our framework is: "leave the programming model as much as possible" so that we can reuse many of our standard VB components with few modifications and most of the skill already present.

Who knows if there will ever be something like that in the COM+ explorer?

If you change the transaction protocol, you only have to modify the two components shown below in a darker shade:

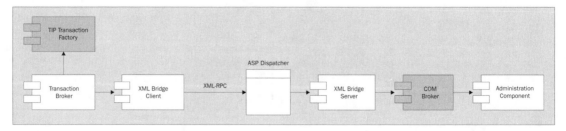

Technology Background

In this section we'd like to talk a bit about two of the technologies we used in the case study. The spectrum of the technologies used is quite wide, ranging from C++ to Visual Basic and from ATL to ASP, all of which are very well covered elsewhere.

On the other hand, XML-RPC and TIP are relatively new technologies, so we'll spend some time talking about them.

XML-RPC

As the name suggests, this is basically a **remote procedure call** system that uses XML and HTTP to invoke function calls on remote hosts. Is it something new at all? RPC (remote procedure calls) is a relatively old method of achieving such a goal. DCOM, CORBA and Java RMI are far newer methods of building networks of communicating distributed applications.

While other technologies are very tightly coupled with the underlying operating system or programming language, the standard on which XML-RPC is based is as solid as that for HTTP as a communication protocol, so it is really portable in almost any environment. Another very important consideration is the fact that it is a very firewall friendly protocol. They are just HTTP packets flowing through the TCP port 80. What could be better?

These important gains are all intrinsic in the use of XML and HTTP. There are other protocols around using these two components and they share the same gains. A very promising protocol in this area is SOAP which you had a look at in Chapter 15.

> *You can find more information about it at* www.develop.com/SOAP.

The main drawback of this technology, in our opinion, is that it is basically stateless. You can't model your distributed hosts as real objects, because from one function call to the next, they can't maintain state. Please don't let stateless fanatics cloud your mind; state is important; the fact that a system or technology cannot maintain state is just unavoidable sometimes.

It is very complex to build a state-aware system over a stateless protocol such as HTTP. An XML based protocol is better suited for macro functions as you don't often need to maintain state in this sort of scenario, as you would typically need to with intra-process function calls.

From a syntactical point of view XML-RPC is just a protocol that lets you wrap your function name and your parameters inside XML tags and brings you back a return value as result. The XML-RPC spec is at www.xmlrpc.com. If you plan to use it for production quality code, you should subscribe to the Dave Winer mailing list on this site.

> *There is also a very nice description of XML-RPC and SOAP in Wrox's "Professional XML" so we won't repeat it here. You can also refer to Chapter 15 for other details on SOAP.*

TIP

TIP is a quite strange piece of technology, to be honest. However, in our opinion, it is potentially a very important one. The strange part is the marketing: who supports it and who doesn't support it. Many software vendors said they would support it in their next product version, but a lot of "next" versions arrived and few have included TIP. At present, as far as we know, it is fully supported in Microsoft COM+, as part of the DTC, and in many Enterprise Java Beans Containers (part of the Java 2 Enterprise Edition specification) whether commercial or free products.

Another odd thing is the apparent lack of documentation about its use. At the time of writing there is virtually nothing. The only real example we managed to lay our hands on, is in the Microsoft Platform SDK. You can find it in the [Microsoft Platform SDK]/Samples/Com/Services/BYOT directory.

We'd like to see TIP implemented by more software developers and documented in many more places, which would enable more users to make use of all its potential advantages. At the moment, there is no other implementation of TIP in the important area of distributed transaction among heterogeneous systems on the Internet. But maybe it is just a matter of time.

Anyway, let's take a step back and talk about what TIP actually is.

First of all it is specified in a Request For Comments (RFC) and this is quite important. You can read it just surfing to www.ietf.org/rfc.html and looking up RFC 2371 and RFC 2372. You will find out that it is really a two-phase commit protocol, designed to manage distributed transactions among heterogeneous systems over the Internet.

OK, but what does that mean?

Distributed transactions are basically a way to compose different pieces of elaboration running on different hosts in the same unit of work, that can succeed or fail in an atomic way. They are not a new concept at all; there are a lot of distributed transaction managers around and there are standards too (www.ietf.cnri.reston.va.us/html.charters/tip-charter.html). The most prominent standard in this field is the X/Open XA specification; you can purchase the complete specification at opengroup.org/public/pubs/catalog/t008.htm. Another important one is OLE transaction from Microsoft, which you can read more about at http://msdn.microsoft.com/library/psdk/cossdk/pgtrans_52wj.htm. And finally, the Java Transaction Service (JTS) http://java.sun.com/products/jts.

All these standards implement the two-phase commit protocol to ensure the transactions are behaving properly. If you want to learn more details about distributed transactions and two-phase commit, you can read "Transaction Processing: Concepts and Techniques" by Gray and Reuter published by Morgan Kaufmann (ISBN 1558601902).

The problem of this kind of standard is twofold: they tend to be complex and homogeneous. They are complex in that they are difficult to implement or adhere to. They are homogeneous in that they usually run only in a specific environment. What is really needed is a transaction protocol so simple that it is easy to implement and heterogeneous so it can mix transactions running on very different platforms and operating systems. TIP is such a thing.

The basis of TIP is its two-pipe architecture. The transaction protocol is totally separate from the application communication protocol. So you can use whatever protocol you like to make your distributed applications communicate and use TIP as an external transaction protocol.

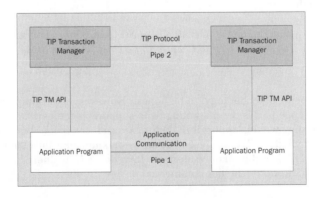

In this use case we used XML-RPC over HTTP as communication protocol, but we could have used DCOM, RMI or whatever you like. This is a real plus of the approach.

From a user point of view TIP is quite simple. There are two ways to operate: **push** and **pull**. We shall use the pull model. In the following text the master application is the one that starts the transaction, the slave application is the one that enlists in the transaction:

- ❑ The master application (the Transaction Broker) starts its own local transaction.

- ❑ It calls a function of the Distributed Transaction Coordinator (DTC) to get back a TIP ID, which is a globally unique identifier (GUID) that refers to just this particular transaction.

- ❑ It gives this identifier to the other distributed applications that need to enlist it in this transaction, passed as a parameter of the remote method it calls.

- ❑ It commits or aborts the local transaction in the usual way (`SetComplete`, `SetAbort`).

At the client side:

- ❑ The slave application (COM Broker) gets the TIP ID.

- ❑ It calls a method of the Distributed Transaction Coordinator (DTC) to create a component that runs under this specific distributed transaction.

- ❑ The component commits or aborts its own transaction as it would do in a usual local transaction, but the outcome influences the outcome of the whole distributed transaction.

This model is called pull because it is the slave application that actually pulls the transaction from the master application.

Take a look at this diagram of how it all works:

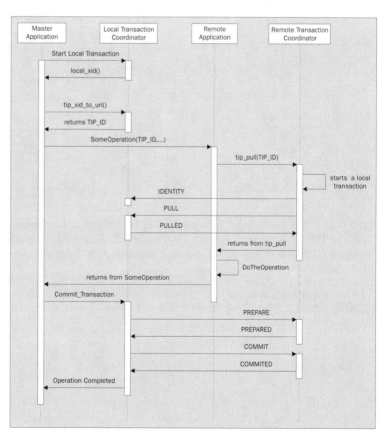

Bear in mind that the code you actually have to write is only a fraction of this. You must only put in your code the instructions for the messages starting from the Local Application and the Remote Application. All the other messages constitute the dialog between the two distributed transaction coordinators, so you don't have to worry about them.

The local application must get the TIP ID from the Local Transaction Coordinator; the remote one must enlist itself in the TIP transaction. They could be the only two function calls, depending on the kind of Transaction Coordinator you use.

If you happen to use the DTC as your transaction coordinator, things are even simpler. Here is the flow of the messages in our case study:

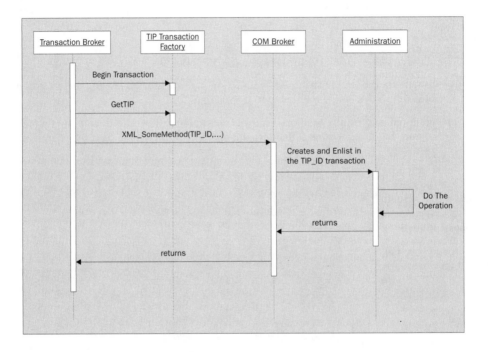

All your components have to do to use TIP is just start a transaction using the TIP Transaction Factory, get the TIP ID and pass it to the COM Broker. Your server component, Administration in this case, is a normal COM+ component without any knowledge of the existence of a TIP transaction surrounding it.

There is another model for TIP to work – the push model. The flow of messages is not too much different from the previous case. Here it is:

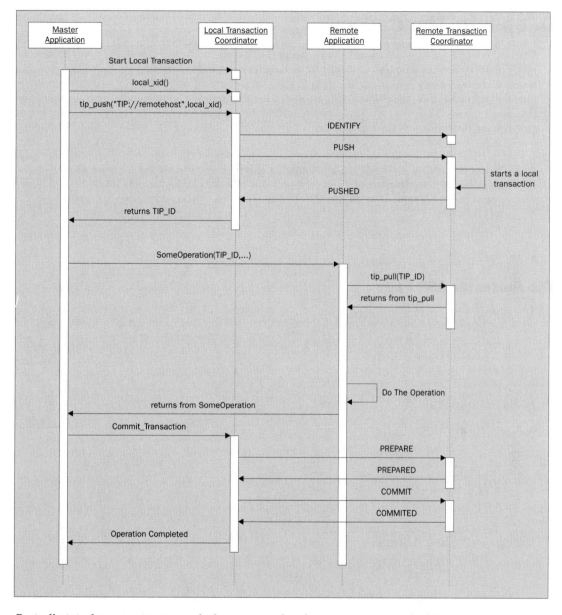

Basically it is the same situation as before, except that the transaction is pushed from the master application to the slave application with the `tip_push` instruction and that the slave `tip_pull` call simply enlists the component in the transaction previously pushed to it.

You can see from this explanation that the user's view of the world is quite simple. This is because the hard work is done by the DTC! Its duty is to recover from bad transactions, manage partial failures, synchronize operations, etc. So, hats off to the DTC.

Deep Into The Code

Up until now we have not discussed any of this project's code at all, and you might think it's time for a code break. With over a dozen components, there is lot of code to examine, and we will not be able to take you through every last detail. We tried to keep the exposition as simple as possible, but at the same time we will present the more interesting slices of C++ code for the "power users" that want to play with the infrastructure. This section is organized to mimic the previous section on Design, so you can easily go back and find your way through the fog.

> A note on code quality: this is not production quality code. We needed to throw away a number of trace instructions and error detection lines to make the code more readable. At the same time all the SQL instructions and connection strings are written into the code.

Here we go...

The Presenter ASP Page

This page is a very simple one. It gets a list of the vehicles in the database using a COM+ component. It waits for the user to click on a car model, then it submits all the data to the confirm.asp page.

```
<%@ Language=VBScript %>
<%
  On error resume next

  Dim Cat
  Dim rsCarlist

  set Cat = Server.CreateObject("Lumacars.Catalog")
  if err.number<>0 then
    Response.Write "Error "
    Response.End
  end if

  Set rsCarList = Cat.getCatalog()
  if err.number<>0 then
    Response.Write "Error"
    Response.End
  end if
%>

<html>
<style>
  A{    FONT-FAMILY: 'MS Sans Serif';
        TEXT-DECORATION: none}
  TD{ FONT-FAMILY: 'MS Sans Serif'}
  H2{ FONT-FAMILY: 'MS Sans Serif'}
  H6{ FONT-FAMILY: 'MS Sans Serif';
        FONT-SIZE: xx-small;
        FONT-WEIGHT: 100;
        COLOR: #0000ff;
        TEXT-DECORATION: none}
```

```
  </style>

<head>
</head>

<body>
<form name="fChoice" method="POST" action="Confirm.asp">
<input type="hidden" name="CarID">
<input type="hidden" name="Price">
<input type="hidden" name="Model">

<table border="0" width="100%">
  <tr>
    <td><img SRC="images/BG1.gif"></td>
    <td width="100%" colspan="2" Align="middle">
      <img SRC="images/Luma.gif">
    </td>
    <td><img SRC="images/BG2.gif"></td>
  </tr>
  <tr>
    <td colspan="4" align="middle">
      <img SRC="images/Buy.gif">
    </td>
  </tr>
  <tr>
    <td> </td>
    <td bgcolor="#d3d3d3"><h4>MODEL</h4></td>
    <td bgcolor="#d3d3d3" align="right"><h4>PRICE</h4></td>
    <td> </td>
  </tr>
<%
  while not rsCarList.EOF
    CarID=rsCarList.Fields("CarID")
    Description=rsCarList.Fields("Description")
    Price=rsCarList.Fields("Price")
%>
  <tr>
    <td> </td>
    <td>
      <a href="javascript:Confirm('<%=CarID%>','<%=Price%>','<%=Description%>')">
        <%=Description%>
      </a>
    </td>
    <td align="right"><%=Price%> </td>
  </tr>
<%
    rsCarList.movenext
  wend
%>
  <tr>
    <td colspan="4"> </td>
  </tr>
  <tr>
    <td valign="top"><img SRC="images/BG4.gif"></td>
    <td width="100%" align="right" colspan="2">
      <h6>Webmaster: joe_bloggs@bloggs.com  </h6>
```

```
     </td>
     <td valign="top"><img SRC="images/BG3.gif"></td>
   </tr>
</table>
</form>
</body>
</html>

<script LANGUAGE="javascript">
<!--
function Confirm (CarID,Price,Model)
{
  document.fChoice.CarID.value=CarID;
  document.fChoice.Price.value=Price;
  document.fChoice.Model.value=Model;
  document.fChoice.submit();
}
//-->
</script>
```

The Confirm ASP Page

This page just gathers the Credit Card ID from the user and submits its data to Submit.asp.

```
<%@ Language=VBScript %>
<%
  Model=Request.Form("Model")
  Price=Request.Form("Price")
  CarID=Request.Form("CarID")
%>

<html>
<style>
  A{  FONT-FAMILY: 'MS Sans Serif';
      TEXT-DECORATION: none}
  TD{ FONT-FAMILY: 'MS Sans Serif'}
  H2{ FONT-FAMILY: 'MS Sans Serif'}
  H6{ FONT-FAMILY: 'MS Sans Serif';
      FONT-SIZE: xx-small;
      FONT-WEIGHT: 100;
      COLOR: #0000ff;
      TEXT-DECORATION: none}
</style>

<head>
</head>

<body>
<form name="fConfirm" method="POST" action="Submit.asp">
<input type="hidden" name="CarID" value="<%=CarID%>">

<table border="0" width="100%">
  <tr>
    <td><img SRC="images/BG1.gif"></td>
    <td width="100%" colspan="3" Align="middle">
      <img SRC="images/Luma.gif">
```

```
        </td>
        <td><img SRC="images/BG2.gif"></td>
      </tr>
      <tr>
        <td colspan="5" align="middle"><img SRC="images/Congrat.gif"></td>
      </tr>
      <tr>
          <td> </td>
          <td colspan="2" bgcolor="#d3d3d3"><h4>MODEL</h4></td>
          <td bgcolor="#d3d3d3" align="right"><h4>PRICE</h4></td>
          <td> </td>
      </tr>
      <tr>
        <td> </td>
        <td align="center"><h3><%=Model%></h3></td>
        <td align="right"><img SRC="images/ferrari.gif"></td>
        <td align="right"><h3><%=Price%></h3></td>
        <td> </td>
      </tr>
      <tr>
        <td colspan="5"> </td>
      </tr>
  </table>

  <center>
  <table>
    <tr>
      <td>Please enter your Credit Card Number</td>
      <td>
        <input type="text" name="CardID">
        <input type="submit" value="Submit" name="submit1">
      </td>
    </tr>
  </table>

  <table>
    <tr>
      <td valign="top"><img SRC="images/BG4.gif"></td>
      <td width="100%" align="right" colspan="3">
        <h6>Webmaster: joe_bloggs@bloggs.com</h6>
      </td>
      <td valign="top"><img SRC="images/BG3.gif"></td>
    </tr>
  </table>
  </center>
  </form>
  </body>
  </html>
```

The Submit ASP Page

This is the page that starts the transaction. It creates the Transaction Broker component and calls its `submitOrder` method. Then it gets a result back and displays it.

```
<%@ Language=VBScript %>
<%
  On error resume next

  Dim ObjSubmit
  Dim Ret
  Dim CardID
  Dim CarID

  CardID = Request.Form("CardID")
  CarID = Request.Form("CarID")

  set ObjSubmit = Server.CreateObject("TransactionBroker.Submit")
  if err.number<>0 then
    Response.Write "Error"
    Response.End
  end if
  ret=ObjSubmit.SubmitOrder(cardID,CarID)
  if err.number<>0 then
    Response.Write "Error"
    Response.End
  end if
%>

<html>
<style>
  TD{ FONT-FAMILY: 'MS Sans Serif';
      TEXT-ALIGN: center}
  A{  FONT-FAMILY: 'MS Sans Serif';
      TEXT-DECORATION: none}
  H6{ FONT-FAMILY: 'MS Sans Serif';
      FONT-SIZE: xx-small;
      FONT-WEIGHT: 100;
      COLOR: #0000ff;
      TEXT-DECORATION: none}
</style>

<head>
<meta NAME="GENERATOR" Content="Microsoft Visual Studio 6.0">
</head>

<body>
<table border="0" width="100%">
  <tr>
    <td><img SRC="images/BG1.gif"></td>
    <td width="100%" Align="middle">
      <img SRC="images/Luma.gif">
    </td>
    <td><img SRC="images/BG2.gif"></td>
  </tr>
  <tr>
    <td colspan="3">
      Your transaction returned the following result:
    </td>
  </tr>
  <tr>
```

```
      <td colspan="3"><h3><%=Ret%></h3></td>
   </tr>
   <tr>
      <td colspan="3"><a HREF="DEFAULT.asp">Order a new car</a></td>
   </tr>
   <tr>
      <td valign="top"><img SRC="images/BG4.gif"></td>
      <td width="100%">
        <h6 align="right">Webmaster: joe_bloggs@bloggs.com  </h6>
      </td>
      <td valign="top"><img SRC="images/BG3.gif"></td>
   </tr>
</table>

</body>
</html>
```

The Cars Catalog

This is a standard Visual Basic COM+ component. It retrieves all the car models from the local database.

```
Public Function getCatalog() As Object
    Dim rds As New ADODB.Recordset
    rds.CursorLocation = adUseClient
    rds.CursorType = adOpenForwardOnly
    rds.LockType = adLockReadOnly

    rds.Open "select * from LUMA_Catalog", _
"Provider=SQLOLEDB.1;Persist Security Info=False;User ID=sa;Initial" & _
"Catalog=LUMA"
    Set rds.ActiveConnection = Nothing
    Set getCatalog = rds
End Function
```

One note here: sometimes programmers don't care about performances and hidden implications of their code; in this case we only want a list of vehicles. To avoid wasting resources on our overloaded server we have to use a disconnected, read-only, and forward-only recordset.

The Transaction Broker

This very simple business component takes as input the car chosen by the user and the user's credit card, starts a transaction, and calls all the separate servers, sending the TIP ID as a parameter of the call.

```
Public Function submitOrder(ByVal creditCardID As String,_
                                    ByVal carID As String) As Variant
    On Error GoTo errTrans ' If an error occurs: Stop and rollback

    Dim TTF As New LUMATransaction
    Dim xmlBridgeClient As New XMLBRIDGELib.Client
    Dim tip As String
    Dim today As Date
    Dim result As Variant
```

```
        today = Date
        Dim rds As New ADODB.Recordset
        rds.CursorLocation = adUseClient
        rds.CursorType = adOpenForwardOnly
        rds.LockType = adLockReadOnly
        Dim strServer, brokerAddress, strComponent As String
        Dim lPort As Long

        rds.ActiveConnection = _
    "Provider=SQLOLEDB.1;Persist Security Info=False;User ID=sa;_
                                                Initial Catalog=LUMA"
        rds.Open "select * from luma_catalog where CarID ='" & carID & "'"

        ' Make an order to Car Producer
        If rds.RecordCount = 0 Then
            submitOrder = "Car not found"
            Exit Function
        End If

        TTF.BeginTransaction ' Start a new transaction

        tip = TTF.tip

        ' Create a connection with a car producer
        strServer = Trim(rds.Fields("Server").Value)
        lPort = Trim(rds.Fields("ServerPort").Value)
        brokerAddress = Trim(rds.Fields("BrokerAddress").Value)
        strComponent = "TIP:" & Trim(rds.Fields("Component").Value) & _
                                                    ".ProcessOrder"

        xmlBridgeClient.Connect strServer, lPort

        result = xmlBridgeClient.execute(brokerAddress, strComponent, _
                        CStr(tip), CStr(creditCardID), CStr(carID), today)
        xmlBridgeClient.Close
        rds.Close

        ' Send the order to all LUMA offices
        rds.Open "select * from LUMA_Offices"

        While rds.EOF = False
            ' Create a connection with a broker
            strServer = Trim(rds.Fields("Server").Value)
            lPort = Trim(rds.Fields("ServerPort").Value)
            brokerAddress = Trim(rds.Fields("BrokerAddress").Value)
            strComponent = "TIP:" & Trim(rds.Fields("Component").Value) & _
                                                    ".ProcessOrder"

            xmlBridgeClient.Connect strServer, lPort

            result = xmlBridgeClient.execute(brokerAddress, strComponent, _
                        CStr(tip), CStr(creditCardID), CStr(carID), today)
            xmlBridgeClient.Close

            rds.MoveNext
        Wend
```

```
    rds.Close

    TTF.Commit ' Commit transaction
    submitOrder = "Your order has been submitted"
    Exit Function

errTrans:
    submitOrder = "Error-" & Err.Description
    TTF.Rollback
End Function
```

This is what this function does:

❑   It retrieves from the local database who the car producer is for this particular model.

❑   It starts a TIP transaction called `BeginTransaction` and gets the TIP ID associated with it.

❑   It calls the car producer to process the order passing the TIP ID as a parameter.

❑   It gets from the local database the LUMA offices that must be notified of this order.

❑   It cycles through the list of offices, calling each one to process the order and giving each one the transaction to enlist.

❑   If everything is OK, it commits the transaction.

❑   In case of an error, it rolls back the transaction.

Please note that all these operations are enlisted in the same TIP transaction started by the TIP Transaction Factory. You can also figure out that all the calls to the LUMA offices are made using XML-RPC, so we don't have to worry about whether the IT systems move to another location or change their operating systems.

The TIP Transaction Factory

This piece of black magic is the component involved in the creation of a new TIP transaction. It must be marked as "**Requires New Transaction**" in COM+ Explorer. Everything happens here, even though you might not think so:

```
STDMETHODIMP CLUMATransaction::BeginTransaction()
{
    return S_OK;
}
```

What actually happens is that at creation time (or better, when someone needs it) a new local transaction will be automatically started. We can then get the TIP ID associated with the transaction:

```
STDMETHODIMP CLUMATransaction::get_TIP(BSTR *pVal)
{
    HRESULT             hr          = S_OK;
    IObjectContext*     pObjCtx     = NULL;
    IObjectContextTip*  pObjCtxTip  = NULL;
    BSTR                bstrTipURL  = NULL;

    if (!pVal)
```

```
                    return E_POINTER;

        hr = GetObjectContext(&pObjCtx);
        if (FAILED(hr))
            goto ErrorExit;

        hr = pObjCtx->QueryInterface (IID_IObjectContextTip, (void**)&pObjCtxTip);
        if (FAILED(hr))
            goto ErrorExit;

        hr = pObjCtxTip->GetTipUrl(&bstrTipURL);
        if (FAILED(hr))
            goto ErrorExit;

    ErrorExit:
        *pVal = bstrTipURL;
        if (pObjCtxTip)
            pObjCtxTip->Release();
        if (pObjCtx)
            pObjCtx->Release ();
        return hr;
    }
```

Later on there is a need to commit or roll back the transaction. Here are the functions that carry out either of these operations:

```
STDMETHODIMP CLUMATransaction::Commit()
{
    HRESULT             hr          = S_OK;
    IObjectContext*     pObjCtx     = NULL;

    hr = GetObjectContext(&pObjCtx);
    if (FAILED(hr))
        return hr;

    hr = pObjCtx->SetComplete ();
    if (FAILED(hr))
        return hr;

    return hr;
}


STDMETHODIMP CLUMATransaction::Rollback()
{
    HRESULT         hr          = S_OK;
    IObjectContext*     pObjCtx     = NULL;

    hr = GetObjectContext(&pObjCtx);
    if (FAILED(hr))
        return hr;

    hr = pObjCtx->SetAbort ();
    if (FAILED(hr))
        return hr;

    return hr;
}
```

You can find a fairly detailed explanation of how it all works in the Microsoft Platform SDK, in the directory named BYOT.

The XML Bridge Client

This component is implemented in C++ using ATL. There are a few classes encompassing the solution. They are by themselves quite reusable, so it makes sense to describe them here.

XMLRPCClient

```
void XMLRPCClient::connect(char* aServer,INTERNET_PORT aPort)
{
    // Initialize the Win32 Internet functions
    _session = ::InternetOpen("LUMABrowser",
            INTERNET_OPEN_TYPE_PRECONFIG, // Use registry settings.
            NULL, // Proxy name. NULL indicates use default.
            NULL, // List of local servers. NULL indicates default.
            0);

    if (_session == NULL)
        throw WininetException(GetLastError(), "Cannot initialize Wininet");

    _connection = InternetConnect(_session, aServer,
            aPort,NULL,NULL,INTERNET_SERVICE_HTTP,
            NULL,NULL);

    if (_connection == NULL)
     throw WininetException(GetLastError(), "Cannot connect to the server");
}
```

```
char* XMLRPCClient::execute(char *anObject, char *aCall)
{
    if(_session == NULL)
        throw WininetException(GetLastError(), "Session not started");

    if (_connection == NULL)
        throw WininetException(GetLastError(), "Connection not started");
    char szSizeBuffer[32];
    DWORD dwLengthSizeBuffer = sizeof(szSizeBuffer);
    DWORD dwFileSize;
    DWORD dwBytesRead;
    LPSTR szContents;

    HINTERNET req = HttpOpenRequest( _connection, "POST", anObject,
            NULL, NULL, NULL,INTERNET_FLAG_NO_CACHE_WRITE,0);

    if (req == NULL)
        throw WininetException(GetLastError(), "Cannot post to this object");

    BOOL sendOK = HttpSendRequest(req, NULL, 0, aCall, strlen(aCall));

    if ( !sendOK )
        throw WininetException(GetLastError(), "Cannot send the post data");

    BOOL bQuery = ::HttpQueryInfo(req,HTTP_QUERY_CONTENT_LENGTH, szSizeBuffer,
                    &dwLengthSizeBuffer, NULL) ;
```

```
        if ( !bQuery )
            throw WininetException(GetLastError(), "Cannot query the Http file");

        // Allocating the memory space for HTTP file contents
        dwFileSize=atol(szSizeBuffer);
        szContents = new char[dwFileSize+1];

        // Read the HTTP file
    BOOL bRead = ::InternetReadFile(req, szContents, dwFileSize, &dwBytesRead);
        szContents[dwFileSize] = '\0';

        if ( !bRead )
            throw WininetException(GetLastError(), "Cannot read the file");

        ::InternetCloseHandle(req); // Close the connection.
        return szContents;
}

_variant_t XMLRPCClient::doACall(char* anObject, const char *aCall,
                                                  SAFEARRAY *parms)
{
    auto_ptr<char> totalCall( _translator.call(aCall, parms) );
    char* reply = execute(anObject, totalCall.get());
    return parseReply(reply);
}
```

These functions are just thin wrappers around the WinInet APIs. They basically let you connect to an Internet host and execute an XML-RPC POST. After we do the call we need to parse the result string to get a variant back.

```
_variant_t XMLRPCClient::parseReply(char *aReply)
{
    try
    {
        XMLPlatformUtils::Initialize();
    }
    catch (const XMLException& toCatch)
    {
        throw WininetException(GetLastError(),
                               StrX(toCatch.getMessage()).localForm());
    }

    const bool doValidation = false;
    const char* gMemBufId = "prodInfo";

    SAXParser parser;
    parser.setDoValidation(doValidation);

    XMLRPCHandler handler(false);
    parser.setDocumentHandler(&handler);
    parser.setErrorHandler(&handler);

    MemBufInputSource* memBufIS = new MemBufInputSource
    (
        (const XMLByte*)aReply, strlen(aReply), gMemBufId, true
    );
    try
    {
```

```
        parser.parse(*memBufIS);
    }
    catch (const XMLException& e)
    {
        throw WininetException(GetLastError(),
                                StrX(e.getMessage()).localForm());
    }
    _variant_t res( handler.getResult() );

    if( handler.isFault() )
    {
        try
        {
            IHashTablePtr hashPtr( res );
            _variant_t msgVar( hashPtr->get("faultString") );
            _bstr_t msg ( msgVar );

            DWORD code = (long)hashPtr->get("faultCode");

            throw WininetException(code, msg);
        }
        catch(_com_error&)
        {
        }
    }
    return res;
}
```

This function is based on the Xerces C++ Parser API.

Xerces C++ is a validating XML parser. It is a very neat product conforming to the XML 1.0 recommendation and associated standards. At the time of writing, it conforms to DOM 1.0, SAX 1.0 and namespaces. It is also one of the few C++ implementations of an XML parser, and it is free. It is available as source code or you can download it as a precompiled shared library, from http://xml.apache.org or from the Wrox site within our source code package. We used it because of its very high quality, and because of its support for SAX.

The explanation of the inner workings of this function is outside the scope of this case study, though anyone involved with SAX can easily understand it. The only things that are different from what is found in the documentation are the use of a MemBufInputSource and the throwing of an exception in case of errors.

For more information on SAX, look up the www.megginson.com/sax/ and the SAX reference (Appendix E).

XMLRPCHandler

This is the core of the component. This is where the real translation from an XML stream to a variant is performed. If you are used to SAX, this is the document handler.

```
void XMLRPCHandler::characters(const XMLCh* const chars,
                                        const unsigned int length)
{
    if(_cdata == "")
    {
        _cdata.append(StrX(chars).localForm(), length);
    }
}
```

```cpp
void XMLRPCHandler::endElement(const XMLCh* const name)
{
    string elemName( StrX(name).localForm() );

    if(elemName == "value")
    {
    if(_currentValue.type != XML_ARRAY && _currentValue.type != XML_STRUCT )
            _currentValue.characterData(_cdata);

        int depth = _values.size();

        if( depth < 2 || (_values[depth-1].hashCode() != XML_STRUCT))
        {
            _Value v = _currentValue;
            if(depth < 2)
            {
                objectParsed(v);
            }
            else
            {
                _currentValue = _values.back();
                _values.pop_back();
                _currentValue.endElement(v);
            }
        }
    }

    if(elemName == "member")
    {
        _Value v = _currentValue;
        _currentValue = _values.back();
        _values.pop_back();
        _currentValue.endElement(v);
    }
    else if(elemName == "name")
    {
        _currentValue.name = _cdata.c_str();
    }
}

void XMLRPCHandler::startElement(const XMLCh* const name,
                                 AttributeList& attributes)
{
    string elemName( StrX(name).localForm() );

    if(elemName == "fault")
    {
        _isFault = true;
    }

    if(elemName == "value")
    {
        _cdata = "";
        _values.push_back(_currentValue);
        _currentValue.type = XML_STRING;
    }
```

```
    if(elemName == "name")
    {
        _cdata = "";
    }

    if(elemName == "i4" || elemName == "int")
    {
        _currentValue.setType(XML_INT);
        return;
    }

    if(elemName == "string")
    {
        _currentValue.setType(XML_STRING);
        return;
    }

    if(elemName == "boolean")
    {
        _currentValue.setType(XML_BOOLEAN);
        return;
    }

    if(elemName == "double")
    {
        _currentValue.setType(XML_DOUBLE);
        return;
    }

    if(elemName == "dateTime.iso8601")
    {
        _currentValue.setType(XML_DATE);
        return;
    }

    if(elemName == "struct")
    {
        _currentValue.setType(XML_STRUCT);
        return;
    }

    if(elemName == "array")
    {
        _currentValue.setType(XML_ARRAY);
        return;
    }

    if(elemName == "base64")
    {
        _currentValue.setType(XML_BASE64);
        return;
    }
}
```

```
_variant_t XMLRPCHandler::getResult()
{
    return _result;
}
```

This class uses a helper class to do its job. This is where a lot of computations are carried on,
so here it is:

```
enum Types
{
    XML_INT,
    XML_STRING,
    XML_DOUBLE,
    XML_BOOLEAN,
    XML_DATE,
    XML_BASE64,
    XML_STRUCT,
    XML_ARRAY,
    XML_NONE
}

class _Value
{
public:

    Types type;
    _variant_t value;
    _bstr_t name;

    IHashTablePtr myStruct;
    IVectorPtr array;
    _Value(): type(XML_STRING), myStruct(), array() {}

    void endElement(const _Value& child)
    {
        switch(type)
        {
        case XML_ARRAY:
            array->addElement(child.value);
            break;
        case XML_STRUCT:
            myStruct->put(name,child.value);
            break;
        }
    }

    void setType(Types aType)
    {
        type = aType;

        if(type == XML_ARRAY)
        {
            array.CreateInstance( __uuidof( Vector ) );
            value = (IDispatch*)array;
        }
```

```
            if(type == XML_STRUCT)
            {
                myStruct.CreateInstance( __uuidof( HashTable ) );
                value = (IDispatch*)myStruct;
            }
    }


    void characterData(string cdata)
    {
        switch(type)
        {
        case XML_INT:
            value = _variant_t( atol( cdata.c_str() ) );
            break;
        case XML_DOUBLE:
            value = _variant_t( atof( cdata.c_str() ) );
            break;
        case XML_BOOLEAN:
            if(atoi( cdata.c_str() ) == -1)
                value = _variant_t( false );
            else
                value = _variant_t( true );
            break;
        case XML_DATE:
        {
            long years = atol(cdata.substr(0,4).c_str());
            long months = atol(cdata.substr(4,2).c_str());
            long days = atol(cdata.substr(6,2).c_str());
            long hours = atol(cdata.substr(9,2).c_str());
            long minutes = atol(cdata.substr(12,2).c_str());
            long seconds = atol(cdata.substr(15,2).c_str());

            CComDATE date(years,months,days,hours,minutes,seconds);

            value = _variant_t(date);
            value.ChangeType(VT_DATE);
        }
        break;
        case XML_BASE64:
        {
            Base64Coder coder;

            coder.Decode(cdata.c_str());
            value = _variant_t(coder.DecodedMessage());
        }
        break;
        case XML_STRING:
            value = _variant_t(cdata.c_str());
            break;
        }
    }

    Types hashCode()
    {
        return type;
    }
};
```

XMLRPCTranslator

This is a class mainly used to convert Variants and SafeArrays to their equivalent XML-RPC representations.

```
string XMLRPCTranslator::translateVariant(const VARIANT& v)
{
    string result;
    _variant_t w(v);

    switch(v.vt)
    {
    case VT_I2:
    case VT_I4:
        result = compose("i4",_bstr_t(w));
        break;
    case VT_BOOL:
        if(w)
            result = compose("boolean","1");
        else
            result = compose("boolean","0");
        break;
    case VT_BSTR:
        result = compose("string",_bstr_t(w));
        break;
    case VT_R8:
    {
        LCID lcid =
        MAKELCID(MAKELANGID(LANG_ENGLISH,SUBLANG_ENGLISH_US), SORT_DEFAULT);

        HRESULT hr = VariantChangeTypeEx(&w,&w,lcid,NULL,VT_BSTR);

        if(SUCCEEDED(hr))
            result = compose("double",_bstr_t(w));
        else
            result = compose("double","0.0");
        break;
    }
    case VT_DATE:
    case VT_DATE|VT_BYREF:
    {
        CComDATE d(w);
        static const char f[] = "%Y%m%dT%H:%M:%S";
        char b[] = "19980717T14:08:55";
        d.Format(b,f);
        result = compose("dateTime.iso8601",b);
        break;
    }
    case VT_UNKNOWN:
    case VT_DISPATCH:
    case VT_DISPATCH|VT_BYREF:
    case VT_UNKNOWN|VT_BYREF:
        result = composeUnknown(w);
        break;
```

```
        }
    return result;
}


string XMLRPCTranslator::compose(const char* aType, const char* aValue)
{
return string("<value><")+aType + ">" + aValue + "</" + aType + "></value>";
}


string XMLRPCTranslator::composeUnknown(const _variant_t &v)
{
    try
    {
        IXMLSourcePtr xml(static_cast<IUnknown*>(v));
        _bstr_t xmlStr = xml->AsXML;
        string result = static_cast<char*>(xmlStr);
        return result;
    }
    catch(...)
    {
        return "";
    }
}


string XMLRPCTranslator::translateSafeArray(SAFEARRAY *anArray)
{
    CSafeArray array(anArray);
    string result("<params>");
    long index[1];
    VARIANT k;
    VARIANT* v = &k;
    VariantInit(v);

    for(long i = array.GetLowerBound(1);i<=array.GetUpperBound(1);i++)
    {
        index[0] = i;
        array.GetElement(index,v);
        result += wrapParameter( translateVariant(*v) );
    }

    VariantClear(v);
    array.Dispose();
    return result += "</params>";
}


string XMLRPCTranslator::wrapParameter(const string &aParm)
{
    return string("<param>") + aParm + "</param>";
}
```

```
char* XMLRPCTranslator::call(const char* aFunc, SAFEARRAY *anArray)
{
    string result("<\?xml version=\"1.0\"\?>");

    result += "<methodCall><methodName>";
    result += aFunc;
    result += "</methodName>";
    result += translateSafeArray(anArray);
    result += "</methodCall>";

    char* buf = new char[result.size() +1];
    strcpy(buf,result.c_str());
    return buf;
}
```

Utility Components

We also wrote two utility components:

- ❑ HashTable
- ❑ Vector

They are just the COM equivalents of the `Struct` and `Array` data structures in XML-RPC. Basically, when we receive one of these back, we need to convert it to something that our components will understand. They are all prototypical implementations and need to be augmented with other useful functionalities, but they suit our needs here.

The `HashTable` component is just a thin wrapper around the STL `map` class. Here it is:

```
STDMETHODIMP CHashTable::put(BSTR aKey, VARIANT aValue)
{
    try
    {
        _map[aKey] = aValue;
        return S_OK;
    }
    catch( ... )
    {
        return Error("Unknown exception");
    }
}

STDMETHODIMP CHashTable::get(BSTR aKey, VARIANT* result)
{
    try
    {
        if(_map.find(aKey) != _map.end())
        {
            *result = _variant_t(_map[aKey]).Detach();
        }
        else
        {
            *result = _variant_t().Detach();
        }
```

```
        return S_OK;
    }
    catch( ... )
    {
        return Error("Unknown exception");
    }
}


STDMETHODIMP CHashTable::size(long *result)
{
    *result = _map.size();
    return S_OK;
}


STDMETHODIMP CHashTable::getKeys(SAFEARRAY** result)
{
    *result = NULL;
    long bounds[2] = { 0, _map.size() };
    long index[1];
    CSafeArray array(1, VT_VARIANT, bounds);
    long counter = 0;

    for(CHashTable::HashTable::const_iterator it =
                                _map.begin();it != _map.end();++it)
    {
        index[0] = counter++;
        array.SetElement(index,_variant_t((*it).first).Detach());
    }
    *result = array;
    array.Dispose();
    return S_OK;
}


// IXMLSource
STDMETHODIMP CHashTable::get_AsXML(BSTR * pVal)
{
    if (pVal == NULL)
        return E_POINTER;

    XMLWriter writer;
    writer.write(GetUnknown());
    *pVal = _bstr_t(writer.getResult()).copy();
    return S_OK;
}
```

As you can see there are only a few functions. You can basically put a value associated with a key, get a value, get the size of the container and get all the keys in the structure.

The `Vector` component is a very simple abstraction of a sequence and it is implemented over the `vector` class of STL. Here is the code:

```
STDMETHODIMP CVector::addElement(VARIANT aValue)
{
    try
    {
        _vector.push_back(aValue);
```

```
            return S_OK;
        }
    catch( ... )
        {
            return Error("Unknown exception");
        }
}

STDMETHODIMP CVector::addElementAt(long anIndex, VARIANT aValue)
{
    try
        {
            _vector[anIndex] = aValue;
            return S_OK;
        }
    catch( ... )
        {
            return Error("Unknown exception");
        }
}

STDMETHODIMP CVector::getElementAt(long anIndex, VARIANT *result)
{
    try
        {
            if(anIndex>=0 && anIndex<_vector.size())
                *result = _variant_t(_vector[anIndex]).Detach();
            else
                *result = _variant_t().Detach();
            return S_OK;
        }
    catch( ... )
        {
            return Error("Unknown exception");
        }
}

STDMETHODIMP CVector::size(long *result)
{
    try
        {
            *result = _vector.size();
            return S_OK;
        }
    catch( ... )
        {
            return Error("Unknown exception");
        }
}

STDMETHODIMP CVector::get_AsXML(BSTR * pVal)
{
    if (pVal == NULL)
        return E_POINTER;
```

```
    XMLWriter writer;
    writer.write(GetUnknown());
    *pVal = _bstr_t(writer.getResult()).copy();
    return S_OK;
}
```

An interesting point in both the components is that they implement the IXMLSource interface along with their default interface. This is due to the fact that we want each component in our framework to be able to expose its state as an XML stream.

Here is the IDL for this interface:

```
[
    object,
    uuid(97940581-CCE8-11d3-BF33-0060086790FB),
    dual,
    helpstring("Provide data as XML stream"),
    pointer_default(unique)
]
interface IXMLSource : IDispatch
{
    [propget, id(1), helpstring("XML rappresentation of the data")]
                HRESULT AsXML([out, retval] BSTR *pVal);
};
```

If you need an object to be marshaled back and forth by our components, the easiest way to do it is to let it implement this interface.

The problem with this approach, though, is that our script clients can't invoke methods on this interface because it is not the default one. There are several solutions to this inconvenience; one of the most interesting is the "DISPID Encoding" which you can read about in Wrox's "Professional ATL COM Programming" by Richard Grimes (ISBN 1-861001-40-1).

We tried to encapsulate his technique and use this versatile piece of code:

```
#define DISPIDENCODE2(LIBRARY,CLASS1,CLASS2)                              \
public:                                                                   \
    enum DISPID_VALUES                                                    \
    {                                                                     \
        INTERFACEMASK    = 0xFFFF0000,                                    \
        DISPIDMASK       = 0x0000FFFF,                                    \
        IDISP##CLASS1    = 0x00010000,                                    \
        IDISP##CLASS2    = 0x00020000,                                    \
    };                                                                    \
                                                                          \
    typedef IDispatchImpl<I##CLASS1, &IID_I##CLASS1, &LIBRARY>            \
        CLASS1##Type;                                                     \
                                                                          \
    typedef IDispatchImpl<I##CLASS2, &IID_I##CLASS2, &LIBRARY>            \
        CLASS2##Type;                                                     \
                                                                          \
    STDMETHODIMP GetIDsOfNames(REFIID riid,                              \
        LPOLESTR* rgszNames, UINT cNames, LCID lcid, DISPID* rgdispid)   \
    {                                                                     \
```

```
            HRESULT hr = DISP_E_UNKNOWNNAME;                            \
                                                                        \
        hr = CLASS1##Type::GetIDsOfNames(riid, rgszNames, cNames,       \
                lcid, rgdispid);                                        \
                                                                        \
        if (SUCCEEDED(hr))                                             \
        {                                                              \
            rgdispid[0] |= IDISP##CLASS1;                              \
            return hr;                                                 \
        }                                                              \
                                                                        \
        hr = CLASS2##Type::GetIDsOfNames(riid, rgszNames, cNames,       \
                lcid, rgdispid);                                        \
        if (SUCCEEDED(hr))                                             \
        {                                                              \
            rgdispid[0] |= IDISP##CLASS2;                              \
            return hr;                                                 \
        }                                                              \
        return hr;                                                     \
    }                                                                  \
                                                                        \
    STDMETHODIMP Invoke(DISPID dispidMember,                           \
        REFIID riid, LCID lcid, WORD wFlags, DISPPARAMS* pdispparams,  \
        VARIANT* pvarResult, EXCEPINFO* pexcepinfo, UINT* puArgErr)    \
    {                                                                  \
        DWORD dwInterface = (dispidMember & INTERFACEMASK);           \
        dispidMember &= DISPIDMASK;                                    \
        switch (dwInterface)                                          \
        {                                                             \
        case IDISP##CLASS1:                                            \
            return CLASS1##Type::Invoke(                              \
                dispidMember, riid, lcid, wFlags, pdispparams,        \
                pvarResult, pexcepinfo, puArgErr);                    \
        case IDISP##CLASS2:                                            \
            return CLASS2##Type::Invoke(                              \
                dispidMember, riid, lcid, wFlags, pdispparams,        \
                pvarResult, pexcepinfo, puArgErr);                    \
        default:                                                      \
            return DISP_E_MEMBERNOTFOUND;                             \
        }                                                             \
    }                                                                 \
```

This macro is good to be placed in the header file of your ATL class like this:

```
DISPIDENCODE2(LIBID_DATASTRUCTURESLib,HashTable,XMLSource)
```

Why?

Well, it is used to expose both the methods of HashTable and of XMLSource from the default interface, and so they can be accessed from a script client.

Overriding the default ATL implementation of the IDispatch interface, we are able to decide whether to forward the function call to one interface or the other. When the client calls GetIDsOfNames we encode in the returned identifier, the notion of the interface to call. Later, when the client calls Invoke, we look at the identifier and decoding it, we decide what interface to direct our request to. It's very simple.

The macro just presented is useful only in the two interfaces case, but it is very easy to extend it to include any number of interfaces. As a client, you don't have to understand how the macro works, you just need to include it in the header file of your class.

Utility Classes

We needed some helper classes to ease our task, so we freely took from the net some useful pieces of code and some pieces we wrote ourselves. We are very grateful to the coders who posted them on the Internet. They are:

- ❏   A Base 64 Coder, from Microsoft.

- ❏   A very simple `SafeArray` wrapper by Praveen S. Kumar, from CodeGuru (www.codeguru.com).

- ❏   Date and Time utility classes from Chris Sells, which you can get from www.sellsbrothers.com/tools.

The ASP Dispatcher

This is the piece of code that has the first grasp on our XML function calls.

```
<%@ Language=VBScript %>

<%
    dim sreq, obj
    Response.ContentType = "text/xml"
    set obj = server.CreateObject("XMLBridge.Server")
    sreq = obj.ExecuteXML(Request)

    Response.Write sreq
%>
```

Isn't it a beauty? So simple!

The XML Bridge Server

This component is binary tied to the XML Bridge Client – it is in the same shared library. This is due to the fact that they share a fair bit of common code and they are semantically related. They do have a different `ProgID` so, at a logical level, they are two different components.

This is the `ExecuteXML` function you call from the client, in our case an ASP broker:

```
STDMETHODIMP CServer::ExecuteXML(VARIANT XMLstring, VARIANT *result)
{
    CComBSTR strFunction;
    CComVariant vRes;
    SAFEARRAYBOUND bound = {0,0};
    SAFEARRAY* pars;
    HRESULT hr;
    USES_CONVERSION;


    strFunction = GetFunctionFromVar(XMLstring);
    pars = SafeArrayCreate(VT_VARIANT,1,&bound);
    strFunction = parseFunctionCall(&strFunction,pars);
```

```
        // Instantiate a COM Broker component
        IBroker* broker;

        hr = CoCreateInstance(CLSID_Broker,
                              NULL,
                              CLSCTX_INPROC_SERVER, // Only in process components
                              IID_IBroker,
                              (void**)&broker);

        if (hr != S_OK)
        {
            // return a XML_RPC ERROR
            vRes = TranslateError(NULL,"Cannot create Broker",hr,IID_NULL);
        }
        else
        {
            hr = broker->Execute(strFunction,&pars,&vRes);
            if( hr != S_OK)
            {
                vRes = TranslateError(broker,
                                      "",
                                      hr,
                                      IID_IBroker);
            }
            else
            {
                // Everithing OK!
                // Translate the result in XML-RPC conformant way
                XMLRPCTranslator trx;
                vRes = trx.translateVariant(vRes).c_str();
            }
            long refCount = broker->Release();
        }
        SafeArrayDestroy(pars);
        *result = vRes; //Result from the broker in XML format;

        // The result is always S_OK the excpetion is eventually in XML-RPC form
        // stored in the result
        return S_OK;
    }
```

About ExecuteXML's parameters: the first parameter is an input parameter and contains the XML stream representing the component to be activated; the second one is the return value.

The XMLString as input parameter is a VARIANT, because we can receive the string in many different ways. When we were writing this code we used a VB test client and the XML string was in BSTR form, but when we started to use ASP as a client, the only way we found to read a POST was using BinaryRead. This function gets all the bytes in the HTTP POST request and returns the data as a SafeArray of Variant Unsigned Int. So, we decided to use a more general way to pass the string and leave it to the C++ code to investigate which kind of stream we are passing to it. In this way we can eventually add a new kind of stream without changing the interface.

This method, unlike some common COM methods, always returns S_OK. This isn't due to a poor programming technique; it's a choice.

Think about this component: we need a translator from COM to XML-RPC and vice versa; this is the vice versa part. If everything involved in the call, business objects, infrastructure, or whatever, needs to throw an exception, we have to propagate this exception in an XML-RPC fashion, not as a COM exception.

This function is actually called from the ASP Dispatcher to execute the right method call on the component. It uses a bunch of helper stuff. Here it is:

```
BSTR CServer::parseFunctionCall(BSTR* strIn,SAFEARRAY* pars)
{
    CComBSTR strFunction="";
    wstring xml = *strIn,str;
    wstring::size_type   startPos,n;
    XMLRPCClient client;
    _variant_t el;
    startPos = xml.find(L"<methodName>",0);
    USES_CONVERSION;

    if (startPos == wstring::npos)
    {
        return strFunction;
    }

    startPos += 12;
    n = xml.find(L"</",startPos);
    str = xml.substr(startPos,n-startPos);
    strFunction = str.data();


    long elements = 0;
    HRESULT hr;
    char* cStr;

    SAFEARRAYBOUND safeBound ;
    safeBound.cElements = elements;
    safeBound.lLbound   = 0;

    char tr1[10];

    while( (startPos = xml.find(L"<param>",startPos)) != wstring::npos)
    {
        ltoa(elements,tr1,10);
        n = xml.find(L"</param>",startPos);
        ltoa(n,tr1,10);
        str = xml.substr(startPos+7,n-startPos-7);

        safeBound.cElements = elements+1;
        hr = SafeArrayRedim(pars,&safeBound);

        cStr = W2A(str.c_str());
        el = client.parseReply(cStr);

        hr = SafeArrayPutElement(pars, &elements, &el);
        startPos = n;
        elements++;
    }
    return strFunction;
}
```

```
BSTR CServer::GetStringFromArray(VARIANT objArray)
{
    VARTYPE vt = VT_ARRAY | VT_UI1;
    char el;
    HRESULT hr;
    long lLBound, lUBound;
    USES_CONVERSION;
    char* strBuf;
    SAFEARRAY*  pSA;

    if (objArray.vt == vt)
    {
        pSA = objArray.parray;
        hr = ::SafeArrayGetUBound(pSA, 1, &lUBound);
        hr = ::SafeArrayGetLBound(pSA, 1, &lLBound);
        strBuf = new char[lUBound-lLBound+2];

        for(long i = lLBound; i <= lUBound ;   i++)
        {
            el = 0;
            hr = ::SafeArrayGetElement(pSA, &i, &el);
            el = el & 0x000000FF;
            if(el>0 && el<255)
                strBuf[i] =el;
            else
                strBuf[i] = ' ';
        }
        strBuf[i]='\0';
    }
    CComBSTR str(A2W(strBuf));
    delete strBuf;
    return str;
}


BSTR CServer::GetFunctionFromVar(VARIANT vXML)
{
    HRESULT hr = S_OK;
    CComBSTR strFunction;

    switch(vXML.vt)
    {
    case (VT_ARRAY | VT_UI1):
        strFunction = GetStringFromArray(vXML);
        break;
    case VT_BSTR:
        strFunction = vXML.bstrVal;
        break;
    default:
        hr = E_NOTIMPL;
        break;
    } // End type supported
    return strFunction;
}
```

```
wstring CServer::Trim(wstring *strIn)
{
    wstring strOut = *strIn;
    wstring::size_type startPos;

    // Trim Left
    startPos = strOut.find_first_not_of(SPACE_CHARS);
    strOut = strOut.substr( startPos );

    // Trim Right
    reverse( strOut.begin(), strOut.end() );
    startPos = strOut.find_first_not_of(SPACE_CHARS);
    strOut = strOut.substr( startPos );
    reverse( strOut.begin(), strOut.end() );

    return strOut;

}
```

```
BSTR CServer::TranslateError(IBroker* objPtr,LPCSTR msg, HRESULT err,REFIID riid)
{
    USES_CONVERSION;
    CComBSTR strErr (msg);
    CComBSTR strRes;
    char tmp[33];
    _ltoa(err,tmp,10);
    CComBSTR desHR(tmp);

if(objPtr!=NULL) // I get a reference I'll see if support ISupportErrorInfo
    {
        CComQIPtr<ISupportErrorInfo>iSEIPtr(objPtr);
        if (iSEIPtr) // Support IErrorInfo
        {
            HRESULT hr = iSEIPtr->InterfaceSupportsErrorInfo(riid);
            if (hr == S_OK)
            {
                IErrorInfo* pErr;
                GetErrorInfo(0,&pErr);
                pErr->GetDescription(&strErr);
                long ref = pErr->Release();
                _ltoa(ref,tmp,10);
            }
        }
        else
            strErr+=A2OLE(" Object not support IErrorInfo");
    }

    // Code indented to show XML structure of string
    strRes ="<?xml version=\"1.0\"?>";
    strRes += "<methodResponse>";
      strRes += "<fault>";
        strRes += "<value>";
          strRes += "<struct>";
            strRes += "<member>";
              strRes += "<name>faultCode</name>";
              strRes += "<value><int>";
```

```
                    strRes += desHR;
                    strRes += "</int></value>";
                strRes += "</member>";
                strRes += "<member>";
                    strRes += "<name>faultString</name>";
                    strRes += "<value><string>";
                    strRes += strErr;
                    strRes += "</string></value>";
                strRes += "</member>";
            strRes += "</struct>";
        strRes += "</value>";
    strRes += "</fault>";
    strRes += "</methodResponse>";
    return strRes;
}
```

The COM Broker

This is the dynamic dispatcher. Here's how it looks:

```
STDMETHODIMP CBroker::Execute(BSTR strFunction,SAFEARRAY** someParameters,
                              VARIANT *result)
{
    HRESULT hr;
    USES_CONVERSION;
    IDispatch* ptrObj;
    DISPID dispID;
    CComVariant res("OK!");
    CComBSTR progID;
    CComBSTR funName;

    std::wstring str;
    EXCEPINFO excepInfo;
    UINT argErr;
    GUID guidObj = {0};
    GUID guidByotServer = {0};

    DISPPARAMS pars;
    progID = getProgID(strFunction);
    funName = getFuncName(strFunction);

    // See if the component exist
    hr = CLSIDFromProgID(progID, &guidObj);
    if (FAILED(hr))
        return MakeError(hr,progID,funName);

    hr = MakeDispParams(*someParameters,&pars);
    if (FAILED(hr))
        return MakeError(hr,L"",funName);

    if ( m_bstrTIP == L"") // Do not require TIP
    {
        hr = CoCreateInstance(guidObj,
                              NULL,
                              CLSCTX_ALL,
```

```
                                    IID_IDispatch,
                                    (void**)&ptrObj);

        if(FAILED(hr))
            return MakeError(hr,progID,funName);
    }
    else // TIP required
    {
        ICreateWithTipTransactionEx* pCreateWithTipTx = NULL;
        hr = CLSIDFromProgID(L"Byot.ByotServerEx", &guidByotServer);

        if (FAILED(hr))
            return MakeError(hr,L"Byot.ByotServerEx",funName);

        hr = CoCreateInstance(guidByotServer,
                              NULL,
                              CLSCTX_ALL,
                              IID_ICreateWithTipTransactionEx,
                              (void**)&pCreateWithTipTx);
        if (FAILED(hr))
            return MakeError(hr,L"Byot.ByotServerEx",funName);

        // Object creation with TIP
        hr = pCreateWithTipTx->CreateInstance(m_bstrTIP,
                                              guidObj,
                                              CLSCTX_ALL,
                                              IID_IDispatch,
                                              (void**)&ptrObj);
        if (FAILED(hr))
            return MakeError(hr,progID,funName);
    }
    hr =
        ptrObj->GetIDsOfNames(IID_NULL,&funName,1,LOCALE_SYSTEM_DEFAULT,&dispID);

    if (FAILED(hr))
    {
        ptrObj->Release();
        return MakeError(hr,progID,funName);
    }
    hr = ptrObj->Invoke(dispID,
                        IID_NULL,
                        LOCALE_SYSTEM_DEFAULT,
                        DISPATCH_METHOD, // Only Method
                        &pars,
                        &res,
                        &excepInfo,
                        &argErr);

    ptrObj->Release();
    *result = res;
    delete[] pars.rgvarg;

    if (FAILED(hr))
        return MakeError(hr,progID,funName,&excepInfo);
    else
        return hr;
}
```

This function is actually a wrapper around an invocation on the `IDispatch` interface. We thought we could use a Visual Basic component for it, but we were wrong. This is due to the signature of the Visual Basic 6 `CallByName` function. If you use it, you must know the type and number of the parameters of the function you want to call at compile time. We only know them at run time, so we need another piece of C++ code here.

The function uses some utility procedures to do its business, which are shown below:

```cpp
STDMETHODIMP CBroker::MakeDispParams(SAFEARRAY* parIn, DISPPARAMS *parOut)
{
    HRESULT hr;
    long i;
    long lLBound, lUBound, lNoElements;
    CComVariant el;
    if (parIn->cDims > 1 )
        return BR_INVALID_DIM; // Only one dimension for now ;)

    hr = SafeArrayGetLBound(parIn, 1, &lLBound);
    hr = SafeArrayGetUBound(parIn, 1, &lUBound);

    parOut->cNamedArgs = 0;
    parOut->rgdispidNamedArgs = NULL;
    if(m_bstrTIP == L"TIP")
    {
        lLBound++;
        // Get First element
        i = 0;
        hr = ::SafeArrayGetElement(parIn, &i, &el);
        m_bstrTIP = el.bstrVal;
    }

    lNoElements = lUBound - lLBound + 1;
    parOut->cArgs = lNoElements;
    parOut->rgvarg = new VARIANTARG[lNoElements];

    // Loop in reverse order to visit the params chain
    for(i = lUBound; i >= lLBound ; i--)
    {
        hr = ::SafeArrayGetElement(parIn, &i, &el);
        if (hr == S_OK)
            parOut->rgvarg[lUBound - i] = el;
        else
            return hr;
    } // End loop over params
    return S_OK;
}
```

This helper function gets the `ProgID` of the component to be instantiated from our `"[TIP:]ProgID.FunctionName"` string. Bear in mind that in the XML-RPC specifications, there are no constraints about the format of the function to be called, so we have chosen the most familiar form to COM programmers.

```
BSTR CBroker::getProgID(BSTR strFunction)
{
    std::wstring::size_type    startPos,n;
    _bstr_t str;

    std::wstring strID(strFunction);
    startPos = strID.find(L":",0);

    if (startPos == std::wstring::npos)
        startPos = 0;
    else // TIP Requested
    {
        m_bstrTIP = strID.substr(0,startPos).data();
        startPos++;
    }

    n = strID.find(L".",startPos);
    n = strID.find(L".",n+1);

    if(n != std::wstring::npos)
    {
        str = strID.substr(startPos,n-startPos).data();
    }
    return str;
}
```

This one gets the name of the function to be invoked:

```
CBroker::getFuncName(BSTR strFunction)
{
    std::wstring::size_type    startPos,n;
    _bstr_t str;

    std::wstring strID(strFunction);
    startPos = strID.find(L":",0);

    if (startPos == std::wstring::npos)
        startPos = 0;

    n = strID.find(L".",startPos);
    n = strID.find(L".",n+1);

    if( n != std::wstring::npos)
    {
        str = strID.substr(n+1).data();
    }
    return str;
}
```

In other parts of the code base, there isn't an accurate error management but, in this case, we have many components at different levels and possibly in different machines, so we'd like to demonstrate how you could propagate errors using XML-RPC.

```
HRESULT CBroker::MakeError(HRESULT hr, BSTR progID, BSTR msg,
                          EXCEPINFO* pExcepInfo)
{
    CComBSTR strError;
    switch(hr)
    {
    case CO_E_CLASSSTRING:
        strError = "The registered CLSID for the ProgID is invalid";
        break;
    case REGDB_E_WRITEREGDB :
        strError = "ProgID cannot be found in the registry";
        break;
    case REGDB_E_CLASSNOTREG :
        strError = "not registered in the registration database"
                   "OR registered as not in-process";
        break;
    case CLASS_E_NOAGGREGATION:
        strError = "This class cannot be created as part of an aggregate";
        break;
    case E_NOINTERFACE:
        strError =
            "The specified class does not implement the requested interface,"
      " or the controlling IUnknown does not expose the requested interface";
        break;
    case E_OUTOFMEMORY:
        strError = "Not enough memory available to instantiate the object.";
        break;
    case E_INVALIDARG:
      strError = "The argument passed in the ppvObj parameter is invalid. ";
        break;
    case DISP_E_BADPARAMCOUNT:
      strError = "The number of elements provided to DISPPARAMS is different"
        " from the number of arguments accepted by the method or property.";
       break;
    case DISP_E_BADVARTYPE:
     strError = "One of the arguments in rgvarg is not a valid variant type.";
        break;
    case DISP_E_EXCEPTION:
        //The application needs to raise an exception.
        if(pExcepInfo)
            strError = pExcepInfo->bstrDescription;
        break;
    case DISP_E_MEMBERNOTFOUND:
      strError = "The requested member does not exist, or the call to Invoke"
                  " tried to set the value of a read-only property";
        break;
    case DISP_E_NONAMEDARGS:
        strError =
        "This implementation of IDispatch does not support named arguments";
        break;
    case DISP_E_OVERFLOW:
        strError = "One of the arguments in rgvarg could not be coerced"
                    " to the specified type.";
        break;
    case DISP_E_PARAMNOTFOUND:
        strError = "One of the parameter DISPIDs does not correspond"
```

```
                              " to a parameter on the method";
            break;
        case DISP_E_TYPEMISMATCH:
            strError = "One or more of the arguments could not be coerced";
            break;
        case DISP_E_UNKNOWNINTERFACE:
          strError = "The interface identifier passed in riid is not IID_NULL.";
            break;
        case DISP_E_UNKNOWNLCID:
            strError = "The locale identifier (LCID) was not recognized";
            break;
        case DISP_E_PARAMNOTOPTIONAL:
            strError = "A required parameter was omitted";
            break;
        case DISP_E_UNKNOWNNAME:
            strError = "One or more of the names were not known";
            break;
        case DISP_E_ARRAYISLOCKED:
            strError = "Array is locked";
            break;
        case DISP_E_BADINDEX:
            strError = "Bad index in array";
            break;
        default:
            strError = "An unexpected error occurred";
            break;
    }
    return Error(strError,IID_IBroker,hr);
}
```

These are all quite reusable pieces of code.

The Car Producer Business Component

This is a standard transactional Visual Basic COM+ configured component. It does its job, to write a record in the Car Producer's database, and calls `SetComplete` or `SetAbort` depending on the result of the operation.

```
Public Sub ProcessOrder(ByVal CreditCardID As String,ByVal carID As String,_
                                                      ByVal orderDate As Date)
    Dim ctx As ObjectContext
    Set ctx = GetObjectContext()
    Dim cmd As New ADODB.Command
    Dim strSQL As String
    On Error GoTo errPO

    strSQL = "INSERT INTO LUMA_ORDERS "
    strSQL = strSQL & "(CarID,CustomerID,date,NumberOfCars)"
    strSQL = strSQL & " VALUES( "
    strSQL = strSQL & "'" & carID & "','" & CreditCardID & "',{d '"
    strSQL = strSQL & Format(orderDate, "yyyy-mm-dd") & "'},1)"

    cmd.ActiveConnection = "Provider=SQLOLEDB.1;Persist Security _
                            Info=False;User ID=sa;Initial Catalog=LUMA"
    cmd.CommandText = strSQL
    cmd.CommandType = adCmdText
```

```
        cmd.Execute

        ctx.SetComplete
        Exit Sub

errPO:
        Set cmd = Nothing
        ctx.SetAbort
        Err.Raise Err.Number, "GetOrder", Err.Description
End Sub
```

You can find the code for the other transactional components on the Wrox site, www.wrox.com. We won't include it here because the functionality is all quite standard.

> **The code download contains the data in an Access file which can be imported into SQL Server using DTS.**

In this example, we have a SQL Server table that represents all the offices in the LUMA Cars organization. For the sake of simplicity, all the component's methods have the same signature (CreditCardId as a string, CarID as a string, orderDate as a Date). In this way we can add any remote offices to the organization or remove them simply by inserting or deleting a row in our database. We can therefore test the transaction to see whether it committed, aborted, failed or whatever you want, in a very simple way, by inserting or deleting some rows.

If you want, you can test the rollback mechanism by calling FaultComponent.SetAbort, which will attempt to add a row in the LUMA_Offices table. And your transaction, distributed among different servers, will be rolled back.

```
Public Sub ProcessOrder(ByVal CreditCardID As String,ByVal carID As String,_
                                              ByVal orderDate As Date)

        GetObjectContext().SetAbort
End Sub
```

Security Wrap Up

Security is a very hard topic to get to grips with. Security in an Internet domain is even harder. We don't have enough space here to give this subject the attention it deserves. So what can we say here?

No chapter of any book and probably no single book by itself can resolve all the problems in the Internet security arena. We have a more modest goal – to show you the security concerns of applying our framework and to point you to some resources you can use to learn how to secure your application.

The problem can be summed up simply – you need to secure two open TCP ports, one for the web server, the other one for the TIP protocol, if you need to use distributed transactions. We can talk for months about how to protect these two ports and I'm sure everybody out there has strong opinions about it. However, we think that current Internet security is all about strong encryption, where strong means "with at least a 128-bit key". A lot of commercial transactions on the Internet are performed with an RC4-Export (40 bit) level of security, which will be hidden from an occasional observer, but will be possible for a more motivated and dedicated hacker to break.

So what you really need is 128 bit encryption protocol. The problem with this kind of protocol is that the USA Government considers them as a sensitive technology and their export is actually quite difficult even though they have eased some restrictions.

One emerging protocol in the area of Internet Security is TLS, as described in the RFC 2246. It is a very flexible protocol that can be used to protect our two ports. It can encrypt web pages and form posts, validate users connecting to the LUMA main portal and XML streams of data to the outer systems, and it can encrypt our TIP communications too. TIP is a protocol that can be used over many communication backbones and take advantage of the existing security mechanisms. So we predict TLS will be used in these kinds of systems to help in tackling the security problem.

This previous section provides the briefest of views of the security problems, which really need to be analysed in much more detail. You can visit http://csrc.nist.gov to find more information.

Summary

Communication among heterogeneous systems is quite an interesting but challenging topic, and it's something we need to understand as more and more companies want to link their information systems to the outside world and perform their tasks in a more automated way.

XML-RPC can be a solution to all the people involved in the interaction between heterogeneous systems. Integrating CORBA, Java, and COM systems can be a nightmare, which is why XML-RPC and its related protocol SOAP, were developed. If you are developing a commercial application that uses such protocols it is even more complicated. ORB producers, COM configurations, data type representations, network configurations, and firewalls, are among other areas to consider.

XML-RPC is simple to understand and to implement, it is based on standard technologies like HTTP and XML and we think it is very neat to use. TIP is a very promising new technology in this area, but there is little documentation and few real-world examples of its use. Our goal in writing this case study was to give you some useful information on TIP and show you how to use it.

Case Study – Data Transfer

Introduction

For the purposes of this case study, we're going to create an online cheese shop. Customers can come to the web site and enter orders for cheese; these are distributed by the web site to various fulfillment centers (local cheese shops, independent franchisees, etc.), which deliver the selected cheese(s) and take payment directly from the customer. Mr. Wensleydale, the web site proprietor, gets a transaction fee for each purchase order fulfilled – not bad for just pushing around XML data!

We're going to use XML as our data repository in this example. Data is collected from an online form and persisted to a file as XML on the server; the fulfillment centers may then query this repository and retrieve the purchase orders that fall in their territory. We'll be using XML, XSLT, and XPath on the server to implement the system – we want our cheese lovers to be able to use Netscape or IE to place their orders. In order to run the examples in this case study, you'll need to install the Microsoft XML technology preview version of MSXML (available from http://msdn.microsoft.com/downloads /webtechnology/xml/msxml.asp), or have a version of IIS installed that provides full XSLT and XPath support (not yet available at press time).

In this case study, we'll design and build two applications: the application that accepts the purchase order from the customer over the Web, and the application that allows fulfillment centers to download the orders for their fulfillment zone (in our example, a postal code).

Online Ordering

The purchase order for the cheese shop looks like this:

<table>
<tr><td colspan="4" align="center">Cheese Shop
Mr. Wensleydale, Proprietor</td></tr>
<tr><td colspan="4">
Customer Name: _____
Shipping Address: _____
_____
_____, __ _____

Telephone: _____
</td></tr>
<tr><td>Cheese</td><td>Amount</td><td>Price</td><td>Cost</td></tr>
<tr><td></td><td></td><td></td><td></td></tr>
<tr><td></td><td></td><td></td><td></td></tr>
<tr><td></td><td></td><td></td><td></td></tr>
<tr><td></td><td></td><td></td><td></td></tr>
<tr><td>Total:</td><td></td><td></td><td></td></tr>
</table>

As we take orders, we'll use ASP to create XML documents representing the purchase orders and persist them to a hard drive cache. Then, an adminstrative tool will be used by the various fulfillment shops to obtain the outstanding orders for their postal code. The information will be transformed as the fulfillment shops require, and the information will be downloaded to them.

First, let's build an XML structure to contain our purchase orders. A sample might look like this:

```
<PurchaseOrder
    CustomerName="Ron Obvious"
    Address1="100 Main Street"
    Address2="Suite 200"
    City="Anywhere"
    State="WV"
    PostalCode="12345"
    Telephone="111-22-3333">
  <LineItem
      CheeseType="1 lb. Cheddar"
      Amount="2"
      Price="4.95"/>
  <LineItem
      CheeseType="1 lb. Venezuelan Beaver Cheese"
      Amount="3"
      Price="7.95"/>
</PurchaseOrder>
```

The XML DTD for this structure would then be:

```
<!ELEMENT PurchaseOrder(LineItem+)>
<!ATTLIST PurchaseOrder
```

```
       CustomerName CDATA #REQUIRED
       Address1     CDATA #REQUIRED
       Address2     CDATA #IMPLIED
       City         CDATA #REQUIRED
       State        CDATA #REQUIRED
       PostalCode   CDATA #REQUIRED
       Telephone    CDATA #REQUIRED>

<!ELEMENT LineItem EMPTY>
<!ATTLIST LineItem
       CheeseType   CDATA #REQUIRED
       Amount       CDATA #REQUIRED
       Price        CDATA #REQUIRED>
```

Now that we have data structures, let's take a look at the online data entry form:

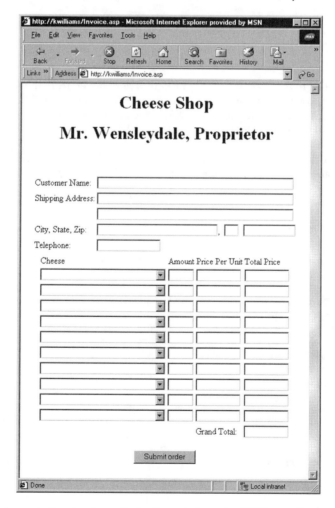

Before we look at the code for this form, let's take a look at the XML that drives it.

The Purchase Order Form

Mr. Wensleydale's inventory changes on a minute-to-minute basis. After all, there's not much call for Cheddar around here, and the cat's eaten all of the Stilton... As a result, we need to be able to dynamically generate the order page based on a changing inventory. Our inventory will be stored in an XML document called `inventory.xml` that looks something like this:

```xml
<?xml version="1.0"?>
<Inventory>
  <Cheese
    Name="1 lb. Cheddar"
    Price="3.99"/>
  <Cheese
    Name="1 lb. Gouda"
    Price="4.99"/>
  <Cheese
    Name="0.5 lb. Venezuelan Beaver Cheese"
    Price="7.99"/>
</Inventory>
```

As new items are added to the inventory, then, or items are removed from it, we want the order form to automatically reflect those changes. We'll accomplish this by generating HTML on the fly from our ASP script – using the DOM to access the inventory XML document – and also by generating Javascript on the fly as well. Let's take a look at the code that accomplishes this.

The first part of our code sets up our purchase order page and the summary information (customer name, etc.) for the purchase order. Since these fields never change, static HTML is used to create this part of the page:

```
<%@ Language=VBScript %>
<HTML>
<HEAD>
<META NAME="GENERATOR" Content="Microsoft Visual Studio 6.0">
<TITLE></TITLE>
</HEAD>
<BODY LANGUAGE=javascript onerror="return window_onerror()">
<H1 align=center>Cheese Shop</H1>
<H1 align=center>Mr. Wensleydale, Proprietor</H1>
<FORM METHOD=post ACTION="submitPurchaseOrder.asp" id=frmPurchaseOrder
          name=frmPurchaseOrder>
<P align=center> </P>
<TABLE align=center>
  <TR>
    <TD>Customer Name:</TD>
    <TD><INPUT NAME="txtName" Id="txtName" maxLength="50" size="50"></TD>
  </TR>
  <TR>
    <TD>Shipping Address:</TD>
    <TD>
      <INPUT NAME="txtAddress1" Id="txtAddress1" maxLength ="50" size ="50">
    </TD>
  </TR>
  <TR>
    <TD></TD>
```

```
        <TD>
          <INPUT NAME="txtAddress2" Id="txtAddress2" maxLength="50" size ="50">
        </TD>
      </TR>
      <TR>
        <TD>City, State, Zip:</TD>
        <TD>
        <INPUT NAME="txtCity" Id="txtCity" maxLength="30" size="30">, 
        <INPUT NAME="txtState" Id="txtState" maxLength="2" size="2"> 
        <INPUT NAME="txtPostalCode" Id="txtPostalCode" maxLength="12" size="12">
        </TD>
      </TR>
      <TR>
        <TD>Telephone:</TD>
        <TD>
          <INPUT TYPE="telephone" NAME="txtTelephone"
                              Id="txtTelephone" maxLength="15" size="15">
        </TD>
      </TR>
    </TABLE>
```

Next, we'll write the header information for the line item portion of the purchase order:

```
<TABLE align=center>
  <TR>
    <TD>Cheese</TD>
    <TD>Amount</TD>
    <TD>Price Per Unit</TD>
    <TD>Total Price</TD>
  </TR>
```

For the next part of the purchase order form, we'll need to dynamically generate SELECT inputs (dropdowns) based on the contents of our inventory.xml file. First, the code creates an XML DOM object and synchronously loads the inventory file:

```
<%
' now, we need to generate ten line entry items
' we can find a list of cheeses in stock at inventory.xml in the current dir
Dim i
Dim rTotalCost
Dim iCheese
Dim xmlDOM
Dim nlCheeses

Set xmlDOM = Server.CreateObject("MSXML2.DOMDocument")
xmlDOM.async = false
xmlDOM.load("inventory.xml")
```

The code then obtains a list of the items that are available for purchase and creates option controls containing the list for each row in the table:

```
Set nlCheeses = xmlDOM.getElementsByTagName("Cheese")

For i = 1 to 10
  Response.Write "<TR><TD>"
```

```
Response.Write "<SELECT Language=" & chr(34) & "JScript" & chr(34) & " "
Response.Write "Name=" & chr(34) & "cboCheese" & i & chr(34) & " "
Response.Write "Id=" & chr(34) & "cboCheese" & i & chr(34)
Response.Write " onchange=" & chr(34)
Response.Write "setCheesePrice(" & i & ")" & chr(34) & ">"
Response.Write "<OPTION value=" & chr(34) & chr(34) & "selected></OPTION>"
For iCheese = 0 to nlCheeses.length - 1
   Response.Write "<OPTION Value=" & chr(34)
   Response.Write nlCheeses.item(iCheese).getAttribute("Name") & _
                  chr(34) & ">"
   Response.Write nlCheeses.item(iCheese).getAttribute("Name") & _
                  "</OPTION>"
Next
```

Note that we've added a JScript function call, `setCheesePrice`, to the `onchange` event for each of the dropdowns – this function will be used to populate the read-only price for that row. This function will be built on the fly in our script using the information in `inventory.xml`, as we'll see a little later in the listing.

The script then goes on to create the other fields in the table: the amount, the price (read-only), and the subtotal (read-only). It also creates a read-only grand total field. The values for these fields will be calculated using another dynamically generated function, `calculateCost`, which we'll also build from the information in `inventory.xml`.

```
Response.Write "</SELECT></TD>"
Response.Write "<TD><INPUT NAME=" & chr(34) & "txtAmount" & i & _
               chr(34) & " "
Response.Write "Id=" & chr(34) & "txtAmount" & i & chr(34)
Response.Write " onchange=" & chr(34) & "calculateCost(" & i & ")"& _
               chr(34)
Response.Write " size=5 maxlength=5></TD>"
Response.Write "<TD><INPUT NAME=" & chr(34) & "txtPrice" & i & _
               chr(34) & " "
Response.Write "Id=" & chr(34) & "txtPrice" & i & chr(34) & _
               " disabled size=10 "
Response.Write "maxlength=10><INPUT TYPE='hidden' NAME="
Response.Write chr(34) & "hiddenPrice" & i & chr(34) & " Id=" & chr(34)
Response.Write "hiddenPrice" & i & chr(34) & "></TD>"
Response.Write "<TD><INPUT NAME=" & chr(34) & "txtTotalPrice" & _
               i & chr(34) & " "
Response.Write "Id=" & chr(34) & "txtTotalPrice" & i & chr(34)& _
               " disabled size=10 "
Response.Write "maxlength=10></TD>"
Response.Write "</TR>"
Next
%>
   </TR>
   <TR>
     <TD></TD>
     <TD></TD>
     <TD>Grand Total:</TD>
     <TD><INPUT NAME="txtGrandTotal" maxlength=10 size=10
            Id="txtGrandTotal" disabled></TD>
   </TR>
</TABLE>
```

```
<P align="center">
  <INPUT type="submit" name="cmdSubmit" id="cmdSubmit" value="Submit order">
</P>
</FORM>
</BODY>
```

Next, let's take a look at the two JScript procedures we mentioned before. The first one, setCheesePrice, sets the value of the price input field based on the product selected in the matching dropdown. It also recalculates the total purchase order amount based on the price and quantity selected of the product in question. The ASP code iterates through all the products in inventory.xml and writes JScript to the Response object based on the information contained there.

```
<%
   Set nlCheeses = xmlDOM.getElementsByTagName("Cheese")
   Response.Write "<SCRIPT ID=setCheesePrice LANGUAGE=javascript>" & vbCRLF
   Response.Write "function setCheesePrice(i) {" & vbCRLF
   Response.Write "switch(frmPurchaseOrder.elements(" & chr(34) & _
                  "cboCheese" & chr(34) & " + i).value) {" & vbCRLF
   For iCheese = 0 to nlCheeses.length - 1
     Response.Write "case " & chr(34)
     Response.Write nlCheeses.item(iCheese).getAttribute("Name") & _
                  chr(34) & ":" & vbCRLF
     Response.Write "frmPurchaseOrder.elements(" & chr(34) & "txtPrice" & _
                  chr(34) & " + i).value = " & chr(34)
     Response.Write nlCheeses.item(iCheese).getAttribute("Price") & _
                  chr(34) & ";" & vbCRLF
     Response.Write "frmPurchaseOrder.elements(" & chr(34) & _
                  "hiddenPrice" & chr(34) & " + i).value = " & chr(34)
     Response.Write nlCheeses.item(iCheese).getAttribute("Price") & _
                  chr(34) & ";" & vbCRLF
     Response.Write "break;" & vbCRLF
   Next
   Response.Write "}" & vbCRLF
   Response.Write "calculateCost(i);"
   Response.Write "}" & vbCRLF
```

Here's the code that gets sent to the client, based on the inventory.xml we saw earlier in the study:

```
function setCheesePrice(i) {
  switch(frmPurchaseOrder.elements("cboCheese" + i).value)
  {
  case "1 lb. Cheddar":
    frmPurchaseOrder.elements("txtPrice" + i).value = "3.99";
    frmPurchaseOrder.elements("hiddenPrice" + i).value = "3.99";
    break;
  case "1 lb. Gouda":
    frmPurchaseOrder.elements("txtPrice" + i).value = "4.99";
    frmPurchaseOrder.elements("hiddenPrice" + i).value = "4.99";
    break;
  case "0.5 lb. Venezuelan Beaver Cheese":
    frmPurchaseOrder.elements("txtPrice" + i).value = "7.99";
    frmPurchaseOrder.elements("hiddenPrice" + i).value = "7.99";
    break;
  }
  calculateCost(i);
}
```

Learning to generate dynamic client-side script like this is a little like having X-ray vision – it's a power that can be used for good or evil. Use care when using this type of technique, and document everything to make it as plain as possible to the next guy that has to modify your code.

The second JScript procedure, `calculateCost`, calculates the total purchase price based on the products and amounts selected. It is called whenever the amount is changed, or (indirectly) whenever a product is changed.

```
Response.Write "function calculateCost(i) {" & vbCRLF
Response.Write "var j;" & vbCRLF
Response.Write "var rTotalCost;" & vbCRLF
Response.Write "rTotalCost = 0;" & vbCRLF
Response.Write "if (frmPurchaseOrder.elements('txtAmount' + i).value > 0)" & _
               " {" & vbCRLF
Response.Write "  if (frmPurchaseOrder.elements('txtPrice' + i).value > 0)" & _
               " {" & vbCRLF
Response.Write "    frmPurchaseOrder.elements('txtTotalPrice' + i).value ="
Response.Write "frmPurchaseOrder.elements('txtPrice' + i).value * "
Response.Write "frmPurchaseOrder.elements('txtAmount' + i).value;" & _
               vbCRLF
Response.Write "  }" & vbCRLF
Response.Write "for (j=1; j<=10; j++) {" & vbCRLF
Response.Write "  rTotalCost = rTotalCost + 1.0 * " & _
               "frmPurchaseOrder.elements('txtTotalPrice' + j).value;" & _
               vbCRLF
Response.Write "  }" & vbCRLF
Response.Write "frmPurchaseOrder.elements('txtGrandTotal').value = " & _
               "rTotalCost;" & vbCRLF
Response.Write "}" & vbCRLF & "}" & vbCRLF
Set nlCheeses = Nothing
set xmlDOM = Nothing
%>
//-->
</HTML>
```

The JScript sent to the client for this function is the following, also indented for easy reading:

```
function calculateCost(i) {
  var j;
  var rTotalCost;
  rTotalCost = 0;
  if (frmInvoice.elements('txtAmount' + i).value > 0)
  {
    if (frmInvoice.elements('txtPrice' + i).value > 0)
    {
      frmInvoice.elements('txtTotalPrice' + i).value =
              frmInvoice.elements('txtPrice' + i).value *
              frmInvoice.elements('txtAmount' + i).value;
    }
    for (j=1; j<=10; j++)
    {
      rTotalCost = rTotalCost + 1.0 *
              frmInvoice.elements('txtTotalPrice' + j).value;
    }
  frmInvoice.elements('txtGrandTotal').value = rTotalCost;
  }
}
```

The full listing of `PurchaseOrder.asp` looks like this:

```asp
<%@ Language=VBScript %>
<HTML>
<HEAD>
<META NAME="GENERATOR" Content="Microsoft Visual Studio 6.0">
<TITLE></TITLE>
</HEAD>
<BODY LANGUAGE=javascript onerror="return window_onerror()">
<H1 align=center>Cheese Shop</H1>
<H1 align=center>Mr. Wensleydale, Proprietor</H1>
<FORM METHOD=post ACTION="submitPurchaseOrder.asp" id=frmPurchaseOrder
  name=frmPurchaseOrder>
<P align=center> </P>
<TABLE align=center>
  <TR>
    <TD>Customer Name:</TD>
    <TD><INPUT NAME="txtName" Id="txtName" maxLength="50" size="50" ></TD>
  </TR>
  <TR>
    <TD>Shipping Address:</TD>
    <TD>
      <INPUT NAME="txtAddress1" Id="txtAddress1" maxLength="50" size="50">
    </TD>
  </TR>
  <TR>
    <TD></TD>
    <TD>
      <INPUT NAME="txtAddress2" Id="txtAddress2" maxLength="50" size="50">
    </TD>
  </TR>
  <TR>
    <TD>City, State, Zip:</TD>
    <TD>
      <INPUT NAME="txtCity" Id="txtCity" maxLength="30" size="30" >, 
      <INPUT NAME="txtState" Id="txtState" maxLength="2" size="2" > 
      <INPUT NAME="txtPostalCode" Id="txtPostalCode" maxLength="12" size="12">
    </TD>
  </TR>
  <TR>
    <TD>Telephone:</TD>
    <TD>
      <INPUT TYPE="telephone" NAME="txtTelephone" Id="txtTelephone"
             maxLength="15"size="15">
    </TD>
  </TR>
</TABLE>
<TABLE align=center>
  <TR>
    <TD>Cheese</TD>
    <TD>Amount</TD>
    <TD>Price Per Unit</TD>
    <TD>Total Price</TD>
  </TR>
<%
' now, we need to generate ten line entry items
```

```
' we can find a list of cheeses in stock at inventory.xml in the current dir
Dim i
Dim rTotalCost
Dim iCheese
Dim xmlDOM
Dim nlCheeses

Set xmlDOM = Server.CreateObject("MSXML2.DOMDocument")
xmlDOM.async = false
xmlDOM.load("inventory.xml")

Set nlCheeses = xmlDOM.getElementsByTagName("Cheese")

For i = 1 to 10
  Response.Write "<TR><TD>"
  Response.Write "<SELECT Language=" & chr(34) & "JScript" & chr(34) & " "
  Response.Write "Name=" & chr(34) & "cboCheese" & i & chr(34) & " "
  Response.Write "Id=" & chr(34) & "cboCheese" & i & chr(34)
  Response.Write " onchange=" & chr(34)
  Response.Write "setCheesePrice(" & i & ")" & chr(34) & ">"
  Response.Write "<OPTION value=" & chr(34) & chr(34) & _
                    " selected></OPTION>"
  For iCheese = 0 to nlCheeses.length - 1
    Response.Write "<OPTION Value=" & chr(34)
    Response.Write nlCheeses.item(iCheese).getAttribute("Name") & _
                    chr(34) & ">"
    Response.Write nlCheeses.item(iCheese).getAttribute("Name") & _
                    "</OPTION>"
  Next
  Response.Write "</SELECT></TD>"
  Response.Write "<TD><INPUT NAME=" & chr(34) & "txtAmount" & i & _
                    chr(34) & " "
  Response.Write "Id=" & chr(34) & "txtAmount" & i & chr(34)
  Response.Write " onchange=" & chr(34) & "calculateCost(" & i & ")" & _
                    chr(34)
  Response.Write " size=5 maxlength=5></TD>"
  Response.Write "<TD><INPUT NAME=" & chr(34) & "txtPrice" & i & _
                    chr(34) & " "
  Response.Write "Id=" & chr(34) & "txtPrice" & i & chr(34) & _
                    " disabled size=10 "
  Response.Write "maxlength=10><INPUT TYPE='hidden' NAME="
  Response.Write chr(34) & "hiddenPrice" & i & chr(34) & " Id=" & chr(34)
  Response.Write "hiddenPrice" & i & chr(34) & "></TD>"
  Response.Write "<TD><INPUT NAME=" & chr(34) & "txtTotalPrice" & _
                    i & chr(34) & " "
  Response.Write "Id=" & chr(34) & "txtTotalPrice" & i & chr(34)& _
                    " disabled size=10 "
  Response.Write "maxlength=10></TD>"
  Response.Write "</TR>"
Next

Set nlCheeses = Nothing
Set xmlDOM = Nothing
%>
  </TR>
  <TR>
```

```
      <TD></TD>
      <TD></TD>
      <TD>Grand Total:</TD>
      <TD><INPUT NAME="txtGrandTotal" maxlength=10 size=10
             Id="txtGrandTotal" disabled></TD>
   </TR>
</TABLE>
<P align="center">
   <INPUT type="submit" name="cmdSubmit" id="cmdSubmit" value="Submit order">
</P>
</FORM>
</BODY>
<%
  Set nlCheeses = xmlDOM.getElementsByTagName("Cheese")
  Response.Write "<SCRIPT ID=setCheesePrice LANGUAGE=javascript>" & vbCRLF
  Response.Write "function setCheesePrice(i) {" & vbCRLF
  Response.Write "switch(frmPurchaseOrder.elements(" & chr(34) & _
                    "cboCheese" & chr(34) & " + i).value) {" & vbCRLF
  For iCheese = 0 to nlCheeses.length - 1
    Response.Write "case " & chr(34)
    Response.Write nlCheeses.item(iCheese).getAttribute("Name") & chr(34) &_
                    ":" & vbCRLF
    Response.Write "frmPurchaseOrder.elements(" & chr(34) & "txtPrice" & _
                    chr(34) & " + i).value = " & chr(34)
    Response.Write nlCheeses.item(iCheese).getAttribute("Price") & _
                    chr(34) & ";" & vbCRLF
    Response.Write "frmPurchaseOrder.elements(" & chr(34) & _
                    "hiddenPrice" & chr(34) & " + i).value = " & chr(34)
    Response.Write nlCheeses.item(iCheese).getAttribute("Price") & _
                    chr(34) & ";" & vbCRLF
    Response.Write "break;" & vbCRLF
  Next
  Response.Write "}" & vbCRLF
  Response.Write "calculateCost(i);"
  Response.Write "}" & vbCRLF

  Response.Write "function calculateCost(i) {" & vbCRLF
  Response.Write "var j;" & vbCRLF
  Response.Write "var rTotalCost;" & vbCRLF
  Response.Write "rTotalCost = 0;" & vbCRLF
  Response.Write "if (frmPurchaseOrder.elements('txtAmount' + i).value > 0)" & _
                    " {" & vbCRLF
  Response.Write "  if (frmPurchaseOrder.elements('txtPrice' + i).value > 0)" & _
                    " {" & vbCRLF
  Response.Write "    frmPurchaseOrder.elements('txtTotalPrice' + i).value = "
  Response.Write "frmPurchaseOrder.elements('txtPrice' + i).value * "
  Response.Write "frmPurchaseOrder.elements('txtAmount' + i).value;" & _
                vbCRLF
  Response.Write "  }" & vbCRLF
  Response.Write "for (j=1; j<=10; j++) {" & vbCRLF
  Response.Write "  rTotalCost = rTotalCost + 1.0 * " & _
                    "frmPurchaseOrder.elements('txtTotalPrice' + j).value;" & _
                vbCRLF
  Response.Write "  }" & vbCRLF
  Response.Write "frmPurchaseOrder.elements('txtGrandTotal').value = " & _
                    "rTotalCost;" & vbCRLF
```

633

```
      Response.Write "}" & vbCRLF & "}" & vbCRLF
      Set nlCheeses = Nothing
      set xmlDOM = Nothing
%>


//-->
</HTML>
```

The Purchase Order Processor

Next, let's take a look at the script we'll be using to receive the submitted order and persist the information to XML files.

First, let's set up our file. This file is pure VBScript – its only purpose is to create the XML document from the purchase order information supplied. After processing is complete, we'll redirect the response to the appropriate HTML page.

```
<%@ Language=VBScript %>

<%
   Dim docPurchaseOrder
   Dim elPurchaseOrder
   Dim elLineItem
   Dim bName, bAddress1, bCity, bState, bZip, bTelephone
   Dim bCheese1, bAmount1, bPrice1
   Dim sFilename
   Dim sOldFilename
   Dim fsoPurchaseOrder
   Dim tsPurchaseOrder
   Dim iDuplicate
   Dim i
```

Next, we check to see that the provided information conforms to the DTD we have defined for our purchase order with regards to required information. This is necessary because the DOM doesn't allow us to set the DTD for a document we are creating. If it did, we could simply attempt to set the values in the DOM document object – it would return errors if the data didn't conform to the supplied DTD. When the DOM level 2 implementations become available, this issue will be addressed. (A better approach to data validation would be to check this on the client side with JScript to reduce the number of round trips to the server – doing so is left as an exercise for the reader.)

```
   bName = false
   bAddress1 = false
   bCity = false
   bState = false
   bZip = false
   bTelephone = false
   bCheese1 = false
   bAmount1 = false
   bPrice1 = false

   ' make sure all the required information is there
   If Request("txtName") > "" Then bName = True
   If Request("txtAddress1") > "" Then bAddress1 = True
```

```
If Request("txtCity") > "" Then bCity = True
If Request("txtState") > "" Then bState = True
If Request("txtPostalCode") > "" Then bZip = True
If Request("txtTelephone") > "" Then bTelephone = True
If Request("cboCheese1") > "" Then bCheese1 = True
If Request("txtAmount1") > "" Then bAmount1 = True
If Request("hiddenPrice1") > "" Then bPrice1 = True
```

Next, we're going to use the DOM to create the document tree in memory. Note that, at least for smaller documents, using the DOM to create the document is almost always a better choice than serializing it to text "by hand" – because documents created using the DOM are guaranteed to be well-formed.

```
If (bName AND bAddress1 AND bCity AND bState AND bZip AND bCheese1 _
                AND bAmount1 AND bPrice1) Then
  ' all required information is present, let's build the document
  Set docPurchaseOrder = Server.CreateObject("MSXML2.DOMDocument")
  Set elPurchaseOrder = docPurchaseOrder.createElement("PurchaseOrder")
  docPurchaseOrder.appendChild elPurchaseOrder
  elPurchaseOrder.setAttribute "CustomerName", Request("txtName")
  elPurchaseOrder.setAttribute "Address1", Request("txtAddress1")
  If Request("txtAddress2") > "" Then
    elPurchaseOrder.setAttribute "Address2", Request("txtAddress2")
  End If
  elPurchaseOrder.setAttribute "City", Request("txtCity")
  elPurchaseOrder.setAttribute "State", Request("txtState")
  elPurchaseOrder.setAttribute "PostalCode", Request("txtPostalCode")
  elPurchaseOrder.setAttribute "Telephone", Request("txtTelephone")
  For i = 1 to 10
    If Request("cboCheese" & i) > "" And Request("txtAmount" & i) > "" Then
      ' this one needs to be added to the order
      Set elLineItem = docPurchaseOrder.createElement("LineItem")
      elPurchaseOrder.appendChild elLineItem
      elLineItem.setAttribute "CheeseType", Request("cboCheese" & i)
      elLineItem.setAttribute "Amount", Request("txtAmount" & i)
      elLineItem.setAttribute "Price", Request("hiddenPrice" & i)
    End If
  Next
```

Now that we have the document in memory, we need to persist it to a file to be operated on by the fulfillment form. We'll place the documents in c:\PurchaseOrders\ (note that you'll have to create a similar directory on your machine to test this code), and we'll create a filename based on when the form was processed:

```
sFilename = "c:\PurchaseOrders\"
sFilename = sFilename & DatePart("yyyy", Now())
sFilename = sFilename & DatePart("m", Now())
sFilename = sFilename & Datepart("d", Now())
sFilename = sFilename & DatePart("h", Now())
sFilename = sFilename & DatePart("n", Now())
sFilename = sFilename & DatePart("s", Now())
sOldFilename = sFilename
sFilename = sFilename & ".xml"
Set fsoPurchaseOrder = Server.CreateObject("Scripting.FileSystemObject")
```

635

```
        iDuplicate = 1
        While fsoPurchaseOrder.FileExists(sFilename)
          sFilename = sOldFilename & "_" & iDuplicate & ".xml"
        Wend
        docPurchaseOrder.save sFilename
```

The last five lines are used to append a suffix to the filename in case two or more requests arrive simultaneously. We could also use the built-in temporary filename generator to create a name for the file, but it's nice having the semantic information built into the filename that is used. However, using the temporary filename generator would be a more robust approach.

Finally, based on whether all the required information was available, we redirect the response to the appropriate page:

```
        Response.Redirect "orderPlaced.htm"
    Else
        ' something was missing
        Response.Redirect "missingInfo.htm"
    End If
%>
```

Here's the entire listing for `submitPurchaseOrder.asp`:

```
<%@ Language=VBScript %>

<%
    Dim docPurchaseOrder
    Dim elPurchaseOrder
    Dim elLineItem
    Dim bName, bAddress1, bCity, bState, bZip, bTelephone
    Dim bCheese1, bAmount1, bPrice1
    Dim sFilename
    Dim sOldFilename
    Dim fsoPurchaseOrder
    Dim tsPurchaseOrder
    Dim iDuplicate
    Dim i

    bName = false
    bAddress1 = false
    bCity = false
    bState = false
    bZip = false
    bTelephone = false
    bCheese1 = false
    bAmount1 = false
    bPrice1 = false

    ' make sure all the required information is there
    If Request("txtName") > "" Then bName = True
    If Request("txtAddress1") > "" Then bAddress1 = True
    If Request("txtCity") > "" Then bCity = True
    If Request("txtState") > "" Then bState = True
    If Request("txtPostalCode") > "" Then bZip = True
```

```
If Request("txtTelephone") > "" Then bTelephone = True
If Request("cboCheese1") > "" Then bCheese1 = True
If Request("txtAmount1") > "" Then bAmount1 = True
If Request("hiddenPrice1") > "" Then bPrice1 = True

If (bName AND bAddress1 AND bCity AND bState AND bZip AND bCheese1 _
        AND bAmount1 AND bPrice1) Then
  ' all required information is present, let's build the document
  Set docPurchaseOrder = Server.CreateObject("MSXML2.DOMDocument")
  Set elPurchaseOrder = docPurchaseOrder.createElement("PurchaseOrder")
  docPurchaseOrder.appendChild elPurchaseOrder
  elPurchaseOrder.setAttribute "CustomerName", Request("txtName")
  elPurchaseOrder.setAttribute "Address1", Request("txtAddress1")
  If Request("txtAddress2") > "" Then
    elPurchaseOrder.setAttribute "Address2", Request("txtAddress2")
  End If
  elPurchaseOrder.setAttribute "City", Request("txtCity")
  elPurchaseOrder.setAttribute "State", Request("txtState")
  elPurchaseOrder.setAttribute "PostalCode", Request("txtPostalCode")
  elPurchaseOrder.setAttribute "Telephone", Request("txtTelephone")
  For i = 1 to 10
   If Request("cboCheese" & i) > "" And Request("txtAmount" & i) > "" Then
      ' this one needs to be added to the order
      Set elLineItem = docPurchaseOrder.createElement("LineItem")
      elPurchaseOrder.appendChild elLineItem
      elLineItem.setAttribute "CheeseType", Request("cboCheese" & i)
      elLineItem.setAttribute "Amount", Request("txtAmount" & i)
      elLineItem.setAttribute "Price", Request("hiddenPrice" & i)
    End If
  Next
  ' now let's persist the document to a file
  ' we'll assume the files are stored locally
  ' in the c:\PurchaseOrders\ directory
  sFilename = "c:\PurchaseOrders\"
  sFilename = sFilename & DatePart("yyyy", Now())
  sFilename = sFilename & DatePart("m", Now())
  sFilename = sFilename & Datepart("d", Now())
  sFilename = sFilename & DatePart("h", Now())
  sFilename = sFilename & DatePart("n", Now())
  sFilename = sFilename & DatePart("s", Now())
  sOldFilename = sFilename
  sFilename = sFilename & ".xml"
  Set fsoPurchaseOrder = Server.CreateObject("Scripting.FileSystemObject")
  iDuplicate = 1
  While fsoPurchaseOrder.FileExists(sFilename)
    sFilename = sOldFilename & "_" & iDuplicate & ".xml"
  Wend
  docPurchaseOrder.save sFilename
  Response.Redirect "orderPlaced.htm"
Else
  ' something was missing
  Response.Write "Redirecting to missingInfo.htm"
End If
%>
```

Here's the code for the `orderPlaced.htm` and `missingInfo.htm` files:

```
<HTML>
<HEAD>
</HEAD>
<BODY>
<H1 align=center>Cheese Shop</H1>
<P align=center>Your order has been successfully submitted. You will be billed for
your order when the delivery arrives, typically within 12 to 24 hours. </P>
<P align=center>Thank you!</P>
<P> </P>
</BODY>
</HTML>
```

```
<HTML>
<HEAD>
</HEAD>
<BODY>
<H1 align=center>Cheese Shop</H1>
<P align=center>You appear to have omitted one or more required fields. Please use
the BACK button on your browser to go back and check your entry.</P>
<P> </P>
</BODY>
</HTML>
```

And this is what the two pages look like; `orderPlaced.htm` is on the left:

The Fulfillment Form

Once we have the XML purchase orders persisted to files, we need to have another interface via which the various fulfillment shops may access the orders for their postal code at any time. The user interface for this screen looks something like this:

Since we're not building anything dynamically on this page, it's simply an HTML form. Here's the code for the form:

```
<HTML>
<HEAD>
</HEAD>
<BODY>
<FORM name="frmFulfillment" id="frmFulfillment" method="post"
            action="submitFulfillment.asp">
<H1 align=center>Cheese Shop Fulfillment</H1>
<P align=center>Enter the postal code being serviced:
  <INPUT id=txtPostalCode name=txtPostalCode maxlength="10" size="10">
</P>
<TABLE align=center>
  <TR>
    <TD>
      <INPUT type="radio" id=rdoFileType name=rdoFileType value="Delimited"
            checked>Download a comma-delimited file
    </TD>
  </TR>
  <TR>
    <TD>
      <INPUT type="radio" id=rdoFileType name=rdoFileType value="XML">
      Download an XML file with summary
    </TD>
  </TR>
</TABLE>
<P align=center>
  <INPUT id=cmdSubmit type=submit value="Download orders" name=cmdSubmit>
</P>
</FORM>
</BODY>
</HTML>
```

Next, let's take a look at the code that will be used to select the appropriate purchase orders from the file repository and generate the response information to the fulfillment shops. The various shops may select the format of the data being downloaded to them; in this example, we'll show how we can use XSLT and XPath to manipulate the information in the documents. The two formats we will show are XML and comma-delimited; it would be a simple matter to add additional formats using different XSLT templates.

First, we instantiate four DOM documents:

❑　docPurchaseOrder to hold each purchase order as it is read from the persisted files

❑　docFulfillment to hold the concatenated purchase order document

❑　docStylesheet to hold the appropriate stylesheet for the desired output

❑　docOutput to hold the transformed output (if that output is XML)

```
<%@ Language=VBScript %>

<%
  ' first let's iterate through all the files queued
  ' and determine which ones we need to use
```

639

```
Dim fso
Dim folderPurchaseOrders
Dim filesPurchaseOrders
Dim filePurchaseOrder
Dim docPurchaseOrder
Dim docFulfillment
Dim docStylesheet
Dim docOutput
Dim elPurchaseOrder
Dim elFulfillment

' FOPur instances of the MSXML3 parser are needed. This parser can do XSLT
Set docPurchaseOrder = Server.CreateObject("MSXML2.DOMDocument.3.0")
docPurchaseOrder.async = false
Set docFulfillment = Server.CreateObject("MSXML2.DOMDocument.3.0")
Set docStylesheet = Server.CreateObject("MSXML2.DOMDocument.3.0")
docStylesheet.async = false
Set docOutput = Server.CreateObject("MSXML2.DOMDocument.3.0")
docOutput.async = false

docFulfillment.setProperty "SelectionLanguage", "XPath"
docStylesheet.setProperty "SelectionLanguage", "XPath"
```

Since our raw aggregated document simply consists of all the purchase orders run together and encapsulated within a Fulfillment element, we create that element for the docFulfillment document:

```
Set elFulfillment = docFulfillment.createElement("Fulfillment")
docFulfillment.appendChild(elFulfillment)
```

Next, we start opening the documents in the **c:/PurchaseOrders/** directory, looking for any that have a postal code matching that entered on the fulfillment form. Note that the code assumes that only XML documents will be found in this directory – other document types will cause problems for the script. If there is a match on the entered postal code, that purchase order is appended to the docFulfillment document as a child of the Fulfillment element.

```
Set fso = Server.CreateObject("Scripting.FileSystemObject")
Set folderPurchaseOrders = fso.GetFolder("c:/PurchaseOrders/")
Set filesPurchaseOrders = folderPurchaseOrders.files

For Each filePurchaseOrder in filesPurchaseOrders
  ' see what the postal code is...
  docPurchaseOrder.load filePurchaseOrder.Path
  Set elPurchaseOrder = docPurchaseOrder.firstChild
  If elPurchaseOrder.getAttribute("PostalCode") = _
                                      Request("txtPostalCode") Then
    ' this is one we need
    elFulfillment.appendChild(elPurchaseOrder)
  End If
Next
```

At this point, our docFulfillment document contains the raw collected purchase orders for the provided postal code. Next, we need to transform this document based on the type of output selected by the user and send the results back to the user:

640

```
    If Request("rdoFileType") = "XML" Then
      docStylesheet.load("http://kwilliams/summary.xsl")
      docFulfillment.transformNodeToObject docStylesheet, docOutput
      Response.ContentType = "text/xml"
      Response.Write docOutput.xml
    Else
      docStylesheet.load("http://kwilliams/delimited.xsl")
      Response.Write docFulfillment.transformNode(docStylesheet)
    End If
    Response.End
%>
```

We'll take a look at the contents of these two XSLT scripts a little later.

The full text of the submitFulfillment.asp script looks like this:

```
<%@ Language=VBScript %>

<%
  ' first let's iterate through all the files queued
  ' and determine which ones we need to use
  Dim fso
  Dim folderPurchaseOrders
  Dim filesPurchaseOrders
  Dim filePurchaseOrder
  Dim docPurchaseOrder
  Dim docFulfillment
  Dim docStylesheet
  Dim docOutput
  Dim elPurchaseOrder
  Dim elFulfillment

  Set docPurchaseOrder = Server.CreateObject("MSXML2.DOMDocument")
  docPurchaseOrder.async = false
  Set docFulfillment = Server.CreateObject("MSXML2.DOMDocument")
  Set docStylesheet = Server.CreateObject("MSXML2.DOMDocument")
  docStylesheet.async = false
  Set docOutput = Server.CreateObject("MSXML2.DOMDocument")
  docOutput.async = false

  docFulfillment.setProperty "SelectionLanguage", "XPath"
  docStylesheet.setProperty "SelectionLanguage", "XPath"

  Set elFulfillment = docFulfillment.createElement("Fulfillment")
  docFulfillment.appendChild(elFulfillment)

  Set fso = Server.CreateObject("Scripting.FileSystemObject")
  Set folderPurchaseOrders = fso.GetFolder("c:/PurchaseOrders/")
  Set filesPurchaseOrders = folderPurchaseOrders.files

  For Each filePurchaseOrder in filesPurchaseOrders
    ' see what the postal code is...
    docPurchaseOrder.load filePurchaseOrder.Path
    Set elPurchaseOrder = docPurchaseOrder.firstChild
```

```
      If elPurchaseOrder.getAttribute("PostalCode") = _
                                          Request("txtPostalCode") Then
        ' this is one we need
        elFulfillment.appendChild(elPurchaseOrder)
      End If
    Next

    If Request("rdoFileType") = "XML" Then
      docStylesheet.load("summary.xsl")
      docFulfillment.transformNodeToObject docStylesheet, docOutput
      Response.ContentType = "text/xml"
      Response.Write docOutput.xml
    Else
      docStylesheet.load("delimited.xsl")
      Response.Write docFulfillment.transformNode(docStylesheet)
    End If
    Response.End
%>
```

As you can see, the script uses two different XSLT scripts to perform translation of the individual purchase order documents. First, it creates an aggregate document by grouping the various purchase orders collected for the appropriate postal code; then, it uses XSLT to transform that document to the desired output. For XML output, the XSLT script performs aggregation, gathering together all the different types of cheeses and providing total amounts that need to be pulled from the fulfillment shop's inventory; for comma-delimited output, the XSLT produces a simple flattened format that the fulfillment shop may read with Excel or some other spreadsheet software.

For the XML output, we summarize the total quantity ordered for each type of cheese in a summary section at the end of the document; this enables the fulfillment shop to easily pull the proper amount of inventory before beginning delivery for the set of purchase orders. The XSLT script used to perform this transformation looks like this:

```xml
<?xml version="1.0"?>
<xsl:stylesheet xmlns:xsl="http://www.w3.org/1999/XSL/Transform" version="1.0">
  <xsl:template match="/">
    <xsl:element name="Fulfillment">
      <xsl:copy-of select="//PurchaseOrder"/>
      <xsl:element name="Summary">
        <xsl:for-each select="//LineItem">
          <xsl:sort select="@CheeseType"/>
          <xsl:variable name="thisCheeseType" select="@CheeseType"/>
          <xsl:if test="generate-id(@CheeseType)=
                        generate-id(//@CheeseType[.=$thisCheeseType])">
            <xsl:element name="LineItem">
              <xsl:attribute name="CheeseType">
                <xsl:value-of select="@CheeseType"/>
              </xsl:attribute>
              <xsl:attribute name="Amount">
                <xsl:value-of
              select="sum(//LineItem[@CheeseType=$thisCheeseType]/@Amount)"/>
              </xsl:attribute>
            </xsl:element>
          </xsl:if>
        </xsl:for-each>
      </xsl:element>
```

```
      </xsl:element>
   </xsl:template>
 </xsl:stylesheet>
```

XSLT tends to be a very dense language, so let's take a look at it more closely. First, we frame the document with a `Fulfillment` element:

```
<xsl:element name="Fulfillment">
```

Then, we write a copy of every purchase order in the raw document, along with that node's children:

```
<xsl:copy-of select="//PurchaseOrder"/>
```

Next, we create a `Summary` element to hold summary information:

```
<xsl:element name="Summary">
```

We need to examine each line item for all the purchase orders in the set to create our summary information. We'll sort them by the type of item being ordered – this will help us create the sums for each type of item:

```
<xsl:for-each select="//LineItem">
  <xsl:sort select="@CheeseType"/>
```

Next, let's set aside the current `CheeseType` being operated on in a variable called `thisCheeseType` – this allows us to perform a distinctness test, as we'll see in a minute:

```
<xsl:variable name="thisCheeseType" select="@CheeseType"/>
```

The next line is the line that ensures we are operating on the data in a distinct manner:

```
<xsl:if test="generate-id(@CheeseType)=
                generate-id(//@CheeseType[.=$thisCheeseType])">
```

This is important, because if two people both ordered a pound of Cheddar, we want to make sure we only see Cheddar once in the output. This test takes advantage of two behaviors of the `generate-id` function: it always returns a unique value for each node (even two nodes that have the same content), and if it is run against a node set, it returns the unique value for the node that appears first in document order. So, this `xsl:if` statement checks to see if the unique ID for the current node is the same as the unique ID for the `CheeseType` attribute that occurs first in document order – in other words, the test will only pass once for each cheese type. Therefore, we are guaranteed that each type will appear only once in the summary section.

Next, we create a `LineItem` element that calculates the sum of all amounts for all line items on all purchase orders with the same cheese type:

```
<xsl:element name="LineItem">
  <xsl:attribute name="CheeseType">
    <xsl:value-of select="@CheeseType"/>
```

```
       </xsl:attribute>
       <xsl:attribute name="Amount">
         <xsl:value-of
     select="sum(//LineItem[@CheeseType=$thisCheeseType]/@Amount)"/>
       </xsl:attribute>
     </xsl:element>
```

Finally, we terminate all of the elements we have started, and processing ends:

```
       </xsl:if>
      </xsl:for-each>
     </xsl:element>
    </xsl:element>
   </xsl:template>
</xsl:stylesheet>
```

An example output document of this stylesheet looks like this (we've added whitespace for readability):

```
<?xml version="1.0"?>
<Fulfillment>
  <PurchaseOrder
      CustomerName="Homer Simpson"
      Address1="742 Evergreen Terrace"
      City="Springfield"
      State="VA"
      PostalCode="11111"
      Telephone="800-555-1212">
    <LineItem
        CheeseType="1 lb. Cheddar"
        Amount="1"
        Price="3.99"/>
  </PurchaseOrder>
  <PurchaseOrder
      CustomerName="Ned Flanders"
      Address1="744 Evergreen Terrace"
      City="Springfield"
      State="VA"
      PostalCode="11111"
      Telephone="800-555-1213">
    <LineItem
        CheeseType="1 lb. Gouda"
        Amount="1"
        Price="5.99"/>
    <LineItem
        CheeseType="1 lb. Cheddar"
        Amount="2"
        Price="3.99"/>
    <LineItem
        CheeseType="0.5 lb. Wensleydale"
        Amount="4"
        Price="2.99"/>
  </PurchaseOrder>
  <PurchaseOrder
      CustomerName="Barney Gumbel"
```

```
                Address1="Above Moe's Tavern"
                City="Springfield"
                State="VA"
                PostalCode="11111"
                Telephone="800-555-1313">
        <LineItem
            CheeseType="1 lb. Cheddar"
            Amount="2"
            Price="3.99"/>
        <LineItem
            CheeseType="0.5 lb. Stilton"
            Amount="1"
            Price="3.99"/>
        <LineItem
            CheeseType="1 lb. Gouda"
            Amount="17"
            Price="5.99"/>
    </PurchaseOrder>
    <Summary>
        <LineItem
            CheeseType="0.5 lb. Stilton"
            Amount="1"/>
        <LineItem
            CheeseType="0.5 lb. Wensleydale"
            Amount="4"/>
        <LineItem
            CheeseType="1 lb. Cheddar"
            Amount="5"/>
        <LineItem
            CheeseType="1 lb. Gouda"
            Amount="18"/>
    </Summary>
</Fulfillment>
```

The stylesheet for the comma-delimited version of the output looks like this:

```
<?xml version="1.0"?>
<xsl:stylesheet xmlns:xsl="http://www.w3.org/1999/XSL/Transform" version="1.0">
  <xsl:output method="text"/>
  <xsl:template match="/">
    <xsl:for-each select="//PurchaseOrder">
      <xsl:text>H,"</xsl:text>
      <xsl:value-of select="@CustomerName"/>
      <xsl:text>","</xsl:text>
      <xsl:value-of select="@Address1"/>
      <xsl:text>","</xsl:text>
      <xsl:value-of select="@Address2"/>
      <xsl:text>","</xsl:text>
      <xsl:value-of select="@City"/>
      <xsl:text>","</xsl:text>
      <xsl:value-of select="@State"/>
      <xsl:text>","</xsl:text>
      <xsl:value-of select="@PostalCode"/>
      <xsl:text>","</xsl:text>
      <xsl:value-of select="@Telephone"/>
```

```
            <xsl:text disable-output-escaping="yes">"&#x0a;&#x0d;</xsl:text>
         <xsl:for-each select="LineItem">
            <xsl:text>D,"</xsl:text>
            <xsl:value-of select="@CheeseType"/>
            <xsl:text>",</xsl:text>
            <xsl:value-of select="@Amount"/>
            <xsl:text>,</xsl:text>
            <xsl:value-of select="@Price"/>
            <xsl:text disable-output-escaping="yes">&#x0a;&#x0d;</xsl:text>
         </xsl:for-each>
      </xsl:for-each>
   </xsl:template>
</xsl:stylesheet>
```

This stylesheet operates in a slightly more straightforward manner than the previous one. First, each purchase order in the document is operated on:

```
      <xsl:for-each select="//PurchaseOrder">
```

A header record is written first. This header record has the literal H in its first position, indicating that it is a header record; it then contains summary information for the purchase order, such as name and address:

```
      <xsl:text>H,"</xsl:text>
      <xsl:value-of select="@CustomerName"/>
      <xsl:text>","</xsl:text>
      <xsl:value-of select="@Address1"/>
      <xsl:text>","</xsl:text>
      <xsl:value-of select="@Address2"/>
      <xsl:text>","</xsl:text>
      <xsl:value-of select="@City"/>
      <xsl:text>","</xsl:text>
      <xsl:value-of select="@State"/>
      <xsl:text>","</xsl:text>
      <xsl:value-of select="@PostalCode"/>
      <xsl:text>","</xsl:text>
      <xsl:value-of select="@Telephone"/>
```

At the end of this record, we'll write a hard CRLF using escaped characters. Note that we have to set the disable-output-escaping flag on the call to xsl:text, otherwise the specified text will be re-escaped before it is sent to the output:

```
      <xsl:text disable-output-escaping="yes">"&#x0a;&#x0d;</xsl:text>
```

Next, a similar set of commands is used to send the detail information (prefixed with a D) for each line item to the output buffer, and to issue a hard CRLF at the end of the line:

```
      <xsl:for-each select="LineItem">
         <xsl:text>D,"</xsl:text>
         <xsl:value-of select="@CheeseType"/>
         <xsl:text>",</xsl:text>
         <xsl:value-of select="@Amount"/>
```

```
        <xsl:text>,</xsl:text>
        <xsl:value-of select="@Price"/>
        <xsl:text disable-output-escaping="yes">&#x0a;&#x0d;</xsl:text>
    </xsl:for-each>
```

Sample output from this transform is shown below:

```
H,"Kevin Williams","100 Every Road","","Everywheresville","WV","11111",""
D,"1 lb. Cheddar",1,3.99
H,"Joe Friday","100 Every Road","","Palookasville","WV","11111",""
D,"1 lb. Gouda",1,5.99
D,"1 lb. Cheddar",2,3.99
D,"0.5 lb. Wensleydale",4,2.99
H,"Fred Jones","102 Every Road","","Everywheresville","WV","11111",""
D,"1 lb. Cheddar",2,3.99
D,"0.5 lb. Stilton",1,3.99
D,"1 lb. Gouda",17,5.99
```

Note that this appears all run together if you look at the output in IE – this is because HTML discards whitespace (including the carriage return and line feed at the end of every line).

Summary

In this case study, we've seen how XML may be used in ASP to address some real-world issues:

❑ Using the DOM to generate XML from a submitted HTML form

❑ Persisting generated XML documents to files

❑ Using XSLT to search an archive of XML files

❑ Using XSLT to transform XML files to formats other than HTML

XML is a good choice for transferring information to non-Windows platforms, as well: in our example, if the fulfillment application were running on a Unix machine, it would be able to handle the generated XML files correctly. If we'd chosen to persist our data in a relational database, on the other hand, more code would be needed to marshal the information and pass it to the Unix machine.

The techniques used in this case study will help you in your efforts to integrate to legacy systems and make XML the backbone of your data transfer technology.

Extensible Markup Language (XML) 1.0 Specification

This appendix is taken from the W3C Recommendation 10-February-1998 available at:

`http://www.w3.org/TR/REC-xml`

The appendix has also been edited in accordance with the list of errata of 17-February-1999 posted at
`http://www.w3.org/XML/xml-19980210-errata`

Editors:

Tim Bray (Textuality and Netscape)   tbray@textuality.com
Jean Paoli (Microsoft)   jeanpa@microsoft.com
C. M. Sperberg-McQueen
(University of Illinois at Chicago)   cmsmcq@uic.edu

Abstract

The Extensible Markup Language (XML) is a subset of SGML that is completely described in this document. Its goal is to enable generic SGML to be served, received, and processed on the Web in the way that is now possible with HTML. XML has been designed for ease of implementation and for interoperability with both SGML and HTML.

Status of this document

This document has been reviewed by W3C Members and other interested parties and has been endorsed by the Director as a W3C Recommendation. It is a stable document and may be used as reference material or cited as a normative reference from another document. W3C's role in making the Recommendation is to draw attention to the specification and to promote its widespread deployment. This enhances the functionality and interoperability of the Web.

This document specifies a syntax created by subsetting an existing, widely used international text processing standard (Standard Generalized Markup Language, ISO 8879:1986(E) as amended and corrected) for use on the World Wide Web. It is a product of the W3C XML Activity, details of which can be found at http://www.w3.org/XML. A list of current W3C Recommendations and other technical documents can be found at http://www.w3.org/TR.

This specification uses the term URI, which is defined by Berners-Lee et al, a work in progress expected to update IETF RFC1738 and IETF RFC1808.

The list of known errors in this specification is available at http://www.w3.org/XML/xml-19980210-errata.

Please report errors in this document to xml-editor@w3.org.

Extensible Markup Language (XML) 1.0

Table of Contents

Appendices

1. Introduction

Extensible Markup Language, abbreviated XML, describes a class of data objects called XML documents and partially describes the behavior of computer programs which process them. XML is an application profile or restricted form of SGML, the Standard Generalized Markup Language [ISO 8879]. By construction, XML documents are conforming SGML documents.

XML documents are made up of storage units called entities, which contain either parsed or unparsed data. Parsed data is made up of characters, some of which form character data, and some of which form markup. Markup encodes a description of the document's storage layout and logical structure. XML provides a mechanism to impose constraints on the storage layout and logical structure.

A software module called an **XML processor** is used to read XML documents and provide access to their content and structure. It is assumed that an XML processor is doing its work on behalf of another module, called the **application**. This specification describes the required behavior of an XML processor in terms of how it must read XML data and the information it must provide to the application.

1.1 Origin and Goals

XML was developed by an XML Working Group (originally known as the SGML Editorial Review Board) formed under the auspices of the World Wide Web Consortium (W3C) in 1996. It was chaired by Jon Bosak of Sun Microsystems with the active participation of an XML Special Interest Group (previously known as the SGML Working Group) also organized by the W3C. The membership of the XML Working Group is given in an appendix. Dan Connolly served as the WG's contact with the W3C. The design goals for XML are:

- ❑ XML shall be straightforwardly usable over the Internet.
- ❑ XML shall support a wide variety of applications.
- ❑ XML shall be compatible with SGML.
- ❑ It shall be easy to write programs which process XML documents.
- ❑ The number of optional features in XML is to be kept to the absolute minimum, ideally zero.
- ❑ XML documents should be human-legible and reasonably clear.
- ❑ The XML design should be prepared quickly.
- ❑ The design of XML shall be formal and concise.
- ❑ XML documents shall be easy to create.
- ❑ Terseness in XML markup is of minimal importance.

This specification, together with associated standards (Unicode and ISO/IEC 10646 for characters, Internet RFC 1766 for language identification tags, ISO 639 for language name codes, and ISO 3166 for country name codes), provides all the information necessary to understand XML Version 1.0 and construct computer programs to process it.

This version of the XML specification may be distributed freely, as long as all text and legal notices remain intact.

1.2 Terminology

The terminology used to describe XML documents is defined in the body of this specification. The terms defined in the following list are used in building those definitions and in describing the actions of an XML processor:

may

Conforming documents and XML processors are permitted to but need not behave as described.

must

Conforming documents and XML processors are required to behave as described; otherwise they are in error.

error

A violation of the rules of this specification; results are undefined. Conforming software may detect and report an error and may recover from it.

fatal error

An error which a conforming XML processor must detect and report to the application. After encountering a fatal error, the processor may continue processing the data to search for further errors and may report such errors to the application. In order to support correction of errors, the processor may make unprocessed data from the document (with intermingled character data and markup) available to the application. Once a fatal error is detected, however, the processor must not continue normal processing (i.e., it must not continue to pass character data and information about the document's logical structure to the application in the normal way).

at user option

Conforming software may or must (depending on the modal verb in the sentence) behave as described; if it does, it must provide users a means to enable or disable the behavior described.

validity constraint

A rule which applies to all valid XML documents. Violations of validity constraints are errors; they must, at user option, be reported by validating XML processors.

well-formedness constraint

A rule which applies to all well-formed XML documents. Violations of well-formedness constraints are fatal errors.

match

(Of strings or names:) Two strings or names being compared must be identical. Characters with multiple possible representations in ISO/IEC 10646 (e.g. characters with both precomposed and base+diacritic forms) match only if they have the same representation in both strings. At user option, processors may normalize such characters to some canonical form. No case folding is performed. (Of strings and rules in the grammar:) A string matches a grammatical production if it belongs to the language generated by that production. (Of content and content models:) An element matches its declaration when it conforms in the fashion described in the constraint "Element Valid".

for compatibility

A feature of XML included solely to ensure that XML remains compatible with SGML.

for interoperability

A non-binding recommendation included to increase the chances that XML documents can be processed by the existing installed base of SGML processors which predate the WebSGML Adaptations Annex to ISO 8879.

2. Documents

A data object is an **XML document** if it is well-formed, as defined in this specification. A well-formed XML document may in addition be valid if it meets certain further constraints.

Each XML document has both a logical and a physical structure. Physically, the document is composed of units called entities. An entity may refer to other entities to cause their inclusion in the document. A document begins in a "root" or document entity. Logically, the document is composed of declarations, elements, comments, character references, and processing instructions, all of which are indicated in the document by explicit markup. The logical and physical structures must nest properly, as described in "**4.3.2 Well-Formed Parsed Entities**".

2.1 Well-Formed XML Documents

A textual object is a well-formed XML document if:

❑   Taken as a whole, it matches the production labeled `document`.

❑   It meets all the well-formedness constraints given in this specification.

❑   Each of the parsed entities which is referenced directly or indirectly within the document is well-formed.

Document			
[1]	document	::=	prolog element Misc*

Matching the `document` production implies that:

❑   It contains one or more elements.

❑   There is exactly one element, called the **root**, or document element, no part of which appears in the content of any other element. For all other elements, if the **start-tag** is in the content of another element, the **end-tag** is in the content of the same element. More simply stated, the elements, delimited by start- and end-tags, nest properly within each other.

As a consequence of this, for each non-root element C in the document, there is one other element P in the document such that C is in the content of P, but is not in the content of any other element that is in the content of P. P is referred to as the **parent** of C, and C as a **child** of P.

2.2 Characters

A parsed entity contains **text**, a sequence of characters, which may represent markup or character data. A **character** is an atomic unit of text as specified by ISO/IEC 10646. Legal characters are tab, carriage return, line feed, and the legal graphic characters of Unicode and ISO/IEC 10646. The use of "compatibility characters", as defined in section 6.8 of Unicode, is discouraged.

Character Range				
[2]	Char	::=	#x9 | #xA | #xD | [#x20-#xD7FF] | [#xE000-#xFFFD] | [#x10000-#x10FFFF]	/*any Unicode character, excluding the surrogate blocks, FFFE, and FFFF. */

Production [2] is normative; in practical terms this means that newly added Unicode characters such as the Euro (€ €) are legal in XML documents.

The mechanism for encoding character code points into bit patterns may vary from entity to entity. All XML processors must accept the UTF-8 and UTF-16 encodings of 10646; the mechanisms for signaling which of the two is in use, or for bringing other encodings into play, are discussed later, in "**4.3.3 Character Encoding in Entities**".

2.3 Common Syntactic Constructs

This section defines some symbols used widely in the grammar.

S (white space) consists of one or more space (#x20) characters, carriage returns, line feeds, or tabs.

White Space		
[3]	S ::=	(#x20 | #x9 | #xD | #xA)+

Characters are classified for convenience as letters, digits, or other characters. Letters consist of an alphabetic or syllabic base character possibly followed by one or more combining characters, or of an ideographic character. Full definitions of the specific characters in each class are given in "**B. Character Classes**".

A **Name** is a token beginning with a letter or one of a few punctuation characters, and continuing with letters, digits, hyphens, underscores, colons, or full stops, together known as name characters. Names beginning with the string "xml", or any string which would match (('X'|'x') ('M'|'m') ('L'|'l')), are reserved for standardization in this or future versions of this specification.

> *NOTE: The colon character within XML names is reserved for experimentation with name spaces. Its meaning is expected to be standardized at some future point, at which point those documents using the colon for experimental purposes may need to be updated. (There is no guarantee that any name-space mechanism adopted for XML will in fact use the colon as a name-space delimiter.) In practice, this means that authors should not use the colon in XML names except as part of name-space experiments, but that XML processors should accept the colon as a name character.*

An Nmtoken (name token) is any mixture of name characters.

Names and Tokens			
[4]	NameChar	::=	Letter | Digit | '.' | '-' | '_' | ':' | CombiningChar | Extender
[5]	Name	::=	(Letter | '_' | ':') (NameChar)*
[6]	Names	::=	Name (S Name)*
[7]	Nmtoken	::=	(NameChar)+
[8]	Nmtokens	::=	Nmtoken (S Nmtoken)*

Literal data is any quoted string not containing the quotation mark used as a delimiter for that string. Literals are used for specifying the content of internal entities (EntityValue), the values of attributes (AttValue), and external identifiers (SystemLiteral). Note that a SystemLiteral can be parsed without scanning for markup.

Literals				
[9]	EntityValue	::=	`'"' ([^%&"] | PEReference | Reference)*`	
			`'"'`	
			`| '"' ([^%&'] | PEReference | Reference)*`	
			`'"'`	
[10]	AttValue	::=	`'"' ([^<&"] | Reference)* '"'`	
			`| '"' ([^<&'] | Reference)* '"'`	
[11]	SystemLiteral	::=	`('"' [^"]* '"')	('"' [^']* '"')`	
[12]	PubidLiteral	::=	`'"' PubidChar* '"'	'"' (PubidChar -`	
			`'"')* '"'`	
[13]	PubidChar	::=	`#x20	#xD	#xA	[a-zA-Z0-9] |`	
			`[-'()+,./:=?;!*#@$_%]`	

2.4 Character Data and Markup

Text consists of intermingled character data and markup. **Markup** takes the form of start-tags, end-tags, empty-element tags, entity references, character references, comments, CDATA section delimiters, document type declarations, and processing instructions.

All text that is not markup constitutes the **character data** of the document.

The ampersand character (&) and the left angle bracket (<) may appear in their literal form *only* when used as markup delimiters, or within a comment, a processing instruction, or a CDATA section. They are also legal within the literal entity value of an internal entity declaration; see "**4.3.2 Well-Formed Parsed Entities**". If they are needed elsewhere, they must be escaped using either numeric character references or the strings "&" and "<" respectively. The right angle bracket (>) may be represented using the string ">", and must, for compatibility, be escaped using ">" or a character reference when it appears in the string "]]>" in content, when that string is not marking the end of a CDATA section.

In the content of elements, character data is any string of characters which does not contain the start-delimiter of any markup. In a CDATA section, character data is any string of characters not including the CDATA-section-close delimiter, "]]>".

To allow attribute values to contain both single and double quotes, the apostrophe or single-quote character (') may be represented as "'", and the double-quote character (") as """.

Character Data			
[14]	CharData	::=	`[^<&]* - ([^<&]* ']]>' [^<&]*)`

2.5 Comments

Comments may appear anywhere in a document outside other markup; in addition, they may appear within the document type declaration at places allowed by the grammar. They are not part of the document's character data; an XML processor may, but need not, make it possible for an application to retrieve the text of comments. For compatibility, the string "--" (double-hyphen) must not occur within comments.

Comments			
[15]	Comment	::=	`'<!--' ((Char - '-')	('-' (Char - '-')))* '-->'`

An example of a comment:

```
<!-- declarations for <head> & <body> -->
```

2.6 Processing Instructions

Processing instructions (PIs) allow documents to contain instructions for applications.

Processing Instructions			
[16]	PI	::=	`'<?' PITarget (S (Char* - (Char* '?>' Char*)))? '?>'`
[17]	PITarget	::=	`Name - (('X' | 'x') ('M' | 'm') ('L' | 'l'))`

PIs are not part of the document's character data, but must be passed through to the application. The PI begins with a target (`PITarget`) used to identify the application to which the instruction is directed. The target names "XML", "xml", and so on are reserved for standardization in this or future versions of this specification. The XML Notation mechanism may be used for formal declaration of PI targets.

2.7 CDATA Sections

CDATA sections may occur anywhere character data may occur; they are used to escape blocks of text containing characters which would otherwise be recognized as markup. CDATA sections begin with the string "`<![CDATA[`" and end with the string "`]]>`":

CDATA Sections			
[18]	CDSect	::=	`CDStart CData CDEnd`
[19]	CDStart	::=	`'<![CDATA['`
[20]	CData	::=	`(Char* - (Char* ']]>' Char*))`
[21]	CDEnd	::=	`']]>'`

Within a CDATA section, only the `CDEnd` string is recognized as markup, so that left angle brackets and ampersands may occur in their literal form; they need not (and cannot) be escaped using "`&lt;`" and "`&amp;`". CDATA sections cannot nest.

An example of a CDATA section, in which "`<greeting>`" and "`</greeting>`" are recognized as character data, not markup:

```
<![CDATA[<greeting>Hello, world!</greeting>]]>
```

2.8 Prolog and Document Type Declaration

XML documents may, and should, begin with an **XML declaration** which specifies the version of XML being used. For example, the following is a complete XML document, well-formed but not valid:

```
<?xml version="1.0"?>
<greeting>Hello, world!</greeting>
```

and so is this:

```
<greeting>Hello, world!</greeting>
```

The version number "1.0" should be used to indicate conformance to this version of this specification; it is an error for a document to use the value "1.0" if it does not conform to this version of this specification. It is the intent of the XML working group to give later versions of this specification numbers other than "1.0", but this intent does not indicate a commitment to produce any future versions of XML, nor if any are produced, to use any particular numbering scheme. Since future versions are not ruled out, this construct is provided as a means to allow the possibility of automatic version recognition, should it become necessary. Processors may signal an error if they receive documents labeled with versions they do not support.

The function of the markup in an XML document is to describe its storage and logical structure and to associate attribute-value pairs with its logical structures. XML provides a mechanism, the document type declaration, to define constraints on the logical structure and to support the use of predefined storage units. An XML document is **valid** if it has an associated document type declaration and if the document complies with the constraints expressed in it.

The document type declaration must appear before the first element in the document.

Prolog			
[22]	prolog	::=	XMLDecl? Misc* (doctypedecl Misc*)?
[23]	XMLDecl	::=	'<?xml' VersionInfo EncodingDecl? SDDecl? S? '?>'
[24]	VersionInfo	::=	S 'version' Eq ("'" VersionNum "'" | '"' VersionNum '"')
[25]	Eq	::=	S? '=' S?
[26]	VersionNum	::=	([a-zA-Z0-9_.:] | '-')+
[27]	Misc	::=	Comment | PI | S

The XML **document type declaration** contains or points to markup declarations that provide a grammar for a class of documents. This grammar is known as a document type definition, or **DTD**. The document type declaration can point to an external subset (a special kind of external entity) containing markup declarations, or can contain the markup declarations directly in an internal subset, or can do both. The DTD for a document consists of both subsets taken together.

A **markup declaration** is an element type declaration, an attribute-list declaration, an entity declaration, or a notation declaration. These declarations may be contained in whole or in part within parameter entities, as described in the well-formedness and validity constraints below. For further information, see "**4. Physical Structures**".

[28]	doctypedecl	::=	`'<!DOCTYPE' S Name`
			`(S ExternalID)? S?`
			`('[' (markupdecl`
			`| PEReference`
			`| S)* ']' S?)? '>'`
				[VC: Root Element Type]

[29]	markupdecl	::=	`elementdecl`
			`| AttlistDecl`
			`| EntityDecl`
			`| NotationDecl`
			`| PI | Comment`
				[VC: Proper Declaration/PE Nesting]

				[WFC: PEs in Internal Subset]

The markup declarations may be made up in whole or in part of the replacement text of parameter entities. The productions later in this specification for individual nonterminals (`elementdecl`, `AttlistDecl`, and so on) describe the declarations *after* all the parameter entities have been included.

Validity Constraint: Root Element Type

The `Name` in the document type declaration must match the element type of the root element.

Validity Constraint: Proper Declaration/PE Nesting

Parameter-entity replacement text must be properly nested with markup declarations. That is to say, if either the first character or the last character of a markup declaration (`markupdecl` above) is contained in the replacement text for a parameter-entity reference, both must be contained in the same replacement text.

Well-Formedness Constraint: PEs in Internal Subset

In the internal DTD subset, parameter-entity references can occur only where markup declarations can occur, not within markup declarations. (This does not apply to references that occur in external parameter entities or to the external subset.)

Like the internal subset, the external subset and any external parameter entities referred to in the DTD must consist of a series of complete markup declarations of the types allowed by the non-terminal symbol `markupdecl`, interspersed with white space or parameter-entity references. However, portions of the contents of the external subset or of external parameter entities may conditionally be ignored by using the conditional section construct; this is not allowed in the internal subset.

External Subset			
[30]	extSubset	::=	`TextDecl? extSubsetDecl`
[31]	extSubsetDecl	::=	`( markupdecl | conditionalSect` `| PEReference | S )*`

The external subset and external parameter entities also differ from the internal subset in that in them, parameter-entity references are permitted *within* markup declarations, not only *between* markup declarations.

An example of an XML document with a document type declaration:

```
<?xml version="1.0"?>
<!DOCTYPE greeting SYSTEM "hello.dtd">
<greeting>Hello, world!</greeting>
```

The system identifier "hello.dtd" gives the URI of a DTD for the document.

The declarations can also be given locally, as in this example:

```
<?xml version="1.0" encoding="UTF-8" ?>
<!DOCTYPE greeting [
  <!ELEMENT greeting (#PCDATA)>
]>
<greeting>Hello, world!</greeting>
```

If both the external and internal subsets are used, the internal subset is considered to occur before the external subset. This has the effect that entity and attribute-list declarations in the internal subset take precedence over those in the external subset.

2.9 Standalone Document Declaration

Markup declarations can affect the content of the document, as passed from an XML processor to an application; examples are attribute defaults and entity declarations. The standalone document declaration, which may appear as a component of the XML declaration, signals whether or not there are such declarations which appear external to the document entity.

Standalone Document Declaration	
[32] SDDecl ::= S 'standalone' Eq (("'" ('yes' | 'no') "'") | ('"' ('yes' | 'no') '"'))	[VC: Standalone Document Declaration]

In a standalone document declaration, the value "yes" indicates that there are no markup declarations external to the document entity (either in the DTD external subset, or in an external parameter entity referenced from the internal subset) which affect the information passed from the XML processor to the application. The value "no" indicates that there are or may be such external markup declarations. Note that the standalone document declaration only denotes the presence of external *declarations*; the presence, in a document, of references to external *entities*, when those entities are internally declared, does not change its standalone status.

If there are no external markup declarations, the standalone document declaration has no meaning. If there are external markup declarations but there is no standalone document declaration, the value "no" is assumed.

Any XML document for which standalone="no" holds can be converted algorithmically to a standalone document, which may be desirable for some network delivery applications.

Validity Constraint: Standalone Document Declaration
The standalone document declaration must have the value "no" if any external markup declarations contain declarations of:

❑ attributes with default values, if elements to which these attributes apply appear in the document without specifications of values for these attributes, or

❑ entities (other than amp, lt, gt, apos, quot), if references to those entities appear in the document, or

❏ attributes with values subject to **normalization**, where the attribute appears in the document with a value which will change as a result of normalization, or

❏ element types with element content, if white space occurs directly within any instance of those types.

An example XML declaration with a standalone document declaration:

```
<?xml version="1.0" standalone='yes'?>
```

2.10 White Space Handling

In editing XML documents, it is often convenient to use "white space" (spaces, tabs, and blank lines, denoted by the nonterminal S in this specification) to set apart the markup for greater readability. Such white space is typically not intended for inclusion in the delivered version of the document. On the other hand, "significant" white space that should be preserved in the delivered version is common, for example in poetry and source code.

An XML processor must always pass all characters in a document that are not markup through to the application. A validating XML processor must also inform the application which of these characters constitute white space appearing in element content.

A special attribute named xml:space may be attached to an element to signal an intention that in that element, white space should be preserved by applications. In valid documents, this attribute, like any other, must be declared if it is used. When declared, it must be given as an enumerated type whose only possible values are "default" and "preserve". For example:

```
<!ATTLIST poem   xml:space (default|preserve) 'preserve'>
```

The value "default" signals that applications' default white-space processing modes are acceptable for this element; the value "preserve" indicates the intent that applications preserve all the white space. This declared intent is considered to apply to all elements within the content of the element where it is specified, unless overriden with another instance of the xml:space attribute.

The root element of any document is considered to have signaled no intentions as regards application space handling, unless it provides a value for this attribute or the attribute is declared with a default value.

2.11 End-of-Line Handling

XML parsed entities are often stored in computer files which, for editing convenience, are organized into lines. These lines are typically separated by some combination of the characters carriage-return (#xD) and line-feed (#xA).

To simplify the tasks of applications, wherever an external parsed entity or the literal entity value of an internal parsed entity contains either the literal two-character sequence "#xD#xA" or a standalone literal #xD, an XML processor must pass to the application the single character #xA. (This behavior can conveniently be produced by normalizing all line breaks to #xA on input, before parsing.)

2.12 Language Identification

In document processing, it is often useful to identify the natural or formal language in which the content is written. A special attribute named xml:lang may be inserted in documents to specify the language used in the contents and attribute values of any element in an XML document. In valid documents, this attribute, like any other, must be declared if it is used. The values of the attribute are language identifiers as defined by IETF RFC 1766, "Tags for the Identification of Languages":

Language Identification			
[33]	LanguageID	::=	Langcode ('-' Subcode)*
[34]	Langcode	::=	ISO639Code | IanaCode | UserCode
[35]	ISO639Code	::=	([a-z] | [A-Z]) ([a-z] | [A-Z])
[36]	IanaCode	::=	('i' | 'I') '-' ([a-z] | [A-Z])+
[37]	UserCode	::=	('x' | 'X') '-' ([a-z] | [A-Z])+
[38]	Subcode	::=	([a-z] | [A-Z])+

The Langcode may be any of the following:

❑ a two-letter language code as defined by ISO 639, "Codes for the representation of names of languages"

❑ a language identifier registered with the Internet Assigned Numbers Authority IANA; these begin with the prefix "i-" (or "I-")

❑ a language identifier assigned by the user, or agreed on between parties in private use; these must begin with the prefix "x-" or "X-" in order to ensure that they do not conflict with names later standardized or registered with IANA

There may be any number of Subcode segments; if the first subcode segment exists and the Subcode consists of two letters, then it must be a country code from ISO 3166, "Codes for the representation of names of countries." If the first subcode consists of more than two letters, it must be a subcode for the language in question registered with IANA, unless the Langcode begins with the prefix "x-" or "X-".

It is customary to give the language code in lower case, and the country code (if any) in upper case. Note that these values, unlike other names in XML documents, are case insensitive.

For example:

```
<p xml:lang="en">The quick brown fox jumps over the lazy dog.</p>
<p xml:lang="en-GB">What colour is it?</p>
<p xml:lang="en-US">What color is it?</p>
<sp who="Faust" desc='leise' xml:lang="de">
  <l>Habe nun, ach! Philosophie,</l>
  <l>Juristerei, und Medizin</l>
  <l>und leider auch Theologie</l>
  <l>durchaus studiert mit heißem Bemüh'n.</l>
</sp>
```

The intent declared with xml:lang is considered to apply to all attributes and content of the element where it is specified, unless overridden with an instance of xml:lang on another element within that content.

A simple declaration for xml:lang might take the form:

```
xml:lang  NMTOKEN  #IMPLIED
```

but specific default values may also be given, if appropriate. In a collection of French poems for English students, with glosses and notes in English, the xml:lang attribute might be declared this way:

```
<!ATTLIST poem   xml:lang NMTOKEN 'fr'>
<!ATTLIST gloss  xml:lang NMTOKEN 'en'>
<!ATTLIST note   xml:lang NMTOKEN 'en'>
```

3. Logical Structures

Each XML document contains one or more **elements**, the boundaries of which are either delimited by start-tags and end-tags, or, for empty elements, by an empty-element tag. Each element has a type, identified by name, sometimes called its "generic identifier" (GI), and may have a set of attribute specifications. Each attribute specification has a name and a value.

Element
[39]   element ::=   EmptyElemTag
| STag content ETag   [WFC: Element Type Match]
[VC: Element Valid]

This specification does not constrain the semantics, use, or (beyond syntax) names of the element types and attributes, except that names beginning with a match to (('X'|'x')('M'|'m')('L'|'l')) are reserved for standardization in this or future versions of this specification.

Well-Formedness Constraint: Element Type Match
The Name in an element's end-tag must match the element type in the start-tag.

❑ **Validity Constraint: Element Valid**
An element is valid if there is a declaration matching elementdecl where the Name matches the element type, and one of the following holds:

❑ The declaration matches EMPTY and the element has no content.

❑ The declaration matches children and the sequence of child elements belongs to the language generated by the regular expression in the content model, with optional white space (characters matching the nonterminal S) between each pair of child elements.

❑ The declaration matches Mixed and the content consists of character data and child elements whose types match names in the content model.

❑ The declaration matches ANY, and the types of any child elements have been declared.

3.1 Start-Tags, End-Tags, and Empty-Element Tags

The beginning of every non-empty XML element is marked by a **start-tag**.

Start-tag				
[40]	STag	::=	`'<' Name (S Attribute)* S? '>'`	[WFC: Unique Att Spec]
[41]	Attribute	::=	`Name Eq AttValue`	[VC: Attribute Value Type]
				[WFC: No External Entity References]
				[WFC: No < in Attribute Values]

The `Name` in the start- and end-tags gives the element's **type**. The `Name-AttValue` pairs are referred to as the **attribute specifications** of the element, with the `Name` in each pair referred to as the **attribute name** and the content of the `AttValue` (the text between the ' or " delimiters) as the **attribute value**.

Well-Formedness Constraint: Unique Att Spec
No attribute name may appear more than once in the same start-tag or empty-element tag.

Validity Constraint: Attribute Value Type
The attribute must have been declared; the value must be of the type declared for it. (For attribute types, see "3.3 Attribute-List Declarations".)

Well-Formedness Constraint: No External Entity References
Attribute values cannot contain direct or indirect entity references to external entities.

Well-Formedness Constraint: No < in Attribute Values
The replacement text of any entity referred to directly or indirectly in an attribute value (other than "`&lt;`") must not contain a <.

An example of a start-tag:

```
<termdef id="dt-dog" term="dog">
```

The end of every element that begins with a start-tag must be marked by an **end-tag** containing a name that echoes the element's type as given in the start-tag:

End-tag			
[42]	ETag	::=	`'</' Name S? '>'`

An example of an end-tag:

```
</termdef>
```

The text between the start-tag and end-tag is called the element's **content**:

Content of Elements			
[43]	content	::=	`(element | CharData | Reference | CDSect | PI | Comment)*`

If an element is **empty**, it must be represented either by a start-tag immediately followed by an end-tag or by an empty-element tag. An **empty-element tag** takes a special form:

Tags for Empty Elements
[44]   EmptyElemTag ::=   '<' Name (S Attribute)* S? '/>' [WFC: Unique Att Spec]

Empty-element tags may be used for any element which has no content, whether or not it is declared using the keyword EMPTY. For interoperability, the empty-element tag must be used, and can only be used, for elements which are declared EMPTY.

Examples of empty elements:

```
<IMG align="left"
 src="http://www.w3.org/Icons/WWW/w3c_home" />
<br></br>
<br/>
```

3.2 Element Type Declarations

The element structure of an XML document may, for validation purposes, be constrained using element type and attribute-list declarations. An element type declaration constrains the element's content.

Element type declarations often constrain which element types can appear as children of the element. At user option, an XML processor may issue a warning when a declaration mentions an element type for which no declaration is provided, but this is not an error.

An **element type declaration** takes the form:

Element Type Declaration
[45]   elementdecl ::=   '<!ELEMENT' S Name S contentspec S? '>'   [VC: Unique Element Type Declaration]
[46]   contentspec ::=   'EMPTY' | 'ANY' | Mixed | children

where the Name gives the element type being declared.

Validity Constraint: Unique Element Type Declaration
No element type may be declared more than once.

Examples of element type declarations:

```
<!ELEMENT br EMPTY>
<!ELEMENT p (#PCDATA|emph)* >
<!ELEMENT %name.para; %content.para; >
<!ELEMENT container ANY>
```

3.2.1 Element Content

An element type has **element content** when elements of that type must contain only child elements (no character data), optionally separated by white space (characters matching the nonterminal S). In this case, the constraint includes a content model, a simple grammar governing the allowed types of the child elements and the order in which they are allowed to appear. The grammar is built on content particles (cps), which consist of names, choice lists of content particles, or sequence lists of content particles:

Element-content Models
[47]   children ::=   (choice | seq) ('?' | '*' | '+')?
[48]   cp   ::=   (Name | choice | seq) ('?' | '*' | '+')?
[49]   choice   ::=   '(' S? cp (S? '|' S? cp)* S? ')'   [VC: Proper Group/PE Nesting]
[50]   seq   ::=   '(' S? cp (S? ',' S? cp)* S? ')'   [VC: Proper Group/PE Nesting]

where each Name is the type of an element which may appear as a child. Any content particle in a choice list may appear in the element content at the location where the choice list appears in the grammar; content particles occurring in a sequence list must each appear in the element content in the order given in the list. The optional character following a name or list governs whether the element or the content particles in the list may occur one or more (+), zero or more (*), or zero or one times (?). The absence of such an operator means that the element or content particle must appear exactly once. This syntax and meaning are identical to those used in the productions in this specification.

The content of an element matches a content model if and only if it is possible to trace out a path through the content model, obeying the sequence, choice, and repetition operators and matching each element in the content against an element type in the content model. For compatibility, it is an error if an element in the document can match more than one occurrence of an element type in the content model. For more information, see **Appendix E. Deterministic Content Models**.

Validity Constraint: Proper Group/PE Nesting

Parameter-entity replacement text must be properly nested with parenthesized groups. That is to say, if either of the opening or closing parentheses in a choice, seq, or Mixed construct is contained in the replacement text for a parameter entity, both must be contained in the same replacement text. For interoperability, if a parameter-entity reference appears in a choice, seq, or Mixed construct, its replacement text should not be empty, and neither the first nor last non-blank character of the replacement text should be a connector (| or ,).

Examples of element-content models:

```
<!ELEMENT spec (front, body, back?)>
<!ELEMENT div1 (head, (p | list | note)*, div2*)>
<!ELEMENT dictionary-body (%div.mix; | %dict.mix;)*>
```

3.2.2 Mixed Content

An element type has **mixed content** when elements of that type may contain character data, optionally interspersed with child elements. In this case, the types of the child elements may be constrained, but not their order or their number of occurrences:

Mixed-content Declaration		
[51]	Mixed ::=	`'(' S? '#PCDATA' (S? '|' S? Name)* S? ')*'` `| '(' S? '#PCDATA' S? ')'` [VC: Proper Group/PE Nesting] [VC: No Duplicate Types]

where the Names give the types of elements that may appear as children. The keyword PCDATA derives historically from the term "parsed character data".

Validity Constraint: No Duplicate Types

The same name must not appear more than once in a single mixed-content declaration.

Examples of mixed content declarations:

```
<!ELEMENT p (#PCDATA|a|ul|b|i|em)*>
<!ELEMENT p (#PCDATA | %font; | %phrase; | %special; | %form;)* >
<!ELEMENT b (#PCDATA)>
```

3.3 Attribute-List Declarations

Attributes are used to associate name-value pairs with elements. Attribute specifications may appear only within start-tags and empty-element tags; thus, the productions used to recognize them appear in "**3.1 Start-Tags, End-Tags, and Empty-Element Tags**". Attribute-list declarations may be used:

❑   To define the set of attributes pertaining to a given element type.

❑   To establish type constraints for these attributes.

❑   To provide default values for attributes.

Attribute-list declarations specify the name, data type, and default value (if any) of each attribute associated with a given element type:

Attribute-list Declaration		
[52]	AttlistDecl ::=	`'<!ATTLIST' S Name AttDef* S? '>'`
[53]	AttDef ::=	`S Name S AttType S DefaultDecl`

The Name in the AttlistDecl rule is the type of an element. At user option, an XML processor may issue a warning if attributes are declared for an element type not itself declared, but this is not an error. The Name in the AttDef rule is the name of the attribute.

When more than one AttlistDecl is provided for a given element type, the contents of all those provided are merged. When more than one definition is provided for the same attribute of a given element type, the first declaration is binding and later declarations are ignored. For interoperability, writers of DTDs may choose to provide at most one attribute-list declaration for a given element type, at most one attribute definition for a given attribute name in an attribute-list declaration, and at least one attribute definition in each attribute-list declaration. For interoperability, an XML processor may at user option issue a warning when more than one attribute-list declaration is provided for a given element type, or more than one attribute definition is provided for a given attribute, but this is not an error.

3.3.1 Attribute Types

XML attribute types are of three kinds: a string type, a set of tokenized types, and enumerated types. The string type may take any literal string as a value; the tokenized types have varying lexical and semantic constraints. The validity constraints noted in the grammar are applied after the attribute value has been normalized as described in **Section 3.3 Attribute-List Declarations**.

Attribute Types				
[54]	AttType	::=	StringType | TokenizedType | EnumeratedType	
[55]	StringType	::=	'CDATA'	
[56]	TokenizedType	::=	'ID'	[VC: ID]
			| 'IDREF'	[VC: One ID per Element Type]
			| 'IDREFS'	[VC: ID Attribute Default]
			| 'ENTITY'	[VC: IDREF]
			| 'ENTITIES'	[VC: IDREF]
			| 'NMTOKEN'	[VC: Entity Name]
			| 'NMTOKENS'	[VC: Entity Name]
				[VC: Name Token]
				[VC: Name Token]

Validity Constraint: ID

Values of type ID must match the Name production. A name must not appear more than once in an XML document as a value of this type; i.e., ID values must uniquely identify the elements which bear them.

Validity Constraint: One ID per Element Type

No element type may have more than one ID attribute specified.

Validity Constraint: ID Attribute Default

An ID attribute must have a declared default of #IMPLIED or #REQUIRED.

Validity Constraint: IDREF

Values of type IDREF must match the Name production, and values of type IDREFS must match Names; each Name must match the value of an ID attribute on some element in the XML document; i.e. IDREF values must match the value of some ID attribute.

Validity Constraint: Entity Name

Values of type ENTITY must match the Name production, values of type ENTITIES must match Names; each Name must match the name of an unparsed entity declared in the DTD.

Validity Constraint: Name Token

Values of type NMTOKEN must match the Nmtoken production; values of type NMTOKENS must match Nmtokens.

Enumerated attributes can take one of a list of values provided in the declaration. There are two kinds of enumerated types:

Enumerated Attribute Types				
[57]	EnumeratedType	::=	NotationType | Enumeration	
[58]	NotationType	::=	'NOTATION' S '(' S? Name (S? '|' S? Name)* S? ')'	[VC: Notation Attributes] [VC: One Notation per Element Type]
[59]	Enumeration	::=	'(' S? Nmtoken (S? '|' S? Nmtoken)* S? ')'	[VC: Enumeration]

A NOTATION attribute identifies a notation, declared in the DTD with associated system and/or public identifiers, to be used in interpreting the element to which the attribute is attached.

Validity Constraint: Notation Attributes
Values of this type must match one of the notation names included in the declaration; all notation names in the declaration must be declared.

Validity Constraint: One Notation per Element Type
No element type may have more than one NOTATION attribute specified.

Validity Constraint: Enumeration
Values of this type must match one of the Nmtoken tokens in the declaration.

For interoperability, the same Nmtoken should not occur more than once in the enumerated attribute types of a single element type.

3.3.2 Attribute Defaults

An attribute declaration provides information on whether the attribute's presence is required, and if not, how an XML processor should react if a declared attribute is absent in a document.

Attribute Defaults				
[60]	DefaultDecl	::=	'#REQUIRED' | '#IMPLIED' | (('#FIXED' S)? AttValue)	[VC: Required Attribute] [VC: Attribute Default Legal] [WFC: No < in Attribute Values] [VC: Fixed Attribute Default]

In an attribute declaration, #REQUIRED means that the attribute must always be provided, #IMPLIED that no default value is provided. If the declaration is neither #REQUIRED nor #IMPLIED, then the AttValue value contains the declared **default** value; the #FIXED keyword states that the attribute must always have the default value. If a default value is declared, when an XML processor encounters an omitted attribute, it is to behave as though the attribute were present with the declared default value.

Validity Constraint: Required Attribute
If the default declaration is the keyword #REQUIRED, then the attribute must be specified for all elements of the type in the attribute-list declaration.

669

Validity Constraint: Attribute Default Legal

The declared default value must meet the lexical constraints of the declared attribute type.

Validity Constraint: Fixed Attribute Default

If an attribute has a default value declared with the #FIXED keyword, instances of that attribute must match the default value.

Examples of attribute-list declarations:

```
<!ATTLIST termdef
          id      ID     #REQUIRED
          name    CDATA  #IMPLIED>
<!ATTLIST list
          type    (bullets|ordered|glossary)   "ordered">
<!ATTLIST form
          method  CDATA  #FIXED "POST">
```

3.3.3 Attribute-Value Normalization

Before the value of an attribute is passed to the application or checked for validity, the XML processor must normalize it as follows:

❑ a character reference is processed by appending the referenced character to the attribute value

❑ an entity reference is processed by recursively processing the replacement text of the entity

❑ a whitespace character (#x20, #xD, #xA, #x9) is processed by appending #x20 to the normalized value, except that only a single #x20 is appended for a "#xD#xA" sequence that is part of an external parsed entity or the literal entity value of an internal parsed entity

❑ other characters are processed by appending them to the normalized value

If the declared value is not CDATA, then the XML processor must further process the normalized attribute value by discarding any leading and trailing space (#x20) characters, and by replacing sequences of space (#x20) characters by a single space (#x20) character.

All attributes for which no declaration has been read should be treated by a non-validating parser as if declared CDATA.

3.4 Conditional Sections

Conditional sections are portions of the document type declaration external subset which are included in, or excluded from, the logical structure of the DTD based on the keyword which governs them.

Conditional Section			
[61]	conditionalSect	::=	includeSect | ignoreSect
[62]	includeSect	::=	'<![' S? 'INCLUDE' S? '[' extSubsetDecl ']]>'
[63]	ignoreSect	::=	'<![' S? 'IGNORE' S? '[' ignoreSectContents* ']]>'
[64]	ignoreSectContents	::=	Ignore ('<![' ignoreSectContents ']]>' Ignore)*
[65]	Ignore	::=	Char* - (Char* ('<![' | ']]>') Char*)

Like the internal and external DTD subsets, a conditional section may contain one or more complete declarations, comments, processing instructions, or nested conditional sections, intermingled with white space.

If the keyword of the conditional section is INCLUDE, then the contents of the conditional section are part of the DTD. If the keyword of the conditional section is IGNORE, then the contents of the conditional section are not logically part of the DTD. Note that for reliable parsing, the contents of even ignored conditional sections must be read in order to detect nested conditional sections and ensure that the end of the outermost (ignored) conditional section is properly detected. If a conditional section with a keyword of INCLUDE occurs within a larger conditional section with a keyword of IGNORE, both the outer and the inner conditional sections are ignored.

If the keyword of the conditional section is a parameter-entity reference, the parameter entity must be replaced by its content before the processor decides whether to include or ignore the conditional section.

An example:

```
<!ENTITY % draft 'INCLUDE' >
<!ENTITY % final 'IGNORE' >

<![%draft;[
<!ELEMENT book (comments*, title, body, supplements?)>
]]>
<![%final;[
<!ELEMENT book (title, body, supplements?)>
]]>
```

4. Physical Structures

An XML document may consist of one or many storage units. These are called **entities**; they all have **content** and are all (except for the document entity, and the external DTD subset) identified by entity **name**. Each XML document has one entity called the **document entity**, which serves as the starting point for the XML processor and may contain the whole document.

Entities may be either parsed or unparsed. A **parsed entity's** contents are referred to as its replacement text; this text is considered an integral part of the document.

An **unparsed entity** is a resource whose contents may or may not be text, and if text, may not be XML. Each unparsed entity has an associated notation, identified by name. Beyond a requirement that an XML processor make the identifiers for the entity and notation available to the application, XML places no constraints on the contents of unparsed entities.

Parsed entities are invoked by name using entity references; unparsed entities by name, given in the value of ENTITY or ENTITIES attributes.

General entities are entities for use within the document content. In this specification, general entities are sometimes referred to with the unqualified term **entity** when this leads to no ambiguity. Parameter entities are parsed entities for use within the DTD. These two types of entities use different forms of reference and are recognized in different contexts. Furthermore, they occupy different namespaces; a parameter entity and a general entity with the same name are two distinct entities.

4.1 Character and Entity References

A **character reference** refers to a specific character in the ISO/IEC 10646 character set, for example one not directly accessible from available input devices.

Character Reference		
[66]	CharRef ::= '&#' [0-9]+ ';'	
	| '&#x' [0-9a-fA-F]+ ';'	[WFC: Legal Character]

Well-Formedness Constraint: Legal Character
Characters referred to using character references must match the production for Char.

If the character reference begins with "&#x", the digits and letters up to the terminating ; provide a hexadecimal representation of the character's code point in ISO/IEC 10646. If it begins just with "&#", the digits up to the terminating ; provide a decimal representation of the character's code point.

An **entity reference** refers to the content of a named entity. References to parsed general entities use ampersand (&) and semicolon (;) as delimiters. **Parameter-entity references** use percent-sign (%) and semicolon (;) as delimiters.

Entity Reference		
[67] Reference ::= EntityRef | CharRef		
[68] EntityRef ::= '&' Name ';'	[WFC: Entity Declared]	
	[VC: Entity Declared]	
	[WFC: Parsed Entity]	
	[WFC: No Recursion]	
[69] PEReference ::= '%' Name ';'	[VC: Entity Declared]	
	[WFC: No Recursion]	
	[WFC: In DTD]	

Well-Formedness Constraint: Entity Declared
In a document without any DTD, a document with only an internal DTD subset which contains no parameter entity references, or a document with "standalone='yes'", the Name given in the entity reference must match that in an entity declaration, except that well-formed documents need not declare any of the following entities: amp, lt, gt, apos, quot. The declaration of a parameter entity must precede any reference to it. Similarly, the declaration of a general entity must precede any reference to it which appears in a default value in an attribute-list declaration.

Note that if entities are declared in the external subset or in external parameter entities, a non-validating processor is not obligated to read and process their declarations; for such documents, the rule that an entity must be declared is a well-formedness constraint only if standalone='yes'.

Validity Constraint: Entity Declared
In a document with an external subset or external parameter entities with "standalone='no'", the Name given in the entity reference must match that in an entity declaration. For interoperability, valid documents should declare the entities amp, lt, gt, apos, quot, in the form specified in "**4.6 Predefined Entities**". The declaration of a parameter entity must precede any reference to it. Similarly, the declaration of a general entity must precede any reference to it which appears in a default value in an attribute-list declaration.

Well-Formedness Constraint: Parsed Entity

An entity reference must not contain the name of an unparsed entity. Unparsed entities may be referred to only in attribute values declared to be of type ENTITY or ENTITIES.

Well-Formedness Constraint: No Recursion

A parsed entity must not contain a recursive reference to itself, either directly or indirectly.

Well-Formedness Constraint: In DTD

Parameter-entity references may only appear in the DTD.

Examples of character and entity references:

```
Type <key>less-than</key> (&#x3C;) to save options.
This document was prepared on &docdate; and
is classified &security-level;.
```

Example of a parameter-entity reference:

```
<!-- declare the parameter entity "ISOLat2"... -->
<!ENTITY % ISOLat2
        SYSTEM "http://www.xml.com/iso/isolat2-xml.entities" >
<!-- ... now reference it. -->
%ISOLat2;
```

4.2 Entity Declarations

Entities are declared thus:

Entity Declaration			
[70]	EntityDecl	::=	GEDecl | PEDecl
[71]	GEDecl	::=	'<!ENTITY' S Name S EntityDef S? '>'
[72]	PEDecl	::=	'<!ENTITY' S '%' S Name S PEDef S? '>'
[73]	EntityDef	::=	EntityValue | (ExternalID NDataDecl?)
[74]	PEDef	::=	EntityValue | ExternalID

The Name identifies the entity in an entity reference or, in the case of an unparsed entity, in the value of an ENTITY or ENTITIES attribute. If the same entity is declared more than once, the first declaration encountered is binding; at user option, an XML processor may issue a warning if entities are declared multiple times.

4.2.1 Internal Entities

If the entity definition is an EntityValue, the defined entity is called an **internal entity**. There is no separate physical storage object, and the content of the entity is given in the declaration. Note that some processing of entity and character references in the literal entity value may be required to produce the correct replacement text: see "**4.5 Construction of Internal Entity Replacement Text**".

An internal entity is a parsed entity.

Example of an internal entity declaration:

```
<!ENTITY Pub-Status "This is a pre-release of the
specification.">
```

4.2.2 External Entities

If the entity is not internal, it is an **external entity**, declared as follows:

External Entity Declaration			
[75]	ExternalID	::=	'SYSTEM' S SystemLiteral
			| 'PUBLIC' S PubidLiteral S SystemLiteral
[76]	NDataDecl	::=	S 'NDATA' S Name [VC: Notation Declared]

If the NDataDecl is present, this is a general unparsed entity; otherwise it is a parsed entity.

Validity Constraint: Notation Declared
The Name must match the declared name of a notation.

The SystemLiteral is called the entity's **system identifier**. It is a URI, which may be used to retrieve the entity. Note that the hash mark (#) and fragment identifier frequently used with URIs are not, formally, part of the URI itself; an XML processor may signal an error if a fragment identifier is given as part of a system identifier. Unless otherwise provided by information outside the scope of this specification (e.g. a special XML element type defined by a particular DTD, or a processing instruction defined by a particular application specification), relative URIs are relative to the location of the resource within which the entity declaration occurs. A URI might thus be relative to the document entity, to the entity containing the external DTD subset, or to some other external parameter entity.

An XML processor should handle a non-ASCII character in a URI by representing the character in UTF-8 as one or more bytes, and then escaping these bytes with the URI escaping mechanism (i.e., by converting each byte to %HH, where HH is the hexadecimal notation of the byte value).

In addition to a system identifier, an external identifier may include a **public identifier**. An XML processor attempting to retrieve the entity's content may use the public identifier to try to generate an alternative URI. If the processor is unable to do so, it must use the URI specified in the system literal. Before a match is attempted, all strings of white space in the public identifier must be normalized to single space characters (#x20), and leading and trailing white space must be removed.

Examples of external entity declarations:

```
<!ENTITY open-hatch
         SYSTEM "http://www.textuality.com/boilerplate/OpenHatch.xml">
<!ENTITY open-hatch
         PUBLIC "-//Textuality//TEXT Standard open-hatch boilerplate//EN"
         "http://www.textuality.com/boilerplate/OpenHatch.xml">
<!ENTITY hatch-pic
         SYSTEM "../grafix/OpenHatch.gif"
         NDATA gif >
```

4.3 Parsed Entities

4.3.1 The Text Declaration

External parsed entities may each begin with a **text declaration**.

Text Declaration	
[77] TextDecl ::=	`'<?xml' VersionInfo? EncodingDecl S? '?>'`

The text declaration must be provided literally, not by reference to a parsed entity. No text declaration may appear at any position other than the beginning of an external parsed entity.

4.3.2 Well-Formed Parsed Entities

The document entity is well-formed if it matches the production labeled `document`. An external general parsed entity is well-formed if it matches the production labeled `extParsedEnt`. An external parameter entity is well-formed if it matches the production labeled `extPE`.

Well-Formed External Parsed Entity		
[78]	extParsedEnt ::=	TextDecl? content
[79]	extPE ::=	TextDecl? extSubsetDecl

An internal general parsed entity is well-formed if its replacement text matches the production labeled `content`. All internal parameter entities are well-formed by definition.

A consequence of well-formedness in entities is that the logical and physical structures in an XML document are properly nested; no start-tag, end-tag, empty-element tag, element, comment, processing instruction, character reference, or entity reference can begin in one entity and end in another.

4.3.3 Character Encoding in Entities

Each external parsed entity in an XML document may use a different encoding for its characters. All XML processors must be able to read entities in either UTF-8 or UTF-16.

Entities encoded in UTF-16 must begin with the Byte Order Mark described by ISO/IEC 10646 Annex E and Unicode Appendix B (the ZERO WIDTH NO-BREAK SPACE character, #xFEFF). This is an encoding signature, not part of either the markup or the character data of the XML document. XML processors must be able to use this character to differentiate between UTF-8 and UTF-16 encoded documents.

Although an XML processor is required to read only entities in the UTF-8 and UTF-16 encodings, it is recognized that other encodings are used around the world, and it may be desired for XML processors to read entities that use them. Parsed entities which are stored in an encoding other than UTF-8 or UTF-16 must begin with a text declaration containing an encoding declaration:

Encoding Declaration		
[80]	EncodingDecl ::=	S 'encoding' Eq ('"' EncName '"' | "'" EncName "'")
[81]	EncName ::=	[A-Za-z] /*Encoding name ([A-Za-z0-9._] | '-')* contains only Latin characters */

In the document entity, the encoding declaration is part of the XML declaration. The `EncName` is the name of the encoding used.

In an encoding declaration, the values "`UTF-8`", "`UTF-16`", "`ISO-10646-UCS-2`", and "`ISO-10646-UCS-4`" should be used for the various encodings and transformations of Unicode / ISO/IEC 10646, the values "`ISO-8859-1`", "`ISO-8859-2`", ... "`ISO-8859-9`" should be used for the parts of ISO 8859, and the values "`ISO-2022-JP`", "`Shift_JIS`", and "`EUC-JP`" should be used for the various encoded forms of JIS X-0208-1997. XML processors may recognize other encodings; it is recommended that character encodings registered (as *charsets*) with the Internet Assigned Numbers Authority [IANA], other than those just listed, should be referred to using their registered names. Note that these registered names are defined to be case-insensitive, so processors wishing to match against them should do so in a case-insensitive way.

In the absence of information provided by an external transport protocol (e.g. HTTP or MIME), it is an error for an entity including an encoding declaration to be presented to the XML processor in an encoding other than that named in the declaration, or for an entity which begins with neither a Byte Order Mark nor an encoding declaration to use an encoding other than UTF-8. Note that since ASCII is a subset of UTF-8, ordinary ASCII entities do not strictly need an encoding declaration.

It is an error for a `TextDecl` to occur other than at the beginning of an external entity.

It is a fatal error when an XML processor encounters an entity with an encoding that it is unable to process.

Examples of encoding declarations:

```
<?xml encoding='UTF-8'?>
<?xml encoding='EUC-JP'?>
```

4.4 XML Processor Treatment of Entities and References

The table below summarizes the contexts in which character references, entity references, and invocations of unparsed entities might appear and the required behavior of an XML processor in each case. The labels in the leftmost column describe the recognition context:

Reference in Content

as a reference anywhere after the start-tag and before the end-tag of an element; corresponds to the nonterminal `content`.

Reference in Attribute Value

as a reference within either the value of an attribute in a start-tag, or a default value in an attribute declaration; corresponds to the nonterminal `AttValue`.

Occurs as Attribute Value

as a `Name`, not a reference, appearing either as the value of an attribute which has been declared as type `ENTITY`, or as one of the space-separated tokens in the value of an attribute which has been declared as type `ENTITIES`.

Reference in Entity Value

as a reference within a parameter or internal entity's literal entity value in the entity's declaration; corresponds to the nonterminal `EntityValue`.

Reference in DTD

as a reference within either the internal or external subsets of the DTD, but outside of an `EntityValue` or `AttValue`.

	Entity Type				Character
	Parameter	Internal General	External Parsed General	Unparsed	
Reference in Content	Not recognized	Included	Included if validating	Forbidden	Included
Reference in Attribute Value	Not recognized	Included in literal	Forbidden	Forbidden	Included
Occurs as Attribute Value	Not recognized	Forbidden	Forbidden	Notify	Not recognized
Reference in EntityValue	Included in literal	Bypassed	Bypassed	Forbidden	Included
Reference in DTD	Included as PE	Forbidden	Forbidden	Forbidden	Forbidden

4.4.1 Not Recognized

Outside the DTD, the % character has no special significance; thus, what would be parameter entity references in the DTD are not recognized as markup in content. Similarly, the names of unparsed entities are not recognized except when they appear in the value of an appropriately declared attribute.

4.4.2 Included

An entity is **included** when its replacement text is retrieved and processed, in place of the reference itself, as though it were part of the document at the location the reference was recognized. The replacement text may contain both character data and (except for parameter entities) markup, which must be recognized in the usual way, except that the replacement text of entities used to escape markup delimiters (the entities amp, lt, gt, apos, quot) is always treated as data. (The string "AT&T;" expands to "AT&T;" and the remaining ampersand is not recognized as an entity-reference delimiter.) A character reference is **included** when the indicated character is processed in place of the reference itself.

4.4.3 Included If Validating

When an XML processor recognizes a reference to a parsed entity, in order to validate the document, the processor must include its replacement text. If the entity is external, and the processor is not attempting to validate the XML document, the processor may, but need not, include the entity's replacement text. If a non-validating parser does not include the replacement text, it must inform the application that it recognized, but did not read, the entity.

This rule is based on the recognition that the automatic inclusion provided by the SGML and XML entity mechanism, primarily designed to support modularity in authoring, is not necessarily appropriate for other applications, in particular document browsing. Browsers, for example, when encountering an external parsed entity reference, might choose to provide a visual indication of the entity's presence and retrieve it for display only on demand.

677

4.4.4 Forbidden

The following are forbidden, and constitute fatal errors:

- ❑ the appearance of a reference to an unparsed entity.

- ❑ the appearance of any character or general-entity reference in the DTD except within an `EntityValue` or `AttValue`.

- ❑ a reference to an external entity in an attribute value.

4.4.5 Included in Literal

When an entity reference appears in an attribute value, or a parameter entity reference appears in a literal entity value, its replacement text is processed in place of the reference itself as though it were part of the document at the location the reference was recognized, except that a single or double quote character in the replacement text is always treated as a normal data character and will not terminate the literal. For example, this is well-formed:

```
<!ENTITY % YN '"Yes"' >
<!ENTITY WhatHeSaid "He said %YN;" >
```

while this is not:

```
<!ENTITY EndAttr "27'" >
<element attribute='a-&EndAttr;'>
```

4.4.6 Notify

When the name of an unparsed entity appears as a token in the value of an attribute of declared type `ENTITY` or `ENTITIES`, a validating processor must inform the application of the system and public (if any) identifiers for both the entity and its associated notation.

4.4.7 Bypassed

When a general entity reference appears in the `EntityValue` in an entity declaration, it is bypassed and left as is.

4.4.8 Included as PE

Just as with external parsed entities, parameter entities need only be included if validating. When a parameter-entity reference is recognized in the DTD and included, its replacement text is enlarged by the attachment of one leading and one following space (#x20) character; the intent is to constrain the replacement text of parameter entities to contain an integral number of grammatical tokens in the DTD.

4.5 Construction of Internal Entity Replacement Text

In discussing the treatment of internal entities, it is useful to distinguish two forms of the entity's value. The **literal entity value** is the quoted string actually present in the entity declaration, corresponding to the non-terminal `EntityValue`. The **replacement text** is the content of the entity, after replacement of character references and parameter-entity references.

The literal entity value as given in an internal entity declaration (EntityValue) may contain character, parameter-entity, and general-entity references. Such references must be contained entirely within the literal entity value. The actual replacement text that is included as described above must contain the *replacement text* of any parameter entities referred to, and must contain the character referred to, in place of any character references in the literal entity value; however, general-entity references must be left as-is, unexpanded. For example, given the following declarations:

```
<!ENTITY % pub     "&#xc9;ditions Gallimard" >
<!ENTITY   rights "All rights reserved" >
<!ENTITY   book   "La Peste: Albert Camus,
&#xA9; 1947 %pub;. &rights;" >
```

then the replacement text for the entity "book" is:

```
La Peste: Albert Camus,
© 1947 Éditions Gallimard. &rights;
```

The general-entity reference "&rights;" would be expanded should the reference "&book;" appear in the document's content or an attribute value.

These simple rules may have complex interactions; for a detailed discussion of a difficult example, see "**D. Expansion of Entity and Character References**".

4.6 Predefined Entities

Entity and character references can both be used to **escape** the left angle bracket, ampersand, and other delimiters. A set of general entities (amp, lt, gt, apos, quot) is specified for this purpose. Numeric character references may also be used; they are expanded immediately when recognized and must be treated as character data, so the numeric character references "<" and "&" may be used to escape < and & when they occur in character data.

All XML processors must recognize these entities whether they are declared or not. For interoperability, valid XML documents should declare these entities, like any others, before using them. If the entities in question are declared, they must be declared as internal entities whose replacement text is the single character being escaped or a character reference to that character, as shown below.

```
<!ENTITY lt      "&#38;#60;">
<!ENTITY gt      "&#62;">
<!ENTITY amp     "&#38;#38;">
<!ENTITY apos    "&#39;">
<!ENTITY quot    "&#34;">
```

Note that the < and & characters in the declarations of "lt" and "amp" are doubly escaped to meet the requirement that entity replacement be well-formed.

4.7 Notation Declarations

Notations identify by name the format of unparsed entities, the format of elements which bear a notation attribute, or the application to which a processing instruction is addressed.

Notation declarations provide a name for the notation, for use in entity and attribute-list declarations and in attribute specifications, and an external identifier for the notation which may allow an XML processor or its client application to locate a helper application capable of processing data in the given notation.

Notation Declarations			
[82]	NotationDecl	::=	'<!NOTATION' S Name S (ExternalID | PublicID) S? '>'
[83]	PublicID	::=	'PUBLIC' S PubidLiteral

XML processors must provide applications with the name and external identifier(s) of any notation declared and referred to in an attribute value, attribute definition, or entity declaration. They may additionally resolve the external identifier into the system identifier, file name, or other information needed to allow the application to call a processor for data in the notation described. (It is not an error, however, for XML documents to declare and refer to notations for which notation-specific applications are not available on the system where the XML processor or application is running.)

4.8 Document Entity

The **document entity** serves as the root of the entity tree and a starting-point for an XML processor. This specification does not specify how the document entity is to be located by an XML processor; unlike other entities, the document entity has no name and might well appear on a processor input stream without any identification at all.

5. Conformance

5.1 Validating and Non-Validating Processors

Conforming XML processors fall into two classes: validating and non-validating.

Validating and non-validating processors alike must report violations of this specification's well-formedness constraints in the content of the document entity and any other parsed entities that they read.

Validating processors must report violations of the constraints expressed by the declarations in the DTD, and failures to fulfill the validity constraints given in this specification. To accomplish this, validating XML processors must read and process the entire DTD and all external parsed entities referenced in the document.

Non-validating processors are required to check only the document entity, including the entire internal DTD subset, for well-formedness. While they are not required to check the document for validity, they are required to **process** all the declarations they read in the internal DTD subset and in any parameter entity that they read, up to the first reference to a parameter entity that they do *not* read; that is to say, they must use the information in those declarations to *normalize* attribute values, *include* the replacement text of internal entities, and supply *default attribute values*. They must not process entity declarations or attribute-list declarations encountered after a reference to a parameter entity that is not read, since the entity may have contained overriding declarations.

5.2 Using XML Processors

The behavior of a validating XML processor is highly predictable; it must read every piece of a document and report all well-formedness and validity violations. Less is required of a non-validating processor; it need not read any part of the document other than the document entity. This has two effects that may be important to users of XML processors:

❑ Certain well-formedness errors, specifically those that require reading external entities, may not be detected by a non-validating processor. Examples include the constraints entitled Entity Declared, Parsed Entity, and No Recursion, as well as some of the cases described as forbidden in "**4.4 XML Processor Treatment of Entities and References**".

❑ The information passed from the processor to the application may vary, depending on whether the processor reads parameter and external entities. For example, a non-validating processor may not *normalize* attribute values, *include* the replacement text of internal entities, or supply *default attribute values*, where doing so depends on having read declarations in external or parameter entities.

For maximum reliability in interoperating between different XML processors, applications which use non-validating processors should not rely on any behaviors not required of such processors. Applications which require facilities such as the use of default attributes or internal entities which are declared in external entities should use validating XML processors.

6. Notation

The formal grammar of XML is given in this specification using a simple Extended Backus-Naur Form (EBNF) notation. Each rule in the grammar defines one symbol, in the form

```
symbol ::= expression
```

Symbols are written with an initial capital letter if they are defined by a regular expression, or with an initial lower case letter otherwise. Literal strings are quoted.

Within the expression on the right-hand side of a rule, the following expressions are used to match strings of one or more characters:

#xN
where N is a hexadecimal integer, the expression matches the character in ISO/IEC 10646 whose canonical (UCS-4) code value, when interpreted as an unsigned binary number, has the value indicated. The number of leading zeros in the #xN form is insignificant; the number of leading zeros in the corresponding code value is governed by the character encoding in use and is not significant for XML.
[a-zA-Z], [#xN-#xN]
matches any character with a value in the range(s) indicated (inclusive).
[^a-z], [^#xN-#xN]
matches any character with a value *outside* the range indicated.
[^abc], [^#xN#xN#xN]
matches any character with a value not among the characters given.
"string"
matches a literal string matching that given inside the double quotes.
'string'
matches a literal string matching that given inside the single quotes.

These symbols may be combined to match more complex patterns as follows, where A and B represent simple expressions:

(**expression**)
expression is treated as a unit and may be combined as described in this list.

([-'()+,./:=?;!*#@$_%])
characters matching this list are treated as an expression.

A?
matches A or nothing; optional A.

A B
matches A followed by B.

A | B
matches A or B but not both.

A - B
matches any string that matches A but does not match B.

A+
matches one or more occurrences of A.

A*
matches zero or more occurrences of A.

Other notations used in the productions are:

/* ... */
comment.

[wfc: ...]
well-formedness constraint; this identifies by name a constraint on well-formed documents associated with a production.

[vc: ...]
validity constraint; this identifies by name a constraint on valid documents associated with a production.

Appendices

A. References

A.1 Normative References

(Internet Assigned Numbers Authority) *Official Names for Character Sets*, ed. Keld Simonsen et al. See ftp://ftp.isi.edu/in-notes/iana/assignments/character-sets.

IETF (Internet Engineering Task Force). *RFC 1766: Tags for the Identification of Languages*, ed. H. Alvestrand. 1995.

(International Organization for Standardization). *ISO 639:1988 (E). Code for the representation of names of languages.* [Geneva]: International Organization for Standardization, 1988.

(International Organization for Standardization). *ISO 3166-1:1997 (E). Codes for the representation of names of countries and their subdivisions - Part 1: Country codes* [Geneva]: International Organization for Standardization, 1997.

ISO (International Organization for Standardization). *ISO/IEC 10646-1993 (E). Information technology -- Universal Multiple-Octet Coded Character Set (UCS) - Part 1: Architecture and Basic Multilingual Plane.* [Geneva]: International Organization for Standardization, 1993 (plus amendments AM 1 through AM 7).

The Unicode Consortium. *The Unicode Standard, Version 2.0.* Reading, Mass.: Addison-Wesley Developers Press, 1996.

A.2 *Other References*

Aho, Alfred V., Ravi Sethi, and Jeffrey D. Ullman. *Compilers: Principles, Techniques, and Tools.* Reading: Addison-Wesley, 1986, rpt. corr. 1988.

Berners-Lee, T., R. Fielding, and L. Masinter. *Uniform Resource Identifiers (URI): Generic Syntax and Semantics.* 1997. (Work in progress; see updates to RFC1738.)

Brüggemann-Klein, Anne. Formal Models in Document Processing. Habilitationsschrift. Faculty of Mathematics at the University of Freiburg, 1993, available at `ftp://ftp.informatik.uni-freiburg.de/documents/papers/brueggem/habil.ps`.

Brüggemann-Klein, Anne, and Derick Wood. *Deterministic Regular Languages.* Extended abstract in A. Finkel, M. Jantzen, Hrsg., STACS 1992, S. 173-184. Springer-Verlag, Berlin 1992. Lecture Notes in Computer Science 577. Full version titled *One-Unambiguous Regular Languages* in Information and Computation 140 (2): 229-253, February 1998.

James Clark. Comparison of SGML and XML.
See `http://www.w3.org/TR/NOTE-sgml-xml-971215`.

IETF (Internet Engineering Task Force).
RFC 1738: Uniform Resource Locators (URL), ed. T. Berners-Lee, L. Masinter, M. McCahill. 1994.

IETF (Internet Engineering Task Force).
RFC 1808: Relative Uniform Resource Locators, ed. R. Fielding. 1995.

IETF (Internet Engineering Task Force).
RFC 2141: URN Syntax, ed. R. Moats. 1997.

ISO (International Organization for Standardization). *ISO 8879:1986(E). Information processing - Text and Office Systems - Standard Generalized Markup Language (SGML).* First edition - 1986-10-15. [Geneva]: International Organization for Standardization, 1986.

ISO (International Organization for Standardization). *ISO/IEC 10744-1992 (E). Information technology - Hypermedia/Time-based Structuring Language (HyTime).* [Geneva]: International Organization for Standardization, 1992. *Extended Facilities Annexe.* [Geneva]: International Organization for Standardization, 1996.

B. Character Classes

Following the characteristics defined in the Unicode standard, characters are classed as base characters (among others, these contain the alphabetic characters of the Latin alphabet, without diacritics), ideographic characters, and combining characters (among others, this class contains most diacritics); these classes combine to form the class of letters. Digits and extenders are also distinguished.

Characters

[84]	Letter	::=	BaseChar | Ideographic

[85]   BaseChar   ::=   [#x0041-#x005A] | [#x0061-#x007A] | [#x00C0-#x00D6] | [#x00D8-#x00F6] | [#x00F8-#x00FF]
| [#x0100-#x0131] | [#x0134-#x013E]
| [#x0141-#x0148] | [#x014A-#x017E]
| [#x0180-#x01C3] | [#x01CD-#x01F0]
| [#x01F4-#x01F5] | [#x01FA-#x0217]
| [#x0250-#x02A8] | [#x02BB-#x02C1] | #x0386
| [#x0388-#x038A] | #x038C | [#x038E-#x03A1]
| [#x03A3-#x03CE] | [#x03D0-#x03D6] | #x03DA
| #x03DC | #x03DE | #x03E0 | [#x03E2-#x03F3]
| [#x0401-#x040C] | [#x040E-#x044F]
| [#x0451-#x045C] | [#x045E-#x0481]
| [#x0490-#x04C4] | [#x04C7-#x04C8]
| [#x04CB-#x04CC] | [#x04D0-#x04EB]
| [#x04EE-#x04F5] | [#x04F8-#x04F9]
| [#x0531-#x0556] | #x0559 | [#x0561-#x0586]
| [#x05D0-#x05EA] | [#x05F0-#x05F2]
| [#x0621-#x063A] | [#x0641-#x064A]
| [#x0671-#x06B7] | [#x06BA-#x06BE]
| [#x06C0-#x06CE] | [#x06D0-#x06D3] | #x06D5
| [#x06E5-#x06E6] | [#x0905-#x0939] | #x093D
| [#x0958-#x0961] | [#x0985-#x098C]
| [#x098F-#x0990] | [#x0993-#x09A8]
| [#x09AA-#x09B0] | #x09B2 | [#x09B6-#x09B9]
| [#x09DC-#x09DD] | [#x09DF-#x09E1]
| [#x09F0-#x09F1] | [#x0A05-#x0A0A]
| [#x0A0F-#x0A10] | [#x0A13-#x0A28]
| [#x0A2A-#x0A30] | [#x0A32-#x0A33]
| [#x0A35-#x0A36] | [#x0A38-#x0A39]
| [#x0A59-#x0A5C] | #x0A5E | [#x0A72-#x0A74]
| [#x0A85-#x0A8B] | #x0A8D | [#x0A8F-#x0A91]
| [#x0A93-#x0AA8] | [#x0AAA-#x0AB0]
| [#x0AB2-#x0AB3] | [#x0AB5-#x0AB9] | #x0ABD
| #x0AE0 | [#x0B05-#x0B0C] | [#x0B0F-#x0B10]
| [#x0B13-#x0B28] | [#x0B2A-#x0B30]
| [#x0B32-#x0B33] | [#x0B36-#x0B39] | #x0B3D
| [#x0B5C-#x0B5D] | [#x0B5F-#x0B61]
| [#x0B85-#x0B8A] | [#x0B8E-#x0B90]
| [#x0B92-#x0B95] | [#x0B99-#x0B9A] | #x0B9C
| [#x0B9E-#x0B9F] | [#x0BA3-#x0BA4]
| [#x0BA8-#x0BAA] | [#x0BAE-#x0BB5]
| [#x0BB7-#x0BB9] | [#x0C05-#x0C0C]
| [#x0C0E-#x0C10] | [#x0C12-#x0C28]
| [#x0C2A-#x0C33] | [#x0C35-#x0C39]
| [#x0C60-#x0C61] | [#x0C85-#x0C8C]
| [#x0C8E-#x0C90] | [#x0C92-#x0CA8]
| [#x0CAA-#x0CB3] | [#x0CB5-#x0CB9] | #x0CDE
| [#x0CE0-#x0CE1] | [#x0D05-#x0D0C]
| [#x0D0E-#x0D10] | [#x0D12-#x0D28]
| [#x0D2A-#x0D39] | [#x0D60-#x0D61]
| [#x0E01-#x0E2E] | #x0E30 | [#x0E32-#x0E33]
| [#x0E40-#x0E45] | [#x0E81-#x0E82] | #x0E84
| [#x0E87-#x0E88] | #x0E8A | #x0E8D
| [#x0E94-#x0E97] | [#x0E99-#x0E9F]
| [#x0EA1-#x0EA3] | #x0EA5 | #x0EA7
| [#x0EAA-#x0EAB] | [#x0EAD-#x0EAE] | #x0EB0
| [#x0EB2-#x0EB3] | #x0EBD | [#x0EC0-#x0EC4]
| [#x0F40-#x0F47] | [#x0F49-#x0F69]
| [#x10A0-#x10C5]

Characters

		[#x10D0-#x10F6]	#x1100	[#x1102-#x1103]
		[#x1105-#x1107]	#x1109	[#x110B-#x110C]
		[#x110E-#x1112]	#x113C	#x113E | #x1140
		#x114C | #x114E	#x1150	[#x1154-#x1155]
		#x1159 | [#x115F-#x1161]	#x1163 | #x1165	
		#x1167 | #x1169 | [#x116D-#x116E]		
		[#x1172-#x1173] | #x1175	#x119E | #x11A8	
		#x11AB | [#x11AE-#x11AF]	[#x11B7-#x11B8]	
		#x11BA | [#x11BC-#x11C2]	#x11EB | #x11F0	
		#x11F9 | [#x1E00-#x1E9B]	[#x1EA0-#x1EF9]	
		[#x1F00-#x1F15]	[#x1F18-#x1F1D]	
		[#x1F20-#x1F45]	[#x1F48-#x1F4D]	
		[#x1F50-#x1F57]	#x1F59 | #x1F5B | #x1F5D	
		[#x1F5F-#x1F7D]	[#x1F80-#x1FB4]	
		[#x1FB6-#x1FBC]	#x1FBE | [#x1FC2-#x1FC4]	
		[#x1FC6-#x1FCC]	[#x1FD0-#x1FD3]	
		[#x1FD6-#x1FDB]	[#x1FE0-#x1FEC]	
		[#x1FF2-#x1FF4]	[#x1FF6-#x1FFC] | #x2126	
		[#x212A-#x212B]	#x212E | [#x2180-#x2182]	
		[#x3041-#x3094]	[#x30A1-#x30FA]	
		[#x3105-#x312C]	[#xAC00-#xD7A3]	

[86]   Ideographic   ::=   [#x4E00-#x9FA5] | #x3007 | [#x3021-#x3029]

[87]   Combining   ::=   [#x0300-#x0345] | [#x0360-#x0361] | [#x0483-
         Char   #x0486] | [#x0591-#x05A1] | [#x05A3-#x05B9]
                                 [#x05BB-#x05BD] | #x05BF | [#x05C1-#x05C2]
                                 #x05C4 | [#x064B-#x0652] | #x0670
                                 [#x06D6-#x06DC] | [#x06DD-#x06DF]
                                 [#x06E0-#x06E4] | [#x06E7-#x06E8]
                                 [#x06EA-#x06ED] | [#x0901-#x0903] | #x093C
                                 [#x093E-#x094C] | #x094D | [#x0951-#x0954]
                                 [#x0962-#x0963] | [#x0981-#x0983] | #x09BC
                                 #x09BE | #x09BF | [#x09C0-#x09C4]
                                 [#x09C7-#x09C8] | [#x09CB-#x09CD] | #x09D7
                                 [#x09E2-#x09E3] | #x0A02 | #x0A3C | #x0A3E
                                 #x0A3F | [#x0A40-#x0A42] | [#x0A47-#x0A48]
                                 [#x0A4B-#x0A4D] | [#x0A70-#x0A71]
                                 [#x0A81-#x0A83] | #x0ABC | [#x0ABE-#x0AC5]
                                 [#x0AC7-#x0AC9] | [#x0ACB-#x0ACD]
                                 [#x0B01-#x0B03] | #x0B3C | [#x0B3E-#x0B43]
                                 [#x0B47-#x0B48] | [#x0B4B-#x0B4D]
                                 [#x0B56-#x0B57] | [#x0B82-#x0B83]
                                 [#x0BBE-#x0BC2] | [#x0BC6-#x0BC8]
                                 [#x0BCA-#x0BCD] | #x0BD7 | [#x0C01-#x0C03]
                                 [#x0C3E-#x0C44] | [#x0C46-#x0C48]
                                 [#x0C4A-#x0C4D] | [#x0C55-#x0C56]
                                 [#x0C82-#x0C83] | [#x0CBE-#x0CC4]
                                 [#x0CC6-#x0CC8] | [#x0CCA-#x0CCD]
                                 [#x0CD5-#x0CD6] | [#x0D02-#x0D03]
                                 [#x0D3E-#x0D43] | [#x0D46-#x0D48]
                                 [#x0D4A-#x0D4D] | #x0D57 | #x0E31
                                 [#x0E34-#x0E3A] | [#x0E47-#x0E4E] | #x0EB1
                                 [#x0EB4-#x0EB9] | [#x0EBB-#x0EBC]
                                 [#x0EC8-#x0ECD] | [#x0F18-#x0F19] | #x0F35
                                 #x0F37 | #x0F39 | #x0F3E | #x0F3F
                                 [#x0F71-#x0F84] | [#x0F86-#x0F8B]
                                 [#x0F90-#x0F95] | #x0F97 | [#x0F99-#x0FAD]
                                 [#x0FB1-#x0FB7] | #x0FB9 | [#x20D0-#x20DC]
                                 #x20E1 | [#x302A-#x302F] | #x3099 | #x309A

Table continued on following page

Characters			
[88]	Digit	::=	[#x0030-#x0039] | [#x0660-#x0669] | [#x06F0-#x06F9] | [#x0966-#x096F] | [#x09E6-#x09EF] [#x0A66-#x0A6F] | [#x0AE6-#x0AEF] [#x0B66-#x0B6F] | [#x0BE7-#x0BEF] [#x0C66-#x0C6F] | [#x0CE6-#x0CEF] [#x0D66-#x0D6F] | [#x0E50-#x0E59] [#x0ED0-#x0ED9] | [#x0F20-#x0F29]
[89]	Extender	::=	#x00B7 | #x02D0 | #x02D1 | #x0387 | #x0640 #x0E46 | #x0EC6 | #x3005 | [#x3031-#x3035] | [#x309D-#x309E] | [#x30FC-#x30FE]

The character classes defined here can be derived from the Unicode character database as follows:

- Name start characters must have one of the categories Ll, Lu, Lo, Lt, Nl.

- Name characters other than Name-start characters must have one of the categories Mc, Me, Mn, Lm, or Nd.

- Characters in the compatibility area (i.e. with character code greater than #xF900 and less than #xFFFE) are not allowed in XML names.

- Characters which have a font or compatibility decomposition (i.e. those with a "compatibility formatting tag" in field 5 of the database - marked by field 5 beginning with a "<") are not allowed.

- The following characters are treated as name-start characters rather than name characters, because the property file classifies them as Alphabetic: [#x02BB-#x02C1], #x0559, #x06E5, #x06E6.

- Characters #x20DD-#x20E0 are excluded (in accordance with Unicode, section 5.14).

- Character #x00B7 is classified as an extender, because the property list so identifies it.

- Character #x0387 is added as a name character, because #x00B7 is its canonical equivalent.

- Characters ':' and '_' are allowed as name-start characters.

- Characters '-' and '.' are allowed as name characters.

C. XML and SGML (Non-Normative)

XML is designed to be a subset of SGML, in that every valid XML document should also be a conformant SGML document. For a detailed comparison of the additional restrictions that XML places on documents beyond those of SGML, see Clark.

D. Expansion of Entity and Character References (Non-Normative)

This appendix contains some examples illustrating the sequence of entity- and character-reference recognition and expansion, as specified in "**4.4 XML Processor Treatment of Entities and References**".

If the DTD contains the declaration:

```
<!ENTITY example "<p>An ampersand (&#38;#38;) may be escaped
numerically (&#38;#38;#38;) or with a general entity
(&amp;amp;). </p>" >
```

then the XML processor will recognize the character references when it parses the entity declaration, and resolve them before storing the following string as the value of the entity "example":

```
<p>An ampersand (&#38;) may be escaped
numerically (&#38;#38;) or with a general entity
(&amp;amp;).</p>
```

A reference in the document to "&example;" will cause the text to be reparsed, at which time the start- and end-tags of the "p" element will be recognized and the three references will be recognized and expanded, resulting in a "p" element with the following content (all data, no delimiters or markup):

```
An ampersand (&) may be escaped
numerically (&#38;) or with a general entity
(&amp;).
```

A more complex example will illustrate the rules and their effects fully. In the following example, the line numbers are solely for reference.

```
1 <?xml version='1.0'?>
2 <!DOCTYPE test [
3 <!ELEMENT test (#PCDATA) >
4 <!ENTITY % xx '&#37;zz;'>
5 <!ENTITY % zz '&#60;!ENTITY tricky "error-prone" >' >
6 %xx;
7 ]>
8 <test>This sample shows a &tricky; method.</test>
```

This produces the following:

❑ in line 4, the reference to character 37 is expanded immediately, and the parameter entity "xx" is stored in the symbol table with the value "%zz;". Since the replacement text is not rescanned, the reference to parameter entity "zz" is not recognized. (And it would be an error if it were, since "zz" is not yet declared.)

❑ in line 5, the character reference "<" is expanded immediately and the parameter entity "zz" is stored with the replacement text "<!ENTITY tricky "error-prone" >", which is a well-formed entity declaration.

❑ in line 6, the reference to "xx" is recognized, and the replacement text of "xx" (namely "%zz;") is parsed. The reference to "zz" is recognized in its turn, and its replacement text ("<!ENTITY tricky "error-prone" >") is parsed. The general entity "tricky" has now been declared, with the replacement text "error-prone".

❑ in line 8, the reference to the general entity "tricky" is recognized, and it is expanded, so the full content of the "test" element is the self-describing (and ungrammatical) string *This sample shows an error-prone method.*

E. Deterministic Content Models (Non-Normative)

For compatibility, it is required that content models in element type declarations be deterministic.

SGML requires deterministic content models (it calls them "unambiguous"); XML processors built using SGML systems may flag non-deterministic content models as errors.

For example, the content model ((b, c) | (b, d)) is non-deterministic, because given an initial b the parser cannot know which b in the model is being matched without looking ahead to see which element follows the b. In this case, the two references to b can be collapsed into a single reference, making the model read (b, (c | d)). An initial b now clearly matches only a single name in the content model. The parser doesn't need to look ahead to see what follows; either c or d would be accepted.

More formally: a finite state automaton may be constructed from the content model using the standard algorithms, e.g. algorithm 3.5 in section 3.9 of Aho, Sethi, and Ullman. In many such algorithms, a follow set is constructed for each position in the regular expression (i.e., each leaf node in the syntax tree for the regular expression); if any position has a follow set in which more than one following position is labeled with the same element type name, then the content model is in error and may be reported as an error.

Algorithms exist which allow many but not all non-deterministic content models to be reduced automatically to equivalent deterministic models; see Brüggemann-Klein 1991.

F. Autodetection of Character Encodings (Non-Normative)

The XML encoding declaration functions as an internal label on each entity, indicating which character encoding is in use. Before an XML processor can read the internal label, however, it apparently has to know what character encoding is in use - which is what the internal label is trying to indicate. In the general case, this is a hopeless situation. It is not entirely hopeless in XML, however, because XML limits the general case in two ways: each implementation is assumed to support only a finite set of character encodings, and the XML encoding declaration is restricted in position and content in order to make it feasible to autodetect the character encoding in use in each entity in normal cases. Also, in many cases other sources of information are available in addition to the XML data stream itself. Two cases may be distinguished, depending on whether the XML entity is presented to the processor without, or with, any accompanying (external) information. We consider the first case first.

Because each XML entity not in UTF-8 or UTF-16 format *must* begin with an XML encoding declaration, in which the first characters must be '<?xml', any conforming processor can detect, after two to four octets of input, which of the following cases apply. In reading this list, it may help to know that in UCS-4, '<' is "#x0000003C" and '?' is "#x0000003F", and the Byte Order Mark required of UTF-16 data streams is "#xFEFF".

- ❑ 00 00 00 3C: UCS-4, big-endian machine (1234 order)

- ❑ 3C 00 00 00: UCS-4, little-endian machine (4321 order)

- ❑ 00 00 3C 00: UCS-4, unusual octet order (2143)

- ❑ 00 3C 00 00: UCS-4, unusual octet order (3412)

❏   FE FF: UTF-16, big-endian

❏   FF FE: UTF-16, little-endian

❏   00 3C 00 3F: UTF-16, big-endian, no Byte Order Mark (and thus, strictly speaking, in error)

❏   3C 00 3F 00: UTF-16, little-endian, no Byte Order Mark (and thus, strictly speaking, in error)

❏   3C 3F 78 6D: UTF-8, ISO 646, ASCII, some part of ISO 8859, Shift-JIS, EUC, or any other 7-bit, 8-bit, or mixed-width encoding which ensures that the characters of ASCII have their normal positions, width, and values; the actual encoding declaration must be read to detect which of these applies, but since all of these encodings use the same bit patterns for the ASCII characters, the encoding declaration itself may be read reliably

❏   4C 6F A7 94: EBCDIC (in some flavor; the full encoding declaration must be read to tell which code page is in use)

❏   other: UTF-8 without an encoding declaration, or else the data stream is corrupt, fragmentary, or enclosed in a wrapper of some kind

This level of autodetection is enough to read the XML encoding declaration and parse the character-encoding identifier, which is still necessary to distinguish the individual members of each family of encodings (e.g. to tell UTF-8 from 8859, and the parts of 8859 from each other, or to distinguish the specific EBCDIC code page in use, and so on).

Because the contents of the encoding declaration are restricted to ASCII characters, a processor can reliably read the entire encoding declaration as soon as it has detected which family of encodings is in use. Since in practice, all widely used character encodings fall into one of the categories above, the XML encoding declaration allows reasonably reliable in-band labeling of character encodings, even when external sources of information at the operating-system or transport-protocol level are unreliable.

Once the processor has detected the character encoding in use, it can act appropriately, whether by invoking a separate input routine for each case, or by calling the proper conversion function on each character of input.

Like any self-labeling system, the XML encoding declaration will not work if any software changes the entity's character set or encoding without updating the encoding declaration. Implementors of character-encoding routines should be careful to ensure the accuracy of the internal and external information used to label the entity.

The second possible case occurs when the XML entity is accompanied by encoding information, as in some file systems and some network protocols. When multiple sources of information are available, their relative priority and the preferred method of handling conflict should be specified as part of the higher-level protocol used to deliver XML. Rules for the relative priority of the internal label and the MIME-type label in an external header, for example, should be part of the RFC document defining the text/xml and application/xml MIME types. In the interests of interoperability, however, the following rules are recommended.

❑ If an XML entity is in a file, the Byte-Order Mark and encoding-declaration PI are used (if present) to determine the character encoding. All other heuristics and sources of information are solely for error recovery.

❑ If an XML entity is delivered with a MIME type of text/xml, then the `charset` parameter on the MIME type determines the character encoding method; all other heuristics and sources of information are solely for error recovery.

❑ If an XML entity is delivered with a MIME type of application/xml, then the Byte-Order Mark and encoding-declaration PI are used (if present) to determine the character encoding. All other heuristics and sources of information are solely for error recovery.

This algorithm does not work for UTF-7.

These rules apply only in the absence of protocol-level documentation; in particular, when the MIME types text/xml and application/xml are defined, the recommendations of the relevant RFC will supersede these rules.

G. W3C XML Working Group (Non-Normative)

This specification was prepared and approved for publication by the W3C XML Working Group (WG). WG approval of this specification does not necessarily imply that all WG members voted for its approval. The current and former members of the XML WG are:

Jon Bosak, Sun (Chair); James Clark (Technical Lead); Tim Bray, Textuality and Netscape (XML Co-editor); Jean Paoli, Microsoft (XML Co-editor); C. M. Sperberg-McQueen, U. of Ill. (XML Co-editor); Dan Connolly, W3C (W3C Liaison); Paula Angerstein, Texcel; Steve DeRose, INSO; Dave Hollander, HP; Eliot Kimber, ISOGEN; Eve Maler, ArborText; Tom Magliery, NCSA; Murray Maloney, Muzmo and Grif; Makoto Murata, Fuji Xerox Information Systems; Joel Nava, Adobe; Conleth O'Connell, Vignette; Peter Sharpe, SoftQuad; John Tigue, DataChannel
Copyright © 1998 W3C (MIT, INRIA, Keio), All Rights Reserved. W3C liability, trademark, document use and software licensing rules apply.

B

Microsoft XML v3.0 Reference

(March 15 2000 Web Release)

Object, method and property names shown *italicized* are Microsoft extensions.

Objects

Object	Description
DSOControl	XML Data Island (implement with the <XML> tag).
IXMLDOMAttribute	Represents an attribute of an element.
IXMLDOMCDATASection	Represents the CDATA section.
IXMLDOMCharacterData	A base object for higher level objects, including IXMLDOMText and IXMLDOMCDATASection.
IXMLDOMComment	Represents an XML comment.
IXMLDOMDocument	The root object for an XML document.
IXMLDOMDocument2	An extension to the DOMDocument with additional methods and properties.
IXMLDOMDocumentFragment	A lightweight object representing a fragment of an XML document.
IXMLDOMDocumentType	Represents the DOCTYPE section.

Object	Description
IXMLDOMElement	Represents an XML element.
IXMLDOMEntity	Represents an ENTITY section.
IXMLDOMEntityReference	Represents an entity reference node.
IXMLDOMImplementation	Represents implementation specific properties and methods.
IXMLDOMNamedNodeMap	A collection of Node objects, allowing access by name.
IXMLDOMNode	Represents a node in the DOM.
IXMLDOMNodeList	Contains a collection of Node objects.
IXMLDOMNotation	Represents the NOTATION section.
IXMLDOMParseError	Contains details of the last parse error that occurred.
IXMLDOMProcessing Instruction	Represents the <?...?> instructions.
IXMLDOMSchemaCollection	Represents a set of namespace URIs.
IXMLDOMSelection	A list of nodes that match a patter search.
IXMLDOMText	Represents the text content of an element.
IXMLHTTPRequest	Provides client side HTTP requests that are received by the parser.
IXSLProcessor	Represents the XSL parser.
IXSLTemplate	Represents a cached XSL stylesheet.
IXTLRuntime	Represents the methods that are callable from stylesheets.

DSOControl

Properties

Name	Returns	Description
JavaDSOCompatible	Long	A flag indicating whether the DSO should be compatible with the parsing methods used in the Java DSO.
readyState	Long	Indicates the current state of the document. Read only.
XMLDocument	IXMLDOMDocument	Returns the DOM document object.

IXMLDOMAttribute

Methods

Name	Returns	Description
appendChild	IXMLDOMNode	Appends a child node to the current node.
cloneNode	IXMLDOMNode	Creates a clone of the current node.
hasChildNodes	Boolean	Indicates whether or not the current node has child nodes.
insertBefore	IXMLDOMNode	Inserts a child node.
removeChild	IXMLDOMNode	Removes a child node.
replaceChild	IXMLDOMNode	Replaces a child node.
selectNodes	IXMLDOMNodeList	Executes a query on the subtree and returns a list of matching nodes.
selectSingleNode	IXMLDOMNode	Executes a query on the subtree and returns the first matching node.
transformNode	String	Applies the stylesheet to the subtree.
transformNodeTo Object		Applies the stylesheet to the subtree, returning the result through a document or a stream.

Properties

Name	Returns	Description
attributes	IXMLDOMNamedNodeMap	Returns a collection of the node's attributes. Read only.
baseName	String	Returns the base name of the node (nodename with the prefix stripped off). Read only.
childNodes	IXMLDOMNodeList	Returns a collection of the node's children. Read only.
dataType	Variant	Identifies the data type of the node.
definition	IXMLDOMNode	Returns a node that points to the definition of the node in the DTD or schema. Read only.
firstChild	IXMLDOMNode	Returns the first child of the node. Read only.

Table continued on following page

Name	Returns	Description
lastChild	IXMLDOMNode	Returns the last child of the node. Read only.
name	String	Get name of the attribute. Read only.
namespaceURI	String	Returns the URI for the namespace applying to the node. Read only.
nextSibling	IXMLDOMNode	Returns the next (right) sibling of the node. Read only.
nodeName	String	Returns the name of the node. Read only.
nodeType	tagDOMNodeType	The node's type. Read only.
nodeTypedValue	Variant	Get the strongly typed value of the node.
nodeTypeString	String	Returns the type of node in string form (see the list at the end of the appendix). Read only.
nodeValue	Variant	Identifies the value stored in the node.
ownerDocument	IXMLDOMDocument	Returns the root node of the document that contains the node. Read only.
parentNode	IXMLDOMNode	Returns the parent of the node. Read only.
parsed	Boolean	Indicates whether or not the subtree been completely parsed. Read only.
prefix	String	Returns the prefix for the namespace applying to the node. Read only.
previousSibling	IXMLDOMNode	Returns the previous (left) sibling of the node. Read only.
specified	Boolean	Indicates whether node is explicitly specified or is derived from a default value. Read only.
text	String	Identifies the text content of the node and subtree.
value	Variant	Identifies the sring value of the attribute.
xml	String	Rturns the XML source for the node and each of its descendants. Read only.

IXMLDOMCDATASection

Methods

Name	Returns	Description
appendChild	IXMLDOMNode	Appends a child node to the current node.
appendData		Appends a string to value.
cloneNode	IXMLDOMNode	Creates a new copy of the selected node.
deleteData		Deletes a string from within the value
hasChildNodes	Boolean	Indicates whether or not the node has any child nodes.
insertBefore	IXMLDOMNode	Inserts a child node.
insertData		Inserts a string into value
removeChild	IXMLDOMNode	Removes a child node.
replaceChild	IXMLDOMNode	Replaces a child node.
replaceData		Replaces a string within the value.
selectNodes	IXMLDOMNodeList	Executes a query on the subtree and returns a list of matching nodes.
selectSingleNode	IXMLDOMNode	Executes a query on the subtree and returns the first matching node.
splitText	IXMLDOMText	Splits the text node into two text nodes at the position specified.
substringData	String	Retrieves a substring of the value.
transformNode	String	Applies the stylesheet to the subtree.
transformNodeTo Object		Applies the stylesheet to the subtree, returning the result through a document or a stream.

Properties

Name	Returns	Description
attributes	IXMLDOMNamedNodeMap	Returns a collection of the node's attributes. Read only.
baseName	String	Returns the base name of the node (nodename with the prefix stripped off). Read only.

Table continued on following page

Name	Returns	Description
childNodes	IXMLDOMNodeList	Returns a collection of the node's children. Read only.
data	String	Identifies the value of the node.
dataType	Variant	Identifies the data type of the node.
definition	IXMLDOMNode	Returns a node pointing to the definition of the node in the DTD or schema. Read only.
firstChild	IXMLDOMNode	Returns the first child of the node. Read only.
lastChild	IXMLDOMNode	Returns the last child of the node. Read only.
length	Long	Identifies the number of characters in value. Read only.
namespaceURI	String	Returns the URI for the namespace applying to the node. Read only.
nextSibling	IXMLDOMNode	Returns the next (right) sibling of the node. Read only.
nodeName	String	Returns the name of the node. Read only.
nodeType	tagDOMNodeType	Returns the node's type. Read only.
nodeTypedValue	Variant	Identifies the strongly typed value of the node.
nodeTypeString	String	Returns the type of node in string form (see the list at the end of the appendix). Read only.
nodeValue	Variant	Identifies the value stored in the node.
ownerDocument	IXMLDOMDocument	Returns the root node of the document that contains the node. Read only.
parentNode	IXMLDOMNode	Returns the parent of the node. Read only.
parsed	Boolean	Indicates whether or not the subtree has been completely parsed. Read only.
prefix	String	Returns the prefix for the namespace applying to the node. Read only.
previousSibling	IXMLDOMNode	Returns the previous (left) sibling of the node. Read only.

Name	Returns	Description
specified	Boolean	Indicates whether the value was specified or is derived from a default value. Read only.
text	String	Identifies the text content of the node and subtree.
xml	String	Returns the XML source for the node and each of its descendants. Read only.

IXMLDOMCharacterData

Methods

Name	Returns	Description
appendChild	IXMLDOMNode	Appends a child node to the current node.
appendData		Appends a string to value.
cloneNode	IXMLDOMNode	Creates a new copy of the selected node.
deleteData		Deletes a string from within the value.
hasChildNodes	Boolean	Indicates whether or not the node has any child nodes.
insertBefore	IXMLDOMNode	Inserts a child node.
insertData		Inserts a string into value.
removeChild	IXMLDOMNode	Removes a child node.
replaceChild	IXMLDOMNode	Replaces a child node.
replaceData		Replaces a string within the value.
selectNodes	IXMLDOMNodeList	Executes a query on the subtree and returns a list of matching nodes.
selectSingleNode	IXMLDOMNode	Executes a query on the subtree and returns the first matching node.
substringData	String	Retrieves a substring of the value.
transformNode	String	Applies the stylesheet to the subtree.
transformNodeTo Object		Applies the stylesheet to the subtree, returning the result through a document or a stream.

Properties

Name	Returns	Description
attributes	IXMLDOMNamedNodeMap	Returns a collection of the node's attributes. Read only.
baseName	String	Returns the base name of the node (nodename with the prefix stripped off). Read only.
childNodes	IXMLDOMNodeList	Returns a collection of the node's children. Read only.
data	String	Identifies the value of the node.
dataType	Variant	Identifies the data type of the node.
definition	IXMLDOMNode	Returns a node pointing to the definition of the node in the DTD or schema. Read only.
firstChild	IXMLDOMNode	Returns the first child of the node. Read only.
lastChild	IXMLDOMNode	Returns the last child of the node. Read only.
length	Long	Identifies the number of characters in value. Read only.
namespaceURI	String	Returns the URI for the namespace applying to the node. Read only.
nextSibling	IXMLDOMNode	Returns the next (right) sibling of the node. Read only.
nodeName	String	Returns the name of the node. Read only.
nodeType	tagDOMNodeType	Returns the node's type. Read only.
nodeTypedValue	Variant	Identifies the strongly typed value of the node.
nodeTypeString	String	Returns the type of node in string form (see the list at the end of the appendix). Read only.
nodeValue	Variant	Identifies the value stored in the node.
ownerDocument	IXMLDOMDocument	Returns the root node of the document that contains the node. Read only.
parentNode	IXMLDOMNode	Returns the parent of the node. Read only.

Name	Returns	Description
parsed	Boolean	Indicates whether or not the sub-tree has been completely parsed. Read only.
prefix	String	Returns the prefix for the namespace applying to the node. Read only.
previousSibling	IXMLDOMNode	Returns the previous (left) sibling of the node. Read only.
specified	Boolean	Indicates whether the value was specified or is derived from a default value. Read only.
text	String	Identifies the text content of the node and subtree.
xml	String	Returns the XML source for the node and each of its descendants. Read only.

IXMLDOMComment

Methods

Name	Returns	Description
appendChild	IXMLDOMNode	Appends a child node to the current node.
appendData		Appends a string to value.
cloneNode	IXMLDOMNode	Creates a new copy of the selected node.
deleteData		Deletes a string from within the value.
hasChildNodes	Boolean	Indicates whether or not the node has any child nodes.
insertBefore	IXMLDOMNode	Inserts a child node.
insertData		Inserts a string into value.
removeChild	IXMLDOMNode	Removes a child node.
replaceChild	IXMLDOMNode	Replaces a child node.
replaceData		Replaces a string within the value.
selectNodes	IXMLDOMNodeList	Executes a query on the subtree and returns a list of matching nodes.
selectSingleNode	IXMLDOMNode	Executes a query on the subtree and returns the first matching node.

Table continued on following page

Name	Returns	Description
substringData	String	Retrieves a substring of the value.
transformNode	String	Applies the stylesheet to the subtree.
transformNodeTo Object		Applies the stylesheet to the subtree, returning the result through a document or a stream.

Properties

Name	Returns	Description
attributes	IXMLDOMNamedNodeMap	Returns a collection of the node's attributes. Read only.
baseName	String	Returns the base name of the node (nodename with the prefix stripped off). Read only.
childNodes	IXMLDOMNodeList	Returns a collection of the node's children. Read only.
data	String	Identifies the value of the node.
dataType	Variant	Identifies the data type of the node.
definition	IXMLDOMNode	Returns a node pointing to the definition of the node in the DTD or schema. Read only.
firstChild	IXMLDOMNode	Returns the first child of the node. Read only.
lastChild	IXMLDOMNode	Returns the last child of the node. Read only.
length	Long	Identifies the number of characters in value. Read only.
namespaceURI	String	Returns the URI for the namespace applying to the node. Read only.
nextSibling	IXMLDOMNode	Returns the next (right) sibling of the node. Read only.
nodeName	String	Returns the name of the node. Read only.
nodeType	tagDOMNodeType	Returns the node's type. Read only.
nodeTypedValue	Variant	Identifies the strongly typed value of the node.

Name	Returns	Description
nodeTypeString	String	Returns the type of node in string form (see the list at the end of the appendix). Read only.
nodeValue	Variant	Identifies the value stored in the node.
ownerDocument	IXMLDOMDocument	Returns the root node of the document that contains the node. Read only.
parentNode	IXMLDOMNode	Returns the parent of the node. Read only.
parsed	Boolean	Indicates whether or not the subtree has been completely parsed. Read only.
prefix	String	Returns the prefix for the namespace applying to the node. Read only.
previousSibling	IXMLDOMNode	Returns the previous (left) sibling of the node. Read only.
specified	Boolean	Indicates whether the value was specified or is derived from a default value. Read only.
text	String	Identifies the text content of the node and subtree.
xml	String	Returns the XML source for the node and each of its descendants. Read only.

IXMLDOMDocument

Methods

Name	Returns	Description
abort		Aborts an asynchronous download.
appendChild	IXMLDOMNode	Appends a string to value.
cloneNode	IXMLDOMNode	Creates a new copy of the selected node.
createAttribute	IXMLDOMAttribute	Creates an Attribute node.
createCDATA Section	IXMLDOMCDATA Section	Creates a CDATA section node.
createComment	IXMLDOMComment	Creates a Comment node.
createDocument Fragment	IXMLDOMDocument Fragment	Creates a DocumentFragment node.
createElement	IXMLDOMElement	Creates an Element node.

Table continued on following page

Name	Returns	Description
createEntity Reference	IXMLDOMEntity Reference	Creates an EntityReference node.
createNode	IXMLDOMNode	Creates a node of the specified node type and name.
createProcessing Instruction	IXMLDOMProcessing Instruction	Creates a processing instruction (PI) node.
createTextNode	IXMLDOMText	Creates a Text node.
getElementsBy Tag Name	IXMLDOMNodeList	Builds a list of elements by name.
hasChildNodes	Boolean	Indicates whether or not the node has any child nodes.
insertBefore	IXMLDOMNode	Inserts a child node.
load	Boolean	Loads document from the specified XML source.
loadXML	Boolean	Loads the document from a string.
nodeFromID	IXMLDOMNode	Retrieve node from its ID.
removeChild	IXMLDOMNode	Removes a child node.
replaceChild	IXMLDOMNode	Replaces a child node.
save		Saves the document to a specified destination.
selectNodes	IXMLDOMNodeList	Executes a query on the subtree and returns a list of matching nodes.
selectSingleNode	IXMLDOMNode	Executes a query on the subtree and returns the first matching node.
transformNode	String	Applies the stylesheet to the subtree.
transformNodeTo Object		Applies the stylesheet to the subtree, returning the result through a document or a stream.
validate		Validates the currently loaded document, using the current DTD, schema, or schema collection.

Properties

Name	Returns	Description
async	Boolean	Indicates whether or not the document should be loaded asynchronously.

Name	Returns	Description
attributes	IXMLDOMNamedNodeMap	Returns a collection of the node's attributes. Read only.
baseName	String	Returns the base name of the node (nodename with the prefix stripped off). Read only.
childNodes	IXMLDOMNodeList	Returns a collection of the node's children. Read only.
dataType	Variant	Identifies the data type of the node.
definition	IXMLDOMNode	Returns a node pointing to the definition of the node in the DTD or schema. Read only.
doctype	IXMLDOMDocumentType	Returns the node corresponding to the DOCTYPE. Read only.
documentElement	IXMLDOMElement	Identifies the root of the tree.
firstChild	IXMLDOMNode	Returns the first child of the node. Read only.
implementation	IXMLDOMImplementation	Returns information on this DOM implementation. Read only.
lastChild	IXMLDOMNode	Returns the last child of the node. Read only.
namespaces	IXMLSchemaCache	Returns a collection of all schemas associated with this document.
namespaceURI	String	Returns the URI for the namespace applying to the node. Read only.
nextSibling	IXMLDOMNode	Returns the next (right) sibling of the node. Read only.
nodeName	String	Returns the name of the node. Read only.
nodeType	tagDOMNodeType	Returns the node's type. Read only.
nodeTypedValue	Variant	Identifies the strongly typed value of the node.
nodeTypeString	String	Returns the type of node in string form (see the list at the end of the appendix). Read only.
nodeValue	Variant	Identifies the value stored in the node.
ownerDocument	IXMLDOMDocument	Returns the root node of the document that contains the node. Read only.

Table continued on following page

Name	Returns	Description
parentNode	IXMLDOMNode	Returns the parent of the node. Read only.
parsed	Boolean	Indicates whether or not the subtree has been completely parsed. Read only.
parseError	IXMLDOM ParseError	Returns the last parser error. Read only.
prefix	String	Returns the prefix for the namespace applying to the node. Read only.
preserve WhiteSpace	Boolean	Indicates whether or not the parser preserves whitespace.
previousSibling	IXMLDOMNode	Returns the previous (left) sibling of the node. Read only.
readyState	Long	Returns the state of the XML document. Read only.
resolveExternals	Boolean	Indicates whether or not the parser resolves references to external DTD/Entities/Schema.
schemas	Variant	Uses the schema cache to find schemas.
specified	Boolean	Indicates whether the value was specified or is derived from a default value. Read only.
text	String	Identifies the text content of the node and subtree.
url	String	Returns the URL for the loaded XML document. Read only.
validateOnParse	Boolean	Indicates whether or not the parser performs validation.
xml	String	Returns the XML source for the node and each of its descendants. Read only.

Events

Name	Returns	Description
ondataavailable	Variant	Registers the code to be run when the data becomes available after being loaded. Write Only.
onreadystatechange	Variant	Registers the code to be run when the state of the document changes. Write Only.
ontransformnode	Variant	Registers the code to be run when the node has been transformed with a stylesheet. Write Only.

IXMLDOMDocumentFragment

Methods

Name	Returns	Description
appendChild	IXMLDOMNode	Aborts an asynchronous download.
cloneNode	IXMLDOMNode	Appends a string to value.
hasChildNodes	Boolean	Indicates whether or not the node has any child nodes.
insertBefore	IXMLDOMNode	Inserts a child node.
removeChild	IXMLDOMNode	Removes a child node.
replaceChild	IXMLDOMNode	Replaces a child node.
selectNodes	IXMLDOMNodeList	Executes a query on the subtree and returns a list of matching nodes.
selectSingleNode	IXMLDOMNode	Executes a query on the subtree and returns the first matching node.
transformNode	String	Applies the stylesheet to the subtree.
transformNodeTo Object		Applies the stylesheet to the subtree, returning the result through a document or a stream.

Properties

Name	Returns	Description
attributes	IXMLDOMNamedNodeMap	Returns a collection of the node's attributes. Read only.
baseName	String	Returns the base name of the node (nodename with the prefix stripped off). Read only.
childNodes	IXMLDOMNodeList	Returns a collection of the node's children. Read only.
dataType	Variant	Identifies the data type of the node.
definition	IXMLDOMNode	Returns a node pointing to the definition of the node in the DTD or schema. Read only.
firstChild	IXMLDOMNode	Returns the first child of the node. Read only.
lastChild	IXMLDOMNode	Returns the last child of the node. Read only.

Table continued on following page

Name	Returns	Description
namespaceURI	String	Returns the URI for the namespace applying to the node. Read only.
nextSibling	IXMLDOMNode	Returns the next (right) sibling of the node. Read only.
nodeName	String	Returns the name of the node. Read only.
nodeType	tagDOMNodeType	Returns the node's type. Read only.
nodeTypedValue	Variant	Identifies the strongly typed value of the node.
nodeTypeString	String	Returns the type of node in string form (see the list at the end of the appendix). Read only.
nodeValue	Variant	Identifies the value stored in the node.
ownerDocument	IXMLDOMDocument	Returns the root node of the document that contains the node. Read only.
parentNode	IXMLDOMNode	Returns the parent of the node. Read only.
parsed	Boolean	Indicates whether or not the subtree has been completely parsed. Read only.
prefix	String	Returns the prefix for the namespace applying to the node. Read only.
previousSibling	IXMLDOMNode	Returns the previous (left) sibling of the node. Read only.
specified	Boolean	Indicates whether the value was specified or is derived from a default value. Read only.
text	String	Identifies the text content of the node and subtree.
xml	String	Returns the XML source for the node and each of its descendants. Read only.

IXMLDOMDocumentType

Methods

Name	Returns	Description
appendChild	IXMLDOMNode	Appends a child node to the current node.
cloneNode	IXMLDOMNode	Creates a new copy of the selected node.

Name	Returns	Description
hasChildNodes	Boolean	Indicates whether or not the node has any child nodes.
insertBefore	IXMLDOMNode	Inserts a child node.
removeChild	IXMLDOMNode	Removes a child node.
replaceChild	IXMLDOMNode	Replaces a child node.
selectNodes	IXMLDOMNodeList	Executes a query on the subtree and returns a list of matching nodes.
selectSingleNode	IXMLDOMNode	Executes a query on the subtree and returns the first matching node.
transformNode	String	Applies the stylesheet to the subtree.
transformNodeTo Object		Applies the stylesheet to the subtree, returning the result through a document or a stream.

Properties

Name	Returns	Description
attributes	IXMLDOMNamedNodeMap	Returns a collection of the node's attributes. Read only.
baseName	String	Returns the base name of the node (nodename with the prefix stripped off). Read only.
childNodes	IXMLDOMNodeList	Returns a collection of the node's children. Read only.
dataType	Variant	Identifies the data type of the node.
definition	IXMLDOMNode	Returns a node pointing to the definition of the node in the DTD or schema. Read only.
entities	IXMLDOMNamedNodeMap	Returns a list of entities in the document. Read only.
firstChild	IXMLDOMNode	Returns the first child of the node. Read only.
lastChild	IXMLDOMNode	Returns the last child of the node. Read only.
name	String	Returns the name of the document type (root of the tree). Read only.
namespaceURI	String	Returns the URI for the namespace applying to the node. Read only.

Table continued on following page

Name	Returns	Description
nextSibling	IXMLDOMNode	Returns the next (right) sibling of the node. Read only.
nodeName	String	Returns the name of the node. Read only.
nodeType	tagDOMNodeType	Returns the node's type. Read only.
nodeTypedValue	Variant	Identifies the strongly typed value of the node.
nodeTypeString	String	Returns the type of node in string form (see the list at the end of the appendix). Read only.
nodeValue	Variant	Identifies the value stored in the node.
notations	IXMLDOMNamedNodeMap	Returns a list of notations in the document. Read only.
ownerDocument	IXMLDOMDocument	Returns the root node of the document that contains the node. Read only.
parentNode	IXMLDOMNode	Returns the parent of the node. Read only.
parsed	Boolean	Indicates whether or not the subtree has been completely parsed. Read only.
prefix	String	Returns the prefix for the namespace applying to the node. Read only.
previousSibling	IXMLDOMNode	Returns the previous (left) sibling of the node. Read only.
specified	Boolean	Indicates whether the value was specified or is derived from a default value. Read only.
text	String	Identifies the text content of the node and subtree.
xml	String	Returns the XML source for the node and each of its descendants. Read only.

IXMLDOMElement

Methods

Name	Returns	Description
appendChild	IXMLDOMNode	Appends a child node to the current node.

Name	Returns	Description
cloneNode	IXMLDOMNode	Creates a new copy of the selected node.
getAttribute	Variant	Looks up the string value of an attribute by name.
getAttributeNode	IXMLDOMAttribute	Looks up the attribute node by name.
getElements ByTag Name	IXMLDOMNodeList	Builds a list of elements by name.
hasChildNodes	Boolean	Indicates whether or not the node has any child nodes.
insertBefore	IXMLDOMNode	Inserts a child node.
normalize		Collapses all adjacent text nodes in sub-tree.
removeAttribute		Removes an attribute by name.
removeAttributeNode	IXMLDOMAttribute	Removes the specified attribute.
removeChild	IXMLDOMNode	Removes a child node.
replaceChild	IXMLDOMNode	Replaces a child node.
selectNodes	IXMLDOMNodeList	Executes a query on the subtree and returns a list of matching nodes.
selectSingleNode	IXMLDOMNode	Executes a query on the subtree and returns the first matching node.
setAttribute		Sets the string value of an attribute by name.
setAttributeNode	IXMLDOMAttribute	Sets the specified attribute on the element.
transformNode	String	Applies the stylesheet to the subtree.
transformNodeTo Object		Applies the stylesheet to the subtree, returning the result through a document or a stream.

Properties

Name	Returns	Description
attributes	IXMLDOMNamedNode Map	Returns a collection of the node's attributes. Read only.
baseName	String	Returns the base name of the node (nodename with the prefix stripped off). Read only.

Table continued on following page

Name	Returns	Description
childNodes	IXMLDOMNodeList	Returns a collection of the node's children. Read only.
dataType	Variant	Identifies the data type of the node.
definition	IXMLDOMNode	Returns a node pointing to the definition of the node in the DTD or schema. Read only.
firstChild	IXMLDOMNode	Returns the first child of the node. Read only.
lastChild	IXMLDOMNode	Returns the last child of the node. Read only.
namespaceURI	String	Returns the URI for the namespace applying to the node. Read only.
nextSibling	IXMLDOMNode	Returns the next (right) sibling of the node. Read only.
nodeName	String	Returns the name of the node. Read only.
nodeType	tagDOMNodeType	Returns the node's type. Read only.
nodeTypedValue	Variant	Identifies the strongly typed value of the node.
nodeTypeString	String	Returns the type of node in string form (see the list at the end of the appendix). Read only.
nodeValue	Variant	Identifies the value stored in the node.
ownerDocument	IXMLDOMDocument	Returns the root node of the document that contains the node. Read only.
parentNode	IXMLDOMNode	Returns the parent of the node. Read only.
parsed	Boolean	Indicates whether or not the subtree has been completely parsed. Read only.
prefix	String	Returns the prefix for the namespace applying to the node. Read only.
previousSibling	IXMLDOMNode	Returns the previous (left) sibling of the node. Read only.
specified	Boolean	Indicates whether the value was specified or is derived from a default value. Read only.
tagName	String	Returns the tagName of the element. Read only.
text	String	Identifies the text content of the node and subtree.
xml	String	Returns the XML source for the node and each of its descendants. Read only.

IXMLDOMEntity

Methods

Name	Returns	Description
appendChild	IXMLDOMNode	Appends a child node to the current node.
cloneNode	IXMLDOMNode	Creates a new copy of the selected node.
hasChildNodes	Boolean	Indicates whether or not the node has any child nodes.
insertBefore	IXMLDOMNode	Inserts a child node.
removeChild	IXMLDOMNode	Removes a child node.
replaceChild	IXMLDOMNode	Replaces a child node.
selectNodes	IXMLDOMNodeList	Executes a query on the subtree and returns a list of matching nodes.
selectSingleNode	IXMLDOMNode	Executes a query on the subtree and returns the first matching node.
transformNode	String	Applies the stylesheet to the subtree.
transformNodeTo Object		Applies the stylesheet to the subtree, returning the result through a document or a stream.

Properties

Name	Returns	Description
attributes	IXMLDOMNamed NodeMap	Returns a collection of the node's attributes. Read only.
baseName	String	Returns the base name of the node (nodename with the prefix stripped off). Read only.
childNodes	IXMLDOMNodeList	Returns a collection of the node's children. Read only.
dataType	Variant	Identifies the data type of the node.
definition	IXMLDOMNode	Returns a node pointing to the definition of the node in the DTD or schema. Read only.
firstChild	IXMLDOMNode	Returns the first child of the node. Read only.
lastChild	IXMLDOMNode	Returns the last child of the node. Read only.

Table continued on following page

Name	Returns	Description
namespaceURI	String	Returns the URI for the namespace applying to the node. Read only.
nextSibling	IXMLDOMNode	Returns the next (right) sibling of the node. Read only.
nodeName	String	Returns the name of the node. Read only.
nodeType	tagDOMNodeType	Returns the node's type. Read only.
nodeTypedValue	Variant	Identifies the strongly typed value of the node.
nodeTypeString	String	Returns the type of node in string form (see the list at the end of the appendix). Read only.
nodeValue	Variant	Identifies the value stored in the node.
notationName	String	The name of the notation. Read only.
ownerDocument	IXMLDOMDocument	Returns the root node of the document that contains the node. Read only.
parentNode	IXMLDOMNode	Returns the parent of the node. Read only.
parsed	Boolean	Indicates whether or not the subtree has been completely parsed. Read only.
prefix	String	Returns the prefix for the namespace applying to the node. Read only.
previousSibling	IXMLDOMNode	Returns the previous (left) sibling of the node. Read only.
publicId	Variant	Returns the public ID. Read only.
specified	Boolean	Indicates whether the value was specified or is derived from a default value. Read only.
systemId	Variant	Returns the system ID. Read only.
text	String	Identifies the text content of the node and subtree.
xml	String	Returns the XML source for the node and each of its descendants. Read only.

IXMLDOMEntityReference

Methods

Name	Returns	Description
appendChild	IXMLDOMNode	Appends a child node to the current node.
cloneNode	IXMLDOMNode	Creates a new copy of the selected node.
hasChildNodes	Boolean	Indicates whether or not the node has any child nodes.
insertBefore	IXMLDOMNode	Inserts a child node.
removeChild	IXMLDOMNode	Removes a child node.
replaceChild	IXMLDOMNode	Replaces a child node.
selectNodes	IXMLDOMNodeList	Executes a query on the subtree and returns a list of matching nodes.
selectSingleNode	IXMLDOMNode	Executes a query on the subtree and returns the first matching node.
transformNode	String	Applies the stylesheet to the subtree.
transformNodeTo Object		Applies the stylesheet to the subtree, returning the result through a document or a stream.

Properties

Name	Returns	Description
attributes	IXMLDOMNamed NodeMap	Returns a collection of the node's attributes. Read only.
baseName	String	Returns the base name of the node (nodename with the prefix stripped off). Read only.
childNodes	IXMLDOMNodeList	Returns a collection of the node's children. Read only.
dataType	Variant	Identifies the data type of the node.
definition	IXMLDOMNode	Returns a node pointing to the definition of the node in the DTD or schema. Read only.
firstChild	IXMLDOMNode	Returns the first child of the node. Read only.
lastChild	IXMLDOMNode	Returns the last child of the node. Read only.

Table continued on following page

Name	Returns	Description
namespaceURI	String	Returns the URI for the namespace applying to the node. Read only.
nextSibling	IXMLDOMNode	Returns the next (right) sibling of the node. Read only.
nodeName	String	Returns the name of the node. Read only.
nodeType	tagDOMNodeType	Returns the node's type. Read only.
nodeTypedValue	Variant	Identifies the strongly typed value of the node.
nodeTypeString	String	Returns the type of node in string form (see the list at the end of the appendix). Read only.
nodeValue	Variant	Identifies the value stored in the node.
ownerDocument	IXMLDOMDocument	Returns the root node of the document that contains the node. Read only.
parentNode	IXMLDOMNode	Returns the parent of the node. Read only.
parsed	Boolean	Indicates whether or not the subtree has been completely parsed. Read only.
prefix	String	Returns the prefix for the namespace applying to the node. Read only.
previousSibling	IXMLDOMNode	Returns the previous (left) sibling of the node. Read only.
specified	Boolean	Indicates whether the value was specified or is derived from a default value. Read only.
text	String	Identifies the text content of the node and subtree.
xml	String	Returns the XML source for the node and each of its descendants. Read only.

IXMLDOMImplementation

Methods

Name	Returns	Description
hasFeature	Boolean	Identifies whether the parser implementation has a specific feature.

IXMLDOMNamedNodeMap

Methods

Name	Returns	Description
getNamedItem	IXMLDOMNode	Looks up item by name.
getQualifiedItem	IXMLDOMNode	Looks up the item by name and namespace.
nextNode	IXMLDOMNode	Gets next node from iterator.
removeNamedItem	IXMLDOMNode	Removes item by name.
removeQualified Item	IXMLDOMNode	Removes the item by name and namespace.
reset		Resets the position of iterator.
setNamedItem	IXMLDOMNode	Sets item by name.

Properties

Name	Returns	Description
item	IXMLDOMNode	Default collection of nodes. Read only.
length	Long	Identifies the number of nodes in the collection. Read only.

IXMLDOMNode

Methods

Name	Returns	Description
appendChild	IXMLDOMNode	Appends a child node to the current node.
cloneNode	IXMLDOMNode	Creates a new copy of the selected node.
hasChildNodes	Boolean	Indicates whether or not the node has any child nodes.
insertBefore	IXMLDOMNode	Inserts a child node.
removeChild	IXMLDOMNode	Removes a child node.
replaceChild	IXMLDOMNode	Replaces a child node.
selectNodes	IXMLDOMNode List	Executes a query on the subtree and returns a list of matching nodes.

Table continued on following page

Name	Returns	Description
selectSingleNode	IXMLDOMNode	Executes a query on the subtree and returns the first matching node.
transformNode	String	Applies the stylesheet to the subtree.
transformNodeTo Object		Applies the stylesheet to the subtree, returning the result through a document or a stream.

Properties

Name	Returns	Description
attributes	IXMLDOMNamed NodeMap	Returns a collection of the node's attributes. Read only.
baseName	String	Returns the base name of the node (nodename with the prefix stripped off). Read only.
childNodes	IXMLDOMNodeList	Returns a collection of the node's children. Read only.
dataType	Variant	Identifies the data type of the node.
definition	IXMLDOMNode	Returns a node pointing to the definition of the node in the DTD or schema. Read only.
firstChild	IXMLDOMNode	Returns the first child of the node. Read only.
lastChild	IXMLDOMNode	Returns the last child of the node. Read only.
namespaceURI	String	Returns the URI for the namespace applying to the node. Read only.
nextSibling	IXMLDOMNode	Returns the next (right) sibling of the node. Read only.
nodeName	String	Returns the name of the node. Read only.
nodeType	tagDOMNodeType	Returns the node's type. Read only.
nodeTypedValue	Variant	Identifies the strongly typed value of the node.
nodeTypeString	String	Returns the type of node in string form (see the list at the end of the appendix). Read only.
nodeValue	Variant	Identifies the value stored in the node.

Name	Returns	Description
ownerDocument	IXMLDOMDocument	Returns the root node of the document that contains the node. Read only.
parentNode	IXMLDOMNode	Returns the parent of the node. Read only.
parsed	Boolean	Indicates whether or not the subtree has been completely parsed. Read only.
prefix	String	Returns the prefix for the namespace applying to the node. Read only.
previousSibling	IXMLDOMNode	Returns the previous (left) sibling of the node. Read only.
specified	Boolean	Indicates whether the value was specified or is derived from a default value. Read only.
text	String	Identifies the text content of the node and subtree.
xml	String	Returns the XML source for the node and each of its descendants. Read only.

IXMLDOMNodeList

Methods

Name	Returns	Description
nextNode	IXMLDOMNode	Gets next node from iterator.
reset		Resets the position of iterator.

Properties

Name	Returns	Description
item	IXMLDOMNode	The default collection of nodes. Read only.
length	Long	Identifies the number of nodes in the collection. Read only.

IXMLDOMNotation

Methods

Name	Returns	Description
appendChild	IXMLDOMNode	Appends a child node to the current node.

Table continued on following page

719

Name	Returns	Description
cloneNode	IXMLDOMNode	Creates a new copy of the selected node.
hasChildNodes	Boolean	Indicates whether or not the node has any child nodes.
insertBefore	IXMLDOMNode	Inserts a child node.
removeChild	IXMLDOMNode	Removes a child node.
replaceChild	IXMLDOMNode	Replaces a child node.
selectNodes	IXMLDOMNodeList	Executes a query on the subtree and returns a list of matching nodes.
selectSingleNode	IXMLDOMNode	Executes a query on the subtree and returns the first matching node.
transformNode	String	Applies the stylesheet to the subtree.
transformNodeTo Object		Applies the stylesheet to the subtree, returning the result through a document or a stream.

Properties

Name	Returns	Description
attributes	IXMLDOMNamed NodeMap	Returns a collection of the node's attributes. Read only.
baseName	String	Returns the base name of the node (nodename with the prefix stripped off). Read only.
childNodes	IXMLDOMNodeList	Returns a collection of the node's children. Read only.
dataType	Variant	Identifies the data type of the node.
definition	IXMLDOMNode	Returns a node pointing to the definition of the node in the DTD or schema. Read only.
firstChild	IXMLDOMNode	Returns the first child of the node. Read only.
lastChild	IXMLDOMNode	Returns the last child of the node. Read only.
namespaceURI	String	Returns the URI for the namespace applying to the node. Read only.
nextSibling	IXMLDOMNode	Returns the next (right) sibling of the node. Read only.

Name	Returns	Description
nodeName	String	Returns the name of the node. Read only.
nodeType	tagDOMNodeType	Returns the node's type. Read only.
nodeTypedValue	Variant	Identifies the strongly typed value of the node.
nodeTypeString	String	Returns the type of node in string form (see the list at the end of the appendix). Read only.
nodeValue	Variant	Identifies the value stored in the node.
ownerDocument	IXMLDOMDocument	Returns the root node of the document that contains the node. Read only.
parentNode	IXMLDOMNode	Returns the parent of the node. Read only.
parsed	Boolean	Indicates whether or not the subtree has been completely parsed. Read only.
prefix	String	Returns the prefix for the namespace applying to the node. Read only.
previousSibling	IXMLDOMNode	Returns the previous (left) sibling of the node. Read only.
publicId	Variant	Returns the public ID. Read only.
specified	Boolean	Indicates whether the value was specified or is derived from a default value. Read only.
systemId	Variant	Returns the system ID. Read only.
text	String	Identifies the text content of the node and subtree.
xml	String	Returns the XML source for the node and each of its descendants. Read only.

IXMLDOMParseError

Properties

Name	Returns	Description
errorCode	Long	Returns the error code. Read only.
filepos	Long	Returns the absolute file position in the XML document containing the error. Read only.
line	Long	Returns the line number in the XML document where the error occurred. Read only.

Name	Returns	Description
linepos	Long	Returns the character position in the line containing the error. Read only.
reason	String	Returns the cause of the error. Read only.
srcText	String	Returns the data where the error occurred. Read only.
url	String	Returns the URL of the XML document containing the error. Read only.

IXMLDOMProcessingInstruction

Methods

Name	Returns	Description
appendChild	IXMLDOMNode	Appends a child node to the current node.
cloneNode	IXMLDOMNode	Creates a new copy of the selected node.
hasChildNodes	Boolean	Indicates whether or not the node has any child nodes.
insertBefore	IXMLDOMNode	Inserts a child node.
removeChild	IXMLDOMNode	Removes a child node.
replaceChild	IXMLDOMNode	Replaces a child node.
selectNodes	IXMLDOMNodeList	Executes a query on the subtree and returns a list of matching nodes.
selectSingleNode	IXMLDOMNode	Executes a query on the subtree and returns the first matching node.
transformNode	String	Applies the stylesheet to the subtree.
transformNodeTo Object		Applies the stylesheet to the subtree, returning the result through a document or a stream.

Properties

Name	Returns	Description
attributes	IXMLDOMNamed NodeMap	Returns a collection of the node's attributes. Read only.
baseName	String	Returns the base name of the node (nodename with the prefix stripped off). Read only.

Name	Returns	Description
childNodes	IXMLDOMNodeList	Returns a collection of the node's children. Read only.
data	String	Identifies the value of the node.
dataType	Variant	Identifies the data type of the node.
definition	IXMLDOMNode	Returns a node pointing to the definition of the node in the DTD or schema. Read only.
firstChild	IXMLDOMNode	Returns the first child of the node. Read only.
lastChild	IXMLDOMNode	Returns the last child of the node. Read only.
namespaceURI	String	Returns the URI for the namespace applying to the node. Read only.
nextSibling	IXMLDOMNode	Returns the next (right) sibling of the node. Read only.
nodeName	String	Returns the name of the node. Read only.
nodeType	tagDOMNodeType	Returns the node's type. Read only.
nodeTypedValue	Variant	Identifies the strongly typed value of the node.
nodeTypeString	String	Returns the type of node in string form (see the list at the end of the appendix). Read only.
nodeValue	Variant	Identifies the value stored in the node.
ownerDocument	IXMLDOMDocument	Returns the root node of the document that contains the node. Read only.
parentNode	IXMLDOMNode	Returns the parent of the node. Read only.
parsed	Boolean	Indicates whether or not the subtree has been completely parsed. Read only.
prefix	String	Returns the prefix for the namespace applying to the node. Read only.
previousSibling	IXMLDOMNode	Returns the previous (left) sibling of the node. Read only.
specified	Boolean	Indicates whether the value was specified or is derived from a default value. Read only.
target	String	Specifies the application to which this instruction is directed. Read only.
text	String	Identifies the text content of the node and subtree.
xml	String	Returns the XML source for the node and each of its descendants. Read only.

IXMLDOMSchemaCollection

Methods

Name	Returns	Description
add		Adds a new schema to the collection.
addCollection		Copies and merges another collection into this one.
get	IXMLDOMNode	Looks up schema by namespaceURI.
remove		Remove schema by namespaceURI.

Properties

Name	Returns	Description
length	Long	Indicates the number of schemas in collection. Read only.
namespaceURI	String	Gets namespaceURI for schema by index. Read only.

IXMLDOMSelection

Methods

Name	Returns	Description
clone	IXMLDOM Selection	Clones this object with the same position and context.
getProperty	Variant	Gets the value of the named property.
matches	IXMLDOMNode	Checks to see if the node matches the pattern.
nextNode	IXMLDOMNode	Gets next node from iterator.
peekNode	IXMLDOMNode	Gets the next node without advancing the list position.
removeAll		Removes all the nodes that match the selection.
removeNext	IXMLDOMNode	Removes the next node.
reset		Resets the position of iterator.

Properties

Name	Returns	Description
context	IXMLDOMNode	Identifies the nodes to apply selection expression to.

Name	Returns	Description
expr	String	The selection expression.
item	IXMLDOMNode	The default collection of nodes. Read only.
length	Long	Indicates the number of nodes in the collection. Read only.

IXMLDOMText

Methods

Name	Returns	Description
appendChild	IXMLDOMNode	Appends a child node to the current node.
appendData		Appends a string to value.
cloneNode	IXMLDOMNode	Creates a new copy of the selected node.
deleteData		Deletes a string from within the value.
hasChildNodes	Boolean	Indicates whether or not the node has any child nodes.
insertBefore	IXMLDOMNode	Inserts a child node.
insertData		Inserts a string into the value.
removeChild	IXMLDOMNode	Removes a child node.
replaceChild	IXMLDOMNode	Replaces a child node.
replaceData		Replaces a string within the value.
selectNodes	IXMLDOMNodeList	Executes a query on the subtree and returns a list of matching nodes.
selectSingleNode	IXMLDOMNode	Executes a query on the subtree and returns the first matching node.
splitText	IXMLDOMText	Split the text node into two text nodes at the position specified.
substringData	String	Retrieves a substring of the value.
transformNode	String	Applies the stylesheet to the subtree.
transformNodeTo Object		Applies the stylesheet to the subtree, returning the result through a document or a stream.

Properties

Name	Returns	Description
attributes	IXMLDOMNamedNodeMap	Returns a collection of the node's attributes. Read only.
baseName	String	Returns the base name of the node (nodename with the prefix stripped off). Read only.
childNodes	IXMLDOMNodeList	Returns a collection of the node's children. Read only.
data	String	Identifies the value of the node.
dataType	Variant	Identifies the data type of the node.
definition	IXMLDOMNode	Returns a node pointing to the definition of the node in the DTD or schema. Read only.
firstChild	IXMLDOMNode	Returns the first child of the node. Read only.
lastChild	IXMLDOMNode	Returns the last child of the node. Read only.
length	Long	Identifies the number of characters in value. Read only.
namespaceURI	String	Returns the URI for the namespace applying to the node. Read only.
nextSibling	IXMLDOMNode	Returns the next (right) sibling of the node. Read only.
nodeName	String	Returns the name of the node. Read only.
nodeType	tagDOMNodeType	Returns the node's type. Read only.
nodeTypedValue	Variant	Identifies the strongly typed value of the node.
nodeTypeString	String	Returns the type of node in string form (see the list at the end of the appendix). Read only.
nodeValue	Variant	Identifies the value stored in the node.
ownerDocument	IXMLDOMDocument	Returns the root node of the document that contains the node. Read only.
parentNode	IXMLDOMNode	Returns the parent of the node. Read only.
parsed	Boolean	Indicates whether or not the subtree has been completely parsed. Read only.

Name	Returns	Description
prefix	String	Returns the prefix for the namespace applying to the node. Read only.
previousSibling	IXMLDOMNode	Returns the previous (left) sibling of the node. Read only.
specified	Boolean	Indicates whether the value was specified or is derived from a default value. Read only.
text	String	Identifies the text content of the node and subtree.
xml	String	Returns the XML source for the node and each of its descendants. Read only.

IXMLElement

Methods

Name	Returns	Description
addChild		Adds a child element.
getAttribute	Variant	Gets an attribute from the element.
removeAttribute		Removes attribute from the element.
removeChild		Removes a child element.
setAttribute		Sets an attribute on the element.

Properties

Name	Returns	Description
children	IXMLElement Collection	Returns a collection of children. Read only.
parent	IXMLElement	Returns the parent element. Read only.
tagName	String	Identifies the element tag name.
text	String	Identifies the element text.
type	Long	Returns the type of the element. Read only.

IXMLElementCollection

Methods

Name	Returns	Description
item	Object	Returns the current item, or (optional) by index and name.

Properties

Name	Returns	Description
length	Long	Indicates the number of elements in the collection.

IXMLHTTPRequest

Methods

Name	Returns	Description
abort		Aborts HTTP request.
getAllResponseHeaders	String	Gets all HTTP response headers.
getResponseHeader	String	Gets HTTP response header.
open		Opens HTTP connection.
send		Sends HTTP request.
setRequestHeader		Adds HTTP request header.

Properties

Name	Returns	Description
readyState	Long	Gets ready state. Read only.
responseBody	Variant	Gets response body. Read only.
responseStream	Variant	Gets response body. Read only.
responseText	String	Gets response body. Read only.
responseXML	Object	Gets response body. Read only.
status	Long	Gets HTTP status code. Read only.
statusText	String	Gets HTTP status text. Read only.

Events

Name	Returns	Description
onreadystatechange	Object	Registers a complete event handler. Write Only.

IXSLProcessor

Methods

Name	Returns	Description
addObject		Passes object to stylesheet.
addParameter		Sets <xsl:param> values.
reset		Resets state of processor and abort current transform.
setStartMode		Sets XSL mode and its namespace.
transform	Boolean	Starts or resumes the XSL transformation process.

Properties

Name	Returns	Description
input	Variant	XML input tree to transform.
output	Variant	Custom stream object for transform output.
ownerTemplate	IXSLTemplate	Template object used to create this processor object. Read only.
readyState	Long	Identifies the current state of the processor. Read only.
startMode	String	Identifies starting XSL mode. Read only.
startModeURI	String	Identifies the namespace of starting XSL mode. Read only.
stylesheet	IXMLDOMNode	The current stylesheet being used. Read only.

IXSLTemplate

Methods

Name	Returns	Description
createProcessor	IXSLProcessor	Creates a new processor object.

Properties

Name	Returns	Description
stylesheet	IXMLDOMNode	Identifies the stylesheet to use with processors.

IXTLRuntime

Methods

Name	Returns	Description
absoluteChildNumber	Long	Returns the absolute number of the child.
ancestorChildNumber	Long	Returns the absolute number of the nearest ancestor.
appendChild	IXMLDOMNode	Appends a child node to this node.
childNumber	Long	Returns the node number, relative to siblings.
cloneNode	IXMLDOMNode	Creates a new copy of the selected node.
depth	Long	Returns the depth at which the node appears.
formatDate	String	Formats the supplied date.
formatIndex	String	Formats the supplied index number.
formatNumber	String	Formats the supplied number.
formatTime	String	Formats the supplied time.
hasChildNodes	Boolean	Indicates whether or not the node has any child nodes.
insertBefore	IXMLDOMNode	Inserts a child node.
removeChild	IXMLDOMNode	Removes a child node.
replaceChild	IXMLDOMNode	Replaces a child node.
selectNodes	IXMLDOMNode List	Executes a query on the subtree and returns a list of matching nodes.
selectSingleNode	IXMLDOMNode	Executes a query on the subtree and returns the first matching node.
transformNode	String	Applies the stylesheet to the subtree.
transformNodeTo Object		Applies the stylesheet to the subtree, returning the result through a document or a stream.
UniqueID	Long	Returns the Unique Identifier for the node.

Properties

Name	Returns	Description
attributes	IXMLDOM NamedNode Map	Returns a collection of the node's attributes. Read only.

Name	Returns	Description
baseName	String	Returns the base name of the node (nodename with the prefix stripped off). Read only.
childNodes	IXMLDOMNodeList	Returns a collection of the node's children. Read only.
dataType	Variant	Identifies the data type of the node.
definition	IXMLDOMNode	Returns a node pointing to the definition of the node in the DTD or schema. Read only.
firstChild	IXMLDOMNode	Returns the first child of the node. Read only.
lastChild	IXMLDOMNode	Returns the last child of the node. Read only.
namespaceURI	String	Returns the URI for the namespace applying to the node. Read only.
nextSibling	IXMLDOMNode	Returns the next (right) sibling of the node. Read only.
nodeName	String	Returns the name of the node. Read only.
nodeType	tagDOMNodeType	Returns the node's type. Read only.
nodeTypedValue	Variant	Identifies the strongly typed value of the node.
nodeTypeString	String	Returns the type of node in string form (see the list at the end of the appendix). Read only.
nodeValue	Variant	Identifies the value stored in the node.
ownerDocument	IXMLDOMDocument	Returns the root node of the document that contains the node. Read only.
parentNode	IXMLDOMNode	Returns the parent of the node. Read only.
parsed	Boolean	Indicates whether or not the subtree has been completely parsed. Read only.
Prefix	String	Returns the prefix for the namespace applying to the node. Read only.
previousSibling	IXMLDOMNode	Returns the previous (left) sibling of the node. Read only.
specified	Boolean	Indicates whether the value was specified or is derived from a default value. Read only.
text	String	Identifies the text content of the node and subtree.
xml	String	Returns the XML source for the node and each of its descendants. Read only.

Constants

tagDOMNodeType

Name	Value	IE5 nodeTypeString	Description
NODE_ATTRIBUTE	2	attribute	The node is an attribute.
NODE_CDATA_SECTION	4	CDATA section	The node is a CDATA section.
NODE_COMMENT	8	comment	The node is a COMMENT section
NODE_DOCUMENT	9	document	The node is the document section.
NODE_DOCUMENT_FRAGMENT	11	document fragment	The node represents a document fragment.
NODE_DOCUMENT_TYPE	10	document type	The node is a document type description.
NODE_ELEMENT	1	element	The node is an element.
NODE_ENTITY	6	entity	The node is an entity description.
NODE_ENTITY_REFERENCE	5	entity reference	The node is an entity reference.
NODE_INVALID	0		The node is invalid.
NODE_NOTATION	12	notation	The node is a notation.
NODE_PROCESSING_ INSTRUCTION	7	processing instruction	The node is a processing instruction.
NODE_TEXT	3	text	The node is a text node.

tagXMLELEM_TYPE

Name	Value	Description
XMLELEMTYPE_COMMENT	2	The element is a comment.
XMLELEMTYPE_DOCUMENT	3	The element is a document.
XMLELEMTYPE_DTD	4	The element is a DTD or Schema.
XMLELEMTYPE_ELEMENT	0	The element is a plain element.
XMLELEMTYPE_OTHER	6	The element is another element type.
XMLELEMTYPE_PI	5	The element is a processing instruction.
XMLELEMTYPE_TEXT	1	The element is a text value.

Method Calls

IXMLDOMAttribute

```
IXMLDOMNode = IXMLDOMAttribute.appendChild(newChild As IXMLDOMNode)
IXMLDOMNode = IXMLDOMAttribute.cloneNode(deep As Boolean)
Boolean = IXMLDOMAttribute.hasChildNodes
IXMLDOMNode = IXMLDOMAttribute.insertBefore(newChild As IXMLDOMNode, refChild As
            Variant)
IXMLDOMNode = IXMLDOMAttribute.removeChild(childNode As IXMLDOMNode)
IXMLDOMNode = IXMLDOMAttribute.replaceChild(newChild As IXMLDOMNode, oldChild As
            IXMLDOMNode)
IXMLDOMNodeList = IXMLDOMAttribute.selectNodes(queryString As String)
IXMLDOMNode = IXMLDOMAttribute.selectSingleNode(queryString As String)
String = IXMLDOMAttribute.transformNode(stylesheet As IXMLDOMNode)
IXMLDOMAttribute.transformNodeToObject(stylesheet As IXMLDOMNode, outputObject As
            Variant)
```

IXMLDOMCDATASection

```
IXMLDOMNode = IXMLDOMCDATASection.appendChild(newChild As IXMLDOMNode)
IXMLDOMCDATASection.appendData(data As String)
IXMLDOMNode = IXMLDOMCDATASection.cloneNode(deep As Boolean)
IXMLDOMCDATASection.deleteData(offset As Long, count As Long)
Boolean = IXMLDOMCDATASection.hasChildNodes
IXMLDOMNode = IXMLDOMCDATASection.insertBefore(newChild As IXMLDOMNode, refChild
            As Variant)
IXMLDOMCDATASection.insertData(offset As Long, data As String)
IXMLDOMNode = IXMLDOMCDATASection.removeChild(childNode As IXMLDOMNode)
IXMLDOMNode = IXMLDOMCDATASection.replaceChild(newChild As IXMLDOMNode, oldChild
            As IXMLDOMNode)
IXMLDOMCDATASection.replaceData(offset As Long, count As Long, data As String)
IXMLDOMNodeList = IXMLDOMCDATASection.selectNodes(queryString As String)
IXMLDOMNode = IXMLDOMCDATASection.selectSingleNode(queryString As String)
IXMLDOMText = IXMLDOMCDATASection.splitText(offset As Long)
String = IXMLDOMCDATASection.substringData(offset As Long, count As Long)
String = IXMLDOMCDATASection.transformNode(stylesheet As IXMLDOMNode)
IXMLDOMCDATASection.transformNodeToObject(stylesheet As IXMLDOMNode, outputObject
            As Variant)
```

IXMLDOMCharacterData

```
IXMLDOMNode = IXMLDOMCharacterData.appendChild(newChild As IXMLDOMNode)
IXMLDOMCharacterData.appendData(data As String)
IXMLDOMNode = IXMLDOMCharacterData.cloneNode(deep As Boolean)
IXMLDOMCharacterData.deleteData(offset As Long, count As Long)
Boolean = IXMLDOMCharacterData.hasChildNodes
IXMLDOMNode = IXMLDOMCharacterData.insertBefore(newChild As IXMLDOMNode, refChild
            As Variant)
IXMLDOMCharacterData.insertData(offset As Long, data As String)
IXMLDOMNode = IXMLDOMCharacterData.removeChild(childNode As IXMLDOMNode)
IXMLDOMNode = IXMLDOMCharacterData.replaceChild(newChild As IXMLDOMNode, oldChild
            As IXMLDOMNode)
```

```
IXMLDOMCharacterData.replaceData(offset As Long, count As Long, data As String)
IXMLDOMNodeList = IXMLDOMCharacterData.selectNodes(queryString As String)
IXMLDOMNode = IXMLDOMCharacterData.selectSingleNode(queryString As String)
String = IXMLDOMCharacterData.substringData(offset As Long, count As Long)
String = IXMLDOMCharacterData.transformNode(stylesheet As IXMLDOMNode)
IXMLDOMCharacterData.transformNodeToObject(stylesheet As IXMLDOMNode, outputObject
As Variant)
```

IXMLDOMComment

```
IXMLDOMNode = IXMLDOMComment.appendChild(newChild As IXMLDOMNode)
IXMLDOMComment.appendData(data As String)
IXMLDOMNode = IXMLDOMComment.cloneNode(deep As Boolean)
IXMLDOMComment.deleteData(offset As Long, count As Long)
Boolean = IXMLDOMComment.hasChildNodes
IXMLDOMNode = IXMLDOMComment.insertBefore(newChild As IXMLDOMNode, refChild As
                Variant)
IXMLDOMComment.insertData(offset As Long, data As String)
IXMLDOMNode = IXMLDOMComment.removeChild(childNode As IXMLDOMNode)
IXMLDOMNode = IXMLDOMComment.replaceChild(newChild As IXMLDOMNode, oldChild As
                IXMLDOMNode)
IXMLDOMComment.replaceData(offset As Long, count As Long, data As String)
IXMLDOMNodeList = IXMLDOMComment.selectNodes(queryString As String)
IXMLDOMNode = IXMLDOMComment.selectSingleNode(queryString As String)
String = IXMLDOMComment.substringData(offset As Long, count As Long)
String = IXMLDOMComment.transformNode(stylesheet As IXMLDOMNode)
IXMLDOMComment.transformNodeToObject(stylesheet As IXMLDOMNode, outputObject As
                Variant)
```

IXMLDOMDocument

```
IXMLDOMDocument.abort
IXMLDOMNode = IXMLDOMDocument.appendChild(newChild As IXMLDOMNode)
IXMLDOMNode = IXMLDOMDocument.cloneNode(deep As Boolean)
IXMLDOMAttribute = IXMLDOMDocument.createAttribute(name As String)
IXMLDOMCDATASection = IXMLDOMDocument.createCDATASection(data As String)
IXMLDOMComment = IXMLDOMDocument.createComment(data As String)
IXMLDOMDocumentFragment = IXMLDOMDocument.createDocumentFragment
IXMLDOMElement = IXMLDOMDocument.createElement(tagName As String)
IXMLDOMEntityReference = IXMLDOMDocument.createEntityReference(name As String)
IXMLDOMNode = IXMLDOMDocument.createNode(type As Variant, name As String,
                namespaceURI As String)
IXMLDOMProcessingInstruction = IXMLDOMDocument.createProcessingInstruction(target
                As String, data As String)
IXMLDOMText = IXMLDOMDocument.createTextNode(data As String)
IXMLDOMNodeList = IXMLDOMDocument.getElementsByTagName(tagName As String)
Boolean = IXMLDOMDocument.hasChildNodes
IXMLDOMNode = IXMLDOMDocument.insertBefore(newChild As IXMLDOMNode, refChild As
                Variant)
Boolean = IXMLDOMDocument.load(xmlSource As Variant)
Boolean = IXMLDOMDocument.loadXML(bstrXML As String)
IXMLDOMNode = IXMLDOMDocument.nodeFromID(idString As String)
IXMLDOMNode = IXMLDOMDocument.removeChild(childNode As IXMLDOMNode)
IXMLDOMNode = IXMLDOMDocument.replaceChild(newChild As IXMLDOMNode, oldChild As
                IXMLDOMNode)
```

```
IXMLDOMDocument.save(desination As Variant)
IXMLDOMNodeList = IXMLDOMDocument.selectNodes(queryString As String)
IXMLDOMNode = IXMLDOMDocument.selectSingleNode(queryString As String)
String = IXMLDOMDocument.transformNode(stylesheet As IXMLDOMNode)
IXMLDOMDocument.transformNodeToObject(stylesheet As IXMLDOMNode, outputObject As
        Variant)
IXMLDOMDocument.validate
```

IXMLDOMDocumentFragment

```
IXMLDOMNode = IXMLDOMDocumentFragment.appendChild(newChild As IXMLDOMNode)
IXMLDOMNode = IXMLDOMDocumentFragment.cloneNode(deep As Boolean)
Boolean = IXMLDOMDocumentFragment.hasChildNodes
IXMLDOMNode = IXMLDOMDocumentFragment.insertBefore(newChild As IXMLDOMNode,
             refChild As Variant)
IXMLDOMNode = IXMLDOMDocumentFragment.removeChild(childNode As IXMLDOMNode)
IXMLDOMNode = IXMLDOMDocumentFragment.replaceChild(newChild As IXMLDOMNode,
             oldChild As IXMLDOMNode)
IXMLDOMNodeList = IXMLDOMDocumentFragment.selectNodes(queryString As String)
IXMLDOMNode = IXMLDOMDocumentFragment.selectSingleNode(queryString As String)
String = IXMLDOMDocumentFragment.transformNode(stylesheet As IXMLDOMNode)
IXMLDOMDocumentFragment.transformNodeToObject(stylesheet As IXMLDOMNode,
             outputObject As Variant)
```

IXMLDOMDocumentType

```
IXMLDOMNode = IXMLDOMDocumentType.appendChild(newChild As IXMLDOMNode)
IXMLDOMNode = IXMLDOMDocumentType.cloneNode(deep As Boolean)
Boolean = IXMLDOMDocumentType.hasChildNodes
IXMLDOMNode = IXMLDOMDocumentType.insertBefore(newChild As IXMLDOMNode, refChild
             As Variant)
IXMLDOMNode = IXMLDOMDocumentType.removeChild(childNode As IXMLDOMNode)
IXMLDOMNode = IXMLDOMDocumentType.replaceChild(newChild As IXMLDOMNode, oldChild
             As IXMLDOMNode)
IXMLDOMNodeList = IXMLDOMDocumentType.selectNodes(queryString As String)
IXMLDOMNode = IXMLDOMDocumentType.selectSingleNode(queryString As String)
String = IXMLDOMDocumentType.transformNode(stylesheet As IXMLDOMNode)
IXMLDOMDocumentType.transformNodeToObject(stylesheet As IXMLDOMNode, outputObject
             As Variant)
```

IXMLDOMElement

```
IXMLDOMNode = IXMLDOMElement.appendChild(newChild As IXMLDOMNode)
IXMLDOMNode = IXMLDOMElement.cloneNode(deep As Boolean)
Variant = IXMLDOMElement.getAttribute(name As String)
IXMLDOMAttribute = IXMLDOMElement.getAttributeNode(name As String)
IXMLDOMNodeList = IXMLDOMElement.getElementsByTagName(tagName As String)
Boolean = IXMLDOMElement.hasChildNodes
IXMLDOMNode = IXMLDOMElement.insertBefore(newChild As IXMLDOMNode, refChild As
             Variant)
IXMLDOMElement.normalize
IXMLDOMElement.removeAttribute(name As String)
IXMLDOMAttribute = IXMLDOMElement.removeAttributeNode(DOMAttribute As
IXMLDOMAttribute)
IXMLDOMNode = IXMLDOMElement.removeChild(childNode As IXMLDOMNode)
```

```
IXMLDOMNode = IXMLDOMElement.replaceChild(newChild As IXMLDOMNode, oldChild As
IXMLDOMNode)
IXMLDOMNodeList = IXMLDOMElement.selectNodes(queryString As String)
IXMLDOMNode = IXMLDOMElement.selectSingleNode(queryString As String)
IXMLDOMElement.setAttribute(name As String, value As Variant)
IXMLDOMAttribute = IXMLDOMElement.setAttributeNode(DOMAttribute As
            IXMLDOMAttribute)
String = IXMLDOMElement.transformNode(stylesheet As IXMLDOMNode)
IXMLDOMElement.transformNodeToObject(stylesheet As IXMLDOMNode, outputObject As
            Variant)
```

IXMLDOMEntity

```
IXMLDOMNode = IXMLDOMEntity.appendChild(newChild As IXMLDOMNode)
IXMLDOMNode = IXMLDOMEntity.cloneNode(deep As Boolean)
Boolean = IXMLDOMEntity.hasChildNodes
IXMLDOMNode = IXMLDOMEntity.insertBefore(newChild As IXMLDOMNode, refChild As
            Variant)
IXMLDOMNode = IXMLDOMEntity.removeChild(childNode As IXMLDOMNode)
IXMLDOMNode = IXMLDOMEntity.replaceChild(newChild As IXMLDOMNode, oldChild As
            IXMLDOMNode)
IXMLDOMNodeList = IXMLDOMEntity.selectNodes(queryString As String)
IXMLDOMNode = IXMLDOMEntity.selectSingleNode(queryString As String)
String = IXMLDOMEntity.transformNode(stylesheet As IXMLDOMNode)
IXMLDOMEntity.transformNodeToObject(stylesheet As IXMLDOMNode, outputObject As
            Variant)
```

IXMLDOMEntityReference

```
IXMLDOMNode = IXMLDOMEntityReference.appendChild(newChild As IXMLDOMNode)
IXMLDOMNode = IXMLDOMEntityReference.cloneNode(deep As Boolean)
Boolean = IXMLDOMEntityReference.hasChildNodes
IXMLDOMNode = IXMLDOMEntityReference.insertBefore(newChild As IXMLDOMNode,
            refChild As Variant)
IXMLDOMNode = IXMLDOMEntityReference.removeChild(childNode As IXMLDOMNode)
IXMLDOMNode = IXMLDOMEntityReference.replaceChild(newChild As IXMLDOMNode,
            oldChild As IXMLDOMNode)
IXMLDOMNodeList = IXMLDOMEntityReference.selectNodes(queryString As String)
IXMLDOMNode = IXMLDOMEntityReference.selectSingleNode(queryString As String)
String = IXMLDOMEntityReference.transformNode(stylesheet As IXMLDOMNode)
IXMLDOMEntityReference.transformNodeToObject(stylesheet As IXMLDOMNode,
            outputObject As Variant)
```

IXMLDOMImplementation

```
Boolean = IXMLDOMImplementation.hasFeature(feature As String, version As String)
```

IXMLDOMNamedNodeMap

```
IXMLDOMNode = IXMLDOMNamedNodeMap.getNamedItem(name As String)
IXMLDOMNode = IXMLDOMNamedNodeMap.getQualifiedItem(baseName As String,
            namespaceURI As String)
IXMLDOMNode = IXMLDOMNamedNodeMap.nextNode
IXMLDOMNode = IXMLDOMNamedNodeMap.removeNamedItem(name As String)
```

```
IXMLDOMNode = IXMLDOMNamedNodeMap.removeQualifiedItem(baseName As String,
              namespaceURI As String)
IXMLDOMNamedNodeMap.reset
IXMLDOMNode = IXMLDOMNamedNodeMap.setNamedItem(newItem As IXMLDOMNode)
```

IXMLDOMNode

```
IXMLDOMNode = IXMLDOMNode.appendChild(newChild As IXMLDOMNode)
IXMLDOMNode = IXMLDOMNode.cloneNode(deep As Boolean)
Boolean = IXMLDOMNode.hasChildNodes
IXMLDOMNode = IXMLDOMNode.insertBefore(newChild As IXMLDOMNode, refChild As
              Variant)
IXMLDOMNode = IXMLDOMNode.removeChild(childNode As IXMLDOMNode)
IXMLDOMNode = IXMLDOMNode.replaceChild(newChild As IXMLDOMNode, oldChild As
IXMLDOMNode)
IXMLDOMNodeList = IXMLDOMNode.selectNodes(queryString As String)
IXMLDOMNode = IXMLDOMNode.selectSingleNode(queryString As String)
String = IXMLDOMNode.transformNode(stylesheet As IXMLDOMNode)
IXMLDOMNode.transformNodeToObject(stylesheet As IXMLDOMNode, outputObject As
              Variant)
```

IXMLDOMNodeList

```
IXMLDOMNode = IXMLDOMNodeList.nextNode
IXMLDOMNodeList.reset
```

IXMLDOMNotation

```
IXMLDOMNode = IXMLDOMNotation.appendChild(newChild As IXMLDOMNode)
IXMLDOMNode = IXMLDOMNotation.cloneNode(deep As Boolean)
Boolean = IXMLDOMNotation.hasChildNodes
IXMLDOMNode = IXMLDOMNotation.insertBefore(newChild As IXMLDOMNode, refChild As
              Variant)
IXMLDOMNode = IXMLDOMNotation.removeChild(childNode As IXMLDOMNode)
IXMLDOMNode = IXMLDOMNotation.replaceChild(newChild As IXMLDOMNode, oldChild As
IXMLDOMNode)
IXMLDOMNodeList = IXMLDOMNotation.selectNodes(queryString As String)
IXMLDOMNode = IXMLDOMNotation.selectSingleNode(queryString As String)
String = IXMLDOMNotation.transformNode(stylesheet As IXMLDOMNode)
IXMLDOMNotation.transformNodeToObject(stylesheet As IXMLDOMNode, outputObject As
              Variant)
```

IXMLDOMProcessingInstruction

```
IXMLDOMNode = IXMLDOMProcessingInstruction.appendChild(newChild As IXMLDOMNode)
IXMLDOMNode = IXMLDOMProcessingInstruction.cloneNode(deep As Boolean)
Boolean = IXMLDOMProcessingInstruction.hasChildNodes
IXMLDOMNode = IXMLDOMProcessingInstruction.insertBefore(newChild As IXMLDOMNode,
              refChild As Variant)
IXMLDOMNode = IXMLDOMProcessingInstruction.removeChild(childNode As IXMLDOMNode)
IXMLDOMNode = IXMLDOMProcessingInstruction.replaceChild(newChild As IXMLDOMNode,
              oldChild As IXMLDOMNode)
IXMLDOMNodeList = IXMLDOMProcessingInstruction.selectNodes(queryString As String)
IXMLDOMNode = IXMLDOMProcessingInstruction.selectSingleNode(queryString As String)
```

```
String = IXMLDOMProcessingInstruction.transformNode(stylesheet As IXMLDOMNode)
IXMLDOMProcessingInstruction.transformNodeToObject(stylesheet As IXMLDOMNode,
          outputObject As Variant)
```

IXMLDOMSchemaCollection

```
IXMLDOMSchemaCollection.add(namespaceURI As String, var As Variant)
IXMLDOMSchemaCollection.addCollection(otherCollection As IXMLDOMSchemaCollection)
IXMLDOMNode = IXMLDOMSchemaCollection.get(namespaceURI As String)
IXMLDOMSchemaCollection.remove(namespaceURI As String)
```

IXMLDOMSelection

```
IXMLDOMSelection = IXMLDOMSelection.clone
Variant = IXMLDOMSelection.getProperty(name As String)
IXMLDOMNode = IXMLDOMSelection.matches(pNode As IXMLDOMNode)
IXMLDOMNode = IXMLDOMSelection.nextNode
IXMLDOMNode = IXMLDOMSelection.peekNode
IXMLDOMSelection.removeAll
IXMLDOMNode = IXMLDOMSelection.removeNext
IXMLDOMSelection.reset
```

IXMLDOMText

```
IXMLDOMNode = IXMLDOMText.appendChild(newChild As IXMLDOMNode)
IXMLDOMText.appendData(data As String)
IXMLDOMNode = IXMLDOMText.cloneNode(deep As Boolean)
IXMLDOMText.deleteData(offset As Long, count As Long)
Boolean = IXMLDOMText.hasChildNodes
IXMLDOMNode = IXMLDOMText.insertBefore(newChild As IXMLDOMNode, refChild As
          Variant)
IXMLDOMText.insertData(offset As Long, data As String)
IXMLDOMNode = IXMLDOMText.removeChild(childNode As IXMLDOMNode)
IXMLDOMNode = IXMLDOMText.replaceChild(newChild As IXMLDOMNode, oldChild As
          IXMLDOMNode)
IXMLDOMText.replaceData(offset As Long, count As Long, data As String)
IXMLDOMNodeList = IXMLDOMText.selectNodes(queryString As String)
IXMLDOMNode = IXMLDOMText.selectSingleNode(queryString As String)
IXMLDOMText = IXMLDOMText.splitText(offset As Long)
String = IXMLDOMText.substringData(offset As Long, count As Long)
String = IXMLDOMText.transformNode(stylesheet As IXMLDOMNode)
IXMLDOMText.transformNodeToObject(stylesheet As IXMLDOMNode, outputObject As
          Variant)
```

IXMLElement

```
IXMLElement.addChild(pChildElem As IXMLElement, lIndex As Long, lReserved As Long)
Variant = IXMLElement.getAttribute(strPropertyName As String)
IXMLElement.removeAttribute(strPropertyName As String)
IXMLElement.removeChild(pChildElem As IXMLElement)
IXMLElement.setAttribute(strPropertyName As String, PropertyValue As Variant)
```

IXMLHTTPRequest

```
IXMLHTTPRequest.abort
String = IXMLHTTPRequest.getAllResponseHeaders
String = IXMLHTTPRequest.getResponseHeader(bstrHeader As String)
IXMLHTTPRequest.open(bstrMethod As String, bstrUrl As String, [varAsync As
Variant], [bstrUser As Variant], [bstrPassword As Variant])
IXMLHTTPRequest.send([varBody As Variant])
IXMLHTTPRequest.setRequestHeader(bstrHeader As String, bstrValue As String)
```

IXSLProcessor

```
IXSLProcessor.addObject(obj As Object, namespaceURI As String)
IXSLProcessor.addParameter(baseName As String, parameter As Variant, namespaceURI
            As String)
IXSLProcessor.reset
IXSLProcessor.setStartMode(mode As String, namespaceURI As String)
Boolean = IXSLProcessor.transform
```

IXSLTemplate

```
IXSLProcessor = IXSLTemplate.createProcessor
```

IXTLRuntime

```
Long = IXTLRuntime.absoluteChildNumber(pNode As IXMLDOMNode)
Long = IXTLRuntime.ancestorChildNumber(bstrNodeName As String, pNode As
            IXMLDOMNode)
IXMLDOMNode = IXTLRuntime.appendChild(newChild As IXMLDOMNode)
Long = IXTLRuntime.childNumber(pNode As IXMLDOMNode)
IXMLDOMNode = IXTLRuntime.cloneNode(deep As Boolean)
Long = IXTLRuntime.depth(pNode As IXMLDOMNode)
String = IXTLRuntime.formatDate(varDate As Variant, bstrFormat As String,
[varDestLocale As Variant])
String = IXTLRuntime.formatIndex(lIndex As Long, bstrFormat As String)
String = IXTLRuntime.formatNumber(dblNumber As Double, bstrFormat As String)
String = IXTLRuntime.formatTime(varTime As Variant, bstrFormat As String,
[varDestLocale As Variant])
Boolean = IXTLRuntime.hasChildNodes
IXMLDOMNode = IXTLRuntime.insertBefore(newChild As IXMLDOMNode, refChild As
            Variant)
IXMLDOMNode = IXTLRuntime.removeChild(childNode As IXMLDOMNode)
IXMLDOMNode = IXTLRuntime.replaceChild(newChild As IXMLDOMNode, oldChild As
            IXMLDOMNode)
IXMLDOMNodeList = IXTLRuntime.selectNodes(queryString As String)
IXMLDOMNode = IXTLRuntime.selectSingleNode(queryString As String)
String = IXTLRuntime.transformNode(stylesheet As IXMLDOMNode)
IXTLRuntime.transformNodeToObject(stylesheet As IXMLDOMNode, outputObject As
            Variant)
Long = IXTLRuntime.uniqueID(pNode As IXMLDOMNode)
```

IE5 XSL Reference

IE5 broadly supports the **Transformations** section of the working draft of XSL released by W3C on 16th December 1998, though there are some minor differences. It does *not* support the proposals for **Formatting Objects** or **Flow Objects**. This reference section details the XSL support available in IE5 final release.

XSL defines a set of XML elements that have special meaning within the xsl namespace (that is, each is prefixed with the xsl namespace identifier). These elements perform the transformation of the document into a new format. From here, under the W3C proposals, Formatting Objects would be used to define the actual output format for each element transformation. In IE5, we will generally use HTML within the transformations to define the new document format.

Bear in mind that XSL can also be used to transform *any* XML document into another (different) XML document, or into a document in almost any other format. This means, for example, that it can be used to transform an XSL stylesheet document into another XSL stylesheet document, or into some custom format that defines the styling in a way suited to some other application.

The IE5 XSL Elements

XSL in IE5 provides twenty elements that are used to create XSL stylesheets, or style sections within an XML document. The elements are:

Name	Description
xsl:apply-templates	Used inside a template to indicate that XSL should look for and apply another specific template to this node. The attributes are: order-by="[+|-] xsl-pattern" select="xsl-pattern"

Table continued on following page

Name	Description
xsl:attribute	Used to create a new Attribute node and attach it to the current element. The single attribute is:
	name="*attribute-name*"
xsl:cdata	Used to create a new CDATASection at this point in the output. Has no attributes.
xsl:choose	Used with the xsl:when and xsl:otherwise to provide a selection mechanism based on individual conditions for the same or different nodes. Similar to an If...ElseIf...Else construct. Has no attributes.
xsl:comment	Used to create a new Comment node at this point in the output. Has no attributes.
xsl:copy	Used to copy the current node in its entirety to the output. Has no attributes.
xsl:define-template-set	Used to define a set of templates that have a specific scope in the stylesheet. Has no attributes.
xsl:element	Used to create a new Element node at this point in the output. The single attribute is:
	name="*element-name*"
xsl:entity-ref	Used to create a new EntityReference node at this point in the output. The single attribute is:
	name="*entity-reference-name*"
xsl:eval	Used to evaluate a string expression and insert the result into the output. The string can be a mathematical or logical expression, an XSL function or a custom script function. The single attribute is:
	language="*language-name*"
xsl:for-each	Used to create a loop construct similar to a For...Next loop, allowing the same template to be applied to more than one node. The attributes are:
	order-by="[+|-] *xsl-pattern*" select="*xsl-pattern*"
xsl:if	Used to create conditional branches within a template, in the same way as an If...Then construct, to allow a template to provide different output based on a condition. The single attribute is:
	match="*condition-pattern*"
xsl:node-name	Used to insert the name of the current node into the output as a text string. Has no attributes.
xsl:otherwise	*see* xsl:choose (above). Has no attributes.
xsl:pi	Used to create a new ProcessingInstruction node at this point in the output. The single attribute is:
	name="*processing-instruction-name*"
xsl:script	Used to define an area of the template that contains global variable declarations and script code functions. The single attribute is:
	language="*language-name*"

Name	Description
xsl:stylesheet	Used to define the 'root' element of an XSL stylesheet, the scripting language used, whether to preserve any white space in the input document when creating the output document, and a namespace declaration for the `xsl` prefix. The attributes are:
	`xmlns:xml="http://www.w3.org/TR/WD-xsl"`
	`language="language-name"`
	`indent-result="[yes|no]"` (default is `"no"`)
	NOTE: The namespace **must** be as shown here for XSL to work in IE5.
xsl:template	Used to define a template containing the instructions for transforming the XML input into the output for nodes that match a specific pattern. The attributes are:
	`language="language-name"`
	`match="xsl-pattern"`
xsl:value-of	Used to evaluate an XSL pattern in the `select` attribute, and insert into the template as text the value of the matching node and its descendants. The single attribute is:
	`select="xsl-pattern"`
xsl:when	*see* `xsl:choose` (above). The single attribute is:
	`match="xsl-pattern"`

XSL Stylesheet Structure

The following shows the more common ways in which the XSL elements are used to construct an XSL stylesheet, showing the kinds of structures that can be created. This isn't by any means the only combination, as most of the elements can be nested within most of the other elements. However, in general, each stylesheet will consist of one template that matches the root element in the document, followed by others that apply specific style and formatting to specific elements within the document.

```
<xsl:stylesheet xmlns:xsl="http://www.w3.org/TR/WD-xsl">

    <xsl:template match="...">
        <xsl:value-of select="..." />
        <xsl:eval> ...      </xsl:eval>
        <xsl:if match="..."> ... </xsl:if>
        <xsl:copy />

        <xsl:choose>
            <xsl:when match="..."> ... </xsl:when>
            <xsl:otherwise> ... </xsl:otherwise>
        </xsl:choose>

        <xsl:for-each select="...">
            <xsl:value-of select="..." />
            <xsl:eval> ... </xsl:eval>
            <xsl:if match="..."> ... </xsl:if>
            <xsl:copy />
            <xsl:apply-templates />
        </xsl:for-each>
```

```
      <xsl:apply-templates select="..." />
   </xsl:template>

   <xsl:define-template-set>
      <xsl:template match="..."> ... </xsl:template>
      <xsl:template match="..."> ... </xsl:template>
   </xsl:define-template-set>

   <xsl:script> ... </xsl:script>

</xsl:stylesheet>
```

Creating New Nodes in XSL

The XSL elements that create new nodes in the output document are xsl:attribute, xsl:cdata, xsl:comment, xsl:element, xsl:entity-ref, and xsl:pi.

To create the XML node <![CDATA[This is a CDATA section]]> we could use:

```
<xsl:cdata>This is a CDATA section</xsl:cdata>
```

To create the XML node <!ENTITY copy "©"> we could use:

```
<xsl:entity-ref name="copy">©</entity-ref>
```

To create the XML node <!--This is the comment text--> we could use:

```
<xsl:comment>This is the comment text</xsl:comment>
```

To create the XML node <?WroxFormat="StartParagraph"?> we could use:

```
<xsl:pi name="WroxFormat">StartParagraph</xsl:pi>
```

To create the XML element <title>Instant JavaScript</title> we could use:

```
<xsl:element name="title">Instant JavaScript</xsl:element>
```

And to add a print-date attribute to it we could use:

```
<xsl:attribute name="print_date">1998-02-07</xsl:attribute>
```

This gives us the XML result:

```
<title print_date="1998-02-07">Instant JavaScript</title>
```

XSL Stylesheet Runtime Methods

The xsl:eval element can be used to execute a number of built-in methods available in XSL in IE5. The IXTLRuntime object provides these methods:

Name	Description
absoluteChildNumber (this_node)	Returns the index of a specified node within its parent's childNodes list. Values start from "1".
ancestorChildNumber (node_name, this_node)	Finds the first ancestor node of a specified node that has the specified name, and returns the index of that node within its parent's childNodes list. Values start from "1". Returns 0 if there is no ancestor.

Name	Description
childNumber (this_node)	Returns the index of the specified node within its parent's childNodes list of children with the same name (that is, its index within the list of the node's identically named siblings) or 0 if not found. Values start from "1".
depth(start_node)	Returns the depth or level within the document tree at which the specified node appears. The XMLDocument or root node is at level 0.
elementIndexList (this_node, node_name)	Returns an array of node index numbers for the specified node and all its ancestors up to and including the document root node, indicating each node's position within their parent's childNodes list. The ordering of the array starts from the root document node. When the node_name parameter is not supplied, the method returns an array of integers that indicates the index of the specified node with respect to all of its siblings, the index of that node's parent with respect to all of its siblings, and so on until the document root is reached. When the node_name parameter is specified, the returned array contains entries only for nodes of the specified name, and the indices are evaluated relative to siblings with the specified name. Zero is supplied for levels in the tree that do not have children with the supplied name. Although this method is included in the Microsoft documentation, it was not supported by IE5 at the time of writing.
formatDate(date, format, locale)	Formats the value in the date parameter using the specified formatting options. The following format codes are supported: m - Month (1-12) mm - Month (01-12) mmm - Month (Jan-Dec) mmmm - Month (January-December) mmmmm - Month as the first letter of the month d - Day (1-31) dd - Day (01-31) ddd - Day (Sun-Sat) dddd - Day (Sunday-Saturday) yy -Year (00-99) yyyy - Year (1900-9999) The locale to use in determining the correct sequence of values in the date. If omitted the sequence month-day-year is used.

Table continued on following page

Name	Description
`formatIndex (number, format)`	Formats the integer number using the specified numerical system.
	`1` - Standard numbering system
	`01` - Standard numbering with leading zeros
	`A` - Uppercase letter sequence "A" to "Z" then "AA" to"ZZ".
	`a` - Lowercase letter sequence "a" to "z" then "aa" to "zz".
	`I` - Uppercase Roman numerals: "I", "II", "III", "IV", etc.
	`i` - Lowercase Roman numerals: "i", "ii", "iii", "iv", etc.
`formatNumber (number, format)`	Formats the value number using the specified format. Zero or more of the following values can be present in the format string:
	`#` (pound) – Display only significant digits and omit insignificant zeros.
	`0` (zero) – Display insignificant zeros in these positions.
	`?` (question) – Adds spaces for insignificant zeros on either side of the decimal point, so that decimal points align with a fixed-point font. You can also use this symbol for fractions that have varying numbers of digits.
	`.` (period) – Indicates the position of the decimal point.
	`,` (comma) – Display a thousands separator or scale a number by a multiple of one thousand.
	`%` (percent) – Display number as a percentage.
	`E` or `e` – Display number in scientific (exponential) format. If format contains a zero or # to the right of an exponent code, display the number in scientific format and inserts an "E" or "e". The number of 0 or # characters to the right determines the number of digits in the exponent.
	`E-` or `e-` Place a minus sign by negative exponents.
	`E+` or `e+` Place a minus sign by negative exponents and a plus sign by positive exponents.
`formatTime(time, format, locale)`	Formats the value in the time parameter using the specified formatting options. The following format codes are supported:
	`h` - Hours (0-23)
	`hh` - Hours (00-23)
	`m` - Minutes (0-59)
	`mm` - Minutes (00-59)
	`s` - Seconds (0-59)
	`ss` - Seconds (00-59)
	`AM/PM` - Add "AM" or "PM" and display in 12 hour format
	`am/pm` - Add "am" or "pm" and display in 12 hour format

Name	Description
	A/P - Add "A" or "P" and display in 12 hour format
	a/p - Add "a" or "p" and display in 12 hour format
	[h]:mm – Display elapsed time in hours, as in "25.02"
	[mm]:ss - Display elapsed time in minutes, as in "63:46"
	[ss] - Display elapsed time in seconds
	ss.00 - Display fractions of a second
	The locale is used to determine the correct separator characters.
uniqueID(this_node)	Returns the unique identifier for the specified node.

As an example, this code transforms a number which is the content of the current element into Roman numerals using the built-in formatIndex() method:

```
<xsl:eval>
    intNumber=parseInt(this.text);
    formatIndex(intNumber, "i");
</xsl:eval>
```

Note that the content of the element must first be transformed from string format (which is the default for all XML content, unless we specify otherwise in the XML document's schema using data types).

The IE5 XSL Pattern-Matching Syntax

Using the elements described earlier, XSL can create a stylesheet document that contains one or more XSL template elements. These templates are applied to individual elements or sets of elements in the source document to create a particular section of the output document. To define which template applies to which of the source elements or nodes, a **pattern** is used. This pattern has one of two generic forms, and can define the node or nodes that match through:

❑ The **position** and **hierarchy** of the node or nodes within the source document

❑ The application of a **filter** that selectively targets one or more nodes

Node Position and Hierarchy

To select or match nodes (i.e. elements) through their position and hierarchy within the source document, we use a series of **path operators** to build up a pattern string. The path operators are:

Operator	Description
/	A forward slash is the **child** path operator. It selects elements that are direct children of the specified node, in much the same way as we use it to specify paths in a URL. For example, we use book/category to select all <category> elements that are children of <book> elements. To indicate the root node, we place this operator at the start of the pattern, for example: /booklist/book.

Table continued on following page

Operator	Description
//	Two forward slashes indicate the **recursive descent** path operator. It selects all matching nodes at any depth below the current node (all descendants), for example: `booklist//title` to select all `<title>` elements that are descendants at any level of the `<booklist>` element. When it appears at the start of the pattern, it indicates recursive descent from the root node, that is, all elements in the document.
.	The period or 'full stop' is the **current context** path operator. It is used to indicate specifically the current node or 'context', for example: `.//title` to select all `<title>` elements at any level below the current element. The combination `./` always indicates the current context and is usually superfluous – for example `./book/category` is the same as `book/category`.
@	The 'at' operator is the **attribute** path operator. It indicates that this part of the pattern refers to attributes of the current element. For example, `book/@print_date` selects the `print_date` attributes of all `<book>` elements.
*	The asterisk is a **wildcard** path operator, and is used when we want to select all elements or attributes regardless of their name, for example `book/*` to select all child elements of all `book` elements, or `book/@*` to select all the attributes of all `<book>` elements.

Node Index Position

The path operators always return all elements or nodes that match the pattern. The node **index** can be used to specify a particular node within the set (or collection) of matching nodes, and the special XSL `end()` function can be used to specify the last node:

```
/booklist/book[0]        'first <book> element in root <booklist> element
/booklist/book[2]        'third <book> element in root <booklist> element
/booklist/book[end()]    'last <book> element in root <booklist> element
```

Note that the following three examples select different nodes within the same document:

```
book/category[2]         'second <category> element from all <book> elements
book[2]/category[2]      'second <category> element in second <book> element
(book/category)[2]       'second <category> element within the set of all ...
                         '... <category> elements from all <book> elements
```

In the last example, think of the pattern within the parentheses being applied first to create the set of all category elements from all book elements, followed by the index operator selecting just the second one.

XSL Filters and Filter Patterns

An **XSL filter** has the generic form `[operator pattern]` where `operator` is an optional **filter operator** that defines how the pattern is applied, and `pattern` is the required XSL **filter pattern** that selects one or more elements based on a range of criteria. One or more whitespace characters separate the filter operator and the filter pattern. The optional `operator` part can also consist of more than one filter operator expression if required. If omitted, any or all nodes that match the criteria in the filter pattern will be selected.

Filter Patterns

XSL filter patterns are very powerful, and offer an almost infinite number of pattern combinations. The following is a broad guide to the different kinds of ways that they can be used. The examples cover:

❑   Selecting by **child node name**

❑   Selecting by **node value**

❑   Selecting by **attribute existence**

❑   Selecting by **attribute value**

❑   Selecting by a **combination** of these

Selecting by Child Node Name

The position and hierarchy syntax we looked at earlier works by selecting elements based on their name as well as their position within the document. For example, `book/category` selects all `<category>` elements that are child elements of `<book>` elements. This is equivalent to the filter:

```
book[category]/category
```

because the filter `book/category` is actually a shorthand way of saying we want to select all `<book>` elements that have a `<category>` element (equivalent to `book[category]`), and then select the `<category>` element. A more useful way of using the longhand technique is when you want to specify a *different* child element to return. For example,

```
book[title]/category
```

means select only the `<category>` elements of books that have a `<title>` child element. To find all books that have both a `<category>` and a `<title>` child element, we use two filters:

```
book[title][category]
```

Selecting by Node Value

Extending the filter pattern that selects a node by its name, we can also select by value:

```
book[category = 'Scripting']
```

will select all `<book>` elements that have a `<category>` element with the value 'Scripting'. If we want to get the titles of books in this category, we would use:

```
book[category = 'Scripting']/title
```

To specify a value for the current element, we can include the period path operator. For example:

```
book/title[. = 'Instant JavaScript']
```

selects the title of the book 'Instant JavaScript'.

Selecting by Attribute Existence

The '@' attribute operator can also be used in a filter pattern to specify that the element must have a matching attribute:

```
book[@print_date]
```

selects only `book` elements that have a `print_date` attribute.

Selecting by Attribute Value

We can also specify the value that the attribute must have in order to match the pattern:

```
book[@print_date = '1998-05-02']
```

Selecting by a Combination of Methods

And, of course, we can combine all these methods to select exactly the element or node we require. For example:

```
book[@print_date = '1998-05-02']/title[. = 'Instant JavaScript']
```

to find the book titled 'Instant JavaScript' that was printed on 2nd May 1998, or:

```
/booklist//cover_design[issue = "final"]/*[@url = 'images']
```

to select all elements that:

❑ Have *any* name, but also have an attribute named `url` that has the value 'images' (from the `*[@url = 'images']` part);

❑ Are child elements of `cover_design` elements that themselves also have a child element named `issue` with the value 'final' (from the of `cover_design[issue = "final"]` part);

❑ Are descendants of the root `booklist` element (from the `/booklist//` part).

Note that the values of elements and attributes can be enclosed in single or double quotes.

Comparison Operators

The above examples all use the normal equality operator '=' to test if two values are equal. This works for numbers as well as strings. All XML values are strings by default, but IE5 casts them to appropriate data types before carrying out the comparison if possible. The data type chosen is based either on the content of the node value string, or on a **schema** (if one is present) that specifies the data type. This means that a comparison such as [price = 29.95] (without quotes around the numeric value) is perfectly valid.

> *If a schema is present and the content of the node cannot be cast into the type specified in the schema, for example if it contains characters that are illegal for that data type, such as letters in a numeric value, it is omitted from the set of matching nodes.*

As well as the equality operator, there is a full set of other comparison operators:

Shortcut	Operator	Description
=	eq	Case-sensitive equality, for example: [price = 29.95]
!=	ne	Case-sensitive inequality, for example: [category != 'Script']
< *	lt	Case-sensitive less than, for example: [radius lt 14.73]

Shortcut	Operator	Description
<= *	le	Case-sensitive less than or equal, for example: `[age $le$ 18]`
>	gt	Case-sensitive greater than, for example: `[name > 'H']`
>=	ge	Case-sensitive greater than or equal, for example: `[speed >= 55]`
	ieq	Case-insensitive equality
	ine	Case-insensitive inequality
	ilt	Case-insensitive less than
	ile	Case-insensitive less than or equal
	igt	Case-insensitive greater than
	ige	Case-insensitive greater than or equal

** Note that the '<' and '<=' operators cannot be used 'un-escaped' in XSL attributes, because these have to follow XML standards of well formedness. Instead, it is better to use the equivalent lt and le. Also note that all filter operator **names** (such as eq) are case sensitive, that is, they must be all lower-case.*

The shortcut operators perform exactly the same operation as the longer version, so the following are equivalent:

```
[category = 'Scripting']
[category $eq$ 'Scripting']
```

as are:

```
[category != 'Scripting']
[category $ne$ 'Scripting']
```

The case-insensitive operators have no shortcut operator syntax. They are useful, however, when you need to match irrespective of case. There is no UCase or LCase function included in XSL (unless you provide your own script function), so it saves having to do multiple tests, e.g.:

```
[category = 'html' $or$ category = 'HTML']
```

Instead, we just use:

```
[category $ieq$ 'html']
```

Logical Filter Operators

As well as single comparison tests, we can use logical operators to combine patterns to build up more complex ones (as seen in the final example in the previous section). The logical operators are:

Shortcut	Operator	Description
&&	and	Logical AND
||	or	Logical OR
	not	Negation, logical NOT

So, using these we can do things like selecting books that have a `<category>` element that is either 'Scripting' or 'HTML':

```
book/[category = 'Scripting' $or$ category = 'HTML']
```

or which have the title 'Instant JavaScript' (case-insensitive match), but are not in the category 'Scripting':

```
book/[category $ne$ 'Scripting' $and$ title $ieq$ 'Instant JavaScript']
```

The `$not$` operator simply changes the 'truth' of the match, so the following are equivalent, and match `<book>` elements which have a child `<category>` element with the value 'Scripting' but no child `<category>` element with the value 'HTML' (thus excluding `<book>` elements which have child `<category>` elements with both values):

```
book/[category = 'Scripting' $and$ category $ne$ 'HTML']
book/[category = 'Scripting' $and$ $not$ category = 'HTML']
```

Filter Set Operators

Remember that all the above examples of filter patterns that use comparison operators rely on the fact that the default filter action, if no operator is specified in the filter, is to return any or all nodes that match the pattern. However, there are ways that we can specify more exactly which of the matching elements we want, in a similar way to using an index to specify the first element. We use the **set** operators, `$any$` and `$all$`:

Operator	Description
`$all$`	Returns `True` only if the specified pattern matches all of the items in the collection.
`$any$`	Returns `True` if the specified pattern matches any of the items in the collection.

The easiest way to appreciate the difference is to think about the way that elements are selected. For an element named `<book>`, we can specify that we want it to be included in the results if it has a `<category>` child element with the value 'HTML' by using the pattern:

```
book[category = 'HTML']
```

However, this will only match the `<book>` element if the *first* `<category>` element has the value 'HTML'. If it doesn't have this value, even if other (later) child elements do, the `<book>` element will not be selected. However, if we use the pattern:

```
book[$any$ category = 'HTML']
```

we will get a match for this `<book>` element, because we specified that we want the `<book>` elements where *any* of the child elements has the value 'HTML'. If we use the alternative set operator, `$all$`, we are specifying that we only want to select `<book>` elements where *all* of their category child elements have the value 'HTML', not just the first one or any one or more of them. For the book to be included in the results, they must all have the value 'HTML':

```
book[$all$ category = 'HTML']
```

Of course, if the book only has one `<category>` child element, with the value 'HTML', all three of these filters will return this book element. The differences only appear when the pattern specifies elements with more than one matching child (or other) element.

XSL Built-In Methods

We saw one of the built-in methods of XSL earlier on when looking at selecting elements by their index. The last node in a collection of matching nodes is returned by the `end()` method:

```
booklist/category[end()]
```

The Information Methods

Other **information** methods are available to help isolate a specific node in a collection:

Name	Description
end()	Selects and returns the last node in a collection.
index()	Selects and returns the index (number) of the current node within its collection.
nodeName()	Selects and returns the tag name of the current node, including any namespace prefix.
nodeType()	Selects and returns as a number the type of the node (as used in the DOM).
date()	Returns a value in date format.
text()	Selects and returns the text content of the current node.
value()	Returns a type cast version of the value of the current node.

The `value()` method is the default, so the following are equivalent:

```
book[category!value() = "Script"]
book[category = "Script"]
```

> *The exclamation mark operator (sometimes called the **'bang'** operator) denotes that* `value()` *is a method of the* `<category>` *element. The normal use of a period here is not legal. It would be confused with the **current path** operator.*

The `index()` method is also optional when we want a specific element:

```
book[index() = 5]
book[5]
```

However, it is useful for selecting several elements, for example the fourth and fifth `<book>` elements only:

```
book[index() > 3 $and$ index() < 6]
```

The Collection Methods

It's also possible to select elements or other nodes using the **collection** methods supported by XSL in IE5:

Name	Description
ancestor()	Selects the ancestor node nearest to the current node that matches the pattern, starting at the parent node and working back up the document hierarchy. Returns a single element or `null` if none matches.

Name	Description
attribute()	Selects all attribute nodes of the current node, returning them as a collection. The optional parameter can specify the attribute name to match.
comment()	Selects and returns as a collection all child comment nodes.
element()	Selects all child element nodes of the current node, returning them as a collection. The optional parameter can specify the element name to match.
node()	Selects and returns as a collection all child nodes that are not attributes.
pi()	Selects and returns as a collection all child processing instruction nodes.
textnode()	Selects and returns as a collection all child text nodes.

As an example, we can select all of the comment elements within our `<book>` elements using:

```
book/comment()
```

The `attribute()` and `element()` methods accept a text parameter that can be used to limit the matching nodes:

```
book/attribute('print_date')
```

Of course, this is equivalent to the `'@'` operator we saw earlier, so these provide the same result:

```
book/attribute('print_date')
book/@print_date
```

And the `element()` method is equivalent to the earlier syntax as well – these two provide the same result:

```
book/element('category')
book/category
```

The `ancestor()` method also accepts a text parameter containing the pattern to be matched. For example:

```
ancestor(book/category)
```

will match the nearest `<category>` ancestor node which is a child of a `<book>` element. Note that this method cannot occur to the right of a `'/'` or `'//'` in the pattern, and that, unlike the `attribute()` and `element()` methods, the name of the node to be matched should not be placed in quotes.

Important Note

Remember that, of all of the XML-related technologies, XSL is probably the most volatile at the moment, in terms of changes that will come about in the language and syntax. There are subtle differences between the W3C working draft and Microsoft's implementation of XSL in IE5. You may wish to confine your development effort to experimental and induction projects until the future standards are more firmly established.

D

Style Sheet Properties

Over 70 Cascading Style Sheets properties are used in the major browsers. Most of them are in the CSS1 recommendations, but a few have only recently been introduced in the CSS2 public drafts. We've broken up the properties into several major 'groups' and listed which are new in CSS2. We've listed all the properties below (by group), with some of the crucial information for each. We start with a summary of the units of measurement.

Units of Measurement

There are two basic categories of unit: relative and absolute. As a general rule, relative measures are preferred, as using absolute measures requires familiarity with the actual mechanism of display (e.g. what kind of printer, what sort of monitor, etc.).

Relative Units

Values: em, en, ex, px

em, en and ex are typographic terms, and refer to the sizes of other characters on display (the m, n, and x characters).

px refers to a measurement in screen pixels, which is generally only meaningful for display on computer monitors and depends on the user's display resolution setting.

In IE4/5, em and ex are the same as pt, and en is the same as px.

Absolute Units

Values: in, cm, mm, pt, pc

in gives the measurement in inches, cm gives it in centimetres, mm in millimetres, pt is in typeface points (72 to an inch), and pc is in picas (1 pica equals 12 points). These units are generally only useful when you know what the output medium is going to be, since browsers are allowed to approximate if they must.

Percentage

Values: Numeric

This is given as a number (with or without a decimal point), and is relative to a length unit (which is usually the font size of the current element).

Listing of Properties

There follows a listing of all the properties for use in Dynamic HTML, together with their JavaScript Style Sheet equivalent, the equivalent scripting property in IE4/5, possible values, defaults, and other useful information. The properties are divided up into categories – **font** properties, **color** and **background** properties, **text** properties, **size** and **position** properties, **printing** properties, **filter** properties and **other** properties.

Font Properties

font

IE4/5 Scripting Property:	font
Values:	<font-size>, [/<line-height>], <font-family>
Default:	Not defined
Applies to:	All elements
Inherited:	Yes
Percentage?:	Only on <font-size> and <line-height>

This allows you to set several font properties all at once, with the initial values being determined by the properties being used (e.g. the default for font-size is different to the default for font-family). This property should be used with multiple values separated by spaces, or a comma if specifying multiple font-families.

font-family

IE4/5 Scripting Property:	fontFamily
Values:	Name of a font family (e.g. New York) or a generic family (e.g. Serif)
Default:	Set by browser
Applies to:	All elements
Inherited:	Yes
Percentage?:	No

You can specify multiple values in order of preference (in case the browser doesn't have the font you want). To do so, simply specify them and separate multiple values with commas. You should end with a generic font-family (allowable values would then be serif, sans-serif, cursive, fantasy, or monospace). If the font name has spaces in it, you should enclose the name in quotation marks.

font-size

IE4/5 Scripting Property:	fontSize
Values:	<absolute>, <relative>, <length>, <percentage>
Default:	medium
Applies to:	All elements
Inherited:	Yes
Percentage?:	Yes, relative to parent font size

The values for this property can be expressed in several ways:

❏ Absolute size: legal values are xx-small, x-small, small, medium, large, x-large, xx-large

❏ Relative size: values are larger, smaller

❏ Length: values are in any unit of measurement, as described at the beginning of this Appendix.

❏ Percentage: values are a percentage of the parent font size

font-style

IE4/5 Scripting Property:	fontStyle
Values:	normal, italic, or oblique
Default:	normal
Applies to:	All elements
Inherited:	Yes
Percentage?:	No

This is used to apply styling to your font – if a pre-rendered font is available (e.g. New York Oblique) then that will be used if possible. If not, the styling will be applied electronically.

font-variant

IE4/5 Scripting Property:	fontVariant
Values:	normal, small-caps
Default:	normal
Applies to:	All elements
Inherited:	Yes
Percentage?:	No

Normal is the standard appearance, and is therefore set as the default. Small-caps uses capital letters that are the same size as normal lowercase letters.

font-weight

IE4/5 Scripting Property:	fontWeight
Values:	normal, bold, bolder, lighter—or numeric values from 100 to 900
Default:	normal
Applies to:	All elements
Inherited:	Yes
Percentage?:	No

Specifies the 'boldness' of text, which is usually expressed by stroke thickness. If numeric values are used, they must proceed in 100-unit increments (e.g. 250 isn't legal). 400 is the same as normal, and 700 is the same as bold.

Color and Background Properties

color

IE4/5 Scripting Property:	color
Values:	Color name or RGB value
Default:	Depends on browser

Applies to:	All elements
Inherited:	Yes
Percentage?:	No

Sets the text color of any element. The color can be specified by name (e.g. green) or by RGB-value. The RGB value can be expressed in several ways.

background

IE4/5 Scripting Property:	background
Values:	transparent, <color>, <URL>, <repeat>, <scroll>, <position>
Default:	transparent
Applies to:	All elements
Inherited:	No
Percentage?:	Yes, will refer to the dimension of the element itself

Specifies the background of the document. Transparent is the same as no defined background. You can use a solid color, or you can specify the URL for an image to be used. The URL can be absolute or relative, but must be enclosed in parentheses and immediately preceded by url:

```
BODY { background: url(http://foo.bar.com/image/small.gif) }
```

It is possible to use a color and an image, in which case the image will be overlaid on top of the color. The color can be a single color, or two colors that will be blended together. Images can have several properties set:

❑   <repeat> can be repeat, repeat-x, repeat-y and no-repeat. If no repeat value is given, then repeat is assumed.

❑   <scroll> determines whether the background image will remain fixed, or scroll when the page does. Possible values are fixed or scroll.

❑   <position> specifies the location of the image on the page. Values are by percentage (horizontal, vertical), by absolute distance (in a unit of measurement, horizontal then vertical), or by keyword (values are top, middle, bottom, left, center, right).

❑   It is also possible to specify different parts of the background properties separately using the next five properties:

background-attachment

IE4/5 Scripting Property:	backgroundAttachment
Values:	fixed, scroll
Default:	scroll
Applies to:	All elements
Inherited:	No
Percentage?:	No

Determines whether the background will remain fixed, or scroll when the page does.

background-color

IE4/5 Scripting Property:	backgroundColor
Values:	transparent, <color>
Default:	transparent

Applies to:	All elements
Inherited:	No
Percentage?:	No

Sets a color for the background. This can be a single color, or two colors blended together. The colors can be specified by name (e.g. green) or by RGB-value (which can be stated in hex "#FFFFFF", by percentage "80%, 20%, 0%", or by value "255,0,0"). The syntax for using two colors is:

```
BODY { background-color: red / blue }
```

background-image

IE4/5 Scripting Property:	backgroundImage
Values:	<URL>, none
Default:	none
Applies to:	All elements
Inherited:	No
Percentage?:	No

You can specify the URL for an image to be used as the background. The URL can be absolute or relative, but must be enclosed in parentheses and immediately preceded by url.

background-position

Scripting Properties:	backgroundPosition, backgroundPositionX, backgroundPositionY
Values:	<position> <length> top, center, bottom, left, right.
Default:	top, left
Applies to:	All elements
Inherited:	No
Percentage?:	No

Specifies the initial location of the background image on the page using two values, which are defined as a percentage (horizontal, vertical), an absolute distance (in a unit of measurement, horizontal then vertical), or using two of the available keywords.

background-repeat

IE4/5 Scripting Property:	backgroundRepeat
Values:	repeat, repeat-x, repeat-y, no-repeat.
Default:	repeat
Applies to:	All elements
Inherited:	No
Percentage?:	No

Determines whether the image is repeated to fill the page or element. If repeat-x or repeat-y are used, the image is repeated in only one direction. The default is to repeat the image in both directions.

Text Properties

letter-spacing

IE4/5 Scripting Property:	letterSpacing

Values:	normal, <length>
Default:	normal
Applies to:	All elements
Inherited:	Yes
Percentage?:	No

Sets the distance between letters. The length unit indicates an addition to the default space between characters. Values, if given, should be in units of measurement.

line-height

IE4/5 Scripting Property:	lineHeight
Values:	<number>, <length>, <percentage>, normal
Default:	Depends on browser
Applies to:	All elements
Inherited:	Yes
Percentage?:	Yes, relative to the font-size of the current element

Sets the height of the current line. Numerical values are expressed as the font size of the current element multiplied by the value given (for example, 1.2 would be valid). If given by length, a unit of measurement must be used. Percentages are based on the font-size of the current font size, and should normally be more than 100%.

list-style

IE4/5 Scripting Property:	listStyle
Values:	<keyword>, <position>, <url>
Default:	Depends on browser
Applies to:	All elements
Inherited:	Yes
Percentage?:	No

Defines how list items are displayed. Can be used to set all the properties, or the individual styles can be set independently using the following styles.

list-style-image

IE4/5 Scripting Property:	listStyleImage
Values:	none, <url>
Default:	none
Applies to:	All elements
Inherited:	Yes
Percentage?:	No

Defines the URL of an image to be used as the 'bullet' or list marker for each item in a list.

list-style-position

IE4/5 Scripting Property:	listStylePosition
Values:	inside, outside
Default:	outside
Applies to:	All elements
Inherited:	Yes
Percentage?:	No

Indicates if the list marker should be placed indented or extended in relation to the list body.

list-style-type

IE4/5 Scripting Property:	`listStyleType`
Values:	`none`, `circle`, `disk`, `square`, `decimal`, `lower-alpha`, `upper-alpha`, `lower-roman`, `upper-roman`
Default:	`disk`
Applies to:	All elements
Inherited:	Yes
Percentage?:	No

Defines the type of 'bullet' or list marker used to precede each item in the list.

text-align

IE4/5 Scripting Property:	`textAlign`
Values:	`left`, `right`, `center`, `justify`
Default:	Depends on browser
Applies to:	All elements
Inherited:	Yes
Percentage?:	No

Describes how text is aligned within the element. Essentially replicates the <DIV ALIGN=> tag.

text-decoration

Scripting Properties:	`textDecoration`, `textDecorationLineThrough`, `textDecorationUnderline`, `textDecorationOverline`
Values:	`none`, `underline`, `overline`, `line-through`
Default:	`none`
Applies to:	All elements
Inherited:	No
Percentage?:	No

Specifies any special appearance of the text. Open to extension by vendors, with unidentified extensions rendered as an underline. This property is not inherited, but will usually span across any 'child' elements.

text-indent

IE4/5 Scripting Property:	`textIndent`
Values:	<length>, <percentage>
Default:	Zero
Applies to:	All elements
Inherited:	Yes
Percentage?:	Yes, refers to width of parent element

Sets the indentation values, in units of measurement, or as a percentage of the parent element's width.

text-transform

IE4/5 Scripting Property:	`textTransform`
Values:	`capitalize`, `uppercase`, `lowercase`, `none`
Default:	`none`

Applies to:	All elements
Inherited:	Yes
Percentage?:	No

❏ `capitalize` will set the first character of each word in the element as uppercase.

❏ `uppercase` will set every character in the element in uppercase.

❏ `lowercase` will place every character in lowercase.

❏ `none` will neutralize any inherited settings.

vertical-align

IE4/5 Scripting Property:	`verticalAlign`
Values:	`baseline, sub, super, top, text-top, middle, bottom, text-bottom, <percentage>`
Default:	`baseline`
Applies to:	Inline elements
Inherited:	No
Percentage?:	Yes, will refer to the line-height itself

Controls the vertical positioning of any affected element.

❏ `baseline` sets the alignment with the base of the parent.

❏ `middle` aligns the vertical midpoint of the element with the baseline of the parent plus half of the vertical height of the parent.

❏ `sub` makes the element a subscript.

❏ `super` makes the element a superscript.

❏ `text-top` aligns the element with the top of text in the parent element's font.

❏ `text-bottom` aligns with the bottom of text in the parent element's font.

❏ `top` aligns the top of the element with the top of the tallest element on the current line.

❏ `bottom` aligns with the bottom of the lowest element on the current line.

Size and Border Properties

These values are used to set the characteristics of the layout 'box' that exists around elements. They can apply to characters, images, and so on.

border-top-color, border-right-color, border-bottom-color, border-left-color, border-color

Scripting Properties:	`borderTopColor, borderRightColor, borderBottomColor, borderLeftColor, borderColor`
Values:	`<color>`
Default:	`<none>`
Applies to:	Block and replaced elements
Inherited:	No
Percentage?:	No

Sets the color of the four borders. By supplying the URL of an image instead, the image itself is repeated to create the border.

border-top-style, border-right-style, border-bottom-style, border-left-style, border-style

Scripting Properties:	`borderTopStyle, borderRightStyle, borderBottomStyle,` `borderLeftStyle, borderStyle`
Values:	`none, solid, double, groove, ridge, inset, outset`
Default:	`none`
Applies to:	Block and replaced elements
Inherited:	No
Percentage?:	No

Sets the style of the four borders.

border-top, border-right, border-bottom, border-left, border

Scripting Properties:	`borderTop, borderRight, borderBottom, borderLeft, border`
Values:	`<border-width>, <border-style>, <color>`
Default:	`medium, none, <none>`
Applies to:	Block and replaced elements
Inherited:	No
Percentage?:	No

Sets the properties of the border element (box drawn around the affected element). Works roughly the same as the margin settings, except that it can be made visible.

- ❑ `<border-width>` can be thin, `medium`, `thick`, or as a unit of measurement.

- ❑ `<border-style>` can be none, `solid`.

The color argument is used to fill the background of the element while it loads, and behind any transparent parts of the element. By supplying the URL of an image instead, the image itself is repeated to create the border. It is also possible to specify values for attributes of the border property separately using the `border-width`, `border-style` and `border-color` properties.

border-top-width, border-right-width, border-bottom-width, border-left-width, border-width

Scripting Properties:	`borderTopWidth, borderRightWidth, borderBottomWidth,` `borderLeftWidth, borderWidth`
Values:	`thin, medium, thick <length>`
Default:	`medium`
Applies to:	Block and replaced elements
Inherited:	No
Percentage?:	No

Sets the width of the border for the element. Each side can be set individually, or the `border-width` property used to set all of the sides. You can also supply up to four arguments for the border-width property to set individual sides, in the same way as with the `margin` property.

clear

IE4/5 Scripting Property:	`clear`
Values:	`none, both, left, right`
Default:	`none`
Applies to:	All elements
Inherited:	No
Percentage?:	No

Forces the following elements to be displayed below an element which is aligned. Normally, they would wrap around it.

clip

IE4/5 Scripting Property:	`clip`
Values:	`rect(<top><right><bottom><left>)`, `auto`
Default:	`auto`
Applies to:	All elements
Inherited:	No
Percentage?:	No

Controls which part of an element is visible. Anything that occurs outside the clip area is not visible.

display

IE4/5 Scripting Property:	`display`
Values:	`""`, `none`
Default:	`""`
Applies to:	All elements
Inherited:	No
Percentage?:	No

This property indicates whether an element is rendered. If set to `none` the element is not rendered, if set to `""` it is rendered.

float

IE4/5 Scripting Property:	`styleFloat`
Values:	`none, left, right`
Default:	`none`
Applies to:	DIV, SPAN and replaced elements
Inherited:	No
Percentage?:	No

Causes following elements to be wrapped to the left or right of the element, rather than being placed below it.

height

Scripting Properties:	`height, pixelHeight, posHeight`
Values:	`auto, <length>`
Default:	`auto`
Applies to:	DIV, SPAN and replaced elements
Inherited:	No
Percentage?:	No

Sets the vertical size of an element, and will scale the element if necessary. The value is returned as a string including the measurement type (px, %, etc.). To retrieve the value as a number, query the `posHeight` property.

left – New in CSS2

Scripting Properties:	`left, pixelLeft, posLeft`
Values:	`auto, <length>, <percentage>`
Default:	`auto`
Applies to:	All elements

Inherited:	No
Percentage?:	Yes, refers to parent's width

Sets or returns the left position of an element when displayed in 2D canvas mode, allowing accurate placement and animation of individual elements. The value is returned as a string including the measurement type (px, %, etc.). To retrieve the value as a number, query the posLeft property.

margin-top, margin-right, margin-bottom, margin-left, margin

Scripting Properties:	marginTop, marginRight, marginBottom, marginLeft, margin
Values:	auto, <length>, <percentage>
Default:	Zero
Applies to:	Block and replaced elements
Inherited:	No
Percentage?:	Yes, refers to parent element's width

Sets the size of margins around any given element. You can use margin as shorthand for setting all of the other values (as it applies to all four sides). If you use multiple values in margin but use less than four, opposing sides will try to be equal. These values all set the effective minimum distance between the current element and others.

overflow – New in CSS2

IE4/5 Scripting Property:	overflow
Values:	none, clip, scroll
Default:	none
Applies to:	All elements
Inherited:	No
Percentage?:	No

This controls how a container element will display its content if this is not the same size as the container.

❑ none means that the container will use the default method. For example, as in an image element, the content may be resized to fit the container.

❑ clip means that the contents will not be resized, and only a part will be visible.

❑ scroll will cause the container to display scroll bars so that the entire contents can be viewed by scrolling.

padding-top, padding-right, padding-bottom, padding-left, padding

Scripting Properties:	paddingTop, paddingRight, paddingBottom, paddingLeft, padding
Values:	auto, <length>, <percentage>
Default:	Zero
Applies to:	Block and replaced elements
Inherited:	No
Percentage?:	Yes, refers to parent element's width

Sets the distance between the content and border of an element. You can use padding as shorthand for setting all of the other values (as it applies to all four sides). If you use multiple values in padding but use less than four, opposing sides will try to be equal. These values all set the effective minimum distance between the current element and others.

position – New in CSS2

IE4/5 Scripting Property:	`position`
Values:	`absolute, relative, static`
Default:	`relative`
Applies to:	All elements
Inherited:	No
Percentage?:	No

Specifies if the element can be positioned directly on the 2-D canvas.

❑ `absolute` means it can be fixed on the background of the page at a specified location, and move with it.

❑ `static` means it can be fixed on the background of the page at a specified location, but not move when the page is scrolled.

❑ `relative` means that it will be positioned normally, depending on the preceding elements.

top – New in CSS2

Scripting Properties:	`top, pixelTop, posTop`
Values:	`auto, <percentage> <length>`
Default:	`auto`
Applies to:	All elements
Inherited:	No
Percentage?:	Yes, refers to parent's width

Sets or returns the vertical position of an element when displayed in 2-D canvas mode, allowing accurate placement and animation of individual elements. Value is returned as a string including the measurement type (px, %, etc.). To retrieve the value as a number, query the `posTop` property.

visibility – New in CSS2

IE4/5 Scripting Property:	`visibility`
Values:	`visible, hidden, inherit`
Default:	`inherit`
Applies to:	All elements
Inherited:	No
Percentage?:	No

Allows the element to be displayed or hidden on the page. Elements which are hidden still take up the same amount of space, but are rendered transparently. Can be used to dynamically display only one of several overlapping elements

❑ `visible` means that the element will be visible.

❑ `hidden` means that the element will not be visible.

❑ `inherit` means that the element will only be visible when its parent or container element is visible.

white-space

IE4/5 Scripting Property:	not supported
Values:	`<length>, <percentage>`
Default:	`Zero`

Applies to:	Block-level elements
Inherited:	No
Percentage?:	Yes, refers to parent's width

Sets the spacing between elements. Using a `<percentage>` value will base the spacing on the parent element or default spacing for that element.

width

Scripting Properties:	width, pixelWidth, posWidth
Values:	auto, `<length>`, `<percentage>`
Default:	auto, except for any element with an intrinsic dimension
Applies to:	DIV, SPAN and replaced elements
Inherited:	No
Percentage?:	Yes, refers to parent's width

Sets the horizontal size of an element, and will scale the element if necessary. The value is returned as a string including the measurement type (px, %, etc.). To retrieve the value as a number, query the posWidth property.

z-index – New in CSS2

IE4/5 Scripting Property:	zIndex
Values:	`<number>`
Default:	Depends on the HTML source
Applies to:	All elements
Inherited:	No
Percentage?:	No

Controls the ordering of overlapping elements, and defines which will be displayed 'on top'. Positive numbers are above the normal text on the page, and negative numbers are below. Allows a 2.5-D appearance by controlling the layering of the page's contents.

Printing Properties

page-break-after

IE4/5 Scripting Property:	pageBreakAfter
Values:	`<auto>`, `<always>`, `<left>`, `<right>`
Default:	`<auto>`
Applies to:	All elements
Inherited:	No
Percentage?:	No

Controls when to set a page break and on what page the content will resume, i.e. either the left or the right.

page-break-before

IE4/5 Scripting Property:	pageBreakBefore
Values:	`<auto>`, `<always>`, `<left>`, `<right>`
Default:	`<auto>`
Applies to:	All elements
Inherited:	No
Percentage?:	No

Controls when to set a page break and on what page the content will resume, i.e. either the left or the right.

Other Properties

cursor

IE4/5 Scripting Property:	cursor
Values:	auto, crosshair, default, hand, move, e-resize, ne-resize, nw-resize, n-resize, se-resize, sw-resize, s-resize, w-resize, text, wait, help
Default:	auto
Applies to:	All elements
Inherited:	No
Percentage?:	No

Specifies the type of cursor the mouse pointer should be.

IE4/5 Unsupported CSS Properties

Internet Explorer 4 doesn't support the following CSS1 properties:

```
word-spacing
!important
first-letter pseudo
first-line pseudo
white-space
```

Navigator 4 Unsupported CSS Properties

Navigator 4 doesn't support the following CSS1 properties:

```
word-spacing
!important
first-letter pseudo
first-line pseudo
font
font-variant
letter-spacing
list-style-image,list-style-position,list-style
background-attachment,background-position,background-repeat,background
border-top-color,border-right-color,border-left-color,border-bottom-color
border-top,border-right,border-bottom,border-left
clip
overflow
@import
```

SAX 1.0: The Simple API for XML

This appendix contains the specification of the SAX interface. It is taken largely verbatim from the definitive specification to be found on http://www.megginson.com/sax/, with editorial comments added in *italics*.

The classes and interfaces are described in alphabetical order; within each class, the methods are also listed alphabetically.

The SAX specification is in the public domain: see the web site quoted above for a statement of policy on copyright. Essentially the policy is: do what you like with it, copy it as you wish, but no-one accepts any liability for errors or omissions.

The SAX distribution also includes three "helper classes":

- ❑ AttributeListImpl is an implementation of the AttributeList interface
- ❑ LocatorImpl is an implementation of the Locator interface
- ❑ ParserFactory is a class that enables you to load a parser identified by a parameter at run-time.

The documentation of these helper classes is not included here. For this, and for SAX sample applications, see the SAX distribution available from http://www.megginson.com.

Class Hierarchy

```
class java.lang.Object
    interface org.xml.sax.AttributeList
    class org.xml.sax.helpers.AttributeListImpl
```

```
        (implements org.xml.sax.AttributeList)
   interface org.xml.sax.DTDHandler
   interface org.xml.sax.DocumentHandler
   interface org.xml.sax.EntityResolver
   interface org.xml.sax.ErrorHandler
   class org.xml.sax.HandlerBase
        (implements org.xml.sax.EntityResolver,
                org.xml.sax.DTDHandler,
                org.xml.sax.DocumentHandler,
                org.xml.sax.ErrorHandler)
   class org.xml.sax.InputSource
   interface org.xml.sax.Locator
   class org.xml.sax.helpers.LocatorImpl
        (implements org.xml.sax.Locator)
   interface org.xml.sax.Parser
   class org.xml.sax.helpers.ParserFactory
class java.lang.Throwable (implements java.io.Serializable)
   class java.lang.Exception
   class org.xml.sax.SAXException
   class org.xml.sax.SAXParseException
```

Interface org.xml.sax.AttributeList

An AttributeList is a collection of attributes appearing on a particular start tag. The Parser supplies the DocumentHandler with an AttributeList as part of the information available on the startElement event. The AttributeList is essentially a set of name-value pairs for the supplied attributes; if the parser has analyzed the DTD it may also provide information about the type of each attribute.

Interface for an element's attribute specifications

The SAX parser implements this interface and passes an instance to the SAX application as the second argument of each startElement event.

The instance provided will return valid results only during the scope of the startElement invocation (to save it for future use, the application must make a copy: the AttributeListImpl helper class provides a convenient constructor for doing so).

An AttributeList includes only attributes that have been specified or defaulted: #IMPLIED attributes will not be included.

There are two ways for the SAX application to obtain information from the AttributeList. First, it can iterate through the entire list:

```
public void startElement (String name, AttributeList atts) {
  for (int i = 0; i < atts.getLength(); i++) {
    String name = atts.getName(i);
    String type = atts.getType(i);
    String value = atts.getValue(i);
    [...]
  }
}
```

(Note that the result of getLength() will be zero if there are no attributes.)

As an alternative, the application can request the value or type of specific attributes:

```
public void startElement (String name, AttributeList atts) {
   String identifier = atts.getValue("id");
   String label = atts.getValue("label");
   [...]
}
```

The `AttributeListImpl` helper class provides a convenience implementation for use by parser or application writers.

Method Name	Description
getLength()	The SAX parser may provide attributes in any arbitrary order, regardless of the order in which they were declared or specified. The number of attributes may be zero. Returns the number of attributes in this list.
getName(index)	The names must be unique: the SAX parser shall not include the same attribute twice. Attributes without values (those declared #IMPLIED without a value specified in the start tag) will be omitted from the list. Returns the name of an attribute in this list (by position). If the attribute name has a namespace prefix, the prefix will still be attached. Parameter: the index of the attribute in the list starting at zero (int).
getType(index)	The attribute type is one of the strings "CDATA", "ID", "IDREF", "IDREFS", "NMTOKEN", "NMTOKENS", "ENTITY", "ENTITIES", or "NOTATION" (always in upper case). If the parser has not read a declaration for the attribute, or if the parser does not report attribute types, then it must return the value "CDATA" as stated in the XML 1.0 Recommendation (clause 3.3.3, "Attribute-Value Normalization"). For an enumerated attribute that is not a notation, the parser will report the type as "NMTOKEN". Returns the type of an attribute in the list (by position). Parameter: the index of the attribute in the list starting at zero (int).
getType(name)	The return value is the same as the return value for getType(index). If the attribute name has a namespace prefix in the document, the application must include the prefix here. Returns the type of an attribute in the list (by name). Parameter: the name of the attribute (String).
getValue(index)	If the attribute value is a list of tokens (IDREFS, ENTITIES, or NMTOKENS), the tokens will be concatenated into a single string separated by whitespace. Returns the value of an attribute in the list (by position). Parameter: the index of the attribute in the list starting at zero (int).

Table continued on following page

Method Name	Description
getValue(name)	The return value is the same as the return value for getValue(index). If the attribute name has a namespace prefix in the document, the application must include the prefix here. Returns the value of an attribute in the list (by name). Parameter: the name of the attribute (String).

Interface org.xml.sax.DocumentHandler

Every SAX application is likely to include a class that implements this interface, either directly or by subclassing the supplied class HandlerBase.

Receive notification of general document events

This is the main interface that most SAX applications implement: if the application needs to be informed of basic parsing events, it implements this interface and registers an instance with the SAX parser using the setDocumentHandler method. The parser uses the instance to report basic document-related events like the start and end of elements and character data.

The order of events in this interface is very important, and mirrors the order of information in the document itself. For example, all of an element's content (character data, processing instructions, and/or subelements) will appear, in order, between the startElement event and the corresponding endElement event.

Application writers who do not want to implement the entire interface can derive a class from HandlerBase, which implements the default functionality; parser writers can instantiate HandlerBase to obtain a default handler. The application can find the location of any document event using the Locator interface supplied by the parser through the setDocumentLocator method.

Method Name	Description
characters (ch[], start, length) throws SAXException	Receives notification of character data. The parser will call this method to report each chunk of character data. SAX parsers may return all contiguous character data in a single chunk, or they may split it into several chunks; however, all of the characters in any single event must come from the same external entity, so that the Locator provides useful information. The application must not attempt to read from the array outside of the specified range *and must not attempt to write to the array*. Note that some parsers will report whitespace using the ignorableWhitespace() method rather than this one (validating parsers must do so). Parameters: ch – the characters from the XML document (char array). start – the start position in the array (int). length – the number of characters to read from the array (int).

Method Name	Description
endDocument() throws SAXException	Throws: SAXException – any SAX exception, possibly wrapping another exception. Receives notification of the end of a document. The SAX parser will invoke this method only once *for each document*, and it will be the last method invoked during the parse. The parser shall not invoke this method until it has either abandoned parsing (because of an unrecoverable error) or reached the end of input. Throws: SAXException – any SAX exception, possibly wrapping another exception.
endElement(name) throws SAXException	Receives notification of the end of an element. The SAX parser will invoke this method at the end of every element in the XML document; there will be a corresponding startElement() event for every endElement() event (even when the element is empty). If the element name has a namespace prefix, the prefix will still be attached to the name. Parameter: the element type name (String). Throws: SAXException – any SAX exception, possibly wrapping another exception.
ignorableWhitespace (ch[], start, length) throws SAXException	Receives notification of ignorable whitespace in element content. Validating parsers must use this method to report each chunk of ignorable whitespace (see the W3C XML 1.0 recommendation, section 2.10): non-validating parsers may also use this method if they are capable of parsing and using content models. SAX parsers may return all contiguous whitespace in a single chunk, or they may split it into several chunks; however, all of the characters in any single event must come from the same external entity, so that the Locator provides useful information. The application must not attempt to read from the array outside of the specified range. Parameters: ch – The characters from the XML document (char array). start – The start position in the array (int). length – The number of characters to read from the array (int). Throws: SAXException – any SAX exception, possibly wrapping another exception.

Table continued on following page

Method Name	Description

`processingInstruction (target, data)`
 	
`throws SAXException`
	Receives notification of a processing instruction. The parser will invoke this method once for each processing instruction found: note that processing instructions may occur before or after the main document element.
	
	A SAX parser should never report an XML declaration (XML 1.0, section 2.8) or a text declaration (XML 1.0, section 4.3.1) using this method.
	
	Parameters:
	`target` – The processing instruction target (`String`).
	`data` – The processing instruction data, or `null` if none was supplied (`String`).
	
	Throws: `SAXException` – any SAX exception, possibly wrapping another exception.

`setDocumentLocator (locator)`	Receives an object for locating the origin of SAX document events. A SAX parser is strongly encouraged (though not absolutely required) to supply a locator: if it does so, it must supply the locator to the application by invoking this method before invoking any of the other methods in the `DocumentHandler` interface. The locator allows the application to determine the end position of any document-related event, even if the parser is not reporting an error. Typically, the application will use this information for reporting its own errors (such as character content that does not match an application's business rules). The information returned by the locator is probably not sufficient for use with a search engine. In practice, some implementations report the start position of the event (e.g. the column number where a tag starts) rather than the end position. Note that the locator will return correct information only during the invocation of the events in this interface. The application should not attempt to use it at any other time. Parameter: `locator` – An object that can return the location of any SAX document event (of type `Locator`).

`startDocument()`
 	
`throws SAXException`
	Receives notification of the beginning of a document. The SAX parser will invoke this method only once *for each document*, before any other methods in this interface or in `DTDHandler` (except for `setDocumentLocator`).
	
	Throws: `SAXException` – any SAX exception, possibly wrapping another exception.

Method Name	Description

`startElement`
`(name, atts)`
 	
`throws SAXException`
	Receives notification of the beginning of an element. The parser will invoke this method at the beginning of every element in the XML document; there will be a corresponding `endElement()` event for every `startElement()` event (even when the element is empty). All of the element's content will be reported, in order, before the corresponding `endElement()` event.
	
	If the element name has a namespace prefix, the prefix will still be attached. Note that the attribute list provided will contain only attributes with explicit values (specified or defaulted): `#IMPLIED` attributes will be omitted.
	
	Parameters:
	`name` – The element type name (`String`).
	`atts` – The attributes attached to the element (of type `AttributeList`).
	
	Throws: SAXException – any SAX exception, possibly wrapping another exception.

Interface org.xml.sax.DTDHandler

This interface should be implemented by the application, if it wants to receive notification of events related to the DTD. SAX does not provide full details of the DTD, but this interface is available because, without it, it would be impossible to access notations and unparsed entities referenced in the body of the document.

Notations and unparsed entities are rather specialized facilities in XML, so most SAX applications will not need to use this interface.

Receive notification of basic DTD-related events

If a SAX application needs information about notations and unparsed entities, then the application implements this interface and registers an instance with the SAX parser using the parser's `setDTDHandler` method. The parser uses the instance to report notation and unparsed entity declarations to the application.

The SAX parser may report these events in any order, regardless of the order in which the notations and unparsed entities were declared; however, all DTD events must be reported after the document handler's `startDocument` event, and before the first `startElement` event.

It is up to the application to store the information for future use (perhaps in a hash table or object tree). If the application encounters attributes of type `"NOTATION"`, `"ENTITY"`, or `"ENTITIES"`, it can use the information that it obtained through this interface to find the entity and/or notation corresponding with the attribute value.

The `HandlerBase` class provides a default implementation of this interface, which simply ignores the events.

Method Name	Description
`notationDecl` `(name, publicId, systemId)` `throws SAXException`	Receives notification of a notation declaration event. It is up to the application to record the notation for later reference, if necessary. If a system identifier is present, and it is a URL, the SAX parser must resolve it fully before passing it to the application.
	Parameters: `name` – The notation name (`String`). `publicId` – The notation's public identifier, or `null` if none was given (`String`). `systemId` – The notation's system identifier, or `null` if none was given (`String`).
	Throws: `SAXException` – any SAX exception, possibly wrapping another exception.
`unparsedEntityDecl` `(name, publicId, systemId, notationName)` `throws SAXException`	Receives notification of an unparsed entity declaration event. Note that the notation name corresponds to a notation reported by the `notationDecl()` event. It is up to the application to record the entity for later reference, if necessary.
	If the system identifier is a URL, the parser must resolve it fully before passing it to the application.
	Parameters: `name` – The unparsed entity's name (`String`). `publicId` – The entity's public identifier, or `null` if none was given (`String`). `systemId` – The entity's system identifier (it must always have one) (`String`). `notation` – The name of the associated notation (`String`).
	Throws: `SAXException` – any SAX exception, possibly wrapping another exception.

Interface org.xml.sax.EntityResolver

When the XML document contains references to external entities, the URL will normally be automatically analyzed by the parser. The relevant file will be located and parsed where appropriate. This interface allows an application to override this behavior. This might be needed, for example, if you want to retrieve a different version of the entity from a local server, or if the entities are cached in memory or stored in a database, or if the entity is really a reference to variable information such as the current date.

When the parser needs to obtain an entity, it calls this interface, which can respond by supplying any `InputSource` object.

Basic interface for resolving entities

If a SAX application needs to implement customized handling for external entities, it must implement this interface and register an instance with the SAX parser using the parser's `setEntityResolver` method.

The parser will then allow the application to intercept any external entities (including the external DTD subset and external parameter entities, if any) before including them.

Many SAX applications will not need to implement this interface, but it will be especially useful for applications that build XML documents from databases or other specialized input sources, or for applications that use URI types other than URLs.

The following resolver would provide the application with a special character stream for the entity with the system identifier "http://www.myhost.com/today":

```
import org.xml.sax.EntityResolver;
import org.xml.sax.InputSource;

public class MyResolver implements EntityResolver {
    public InputSource resolveEntity (String publicId, String systemId)
    {
            if (systemId.equals("http://www.myhost.com/today")) {
                // return a special input source
            MyReader reader = new MyReader();
            return new InputSource(reader);
        } else {
                // use the default behaviour
            return null;
        }
    }
}
```

The application can also use this interface to redirect system identifiers to local URIs or to look up replacements in a catalog (possibly by using the public identifier).

The `HandlerBase` class implements the default behavior for this interface, which is simply always to return null (to request that the parser use the default system identifier).

Method Name	Description
resolveEntity (publicId, systemId) throws SAXException, IOException	Allows the application to resolve external entities. The parser will call this method before opening any external entity except the top-level document entity (including the external DTD subset, external entities referenced within the DTD, and external entities referenced within the document element): the application may request that the parser resolve the entity itself, that it use an alternative URI, or that it use an entirely different input source. Application writers can use this method to redirect external system identifiers to secure and/or local URIs, to look up public identifiers in a catalog, or to read an entity from a database or other input source (including, for example, a dialog box). If the system identifier is a URL, the SAX parser must resolve it fully before reporting it to the application. Returns an `InputSource` object describing the new input source, or null to request that the parser open a regular URI connection to the system identifier.

Table continued on following page

Method Name	Description
	Parameters: publicId – The public identifier of the external entity being referenced, or null if none was supplied (String). systemId – The system identifier of the external entity being referenced (String). Throws: SAXException – any SAX exception, possibly wrapping another exception. Throws: IOException – a Java-specific IO exception, possibly the result of creating a new InputStream or reader for the InputSource.

Interface org.xml.sax.ErrorHandler

You may implement this interface in your application if you want to take special action to handle errors. There is a default implementation provided within the HandlerBase class.

Basic interface for SAX error handlers

If a SAX application needs to implement customized error handling, it must implement this interface and then register an instance with the SAX parser using the parser's setErrorHandler method. The parser will then report all errors and warnings through this interface.

The parser shall use this interface instead of throwing an exception: it is up to the application whether to throw an exception for different types of errors and warnings. Note, however, that there is no requirement that the parser continue to provide useful information after a call to fatalError (in other words, a SAX driver class could catch an exception and report a fatalError).

The HandlerBase class provides a default implementation of this interface, ignoring warnings and recoverable errors and throwing a SAXParseException for fatal errors. An application may extend that class rather than implementing the complete interface itself.

Method Name	Description
error(exception) throws SAXException	Receives notification of a recoverable error. This corresponds to the definition of "error" in section 1.2 of the W3C XML 1.0 Recommendation. For example, a validating parser would use this callback to report the violation of a validity constraint. The default behavior is to take no action. The SAX parser must continue to provide normal parsing events after invoking this method: it should still be possible for the application to process the document through to the end. If the application cannot do so, then the parser should report a fatal error even if the XML 1.0 recommendation does not require it to do so.

Method Name	Description
	Parameter: `exception` – the error information encapsulated in a `SAXParseExeption`.
	Throws: `SAXException` – any SAX exception, possibly wrapping another exception.
`fatalError(exception)` `throws SAXException`	Receives notification of a non-recoverable error. This corresponds to the definition of "fatal error" in section 1.2 of the W3C XML 1.0 Recommendation. For example, a parser would use this callback to report the violation of a well-formedness constraint.
	The application must assume that the document is unusable after the parser has invoked this method, and should continue (if at all) only for the sake of collecting additional error messages: in fact, SAX parsers are free to stop reporting any other events once this method has been invoked.
	Parameter: `exception` – the error information encapsulated in a `SAXParseExeption`.
	Throws: `SAXException` – any SAX exception, possibly wrapping another exception.
`warning(exception)` `throws SAXException`	Receives notification of a warning. SAX parsers will use this method to report conditions that are not errors or fatal errors as defined by the XML 1.0 recommendation. The default behavior is to take no action.
	The SAX parser must continue to provide normal parsing events after invoking this method: it should still be possible for the application to process the document through to the end.
	Parameter: `exception` – the error information encapsulated in a `SAXParseExeption`.
	Throws: `SAXException` – any SAX exception, possibly wrapping another exception.

Class org.xml.sax.HandlerBase

This class is supplied with SAX itself: it provides default implementations of most of the methods that would otherwise need to be implemented by the application. If you write classes in your application as subclasses of `HandlerBase`, you need only code those methods where you want something other than the default behavior.

Default Base Class for Handlers

This class implements the default behavior for four SAX interfaces: `EntityResolver`, `DTDHandler`, `DocumentHandler`, and `ErrorHandler`.

Application writers can extend this class when they need to implement only part of an interface; parser writers can instantiate this class to provide default handlers when the application has not supplied its own.

Note that the use of this class is optional.

In the description below, only the behavior of each method is described. For the parameters and return values, see the corresponding interface definition.

Method Name	Description
`characters` `(ch[], start, length)` `throws SAXException`	By default, do nothing. Application writers may override this method to take specific actions for each chunk of character data (such as adding the data to a node or buffer, or printing it to a file).
`endDocument ()` `throws SAXException`	By default, do nothing. Application writers may override this method in a subclass to take specific actions at the end of a document (such as finalizing a tree or closing an output file).
`endElement (name)` `throws SAXException`	By default, do nothing. Application writers may override this method in a subclass to take specific actions at the end of each element (such as finalizing a tree node or writing output to a file).
`error (exception)` `throws SAXException`	The default implementation does nothing. Application writers may override this method in a subclass to take specific actions for each error, such as inserting the message in a log file or printing it to the console.
`fatalError (exception)` `throws SAXException`	The default implementation throws a `SAXParseException`. Application writers may override this method in a subclass if they need to take specific actions for each fatal error (such as collecting all of the errors into a single report): in any case, the application must stop all regular processing when this method is invoked, since the document is no longer reliable, and the parser may no longer report parsing events.
`ignorableWhitespace` `(ch[], start, length)` `throws SAXException`	By default, do nothing. Application writers may override this method to take specific actions for each chunk of ignorable whitespace (such as adding data to a node or buffer, or printing it to a file).
`notationDecl` `(name, publicId, systemId)`	By default, do nothing. Application writers may override this method in a subclass if they wish to keep track of the notations declared in a document.

Method Name	Description
`processingInstruction (target, data)` `throws SAXException`	By default, do nothing. Application writers may override this method in a subclass to take specific actions for each processing instruction, such as setting status variables or invoking other methods.
`resolveEntity (publicId, systemId)` `throws SAXException`	Always return null, so that the parser will use the system identifier provided in the XML document. This method implements the SAX default behavior: application writers can override it in a subclass to do special translations such as catalog lookups or URI redirection.
`setDocumentLocator (locator)`	By default, do nothing. Application writers may override this method in a subclass if they wish to store the locator for use with other document events.
`startDocument()` `throws SAXException`	By default, do nothing. Application writers may override this method in a subclass to take specific actions at the beginning of a document (such as allocating the root node of a tree or creating an output file).
`startElement (name, attributes)` `throws SAXException`	By default, do nothing. Application writers may override this method in a subclass to take specific actions at the start of each element (such as allocating a new tree node or writing output to a file).
`unparsedEntityDecl (name, publicId, systemId, notationName)`	By default, do nothing. Application writers may override this method in a subclass to keep track of the unparsed entities declared in a document.
`warning(exception)` `throws SAXException`	The default implementation does nothing. Application writers may override this method in a subclass to take specific actions for each warning, such as inserting the message in a log file or printing it to the console.

Class org.xml.sax.InputSource

An `InputSource` object represents a container for the XML document or any of the external entities it references (technically, the main document is itself an entity). The `InputSource` class is supplied with SAX: generally the application instantiates an `InputSource` and updates it to say where the input is coming from, and the parser interrogates it to find out where to read the input from.

The `InputSource` object provides three ways of supplying input to the parser: a system identifier (or URL), a reader (which delivers a stream of Unicode characters), or an `InputStream` (which delivers a stream of uninterpreted bytes).

A single input source for an XML entity

This class allows a SAX application to encapsulate information about an input source in a single object, which may include a public identifier, a system identifier, a byte stream (possibly with a specified encoding), and/or a character stream.

There are two places that the application will deliver this input source to the parser: as the argument to the Parser.parse method, or as the return value of the EntityResolver.resolveEntity method.

The SAX parser will use the InputSource object to determine how to read XML input. If there is a character stream available, the parser will read that stream directly; if not, the parser will use a byte stream, if available; if neither a character stream nor a byte stream is available, the parser will attempt to open a URI connection to the resource identified by the system identifier.

An InputSource object belongs to the application: the SAX parser shall never modify it in any way (it may modify a copy if necessary).

If you supply input in the form of a reader or InputStream, it may be useful to supply a system identifier as well. If you do this, the URI will not be used to obtain the actual XML input, but it will be used in diagnostics, and more importantly to resolve any relative URIs within the document, for example entity references.

Method Name	Description
InputSource()	Zero-argument default constructor.
InputSource (systemId)	Creates a new input source with a system identifier.
	Applications may use setPublicId to include a public identifier as well, or setEncoding to specify the character encoding, if known. If the system identifier is a URL, it must be full resolved.
	Parameters: systemId – the system identifier (String).
InputSource (byteStream)	Creates a new input source with a byte stream.
	Application writers may use setSystemId to provide a base for resolving relative URIs, setPublicId to include a public identifier, and/or setEncoding to specify the object's character encoding.
	Parameter: byteStream – the raw byte stream containing the document, of type InputStream.
InputSource (characterStream)	Creates a new input source with a character stream.
	Application writers may use setSystemId to provide a base for resolving relative URIs, and setPublicId to include a public identifier. The character stream should not include a byte order mark.
	Parameter: characterStream the character stream containing the document, of type Reader.
setPublicId (publicId)	Sets the public identifier for this input source.
	The public identifier is always optional: if the application writer includes one, it will be provided as part of the location information.
	Parameters: publicId – the public identifier as a String.

Method Name	Description
getPublicId()	Gets the public identifier for this input source. Returns the public identifier (String), or null if none was supplied.
setSystemId (systemId)	Sets the system identifier for this input source. The system identifier is optional if there is a byte stream or a character stream, but it is still useful to provide one, since the application can use it to resolve relative URIs and can include it in error messages and warnings (the parser will attempt to open a connection to the URI only if there is no byte stream or character stream specified). If the application knows the character encoding of the object pointed to by the system identifier, it can register the encoding using the setEncoding method. If the system ID is a URL, it must be fully resolved. Parameter: systemId – the system identifier as a String.
getSystemId()	Gets the system identifier for this input source. The getEncoding method will return the character encoding of the object pointed to, or null if unknown. If the system ID is a URL, it will be fully resolved. Returns the system identifier as a String.
setByteStream (byteStream)	Sets the byte stream for this input source. The SAX parser will ignore this if there is also a character stream specified, but it will use a byte stream in preference to opening a URI connection itself. If the application knows the character encoding of the byte stream, it should set it with the setEncoding method. Parameter: byteStream – a byte stream containing an XML document or other entity, of type InputStream.
getByteStream()	Gets the byte stream for this input source. The getEncoding method will return the character encoding for this byte stream, or null if unknown. Returns the byte stream (as an InputStream object), or null if none was supplied.
setEncoding (encoding)	Sets the character encoding, if known. The encoding must be a string acceptable for an XML encoding declaration (see section 4.3.3 of the XML 1.0 recommendation). This method has no effect when the application provides a character stream. Parameter: encoding – a string describing the character encoding.
getEncoding()	Gets the character encoding for a byte stream or URI. Returns the encoding as a String, or null if none was supplied.

Table continued on following page

Method Name	Description
setCharacterStream (characterStream)	Sets the character stream for this input source.
	If there is a character stream specified, the SAX parser will ignore any byte stream and will not attempt to open a URI connection to the system identifier.
	Parameter: characterStream – The character stream containing the XML document or other entity, of type Reader.
getCharacterStream()	Gets the character stream for this input source. Returns the character stream (as a Reader object), or null if none was supplied.

Interface org.xml.sax.Locator

This interface provides methods that the application can use to determine the current position in the source XML document.

Interface for associating a SAX event with a document location

If a SAX parser provides location information to the SAX application, it does so by implementing this interface and then passing an instance to the application using the document handler's setDocumentLocator method. The application can use the object to obtain the location of any other document handler event in the XML source document.

Note that the results returned by the object will be valid only during the scope of each document handler method: the application will receive unpredictable results if it attempts to use the locator at any other time.

SAX parsers are not required to supply a locator, but they are very strong encouraged to do so. If the parser supplies a locator, it must do so before reporting any other document events. If no locator has been set by the time the application receives the startDocument event, the application should assume that a locator is not available.

Method Name	Description
getPublicId()	Returns the public identifier for the current document event as a String, or null if none is available.
getSystemId()	Returns the system identifier for the current document event as a String, or null if none is available.
	If the system identifier is a URL, the parser must resolve it fully before passing it to the application.

Method Name	Description
getLineNumber()	Returns the line number where the current document event ends or -1 if none is available.
	In practice some parsers report the line number and column number where the event starts. Note that this is the line position of the first character after the text associated with the document event.
getColumnNumber()	Returns the column number where the current document event ends, or -1 if none is available.
	Note that this is the column number of the first character after the text associated with the document event. The first column in a line is position 1.

Interface org.xml.sax.Parser

Every SAX parser must implement this interface. An application parses an XML document by creating an instance of a parser (that is, a class that implements this interface) and calling one of its parse() methods.

Basic interface for SAX (Simple API for XML) parsers

All SAX parsers must implement this basic interface: it allows applications to register handlers for different types of events and to initiate a parse from a URI, or a character stream.

All SAX parsers must also implement a zero-argument constructor (though other constructors are also allowed).

SAX parsers are reusable but not re-entrant: the application may reuse a parser object (possibly with a different input source) once the first parse has completed successfully, but it may not invoke the parse() methods recursively within a parse.

Method Name	Description
parse(source)	Parses an XML document.
throws SAXException, IOException	The application can use this method to instruct the SAX parser to begin parsing an XML document from any valid input source (a character stream, a byte stream, or a URI).
	Applications may not invoke this method while a parse is in progress (they should create a new Parser instead for each additional XML document). Once a parse is complete, an application may reuse the same Parser object, possibly with a different input source.
	Parameter: source – the input source for the top-level of the XML document, of type InputSource.

Table continued on following page

Method Name	Description
	Throws: SAXException – any SAX exception, possibly wrapping another exception.
	Throws: IOException – an IO exception from the parser, possibly from a byte stream or character stream supplied by the application.
parse(systemId)	Parses an XML document from a system identifier (URI).
throws SAXException, IOException	This method is a shortcut for the common case of reading a document from a system identifier. It is the exact equivalent of the following: `parse(new InputSource(systemId));` If the system identifier is a URL, it must be fully resolved by the application before it is passed to the parser. Parameter: systemId – The system identifier as a String. Throws: SAXException – any SAX exception, possibly wrapping another exception. Throws: IOException – an IO exception from the parser, possibly from a byte stream or character stream supplied by the application.
setDocumentHandler (handler)	Allows an application to register a document event handler. If the application does not register a document handler, all document events reported by the SAX parser will be silently ignored (this is the default behavior implemented by HandlerBase). Applications may register a new or different handler in the middle of a parse, and the SAX parser must begin using the new handler immediately. Parameter: handler – The document handler, of type DocumentHandler.
setDTDHandler (handler)	Allows an application to register a DTD event handler. If the application does not register a DTD handler, all DTD events reported by the SAX parser will be silently ignored (this is the default behavior implemented by HandlerBase). Applications may register a new or different handler in the middle of a parse, and the SAX parser must begin using the new handler immediately. Parameter: handler – The DTD handler, of type DTDHandler.

Method Name	Description
setEntityResolver (resolver)	Allows an application to register a custom entity resolver.
	If the application does not register an entity resolver, the SAX parser will resolve system identifiers and open connections to entities itself (this is the default behavior implemented in HandlerBase).
	Applications may register a new or different entity resolver in the middle of a parse, and the SAX parser must begin using the new resolver immediately.
	Parameter: resolver – The object for resolving entities, of type EntityResolver.
setErrorHandler (handler)	Allows an application to register an error event handler.
	If the application does not register an error event handler, all error events reported by the SAX parser will be silently ignored, except for fatalError, which will throw a SAXException (this is the default behavior implemented by HandlerBase).
	Applications may register a new or different handler in the middle of a parse, and the SAX parser must begin using the new handler immediately.
	Parameter: handler – the error handler, of type ErrorHandler.
setLocale(locale) throws SAXException	Allows an application to request a locale for errors and warnings.
	SAX parsers are not required to provide localization for errors and warnings; if they cannot support the requested locale, however, they must throw a SAX exception. Applications may not request a locale change in the middle of a parse.
	Parameter: locale – a Java Locale object.
	Throws: SAXException – throws an exception (using the previous or default locale) if the requested locale is not supported.

Class org.xml.sax.SAXException

This class is used to represent an error detected during processing either by the parser or by the application.

Encapsulate a general SAX error or warning

This class can contain basic error or warning information from either the XML parser or the application: a parser writer or application writer can subclass it to provide additional functionality. SAX handlers may throw this exception or any exception subclassed from it.

If the application needs to pass through other types of exceptions, it must wrap those exceptions in a SAXException or an exception derived from a SAXException.

If the parser or application needs to include information about a specific location in an XML document, it should use the SAXParseException subclass.

Method Name	Description
getMessage()	Returns a detailed error or warning message for this exception as a String.
	If there is a embedded exception, and if the SAXException has no detail message of its own, this method will return the detail message from the embedded exception.
getException()	Returns the embedded exception, or null if there is none.
toString()	Converts the exception to a String.

Class org.xml.sax.SAXParseException

This exception class represents an error or warning condition detected by the parser or by the application. In addition to the basic capability of SAXException, a SAXParseException allow information to be retained about the location in the source document where the error occurred. For an application-detected error, this information might be obtained from the Locator object.

Encapsulate an XML parse error or warning

This exception will include information for locating the error in the original XML document. Note that although the application will receive a SAXParseException as the argument to the handlers in the ErrorHandler interface, the application is not actually required to throw the exception; instead, it can simply read the information in it and take a different action.

Since this exception is a subclass of SAXException, it inherits the ability to wrap another exception.

Method Name	Description
SAXParseException (message, locator)	Creates a new SAXParseException from a message and a locator.
	This constructor is especially useful when an application is creating its own exception from within a DocumentHandler callback.
	Parameters:
	message – The error or warning message as a String.
	locator – The locator object for the error or warning, of type Locator.

Method Name	Description
SAXParseException (message, locator, e)	Wraps an existing exception in a SAXParseException. This constructor is especially useful when an application is creating its own exception from within a DocumentHandler callback, and needs to wrap an existing exception that is not a subclass of SAXException. Parameters: message – The error or warning message as a String, or null to use the message from the embedded exception. locator – The locator object for the error or warning, of type Locator. e – any exception
SAXParseException (message, publicId, systemId, lineNumber, columnNumber)	Creates a new SAXParseException. This constructor is most useful for parser writers. If the system identifier is a URL, the parser must resolve it fully before creating the exception. Parameters: message – The error or warning message. publicId – The public identifier of the entity that generated the error or warning. systemId – The system identifier of the entity that generated the error or warning. The first three parameters are all Strings. lineNumber – The line number of the end of the text that caused the error or warning. columnNumber – The column number of the end of the text that cause the error or warning. These last two parameters are integers.
SAXParseException (message, publicId, systemId, lineNumber, columnNumber, e)	Creates a new SAXParseException with an embedded exception. This constructor is most useful for parser writers who need to wrap an exception that is not a subclass of SAXException. If the system identifier is a URL, the parser must resolve it fully before creating the exception. Parameters: message – The error or warning message, or null to use the message from the embedded exception. publicId – The public identifier of the entity that generated the error or warning. systemId – The system identifier of the entity that generated the error or warning.

Table continued on following page

793

Method Name	Description
	The first three parameters are all `Strings`.
	`lineNumber` – The line number of the end of the text that caused the error or warning.
	`columnNumber` – The column number of the end of the text that cause the error or warning.
	These two parameters are integers.
	`e` – another exception to embed in this one.
`getPublicId()`	Gets a string containing the public identifier of the entity where the exception occurred, or `null` if none is available.
`getSystemId()`	Gets a string containing the system identifier of the entity where the exception occurred, or `null` if none is available.
	If the system identifier is a URL, it will be resolved fully.
`getLineNumber()`	Gets the line number of the end of the text where the exception occurred, or -1 if none is available.
`getColumnNumber()`	Gets the column number of the end of the text where the exception occurred, or -1 if none is available. The first column in a line is position 1.

XPath, XLink, and XPointer

We are now going to look at the mechanisms which are being developed to allow linking of XML and how we can address parts of an XML document. In particular, we are going to look at

- Selecting particular parts of an XML document using XPath
- Reviewing the current limitation imposed by traditional HTML hyperlinks
- The XLink specification that is intended to address these problems, namely:
  - Simple Links which are similar to HTML links
  - Extended Links for linking multiple resources
- Using XPointer to point to particular fragments of XML documents

XPath

The W3C XPath recommendation can be found at http://www.w3.org/TR/XPath, and its current version is a Recommendation, and so will not change. (XLink and XPointer are, at the time of publication, still in draft status.) The XPath specification defines the way that a single node or a subset of nodes can be selected in an XML document. XPath can be used to query nodes, or it can be used to transform nodes and entire documents. XSLT extends XPath to include the necessary functionality to perform transactions. XPath forms the basis of the newer technology XPointer, which we will discuss later on in this Appendix.

Basic XPath syntax takes this form:

```
axis::node-test [predicate]
```

where:

- ❏ axis – a part of the document defined from the perspective of the context node.

- ❏ node-test – a selection from the nodes contained in the axis.

- ❏ predicate – an expression, enclosed in square brackets, containing functions to fine-tune the selection of nodes. The predicate may contain other XPaths and/or other predicates.

Each will be explained in turn.

The Context Node

This term appears many times in this section. It basically refers to the current node or collection of nodes (node set) that are being worked with. All location steps operate relative to the context node.

Axes

Axes are defined relative to the current node and form the basis of all other XPath operations – the node tests and predicates. Some refer to just one node only (such as parent) whereas others can refer to a node set (such as preceding); others are combinations of two other axes (descendant-or-self).

A full list of axes is given below:

Axes	Definition
ancestor	Collection containing the parent and its parent etc., all the way back to the root node.
ancestor-or-self	Union of ancestor node and self node.
attribute	Attribute collection of context node.
child	Collection of children of context node.
descendant	Collection of all children, children's children, etc.
descendant-or-self	Union of descendant node and self node.
following	All nodes after the context node in document order.
following-sibling	Following siblings of the context node.
namespace	Namespace collection of context node.
parent	Parent of context node.
preceding	All nodes before the context node in document order.
preceding-sibling	Preceding siblings of the context node.
self	The context node.

Node-Tests

When we have used the above, we will have a node or collection of nodes that will allow us to apply tests to the nodes.

Node Test	Definition
element name	Matches nodes with the specified element name.
`*`	Matches all elements in axis.
`comment()`	Matches all comment nodes in the axis.
`node()`	Matches all nodes in the axis.
`processing-instruction()`	Matches all processing instructions in the axis.
`text()`	Matches all text nodes in the axis.

Some XPath Examples

This selects all elements that are ancestors of the context node:

```
ancestor::*
```

This selects all nodes that precede the context node in document order that have an element called `future`:

```
preceding::future
```

This selects all the text nodes that are a descendants of the context node:

```
descendant::text()
```

Simple XPath expressions can be built up into longer, more complicated ones. The first expression in the sequence is evaluated, and the results form the context for the second expression, and so on. So, in the following example, all the `text()` nodes are selected from `information` elements, which are children of `mobilephone` elements, which are children of the context node. Or, as far as XPath is concerned, starting at the context node, all the `mobilephone` child elements are selected, from those, all the `information` child elements are selected, and finally all the `text()` nodes are evaluated. This is a very fine way of homing in on your information in a very specific way.

Each XPath expression is separated by a slash (/):

```
child::mobilephone/child::info/child::text()
```

Absolute and Relative Paths

The document root is referenced by just a forward slash (/), and any axes preceded by / are treated as absolute paths, i.e. they start at the document root rather than the context node. So the XPath expression:

```
/child::*
```

refers to the child of the document root, which is the root element. However, this expression:

```
/child::*/attribute::*
```

selects all the attributes on the root element.

Shorthand Forms

Some axes have abbreviated forms (which are the only axes understood by the original release of IE 5). The updated versions of the MSXML parser support all the axes.

Shorthand form	Meaning	Example
nothing	`child::`	`article` is equivalent to `child::article`
@	`attribute::`	`@name` is equivalent to `attribute::name`
.	`self`	`.` is equivalent to `self::*`
..	`parent`	`..` is equivalent to `parent::*`
//	`descendant::`	`//*` is equivalent to `/descendant::*` (absolute path) `.//*` is equivalent to `descendant::*` (relative path)

Predicates

Predicates are used to filter nodes down further and these return Boolean values, using various operators in conjunction with XPath functions. The Boolean operators are =, !=, <, <=, >, and >=. Logical operators are and and or. Mathematical operators are +, -, *, div, mod, and |. Most of these are self-explanatory; however, div refers to floating point division, whereas mod returns the remainder after division. The | (pipe) character creates a union of two node sets. Some examples of using predicates follow:

This expression selects only the fourth chapter element among the children of the context node:

```
child::chapter[4]
```

However this expression selects all the chapter elements that are children of the context node that themselves have subtitle elements:

```
child::chapter[child::subtitle]
```

This selects all haspaid attributes of any or all of the descendants of the context node that have a value of no:

```
descendant::*[attribute::haspaid='no']
```

XPath Functions

XPath functions can be divided into four groups as follows:

❑   numbers – return true if non-zero, or NAN (not a number).

❑   node-sets – return true if they are not empty.

❑   strings – return `true` if the length is non-zero.

❑   Boolean – return only `true` or `false`.

Number Functions

All these functions return a number:

Function Name (Parameters)	Definition
`number(object?)`	Converts strings to numerical equivalent.
`sum(node-set?)`	Returns the sum of the numbers presented in the node set.
`floor(number)`	Returns the largest integer that is not greater than the argument.
`ceiling(number)`	Returns the smallest integer that is not greater than the argument.
`round(number)`	Returns integer closest to the argument.

Node Set Functions

Function Name (Parameters)	Definition
`last()`	Number of nodes (or context size) in the axis. Return type: `number`.
`position()`	Context position of node within nodes collection. Return type: `number`.
`count(node-set)`	Number of nodes in node-set argument. Return type: `number`.
`id(object)`	Collection of all parent nodes. Return type: `node-set`.
`local-name (node-set?)`	Returns local part of the expanded-name of the supplied node, or the context node if no argument. Return type: `string`.
`namespace-uri (node-set?)`	Returns namespace part of the expanded name of the supplied node, or the context node if no argument. Return type: `string`.
`name(node-set?)`	Returns fully qualified name (Qname) of the expanded-name of the first-node of the supplied node-set, or the context node if no argument. Return type: `string`.

String Functions

Function Name (Parameters)	Definition
`string(object?)`	Returns a string version of he object specified. Return type: `string`.
`concat (string,string, string*)`	Returns concatenation of arguments. Return type: `string`.

Table continued on following page

Function Name (Parameters)	Definition
starts-with(string,string)	True only if the first string starts with the second string and false otherwise. Return type: boolean.
contains(string,string)	True if the first string contains the second string, otherwise false. Return type: boolean.
substring-before(string,string)	Returns the part of the first string which occurs before the second string, if it contains the second string, otherwise a empty string is returned. Return type: string.
substring-after(string,string)	Returns the part of the first string which occurs after the second string, if it contains the second string, otherwise a empty string is returned. Return type: string.
substring (string,number, number)	Returns the section from the first string indexed by the first number passed of length defined by the second number. Return type: string.
string-length(string?)	Returns the length of the string argument or context node if an argument of not passed. Return type: number.
normalize-space(string?)	Removes leading and trailing white spaces of argument or of context node string. Return type: number.
translate (string,string,string)	Returns Qname of the expanded-name of the first-node of the supplied node-set, or the context node if no argument. Return type: string.

Boolean Functions

Function Name (Parameters)	Definition
boolean(object)	Returns a Boolean depending on the object supplied.
not(object)	Returns true if argument is false, and vice versa.
true()	Returns true.
false()	Returns false.
lang(string)	Returns true if the language of the context node (specified by the xml:lang attribute) is the same as the language specified.

Some examples of using XPath functions are as follows:

This returns the sum of the age attributes of all the person elements:

```
descendant::*[sum(person/@age)]
```

This selects the article children of the context node that have a fifth paragraph element:

```
child::article[paragraph[position() = 5]]
```

This returns all person elements that are children of the context node that have a last name attribute beginning with 'S':

```
child::person[start-with(@last-name, "S")]
```

XLink

The growth of the Internet has largely been due to the ease of being able to insert a hyperlink into a web document to link to an external resource, such as a web page, image or document. In the XML world, we need a way of linking documents together also, but as we will see, this is taken to another level, allowing us to define multiple links between documents, specify traversal paths between participating resources with particular roles, and even define links between documents in an external document.

> It should be noted that XLink only provides a way to specify linkages, not how they are rendered.

Let's first look at the limitations of linking in HTML documents.

HTML Linking Limitations

The anchor tag (<A>) in HTML is used as a hyperlink between documents and is specified as follows:

```
<A HREF="http://www.xml.com/index.html">XML homepage</A>
```

This tells us the link defined by the text "XML homepage" connects the resource defined at http://www.xml.com/index.html. This is illustrated in the figure below:

One problem with HTML documents is that we have to embed the links within the actual source document. This works fine for HTML documents, but lacks support for files such as images or Office documents. It would be much better if we could define the links external to the source file, enabling us to manage the links in a central repository, such as a file or a database.

Also, an HTML link acts in one direction. If we want to have a relationship between document A and document B, we have to embed links in both documents, linking to each other. It would be nice if we could define one link which implied that there is a relationship between each document.

HTML links also limit us to connections between two resources, so that if we have a similar list of links (e.g. a menu) between multiple pages, then a link would have to be embedded in each and every document. Ideally, we could put all of the links in one document which would define the relationships between all pages and have the browser take care of navigation.

Finally, in HTML, a link is followed by clicking on it, and it is either immediately displayed in the current window or a new window is opened. Ideally, we would be able to tell the rendering engine whether it should automatically follow the link or wait for it to be clicked on, and furthermore if it should be opened in a new window or directly embedded in the current document.

XML linking dramatically improves on the HTML link functionality.

XLink Design

The XLink namespace is defined by the following URI:

```
http://www.w3.org/1999/xlink
```

Now, to make use of XLink attributes and elements we are required to define the XLink namespace, and so the following would make the prefix XLink available within the element WroxElement to represent the XLink namespace.

```
<WroxElement
  xmlns:xlink="http://www.w3.org/1999/xlink">
  ...
</WroxElement >
```

There are also a number of attributes which can be applied to XLink elements. We will look at the different types of XLink elements we can have later in the appendix, but for now we should understand each of the attributes that will be applicable.

XLink Attributes

XLink provide a series of global attributes as defined below:

Attribute	Meaning
type	Specifies the type of link (simple or extended).
href	The destination of the URI link.
role	The function of the link's content.
title	A human readable description of the function of the link.
actuate	Defines how the link should be triggered and can be onRequest (the user must take an action to trigger the link – similar to an HTML link) or onLoad (the link is automatically triggered when the document is loaded).
show	Describes how the link target resource should be displayed when it is retrieved. This can be one of new (in a separate context), replace (the target content should replace the current content – similar to an HTML link) and embedded (the content is embedded directly in the document at the position of the link).
from	Defines the value of the role attribute of the locator or resource element defining the *start point* of the link.
to	Defines the value of the role attribute of the locator or resource attribute defining the *end point* of the link.

The type Attribute

The `type` attribute actually identifies the XLink element and for the moment, it must have one of the following values: `simple` and `extended`. They are explained in more detail below.

So, the syntax for a simple type attribute could be:

```
<Link xlink:type="simple">Wrox</Link>
```

And for an extended link, it would be:

```
<Link xlink:type="extended"><!--extended link details--></Link>
```

The href Attribute

The `href` attribute or `locator` attribute specifies the URI of the resource the source document is linking to, for example:

```
<Link xlink:type="simple" xlink:href="http://www.wrox.com">Wrox</Link>
```

The Semantic Attributes: role and title

The `role` attribute is used on an XLink element to describe in a machine-readable fashion the function of the remote resource. It must be a fully qualified name (QName) and therefore we must use a namespace which contains the role element, hence allowing us to distinguish between it and any other role of a similar name.

In addition, the `title` attribute is used to describe the function of a resource in a human readable fashion. This functions in the same way as the HTML `TITLE` element.

So, we could expand our example above to the following:

```
<Link xlink:type="simple"
  xlink:href="http://www.wrox.com"
  xmlns:wrox="http://www/wrox.com/"
  xlink:role="wrox:publisher"
  xlink:title="Publisher of technical books">
  Wrox
</Link>
```

The Behavior Attributes: actuate and show

The behavior attributes can be used on simple and `arc` (see `arc` section below) type elements. On a simple link, they determine the behavior intentions when traversing to the single destination resource. However, on an arc-type element, they determine the intentions for traversal among the multiple links specified by the arc.

The `show` attribute can be one you define yourself, as long as it is a qualified name (QName) with a prefix linking to a namespace. If you do not specify a QName, the value must be one of the following:

❑   new – an application should display the end resource in a new window (similar to the HTML fragment `target="_blank"`).

❑   replace – the end resource should be displayed in the same window as the source resource (similar to the HTML fragment `target="_self"`).

❑   embed – the end resource should be displayed in place of the source resource (similar to the HTML fragment `<IMG>` tag in an HTML document).

In a similar way to the show attribute, the actuate attribute may have a QName specified and, if not, one of the following values should be specified:

❏ onLoad – the resource is retrieved immediately, like the < IMG > tag in an HTML document.

❏ onRequest – the resource is retrieved when the user of a XLink-aware processor requests it.

Types of Links

The W3C XLink specification allows for two types of links, simple and extended:

Simple Link

A **simple link** is a link that associates exactly two resources, one local and one remote. Because it involves a local resource, a simple link is always inline. It essentially provides the same functionality as an HTML <A> tag and provides a one-way link involving a source resource and a destination resource. So, a simple link could be defined as follows:

```
<simpleLink xlink:type="simple" xlink:href="http://www.wrox.com">Wrox</simpleLink>
```

This link can be described by the following diagram:

Of course, there is much more we can do with adding simple links using the selection of XLink attributes, so let's examine this through as series of examples.

Our first example is a simple link which is very much like a traditional HTML link and replaces the source page with the new resource when the user clicks the link:

```
<BookLink xlink:href="http://www.wrox.com/xml/proxml.asp"
    xlink:title="Advanced XML title covering all aspects of XML/XSL, E-Commerce and
    XML RPC">
    Pro XML
</BookLink>
```

We may then want to extend this example to display some information about the book immediately, by displaying a picture of the book when the user clicks on the "View Picture" link. Finally, we could include a link back to the XML list of books. Notice that the link to the picture has an actuate value of onRequest and a show value of embed, which means that it will be displayed at the position of the link when the user actually clicks the link. The final link to the list of XML books is also activated when the user clicks the link, but, in a similar way to an HTML link, replaces the page completely.

```
<?xml version="1.0"?>
<person xmlns:xlink="http://www.w3.org/1999/xlink/namespace/">
  <name xlink:type="simple"
        xlink:href="http://www.wrox.com/xml/proxml.asp"
        xlink:actuate="onLoad"
        xlink:show="embed"/>
  <picture xlink:type="simple"
```

```
            xlink:href="proxml.jpg"
            xlink:actuate="onRequest"
            xlink:show="embed"
            xlink:title="View picture">
   View picture.
  </picture>
  <homepage xlink:type="simple"
            xlink:href="http://www.wrox.com/xml/default.asp"
            xlink:actuate="onRequest"
            xlink:show="replace">
    XML Book List.
  </homepage>
</person>
```

Now we have examined simple links, let's look at extended links.

Extended Link

An **extended link** is a link that associates an arbitrary number of resources. The participating resources may be any combination of remote and local. If all the resources are remote, the link is out of line. If any of the resources are local, then the link is inline.

Let's look in a bit more detail at what this implies.

An extended link offers the full functionality of XLink and can be out of line or describe links participating in multiple resources. If the content of the current document participates as one of the resources, then the extended link can be inline, similar to simple types. Alternatively, an extended link can be out of line, which implies that all of the link's resources are remote and allows us to define the links in an external file as illustrated below:

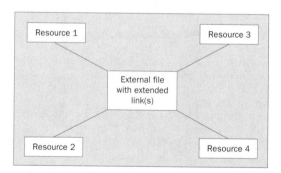

This allows us to be able to store information about a document which is either read-only or would be expensive to modify, or even entities such as images which have no support for embedding links.

In fact, extended links also contain a combination of the following four element types:

- ❑ resource –which address local resources participating in the link
- ❑ locator – which address the remote resources participating in the link
- ❑ arc – which describe the traversal rules of the resources participating in the link
- ❑ title – which have human readable descriptions of the link

Extended links are indicated as follows:

```
xlink:type="extended"
```

Extended links should have one or more child elements. Let's now look at the elements that construct a valid extended link.

xlink:type="resource"

If an extended link contains one or more local resources, it is an inline link; the type attribute has the value `resource` and means that there are special sub-elements within the extended link itself. This kind of extended links may only use the semantic attributes `role` and `title`.

The following example could describe the title of a book and its ISBN number. This could serve as the starting resource for links of lists of books.

```
<item xlink:type="resource"
      xlink:role="order:item"
      xlink:title="Book">
  <title>Professional Site Server Commerce Edition</title>
  <isbn>B76253776</isbn>
</item>
```

xlink:type="locator"

Remote resources taking part in an extended link are indicated by the `type` attribute having the value `locator`. The only other attribute required in such a link, is the `href` attribute to indicated the URI of the resource, although the `role` and `title` attributes may also be present if required.

The following example two extended links; one provides a link for finding out a bit more about a book, and the second allows the book to be purchased:

```
<BookLink xlink:type="extended" xmlns:WroxBooks="http://www.wrox.com/Books">
  <resource xlink:type="locator"
            xlink:href="http://www.wrox.com/XML/proxml.xml"
            xlink:role="WroxBooks:book"
            xlink:title="Book"/>
  <resource xlink:type="locator"
            xlink:href="http://www.wroxOrders.com/XML/proxml.xml"
            xlink:role="WroxBooks:purchase"
            xlink:title="Purchase"/>
</BookLink>
```

Beyond defining our extended links, we can indicate rules for their traversal using `arc` elements.

xlink:type="arc"

An `arc` element is defined by the value of the type attribute being `arc` and this entity groups the rules for traversal among the extended links you have defined. The `arc` elements define the direction the link must traverse using the traversal attributes, `from` and `to`, and the behavior activated when the link is followed using the behavior attributes `show` and `actuate`.

The `arc` element can also use the semantic attributes, role and title and describe the *meaning of the resource being traverse to in the context of that arc.* For example, we may have two resources representing XML books, but a particular link between them may be called "Advanced Users" and a link in the inverse direction be called "Beginners".

We use the `from` attribute to define resources from which a traversal may be initiated, and the `to` attribute indicates resources which can be traversed to, i.e. the end-point of a `from` link.

The following example extends our previous example. You can see we have now defined two arcs which allow us to go in either direction between the book and order links. This would therefore allow us to get the book name for a particular order or get the order details for a particular book.

```
<BookLink xlink:type="extended"
          xmlns:WroxBooks="http://www.wrox.com/Books">
  <resource xlink:type="locator"
            xlink:href="http://www.wrox.com/XML/proxml.xml"
            xlink:role="WroxBooks:book"
            xlink:title="Book"/>
  <resource xlink:type="locator"
            xlink:href="http://www.wroxOrders.com/XML/proxml.xml"
            xlink:role="WroxBooks:purchase"
            xlink:title="Purchase"/>
  <go xlink:type="arc"
      xlink:from=" WroxBooks:book"
      xlink:to=" WroxBooks:purchase"
      xlink:show="replace"
      xlink:actuate="onRequest"
      xlink:role=" WroxBooks:GetBookOrder"
      xlink:title="Book Order"/>
  <go xlink:type="arc"
      xlink:from=" WroxBooks:purchase"
      xlink:to=" WroxBooks:book"
      xlink:show="replace"
      xlink:actuate="onRequest"
      xlink:role=" WroxBooks:GetBookName"
      xlink:title="Book Name"/>
</BookLink>
```

xlink:type="title"

We previously discussed how we can use the `title` attribute to define some human-readable information to users. In instances where we want to add more information to the title, such as further markup, we can instead use a `title` element.

Therefore, from our previous example, we could redefine the fragment:

```
<go xlink:type="arc"
    xlink:from=" WroxBooks:purchase"
    xlink:to=" WroxBooks:book"
    xlink:show="replace"
    xlink:actuate="onRequest"
    xlink:role=" WroxBooks:GetBookName"
    xlink:title="Book Name"/>
```

as the following:

```
<go xlink:type="arc"
    xlink:from=" WroxBooks:purchase"
    xlink:to=" WroxBooks:book"
```

```
        xlink:show="replace"
        xlink:actuate="onRequest"
        xlink:role=" WroxBooks:GetBookName">
    <BookTitle xlink:type="title">
      <Name>Professional XML</Name>
      <isbn>IN 8729728</isbn>
      <Publisher>Wrox Press</Publisher>
    </BookTitle>
  </go>
```

XPointer

The XLink specification deals mainly with linking to entire documents, but it would also be very useful if we could point to document fragments within a resource. The W3C has defined XPointer as a mechanism for doing this and we are going to cover it in this section.

Pointers in HTML

We currently have a limited way of pointing to fragments within HTML documents using the anchor element <A>. This requires us to do two things:

❏   To define the target area within the resource document, which is called books.htm:

```
<HTML>
  <BODY>
    <A NAME="book1">Advanced XML Book<BR/></A>
    <A NAME="book2">General XML 1.0 reference book<BR/></A>
  </BODY>
</HTML>
```

❏   Then create the link in the source document

```
<HTML>
  <BODY>
    <A HREF="books.htm#book1">Info about Pro XML<BR/></A>
    <A HREF="books.htm#book2"> Info about XML Reference<BR/></A>
  </BODY>
</HTML>
```

There are some obvious problems with this method. Firstly, we have to create the target areas for every document we want to link to – this is more work than should be necessary and even more of a problem if you do not have write access to the document. Also, the entire document has to be rendered in order to access a part of that document.

Let's look at how XPointer solves this.

Using XPointer

The XPointer specification is available from http://www.w3.org/TR/xptr and is currently Working Draft in last call status. It extends XPath by providing syntax to state address information in a link to an XML document and extends the features of XPath.

However, XPointer refers to locations rather than to the XPath nodes; these can be any of the node types found in XPath, but in addition, can also be `points` and `ranges`.

XPointer provides us with syntax to not only specify a particular document, but also obtain a particular part of the document by appending the details to a URI.

So, consider the following file called `books.xml`:

```
<Books>
  <Book ID="98773">
    <Title>Pro XML</Title>
    <Publisher>Wrox</Publisher>
    <isbn>8723213890</isbn>
  </Book>
  <Book ID="98773">
    <Title>Pro Site Server 3.0</Title>
    <Publisher>Wrox</Publisher>
    <isbn>029302323</isbn>
  </Book>
</Books>
```

We could then access the first book (Pro XML) with the following link fragment:

```
    <resource xlink:type="locator"

xlink:href="http://www.wrox.com/books.xml#xpointer(//Book[.@ID='98773'])"
            xlink:role="WroxBooks:name"
            xlink:title="Book"/>
```

Notice that we take the XPath expression, `//Book[.@ID='98773']`, which asks to return the `<Book>` element that has an ID attribute of value 98773, and append it to the `#xpointer` syntax.

XPointer Extensions to XPath

The XPointer specification adds to the XPath specification the concepts of `points` and `ranges`.

A **point** location can be a node as well as a location defined by its character content, like the first letter of the `isbn` element in our example above.

A **range** however, is defined by a start point and an end point and is specified as follows:

```
    #xpointer(<locatorElement> to <locatorElement>)
```

And so, if we consider the following structure:

```
<Books>
  <Book ID="98773">
    <Title>Pro XML</Title>
    <Publisher>Wrox</Publisher>
    <isbn>8723213890</isbn>
    <author>Steven Livingstone</author>
```

```
      <author>Steven Howard</author>
    </Book>
    <Book ID="98773">
      <Title>Pro Site Server 3.0</Title>
      <Publisher>Wrox</Publisher>
      <isbn>029302323</isbn>
      <author>Didier Martin</author>
      <author>Steven Livingstone</author>
      <author>Michael Kay</author>
    </Book>
  </Books>
```

Then if we selected the range according to the following XPointer:

```
  xpointer(//Book to author[2])
```

we would get the following result:

```
<Book ID="98773">
  <author>Steven Howard</author>
<Book ID="98773">
  <author>Steven Livingstone</author>
```

This is because the first expression is evaluated (//Book) and returns the <Book> elements and the second expression will iterate through each of these expressions and return the second author element.

XPointer Functions

There are further XPointer extension functions that we will briefly look at here.

Function	Description
end-point()	Takes a location set and returns a location set containing all the end points of the locations in the argument location set, e.g. end-point(//child[1]) returns the end point of the first child in the document.
here()	Returns the element which contains the XPointer allowing pointing relative to the current element, e.g. here()/.. points to the parent of the XPointer element itself.
start-point()	Takes a location set and returns a location set containing all the start points of the locations in the argument location set, e.g. start-point(//child[2]) returns the start point of the second child in the document.
string-range()	Searches the target document returning range locations for each instance that was found of the string in the target instance, e.g. string-range(/,"Wrox") returns instances of Wrox in document.
unique()	Returns a Boolean value of true if the location set contains on one item (useful to know for pointing to).

Summary

We reviewed the structure and syntax of the XPath specification, that is, axes, node tests, and predicates and illustrated how to construct and use XPath expressions with some simple examples.

We have given a thorough overview of XLink, and the various ways you can create both simple and extended links. We saw how much of an advantage these techniques will have over the HTML anchor tags that we currently work with.

We also looked at XPointer to see how we will further be able to improve on the anchor tag, by being able to point to document fragments, and even use XPath to have a dynamic link. Finally, we looked at the extensions to XPath introduced by XPointer.

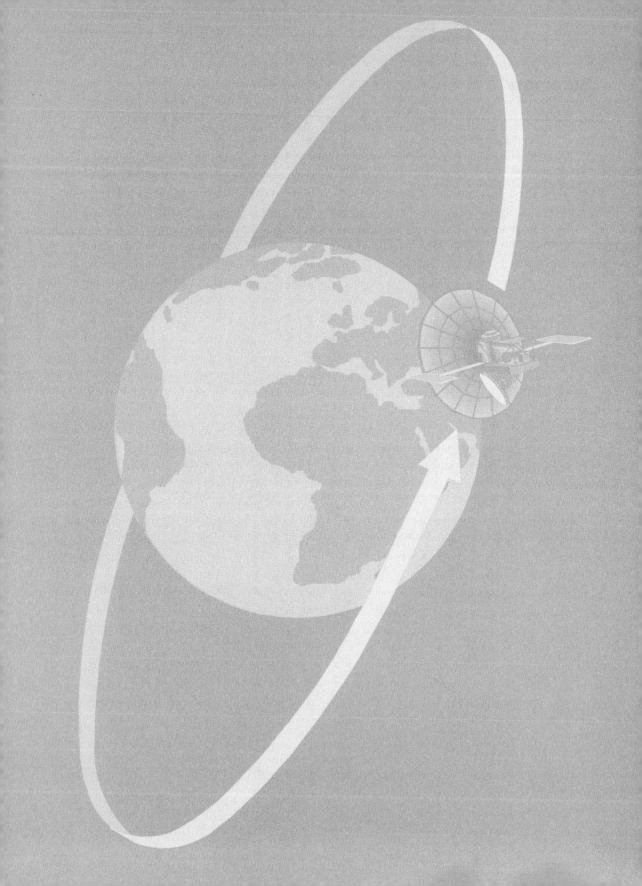

IE5 XML Schemas and Data Types

While XML documents can be successfully defined using a **Document Type Definition** (DTD), there is felt to be a requirement for a more flexible way of defining the structure of XML documents. It is also accepted that there needs to be a way for the data type to be indicated within the design of the XML document to make it easier for the handling of XML documents to be mechanized.

To this end, the W3C is – at the time of writing – working on a group of proposals that come under the general heading of **XML Schemas and Data Types**. This includes the proposed **Document Content Definition** (DCD) language. Internet Explorer 5 supports a reasonably standard implementation of XML Schemas and Data Types, as described in this reference section. This technology is still developing in IE5 and not all of the attributes listed here may work as described at the present time.

XML Schemas

An **XML Schema** is a description or definition of the structure of an XML document. The schema is itself written in XML. This makes it easier for newcomers to understand, when compared to the need to learn the SGML-like syntax of the Document Type Definition (DTD).

Internet Explorer 5 includes an implementation of XML Schemas that provides eight predefined elements for use in defining XML documents:

Name	Description
Schema	The overall enclosing element of the schema, which defines the schema name.
ElementType	Defines a type of element that will be used within the schema.
element	Defines an instance of an element declared for use within an `<ElementType>` element.
AttributeType	Defines a type of attribute that will be used within the schema.

Table continued on following page

Name	Description
attribute	Defines an instance of an attribute declared for use within an `<ElementType>` element.
datatype	Defines the type of data that an attribute or element can contain.
description	Used to provide information about an attribute or element.
group	Used to collect elements together to define specific sequences of elements.

IE5 XML Schema Elements

This section describes each of the XML Schema elements in alphabetical order, complete with its attributes.

The attribute Element

The `<attribute>` element is used to define specific instances of an attribute that is used within an `<AttributeType>` or `<ElementType>` element.

Element Name	Attribute	Description
attribute	default	The default value for the attribute, used when `required` is `"no"`. If `required` is `"yes"` then the value provided in the document must be the same as the default value.
	required	Specifies if a value for this attribute is required. Can be either `"yes"` or `"no"`.
	type	Specifies the `<AttributeType>` of which the attribute is an instance.

The AttributeType Element

The `<AttributeType>` element is used to define a type of attribute that is used within elements in the schema. Specific instances of the attribute can be further specified using the `<attribute>` element.

Element Name	Attribute	Description
AttributeType	default	The default value for the attribute. If the attribute is an enumerated type, the value must appear in the list.
	dt:type	The data type that the attribute will accept.
	dt:values	A set of values that form an enumerated type, for example `"roses carnations daisies"`
	name	A unique string that identifies the `<AttributeType>` element within the schema and provides the attribute name.
	model	Defines whether the attribute can accept content that is not defined in the schema. The value `"open"` allows undefined content to appear, while the value `"closed"` allows only content defined in the schema to appear.
	required	Specifies if a value for this attribute is required. Can be either `"yes"` or `"no"`. This and `default` are mutually exclusive when `required` is `"yes"`.

The `dt:type` and `dt:values` are used in the same way as in the `<datatype>` element:

```
<AttributeType name="flowername"
               default="rose"
               dt:type="enumeration"
               dt:values="rose carnation daisy lilac" />
```

Note that, although `dt` is the usual namespace prefix for data types, we can replace it with a different prefix.

The datatype Element

The `<datatype>` element is used to define the type of data that an attribute or element can contain. At the time of writing, support for this element was particularly limited.

Element Name	Attribute	Description
datatype	dt:max	The maximum (inclusive) value that the element or attribute can accept.
	dt:maxExclusive	The maximum exclusive value that the element or attribute can accept, that is, the value must be less than this value.
	dt:maxlength	The maximum length of the element or attribute value. For strings this is the number of characters. For number and binary values this is the number of bytes required to store the value.
	dt:min	The minimum (inclusive) value that the element or attribute can accept.
	dt:minExclusive	The minimum exclusive value that the element or attribute can accept, that is, the value must be more than this value.
	dt:type	One of the specific or primitive data types listed at the end of this appendix.
	dt:values	For an `enumeration`, the list of values in the enumeration.

The description Element

The `<description>` element is used to provide information about an attribute or element.

Element Name	Attribute	Description
description	none	The descriptive text for the element or attribute.

The element Element

The `<element>` element is used to define specific instances of an element that are used within an `<ElementType>` element.

Element Name	Attribute	Description
element	type	The name of an element type defined in this or another schema, and of which this element is an instance.
element	minOccurs	Defines whether the element is optional in documents based on the schema. `"0"` denotes that it is optional and does not need to appear, while `"1"` denotes that the element must appear at least once. The default if omitted is `"1"`.
	maxOccurs	Defines the maximum number of times that the element can appear at this point within documents based on the schema. `"1"` means only once, while `"*"` means any number of times. The default if omitted is `"1"`.

The ElementType Element

The `<ElementType>` element is used to define a type of element that is used within the schema. Specific instances of the element can be further specified using the `<element>` element.

Element Name	Attribute	Description
ElementType	content	Defines the type of content that the element can contain. `"empty"` means no content, `"textOnly"` means it can contain only text (unless the model is `"open"`), `"eltOnly"` means it can contain only other elements and no free text, and `"mixed"` means it can contain any mixture of content.
	dt:type	One of the specific or primitive data types listed at the end of this appendix.
	model	Defines whether the element can accept content that is not defined in the schema. The value `"open"` allows undefined content to appear, while the value `"closed"` allows only content defined in the schema to appear.
	name	A unique string that identifies the `<ElementType>` element within the schema and provides the element name.
	order	Defines how sequences of the element can appear. The value `"one"` means that only one of the set of enclosed element elements can appear, `"seq"` means that all the enclosed elements must appear in the order that they are specified, and `"many"` means that none, any or all of the enclosed elements can appear in any order.

For examples of the content and order attributes, see the section on the `<group>` element next.

The group Element

The `<group>` element is used to collect series of `<element>` and/or `<attribute>` elements together so that they can be assigned a specific sequence in the schema. This can precisely control the order that they can appear in documents that are based on this schema.

Element Name	Attribute	Description
group	minOccurs	Defines whether the group is optional in documents based on the schema. `"0"` denotes that it is optional and does not need to appear, while `"1"` denotes that the group must appear at least once. The default if omitted is `"1"`.
	maxOccurs	Defines the maximum number of times that the group can appear at this point within documents based on the schema. `"1"` means only once, while `"*"` means any number of times. The default if omitted is `"1"`.
	order	Defines how sequences of the groups and element types contained in this group can appear. `"one"` means that only one of the set of enclosed groups or element types can appear, `"seq"` means that all the enclosed groups or element types must appear in the order that they are specified, and `"many"` means that none, any or all of the enclosed groups or element types can appear in any order.

The next example shows some of the ways that groups and element types can be used to define the ordering and appearance of elements in a document:

```
<ElementType name="first" content="empty" />
<ElementType name="second" content="textOnly" dt:type="string" />
<ElementType name="thirdEqual" content="empty" />

<ElementType name="third" content="eltOnly" order="many">
   <element type="thirdEqual" />
</ElementType>

<ElementType name="fallen" content="empty" />
<ElementType name="unplaced" content="empty" />
<ElementType name="last" content="empty" />

<ElementType name="raceorder" order="seq">

   <element type="first" />
   <element type="second" />
   <element type="third" />

   <group minOccurs="1" maxOccurs="1" order="one">
      <element type="fallen" />
      <element type="unplaced" />
      <element type="last" />
   </group>

</ElementType>
```

Because the main element raceorder has the attribute order="seq", the <first>, <second> and <third> elements must appear at least once in the order shown. This also applies to the group element; however, of the three elements that are defined within the group, only one can occur in the document. So, the following combinations are some of the legal and valid possibilities:

```
<first />
<second>too slow again</second>
<third />
<fallen />
<first />
<second />
<third>
    <thirdEqual />
</third>
<unplaced />
<first />
<second>still too slow</second>
<third>
    <thirdEqual />
    <thirdEqual />
    <thirdEqual />
</third>
<last />
```

The Schema Element

The <Schema> element is the enclosing element of the schema. It defines the schema name and the namespaces that the schema uses.

Element Name	Attribute	Description
Schema	name	Defines a name by which the schema will be referred to.
	xmlns	Specifies the default namespace URI for the elements and attributes in the schema.
	xmlns:dt	Specifies the namespace URI for the datatype attributes in the schema.

```
<Schema name="myschema"
        xmlns="urn:schemas-microsoft-com:xml-data"
        xmlns:dt="urn:schemas-microsoft-com:datatypes">
```

As we noted above, the datatype namespace prefix does not have to be dt, but this is the usual value, and clearly indicates to a (human) reader that the attributes prefixed by it belong to the datatype namespace. However, the namespace definitions (the URN parts) *must* be as they appear here.

The IE5 XML Schema Structure

The following code shows the overall structure of an IE5 XML Schema, with the type of value expected for each attribute. Where elements can appear in more than one place, the subsequent occurrences have the attribute list removed to avoid excessive duplication:

```
<Schema name="schema_name"
        xmlns="namespace_URI"
        xmlns:dt="namespace_URI" >

   <AttributeType default="default_value"
                  dt:type="xml_data_type"
                  dt:values="enumerated_value_list"
                  name="name_or_id"
                  model="open"|"closed"
                  required="yes"|"no">
      <datatype dt:max="maximum_value"
                dt:maxExclusive="maximum_value_exclusive"
                dt:maxlength="maximum_length"
                dt:min="minimum_value"
                dt:minExclusive="minimum_value_exclusive"
                dt:type="xml_data_type" />
                dt:values="enumerated_value_list" />

      <description>description_text</description>
   </AttributeType>

   <AttributeType>
      ... etc ...
   </AttributeType>

   <ElementType content="empty"|"textOnly"|"eltOnly"|"mixed"
                dt:type="xml_data_type"
                model="open|"closed"
                name="name_or_id"
                order="one"|"seq"|"many" >

      <description>description_text</description>

      <datatype ... etc ... />

      <element type="element_type"
               minOccurs="0"|"1"
               maxOccurs="1"|"*" />

      <attribute default="default_value"
                 required="yes"|"no" />

      <attribute ... etc ... />

      <group minOccurs="0"|"1"
             maxOccurs="1"|"*"
             order="one"|"seq"|"many" >

         <attribute ... etc ... />

         <element ... etc ... />

      </group>

   </ElementType>

</Schema>
```

XML Datatypes

Data types are referenced from the data type namespace, which is declared within the XML `<Schema>` element of the schema using the `xmlns`: *datatypename* attribute.

The data types that are proposed by W3C, and supported in Internet Explorer 5, are shown in the next table, which includes all highly popular types and all the built-in types of popular database and programming languages and systems such as SQL, Visual Basic, C, C++ and Java.

This table is taken from the W3C note at http://www.w3.org/TR/1998/NOTE-XML-data/

Name	Parse type	Storage type	Example
string	pcdata	string (Unicode)	Ομωνυμα λεγαται ων ονομα μονον κοινον, ο δε κατα τουνομα λογος της ουσιας ετερος, οιον ζυον ο τε ανθροπος και το γεγραμμενον.
number	A number, with no limit on digits, may potentially have a leading sign, fractional digits, and optionally an exponent. Punctuation as in US English.	string	15, 3.14, -123.456E+10
int	A number, with optional sign, no fractions, no exponent.	32-bit signed binary	1, 58502, -13
float	Same as for number	64-bit IEEE 488	.314159265358979E+1
fixed. 14.4	Same as number but no more than 14 digits to the left of the decimal point, and no more than 4 to the right.	64-bit signed binary	12.0044
boolean	"1" or "0"	bit	0, 1 (1=="true")
dateTime. iso8601	A date in ISO 8601 format, with optional time and no optional zone. Fractional seconds may be as precise as nanoseconds.	Structure or object containing year, month, hour, minute, second, nanosecond.	19941105T 08:15:00301

Name	Parse type	Storage type	Example
dateTime. iso8601.tz	A date in ISO 8601 format, with optional time and optional zone. Fractional seconds may be as precise as nanoseconds.	Structure or object containing year, month, hour, minute, second, nanosecond, zone.	19941105T 08:15:5+03
date. iso8601	A date in ISO 8601 format (no time).	Structure or object containing year, month, day.	19541022
time. iso8601	A time in ISO 8601 format, with no date and no time zone.	Structure or object exposing day, hour, minute.	
time. iso8601. tz	A time in ISO 8601 format, with no date but optional time zone.	Structure or object containing day, hour, minute, zone-hours, zoneminutes.	08:15-05:00
i1	A number, with optional sign, no fractions, no exponent.	8-bit binary	1, 255
i2	as above	16-bit binary	1, 703, -32768
i4	as above	32-bit binary	
i8	as above	64-bit binary	
ui1	A number, unsigned, no fractions, no exponent.	8-bit unsigned binary	1, 255
ui2	as above	16-bit unsigned binary	1, 703, -32768
ui4	as above	32-bit unsigned binary	
ui8	as above	64-bit unsigned binary	
r4	Same as number	IEEE 488 4-byte float	
r8	as above	IEEE 488 8-byte float	
float. IEEE.754. 32	as above	IEEE 754 4-byte float	

Table continued on following page

823

Name	Parse type	Storage type	Example
`float. IEEE.754. 64`	as above	IEEE 754 8-byte float	
`uuid`	Hexadecimal digits representing octets. Optional embedded hyphens should be ignored.	128-bytes Unix UUID structure	F04DA480-65B9-11d1-A29F-00AA00C14882
`uri`	Universal Resource Identifier	Per W3C spec	http://www.ics.uci.edu/pub/ietf/uri/draft-fielding-uri-syntax-00.txt http://www.ics.uci.edu/pub/ietf/uri/ http://www.ietf.org/html.charters/urn-charter.html
`bin.hex`	Hexadecimal digits representing octets	no specified size	
`char`	String	1 Unicode character (16 bits)	
`string. ansi`	String containing only ASCII characters <= 0xFF.	Unicode or single-byte string.	This does not look Greek to me.

The dates and times above reading `iso8601`*xxx* actually use a restricted subset of the formats defined by ISO 8601. Years, if specified, must have four digits. Ordinal dates are not used. Of formats employing week numbers, only those that truncate year and month are allowed.

Primitive XML Data Types

The W3C also recommends tokenized data types for use in XML 1.0. These are sometimes referred to as **primitive types**. The primitive types supported in Internet Explorer 5 are:

Name	Description
entity	The XML ENTITY type.
entities	The XML ENTITIES type.
enumeration	An enumerated type, i.e. a list of permissible values.
id	The XML ID type.
idref	The XML IDREF type.
idrefs	The XML IDREFS type.
nmtoken	The XML NMTOKEN type.
nmtokens	The XML NMTOKENS type.
notation	A NOTATION type.
string	Represents a generic String data type.

XML Preview for SQL Server

Well, if you have made it this far, it must be pretty clear that XML is very important to Microsoft. It seems every one of their products is getting an XML makeover (though the delivery date on the new XML-enabled Barney has yet to be determined). Kidding aside, XML plays a large role in Microsoft's view of the future. SQL Server is no exception. Although this book focuses on ASP development, a brief look at other technologies is appropriate. This appendix will focus on the SQL Server Technology Preview that Microsoft has made available. I will walk through the installation and setup of the Preview and then dive into some examples of how to use it.

We have to wait for SQL Server 2000 to experience tight XML integration, but a technology preview is available for download. This code (which works in SQL Server version 7.0) is a preview and therefore is of questionable stability. However, it does show what will be possible with the next version of SQL Server due in mid-2000. You will need Microsoft SQL Server 7.0 with at least Service Pack 1 running on either Windows NT (SP5) and IIS 4.0 or Windows 2000 and IIS 5.0. Windows 98 and Personal Web Server are not supported at this time as only the Desktop edition of SQL Server can be installed on Windows 98. You can find the Microsoft SQL Server XML Technology Preview at http://msdn.Microsoft.com/workshop/xml/articles/xmlsql/sqlxml_prev.asp.

This preview shows us what is in store for the future of databases over the Web. The preview provides XML integration with SQL Server version 7.0, as well as allowing direct access via a SQL-compliant URL. We can then query a database directly from the Web and have the results returned as XML formatted documents. In fact, you could even update, insert, or delete records from the URL. SQL Server will be exposed to IIS via an ISAPI DLL. You will be able to call not only predefined queries (and stored procedures) but also *ad hoc* queries.

Installation

This appendix was written using version 1.0.1.0 of the SQL XML Technology Preview. Because this product is only a preview, new versions are released fairly frequently, and subsequent versions may be slightly different from the setup described here.

The preview is contained in a self-installing compressed executable named `sqlxmlsetup.exe`. You may be surprised by its small size, only 334KB. Running the install is a quick and painless process, and when it is finished, it displays the `readme` file in your browser.

The next step requires you to configure a Virtual Directory for SQL Server. A registration tool is installed for this purpose, and can be found in the **XML Technology Preview for SQL Server** program group on the **Start** menu. It looks similar to other Microsoft Management Console snap-ins:

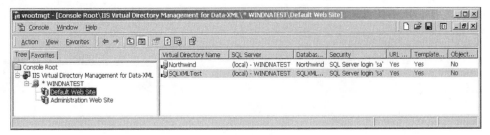

The tree-view pane shows a list of Web Servers (Sites) currently installed on your server. To create a new Virtual Directory, you can right-click on a Server name and then click **New Virtual Directory** from the menu, or click on **New Virtual Directory** from the **Action** menu. You will see the new directory in the right-hand Virtual Directory listing. The next step is to start entering parameters for the new directory, such as name, source database, etc. as described in the following section. In the screenshot above, you will notice that I created a new directory named `SQLXMLTest`.

Virtual Directory Configuration

The Virtual Directory that the SQL XML Preview uses is not the same as a typical IIS Virtual Directory. Any `.htm` or `.asp` pages will not be accessible through the URL. Only SQL Server or XML template files stored in this directory can be accessed. Let's take the example of the `SQLXMLTest` directory that I set up above and look at how it is configured.

To configure the Virtual Directory, either right-click on the Virtual Directory name and choose **Properties** or just double-click on the name. You will see the following:

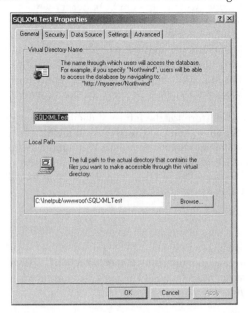

Firstly, give your Virtual Directory a name that you want to refer to it by, in this case SQLXMLTest, and select a path for your files. Now remember, this is the physical path of the Virtual Directory. It will not allow you to serve up HTML or ASP, only XML query templates (.xml files) and their style information (.xsl files), even if you've specified a directory on your web server. You will also see the Security, Data Source, Settings and Advanced tabs; I will look at each of these in turn.

Security

The Security tab on the Properties dialog allows you to configure who can gain access to your data:

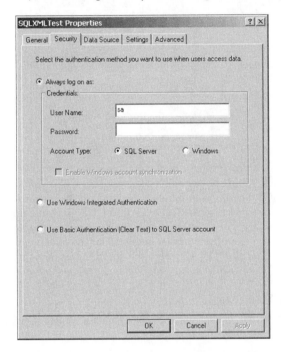

If you choose the Always log on as option, any query submitted to SQL Server will use that SQL User Account. (Note: this is not an NT Account but a SQL Server Account.) You must be very careful when using this option. If the specified user, as in my example, has administrative rights, they can do just about anything to your database. When constructing a solution for the Internet, the security design for SQL Server will be very important to avoid malicious and accidental attacks.

Windows Integrated Authentication will only work through Microsoft Internet Explorer. The user's credentials will be passed along with the request and authenticated against a Windows NT user account. Basic Authentication passes the user's name and password in clear text across the network; the user is validated against a SQL Server User Account. If the number of users is relatively small, Basic Authentication works, and is not network dependent. For a corporate intranet application, Windows Integrated Authentication is your best bet.

Data Source

Since we have now set up the IIS and security properties, it is time to actually point at a data source. The third tab on the Properties dialog looks like this:

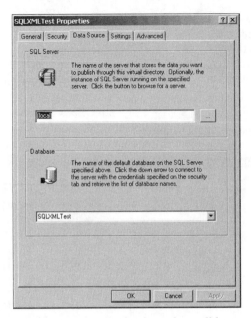

The first thing to do is pick a SQL Server and a database that will be exposed via IIS. I am running IIS on the same box as my SQL Server, and therefore pick [local]. However, any SQL Server on the network could be accessed. The sqlxml.dll runs on the IIS machine, not on the SQL Server machine. This allows tremendous power. For most large, and even not so large, enterprise applications, the web server is completely separate from the database server. This also fits in well with Microsoft's Distributed interNet Applications architecture (DNA), where the components of a complete system are separated into logical parts.

Access Type Settings

Now we are in the home stretch for getting SQL Server XML-aware. Setting the allowable actions is the last task in completing the installation:

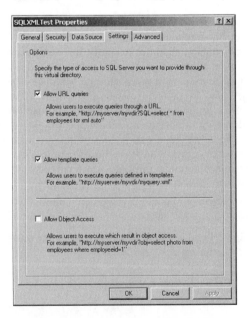

There are three access types that can be specified:

❏ Allow URL queries: This allows you to treat the URL like a command line and issue SQL commands directly to SQL Server:
http://localhost/Northwind?sql=SELECT+*+FROM+pubs+FOR+XML+RAW

❏ Allow template queries: This allows you to create query template files in XML and store them in the Virtual Directory. These are invoked by calling the XML file name in the URL:
http://localhost/Northwind/getpubs.xml

❏ Allow Object access: This allows access via the SQLXML object model in code or script.

If you plan on using only the URL to submit SQL Statements, then you would choose Allow URL queries. If you would also like to use XML template files then you would also check Allow template queries. If you want to utilize the SQLXML object model in your code or script, then you must check Allow Object access.

Advanced

You may notice a fifth tab, Advanced, which allows you to specify the path to sqlxml.dll. If you installed sqlxml.dll in a different directory than the default, then you will need to make sure the path is set correctly here.

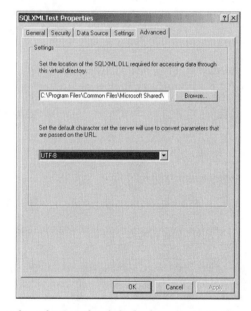

The final option available is for selecting the default character set to be used.

URL Queries

Now that SQL is set up for web access, we can submit queries directly from a URL, such as:http://localhost/SQLXMLTest?sql=SELECT+*FROM+pubs+FOR+XML+RAW

In the example above, SQLXMLTest refers to a Virtual Directory that is explicitly created to deliver access to SQL Server. As noted in the installation instructions, the SQL Server machine does not have to be the same as the one where IIS and the Virtual Directory are located.

You may notice that any spaces are replaced by '+'. Characters such as /, ?, #, %, and & have unique meanings in the URL. To properly use these characters they must be replaced by escape sequences. The following table shows the proper escape sequences:

Character	Escape sequence (% followed by the character's hex value)
/	%2F
?	%3F
#	%23
%	%25
&	%26

You will also notice the new directive FOR XML RAW lets the ISAPI DLL know the format for the results. By specifying the keyword RAW each record is built with the <row . . ./> tag. If FOR XML AUTO is specified, each record is built using the table name as the tag (e.g. <pubs . . . />). The difference may seem immaterial however, using RAW will generate XML that is consistent across tables. Generic XSL files can then be used to format the output, regardless of the underlying structure. There is a third option for specifying the XML format and that is FOR XML EXPLICIT. Using this option you are in full control of what the returned XML looks like. It also requires that you guarantee the XML is valid and well-formed. Since most of a book could be devoted to the uses of FOR XML EXPLICIT, it will suffice to say that it exists, and if you need generic data interchange between many systems it certainly bears further study.

You can also further specify the way data is returned, by adding a definition clause of DTD or XMLDATA. These commands include the XML document definition within the results. If we run the query:

http://localhost/SQLXMLTest?sql=SELECT+*+FROM+Contacts+FOR+XML+RAW,XMLDATA

We see the following results:

```
<?xml version="1.0" encoding="UTF-8" ?>
<root>
<Schema xmlns="urn:schemas-microsoft-com:xml-data" xmlns:dt="urn:schemas-
microsoft-com:datatypes">
  <ElementType name="row" content="textOnly" model="closed">
    <AttributeType name="first__name" dt:type="string" />
    <AttributeType name="last__name" dt:type="string" />
    <AttributeType name="street__info" dt:type="string" />
    <AttributeType name="city" dt:type="string" />
    <AttributeType name="state" dt:type="string" />
    <AttributeType name="zip" dt:type="string" />
    <AttributeType name="phone" dt:type="string" />
    <AttributeType name="type" dt:type="string" />
    <attribute type="first__name" required="no" />
    <attribute type="last__name" required="no" />
    <attribute type="street__info" required="no" />
    <attribute type="city" required="no" />
    <attribute type="state" required="no" />
    <attribute type="zip" required="no" />
    <attribute type="phone" required="no" />
    <attribute type="type" required="no" />
```

```
    </ElementType>
</Schema>
<row first__name="John" last__name="Doe" street__info="103 Easter Avenue"
city="Pleasantville" state="Indiana" zip="30113" phone="555-5555" type="personal"
/>
<row first__name="Alice" last__name="Smith" street__info="52B Wilkens Street"
city="Pleasantville" state="Indiana" zip="30113" phone="555-6666" type="personal"
/>
<row first__name="Richard" last__name="Blair" street__info="123 North Main Steet"
city="Dearborn" state="Michigan" zip="48124" phone="555-4981" type="business" />
<row first__name="William M." last__name="Kropog" street__info="80698 Matthew
Street" city="Covington" state="Louisiana" zip="70533" phone="555-0713"
type="business" />
<row first__name="Bill" last__name="Gates" street__info="1 Microsoft Way"
city="Redmond" state="Washington" zip="97811" phone="555-1212" type="business" />
</root>
```

There is no file behind this XML. SQL Server generated the results and they were formatted in XML by the ISAPI filter. ADO was not used at all. In fact, there was absolutely no code whatsoever. You can send a query via a URL and get back data in XML format. This will make integrating dissimilar systems a little easier. You will notice that the Schema information that is returned is a little different than the XML-Data Schema information provided by ADO. The SQL Server version is much simpler, as it does not need to include recordset information.

If we run the a query with the DTD directive:

http://localhost/SQLXMLTest?sql=SELECT+first_name+FROM+Contacts+FOR+XML+RAW,DTD

We receive the following:

```
<?xml version="1.0" encoding="UTF-8" ?>
<!DOCTYPE root [<!ELEMENT root (Contacts)*><!ELEMENT Contacts EMPTY><!ATTLIST
Contacts first__name CDATA #IMPLIED>]>
<root>
  <Contacts first__name="John"/>
  <Contacts first__name="Alice"/>
  <Contacts first__name="Richard"/>
  <Contacts first__name="William M."/>
  <Contacts first__name="Bill"/>
</root>
```

If you actually run this query on your own, you will notice that in order to view the DTD information you have to view the source code for the page.

If the FOR XML directive is left off, the receiving container must know how to deal with the results. If a query only returns one column, the first record's value would appear in the browser window. Source information can also be specified for an image tag, such as:

```
<img src="http://localhost/SQLXMLTest?sql=SELECT photo FROM Contacts WHERE ID=1">
```

If this appeared in an HTML page, the photo would be retrieved from the database and properly inserted.

SELECT statements are not the only commands that can be issued via the URL. Stored procedures can also be directly called. If a stored procedure is created to return all of the contacts in the table, it can be called using:

http://localhost/SQLXMLTest?sql=execute+spContacts+FOR+XML+RAW,XMLDATA

This returns exactly the same results as calling the SELECT statement. The one advantage of the stored procedure is its compiled nature. Also, there are a number of things you can do in a stored procedure that would be prohibitive at the URL level, such as multi-table joins, and complex grouping and summary commands.

It might appear that by passing the SQL string on the URL you would have to publish your table names and columns to allow more productive queries than "SELECT * FROM *sometable*". Not only would this be a dangerous notion, since it would make it incredibly easy to infiltrate your data store, but it would also be difficult to teach the proper SQL/XML syntax to anyone who needed access. Fortunately, there is a solution in the form of template queries.

Template Queries

Well, it turns out those templates are stored in XML format. They are simply text files containing a SQL query wrapped up inside XML. So, to insulate the user from having to type the query in the URL, you can create a file like this:

```
<root xmlns:sql="urn:schemas-microsoft-com:xml-sql">
<sql:query >
SELECT * FROM Contacts FOR XML AUTO
</sql:query>
</root>
```

The query syntax is contained within the <root> element, which, of course, is the root node for this XML document. The <sql:query> tag is based on the schema defined in the namespace urn:schemas-microsoft-com:xml-sql. Since this is a template that is being called and not a SQL statement passed on the URL, we do not need to use + instead of spaces. If this is saved in a SQL-enabled Virtual Directory, it can be called just like any other XML file:

http://localhost/SQLXMLTest/mycontacts.xml

This query is similar to the example above, but a data definition directive was not included. Therefore, only the data is returned in XML, with no schema information. Since the query portion is identical to the previous URL-based query, the resulting XML data is the same. However, I have now insulated my data structure from the user. It is then possible to change the structure of the table, or explicitly select columns without the user having to be aware of what is happening at the database level. They can simply continue calling mycontacts.xml.

Another advantage of using a template file is the ease of specifying the XSL file. I could change the template to look like:

```
<?xsl-serverstylesheet xslfile="mycontacts.xsl" ?>
<root xmlns:sql="urn:schemas-microsoft-com:xml-sql">
  <sql:query >
```

```
        SELECT * FROM Contacts FOR XML AUTO
    </sql:query>
</root>
```

Now whenever the user calls the mycontacts.xml file, the data is transformed using the mycontacts.xsl file:

```
<xsl:stylesheet xmlns:xsl="http://www.w3.org/TR/WD-xsl">
  <xsl:template match = "*">
    <xsl:apply-templates />
  </xsl:template>

  <xsl:template match="/">
   <HTML>
     <HEAD>
       <TITLE>SQL XML-XSL Test</TITLE>
       <STYLE>
         .Table {background:black}
         .TableHead {font:bold; color:white; background:black}
         .TableColumnHead
               {font:normal 'Verdana' bold; color:white; background:#000000}
         .TableRow {font:x-small 'Verdana'; color:black; background:#CCCCCC}
       </STYLE>
     </HEAD>
     <BODY>
       <DIV STYLE="font-family:Tahoma, Arial, sans-serif;
             font-size:30pt; color:blue;
             text-align:center; font-weight:bold">My Contacts</DIV>
       <HR />
       <TABLE WIDTH="100%" CELLPADDING="3">
         <THEAD>
           <TR CLASS="TableHead">
             <TD CLASS="TableColumnHead">Name</TD>
             <TD CLASS="TableColumnHead">Street</TD>
             <TD CLASS="TableColumnHead">City</TD>
             <TD CLASS="TableColumnHead">State</TD>
             <TD CLASS="TableColumnHead">Zip</TD>
             <TD CLASS="TableColumnHead">Phone</TD>
           </TR>
         </THEAD>
         <xsl:apply-templates select="root" />
       </TABLE>
     </BODY>
   </HTML>
  </xsl:template>

  <xsl:template match="Contacts">
    <TR CLASS="TableRow">
      <TD>
      <xsl:value-of select="@first_name"/>
      <xsl:value-of select="@last_name"/>
      </TD>
      <TD><xsl:value-of select="@street_info" /></TD>
      <TD><xsl:value-of select="@city" /></TD>
      <TD><xsl:value-of select="@state" /></TD>
```

835

```
        <TD><xsl:value-of select="@zip" /></TD>
        <TD><B><xsl:value-of select="@phone" /></B></TD>
     </TR>
   </xsl:template>
 </xsl:stylesheet>
```

The output can now be nicely formatted to be pleasant to look at, and the user is completely insulated from the possible back-end complexities of generating the data view. By including the XSL call in the template it will always be used; the user cannot forget to pick that particular XSL file. The results look like this:

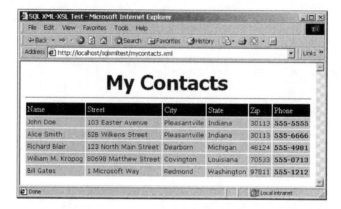

One problem I found when developing the code for this book was the lack of feedback that the preview has built in. I thought I created a valid XML template and XSL file, however nothing would appear in my browser, except an Illegal Operation error. Once I called a stand-alone XML sample file that referenced the XSL file, I realized I had forgotten a closing tag. However, I did not get any error message when calling through the template.

Using Parameters

In the examples so far, I have always returned the whole contents of a table. This may be fine to demonstrate a new technology, but it certainly isn't useful in the real world. Thankfully, templates can utilize parameters. It is also possible to specify default values for the parameters.

```
<?xsl-serverstylesheet xslfile="mycontacts.xsl" ?>
<root xmlns:sql="urn:schemas-microsoft-com:xml-sql">
  <sql:query State="">
    exec spGetContacts ? FOR XML AUTO
  </sql:query>
</root>
```

This template allows the filtering of the contact list. Notice that I can reuse the XSL stylesheet from the previous example. Also notice that the State parameter is assigned an empty string. I could specify a default value by: `<sql:query State="Michigan">` Then if I forgot to pass the parameter value the contacts from Michigan would be returned by default. To call this new template and specify a parameter, I just add the parameter's name to the URL with a value, like a standard GET:

http://localhost/SQLXMLTest/getcontacts.xml?State=Michigan

This will execute the stored procedure spGetContacts with the parameter Michigan and return only those contacts in that state.

So far the select statements have been very simple. Using templates, you can facilitate much more complex queries. For truly complex queries you probably want to use a stored procedure for speed, but you could just use a template file. For example, say you have a table of Projects and a separate table that associates these Projects with your contacts. To view names with projects, the following template could be used:

```
<?xsl-serverstylesheet xslfile="projcontacts.xsl" ?>
<root xmlns:sql="urn:schemas-microsoft-com:xml-sql">
  <sql:query ProjectID="">
    SELECT first_name, last_name, Description
    FROM Contacts
    INNER JOIN ProjectContacts
    INNER JOIN Projects ON ProjectContacts.ProjectID = Projects.ProjectID
    ON Contacts.ID = ProjectContacts.ContactID
    WHERE ProjectContacts.ProjectID = ? FOR XML RAW
  </sql:query>
</root>
```

Three tables are being joined together, and a parameter is passed specifying the project ID linking to the contacts that are to be displayed. This template would be called on the URL using the following:

http://localhost/SQLXMLTest/ProjectPeople.xml?ProjectID=3

You might note that FOR XML RAW has been specified instead of FOR XML AUTO here. By using the RAW directive the results are all contained within the same <row /> tag. If AUTO had been used, a hierarchical structure of <contact><project /></contact> would have been returned for each name. Although the hierarchical structure would make sense if data were being passing to a third party (as it maintains the true view of the data), it makes the XSL for display more complicated, as child nodes for each contact's project have to be dealt with. With the RAW directive set, the XSL only has to process <row /> elements, in much the same way as Contacts was searched for in the previous example. The formatted output from this template looks like this:

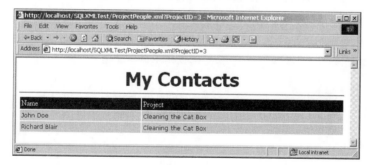

Object Access

Besides the ISAPI DLL file, sqlxml.dll, the preview also installs osqlxml.dll by default. This DLL allows us to access the features that the ISAPI extension exports. Since this is a preview, be warned that the object model is not at all finalized; there may be changes that could affect your code's stability. That said, let's take a brief look at how to implement this object on the server:

```
<%@ LANGUAGE="VBScript" %>
<% Response.ContentType = "text/xml"%>   ' Remember we have to let the server
                                         ' know what's coming

<%
Dim objSQLXML
Set objSQLXML = Server.CreateObject("Microsoft.SQLXMLRequest")
ObjSQLXML.Connection = "Driver=SQL Server; _
     Server=CodingCat;Database=SQLXMLTest;uid=sa;pwd=;Outputencoding=UTF-16"
ObjSQLXML.ExecuteQuery("SELECT * FROM Contacts FOR XML AUTO")
Response.BinaryWrite objSQLXML.Result
%>
```

The only thing that looks a little different from other typical database ASP code is using the BinaryWrite method of the Response object. This is because the Result is not a string *per se*. It is encoded by default as UTF-8, which allows non-standard characters to be properly transmitted down the wire. Adding Outputencoding=UTF-16 to the connection string will allow the scripting engines to manipulate the results. UTF-8 is not Unicode and therefore cannot be manipulated in script, UTF-16 converts the results to Unicode and the scripting engines can then make use of them.

Update Grams

Using the URL, templates, and the object model to retrieve data demonstrates some power for future systems. However, this new technology would not be complete without the ability to actually modify the data and get those changes back to the server. The XML returned by the SQLXML object could be sent to the XMLDOM for further manipulation in script. However, another important feature of the SQL Server XML Technology Preview is the ability to have XML-based inserts, updates, and deletes.

There are three additional tags defined in the urn:schemas-microsoft-com:xml-sql namespace to facilitate these actions. The first is: <sql:sync>. This tag let the ISAPI filter know that we need to modify data. The other two tags are <sql:before> and <sql:after>. In order to insert a record you would only use the <sql:after> tag. To delete data, include only the <sql:before> tag. Using both performs an update. When using these tags the resulting XML is referred to as an **Update Gram**.

For example, to insert records into the contacts table, the template would look like:

```
<root xmlns:sql='urn:schemas-microsoft-com:xml-sql'>
  <sql:sync>
    <sql:after>
<Contacts first_name="The" last_name="Tick" street_info="25 Main Street Apt C"
city="The City" state="Confusion" zip="yes" phone="555-0987" type="personal" />
      ... '(more inserts here)
    </sql:after>
  </sql:sync>
</root>
```

You are not restricted to modifying one record at a time. Another nice feature is its transactional nature. The <sql:sync> tag signifies the beginning of the transaction and the </sql:sync> closing tag marks the end. Anything in between is considered that transaction itself, and all of the operations within the <sql:before></sql:before> and <sql:after></sql:after> blocks must be successful for the transaction to be considered a success.

Summary

In this appendix, we have looked at how to get the SQL XML Technology Preview up and running. We looked at ways of retrieving data in a variety of XML 'flavors': from basic queries via the URL, to calling SQL statements encapsulated in XML template files. We also took a brief look at the SQLXML object and Update Grams.

An entire book could be (and I am sure will be) devoted to the subject of XML in SQL Server. What we can see, however, is that Microsoft is taking XML very seriously. The next release of SQL Server will provide substantial power for delivering not only data, but also information. This preview also demonstrates some of the true power of XML. I can certainly see a time in the not too distant future where all data exchanges are handled through XML. Traditional Electronic Data Interchange (EDI) will eventually suffocate under the weight of XML. What is certain is that as businesses utilize the Internet more and more for their communication, XML will be there to support them. I can remember hearing about HTML and thinking, "I don't really see a use for it in my job". Now I couldn't do my job without it. It looks like XML will follow this same path.

Support, Errata and P2P.Wrox.Com

One of the most irritating things about any programming book is when you find that bit of code you've just spent an hour typing simply doesn't work. You check it a hundred times to see if you've set it up correctly, and then you notice the spelling mistake in the variable name on the book page. Of course, you can blame the authors for not taking enough care and testing the code, the editors for not doing their job properly, or the proofreaders for not being eagle-eyed enough, but this doesn't get around the fact that mistakes do happen.

We try hard to ensure no mistakes sneak out into the real world, but we can't promise that this book is 100% error free. What we can do is offer the next best thing by providing you with immediate support and feedback from experts who have worked on the book and try to ensure that future editions eliminate these gremlins. We also now commit to supporting you not just while you read the book, but once you start developing applications as well through our online forums where you can put your questions to the authors, reviewers, and fellow industry professionals.

In this appendix we'll look at how to:

- ❑ Enroll in the peer to peer forums at http://p2p.wrox.com
- ❑ Post and check for errata on our main site, http://www.wrox.com
- ❑ E-mail technical support a query or feedback on our books in general

Between all three support procedures, you should get an answer to your problem in no time flat.

The Online Forums at P2P.Wrox.Com

Join the Pro ASP XML mailing list for author and peer support. Our system provides **programmer to programmer™ support** on mailing lists, forums and newsgroups all in addition to our one-to-one email system, which we'll look at in a minute. Be confident that your query is not just being examined by a support professional, but by the many Wrox authors and other industry experts present on our mailing lists.

How To Enroll For Support

Just follow this four-step system:

1. Go to p2p.wrox.com in your favorite browser.
   Here you'll find any current announcements concerning P2P – new lists created, any removed and so on.

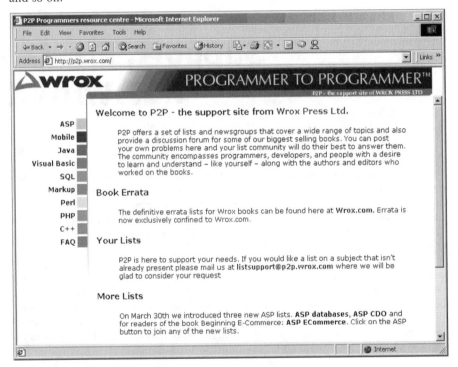

2. Click on the ASP button in the left hand column.

3. Choose to access the asp_xml list.

4. If you are not a member of the list, you can choose to either view the list without joining it or create an account in the list, by hitting the respective buttons.

5. If you wish to join, you'll be presented with a form in which you'll need to fill in your email address, name and a password (of at least 4 digits). Choose how you would like to receive the messages from the list and then hit Save.

6. Congratulations. You're now a member of the asp_xml mailing list.

Why this system offers the best support

You can choose to join the mailing lists or you can receive them as a weekly digest. If you don't have the time or facility to receive the mailing list, then you can search our online archives. You'll find the ability to search on specific subject areas or keywords. As these lists are moderated, you can be confident of finding good, accurate information quickly. Mails can be edited or moved by the moderator into the correct place, making this a most efficient resource. Junk and spam mail are deleted, and your own email address is protected by the unique Lyris system from web-bots that can automatically hoover up newsgroup mailing list addresses. Any queries about joining, leaving lists or any query about the list should be sent to: danielw@wrox.com.

Checking The Errata Online at www.wrox.com

The following section will take you step by step through the process of posting errata to our web site to get that help. The sections that follow, therefore, are:

- ❏ Wrox Developers Membership
- ❏ Finding a list of existing errata on the web site
- ❏ Adding your own errata to the existing list
- ❏ What happens to your errata once you've posted it (why doesn't it appear immediately)?

There is also a section covering how to e-mail a question for technical support. This comprises:

- ❏ What your e-mail should include
- ❏ What happens to your e-mail once it has been received by us

So that you only need view information relevant to yourself, we ask that you register as a Wrox Developer Member. This is a quick and easy process, that will save you time in the long-run. If you are already a member, just update membership to include this book.

Wrox Developer's Membership

To get your FREE Wrox Developer's Membership click on Membership in the top navigation bar of our home site – http://www.wrox.com. This is shown in the following screenshot:

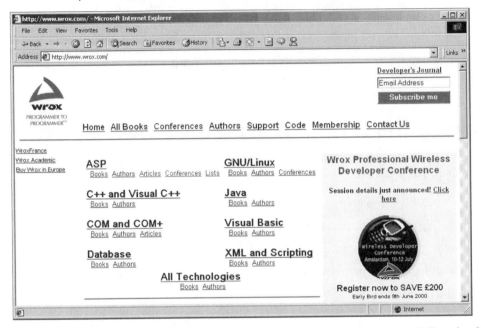

Then, on the next screen (not shown), click on New User. This will display a form. Fill in the details on the form and submit the details using the Register button at the bottom. Before you can say 'The best read books come in Wrox Red' you will get the following screen:

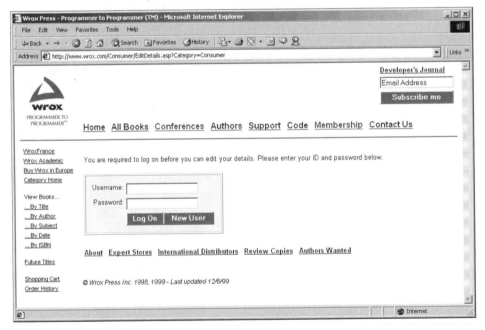

Type in your username and password once again and click Log On. The following page allows you to change your details if you need to, but now you're logged on, you have access to all the source code downloads and errata for the entire Wrox range of books.

Finding an Errata on the Web Site

Before you send in a query, you might be able to save time by finding the answer to your problem on our web site – http://www.wrox.com.

Each book we publish has its own page and its own errata sheet. You can get to any book's page by clicking on Support from the top navigation bar.

Halfway down the main support page is a drop down box called Title Support. Simply scroll down the list until you see Professional ASP XML. Select it and then hit Errata.

This will take you to the errata page for the book. Select the criteria by which you want to view the errata, and click the Apply criteria button. This will provide you with links to specific errata. For an initial search, you are advised to view the errata by page numbers. If you have looked for an error previously, then you may wish to limit your search using dates. We update these pages daily to ensure that you have the latest information on bugs and errors.

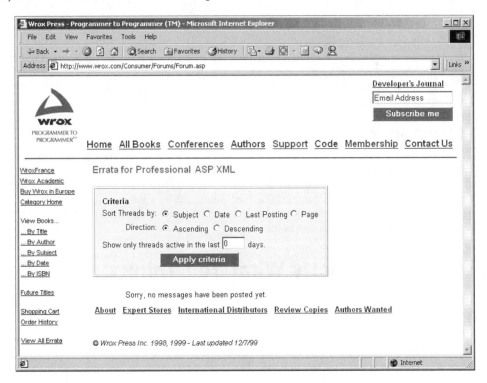

Add an Errata : E-mail Support

If you wish to point out an errata to put up on the website or directly query a problem in the book page with an expert who knows the book in detail then e-mail support@wrox.com, with the title of the book and the last four numbers of the ISBN in the subject field of the e-mail. A typical email should include the following things:

The **name**, **last four digits of the ISBN** and **page number** of the problem in the Subject field.

Your **name**, **contact info** and the **problem** in the body of the message.

We won't send you junk mail. We need the details to save your time and ours. If we need to replace a disk or CD we'll be able to get it to you straight away. When you send an e-mail it will go through the following chain of support:

Customer Support

Your message is delivered to one of our customer support staff who are the first people to read it. They have files on most frequently asked questions and will answer anything general immediately. They answer general questions about the book and the web site.

Editorial

Deeper queries are forwarded to the technical editor responsible for that book. They have experience with the programming language or particular product and are able to answer detailed technical questions on the subject. Once an issue has been resolved, the editor can post the errata to the web site.

The Authors

Finally, in the unlikely event that the editor can't answer your problem, s/he will forward the request to the author. We try to protect the author from any distractions from writing. However, we are quite happy to forward specific requests to them. All Wrox authors help with the support on their books. They'll mail the customer and the editor with their response, and again all readers should benefit.

What We Can't Answer

Obviously with an ever-growing range of books and an ever-changing technology base, there is an increasing volume of data requiring support. While we endeavor to answer all questions about the book, we can't answer bugs in your own programs that you've adapted from our code. So, while you might have loved the chapters on file handling, don't expect too much sympathy if you cripple your company with a routine which deletes the contents of your hard drive. But do tell us if you're especially pleased with the routine you developed with our help.

How to Tell Us Exactly What You Think

We understand that errors can destroy the enjoyment of a book and can cause many wasted and frustrated hours, so we seek to minimize the distress that they can cause.

You might just wish to tell us how much you liked or loathed the book in question. Or you might have ideas about how this whole process could be improved. In which, case you should e-mail feedback@wrox.com. You'll always find a sympathetic ear, no matter what the problem is. Above all you should remember that we do care about what you have to say and we will do our utmost to act upon it.

Index

A guide to the index.

The index is arranged hierarchically, in alphabetical order, with symbols preceding the letter A. Most second-level entries and many third-level entries also occur as first-level entries. This is to ensure that users will find the information they require however they choose to search for it.

M

Q